MOON

D0864685

OREGON
TRAIL
Road Trip

KATRINA EMERY

CONTENTS

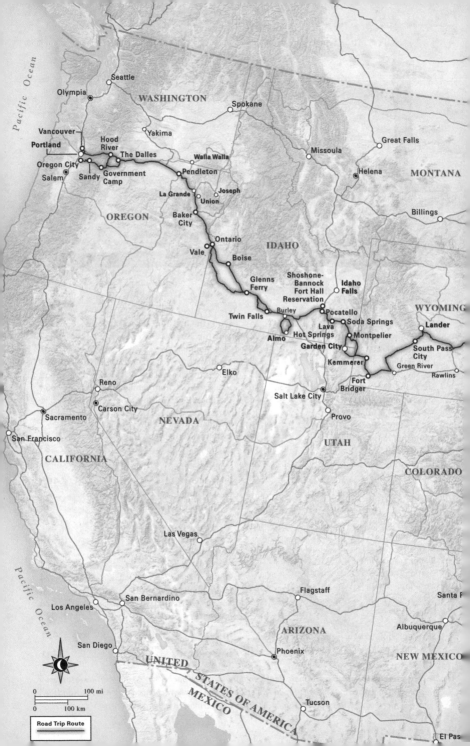

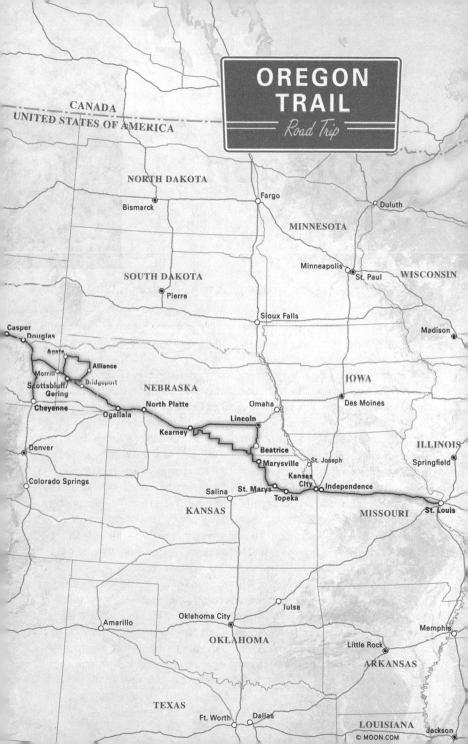

DISCOVER
the Oregon Trail

The Oregon Trail is in many ways the country's original road trip.

Lured by reports of the fertile Willamette Valley, emigrants loaded up their wagons and began heading west in the early 1840s. The first few wagon trains followed trails known to Native Americans, trappers, and traders; lucky ones had guides. By the mid-1850s wagons were leaving Independence, Missouri, by the hundreds every day, setting off across the rugged prairie, the Route 66 of its day. In every region, indigenous peoples watched as the emigrants rolled through their lands, some offering trade and assistance, some fearful. These interactions paved the way for future relationships.

In 2018, the trail celebrated its 175th anniversary. Once part of an unmapped territory, the Oregon Trail still goes through some of the most rural and wild landscapes the United States has to offer. The rolling green of the Kansas and Nebraska prairies gives way to rocky bluffs and high plains as the trail climbs into the rugged Rocky Mountains in Wyoming, where emigrants crossed the Continental Divide. From the western side of the watershed, the trail heads into the dramatic lava-bed canyons of Idaho's Snake River Valley and the high desert of eastern Oregon before the grand finale: the waterfall-pocked Columbia River Gorge or forested Mount Hood, depending on the road taken, leading to the lush lands surrounding Oregon City, the trail's endpoint.

Locations along the route became legendary, and now is the perfect chance to see them with your own eyes. What once took wagons 4-6 months to cover can now be spanned in a 30-hour drive. Following in the footsteps of the pioneers, you'll learn about the complex history of the country while also exploring its natural wonders. Today's road-trippers can marvel at the landmarks the emigrants saw, walk alongside their wagon ruts, and soak in the same hot springs, while also enjoying modern attractions and amusements in parts of the country that are often overlooked. With Wild West culture, small-town charm, breweries, great local cuisine, and outdoor recreation opportunities, this route continues to offer riches. It's still ripe for discovery.

8 TOP
EXPERIENCES

1 **Embark on Your Own Covered-Wagon Adventure:** A ride with **Pioneer Trails Adventures** (page 46) takes you on a tour from the official start of the Oregon Trail in Independence Square in Missouri, while **Historic Trails West** (page 205) in Wyoming takes you on a wagon into the mountainous wild.

2 **Walk Alongside Original Wagon Ruts:** Pioneers left behind traces of their passage, still in evidence today (page 24). The deepest ruts were cut into sandstone by the passage of thousands of wagon wheels.

3 **Spot Pioneer Landmarks:** Celebrate your passage across the country as the emigrants did, marveling at geographical stunners like **Chimney Rock** (page 161), **Scotts Bluff** (page 168), and **Independence Rock** (page 211).

>>>

4 **Soak up the Springs:** In Idaho, do as the emigrants did and dip a cup into the bubbling water at **Soda Springs** (page 248) and enjoy a hot soak at **Lava Hot Springs** (page 252).

5 **Celebrate at Trail-Themed Festivals and Events:** Enjoy pioneer-style fun and a carnival at the **SantaCaliGon Days Festival** (page 49) in Independence Square, where it all began, or toast the trail's official end with a pint at the **Oregon Trail Brewfest** (page 389) in Oregon City.

<<<

6 **Gain a Wider Perspective:** Visit sites along the trail to learn about the histories of the indigenous people who lived on the land prior to the pioneers, free and enslaved black emigrants, Mormon emigrants who embarked on their own journeys west, Chinese settlers, and more (page 28).

>>>

7 **Pick a Scenic Route:** Like the pioneers, once in Oregon on the final stretch you'll need to make a choice—go along the **Columbia River Gorge** (page 356) or follow the Barlow Road route around **Mount Hood** (page 377). Either way, you'll find jaw-dropping landscapes and recreation options.

>>>

8 **Learn at Interactive Museums:** Take a simulated wagon ride guided by living-history actors at the **National Oregon/California Trail Center** (page 245), see reenactments at the **National Historic Oregon Trail Interpretive Center** (page 326), and load your own wagon at the **End of the Oregon Trail Interpretive Center** (page 386).

PLANNING YOUR TRIP

Regions

Missouri and Kansas

The Oregon Trail officially begins in **Independence,** Missouri, where the **National Frontier Trails Museum** makes a good introduction to the trip, as does a visit to **Independence Square,** from which the wagons initially set out. From Independence, you'll continue just west on the route and can catch your first **wagon ruts** on the way to **Kansas City,** where you'll enjoy **barbecue** and lively **nightlife.** On the way through Kansas, take a break at **Alcove Springs,** where emigrants also once rested and where today you can wander terrain still bearing their traces on short hikes. Also stop to check out the route's first **Pony Express Station sites;** many of these were used first as stops on the Oregon Trail.

Alternatively, start your trip in **St. Louis,** 240 miles (386 km) west of Independence and a convenient hub. Known as the Gateway to the West—forebears Lewis and Clark kicked off their explorations here—it's also a fitting starting point and allows you to visit the newly renovated **Gateway Arch National Park,** which has a thoughtful museum on westward expansion, as well as the playful **City Museum**—a completely different type of museum that both kids and adults will love. At night, enjoy **barbecue** and **live music.**

Nebraska

In Nebraska you'll enter the Platte River Valley, one of the most pleasant stretches the emigrants experienced along the trail. Along the way, you can make easy detours to **Beatrice,** to visit the **Homestead National Monument of America,** and the fun college town of **Lincoln.** On the trail in **Kearney,** another college town, enjoy some **steak** and **craft beer,** and learn more about the Great Platte River Road, which we have to thank for the trail as well as the interstate today—at **The Archway** museum. Continuing on, check out the cowboy town of **Ogallala,** keep an eye out for pioneer landmarks such as **Chimney Rock,** and go for a hike at **Scotts Bluff National Monument,** through which emigrants found a navigable pass through rocky formations.

Wyoming

Continuing along the Platte River, you'll find the **Guernsey Ruts,** the best on the trail—cut four feet deep into the rock. Wave to the **jackalopes** in **Douglas** on your way to **Casper,** where you can visit the **National Historic Trails Interpretive Center** to learn more about the overland trails, of which the Oregon Trail was just one, and hop on a tour with **Historic Trails West** for a covered-wagon journey of your own, before crossing the Continental Divide like the pioneers at **South Pass.** Along the way you'll have opportunities to visit **historic forts,** which served as Oregon Trail way stations, among other purposes; learn about the **Mormon Trail** at numerous sites; and examine **pioneer signatures** at places like **Independence Rock.** Those with more time can add a side trip to Wyoming's biggest city, **Cheyenne,** or the outdoorsy town of **Lander;** catch a **rodeo;** or discover the state's rich **fossil history.**

Idaho

Enter Idaho following closely along the Oregon Trail on U.S. 30, or take a short scenic detour through Utah that brings you by pretty **Bear Lake.** Either way, you'll make it to **Montpelier,** where you can embark on a guided living-history tour on a simulated wagon ride at the excellent **National Oregon/California Trail Center.** Continuing west, take advantage of the springs along the trail, as the emigrants did, by drinking the cool mineral

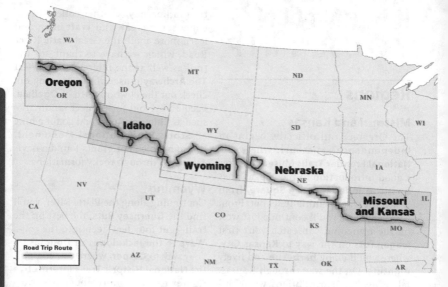

Road Trip Route

water at **Soda Springs** and enjoying a hot soak at **Lava Hot Springs.** Stop at the **Shoshone Bannock Tribal Museum** near Pocatello for an indigenous perspective on the region. In **Twin Falls,** take a walk along the **Snake River** on the **Canyon Rim Trail** to **Shoshone Falls** (or drive there), so pretty that some emigrants made detours just to see it. In Idaho's capital city, trendy **Boise,** enjoy the restaurants—try the local **Basque cuisine**—and **nightlife.** Those with more time along the way through the state might go on a **hike,** get out on the water in a **paddleboard or kayak,** take a side trip to **Idaho Falls,** or check out a quirky museum, like the **Museum of Clean.**

Oregon

At last! On this final leg of the journey, begin with a stop in **Baker City** and head to the nearby **National Historic Oregon Trail Interpretive Center,** possibly the best museum on the trail, with exhibits, ruts, trails, and summer reenactments. Cross the Blue Mountains into the Old West town of **Pendleton** to visit

Tamástslikt Cultural Institute, the only Native American-run museum that looks at the Oregon Trail from an indigenous perspective; take a **Pendleton Underground Tour** to learn about the hidden history of the city's tunnels, built by its Chinese population; and maybe catch the **Pendleton Round-Up** if you've timed it right and booked ahead. You'll soon face the same choice as the pioneers: Head along the **Columbia River Gorge** (though you won't have to float it like they did), where you can explore waterfront towns like **Hood River** and waterfalls like **Multnomah Falls,** or drive the old Barlow Road route around **Mount Hood** to check out the state's tallest mountain and iconic **Timberline Lodge.** Either way brings you to the trail's official endpoint in **Oregon City.** From here, it's a quick jump to vibrant **Portland,** home to great **restaurants, brewpubs,** and **green spaces.** With more time in Oregon, you can add on side trips to the charming town of **Joseph** or hop just over the state line to wine taste in **Walla Walla,** and add on any number of **hikes.**

Clockwise from top left: Shoshone Falls in Twin Falls, Idaho; sunflowers in Nebraska; bison in Wyoming.

When to Go

Most settlers set out from Missouri in early spring—as early as they could manage—and traveled 4-6 months to reach Oregon City. If they reached Independence Rock in Wyoming by July 4th, they knew they were making good time to beat fall snows. For modern travelers, **June** is an ideal month to travel, with warm but not yet too hot temperatures—though note Wyoming might still see some late-season snow. **July-August** are popular as well, though the heat can be intense, averaging 85-90°F (29-32°C), and attractions, hotels, and campsites are busier. **September-October** sees smaller crowds and cooler temperatures, but many smaller museums and attractions are only open Memorial Day-Labor Day, so be aware of **seasonal closures. Snow** can be a real concern, even in late fall, or early spring. **Winter** travelers should be prepared for harsh, cold temperatures averaging 34°F (1°C) across the route. While major highways typically remain open, a snowstorm can cause route closures and dangerous conditions.

Before You Go

During summer, book **accommodations** in the major cities—St. Louis, Kansas City, Boise, and Portland—2-3 months ahead for the best availability. Keep in mind also that the more rural areas of the route won't be as populous, but you also won't have as many choices for accommodations—book at least a month in advance in these areas. Check for **summer festivals and events** that might book out a small town, such as rodeos in Casper,

Wyoming, and Pendleton, Oregon, or the Treefort Music Fest in Boise; for travel during these times, book 3-4 months in advance.

Memorial Day-Labor Day is also high season for camping, and it's recommended you reserve **campsites** 2-3 months in advance for popular state parks, especially in Wyoming, Idaho, and Oregon. If you didn't plan ahead, don't fret—most campgrounds retain a few first-come, first-served spots you can snag.

Some **attractions,** such as experiences at Gateway Arch National Park in St. Louis, or tours like wagon rides, require **advance booking** of a few weeks or up to a month ahead during June-August. Note many attractions along the route are **closed between Labor Day-Memorial Day.**

Rental car or RV reservations should be made at least 2-3 months ahead of time. If you're planning on an out-of-state drop-off, bump that time frame up even earlier to 4-6 months to ensure your request has the best chance of approval—it's dependent on fleet availability.

If you're **driving your own car,** make sure it's in top shape before heading out on the road—change the oil, check the tire pressure, and stock a toolkit and emergency supplies (including a first-aid kit, blanket, and extra food and water).

Note that the Oregon Trail passes through **three time zones.** Missouri, Kansas, and half of Nebraska are in the central time zone; the western half of Nebraska, Wyoming, and Idaho follow mountain standard time; and Oregon is on Pacific standard time, beginning near Ontario in eastern Oregon. Each time zone is an hour earlier ahead as you head west.

Clockwise from top left: sod house in Nebraska; Oregon forest; sign in Oregon.

Driving Guide

Oregon Trail Route Notes

Because the Oregon Trail was not a clear road—wagons often spread out for miles on either side, avoiding each other's dust and potential wagon accidents—the route this guide follows is a close approximation. The drive from Missouri heading into Kansas is mostly along rural roads. Through Kansas, you'll largely follow **I-70.** In Nebraska the route mostly follows **I-80** then joins **U.S 26.** Once in Wyoming, you'll jump from U.S. 26 to **I-25** before veering off onto various **state highways,** and then hitting **U.S. 30** just before Idaho. Soon after you'll connect with to **I-86** and then **I-84** in Idaho. From there, you'll generally follow or parallel I-84 all the way to Oregon City.

The Oregon Trail, along with the Santa Fe Trail and California Trail, all of which originated in Independence, as well as the Pony Express and Mormon Trails, with which they later converge, are designated **National Historic Trails** and under the watch of the **National Park Service** (NPS, www.nps.gov). NPS has installed helpful **Auto Tour Route** signage marking the path of the historic trails and has published guides for each state (although Oregon is still in progress), downloadable as a PDF online or as an app for your smartphone, as well as made available as hard copies at some visitors centers along the way, making a nice supplemental resource.

We haven't attempted to list every roadside sign or way-post marker in this guide, but instead focus on the major or noteworthy sights and landmarks along the way. In addition to historic sights, this book includes suggestions for other unrelated but recommended attractions, recreation, and amenities, as well as **detours,** which take travelers off the main Oregon Trail route being charted to rejoin it later, and **side trips,** out-and-backs from this main trail. If you have more time, take it

slower and stop often for picnics, walks or hikes, and chats with the locals—many of whom will have family stories to tell of the pioneer era. If you have less time, consider tackling the trail in sections, or you'll end up driving pell-mell with little time to stop and see anything.

Getting There and Back

If you have time to road-trip the entire Oregon Trail in one go, the best way to do so is to book a one-way ticket into St. Louis or Kansas City, rent a car or RV, and then drop it off in Portland, and head out from there via one-way ticket. The trail's official start is in Independence, Missouri, part of the Kansas City metropolitan area. If you're coming from farther east, you can choose to start your trip in St. Louis. **Kansas City International Airport** (MCI, 1 International Square, 816/243-5237, www.flykci.com) and **St. Louis Lambert International Airport** (STL, 10701 Lambert International Blvd., 314/426-8000, www.flystl.com) are both hubs where you can easily rent a car or an RV. On the other side of the trail, **Portland International Airport** (PDX, 7000 NE Airport Way, 503/460-4234, www.flypdx.com) makes an easy exit point from the trail's end, Oregon City, 22 miles (35 km) south.

If you have a shorter amount of time, the road trip can easily be split into sections by beginning or ending at different points along the way. The travel hubs of Colorado's **Denver International Airport** (DEN, 8500 Pena Blvd., 303/342-2000, www.flydenver.com), and Utah's **Salt Lake City International Airport** (SLC, 776 N. Terminal Dr., 801/575-2400, www.slcairport.com), are just off the route but can act as entry points to some of the more rural areas of Wyoming and Idaho, respectively.

If you're driving your own car and need to make a quick return trip east, the fastest way from Portland to Kansas City is via the interstates: **I-84** through Oregon and Idaho, **I-80** through Wyoming and

Nebraska, and **I-70** through Kansas and Missouri. This route covers 1,790 miles (2,880 km), a 27-hour drive without stops.

Car and RV Rentals

About half of the route is on interstate highways, and the other half is on smaller two-lane highways through rural areas. Occasionally an accessible dirt road is used. You won't need a car with four-wheel drive, but there are a handful of bumpy dirt roads for which **high clearance** would be helpful.

If you're renting a car, look for the **major brands** with locations throughout the country so you won't have to backtrack to return it, and check for unlimited mileage and low out-of-state drop-off fees.

An RV or camper van makes an excellent vehicle for this trip, with plenty of campsites in beautiful locations along the way. Road conditions unsuitable for an RV are rare and are noted when necessary. Note if you're road-tripping one-way, you'll want to rely on a larger rental company such as **Cruise America,** which allows one-way trips upon request, dependent on fleet availability. Expect a one-way fee of around $650. **Local companies** will be better if you're tackling a shorter section and expect to return to your original location.

Fuel and Services

Gas stations and amenities can be found every 30-40 miles (48-64 km) along the major highways along the route, but there are gaps as wide as 60 miles (97 km) or more on smaller roads in Nebraska, Wyoming, and Idaho.

Cell phone and Wi-Fi service is plentiful in populated areas and along major interstate highways, but in the rural sections—of which there are many, particularly through western Nebraska, Wyoming, and southeastern Idaho—expect to lose a Wi-Fi signal and get spotty service, although you'll still generally be able to make phone calls.

HIT THE ROAD

20 Days on the Oregon Trail

This road trip follows the historic Oregon Trail, the 2,000-mile (3,200-km) overland route popular primarily from the 1840s to the 1860s. The original covered-wagon trip took pioneers 4-6 months, so 20 days is a vast improvement! The trail's official start is in Independence, Missouri, winding through Kansas, Nebraska, Wyoming, and Idaho until its end in Oregon City, Oregon.

Day 1: Missouri
ST. LOUIS

While not the initial starting point for Oregon Trail pioneers, **St. Louis,** Gateway to the West, is a fun, fitting, and convenient place to start. Start the morning off right with breakfast at **Rooster** or a local specialty, gooey butter cake, at **Park Avenue Coffee,** before heading to the main event: **Gateway Arch National Park.** Its beautiful museum offers a perfect introduction to the history of the country's westward expansion. You can also ride to the top of the Gateway Arch for vast views. For lunch, have some barbecue at **Sugarfire Smokehouse** or **Pappy's Smokehouse.** If you have kids—or even if you don't—get the wiggles out with a visit to the fantastically fun **City Museum,** more like a giant playground with a massive slide, tunnels, and cave systems than a museum. For dinner, go for St. Louis-style pie at **Imo's Pizza.** Head out for a night of jazz at **BB's Jazz, Blues & Soups** or catch a show at **The Fabulous Fox Theatre.**

Day 2: Missouri
ST. LOUIS TO KANSAS CITY
275 miles (445 km), 4.5 hours
Today you'll cover the entire state of Missouri on I-70. Stop at the midpoint

of **Arrow Rock** for an early lunch at the historic **J. Huston Tavern,** the oldest continuously operating restaurant west of the Mississippi. Then continue on to **Independence,** the official starting point of the Oregon Trail. Wander **Independence Square,** where emigrants stocked up on supplies before setting off, and make sure to snap a photo with the plaque marking the start of the Oregon Trail. Visit the **National Frontier Trails Museum** or take a covered-wagon ride with **Pioneer Trails Adventures.** Head just outside of town to see your first **wagon ruts** at **85th and Manchester** and **Minor Park/Blue River Crossing.** Instead of returning to Independence, you'll continue the short distance to **Kansas City,** where you can eat at **Arthur Bryant's Barbeque** and spend the night in the historic neighborhood of **Westport** at the **816 Hotel.**

Day 3: Missouri
KANSAS CITY

Explore Westport, the oldest neighborhood in Kansas City and another jumping-off point for the Oregon Trail. Then tour the sunken cargo of a riverboat at the **Arabia Steamboat Museum,** and visit **City Market,** where Oregon Trail emigrants once traded goods and where today you'll find a food and farmers market. In the afternoon, take your pick of Kansas City fun: galleries at **The Nelson-Atkins Museum of Art,** shopping at **Country Club Plaza,** or **fountain-hunting** anywhere. Dinner is back in Westport with excellent modern Mexican at **Port Fonda,** then go out for a night of dancing at the intimate **Riot Room** or cocktails at **Tom's Town** or **SoT.**

Day 4: Kansas-Nebraska
KANSAS CITY TO BEATRICE
215 miles (345 km), 3.75 hours
Your route today heads into and out of Kansas, so get an early start. Continue west via I-70 and stop in **Topeka,** the state capital, to visit the **Old Prairie**

Top: museum at Gateway Arch National Park in St. Louis. **Bottom:** pioneer signatures on Register Cliff in eastern Wyoming.

Best Visible Trail Ruts

ruts near Baker City in Oregon

Historians estimate that about 300 of the original 2,000 miles (480 of 3,200 km) of the Oregon Trail remain untouched. The rest of it has been lost to time or development—in many places, roads and highways were built directly over the popular route, such as Oregon's stretch of U.S. 26 along the Barlow Road route. However, many **ruts**—impressions of the wagon wheels that traversed the land two centuries ago—remain intact. In some places these are known as **swales,** slight sunken depressions that have been

Town or **Kansas Museum of History,** where the many exhibits include displays on the Oregon Trail. Head to Kansas's first craft brewery, **Blind Tiger Brewery,** with hearty meals in addition to beer. Then it's back on the trail via **rural roads** to **Alcove Springs,** a lush green spot that was a favorite of the pioneers and where you can stretch your legs with a short hike that takes you by dramatic **wagon swales.** Find something to eat at the **Wagon Wheel Cafe** in **Marysville** if you're hungry before exploring the town's **Pony Express Barn.** Then head to the nearby **Hollenberg Pony Express Station,** which began as a stop on the Oregon Trail before becoming a Pony Express station and, today, a museum. Drive into Nebraska and end your day in **Beatrice** with dinner at **The Black Crow.** Or you could opt to camp near **Rock Creek Station State Historical Park** and get a jump on tomorrow's itinerary; the total driving time and distance for either endpoint is about the same.

Day 5: Nebraska
BEATRICE TO KEARNEY
180 miles (290 km), 3.25 hours
Learn about the Homestead Act, a primary motivator for the movement out West, at the **Homestead National Monument of America** just outside of Beatrice. Then hike nearby along the wagon ruts at **Rock Creek Station State Historical Park.** From here, the route winds along **rural highways** on its way through the Nebraska farmland. Once in **Kearney,** eat award-winning pizza for lunch at **The Flippin Sweet,** then head to **The Archway** to learn about the Great Platte River Road and the many journeys along it, including the Oregon

overgrown with grass. In most places you can walk or hike along them, but be respectful and never drive on them.

♦ **85th and Manchester Trail Ruts and Minor Park/Blue River Crossing, Missouri:** Leaving Independence, travelers can follow a faint and unique route of ruts left in the urban landscape; the best can be found at Minor Park (page 53) and the small neighborhood corner of 85th and Manchester (page 52). They're both easily viewed right off parking areas.

♦ **Alcove Springs, Kansas:** Springs at this site made a lovely resting spot for pioneers, and short trails take you around them as well as the distinct swales in the grass (page 102).

♦ **Ash Hollow, Nebraska:** A 30-minute loop hike takes you alongside deep ruts and affords excellent views of the hilly terrain that wagons conquered (page 158).

♦ **Guernsey Ruts, Wyoming:** Easily the most impressive ruts along the whole trail, the deep traces of wagon wheels left in the sandstone here are accessible via a short walk (page 180).

♦ **Emigrant Trail, Idaho:** Perfectly preserved inside the Hagerman Fossil Beds National Monument, this strenuous trail takes 3-4 hours to hike but rewards with close-ups of deep ruts that cut through the grass (page 289).

♦ **National Historic Oregon Trail Interpretive Center, Oregon:** Just outside Baker City, this museum has a long set of ruts left in the high desert hills, which has 4 miles (6.4 km) of hiking trails winding around them today (page 326).

Trail. Get out on the **Kearney Water Trail** with a late afternoon kayak. If you don't mind adding an extra 40 minutes of driving to your day, head southwest of town about 30 miles (48 km) for a **steak dinner** at **The Speakeasy.** Or you can stay in town and have steak at **The Alley Rose** instead. Either way, end the day with an all-Nebraska choice of spirits back in Kearney's **McCue's Nebraska Taproom.**

With More Time

Instead of driving via the rural trail roads to Kearney, you can continue driving north from Beatrice 41 miles (65 km) on **U.S. 77** for 45 minutes to detour to Nebraska's capital city, also home to a University of Nebraska campus, lively **Lincoln,** where you may want to spend a night. You can rejoin the trail by heading west on I-80 to Kearney.

Day 6: Nebraska
KEARNEY TO SCOTTSBLUFF AND GERING
280 miles (450 km), 4.5 hours

Get a strong start on you day with breakfast from **Kitt's Kitchen and Coffee,** then get back on the road, heading west via **I-80.** Stop by **North Platte** to see the world's largest railyard from the **Golden Spike** and wander the **Buffalo Bill Ranch State Historical Park.** Get lunch at **Penny's Diner,** an old highway stop that's open 24 hours a day. Then continue west on I 80 to the cowboy town of **Ogallala,** where you can stretch your legs on its historic **Front Street** before continuing on via **U.S. 26** and checking out deep wagon ruts on the **Windlass Hill Trail** at **Ash Hollow.** Back on the road, you'll drive by the pioneer landmarks of **Courthouse and Jail Rocks** and **Chimney Rock** on the way to the sister towns of **Scottsbluff and Gering,** where you can eat dinner

Top: City Market in Kansas City. **Bottom:** Rock Creek Station State Historical Park in Nebraska.

at **The Tangled Tumbleweed,** and sleep well nearby at the **Barn Anew Bed and Breakfast,** a renovated homestead whose owners are highly knowledgeable about the Oregon Trail.

Day 7: Nebraska
SCOTTSBLUFF AND GERING
Fortify yourself with breakfast from **The Mixing Bowl,** then spend the day hiking in the footsteps and wagon ruts of pioneers at the nearby **Scotts Bluff National Monument.** Then learn more about prairie history at the **Legacy of the Plains Museum.** Toast your tired feet with a taster flight from **Flyover Brewing Company**—the Nebraska Pandhandle's only craft brewery, where you can also order a tasty wood-fired pizza.

Day 8: Nebraska-Wyoming
SCOTTSBLUFF TO CASPER
185 miles (300 km), 3.25 hours
Shortly after crossing the border into Wyoming via **U.S. 26,** stop at **Fort Laramie,** once an emigrant supply stop; today you can wander the fort's structures and visit a museum. Then continue west on U.S. 26 to step into the most dramatic ruts along the trail at **Guernsey Ruts** and glimpse some pioneer signatures at **Register Cliff.** Nearby, the Castle at **Guernsey State Park,** just off the route, makes a perfect picnic stop. Just past Guernsey, you'll start heading north via **I-25.** Wave hello to the jackalope statue in **Douglas** before heading into **Casper.** Stop at the **National Historic Trails Interpretive Center** and, if you have enough time, be sure to take an epic covered-wagon ride with **Historic Trails West.** End the day with live music and dinner on the patio at **Yellowstone Garage,** and spend the night at the budget-friendly lodge-like **C'mon Inn Casper.**

With More Time
From the U.S. 26/I-25 junction west of Guernsey, you can take a side trip to Wyoming's biggest city and state capital, **Cheyenne.** The 82-mile (132-km) drive south on **I-25** takes 1.25 hours one-way.

Day 9: Wyoming
CASPER TO LANDER
145 miles (233 km), 2.5 hours
Head southwest on **Highway 220** to see **Independence Rock,** a major landmark for the pioneers; you can stop here and examine some of their signatures carved into the stone as well as climb to the top. Continue on and visit the nearby **Mormon Handcart Historic Site at Martin's Cove,** where you can learn how Mormon pioneers on their way to Utah traveled the trail while marveling at the rugged landscape they struggled through. Pack a picnic lunch, as there's not much to eat along the way. At the midway point of the driving day, you'll come to a highway junction; continue west for a side trip via **U.S. 287** to the pretty, outdoorsy town of **Lander,** where the Wind River Mountains provide stunning scenery as you creep closer to the Continental Divide. Eat at the casual **Gannett Grill** or the more upscale **Cowfish,** which share a patio along the town's Main Street, then finish the day off with a chokecherry shake at **The Scream Shack.** Stay at **The Inn at Lander** for the night, or camp for free in **Lander City Park.**

Day 10: Wyoming
LANDER TO KEMMERER
220 miles (355 km), 3.5 hours
Grab breakfast at **The Middle Fork** in Lander before hitting the road south via **U.S. 287/Highway 28.** Your first stop today is the mining ghost town of **South Pass City,** population 4. Check out the historic buildings, and if you got an early start, tour the old **Carissa Mine** or go for a **creek-side walk.** Continue south on the highway and you'll soon join the pioneers in crossing the Continental Divide at the surprisingly gentle **South Pass.** Stop for a quick lunch at **Farson Mercantile,** then keep on trucking to **Fort Bridger State Historic Site** via

Diverse Perspectives Along the Trail

Mormon Handcart Historic Site at Martin's Cove in Wyoming

While the popular image of covered wagons on the Oregon Trail is dominated by white Christian settlers, the whole story is much more variegated and interesting. Mormon pioneers headed to Utah in such numbers that they created their own alternate route in many places. African American emigrants, both free and enslaved, traveled the trail. Oregon and California saw large numbers of Chinese immigrants, many of whom came to work on the railroad; although they didn't travel via covered wagons on the trail, they left a lasting legacy. And, of course, long before the pioneers, Native Americans made their homes across the West. Along the trail, you'll find opportunities to engage with this diverse history that helps tell the complex and challenging story of our country's becoming.

Missouri

♦ **Gateway Arch National Park:** This park in St. Louis includes a thought-provoking museum on westward expansion that takes into account many perspectives—including Native Americans and free and enslaved African Americans, as well as Mexico, which also had a stake in the West. Also on the grounds is the city's Old Courthouse, where enslaved husband-and-wife Dred and Harriet Scott filed petitions for their freedom during the time of the Oregon Trail, leading to a tipping point in the Civil War (page 59).

Kansas

♦ **Pawnee Indian Museum:** A detour takes you to an intact earth lodge, a rare example of the type of lodging in which the Pawnee people lived in the 1800s (page 107).

Pawnee Indian Museum

Wyoming

♦ **Mormon Handcart Historic Site at Martin's Cove:** Learn about the experiences of Mormon pioneers as they made their way from Illinois to Utah, and try pulling your own handcart, which many used instead of wagons (page 213).

Idaho

♦ **Shoshone Bannock Tribal Museum:** Previously the site of a major stop on the Oregon Trail, this museum at the Shoshone-Bannock Fort Hall Reservation showcases the rich traditions of the area's Indigenous people (page 262).

Oregon

♦ **Kam Wah Chung:** This side trip from the trail to a Chinese grocery and herbal apothecary that dates to 1866 offers a fascinating glimpse into a cultural hub for Chinese Americans in the pioneer area (page 334).

♦ **Tamástslikt Cultural Institute:** The Walla Walla, Umatilla, and Cayuse tribes own and operate this beautiful museum, which tells the story of how they were, how they are, and how they will be (page 344).

♦ **Pendleton Underground Tours:** Many early Chinese immigrants were safer living underground in early settler days; learn about their lives on this city tour (page 345).

♦ **Oregon Historical Society:** The permanent Experience Oregon interactive exhibit showcases stories of Native Americans, African Americans, Chinese Americans, and Japanese Americans, all while asking "What is your Oregon experience?" (page 394).

Top: Fossil Butte National Monument in Wyoming. **Bottom:** geyser in Soda Springs, Idaho.

Highway 372 and I-80, an old emigrant supply stop and military fort. Then drive north on Highway 412 and U.S. 189 to Kemmerer, and grab takeout dinner at Scroungy Moose Pizza.

Day 11: Wyoming-Idaho
KEMMERER TO MONTPELIER
75-85 miles (121-137 km), 1.25-1.5 hours

Eat a hearty breakfast at Caribou Café. On your way west out of Wyoming via U.S. 30, stop at Fossil Butte National Monument to check out the impressive fish fossils. Just west of Fossil Butte, you have a choice at the highway junction: Turn right to follow the old trail via U.S. 30 into Idaho and stop at Big Hill—the longest and one of the steepest descents encountered by the pioneers—or detour and take a slightly longer scenic route by making a left onto Highway 89 for the Bear Lake Scenic Byway, which leads to Idaho through Utah. Either way, you'll end up in Montpelier, where you can take a simulated wagon ride and enjoy a living-history tour at the National Oregon/California Trail Center, then enjoy dinner at the 24-hour favorite Ranch Hand Trail Stop.

With More Time
Stop along the Bear Lake Scenic Byway and spend the day enjoying the outdoors at beautiful Bear Lake, then spend the night at lodgings in lakefront Garden City, Utah.

Day 12: Idaho
MONTPELIER TO LAVA HOT SPRINGS
50 miles (81 km), 1 hour

Today is short on driving and big on fun. Head northwest on U.S. 30 and stop at Soda Springs, where you can literally drink the same water as the pioneers. Dip a cup into the springs and see how you like the mineral taste (it's perfectly safe). Check out the world's only "captive geyser" (city-controlled) in Geyser Park, and then have a meal at Main Street Diner. Continue west on U.S. 30 to Lava Hot Springs, where Oregon Trail emigrants got to enjoy a hot bath and where you can still take a soak today. For more water fun, rent a tube and float the Portneuf River, or go zip-lining through a canyon just outside town. Eat at the Riverwalk Thai Restaurant, set in an old gas station, and stay at Home Hotel or the Riverside Hot Springs Inn & Spa, which have private hot springs for guests to enjoy.

Day 13: Idaho
LAVA HOT SPRINGS TO TWIN FALLS
170 miles (275 km), 2.75 hours

Have breakfast at Café & A'more, then head west out of town on U.S. 30, merging north onto I-15. In Pocatello, learn how to do laundry pioneer-style at the Museum of Clean. Eat some tasty Italian inside another old gas station at Café Tuscano. Then head to the Bannock County Historical Museum, where the highlight is the Fort Hall Replica, a re-creation of what was once a major stop on the Oregon Trail and, in the early days, the point at which parties abandoned their wagons and continued on foot. Just north of town via I-15 is the Shoshone-Bannock Fort Hall Reservation, where the original fort once stood. While the fort is no longer there, the Shoshone Bannock Tribal Museum is a small but worthwhile stop, and provides an indigenous perspective. From Pocatello, head west on I-86/I-84 to Twin Falls. Stop at the Buzz Langdon Visitor Center to get your bearings and stretch your legs along the Canyon Rim Trail. Enjoy fine dining and Snake River views at Elevation 486, then settle into the Blue Lakes Inn for the night.

With More Time
Take a side trip to Idaho Falls, which has some quirky attractions and great breweries; it's only 40 miles (64 km), a

Best for Kids

on a wagon ride along the trail

The Oregon Trail was the original road trip for kids, as families—rather than lone fur trappers and traders—loaded up their wagons and headed west. It was a tough trip, and kids had important jobs along the way, like picking up wood or buffalo chips for making fire. But it also must have been a wild adventure full of exciting sights. Today's journey is perfectly suited to kids, especially grade-schoolers who might have read about the history in class. Older teenagers can learn about the rigors of the trail while they camp and enjoy outdoor adventures in state parks. Almost every large museum along the way will have a kids' section full of toys, games, and activities to help bring the trail's history to life (or just let mom and dad have a quiet hour). Here are some of the best adventures along the way:

Missouri

♦ **Pioneer Trails Adventures:** Kick off the official start of the Oregon Trail with a fun covered-wagon ride from Independence Square, where emigrants also set out (page 46).

♦ **City Museum:** If you start from St. Louis, check out this wondrous playground of a museum; it's not related to the trail, but it boasts a five-story slide, hidden passageways to climb, and so much more (page 61).

35-minute drive farther north via **I-15** from the Shoshone-Bannock Fort Hall Reservation. Or, on the way to Twin Falls, take a scenic detour from Burley, just south of the I-84/Highway 27 junction, through the **City of Rocks,** which also gives you plenty of opportunities to pull over. The **scenic byway** takes two hours without stops and loops you back to the trail.

Day 14: Idaho
TWIN FALLS TO BOISE
135 miles (217 km), 2.5 hours

Have breakfast at **Yellow Brick Café,** then make your way to **Shoshone Falls;** called the "Niagara of the West," the falls also dazzled Oregon Trail emigrants. Depart Twin Falls via **U.S. 30** for the **Thousand Springs Scenic Byway,** where you'll have opportunities to soak in hot

Nebraska

♦ **Harold Warp Pioneer Village:** Spend an afternoon exploring this quirky "village," made up of 28 authentic buildings that tell stories from the pioneer times to the present (page 118).

♦ **The Archway:** This museum uses video, audio, and interactive exhibits to tell the story of travel along the Platte River, from the Oregon Trail to today's interstate, and outside you'll find a fun maze for kids (page 136).

Wyoming

♦ **National Historic Trails Interpretive Center:** Ford a virtual river and pull a handcart like many Mormon emigrants used at this interactive museum (page 203).

♦ **Historic Trails West Tours:** Join a covered-wagon ride and head into the hills outside Casper for a pioneer-style outing (page 205).

♦ **Mormon Handcart Historic Site at Martin's Cove:** Older kids can try pulling their own handcart, while younger folks can take a ride (page 213).

Idaho

♦ **National Oregon/California Trail Center:** Head out on a simulated wagon ride guided by living-history actors at this interactive museum (page 245).

♦ **Lava Hot Springs:** Pioneers soaked in the springs here, and today, so can you and your kids—with the added benefit of water slides (page 252).

Oregon

♦ **Tamástslikt Cultural Institute:** Hear the Walla Walla, Cayuse, and Umatilla tribes' story of creation in the Coyote Theater, then explore the Living Culture Village, which has replicas of tepees and other lodgings that the local tribes have called home (page 344).

♦ **End of the Oregon Trail Interpretive Center:** Pack your wagon, dip a real candle, and dress up like a pioneer at this interactive museum at the official end of the Oregon Trail (page 386).

springs, paddle, and hike along impressive wagon ruts at **Hagerman Fossil Beds National Monument,** depending on how much time you have. Stop for lunch in Hagerman at the **Snake River Grill,** which pulls its trout right from the nearby river. Continue west via **I-84** to **Glenns Ferry,** where you can check out a notorious Snake River fording spot, **Three Island Crossing.** Keep going to **Boise,** and end your day with dinner at **Bittercreek Alehouse** or **Juniper.**

Day 15: Idaho
BOISE

Idaho's capital city has a lot to offer. Get coffee and a pastry from **Slow by Slow,** then head to **Julia Davis Park,** home to many of Boise's major museums. Dive into history at the **Idaho State Museum**

Best of the Rest

In addition to Oregon Trail history, this route affords access to some of today's best of the West.

Food and Drink

Beyond the burgers and steaks, sample delicious regional food and drink.

♦ **Barbecue, Missouri:** Both **St. Louis** (page 69) and **Kansas City** (page 86) have their own meaty traditions.

♦ *Runza,* **Nebraska:** This breaded pocket of meat was brought to the plains by Eastern European immigrants and is now ubiquitous across the state (page 131).

♦ **Basque Cuisine, Idaho:** With a thriving Basque population, Boise is one of the best places to try this cuisine outside of Europe (page 307).

♦ **Craft Beer:** Enjoy local brews along the trail, especially in **Portland,** known as Beervana (page 400).

Recreation

Explore the dramatic landscapes of the West.

♦ **Platte River, Nebraska and Wyoming:** Go kayaking (page 141), try the Nebraskan activity of "tanking (page 150), or fish for trout (page 206) along the length of this river.

♦ **City of Rocks, Idaho:** Unique geological formations create a hiking and rock-climbing playground (page 271).

♦ **Thousand Springs Scenic Byway, Idaho:** Soak in hot springs, hike, and kayak along this lovely stretch (page 284).

♦ **Bruneau Dunes, Idaho:** These sandy dunes offer opportunities for hiking, sandboarding, and stargazing (page 294).

♦ **Wallowa Mountains, Oregon:** Explore this gorgeous region from the gateway town of **Joseph** (page 337).

♦ **Columbia River Gorge, Oregon:** Hike, bike, windsurf, or kiteboard in this National Scenic Area (page 356).

Old West

Get a taste of the Wild West.

♦ **Ogallala, Nebraska:** Known as the Cowboy Capital of Nebraska, Ogallala has a kitschy historical Front Street (page 152).

♦ **South Pass City, Wyoming:** Once a booming mining town, this ghost town is a well-preserved place to explore mines and Old West boardwalks (page 221).

♦ **Pendleton, Oregon:** Slinging whiskey and woolen blankets, and thick with rodeo culture, Pendleton is a cowboy and cowgirl town through and through (page 343).

♦ **Rodeos:** See the show during **NEBRASKAland Days** (page 150), **Cheyenne Frontier Days** (page 192), or the **Pendleton Round-Up** (page 346).

Small-Town Charm

Explore quaint streets and local flavors.

♦ **Lander, Wyoming:** Lander is an outdoorsy town in the shadows of the Wind River Mountains (page 215).

♦ **Idaho Falls, Idaho:** Find a walkable downtown set along the Snake River (page 263).

♦ **Joseph, Oregon:** This scenic town is nestled at the base of the Wallowa Mountains (page 337).

♦ **Walla Walla, Washington:** Enjoy the wine and produce of the Walla Walla Valley in this sweet spot (page 350).

♦ **Hood River, Oregon:** Set along the Columbia River Gorge is this hot spot for windsurfing, kiteboarding, beer, and good food (page 364).

Lively Cities

Enjoy the bustle of the cities.

♦ **St. Louis, Missouri:** Gaze west from the top of Gateway Arch, then enjoy barbecue and jazz in this fun city (page 56).

♦ **Kansas City, Missouri:** Enjoy history, art, and shopping alongside your barbecue and jazz (page 76).

♦ **Lincoln, Nebraska:** Cheer on a college football game, then enjoy a night out in the historic district (page 123).

♦ **Boise, Idaho:** Enjoy the small-town feel of this vibrant city offering great drinks, restaurants, shops, and outdoor fun (page 299).

♦ **Portland, Oregon:** Taste your way through Beervana and enjoy a bike ride or hike in playful Portland (page 392).

Quirk Quotient

Step into something a little weird at these inspired stops.

♦ **City Museum, Missouri:** This fantastic playground for kids and adults is a veritable labyrinth of slides and secret rooms (page 61).

♦ **Carhenge, Nebraska:** See the one-to-one scale ratio of Stonehenge—as built out of automobiles (page 162).

♦ **Douglas, Wyoming:** Get a jackalope hunting certificate in the city from which the mythical creature originates (page 197).

♦ **Museum of Clean, Idaho:** Do some pioneer laundry, among other things, at this fun and interactive museum that explores the history of cleaning (page 259).

♦ **Emu-Z-Um, Idaho:** You'll never see a bigger collection of, well, anything, than at this museum comprised of more than 15 buildings holding all manner of odd antiques (page 295).

or go for a walk or bike ride along the **Boise River Greenbelt,** which cuts through the park. Get lunch and an "ice cream potato" from **Westside Drive-In,** then pick your adventure: Head nearby to see some raptors at **World Center for Birds of Prey,** take a tour of the **Old Idaho Penitentiary,** or go for a hike just behind the penitentiary on the **Table Rock Trail 15.** Back in the city, go to the **Basque Block** for dinner at **Bar Gernika,** and see a show at **Neurolux.**

Day 16: Oregon
BOISE TO BAKER CITY
130 miles (209 km), 2 hours
Continue your journey west on **I-84.** You've made it to Oregon! But you're not done yet. Wave good-bye to the Snake River at **Farewell Bend,** where the pioneers rested before pushing on, then pull into **Baker City.** Have breakfast or lunch at **Lone Pine Cafe,** then visit the fantastic **National Historic Oregon Trail Interpretive Center** and hike around the deep ruts that cut through the surrounding hills. Back in town, grab a pint and a meal at **Barley Brown's Brew Pub.** Head across the street for more beer and maybe some live music at sister property **Barley Brown's Tasting Room.** Then find your room at the historic **Geiser Grand Hotel.**

Day 17: Oregon
BAKER CITY TO PENDLETON
95 miles (153 km), 1.5 hours
Follow the trail up and over the mountains today via **I-84.** Check out some well-preserved ruts and maybe catch some living history reenactments at the **Oregon Trail Interpretive Park at Blue Mountain Crossing.** Then descend into **Pendleton.** Have breakfast or lunch at **The Rainbow Café,** one of the oldest restaurants in the state. Next up is a visit to the **Tamástslikt Cultural Institute,** a history center owned by the Walla Walla, Cayuse, and Umatilla tribes, offering perspective on their history—including

the Oregon Trail—as well as their present and future. Then learn about the secret tunnels built by Chinese settlers with **Pendleton Underground Tours.** Shop for a classic blanket at **Pendleton Woolen Mills,** then enjoy dinner at Hamley Steakhouse. Cap off the night with live music at the **Great Pacific** before ending at the pink **Pendleton House Historic Inn.**

With More Time
Midway between Baker City and Pendleton is the town of **La Grande,** from which you can take a side trip to the bustling little tourist town of **Joseph** at the base of the Wallowa Mountains. The 70-mile (113-km) drive west via **Highway 82** takes 1.5 hours one-way.

Day 18: Oregon
PENDLETON TO HOOD RIVER
160 miles (260 km), 3 hours
On the way out of Pendleton via **I-84,** swing through the tiny town of **Echo** to check out the wagon ruts in **Echo Meadows.** Then continue west to find yourself traveling along the scenic **Columbia River Gorge.** Stop in **The Dalles,** where you can enjoy lunch at the **Sunshine Mill Winery,** in an old grain mill. Just outside town, drive the winding road to **Rowena Crest Viewpoint,** for a breathtaking perspective on the landscape from a bluff high above the gorge. Then roll into the charming town of **Hood River,** where you can play on the water, enjoy great food and beer, or pick your own fruit beneath the watchful eye of Mount Hood.

With More Time
From Pendleton, take a side trip to **Walla Walla, Washington,** where you can visit the **Whitman Mission** and **wineries.** The 40-mile (64-km) drive northwest via **Highway 11/125** takes just under an hour one-way.

Day 19: Oregon
HOOD RIVER TO PORTLAND

I-84: 95 miles (153 km), 1.75 hours

U.S. 30: 100 miles (161 km), 2.25 hours

Hwy. 35 and U.S. 26: 117 miles (188 km), 2.5 hours

It's the final stretch! Enjoy a Scandinavian breakfast at **Broder Øst** before heading out. Then make your choice, just like the pioneers did. Continue west along the **Columbia River Gorge** via either **I-84** or **U.S. 30,** or go around **Mount Hood** on the **Barlow Road** via **Highway 35** and **U.S. 26.** All are beautiful drives with **hiking options** along the way; if you follow the gorge, you can stop at numerous waterfalls, including renowned **Multnomah Falls;** the Barlow Road drive is slightly longer but no less scenic, and you can visit iconic **Timberline Lodge.** Once in **Oregon City,** it's official: You've reach the end of the trail. Celebrate with a visit to the **End of the Trail Interpretive Center** and a gourmet sausage and pint at **Oregon City Brewing Co.,** whose motto is "Pioneering Beer from the Pioneering City." Spend the night in **Portland,** just 15 miles (24 km) north via **Highway 99.**

Day 20: Oregon
PORTLAND

Start your day off downtown with shared plates at **Tasty n Alder.** Then walk the few blocks to find legendary **Powell's City of Books,** where you could spend lifetimes. But continue wandering, heading up to **Washington Park** to find the **International Rose Test Garden** and historic **Pittock Mansion,** former home of two Oregon Trail pioneers and now a museum with amazing views from its hillside perch. For lunch, head across the Willamette River to the east side of town and eat a torta at **Güero,** dumplings at **Kachka,** ramen at **Afuri,** or a gourmet cheese board at **Cheese & Crack.** Make sure to walk through the lovely **Lone Fir Cemetery,** where some early pioneers are buried. Then kick back at some **brewpubs,** and catch a live show at the **Doug Fir Lounge** to end your trip with a bang. You did it!

20 DAYS ON THE OREGON TRAIL

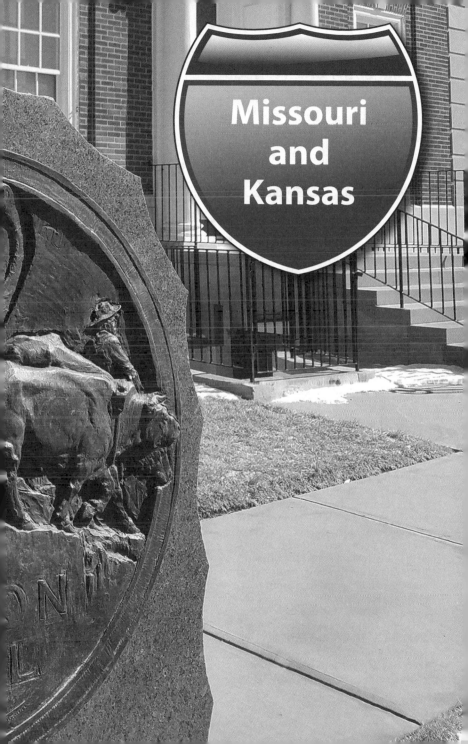

Missouri
and
Kansas

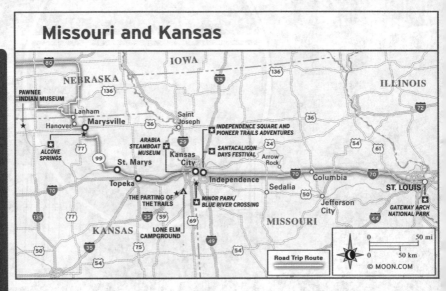

Missouri and Kansas

O regon Fever! The obses-sion gripped the nation as economic failures rippled through farms and banks in the East in the late 1830s.

Lewis and Clark started their explorations from St. Louis, Gateway to the West, but by 1830 the frontier had moved farther west, to towns like Independence, Missouri—the official start of the Oregon Trail. Independence was one of the largest towns west of the Mississippi in the early 1800s; because the Missouri River flowed nearby, emigrants from all over the nation were able to jump riverboats to this westernmost "edge of civilization" before starting their wagon journeys. Supplies were purchased, and then wagons exited Independence Square, bumping along in droves. From there, the gentle plains of Kansas, with resting stops like the bubbling Alcove

Springs, made an easy entry point for the pioneers.

Today's road-trippers can enjoy the fun and festivities of some of Missouri's and Kansas's biggest cities before following trail ruts northwest to Nebraska. The route travels from Independence through the barbecue haven of Kansas City and Kansas's capital city of Topeka before setting out through farmland and the rural towns of northern Kansas.

"This past winter there has been a strange fever raging here (it is the Oregon fever). It seems to be contagious and it is raging terribly, nothing seems to stop it but to tear up and take a six months trip across the plains with ox teams to the Pacific Ocean."

Kit Belknap, 1847, *The Running Commentaries of Keturah Belknap.* Kit nursed her sick toddler while expecting another child along the trail. She made it to Oregon where she had five more children (two of whom died of typhoid), helped her husband with the farm, and lived a long life.

Highlights

★ Start your journey at the same spot as the pioneers did: **Independence Square** (page 44), where you can hop on a covered wagon and retrace the early part of their trip with **Pioneer Trails Adventures** (page 46).

★ Celebrate the three National Historic Trails that originated in Independence at the **SantaCaliGon Days Festival** (page 49).

★ Marvel at some of the first trail ruts carved into the prairie by thousands of wagons at the **Minor Park/Blue River Crossing** (page 53).

★ Visit **Gateway Arch National Park** with its revamped museum, which provides a thoughtful look at westward expansion (page 59).

★ See rescued sunken cargo from the pioneer era at the **Arabia Steamboat Museum** (page 80).

★ See pioneer names carved into stone at **Alcove Springs,** a beautiful natural haven where the Donner Party once rested (page 102).

Planning Your Time

Plan on spending at least three days exploring the Oregon Trail from Missouri through Kansas, budgeting a day each for Independence—the Oregon Trail's official starting point—and Kansas City, Missouri, and accounting for the 208-mile (335-km), 4-hour drive northwest through Kansas to the border with Nebraska. If you're starting in St. Louis, which makes a convenient gateway, plan on an additional 2-3 days if you can: 1-2 days in the city, and another for the 240-mile (386-km) drive west across the state to Independence, which takes 3.5 hours. With more time, you can enjoy the big city offerings of St. Louis and Kansas City, Missouri, each worth a week in their own right. You could also take your time in Topeka and the smaller towns of St. Marys and Marysville in northern Kansas or Arrow Rock in Missouri.

Late spring-early fall is the most popular season to travel in Missouri and Kansas, avoiding the Midwest's brutal winters, when temperatures can get below 20°F (-7°C). You'll want to book attractions and hotels 2-3 months in advance during this time in the bigger cities of Independence, Kansas City, and St. Louis.

Getting There

Starting Points
Oregon Trail Route Notes
On this first section, you'll follow the actual Oregon Trail route as you cut south then west from Independence until the Parting of the Oregon and Santa Fe Trails, and again on the section from St. Marys to Vieux and Cholera Cemeteries in northern Kansas. The rest of the drive follows the closest roads approximating the trail, largely along I-70. After Topeka, most of the rural roads are set in a grid, while the Oregon Trail cuts in a diagonal to the northwest.

Car and RV
Independence, Missouri, is the official start of the Oregon Trail, and Kansas City, Missouri—10 miles (16 km) west— is the closest large city, a 20-minute drive west via I-70. St. Louis, Missouri, east of Independence, is within a day's drive of much of the central and eastern United States, making it a convenient place to start your trip. It's served by the major interstate highways I-55, I-70, and I-64. The 240-mile (386-km) drive from St. Louis to Independence takes about 3.5 hours via I-70.

Some sites along the Oregon Trail are served by dirt roads, which are passable (though bumpy) even for trailers and RVs, but proceed cautiously if it has been rainy, as they can get extremely muddy.

Rentals
Enterprise (www.enterprise.com) is headquartered in St. Louis. Convenient car rentals are available at the St. Louis Lambert International Airport (9305 Natural Bridge Rd., MO, 314/427-7757, 6am-10:30pm daily), in downtown St. Louis (2233 Washington Ave., MO, 314/241-0073, 7:30am-6pm Mon.-Fri., 8am-3pm Sat., 11am-3pm Sun.), and in downtown Kansas City (600 Grand Blvd., MO, 816/842-4700, 7:30am-6pm Mon.-Fri., 9am-noon Sat.). Avis (www. avis.com) has a convenient outpost at the Kansas City International Airport (1 Nassau Circle, MO, 816/464-6200, 24 hours daily).

Get focused customer service at the family-owned Unlimited RV (4400 N. Cobbler Rd., Independence, MO, 816/883-8988, 9am-6pm Mon.-Sat.), which buys, sells, and rents new and pre-owned RVs. They'll answer any questions about your rental and find you the best option from their fleet. Rates for a seven-day trip of around 700 miles (1,100 km) are $1,500-1,900 per week, and include roadside assistance and insurance.

Cruise America (www.cruiseamerica. com) is a nationwide company with a

Best Overnight Stops

★ **St. Louis, Missouri:** Although not part of the official Oregon Trail, this Midwestern city makes an accessible and lively starting point with its delicious food, jazzy tunes, unique museums, and luxurious hotels (page 56).

★ **Kansas City, Missouri:** The biggest city in the state offers fantastic barbecue and vibrant nightlife. It's conveniently close to the Oregon Trail's official starting point in Independence (page 76).

★ **Topeka, Kansas:** Trail ruts, a museum focused on the state's history, and a monument to desegregation are all great reasons to spend some time in the Kansas capital (page 90).

location 21 miles (34 km) southeast of Kansas City (1650 SW Market St., Lee's Summit, MO, 816/671-8042, 8am-5pm Mon.-Sat.) and 25 miles (40 km) northeast of St. Louis (4615 Hedge Rd., Roxana, IL, 618/254-3650, 9am-5pm Mon.-Fri., 9am-2pm Sat.). It offers styles from a truck camper that sleeps three to a large motorhome sleeping seven. For a week, expect to pay $1,300-1,600 total, depending on mileage.

Fuel and Services
Plenty of gas stations are along the route across Missouri and into Kansas. After Topeka, you'll hit smaller towns but will still find amenities every half hour or so. Note that many restaurants close on Sunday, especially in the rural areas between St. Louis and Kansas City, and along the route in northern Kansas after Topeka.

Air
The closest major airport to Independence is the **Kansas City International Airport** (MCI, 1 International Square, MO, 816/243-5237, www.flykci.com), offering nonstop service to 56 cities in the United States, Canada, Mexico, and even Iceland. It's served by Air Canada, Alaska, Allegiant, American, Delta, Frontier, Icelandair, Southwest, Spirit, and United. The airport is 15 miles (24 km) northwest of Kansas City and 30 miles (48 km) northwest of Independence. To

reach downtown Kansas City from the airport, take I-29 southeast for 13 miles (21 km) to exit 2B for U.S. 169. Continue for 1.6 miles (2.6 km), then merge onto Highway 9 into the city. The drive takes 25 minutes.

The **St. Louis Lambert International Airport** (STL, 10701 Lambert International, MO, 314/426-8000, www.flystl.com) offers nonstop service all over the United States, as well as from Canada and Mexico. Airlines include Air Canada, Alaska, American, Delta, Frontier, Southwest, and United. The airport is located about 15 miles (24 km) northwest of St. Louis and 230 miles (370 km) east of Independence. To reach downtown St. Louis from the airport, take I-70 heading east for about 14 miles (23 km) to exit 249B. The drive takes 20 minutes.

Train and Bus
The **St. Louis Gateway Station** (430 S. 15th St., 800/872-7245, 24 hours daily) is in a central downtown location and offers train and bus services. **Amtrak** (800/872-7245, www.amtrak.com) has daily service from St. Louis to Kansas City (5.75 hours, $36-58) on its *Missouri River Runner* route, while its *Texas Eagle* route runs to Chicago, Dallas, San Antonio, and Los Angeles. The station also has **Greyhound** (800/231-2222, www.greyhound.com) bus connections across the country. Popular routes run four times daily from Chicago, Indianapolis, and Kansas City.

Independence, MO

"A multitude of shops had sprung up to furnish emigrants with necessaries for the journey. The streets were thronged with men, horses, mules. There was an incessant hammering and banging from a dozen blacksmiths' sheds, where the heavy wagons were being repaired, and the horses and oxen shod."

Francis Parkman, 1847, *The Oregon Trail: Sketches of Prairie and Rocky-Mountain Life.* Parkman was a noted historian and author who traveled the Oregon Trail by horseback to Fort Laramie and wrote a lyrical and gripping personal narrative of it.

Steps away from the banks of the Missouri River, Independence sprang up to serve travelers on an earlier westward route, the Santa Fe merchant trail. Once those shops and suppliers were established, it made a strategic spot for Oregon-bound emigrants to gear up each spring. After traveling by boat for a week or so, settlers would disembark their steamboats at the landing a few miles north before shopping in Independence. The town had all the wagons, animals, clothing, rifles, food, and supplies they'd need to set out. Once a wagon train was ready, they'd gather in Independence Square before rolling out. Over 175 years after the first large wagon party (known as "The Great Migration") set out in 1843, the route from Independence is rife with proof in the form of trail swales—wagon ruts that have been overgrown with grass, making a gentle swell in the ground.

Independence is proud of its place as the beginning of the Three Trails: Santa Fe, Oregon, and California. Famous former residents of Independence include Jim Bridger, mountain man, trader, and guide; Frank and Jesse James, outlaws and local heroes; and President Harry S. Truman, who always called his hometown "the best town in the world." Today, the town is considered a satellite of Kansas City and is itself the fourth most populous city in the state. Independence Square is the heart of the town, lined with family-owned shops and restaurants that seem to hail from a quieter, quainter era.

Sights
★ Independence Square
After arriving by riverboat from St. Louis on the Missouri River, emigrants headed south to Independence to pitch camp just outside of town. In town, Main Street on Independence Square is where pioneers purchased supplies, including clothing, guns, and food. Many travelers headed west joined larger groups with experienced guides—and when the time came to depart, they would convene at the square to prepare. The Santa Fe Trail was the original route out of town, but later pioneers on the Oregon and California Trails followed the same path, all leaving from Independence Square. Today Independence Square is still the bustling heart of town, lined with a multitude of family-owned businesses. Folks "wind the clock," circling the courthouse like romantic teens of the 1950s as horse-drawn carriages escorting visitors on tours go by.

Historic Truman Courthouse
The centerpiece of Independence Square is the stately brick building that is the **Historic Truman Courthouse** (112 W. Lexington Ave., 816/881-3000, www.jchs. org, 8am-5pm Mon.-Fri., free). Originally built in 1836, it watched over wagons as they departed. A freestanding marker on the exterior west side of the courthouse commemorates the official start of the "Old Oregon Trail." Inside, you can catch a 30-minute film that tells of future president Harry Truman's time here in his hometown as the small county's judge in the 1930s. Poke around the working courthouse on your own and enjoy paintings by George Caleb Bingham, who

Independence

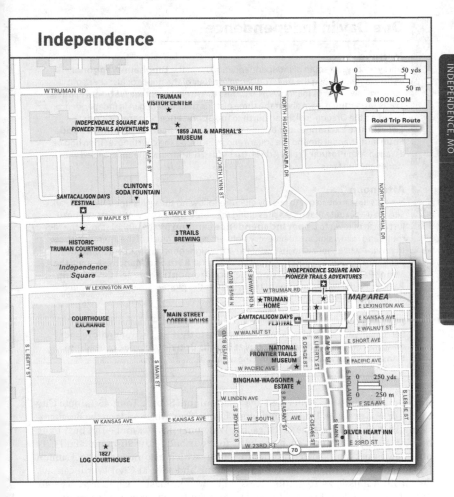

lived in Independence for a time and was known for his depictions of frontier life, or take a guided tour (11am and 2pm Tues.-Fri., free). Guides provide information on local history and the courthouse's paintings, and tell charming stories of Truman's life and work.

1827 Log Courthouse

The **1827 Log Courthouse** (107 W. Kansas, 816/325-7111, 10am-2pm Mon.-Fri., free) was the first government building in the county and the only courthouse between St. Louis and the Pacific when it

was built. As the country began to push west, cases here included land disputes, slave ownership issues, and other growing pains of the expanding territory. The building has been preserved, and visitors can enter to see the rough-hewn log walls and stone fireplaces that made up the early courtroom.

1859 Jail & Marshal's Museum

See how frontier justice was served at the **1859 Jail & Marshal's Museum** (217 N. Main St., 816/252-1892, www.jchs.org, 10am-4pm Mon.-Sat., 1pm-4pm Sun.

One Day in Independence

Morning
Start your day just south of Independence Square at the **Bingham-Waggoner Estate,** a house along the trail. You can take a tour of the house or just check out some trail swales in its meadows. Next, cross the street to visit the **National Frontier Trails Museum** to learn about the three historic trails that began in Independence, including the Oregon Trail. Head north to **Independence Square** for lunch at **Courthouse Exchange,** and be sure to save room for a sundae at **Clinton's Soda Fountain.** Wander around the square and peek inside the courthouse. Then hop on a wagon with **Pioneer Trails Adventures** for a ride around the square filled with stories and fun facts.

Afternoon
Next it's time to head out to nearby environs following the well-signed National Park Service (NPS) route that traces sites along the Three Trails. Completionists can head just north of town to **Upper Independence Landing** for the official start of the NPS route, and follow signage to hit every sight—it will take much of the afternoon to see them all—while those who just want to hit the highlights can head out from Independence Square. The best trail ruts can be seen at **85th and Manchester** and the **Minor Park/Blue River Crossing.** The **Rice-Tremonti Home** and **Cave Spring Park** along the way were some of the first spots the pioneers might have stopped at on their way west.

Evening
For dinner, you can head back to Independence to try the salmon at **Vivilore** and toast your first day on the Oregon Trail at **3 Trails Brewing,** or you can head into **Kansas City,** a lively place to spend the night.

Apr.-Oct., $6 adults, $5 seniors, $3 ages 6-16, free under age 6). Huge iron doors swing shut on 12 limestone cells, each holding countless stories, such as that of outlaw Frank James, older brother to Jesse, and Confederate raider William Quantrill. Admission also grants access to the house next door, historically home to the marshal and his family.

TOP EXPERIENCE

★ Pioneer Trails Adventures
There's no better way to kick off your Oregon Trail journey than with a ride in a covered wagon with **Pioneer Trails Adventures** (217 N. Main St., 816/254-2466, www.pioneertrailsadventures. com, 9am-4:30pm Mon.-Sat. Mar.-Dec., $10-35 over age 12, $7 children). Three different tours cover historical sights in and around Independence Square: the 20-minute Square Tour; 45-minute City Limits Tour, which adds on the Bingham-Waggoner Estate; and—the best bang for your buck—the 90-minute Full City Tour, which also includes the Truman Home and several Civil War locations. The wagon master, who serves as your tour guide, regales you with stories from Independence's past as you pass trail swales, traveling on the actual route that emigrants on the Santa Fe, California, and Oregon Trails followed out of town on their very first day on the trail.

While your wagon will be pulled by horses, oxen, or mules (in fact, the mule is Missouri's state animal), mules were preferred by the pioneers. Horses needed too much water and feed to guarantee survival out in harsher lands.

Tours departs from the parking lot one block north of Independence Square, across from the 1859 Jail & Marshal's

Independence Square Congestion

Independence was the most popular jumping-off point in the early years of the Oregon Trail: Every spring, the small town boomed with commerce as pioneers poured in and then out. They had to time their travels strategically, leaving late enough to ensure melted snow and enough grass for livestock along the way but early enough to make it to Oregon before winter. Late April-early May was usually the best time. Encampments of early arrivals preparing to head out during this peak travel time set up just outside of town, and often swelled to over three square miles.

When a wagon train was getting ready to leave, everyone would mount up in Independence Square. Hundreds of families packing wagons and convincing new oxen to heed them (or learning how to yoke them in the first place) led to chaos. People who had never driven wagons before couldn't get their animals to go in the right direction, or bumped into other wagons or trees. Many tipped over, creating messes and traffic jams. Once on the road, wagons didn't necessarily follow each other—many spread out on either side on the flat prairies, hoping to avoid dust and inexperienced drivers.

Museum, on the corner of Truman Road and Main Street. A wagon with a "Pioneer Trails Adventures" sign marks the spot.

National Frontier Trails Museum

You'll be primed for your own adventure on the trail after the fantastic introduction provided by the **National Frontier Trails Museum** (318 W. Pacific Ave., 816/325-7575, www.ci.independence. mo.us/nftm, 9am-4:30pm Mon.-Sat., 12:30pm-4:30pm Sun., $6 adults, $5 seniors, $3 ages 6-17, free under age 6). It commemorates the three westward expansion trails that began in Independence: the Santa Fe, Oregon, and California Trails. The stories of the trails are told through emigrant and traveler quotes. You'll find artifacts, covered wagons, illustrations, hands-on activities, and an award-winning 17-minute film, *West*. The museum also houses the largest archives of pioneer diaries anywhere.

You can also get a combination ticket ($16) for a covered-wagon ride with Pioneer Trails Adventures at the museum's entrance.

Bingham-Waggoner Estate

One of the most prominent houses at the start of the trail, the **Bingham-Waggoner Estate** (313 W. Pacific Ave., 816/461-3491, www.bwestate.net, 10am-4pm Mon.-Sat.,

1pm-4pm Sun. Apr.-Oct., $6 adults, $5 seniors, $3 ages 6-16) was built in 1852 right along the route of the Santa Fe and Oregon Trails. In 1864 famous Missouri painter George Caleb Bingham bought the house, and he painted many of his most popular works here before it was sold to the Waggoner flour milling family, who owned it for 100 years. A fascinating hour-long tour takes visitors through the large Victorian house, which is full of furniture and decor that belonged to the Waggoner family. See the piano that Harry Truman played when he visited them, and spy an original baseball board game—one of only 10 in the world. Whether you tour the estate or not, it's free to wander the adjoining grounds; take a short walk over the creek near the parking lot to see trail swales in the meadow, proof of the wagons passing by the house on their first day west.

Harry S. Truman National Historic Site

Independence was the hometown of the United States' 33rd president, Harry S. Truman. He once said of his favorite town, "It's just as good a place as there is, and they don't make them any better." Today, Independence is proud of its place in that spotlight, and happily shows visitors anything

The Three Trails

Independence is known as the jumping-off point for three historic trails. Each followed the same route out of town and split off at later points: the Santa Fe just outside of Kansas City, and the California at various points, mostly in Idaho.

♦ **Santa Fe Trail (1821-1880):** The original trail west, the Santa Fe Trail was a commercial venture, busy with merchant traffic. It headed from Missouri across the Southwest to Santa Fe, where merchants could meet up with others who came north from Mexico. Traffic transporting goods went in both directions on the trail.

♦ **Oregon Trail (1843-1869):** The Oregon Trail was the main route that led thousands of emigrants from Missouri to Oregon City, 2,000 miles (3,200 km) west. Unlike the Santa Fe Trail and earlier routes used by trappers and explorers, the Oregon Trail was mostly used by families: men, women, and children who uprooted their lives to move west in hopes of a better life.

♦ **California Trail (1841-1869):** The California Trail stretches a little farther than the Oregon Trail, at about 3,000 miles (4,800 km). After gold was discovered in the state in 1848, miners rushed the trail over the next year to strike it rich. Known as the 49ers, they stayed on the path with their Oregon-bound cohorts until eastern Idaho, when they dipped southwest into Nevada to cross the Sierra Nevada mountain range into California. Unlike emigrants on the Oregon Trail, pioneers headed to California didn't have a main terminus—most spread out across the valleys looking for gold.

that Truman touched. Start out with a visit to the **Harry S. Truman National Historic Site Visitor Center** (223 N. Main St., 816/254-9929, www.nps.gov/hstr, 8am-5pm daily, free), just north of Independence Square, where you can watch an orientation film and see some artifacts. The visitors center is also the place to get tickets to tour the **Truman Home** (219 N. Delaware St., 8am-5pm Tues.-Sun. Nov. 1-Memorial Day, free), located five blocks west. This is the house that Harry Truman and his wife, Bess, lived in before, during, and after his presidency, from 1919 until his death in 1972. Tours last about an hour and are first-come, first-served. A guide takes you through the home.

Down the street, about a 20-minute walk north from the Truman Home, the **Harry S. Truman Library and Museum** (500 W. U.S. 24, 816/268-8200, www.trumanlibrary.gov, 9am-5pm Mon.-Sat., noon-5pm Sun., $8 adults, $7 seniors, $3 ages 6-15, free under age 6) encompasses

the president's official library and his grave site. Exhibits showcase moments in his presidency, as well as a broader range of his life and family history. One of the highlights is an exhibition of letters between Harry and Bess Truman over the years, offering an intimate glimpse into their personal lives.

Upper Independence Landing

There's not a lot to see here today, but the **Wayne City Landing** (1630 Wayne City Rd.), once called the **Upper Independence Landing,** is where Missouri riverboats would offload settlers who would then make their way 3 miles (4.8 km) south to Independence to buy supplies. Today the actual landing site is overrun by industrial buildings, but an overlook off Wayne City Road has an informational plaque near a short walking path along the bluff. This is also the official starting point of the NPS's Auto Route. From here, you can easily follow well-placed NPS signs to Independence

Square and continue onward to numerous trail sights.

From Independence Square, head north on Liberty Street for 2.7 miles (4.3 km). Turn left on Kentucky Road. In 0.5 mile (0.8 km), turn right on River Road, then make a quick slight left onto Wayne City Road. The landing is on the left in 0.2 mile (0.3 km).

Entertainment and Events
Brewpubs
Right on the square is **3 Trails Brewing** (111 N. Main St., 816/886-6256, www.3trailsbrewing.com, 4pm-midnight Mon. and Thurs.-Fri., noon-midnight Sat., noon-7pm Sun.), named for the Oregon, California, and Santa Fe Trails that originated just steps away. The brewery has 10 taps and offers a range of styles, with trail-inspired names like What a Ride, Trail Dragger, and Cali Ruoh. The space is fresh and the service friendly. No food is served, but you're welcome to bring your own.

TOP EXPERIENCE

★ SantaCaliGon Days Festival
The **SantaCaliGon Days Festival** (Independence Square, www.santacaligon.com, Labor Day weekend, free), is one of the oldest and biggest events in the area, attracting over 300,000 people each year over Labor Day weekend in September to celebrate the beginning of the Santa Fe, California, and Oregon Trails. The four-day festival has a carnival with a Ferris wheel and other rides, entertainment at two stages around the square, and 450 arts, crafts, and food booths. The fun evokes the pioneer era with gold panning, old-time photos, crafts like rope-making, a quilt show, and a root beer chugging contest.

Top to bottom: plaque marking the start of the Oregon Trail; inside the Bingham-Waggoner Estate; National Frontier Trails Museum.

Food

Taste a presidential dessert at **Clinton Soda's Fountain** (100 W. Maple Ave., 816/833-2046, www. clintonssodafountain.com, 11am-6pm Mon.-Sat., $6). Harry Truman worked his first job here when it was a drugstore, right across the street from the courthouse he would later preside in. Today, the soda fountain still sells old-fashioned phosphates—an effervescent soft drink—as well as sundaes, ice cream, and malts. Order Harry's Favorite, chocolate ice cream topped with butterscotch, or try Polly's Pop, a local soda made down the street in flavors like black cherry, pineapple, or glazed doughnut.

Courthouse Exchange (113 W. Lexington, 816/252-0344, www. courthouseexchange.com, 11am-9pm Mon.-Thurs., 11am-10pm Fri.-Sat., $10) is a cozy bar-restaurant below street level directly across from the courthouse. Choose from one of three burgers named after each of the trails (the Oregon burger features pulled pork, coleslaw, and fried pickles), a giant fried chicken platter, and a large variety of sandwiches. On the walls are pictures of the courthouse as it has changed over the years.

A 10-minute drive west of Independence Square, **Vivilore** (10815 E. Winner Rd., 816/836-2222, www.vivilore. com, 11am-9pm Tues.-Sat., $18) wows diners with its sumptuous meals, storied antiques, and high-end art. Enjoy dining on salmon, lobster rolls, beef tenderloin, or ancho pork chops in the ivy-covered building or its picturesque courtyard. After your meal, wander through the antiques shop and gallery space on the upper floors of the building to find something special. Reservations are recommended.

Main Street Coffee House (107 S. Main St., 816/503-8388, www.mainstreetcoffeehouse.com, 7:30am-7pm Mon.-Fri., 8:30am-7pm Sat., $3) is just off the square in the southeast corner. Inside the charming storefront is a large wooden counter and plenty of comfortable seats. Start the morning off with a range of hot and iced coffee drinks, including seasonal specials, or smoothies, teas, and hot chocolate. Add something sweet to your pour-over, like a muffin or cookie, or enjoy heartier morning options like quiche, oatmeal, or a breakfast burrito.

Accommodations

The **Silver Heart Inn** (1114 S. Noland Rd., 816/838-9508, http://silverheartinn.com, $115-175) owes its existence to Napolian Stone, a merchant who made his fortune equipping the pioneers headed west. Instead of following the trails himself, he stuck around and built a house in 1856, which today offers three guest rooms and two single-room cottages along with decadent breakfasts starring seasonal dishes. An open-air hot tub adds to the romance. The bed-and-breakfast is a 20-minute walk south of Independence Square.

Located just off I-70 a short drive from the square, **Stoney Creek Hotel** (18011 Bass Pro Dr., 816/908-8600, www. stoneycreekhotels.com, $180-255) has 167 guest rooms that range from king suites to bunk beds. The rustic fireplace in the lobby welcomes travelers to a good night's rest, and the on-site whiskey bar, indoor pool, and hot breakfast adds to the experience.

Along the Trail from Independence to Kansas City

Wagons leaving Independence on the trails headed south before veering southwest and entering the frontier. This was mainly due to geography, and the need to find easy river crossings when tackling the Blue River, among others. The pioneers were leaving the United States behind when they crossed the Missouri border—everything beyond was unregulated territories. The first few days and weeks were likely a time of getting to know their wagons and fellow emigrants, and becoming more comfortable camping and traveling. The prairie provided an easy introduction to the road, and many found it a joyous and exciting time as they struck forth.

When leaving Independence, look for the brown NPS signs to follow this route, which is excellently marked and easy to follow. The 22-mile (35-km) route takes you from Independence south through the suburb of Raytown, then continues southeast to the border of Kansas and Missouri, ending south of Kansas City. It takes just 1 hour to drive, but allow 2-3 hours to cover these notable stops.

Santa Fe Trail Park

Faint trail swales are visible at **Santa Fe Trail Park** (2900 S. Santa Fe Rd., Independence, 5am-midnight daily). The grassy ruts are about 0.25 mile (0.4 km) long and marked by stone columns along Santa Fe Terrace Road. Today, this 45-acre park also features modern amenities like a skateboarding park and picnic tables with barbecue grills.

Getting There

From Independence Square, head south on Noland Road and turn right at the intersection with 23rd Street. In 0.5 mile (0.8 km), turn left onto McCoy Street, which becomes Santa Fe Road. In another 0.5 mile (0.8 km), turn left into the park entrance. After the entrance, watch for a grove of trees in a depression to the right to see the swales. The park is a seven-minute drive from Independence.

Rice-Tremonti Home

The **Rice-Tremonti Home** (8801 E. 66th St., Raytown, 816/358-7423, www.ricetremonti.org, by appointment, free) is in a beautiful white 1844 Gothic Revival farmhouse. Many emigrants' diaries from the trails mention the Rice home, where they were met with generous hospitality: Wagons often camped on the farm, and the family offered bacon, fresh eggs, and milk. Today you can tour the home, as well as "Aunt Sophie's Cabin," which served as living quarters for the family's enslaved workers.

Getting There

From Santa Fe Trail Park, head west on West 31st Street, then left onto Crysler Avenue. Continue on it for 1.5 miles (2.4 km), then turn right onto East 43rd Street. In 0.3 mile (0.4 km), turn left onto Blue Ridge Boulevard and stay on it for 3.1 miles (4.9 km). Turn right on East 63rd Street. In 0.5 mile (0.8 km), turn left onto Elm Avenue, making a right at the first cross street, Blue Ridge Boulevard again. In 0.3 mile (0.4 km), turn left onto Lane Avenue, making a slight right onto East 66th Street. The Rice-Tremonti Home is in 0.2 mile (0.3 km) on your left. The drive takes 15 minutes.

Cave Spring Park

Many wagon trains on all three trails made their first night's camp at **Cave Spring Park** (8701 E. Gregory Blvd., Raytown, 816/659 1945, www.cavespring.org, dawn-dusk daily, free) roughly 10 miles (16 km) from Independence Square. Several pioneer diaries mention the site of the Barnes Enclosure, where owner Jesse Barnes allowed pioneers to camp on his land near

Overpacking on the Trail

Pioneers had a few wagon options when embarking on a long journey. While the Conestoga is well-known and a classic example of a covered wagon—used for transporting heavy goods and military supplies—they were actually too large and unwieldy to use easily on the rough trails, and most pioneers used smaller but sturdier Studebaker wagons. Emigrants had to pack everything they needed, both for their long journey and new lives in Oregon, in a wagon box measuring about 4 by 10 feet with a 1,000-pound capacity. To maximize packing space, most emigrants actually walked alongside their wagons the entire way.

Common items brought along for the journey included food, baking soda,

National Frontier Trails Museum

clothing, rifles, tools, and furniture. But soon after rolling out of Independence, emigrants realized the burden their heavy possessions would be on their oxen and mules. The first dozen miles (20 km) out of town was a veritable junkyard of debris as emigrants quickly lightened their loads and jettisoned heavy butter churns, extra cast-iron pans, chairs, and, in one instance, a piano! Scavengers from town gathered the supplies and brought them back to sell.

> "In procuring supplies for this journey, the emigrant should provide himself with, at least 200 pounds of flour, 150 pounds of bacon, ten pounds of coffee, twenty pounds of sugar, and ten pounds of salt."
>
> Lansford Hastings, 1845, *The Emigrants' Guide to Oregon and California.*
> Hastings wrote one of the earliest guidebooks of the trail, which later become notorious for promoting a spurious shortcut to California, the Hastings Cutoff, which led the Donner Party to tragedy.

the spring and welcomed them into his home. The house itself burned down in 1925, leaving only the stone chimney behind. The chimney and namesake spring inside a cave can still be found on the premises; a walk on the 0.8-mile (1.3-km) **Chimney Trail Loop** that starts at the **interpretive center** (open by appointment) takes you to it. Other easy trails also loop through the park; maps are posted on kiosks near the parking lot.

Getting There

From the Rice-Tremonti Home, continue just a few minutes south on Blue Ridge Boulevard, for 0.6 mile (1 km),

then turn right onto Gregory Boulevard. The parking lot to the park—also known as William M. Klein Park—is on the left.

85th and Manchester Trail Ruts/Wieduwilt Swales

Sometimes referred to as the **Wieduwilt Swales,** hidden in a residential neighborhood in Kansas City, Missouri, at **85th and Manchester,** on the corner of a lot, are some of the state's best ruts, deep and easy to see, dramatically cutting into the ground. The NPS signs direct you here, and a small interpretive panel offers some history on the Oregon, California, and Santa Fe Trails.

Getting There

From Cave Spring Park, continue south on Blue Ridge Boulevard. In 0.8 mile (1.2 km), take a slight right to stay on the road. In another 0.9 mile (1.4 km), turn right onto East 83rd Street, then make the first left onto Manchester Avenue. The road comes to a bend, and you'll find the ruts in the corner lot after the five-minute drive.

Schumacher Park

A pavilion at **Schumacher Park** (6601 E. 93rd St., Kansas City, MO, 5am-midnight daily) has panels that describe the experience of the Oregon, California, and Santa Fe Trails. The meadow surrounding the pavilion is a revitalized native grassland, full of tall grass and seasonal wildflowers like black-eyed Susans, butterfly milkweed, and coneflowers, offering a glimpse of the prairie pioneers might've experienced when they rolled through. Grass was vital to the emigrants, as they needed it to feed their animals—this section of prairie grasses and sedges was planted in recent years expressly to help visitors understand the terrain.

Getting There

From the 85th and Manchester Trail Ruts, continue west and turn left onto Oldham Road. In 0.3 mile (0.5 km), turn right onto East 87th Street. In 0.7 mile (1.1 km), turn left onto Hillcrest Road, then continue 0.8 mile (1.2 km) through two traffic circles to take another left onto 93rd Street. Continue for 0.4 mile (0.6 km) to Schumacher Park. It's a five-minute drive.

★ Minor Park/Blue River Crossing

Some of the most dramatic and easily accessible swales you can see at the beginning of the trail are at **Minor Park** (12235

Top to bottom: *Heading out of Independence* by Charles Goslin; 85th and Manchester; Cave Spring Park.

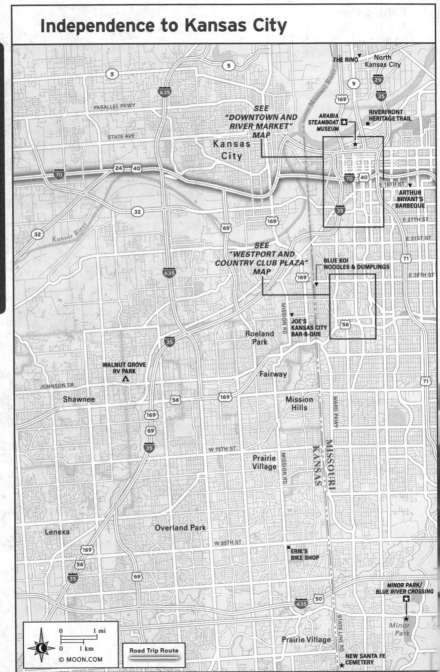

Independence to Kansas City

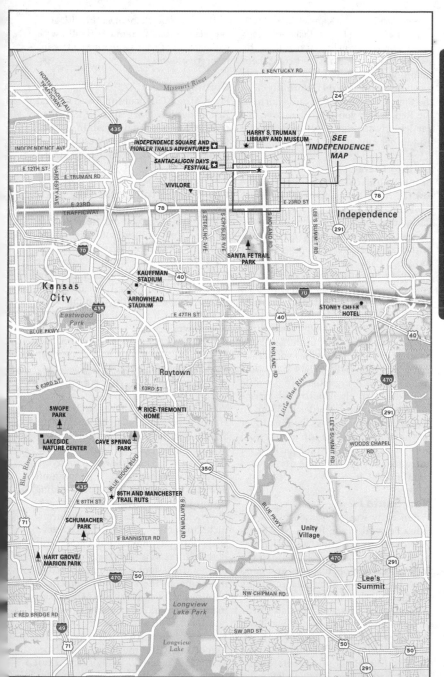

E. Red Bridge Rd., Kansas City, MO). From the parking lot, it's just a few steps to interpretive panels that overlook the swales—you can clearly see two of them spanning the park. This is where wagons on all three trails would historically cross the Blue River, about 300 yards north of the Red Bridge you just drove over. It's particularly striking to see swales in the middle of a city.

Getting There
From Schumacher Park, you can follow the NPS signage to check out **Hart Grove/Marion Park** on the way to Minor Park, but there isn't much to see besides some stone columns marking the path of the trail; I suggest skipping straight to Minor Park. To do so, head east on East 93rd Street for 0.3 mile (0.4 km) and take a right onto Old Santa Fe Road. In 0.2 mile (0.3 km), turn right onto Blue Ridge Boulevard and drive 1 mile (1.9 km), where you'll turn right to merge onto I-470. Stay in the left lane, because in 0.8 mile (1.2 km) you'll take exit 1A for U.S. 71. Stay right and follow signs for Red Bridge Road. In 0.9 mile (1.4 km), turn right onto Red Bridge Road, then drive 2.3 miles (3.7 km) to Minor Park. You'll cross the Blue River on the old Red Bridge—in another 0.3 mile (0.4 km), you'll find a parking lot entrance on your left. The drive takes 10 minutes.

New Santa Fe
When early wagons passed by on the Santa Fe Trail in the 1820s, New Santa Fe didn't exist yet, and the location was simply a nice place to camp along the trail, with wide-open spaces and good grass for livestock. Soon a cabin sprang up, then another, and by the 1840s the village called New Santa Fe had stores, an inn, a saloon, and a post office. It was the last stop in settled land—many pioneers on the three trails bought their last sip of whiskey in the saloon before striking out farther west. All that's left today

of the small settlement is the villagers' **cemetery** (902 W. Santa Fe Trail), with some views of trail swales and a few interpretive signs.

Getting There
From Minor Park, continue west on East Red Bridge Road for 1 mile (1.6 km), then turn left onto Wornall Road. In 1.1 mile (1.7 km), turn right onto West Santa Fe Trail. The cemetery is on the right in 0.7 mile (1.1 km).

Continuing to Kansas City
This is the last stop on this section of the route. From here you can head back to Independence, a 30-minute drive northeast via I-435 and Highway 12 if you drive there directly, or move on to Kansas City for the night. For Kansas City, continue west on Santa Fe Trail, turning right on State Line Road; the road takes you to I-435, which you can take to I-71 for downtown.

Alternate Starting Point: St. Louis, MO

While the official Oregon National Historic Trail begins in Independence, St. Louis makes a convenient and appropriate starting point for those with a little more time. The Gateway to the West, as the city is known, was a jumping-off point for traders and fur trappers heading west prior to the Oregon Trail and seeking their fortunes, as well as explorers, including Lewis and Clark. Music helped shaped the city into the blues crossroads of the nation, as jazz and ragtime drifted up the Mississippi and found a welcoming home. In the 1950s, the hometown legends of Chuck Berry and Miles Davis made their mark. St. Louis today remembers its place in pioneer history with the elegant Gateway Arch and is known for barbecue and live music including blues and jazz. You could easily spend a full week enjoying all the city has to offer,

St. Louis

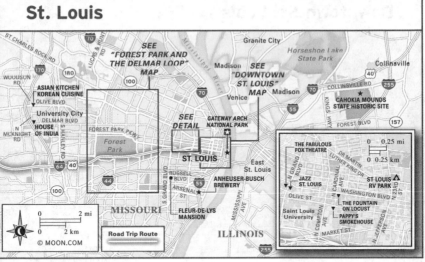

but don't dally too long—the Oregon Trail calls.

Getting There and Around

St. Louis is within manageable driving distance of many central and eastern U.S. cities. Drive from Chicago or Memphis via I-55; Louisville, Kentucky, via I-64; or Indianapolis via I-70. Amtrak trains and Greyhound buses connect to the **St. Louis Gateway Station** (430 S. 15th St., 800/872-7245, 24 hours daily). Flights are available from a variety of U.S. cities to **St. Louis Lambert International Airport** (STL, 10701 Lambert International, 314/426-8000, www.flystl.com). From the airport, you can get downtown on light-rail service via **MetroLink** (www.metrostlouis.org, 4am-1am, $4), which takes about 40 minutes and run approximately every 20 minutes.

Attractions in the city are in largely walkable neighborhoods. A trolley system, **Metro Downtown Trolley** (www.metrostlouis.org, 5am-midnight Mon.-Fri., 7am-midnight Sat., 11am-6:30pm Sun., $2 adults, $1 seniors and ages 5-12, free under age 5), runs every 20 minutes and serves the downtown area with colorful buses that loop to connect Union Station, the City Museum, and more. The **Forest Park Explorer** (www.stladventurepass.com, Mon.-Fri. $2 adults, $1 seniors and children, Sat.-Sun. free) offers access to various attractions in the park as well as the nearby Delmar Loop district. It runs spring-summer 15-30 minutes on weekdays and every 15 minutes on weekends (9am-7pm daily May-Aug.). **Uber** (www.uber.com) and **Lyft** (www.lyft.com) also operate in St. Louis.

Orientation
Downtown

Downtown St. Louis is a tight one square mile, bordered on its western edge by Tucker Boulevard, on its north by Cole Street, and on its south by Chouteau Avenue. It's full of skyscrapers and office workers as well as hotels and restaurants, and the recently revamped Mississippi riverfront along Gateway Arch National Park on its eastern side.

Downtown West, still considered part of downtown, stretches west (of course) another square mile to Jefferson Avenue. It's characterized by tall skyscrapers that

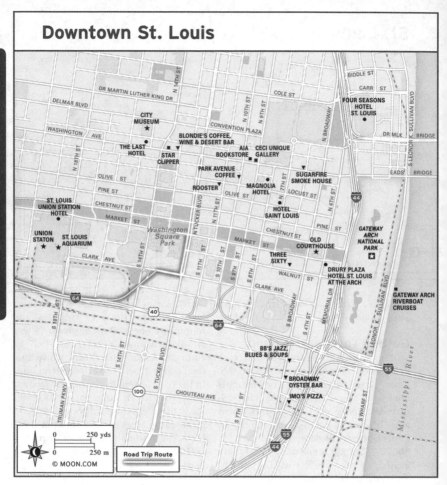

Downtown St. Louis

give way to industrial buildings, like the funky City Museum. Elegant Union Station is here, and walkable Washington Avenue is lined with shops.

Midtown/Grand Center

Midtown is the neighborhood immediately west of Downtown West, and its northern neighbor is Grand Center. Here, about 3 miles (4.8 km) inland from the mighty river, visitors find great food, music, and more, with standout restaurants like Pappy's Smokehouse and The Fountain on Locust, and entertainment

offerings such as Jazz St. Louis and The Fabulous Fox Theatre. Vandeventer Avenue to its west forms its border with the Central West End.

Central West End

The Central West End, neighboring Midtown, is a walkable part of town that includes stately homes and vibrant restaurants and shops. You're steps away from the jewel that is Forest Park. The neighborhood is bounded by Delmar Boulevard to the north and I-64 to the south.

Two Days in St. Louis

Day 1

Start your morning with popovers at **Blondie's Coffee, Wine & Dessert Bar,** then stroll over to **Gateway Arch National Park** for a morning of exploration. Enjoy the excellent **Museum at the Gateway Arch** right beneath the arch itself, which looks into the role St. Louis played in the westward expansion of the United States. Then take the **Tram Ride to the Top** of the arch to enjoy views overlooking the mighty Mississippi on one side and the city on the other. Afterward, walk across the park to the **Old Courthouse** to visit the site where Dred Scott, an enslaved man, sued for his freedom. When you're done, get some St. Louis barbecue at **Sugarfire Smokehouse.** After lunch, kids and kids

the Gateway Arch

at heart will love exploring the creative tunnels and slides at **City Museum,** and beer fans will enjoy a tour of the **Anheuser-Busch Brewery.** Get dinner at **Imo's Pizza** to try St. Louis's version of the pie. Rest up, then head out for some late-night blues at **BB's Jazz, Blues & Soups.**

Day 2

Breakfast this morning is a sweet treat: traditional St. Louis gooey butter cake from **Park Avenue Coffee.** Or if eggs are more up your alley, order some excellent ones at **Rooster.** Drive just outside of town to **Cahokia Mounds State Historic Site** to explore the mysterious city of mounds built by the Mississippian people centuries ago. Spend some time at the interpretive center, then wander around the mounds themselves. Head back to town for tacos with freshly made tortillas at **Mission Taco Joint** in the bustling **Delmar Loop** district, which is great for a post-lunch stroll. From here you can walk to **Forest Park,** where you can choose your own adventure, whether you're interested in visiting a museum or getting active by biking or paddling. Grab dinner or a late-night bite at **The Fountain on Locust,** before or after a show at the nearby **Fabulous Fox Theatre.**

Delmar Loop

Delmar Loop is a cultural entertainment district just north of Forest Park. The main stretch is a walkable six blocks, full of over 100 restaurants, music venues, shops, and businesses, on Delmar Boulevard between Kingsland and Des Peres Avenues.

Sights

★ Gateway Arch National Park

Reopened in 2018 after a long renovation, **Gateway Arch National Park** (11 N. 4th St., 314/655-1600, www.gatewayarch.com, 8am-10pm daily summer, 9am-6pm daily winter, free), formerly known as the Jefferson National Expansion Memorial, encompasses a revamped museum, the Old Courthouse, and 91 acres of beautifully landscaped park fronting the Mississippi River. The park was designated in 1935 by the NPS to commemorate Jefferson's vision of a country stretching west, and to honor St. Louis's role as the Gateway to the West. The arch—designed by Finnish architect Eero

Saarinen—was completed in 1965 and gave a defined form to the mythical "gateway." Constructed of steel and concrete, the arch rises 630 feet (192 m) high, and is the tallest constructed monument in the country. The elegant curves are reflected in the landscape below, which features gently undulating hills and reflecting pools. An Explorer's Garden showcases plants that Lewis and Clark encountered on their expedition. Access to the park, museum, and courthouse is free.

Museum at the Gateway Arch

Head directly under the Gateway Arch to find the **Museum at the Gateway Arch** (8am-10pm daily summer, 9am-6pm daily winter, free). The entrance is just past a reflecting pool and fountain that makes a great place to splash on a hot day. Once inside, start in the mezzanine at the giant terrazzo map on the floor where you can trace the routes of several westward paths, including the Oregon Trail. The museum contains six large exhibit rooms that offer a thoughtful look at St. Louis and the role it played in the United States' westward push. Part of the museum's renovation efforts concentrated on confronting the problematic aspects of the concept of Manifest Destiny, the expansionist belief, popular in the 19th century, that the United States had a God-given right to stretch across the continent and spread their own values and way of life. Attendant complexities and the aftermath are examined in the new museum exhibits, offering viewpoints from the perspective of Native Americans and free and enslaved African Americans, as well as Mexico, which also had a large historical stake in the West.

Tram Ride to the Top

The **Tram Ride to the Top** (8am-10pm daily summer, 9am-6pm daily winter, $12 adults, $8 ages 3-15) is a fun way to get a bird's-eye view of the city. Futuristic five-person pods—not for the claustrophobic—zoom you to the top of the Gateway Arch in four minutes, where views of the city through the small windows can stretch as far as 30 miles (48 km) on a clear day. The trams are a popular attraction, and tickets sell out quickly. Purchase them online (www.gatewayarch.com) a few days prior, especially in spring and summer. The last tram leaves one hour before the park's closing.

You'll walk through the museum to access the tram, so plan to arrive at the park at least 1.5 hours before your ticket entrance to allow time to see it first; while you could wander the museum afterward, it's a nice introduction. There's a large waiting area in the lobby of the tramway, and a café serving burgers, sandwiches, and salads if you get hungry while waiting.

There's also an optional documentary about the arch, **Monument to the Dream** ($7 adults, $3 ages 3-15), that explains more about the history and design process of the park. Various tram combination tickets can save you money if you bundle activities together. For example, the **See Everything Combo** ($32 adults, $18 ages 3-15) includes the tram ride and documentary, as well as a one-hour riverboat cruise that departs from the arch.

Old Courthouse

Missouri entered the Union in 1821 as a slave state, and the **Old Courthouse** (8am-4:30pm daily, free) once hosted sales of enslaved people on its front steps. In 1846, husband-and-wife Dred and Harriet Scott filed separate petitions—later rolled into one by the courts—at the then St. Louis Courthouse, now the Old Courthouse, for their freedom. The case stretched on for 10 years. Finally, in 1857, the Supreme Court ruled that the Scotts and, by extension, all African Americans, were not citizens, and had no rights or privileges—instead of settling the matter, the ruling became a tipping point as the already divided nation descended into Civil War.

An exhibit inside the Old Courthouse

today dives into the struggles of the era and the events leading up to Dred Scott's historic actions. A monument outside the steps of the courthouse depicts Dred and Harriet Scott together, holding hands, facing Gateway Arch. The courthouse also plans to host more local history exhibits in the upcoming years.

City Museum

All your childhood dreams will come true at **City Museum** (750 N. 16th St., 314/231-2489, www.citymuseum.org, 9am-5pm Mon.-Thurs., 9am-midnight Fri.-Sat., 11am-5pm Sun., $16, free under age 3). Housed in an old shoelace factory, this quirky "museum" repurposes architectural and industrial materials from around the city and transforms them into a funhouse playground for the young and young at heart. Wander the space via sculptural stairs and tunnels. Walk through a dragon's mouth. Climb a tree fort and check out the wire castle. Don't miss the 10-story tall slide, the caves system, or the whale room. In the spring and summer, the rooftop hosts a giant Ferris wheel, as well as more slides and tunnels. Whether you have kids or not, this is a must-do while you're in town.

Dress wisely: Long pants make the slides more comfortable, close-toed shoes are required, and a flashlight might be helpful. The museum sells kneepads at the entrance ($6), and they definitely come in handy! Five restaurants on-site serve quick bites like pizza, hot dogs, sandwiches, and cotton candy. Consider going after 5pm Friday-Saturday to beat some of the kiddo crowds. Parking is available in the lot ($10, cash only).

Top to bottom: a covered wagon inside the Museum at the Gateway Arch; the inner dome of the Old Courthouse; Dred and Harriet Scott statue by sculptor Harry Weber in front of the Old Courthouse.

Union Station

"As we plodded our weary way we little expected or realized that many of us would live to see the day when a railroad would be built across that wild, wild country."

B. F. Nichols, 1844, *Across the Plains in 1844: Reminisces of Oregon.* Nichols made it to the area near Salem, Oregon, and published an account of his journey in 1906.

With the construction of the railroad, trains made cross-country travel much more accessible than overland wagon routes. After 1866, those who could afford to bought train tickets for a quick 10-day trip out West rather than an arduous months-long journey. Soon, train travel became an elegant way to cross the country, and St. Louis's **Union Station** (1820 Market St., 314/231-1234, www.stlouisunionstation.com) was one of the most luxurious stations around.

Rail operations continued until 1978, after which the station fell into disrepair. Since then, the former rail station has seen a huge revitalization. Peek into the **Grand Hall**—now part of the Union Station Hotel's lobby and bar—featuring mosaics and stained-glass windows—for a glimpse of this elegance.

If you're around in the evening, catch the fantastic **Grand Hall Experience,** a 3-D light show projected on the lobby's ceiling hourly 5pm-10pm. The free seven-minute show is a work of art featuring flowers, whales, history vignettes, and faux fireworks. Near the entrance on the north side of the building, check out the **Whispering Arch**—discovered when a 1890s worker dropped a hammer under the arch and was heard on the other side of the station. Outside, near Union Station's small lake, you can also enjoy the free breathtaking **Fire and Light Show** (12:30pm, 1:30pm, and hourly 5pm-9pm daily), featuring 25-foot fire plumes, waterfalls, and lights, set to music.

Cahokia Mounds State Historic Site

Newer attractions, replacing a dying 1980s mall incarnation from the recent past, include a giant Ferris wheel, a miniature golf course, a ropes course, dining and shopping, and the **St. Louis Aquarium** (201 S. 18th St., www. stlouisaquarium.com, 10am-6pm daily, $25 adults, $18 ages 3-12), opened in 2019. It houses 13,000 animals, including otters, deep-sea jellyfish, and sharks.

Anheuser-Busch Brewery

Founded in 1852 in St. Louis, **Anheuser-Busch Brewery** (12th St. and Lynch St., 314/577-2626, www.budweisertours. com, tours 11am-4:30pm daily Nov.-Feb., 10am-5pm daily Mar.-Oct.)—maker of Budweiser—has since grown into an international brand. Its **General Brewery Tour** (free) lasts 45 minutes, allowing you to see the brewing process and take a look at the Clydesdale horses, a popular breed known for pulling heavy loads (in this case, historically, beer wagons). The 1.25-hour **Day Fresh Tour** ($10) also shows you the aging cellar and packaging facility. You can get a taste directly from the finishing tank on the 2-hour **Beermaster Tour** (ages 13 and over, $35). Perhaps the best tour for those interested in the brewery history is the **Horses & Heritage Tour** ($25), which focuses on the Clydesdale horses—you can even pet one!—and then guides you into the 1850s-era Schoolhouse Museum to peek into the Anheuser-Busch archives. A sample is also included in this tour. Tours are offered multiple times daily. Walk-in tickets are available on a first-come, first-served basis, but to guarantee your spot, reserve tickets a day ahead online.

You could also just grab a pint from the **Biergarten** (11am-6:30pm daily Jan.-Feb., 11am-7pm daily Mar.-Apr. and Sept.-Oct., 11am-8pm daily May-Aug., 11am-6pm daily Nov.-Dec.). Anheuser-Busch is about 2 miles (3.2 km) from downtown, located in the Soulard neighborhood just south.

Forest Park

The 1,300-acre **Forest Park** is considered one of the crown jewels of the city, and one of the best parks in the nation. The grounds host numerous museums as well as an entire ecosystem of forests, lakes, and streams. Get information and maps at the **Visitor and Education Center** (5595 Grand Dr., 314/561-3288, www.forestparkforever.org, 6am-8pm Mon.-Fri. and 6am-7pm Sat.-Sun. summer, 6am-8pm Mon.-Fri. and 6am-5pm Sat.-Sun. winter, free). The **Forest Park Explorer** (www.stladventurepass.com, spring-summer Mon.-Fri. $1-2, Sat.-Sun. free) offers seasonal access to various attractions in the park and extends to the Delmar Loop entertainment district just north of the park.

Missouri History Museum

The **Missouri History Museum** (5700 Lindell Blvd., 314/746-4599, http://mohistory.org, 10am-5pm Wed.-Mon., 10am-8pm Tues., free) focuses on local

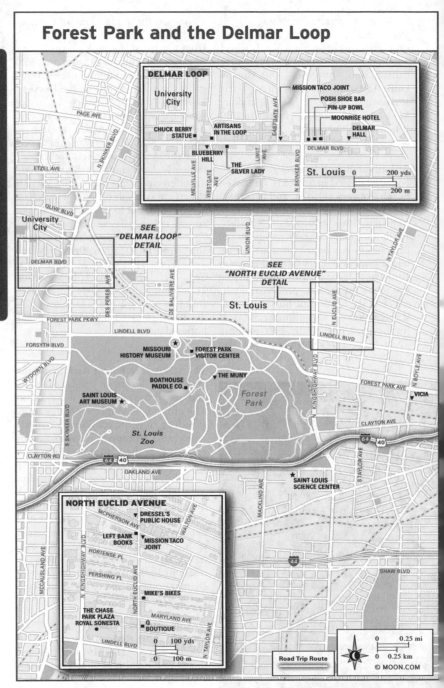

Forest Park and the Delmar Loop

DELMAR LOOP

University City

CHUCK BERRY STATUE ■ ARTISANS IN THE LOOP

BLUEBERRY HILL ■ THE SILVER LADY

MELVILLE AVE WESTGATE AVE LIMIT AVE EASTGATE AVE

MISSION TACO JOINT

POSH SHOE BAR

PIN-UP BOWL

MOONRISE HOTEL

DELMAR HALL

DELMAR BLVD

N SKINKER BLVD

St. Louis   0   200 yds
           0   200 m

PAGE AVE

N SKINKER BLVD

ETZEL AVE

OLIVE BLVD

University City

DELMAR BLVD

SEE "DELMAR LOOP" DETAIL

UNION BLVD

DES PERES AVE

DE BALIVIERE AVE

SEE "NORTH EUCLID AVENUE" DETAIL

N TAYLOR AVE

N EUCLID AVE

St. Louis

LINDELL BLVD

FOREST PARK PKWY

LINDELL BLVD

FORSYTH BLVD

MISSOURI HISTORY MUSEUM ★   ■ FOREST PARK VISITOR CENTER

WYDOWN BLVD

BOATHOUSE PADDLE CO. ■   ▾ THE MUNY

SAINT LOUIS ART MUSEUM ★

Forest Park

S SKINKER BLVD

St. Louis Zoo

N KINGSHIGHWAY BLVD

FOREST PARK AVE

N BOYLE AVE

▾ VICIA

CLAYTON AVE

CLAYTON RD

64 40

OAKLAND AVE

STAYTON AVE

MACKLIND AVE

★ SAINT LOUIS SCIENCE CENTER

NORTH EUCLID AVENUE

MCPHERSON AVE

▾ DRESSEL'S PUBLIC HOUSE

WALTON AVE

LEFT BANK BOOKS ■   ■ MISSION TACO JOINT

HORTENSE PL

N KINGSHIGHWAY BLVD

PERSHING PL

NORTH EUCLID AVE

MCCAUSLAND AVE

■ MIKE'S BIKES

THE CHASE PARK PLAZA ROYAL SONESTA ●

MARYLAND AVE

○ BOUTIQUE

LINDELL BLVD   0   100 yds
               0   100 m

N TAYLOR AVE

44

SHAW BLVD

0   0.25 mi
0   0.25 km

Road Trip Route

© MOON.COM

St. Louis history in the context of the nation. Exhibits cover tragedies in the city's history, such as a cholera epidemic in 1849 and a fire and tornado in 1896. It also examines the split personality of the city during the Civil War, which was officially part of the Union but had many Confederate citizens; the exhibit explores St. Louis's role in the civil rights movement, as well as women's rights, LGBTQ rights, and the rights of people with disabilities.

Saint Louis Art Museum

Located in a beautiful Italian Renaissance building, the **Saint Louis Art Museum** (1 Fine Arts Dr., 314/721-0072, www.slam.org, 10am-5pm Tues.-Sun., free) has a variety of permanent and rotating exhibits. Check out the excellent American gallery, which has a good collection of paintings on the mythic West, where you can get a sense of how the "New World" was romanticized. Notable works include pieces by "Missouri's Artist" George Caleb Bingham and the covered wagons of *Nooning on the Platte* (1859) by prolific painter Albert Bierstadt. These paintings helped popularize the idealized view of the West as a wild, beautiful place full of natural wealth. Look for glimpses of early life in the city with *Saint Louis in 1846* (1846) by Henry Louis and *Mississippi River Landscape* (1845) by Helen M. Kingman.

Saint Louis Science Center

For a day of fun—especially if you have kids—head to the **Saint Louis Science Center** (5050 Oakland Ave., 314/289-4400, www.slsc.org, 9:30am-4:30pm Mon.-Sat., 11am-4:30pm Sun., free) in the park. The hands-on exhibits are both kid- and adult-friendly, interactive but also educational, with a lot of STEM-focused activities. Build the Gateway Arch with foam cushions, discover the mechanics of air by designing a parachute or boat sail, and learn about earthquakes via rumbling floor panels. Huge dinosaurs roar from one of the displays, and the lobby greets you with a continuous motion machine: Make it go by running on a giant hamster wheel. If you're worn out, take some time to relax while you enjoy a show in the Omnimax theater ($10).

Delmar Loop

The **Delmar Loop** has been called one of the country's Best Streets by the American Planning Association. It's a great place to stroll—full of shops, restaurants, bars, and live music venues—and you could easily spend a day here. Here you'll also find the **St. Louis Walk of Fame** (6504 Delmar Blvd., 314/727-7827, www.stlouiswalkoffame.org), which has over 150 brass stars dedicated to famous city folks including Maya Angelou, Miles Davis, Scott Joplin, and Harry Caray. Also look for the bronze **Chuck Berry sculpture** (6555 Delmar Blvd.) with his guitar. Stick around until night falls to watch the neon signs light up the street. Keep your eye peeled for a preening neon peacock, a couple knocking down pins at Pin-Up Bowl, another couple dancing atop the Blueberry Hill music venue, and a giant moon rising above the street.

Cahokia Mounds

Many of the early explorers and fur trappers who ended up around St. Louis in the 1700s thought they were settling new uncharted lands, but the giant earthen structures at **Cahokia Mounds State Historic Site** (30 Ramey St., Collinsville, IL, 618/346-5160, www.cahokiamounds.org, grounds 8am-dusk daily, interpretive center 9am-5pm Wed.-Sun., free) examines some of the history of Native Americans long before their arrival. People known as the Mississippians—ancestors of the Chickasaw, Choctaw, Kansa, Natchez, Osage, and Seminole peoples—built a city here around AD 1200, and the mounds are the remnants. Looking at them today, you might mistake them simply for grassy hills—except for their oddly geometric shapes.

The mounds are thought to have been mostly ceremonial, possibly serving as pedestals for sacred buildings or burial grounds. There is evidence of around 120 mounds in the ancient city, with 72 remaining today, spread out across about 2,000 acres. Cahokia Mounds is the largest prehistoric archaeological site north of Mexico, and it is a UNESCO World Heritage Site.

Begin at the interpretive center, which shows a 15-minute documentary and showcases exhibits on scholarly research and artistic interpretations of the mounds. Then grab a trail map and spend some time exploring the grounds of the Grand Plaza, a leveled-off central plain that was likely used for social gatherings and games. The Twin Mounds are the closest, and Monks Mound is the largest, at 100 feet (30 m) tall. Most impressive, you can walk there—it's about 0.5 mile (0.8 km) from the interpretive center, or you can drive your car to the parking lot at its base. From the top, you'll catch a glimpse of the Gateway Arch.

The Cahokia Mounds State Historic Site is just over the state line in Illinois. From downtown, head east, over the Mississippi River, via Eads Bridge, and turn left onto North 3rd Street to merge onto I-64/I-55. Keep left to stay on I-55, and in 3.5 miles (5.6 km), take exit 6 for Highway 111, and turn right. Turn at the first left onto Collinsville Road. Continue 1.8 miles (2.9 km) to Cahokia Mounds; you'll pass the turnoff to Monks Mound on the left, then reach the sign and turnoff for the interpretive center on the right. The drive takes 15 minutes.

Recreation
Riverboat Cruises
Steamboats once ruled the Mississippi and Missouri Rivers, carrying waves of settlers and supplies farther west.

Top to bottom: Saint Louis Art Museum; butter cake, a St. Louis specialty; interior of The Fountain on Locust.

Enjoy a tour on a real steamboat on the Mississippi with **Gateway Arch Riverboat Cruises** (50 S. Leonor K. Sullivan Blvd., www.gatewayarch.com, Mar.-Dec.). The one-hour **St. Louis Riverfront Cruise** (noon daily Dec.-Feb., noon Mon.-Fri., noon and 1:30pm Sat.-Sun. Mar.-Nov., $22 adults, $11 ages 3-15) gives you a glimpse into the past and present of the busy city's working riverfront, as narrated by an NPS ranger. You'll learn quirky facts about the mighty Mississippi River and its place of importance in St. Louis and the push west. For a special experience, the two-hour **Skyline Dinner Cruise** (Fri.-Sat. May and Sept.-Oct., Fri.-Sun. June-Aug., $49 adults, $20 ages 3-12) offers amazing views of the Gateway Arch as the sun sets over your meal, and you can watch the city light up to the tunes of a Dixieland band. Tip: If you're planning on taking the Gateway Arch Tram Ride to the Top, you can save $3 by booking it with a cruise online.

Walking and Biking

Forest Park is a prime spot for walking and biking. Two paths run parallel to each other around the entire park for 5.8 miles (9.3 km): **Heels Path,** a gravel pedestrian path, and the **Bike Path,** a paved option. They are the primary routes in the park and go past most of the main attractions, with other offshoot paths leading into the center. At a leisurely pace, it'll take about two hours to walk the entire loop, or about 30 minutes to bike it. Kennedy Forest in the southwest corner has routes through a more forested environment; the 60 acres of forest here have 3.5 miles (5.6 km) of walking paths that connect with the main asphalt and gravel ones. The 1-mile (1.6-km) **Kennedy Boardwalk loop,** west of the zoo, is an especially beautiful section for walking.

Find information and maps at the **Visitor and Education Center** (5595 Grand Dr., 314/561-3288, www.forestparkforever.org, 6am-8pm Mon.-Fri., 6am-7pm Sat.-Sun. summer, 6am-8pm Mon.-Fri., 6am-5pm Sat.-Sun. winter, free).

Bike Rentals and Tours

For bike rentals, head to **Mike's Bikes** (324 N. Euclid Ave., 314/875-0080, www.mikesbikesstl.com, 10am-7pm Tues.-Fri., 10am-5pm Sat., noon-5pm Sun., $10 per hour, $40 4-24 hours). The shop is in the Central West End neighborhood, a 1.6-mile (2.5-km) bike ride from the Forest Park Visitor and Education Center, less than a 10-minute ride.

Enjoy a fun and educational guided tour of Forest Park by bike with **City Cycling Tours** (Forest Park Visitor and Education Center, 5595 Grand Dr., 314/616-5724, www.citycyclingtours.com, $25-30 pp). This popular tour takes you cycling about 10 miles (16 km) through the park's beautiful grounds and makes 18 stops over 2.5-3 hours. Tours are offered daily.

Paddling

Mount your own mini expedition by navigating the 22 acres of waterways in Forest Park. Find paddleboat, canoe, kayak, and paddleboard rentals at the **Boathouse Paddle Co.** (6101 Government Dr., www.boathousepaddleco.com, 314/722-6872, 10am-7pm Mon.-Sat., 11am-7pm Sun. Apr.-Sept., $15-22 1st hour, $15 2nd hour), next to the park's Post-Dispatch Lake. Push off from the boathouse and paddle your watercraft through the calm waters.

Bowling

St. Louis has a few popular bowling alley-martini bar combos, and one of the best is **Pin-Up Bowl** (6191 Delmar Blvd., 314/727-5555, www.pinupbowl.com, 3pm-3am Mon.-Thurs., noon-3am Fri.-Sat., bowling $5 pp, shoe rental $3). Located on a happening block of the Delmar Loop, the bowling alley is vintage fun—with retro 1940s decor including pinup girl memorabilia blended with cocktails. It can get busy on weekend evenings, but you can either call ahead for reservations or enjoy the wait with a signature drink.

Entertainment
Bars and Brewpubs

Three Sixty (1 S. Broadway St., 314/241-8439, www.360-stl.com, 4pm-1am Mon.-Thurs., 4pm-2am Fri.-Sat.) is a rooftop bar looming above the city lights. Enjoy your craft beer or expertly mixed cocktail while you gaze over the city and indulge in some people-watching. A fresh menu includes fish tacos, scallops, great burgers, and a perfect selection of finger foods to last all night long. Reservations are recommended.

Find a perfectly crafted cocktail at **Taste** (4584 Laclede Ave., 314/361-1200, www.tastebarstl.com, 5pm-1am Mon.-Sat., 5pm-midnight Sun.) in the Central West End. It's a small and stylish speakeasy, with brick walls and a white-tiled counter with a wooden top. The menu divides modern cocktails by their flavor profile (savory and spicy, aromatic herbal) and also lists classic cocktails according to their historical year. Oregon Trail era? You'll want a whiskey sour, circa 1850.

The Welsh-themed **Dressel's Public House** (419 Euclid Ave., 314/361-1060, http://dresselspublichouse.com, 5pm-10pm daily) has been a mainstay in the city since it opened in the 1980s, offering a casual and comforting place to grab a pint. It offers 14 rotating draft beers as well as a large wine list and cocktail menu. Dressel's also serves food, including a great burger. Be sure to order Dressel's pretzel, covered in the cheesy Welsh rarebit sauce.

4 Hands Brewing Co. (1220 S. 8th St., 314/436-1559, http://4handsbrewery.com, noon-10pm Mon.-Thurs., noon-midnight Fri.-Sat., 11am-9pm Sun.) pairs a roster of locally brewed beer with a casual atmosphere. In its taproom just south of downtown, patrons can enjoy 14 beers on tap while they play free Skee-Ball and arcade games. Get some cans of this St. Louis favorite to go while you're at it.

Live Music

BB's Jazz, Blues & Soups (700 N. Broadway, 314/436-5222, www.bbsjazzbluessoups.com, 6pm-3am Sun.-Fri., 6pm-1:30am Sat., $10 cover) combines the three titular items for a great night out. Get your fill of live music as well as Cajun and creole food in a building that dates to the mid-1800s. Local and touring performers sing the blues while guests enjoy gumbo and catfish po' boys.

The **Broadway Oyster Bar** (736 S. Broadway St. 314/621-8811, wwwbroadwayoysterbar.com, 11am-3am daily, free-$10 cover) is the place to go for live music and a New Orleans-style meal. Twice a night (though just once on Fri.), local and national acts take the stage in a range of styles including rock, folk, reggae, blues, and bluegrass.

A venue world-famous for educating and celebrating the unique style of St. Louis jazz, **Jazz St. Louis** (3536 Washington Ave., 314/571-6000, http://jazzstl.org, box office 10am-5pm Mon.-Fri., 2pm-5pm Sat.-Sun., $10-60) showcases new and classic jazz and boasts top-notch acoustics. The seated space is romantic and intimate—you'll feel like you're dining with the performers, and every seat has an excellent view. Shows typically start at 7:30pm and 9:30pm.

Legendary concert venue **Blueberry Hill** (6504 Delmar Blvd., 314/727-4444, http://blueberryhill.com, 11am-1:30am Mon.-Sat., 11am-midnight Sun., $15-20) has topped too many best-of lists to count. The bar opened in 1972 with a jukebox spinning cool tunes and soon built a stage for live music acts. The father of rock-and-roll Chuck Berry himself performed his famous duck walk on the stage at monthly concerts in the 1990s, and these days, several nights a week, the venue still hosts top performers on multiple stages. Grab a bite to eat and enjoy all the pop culture memorabilia in every corner, including PEZ dispensers, jukeboxes, and historical photos.

The Muny (1 Theatre Dr., 314/361-1900, www.muny.org, mid-June-mid-Aug., $15-105) is an outdoor theater that puts on a roster of concerts in Forest Park during the summer. Tickets are available online, but if you don't grab one ahead of time, keep in mind that the last nine rows of the amphitheater are held on a first-come, first-served basis.

The Arts
Built in 1928 in a palatial style called Siamese Byzantine, **The Fabulous Fox Theatre** (527 N. Grand Blvd., 314/534-1678, www.fabulousfox.com, $29-100) boasts amazing acoustics; it's easily one of the best theaters in the country. The lobby is carpeted in rich red and gold and features large columns. After its early heyday, it seemed doomed for the wrecking ball in the late 1970s, but was saved and carefully renovated to replicate its original glory. Today it's a world-class venue with 4,500 seats featuring Broadway shows, Cirque du Soleil, national bands, and more. You can take a 1.5-hour tour (10:30am Tues., Thurs., and Sat., $10 adults, $8 seniors and ages 2-10, free under age 2) of the theater that takes you behind the stage.

Festivals and Events
Big Muddy Blues Festival (www.bigmuddybluesfestival.com, Labor Day weekend, free) takes place at Laclede's Landing, just north of downtown, along the Mississippi River. The two-day family-friendly event sees beloved local and renowned national bands, all from St. Louis, perform on three outdoor and three indoor stages. It's a big event, with over 65 bands playing to 30,000 people along the banks of the river into the evening.

Over 30 restaurants band together to throw food and drink tasting events and chef competitions at the **Taste of St. Louis** (www.tastestl.com, late Sept., free),

a grand celebration of the city's best food and music. Fun activities for kids include face painting and cooking games. To top it off, some of the city's best entertainers take the stage for live music all weekend.

Food
Barbecue
Get your fix of St. Louie barbecue downtown at the ★ **Sugarfire Smokehouse** (605 Washington Ave., 314/394-1720, http://sugarfiresmokehouse.com, 11am-9pm daily, $13), a local hot spot. Order at the counter, then drench your brisket or pulled pork in the range of sauces kept on each table, like Hot Texan or Sweet St. Louie. For the best bet, get the meat sampler plate rather than a sandwich, and load up with sides like potato salad, mac and cheese, and coleslaw.

Another local favorite, **Pappy's Smokehouse** (3106 Olive St., 314/535-4340, www.pappyssmokehouse.com, 11am-8pm Mon.-Sat., 11am-4pm Sun., $15) slow roasts its meat for over 24 hours before slathering it in sauces and piling it high with sides like baked beans, slaw, and sweet potato fries. Everything is made fresh daily—which means when they're out, they're out.

Creative Contemporary
Have your camera ready when you visit ★ **The Fountain on Locust** (3037 Locust St., 314/535-7800, www.fountainonlocust.com, 11am-10pm Tues.-Thurs., 11am-midnight Fri.-Sat., noon-9pm Sun., $10), easily the most photographed restaurant in the city. When you see the hand-painted walls with art deco chandeliers, you'll understand why. The food is as good as the decor, with sandwiches, delicious soups—47 varieties rotate (pickle is one of the best)—and salads full of colorful veggies. Leave some room for dessert, since the restaurant has what's considered the city's best ice cream. Try the light Pineapple Inside Out Cake in a Cup, or try one of its famous Ice Cream Martinis or the Sparkling Rosé Float.

Vicia (4250 Forest Park Ave., 314/553-9239, www.viciarestaurant.com, 11am-9:30pm Tues.-Thurs., 11am-10pm Fri.-Sat., $16) focuses on seasonal vegetable dishes but throws in some meat to satiate the carnivores. It has rocketed to national acclaim with its light-filled space and menu of beautiful locally sourced dishes like the soft scrambled goose egg and beets fried in beef fat with trumpet mushrooms. Let the bartenders create your perfect cocktail accompaniment with their botanical mixtures.

Pizza

St. Louis has its own style of pizza, a thin crust cooked crisp, covered in provel cheese, and cut into squares. **Imo's Pizza** (904 S. 4th St., 341/421-4667, www.imospizza.com, 10am-midnight Sun.-Thurs., 10am-1am Fri.-Sat., $15) has been slinging it since 1964. Order a specialty pie or choose from plenty of toppings to build your own. Don't forget to add another squared St. Louis tradition from the menu: toasted ravioli with dipping sauce. Imo's has 80 locations throughout the city and also delivers to area hotels. This one is conveniently located just south of the Gateway Arch.

Asian

Find your favorite country's food on Delmar Loop—it offers 46 multinational restaurants in just six blocks. Mexican, Indian, Japanese, Korean, Middle Eastern, Syrian, Thai, and Vietnamese joints are all here slinging delicious bites. It's hard to go wrong, but some good choices are **Asian Kitchen Korean Cuisine** (8423 Olive Blvd., 314/989-9377, 11am-1am Tues.-Sun., $7), offering plenty of *bibimbap* and *banchan* (side dishes) to go around, and **House of India** (8501 Delmar Blvd., 314/567-6850, www.hoistl.com, 11:30am-2:30pm and 5pm-9pm Sun.-Thurs., 11:30am-2pm and 5pm-10pm Fri.-Sat., $14), a longtime favorite for its lunch buffet and some of the best Indian dinner entrées in the city.

Mexican

★ **Mission Taco Joint** (6235 Delmar Blvd., 314/932-5430, www.missiontacojoint.com, 11am-1:30am Mon.-Sat., 11am-midnight Sun., $3.75 per taco) makes its own *masa* daily and presses tortillas fresh after you order—then fills them with ingredients like barbecue duck, *achiote* pork, and pineapple salsa. *Tortas* and burritos are also available, and desserts include churros with dipping chocolate. With *luchador* murals on the wall and a cocktail menu featuring tequila and mescal along with local beer, this is a hip, fresh taste of Mexico. In addition to this Delmar Loop location, the eatery has an outpost in the Central West End.

Breakfast and Lunch

Start the day off at **Rooster** (1104 Locust St., 314/241-8118, www.roosterstl.com, 8am-3pm daily, $10), which stuffs its savory crepes full of locally sourced ingredients like German sausages, smoked sirloin, emmenthaler cheese, and tomato jam. Breakfast and brunch are served all day, and lunch is served from 11am Monday-Friday. A bakery and a butcher shop are on-site, and everything is mixed, cut, baked, and frozen (ice cream!) in-house.

The menu at **Blondie's Coffee, Wine & Dessert Bar** (1301 Washington Ave., 314/241-6100, www.blondiesstl.com, 7:30am-5pm Mon.-Fri., 8am-4pm Sat.-Sun., $8) is good for breakfast, lunch, and dessert. Start the day off with a pastry or egg sandwich, or enjoy one of the soups for lunch. Either way, don't miss a basket of the huge airy popovers served with sweet or savory spreads. You can also enjoy a relaxing afternoon on the patio with a drink from the solid wine and cocktail list.

Coffee and Desserts

Head to **Park Avenue Coffee** (417 N. 10th St., 314/231-5282, http://parkavenuecoffee.com, 7am-6pm Mon.-Sat., 7:30am-6pm Sun., $5) to try a St.

Louis original: gooey butter cake. A mistaken mix-up in butter and flour proportions led to the creation of this dense yellow cake, dusted with powdered sugar, and it's now a city favorite. Park Avenue makes over 70 varieties from scratch, including seasonal flavors, but most folks agree that Mom's Traditional is the best. Get yours with a piping hot coffee to cut the sweetness. Savory breakfast and lunch sandwiches are also served. This venue is right downtown, but there are three other locations throughout the city.

Shopping
Downtown
A walk down Washington Avenue in downtown brings you by plenty of quirky local stops and shops. The **AIA Bookstore** (911 Washington Ave., 314/231-4252, 9am-4pm Mon.-Fri.) is run by the St. Louis Chapter of the American Institute of Architects. It's full of books like *1001 Buildings You Must See before You Die* and guides to local St. Louis treasures. You can also pick up a unique gift for the architect nerd in your life. Washington Avenue itself is a great place to enjoy some of the unique architectural styles of the city. **Ceci Unique Gallery** (901 Washington Ave., 314/241-1113, www. ceciuniquegallery.com, 10am-7pm Mon.-Sat., noon-6pm Sun.) features colorful clothes, blown glass art, and jewelry. **Star Clipper** (1319 Washington Ave., 314/240-5337, www.fantasybooksinc. com, noon-6pm Sun.-Tues., 10am-9pm Wed., noon-7pm Thurs., noon-10pm Fri., 11am-8pm Sat.) is the best spot for all your comic book, manga, graphic novels, and zine needs.

Central West End
The shops at Central West End make for a good afternoon of strolling. Find your new favorite read at **Left Bank Books** (399 N. Euclid St., 314/367-6731, www. left-bank.com, 10am-10pm Mon.-Sat., 11am-6pm Sun.).

Spot the World's Largest Chess Piece (14 feet 6 inches tall!) at the World Chess Hall of Fame, then grab a souvenir at its chess-themed gift store, **Q Boutique** (4652 Maryland Ave., 314/367-7501, www. qboutiquestl.com, 10am-5pm Mon.-Wed. and Sat., 10am-9pm Thurs.-Fri., noon-5pm Sun.).

Delmar Loop
The Delmar Loop has over 145 shops and businesses. **The Silver Lady** (6364 Delmar Blvd., 314/727-0704, www.thesilver-lady. com, 11am-6pm Tues.-Sun.) has unique jewelry with silver and semiprecious stones. **Posh Shoe Bar** (6193 Delmar Blvd., 314/261-4092, www.poshshoebar. com, 11am-7pm Tues.-Sat.) offers a fantastic selection of stylish shoes and women's clothes. **Artisans in the Loop** (6511 Delmar Blvd., 314/833-3540, www. artisansintheloop.com, 11am-5pm Tues.-Sun.) is a boutique gallery showcasing items from local and national artists.

Accommodations
Downtown hotels can book up fast in the summer months, so plan ahead.

$150-250
Topped by a spinning lunar orb, ★ **Moonrise Hotel** (6177 Delmar Blvd., 314/721-1111, http://moonrisehotel.com, $203-288) beckons visitors; get a closer look at it from the rooftop bar. Inside is more moon-themed decor and 125 pet-friendly rooms featuring large-screen TVs and rainfall showers. Located in the heart of the bustling Delmar Loop, you can book quirky rooms devoted to St. Louis celebrities in the Walk of Fame Suites. The ultra-green hotel has solar panels and an electric car charging station.

★ **Hotel Saint Louis** (705 Olive St., 314/241-4300, www.marriott.com, $150-270) was a bank in the 1890s, and has been renovated as part of the Marriot Autograph Collection to incorporate some fun modern design in its 140 rooms. Robes are made of sweatshirt terrycloth, there are televisions inside the mirrors in the huge baths, and every room includes a record player from local company Crosley, along with a few albums by St. Louis artists to enjoy. Pop upstairs to enjoy the rooftop bar and heated outdoor pool. Offering a big bang for your buck, this is a great place to spend a few nights. It's located in central downtown, 0.5 mile (0.8 km) from Gateway Arch.

Stay right next to the Gateway Arch at the **Drury Plaza Hotel St. Louis at the Arch** (2 S. 4th St., 314/231-3003, www. druryhotels.com $159-209). Located inside the renovated International Fur Exchange Building, once the world's largest fur-trading auction floor, it evokes St. Louis's role in westward expansion and has riverfront and arch views. Inside the lobby you'll find Italian marble, granite, crystal chandeliers, and a water feature devoted to the Lewis and Clark expedition. Enjoy a hot breakfast as well as a free drink and appetizers each evening.

Located inside the gorgeously renovated train station, the **St. Louis Union Station Hotel** (1820 Market St., 314/231-1234, www.stlouisunionstation.com/ stay, $174-318), part of the Hilton's Curio Collection, offers a chance to stay in specialty rooms and suites such as those in the Grand Hall wing, or in the base of the Clocktower. You'll feel like you've traveled back to the elegance of the 1800s while retaining the modern amenities, including a fitness room, a pool, and a gourmet restaurant. Expect to pay $40 for valet parking or $27 for self-parking.

Enjoy the utmost luxury at the chandelier-bedecked **Magnolia Hotel** (421 N. 8th St., 314/436-9000, http:// magnoliahotels.com/stlouis, $142-240) in downtown St. Louis, a 15-minute walk from the Gateway Arch. Once serving movie stars like Cary Grant and John Barrymore, the elegant hotel features spacious rooms outfitted in velvet accents and was the first to place chocolates on pillows—allegedly inspired by Grant himself. Enjoy amenities like a made-to-order breakfast, a fitness center, and complimentary bedtime milk and cookies.

Over $250

The Last Hotel (1501 Washington Ave., 314/390-2500, www.thelasthotelstl.com, $194-550) has 142 rooms ranging from studios to VIP suites, with original barrel ceilings, walk-in showers, floor-to-ceilings windows, and a minibar full of local goods. Amenities include concierge services, a fitness room, and regular events by local artists and musicians. On lively Washington Avenue a block from the City Museum, the hotel is in the rejuvenated International Shoe Company building. An on-site restaurant, The Last Kitchen, serves meals, and The Pantry sells jarred goods. At the rooftop bar, patrons can enjoy views from the 11th floor as they rub shoulders with a giant hippo sculpture that once stood on the corner of the City Museum building.

Renowned hospitality and elegant accommodations are at the **Four Seasons Hotel St. Louis** (999 N. 2nd St., 314/881-5800, www.fourseasons.com/stlouis, $311-1,440). Choose from views of the Mississippi River, downtown, or the elegant Gateway Arch in one of 200 rooms and luxury suites. Although you're just a 10-minute walk from the arch, between the rooftop pool and delectable dishes at the on-site restaurant Cinder House, it may be hard to tear yourself away.

Fleur-de-Lys Mansion (3500 Russell Blvd., 314/773-3500, www.thefleurdelys. com, $215-295) is a four-room bed-and-breakfast. With luxurious bedding, en suite baths, and jetted tubs, this makes a romantic destination. A full gourmet breakfast is served each morning, with seasonal items like bananas foster, crab hollandaise, and cheese blintz soufflés. It's a 10-minute drive from attractions like Gateway Arch, Forest Park, and Union Station.

The **Chase Park Plaza Royal Sonesta** (212 Kingshighway Blvd., 314/633-3000, www.sonesta.com, $265-337) is a classically designed hotel in close walking distance to Forest Park. It's a veritable city unto itself, with 339 rooms and suites, fountains, piazzas, three on-site restaurants, a Mediterranean-style outdoor heated swimming pool, a barbershop, and even a shoe shine.

Camping

You can't beat the location: The **St. Louis RV Park** (900 N. 23rd St., 314/241-3330, http://stlouisrvpark.com, $48) is the closest you'll get to the big city's downtown core with an RV, even offering (faint) views of the Gateway Arch. The treeless grounds aren't anything fancy, but you'll be a 10-minute drive to area attractions like the arch and Forest Park. With electric hookups, showers, and an outdoor pool, this is a simple and friendly place to park the rig.

Information

You can find St. Louis information, maps, restaurant guides, and more at a few visitors centers in the city. The most convenient one is in the lobby of the **Gateway Arch Visitor Center** (8am-10pm daily summer, 9am-6pm daily winter), near Luther Ely Smith Square by the west entrance. Informational kiosks are in **St. Louis's Lambert International Airport's Terminal 1** (9am-5pm Sat.-Sun.) and **Terminal 2** (10am-6pm daily), near the baggage claims. Terminal 2's kiosk is staffed by volunteers, and hours can sometimes change. You can also reach St. Louis Visitor Information by phone (314/421-1023).

⚓ Side Trip: Arrow Rock, MO

Just off I-70 between St. Louis and Independence—an extra 15-minute drive off-route each way—Arrow Rock is a great place to stop and break up the 3.5-hour drive west. At one time, the entire

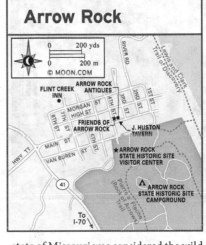

Arrow Rock

state of Missouri was considered the wild frontier. Home to Native Americans and the occasional fur trapper, it took the sons of Daniel Boone himself to push farther west and blaze a trail to a natural salt lick. The Boone's Lick (or Booneslick) Trail soon became a road carrying thousands of settlers into the mid-Missouri region in the early 1800s. Historic towns are left and right, but the oldest and best is Arrow Rock. Indigenous peoples used the flint-loaded point of Arrow Rock—a prominent feature above the river—for arrowheads and tools, and European explorers used it as a landmark. The nearby natural salt licks attracted settlers to the region in the early 1800s, and by the 1820s, wagons headed to trade in Santa Fe would stop by the Big Spring, a well-known watering hole. While Arrow Rock isn't on the official Oregon Trail route, families heading to the promised land of Oregon would certainly have passed by the area on the way to Independence Square, either by wagon on the Booneslick Trail or by riverboat on the "Mighty Mo."

Today, the entire charming village, filled with historic buildings, restaurants, and other venues, is part of the **Arrow Rock State Historic Site,** which has a few dozen full-time residents. On

the Missouri River, it's also a great place for bird-watching and short walks. You'll want at least two hours to eat and poke around the boardwalk-lined Main Street, though you can easily spend a whole day here, or overnight if you have time.

Begin at the **visitors center** (39521 Visitor Center Dr., 660/837-3330, http://mostateparks.com, 10am-4pm daily Mar.-May, 10am-5pm daily June-Aug., 10am-4pm daily Sept.-Nov., 10am-4pm Fri.-Sun. Dec.-Feb.), which has maps and information on tours and current events. A museum inside also gives a good overview of the area's history, with artifacts, dioramas, and a 20-minute documentary.

Getting There and Back

To get to Arrow Rock from St. Louis, head west on I-70 and take exit 98 to follow Highway 41 for 13 miles (21 km). Turn right at the sign for the visitors center; the parking lot here is big enough for RVs and trailers. The next right takes you through the village. Parking is available around town.

To get back on I-70, backtrack on Highway 41 for 5.5 miles (8.9 km), then turn right on Highway K, following signs for Blackwater. Continue through Blackwater and turn left to stay on Highway K. In 2.6 miles (4.2 km), turn left onto Highway M, then in 50 yards, turn right to get back onto I-70 to continue west to Independence, which is 80 miles (129 km) away.

Sights

The **Friends of Arrow Rock** (310 Main St., 660/837-3231, www.friendsofarrowrock.org, 9am-5pm daily Mar.-Dec., 9am-5pm Sat.-Sun. Jan.-Feb., free) have been a vital force in restoring the village, administering the town's museums and keeping a running schedule of events.

Top to bottom: J. Huston Tavern; *Fur Traders Descending the Missouri* by George Caleb Bingham; J. C. Nichols Memorial Fountain, sculpted by Henri Greber, in Kansas City.

Their storefront on the boardwalk is loaded with historical exhibits, books, gifts, and souvenirs. It's also where you can catch a guided 1.25-hour **tram tour** (daily June-Labor Day, Sat.-Sun. May and Sept.-Oct., $10 adults, $3 children) to buildings around town.

A self-guided tour of the village should include a walk down Main Street, as well as visits to a few of the free house museums in town. The **Dr. John Sappington Museum** (108 High St., dawn-dusk, free) recounts the history of one of Arrow Rock's residents, the frontier doctor who popularized the malaria-fighting drug quinine. The **Black History Museum** (608 Morgan St., dawn-dusk, free) recounts the rich history of Arrow Rock's formerly enslaved residents after emancipation, who started their own schools, churches, and communities in the area.

Art history fans will enjoy the **George Caleb Bingham House** (1st St. and High St.), home of "Missouri's Artist," who painted scenes of the frontier's river life and early settlers from the 1830s to the post Civil War years. The inside of the Bingham house is only accessible via the tram tour offered by the Friends of Arrow Rock.

Food and Accommodations

Built in 1834, the **J. Huston Tavern** (305 Main St., 600/837-3200, www.hustontavern.com, 11am-2pm Wed.-Thurs., 11am-2pm and 5pm-8pm Fri.-Sat., 11am-2pm Sun. June-Sept., 11am-2pm and 4:30pm-8pm Fri.-Sat., 11am-2pm Sun. Mar.-May and Oct.-Dec., $13) is the oldest continuously operating restaurant west of the Mississippi. When Huston noticed the numbers of westward-bound emigrants, he began offering lodging and meals to travelers—today it's still the best place in town for a delicious hot meal. The dining areas are spread out around the Huston family house, and the old general store now operates as a bar. Food options include a famous fried chicken, pork tenderloin, biscuits slathered in apple butter, soups, and salads. Take a stroll around the building to see displays of 19th-century life. Reservations are recommended for busy summer weekends.

The **Flint Creek Inn** (507 7th St., 660/837-3352, www.flintcreekinn.com, $110-120) is a relaxed, beautiful bed-and-breakfast. It has five regionally themed rooms that are named after the state birds of spots along the Santa Fe Trail, like the Meadowlark for Kansas or the Bluebird for Missouri. Indeed, bird-watching is a popular activity from the huge windows of the main house, which overlooks a creek and woodlands on the edge of town.

Year-round camping is available at the **Arrow Rock State Historic Site Campground** (39521 Visitor Center Dr., 660/837-3330, http://mostateparks.com, $13-25). Water, showers, and firewood are available April-October. Basic and electric (pull-through and back-in) sites are spread out in grassy, wooded areas with picnic tables. Sites 13-22 are nearest to Big Soldier Lake, which has fishing opportunities. Sites are reservable online, though a good number are held on a first-come, first-served basis.

Kansas City, MO

Kansas City, Missouri, is the biggest city in the state. Nestled between the Missouri and Kansas Rivers, the metropolis has the Oregon Trail to thank, in part, for its success as a city. Although Independence is considered the official start of the Oregon Trail, it was actually one of several jumping-off points along the Missouri River. Westport, now a neighborhood in Kansas City, was one of these. Instead of getting off the riverboats at Upper Independence Landing, some settlers traveled a few miles farther west to the natural bend in the river at Westport Landing; this saved a few precious miles of road travel at the beginning of the trail.

Westport founder John McCoy operated a trading post in 1833 at the corner of Westport Road and Pennsylvania Avenue, where today a sign commemorates its role on the trail. The prosperous business of outfitting wagon trains led to a successful town. In the 20th century, Kansas City grew into a bastion of culture, with jazz, barbecue, and sports scenes exploding. Today, it's a diverse metropolitan city, rooted in Midwestern hospitality yet holding international appeal. Plan to spend at least one full day exploring, eating, drinking, and catching some of the best tunes. If you have more time, you can definitely find more to do in this energetic city.

Getting There and Around

If you're driving **directly from Independence,** the 10-mile (16-km) drive west takes about 20 minutes. From Independence Square, head west on Truman Road. In 7 miles (11.3 km), turn right to merge onto I-70, then drive 1.9 miles (3 km) to exit 2P for downtown.

If you followed the **historic Oregon Trail route from Independence,** head west on Santa Fe Trail from New Santa Fe, turning right at the first cross street, State Line Road. Follow it for 2 miles (3.2 km), then veer right for I-435. In 3.9 miles (6.3 km), use the left lane for exit 71B to U.S. 71. Continue on it for 11.3 miles (18.2 km), then take exit 198 for downtown Kansas City. The drive takes just under 30 minutes.

From **St. Louis,** take I-70 west across the state to Kansas City, 248 miles (399 km). The drive takes 3.75 hours. From the north, you can drive into the city via I-35 from Des Moines, Iowa, or I-29 from Omaha, Nebraska. From the south, you can drive into the city via I-35 from Wichita, Kansas, and I-49 from Springfield, Missouri. I-435 loops around the downtown core, offering access to Independence as well as some of the area's larger suburbs.

You can fly into **Kansas City International Airport** (MCI, 1 International Square, 816/243-5237, www.flykci.com), the closest airport to Independence. From the airport you can get downtown on bus 229 via **RideKC** (http://ridekc.org, 5:30am-11:15pm Mon.-Fri., 6:20am-11:15pm Sat.-Sun., $1.50), which takes about 45 minutes and runs approximately hourly, with less frequent service on early weekday mornings.

An easy way to get around the city is on the free **KC Streetcar** (www.kcstreetcar.org, 6am-midnight Mon.-Thurs., 6am-2am Fri., 7am-2am Sat., 7am-10pm Sun., free) a 2-mile (3.2-km) line that runs north-south from River Market to Union Station. Its 16 stops include Crown Center and the Power and Light District. To reach places farther south, like Westport or Country Club Plaza, drive or jump on the **Kansas City Regional Transit bus** (www.ridekc.org, $1.50 per ride, $3 day pass). The MAX line connects Country Club Plaza, and bus lines 39, 55, and 51 serve Westport. **Uber** (www.uber.com) and **Lyft** (www.lyft.com) also operate in Kansas City.

One Day in Kansas City

Morning
Start the day with a delicious coffee and pastry from **Messenger Coffee Co. + Ibis Bakery,** then head to the **City Market,** where pioneers once traded goods. It's full of fun vendors you can browse, with great shopping and more eats when you get hungry again. If it's a weekend in season you might also catch the farmers market. Next, take a stroll along the **Riverfront Heritage Trail** to locate **Westport Landing,** where riverboats once dropped off pioneers headed west. Back at the River Market area, step into the **Arabia Steamboat Museum** for a look at one of those riverboats' rescued cargoes.

Afternoon
In the afternoon, head to the southern part of the city to check out the free **Nelson-Atkins Museum of Art.** From here it's a short stroll to the **Country Club Plaza,** a shopping district where you can also see some of the city's best **fountains.** Then take a walk around the historic **Westport** neighborhood nearby to see some of the oldest buildings in the city, including **Kelly's Westport Inn,** once a store run by Daniel Boone's grandson and now a bar where you can grab a drink.

Evening
Dine at **Joe's Kansas City Bar-B-Que** for arguably the city's best. And then, if you're still ready for more, hit up the city's hip cocktail scene at **Tom's Town** or **SoT,** or enjoy jazz any night of the week at the **Green Lady Lounge.**

Orientation
Downtown
Downtown Kansas City encompasses a few small walkable districts, including the eclectic Power and Light District, just south of the River Market neighborhood, where visitors will find the original Joe's Kansas City Bar-B-Que and plenty of other dining and bars; the central Crossroads Arts District, home of the Kauffman Center and live music venues like the Green Lady Lounge and Tom's Town; and, farthest south, the Crown Center, where the National WWI Museum and Memorial is located. Downtown is located roughly between U.S. 71 and I-35.

River Market
The River Market neighborhood is sandwiched between downtown and the Missouri River. It's a hip area that centers around City Market, which hosts the region's largest farmers market. Most of the dining and shopping options are found inside the City Market's walls, also home to the excellent Arabia

Steamboat Museum, and you can access the Riverfront Heritage Trail along the Missouri River here.

Westport
The oldest neighborhood in Kansas City traces its roots back to the pioneers and wagons heading west. Today's travelers get to enjoy a booming dining, shopping, and entertainment scene. Westport's central point is the corner of Westport Road and Pennsylvania Avenue, and the district is small and walkable. It's about 2.5 miles (4 km) south of downtown.

Country Club Plaza
With architecture inspired by Kansas City's sister city, Seville, Spain, the Country Club Plaza is a beautiful place to walk around, and it's a hot spot of shopping and dining. The upscale neighborhood features wide avenues for strolling, numerous fountains, and striking Spanish architecture with red-tile roofs. The plaza is about 1 mile (1.6 km) south of Westport.

Downtown Kansas City and River Market

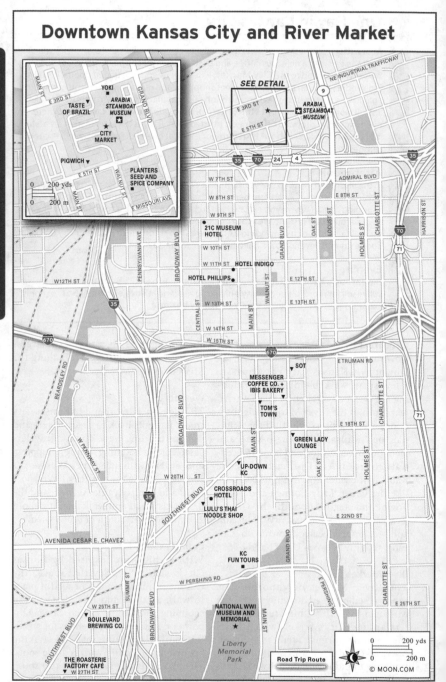

Detail inset:
- MAIN ST
- E 3RD ST
- GRAND BLVD
- YOKI ■
- TASTE OF BRAZIL ▼
- *ARABIA STEAMBOAT MUSEUM* ★
- CITY MARKET
- PIGWICH ▼
- E 5TH ST
- WALNUT ST
- PLANTERS SEED AND SPICE COMPANY
- E MISSOURI AVE
- 0   200 yds
- 0   200 m

Main map labels:
- SEE DETAIL
- NE INDUSTRIAL TRAFFICWAY
- 9
- E 3RD ST
- *ARABIA STEAMBOAT MUSEUM* ★
- E 5TH ST
- 35 70 24 4
- 35
- W 7TH ST
- ADMIRAL BLVD
- W 8TH ST
- E 8TH ST
- CHARLOTTE ST
- W 9TH ST
- OAK ST
- LOCUST ST
- HOLMES ST
- HARRISON ST
- 21C MUSEUM HOTEL ■
- GRAND BLVD
- 70
- PENNSYLVANIA AVE
- BROADWAY BLVD
- W 10TH ST
- 71
- W 11TH ST   HOTEL INDIGO ■
- HOTEL PHILLIPS ■
- E 12TH ST
- WALNUT ST
- W 12TH ST
- CENTRAL ST
- W 13TH ST
- E 13TH ST
- MAIN ST
- 35
- W 14TH ST
- W 15TH ST
- 670
- 670
- BEARDSLEY RD
- E TRUMAN RD
- SOT ▼
- MESSENGER COFFEE CO. + IBIS BAKERY ▼
- CHARLOTTE ST
- TOM'S TOWN ▼
- E 18TH ST
- GREEN LADY LOUNGE ▼
- W PENNWAY ST
- MAIN ST
- OAK ST
- 71
- UP-DOWN KC ▼
- W 20TH   ST
- BROADWAY BLVD
- CROSSROADS HOTEL ■
- LULU'S THAI NOODLE SHOP ▼
- SOUTHWEST BLVD
- E 22ND ST
- HOLMES ST
- 35
- AVENIDA CESAR E. CHAVEZ
- GRAND BLVD
- KC FUN TOURS ■
- W PERSHING RD
- E PERSHING RD
- CHARLOTTE ST
- E 25TH ST
- SUMMIT ST
- W 25TH ST
- BOULEVARD BREWING CO. ▼
- NATIONAL WWI MUSEUM AND MEMORIAL ★
- MAIN ST
- *Liberty Memorial Park*
- Road Trip Route
- 0   200 yds
- 0   200 m
- © MOON.COM
- SOUTHWEST BLVD
- BROADWAY BLVD
- THE ROASTERIE FACTORY CAFÉ ▼
- W 27TH ST

Westport and Country Club Plaza

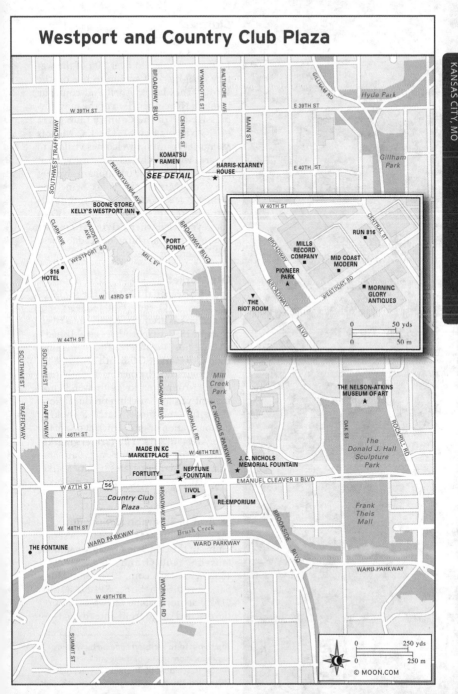

Sights
Kansas City Fountains
Kansas City is known as the City of Fountains, home to over 200 of the watery delights. All spring to life on the second Tuesday of April and continue through November. Two of the most impressive are in the **Country Club Plaza** (47 JC Nichols Pkwy.). The **J. C. Nichols Memorial Fountain** welcomes visitors to the area with four heroic horsemen meant to represent the four triumphant rivers of the world (Mississippi, Volga, Seine, and Rhine). A few blocks down, **Neptune** sits astride a seahorse-pulled chariot. Keep your eye peeled when driving around for your own fountain hunt, or head to www.visitkc.com for a list of them all.

City Market
Shop for seasonal treats at the same location where Oregon Trail pioneers once traded goods after disembarking a riverboat. In 1857, two brothers established a trading post near here. Today, the bustling **City Market** (20 E. 5th St., 816/842-1271, hours vary by merchant, daily, free) is a year-round market with over 30 permanent vendors offering produce, flowers, gifts, and more. Catch a cooking demonstration or grab lunch at one of the many restaurants. The **farmers market** (9am-3pm Sat.-Sun. June-Aug., 9am-3pm Sun. Sept.-Mar.) operates in City Market seasonally, with special events and occasional concerts.

★ Arabia Steamboat Museum
Inside City Market is one of the best museums in the city. The **Arabia Steamboat Museum** (400 Grand Blvd., 816/471-1856, www.1856.com, 10am-5pm Mon.-Sat., noon-5pm Sun., $14.50 adults, $13.50 seniors, $5.50 ages 4-14) houses the rescued cargo from a steamboat—of

Top to bottom: *Westport Landing* by William Henry Jackson; statue of the founders of Westport, sculpted by Thomas L. Beard; Arabia Steamboat Museum.

Beginning the Oregon Trail by Riverboat

Steamboats played an instrumental role in transporting people and supplies as the country pushed west. The first steamboat to travel the full length of the Mississippi was the *New Orleans* in 1811. By the 1830s, steamboats ruled the waters—a trip from St. Louis to New Orleans (about 680 miles/1,094 km) could be done in 6-7 days in comparison to wagons, which moved at a speed of about 15-20 miles (24-32 km) per day; at that rate, the journey would take about a month by land. It made sense, then, that pioneers would want to complete as much of their westward journey as possible by riverboat. A family in Pennsylvania, for example, could get on a riverboat near Pittsburgh and take the Ohio River to the Mississippi River before traveling upstream on the Missouri River to the edge of the frontier at Independence or Westport—before the Missouri curves north and becomes progressively more unnavigable.

the type that emigrants would have traveled on before they set out on the trail—that went down in the Missouri River in 1856. Not only is the story of the group of men who located and excavated the boat a fascinating modern treasure hunt—it was found underground in the middle of a farmer's field, due to the changing course of the river—but the cargo unearthed is the biggest collection of pre-Civil War items ever discovered. The ship was supplying the frontier, and the *Arabia*'s cargo included everything a new town might need: boots, fine china, blacksmith tools, hats, awls, jewelry, buttons, weapons, and more. Visits start with a guided tour and an introductory video, and then you're allowed to tour the display rooms freely. Allow at least an hour for a visit.

Westport Landing

The banks of the Missouri River in the River Market area were once lined with Oregon and California Trail traffic as emigrants disembarked from their boats from St. Louis and beyond to arrive at the edge of the frontier. From here, they traveled a few miles south to the jumping-off point of Westport, where they could stock up on supplies. After Kansas City, the Missouri River turns north, so this was the westernmost part of the country reachable by water; Westport Landing was a few miles west of Upper Independence Landing,

saving travelers some wear on their wagon wheels. You can locate a **marker for Westport Landing** at the observation deck on the **Riverfront Heritage Trail,** an 0.5-mile (0.8-km) walk north via Main Street from City Market.

National WWI Museum and Memorial

An excellent under-the-radar museum is the **National WWI Museum and Memorial** (2 Memorial Dr., www.theworldwar.org, 10am-5pm Tues.-Sun., $18 adults, $14 seniors, $10 ages 6-10, free under age 6), which has the most comprehensive collection of World War I memorabilia in the world. The museum digs deep into the causes and results of World War I and is an educational experience. Admission affords access to the main exhibits, special exhibits, as well as the Liberty Memorial Tower, which has stunning views of Kansas City.

Pioneer Park

Pioneer Park (Westport Rd. and Broadway) is a good place to start a tour of the Westport neighborhood. A large sculpture here commemorates the three men who were instrumental in developing Westport: John C. McCoy, the town founder, is in the center; Alexander Majors, a local business owner and Pony Express partner, faces west; and Jim Bridger, famous mountain man and Westport saloon owner, is on the right, holding a rifle. Nearby you can find a large terrazzo map of the Oregon Trail in the pavement. Bridger was a trapper and early traveler on the Oregon Trail, and he opened a trading post, Fort Bridger, to serve emigrants in southwest Wyoming. In later years, he settled in Westport and was eventually buried in Independence.

Harris-Kearney House

The **Harris-Kearney House** (4000 Baltimore St., 816/561-1821, www. westporthistorical.com, 1pm-5pm Fri.-Sat. Mar.-Oct., or by appointment, $2) is a beautiful two-story Greek Revival home dating from 1855. The Westport Historical Society is housed inside and has extensively renovated the old mansion. It offers tours of the house, which is the oldest brick residence in Kansas City. Special events include Candlelight Ghost Tours and craft demonstrations like lacemaking.

The original owner, Colonel John "Jack" Harris, also owned the former Harris Hotel down the street on the northeast corner of Westport Road and Pennsylvania Avenue. The hotel served pioneers and settlers headed west, offering a chance to stock up on supplies for those headed out on the Oregon, California, and Santa Fe Trails; the hotel no longer stands today, but the location can be found across the street from Kelly's Westport Inn.

The Nelson-Atkins Museum of Art

Just southeast of Westport is **The Nelson-Atkins Museum of Art** (4525 Oak St., 855/830-1482, www.nelson-atkins.org, 10am-5pm Wed. and Sat.-Sun., 10am-9pm Thurs.-Fri., free). The museum, with its giant badminton birdie outdoor sculpture, is a shining light of artistry in the city. The renowned collection is free to visit, so stop in and enjoy European paintings and Imperial Chinese art along with a wide variety of rotating exhibitions.

Recreation
Walking and Biking

The **Riverfront Heritage Trail** (www. kcrivertrails.org), a paved 15-mile (24-km) bicycling and walking path, spans Missouri and Kansas. From the River Market area, you can easily access the Riverfront Heritage Trail by walking north on Main Street, on the west side of City Market. You'll find some route info at each access point. Public artwork and historical information line the trail. A commemorative plaque along the trail marks the Westport Landing, where riverboats deposited pioneers ready to begin their wagon journey west.

Swope Park (3999 Swope Pkwy., 816/513-7500, http://kcparks.org, 5am-midnight daily, free), located 17 miles (27 km) southeast of downtown, is covered in limestone bluffs and has about 12 miles (19 km) of mountain biking trails; the volunteer-run park has plans to increase it to 50 miles (80 km). Most of the routes are downhill-oriented one-way trails. Some are quite technical, including drops and gap jumps. Beginners can try the fun, easy, 3.5-mile (5.6-km) Rancho D-Lux trail, and there's also a 0.5-mile (0.8-km) kid-friendly loop. If you'd rather walk than bike, Swope Park's 2-mile (3.2-km) Fox Hollow Trail is a great option for hiking and enjoying wetland wildlife. Find more trail information at the park's **Lakeside Nature Center** (4701 E. Gregory Blvd., 816/513-8960, 9am-4pm Tues.-Sun., free), Missouri's largest native species rehabilitation center.

Bike Rentals

Rent your bike from the friendly and helpful folks at **Erik's Bike Shop Leawood** (3701 W. 95th St., 913/428-8430, www. eriksbikeshop.com, 10am-7pm Mon.-Fri., 10am-6pm Sat., noon-5pm Sun., $100-120 per day), about 10 miles (16 km) southwest of the park. It has everything from city bikes to mountain bikes.

BCycle (http://kc.bcycle.com, first 30 min. free, $2 per 30 min. thereafter, $7 for 24 hours) is Kansas City's bike-share system. Pick up or drop off a bike at the more than 50 stations around town. Major stations are located downtown, at River Market, Westport, and the Country Club Plaza.

Spectator Sports

Kansas City ranks as one of the best in the Midwest for spectator sports, and fans are passionate—the football stadium is in the Guinness Book of World Records as the loudest in the world! While you're in town, go to a game at one of the town's storied stadiums.

The **Kansas City Royals** (www.mlb.com, Mar.-Sept., $35-150) play at "The K," or **Kauffman Stadium** (1 Royal Way, 800/676-9257). Open since 1973, the stadium has seen its share of fast pitches and stolen bases. Head to Gate A on the Plaza Level to take a look at the **Royals Hall of Fame** (during every home game, free) to see artifacts, photos, and trophies from the baseball team's past.

Possibly the biggest game in town is found at **Arrowhead Stadium** (1 Arrowhead Dr., 816/920-9300), home to NFL football's **Kansas City Chiefs** (Sept.-Jan., $30-150). The stadium broke sound records in 2014. Don't miss out on the ultimate fan experience—tailgating. The parking lot ($60-100 for a parking spot) opens 5 hours before kickoff, and the gates to the stadium open 3.5 hours prior. It's a cultural experience unto itself, with thousands of fans cooking food, playing music, and partying before the game.

Tours

There are several ways to get a feel for Kansas City with excellent guided tours. For a general sightseeing orientation, head out with **KC Fun Tours** (Union Station, 30 W. Pershing Rd., 816/500-5417, www.kcfuntours.com, 10am, noon, and 2pm daily, $20 adults, $18 seniors, $10 under age 13) on a 1.5-hour guided tour via air-conditioned trolley bus. Your guide will regale you with tales about the town's sights, fountains, hot spots, historical sights, and more.

Eat your way through town with **Taste of Kansas City** (913/634-0444, www.tasteofkansascityfoodtours.com, Thurs.-Sat.). It offers a variety of tours, including the **Lip Smacking Foodie Tour** ($60), a 3-hour bus tour with flavor and flair. The **Original Streetcar & Food Tour** ($60) is a 2.5-hour journey with five stops, including tastings and beverages. Or try the 3.5-hour **Prohibition Tour** ($80), including four cocktails from speakeasies, former brothels, and modern distilleries. Advance reservations are required; call or book online.

Entertainment
Bars and Brewpubs

Drink a pint in the oldest building in Kansas City at **Kelly's Westport Inn** (500 Westport Rd., 816/561-5800, http://kellyswestportinn.com, 11am-3am daily). Built in 1850, the former Albert G. Boone Store used to be owned by the grandson of frontiersman Daniel Boone, and supplied covered wagons as they started their journeys west. Find a mural and a plaque on the side of the brick building commemorating this National Historic Landmark. Since 1947, the building has housed Kelly's, an Irish pub. Ireland native Randal Kelly injects his friendly presence and personality into the bar, making for an energetic place with good stories, a lively crowd, and live music. Enjoy happy hour (3pm-7pm Sat.-Sun.).

Kansas City thumbed its nose at Prohibition, so perhaps it's no surprise you can find a stunning cocktail scene here today. Find your new favorite mix at **SoT** (1521 Grand Blvd., 816/842-8292, www.sotkc.com, 4pm-11pm Tues.-Wed., 4pm-1:30am Thurs.-Sat.), which uses unusual ingredients in fantastic ways. The menu changes seasonally, and you can let the bartender create an adventurous drink for you. This is also a place tailored for social media pics, with exposed brick walls accented by rich blue seating and neon pink signs. Reservations are recommended.

An ode to the city's bootlegger past, **Tom's Town** (1701 Main St., 816/541-2400, www.toms-town.com, 4pm-10pm Mon., 4pm-11:30pm Tues.-Thurs., 2pm-midnight Fri.-Sat., 2pm-10pm Sun.) is a distillery offering high-quality spirits. Sip a balanced cocktail from the rich walnut bar in the tasting room. You can also book a tour (45 minutes, Tues.-Sat., $10) to go behind the scenes and learn how your favorite spirit is made, as well as some of the history behind Tom's. It's named for notorious boozy politician Tom Pendergast, who kept the city flush with drinks in the 1920s and openly flouted Prohibition. "The people are thirsty," he famously said.

Boulevard Brewing Co. (2501 Southwest Blvd., 816/474-7095, www.boulevard.com, 11am-8pm Mon.-Wed., 11am-9pm Thurs., 10am-9pm Fri.-Sat., 10am-6pm Sun.) began in 1989 and has grown into a well-known Midwestern brewer and an all-around good place to get a pint. Stop by the pub for a choice of 30 taps. You can also take a tour of the brewery (45 minutes, $5); they're held several times daily and leave from 2504 Madison Avenue, right around the corner—tickets become available on the day and must be purchased in person.

The **Up-Down KC** (101 Southwest Blvd., 816/982-9455, www.updownkc. com, 3pm-1am Mon.-Fri., 11am-1am Sat., 11am-midnight Sun.) is where young Kansas City goes to hang out. The 21-and-up bar has over 50 arcade games and pinball machines, plus a giant *Jenga* and *Connect Four.* Relive your 1980s memories with arcade games like *Mortal Kombat, Tron,* and *Pac-Man,* then cheer your victory (or drown your sorrows) in pizza and local craft beer. There's no entry fee, and games cost $0.25 each.

Live Music
Located above the Missouri River north of downtown, **The Rino** (314 Armour Rd., 816/800-4699, www.therinokc.org, 7am-10pm Mon.-Thurs., 7am-midnight Fri., 8am-midnight Sat., 11am-5pm Sun., $5-15) is a small music venue with a capacity of 150. It offers craft beer and excellent cocktails along with live music most nights of the week. Shows are usually 18 and over and feature up-and-coming artists. During the day, the venue serves as a workspace, complete with great coffee.

Located in Westport and a local favorite, **The Riot Room** (4048 Broadway St., 816/442-8179, www.theriotroom.com, $5-25) is a rock-and-roll bar with plenty of beer, a "reverse happy hour" at midnight, and a rotating cast of diverse acts. The venue is on the small side and holds 300, though even a sold-out show won't feel too crowded. The space is dimly lit, and the sound is big. The Riot Room has a show almost every night of the week. Check the website for tickets and performance schedules.

A romantic venue that focuses exclusively on jazz seven nights a week, the **Green Lady Lounge** (1809 Grand Blvd., 816/215-2954, www.greenladylounge. com, 4pm-3am Sun.-Fri., 2pm-3am Sat., no cover) celebrates the thriving musical scene of Kansas City. With rich red walls covered in oil paintings, servers dressed to the nines, and low lighting, it's a classy place that still manages to be welcoming and unfussy.

The Arts
The **Kauffman Center for the Performing Arts** (1601 Broadway Blvd., 816/994-7222, www.kauffmancenter.org, box office 10am-6pm Mon.-Fri. and 1.5 hours before showtime, $15-100) is home to the city's symphony, opera, and ballet companies, offering an enriching program of events throughout the year. The building itself is a unique architectural wonder created from half-domed concentric arches. Its two performance halls seat 1,600 and 1,800 each. Snag a stunning view of the Kansas City skyline from the lobby before or after your show.

Festivals and Events

Situated in the conservative Midwest, Kansas City is a hot spot of LGBTQ pride year-round, but the biggest celebration is **Kansas City PrideFest** (www.kcpridefest. org, last weekend in May, $10 adults, free under age 12). Kansas City's event was named by the LGBTQ magazine *The Advocate* as one of the top 10 festivals in the nation. The family-friendly event offers a weekend full of fun at Berkeley Riverfront Park in the River Market neighborhood. Performances by national headliners, drag queens, and men's choruses are joined by a kids zone and hangout spaces for LGTBQIA+ teens.

One of the longest-running art festivals in the country, the beloved **Plaza Art Fair** (www.plazaartfair.com, 3rd weekend after Labor Day, free) draws crowds of 250,000 to the Country Club Plaza for three days of fun, with over 240 artists, 3 music stages, and 25 restaurant booths over nine blocks.

Food

Barbecue

Arguably the best barbecue in Kansas City (fighting words!) can be found at ★ **Joe's Kansas City Bar-B-Que** (3002 W. 47th St., 913/722-3366, www.joeskc.com, 11am-9pm Mon.-Thurs., 11am-10pm Fri.-Sat., $9), an award-winning spot that slings its cuts faster than you can order. This original Joe's was born in a gas station, and now has several locations around town. The house specialty is the pulled pork sandwich, served with your choice of sides. Or go with the Z-man Sandwich, including smoked beef brisket, smoked provolone cheese, and two crispy onion rings on a bun. Vegetarian? Get the smoked mushrooms! And take home 20 ounces of Joe's famous sauce for only $5.

Test another city best at ★ **Arthur Bryant's Barbeque** (1727 Brooklyn Ave., 816/231-1123, www.arthurbryantsbbq. com, 10am-9pm Mon.-Sat., 11am-8pm Sun., $11), the legacy of one of the most popular pit masters in history. Try the secret recipe sauce (original or rich and spicy) slathered over any number of slow-roasted meats on Wonder Bread, served with fries or onion rings. And don't miss the burnt ends—a traditional part of Kansas City barbecue; Arthur Bryant's serves up some of the best.

City Market

City Market is a great place to find delicious options. Top of the list is **Taste of Brazil** (25 E. 3rd St., 816/527-0400, http://tasteofbrazilkc.com, 11am-2pm Mon., 11am-6pm Tues.-Sat., 11am-4pm Sun., $10), which has amazing flavorful sandwiches alongside *empadinhas* (Brazilian-style chicken pot pie), *pão de queijo* (cheesy bread rolls), and churros for dessert. **Pigwich** (20 E. 5th St., 816/200-1639, http://thelocalpig.com, 11am-8pm daily, $8) is another local favorite, serving meat-centric sandwiches like a pork brisket, a banh mi, and cheesesteaks. For something sweet head to **Bloom Baking Company** (15 E. 3rd St., 816/283-8427, www.bloombakingco. com, 8am-2pm Mon., 7am-4pm Tues.-Sat., 8am-4pm Sun., $5) with its roster of cream horns, macarons, chocolate tortes, and cupcakes.

Asian

★ **Blue Koi Noodles & Dumplings** (1803 W. 39th St., 816/561-5003, www.bluekoi. net, 11am-9pm Mon.-Thurs., 11am-10pm Fri., noon-10pm Sat., $15) is Chinese comfort food, pure and simple. The eatery offers delicious choices like Ants on a Tree—Chinese noodles tossed with spiced pork and chopped cabbage and carrots—as well as vegetarian and vegan options. Add some steamed dumplings, an almond asparagus rice bowl, and one of the signature bubble teas to round out your meal.

Komatsu Ramen (3951 Broadway Rd., 816/469-5336, www.komatsuramen.co, 11am-1:30am Mon.-Sat., 11am-midnight Sun., $10) is open late for all your postdrinking, noodle-slurping needs. It offers

Kansas City Barbecue

Kansas City is known for its barbecue. This rich tradition harks back to the first outdoor pits of Henry Perry, "The Father of Kansas City Barbecue," in the early 1900s.

So what makes KC's so popular? One answer is the burnt ends, a traditional part of the city's barbecue scene. They're made from the end points of brisket slabs and are exactly what they sound like. A crusty, fatty, juicy vehicle for sauce, they're served as a main dish, side dish, in sandwiches, and sometimes as a topping. Kansas City barbecue traditionally calls for slowly smoked meat (beef, pork, chicken, even fish) slathered in a tomato-based sauce. Usually sweet as well as spicy, Kansas City barbecue sauce typically features a well-balanced flavor profile, though each restaurant has its own secret recipe.

Kansas City barbecue

Over 100 places in the Kansas City area serve barbecue, and the saying goes that if you ask two locals about their favorite place, you'll get three answers.

a wide variety of ramen, from the veggie-forward miso to the hearty *tonkatsu* (breaded deep-fried pork cutlet). Add a steamed bun to your meal to top off the night.

Lulu's Thai Noodle Shop (2030 Central St., 816/474-8424, www.lulusnoodles.com, 11am-10pm Mon.-Sat., noon-9pm Sun., $12) offers a variety of pan-Asian noodles, curries, and street-food bites like Thai hot wings, dumplings, and rolls. The large menu is full of sweet and spicy options, and diners can experiment with the various sauces on the tables.

Mexican

Stop by the bright lights of ★ **Port Fonda** (1414 Pennsylvania Ave., 816/216-6462, www.portfonda.com, 11am-10pm Mon.-Wed., 11am-1am Thurs.-Fri., 9am-1am Sat., 9am-10pm Sun., $12) for award-winning Mexican food. The eclectic restaurant has *luchador* and cowboy decor and a menu brimming with fresh flavors. Vegetarians will find plenty to love, like the jackfruit *al pastor* or the *tlayuda* (a giant Oaxacan-style corn tostada), and

omnivores will love the *barbacoa, pozole verde,* and drool-worthy carnitas.

Coffee and Bakeries

The duo of **Messenger Coffee Co. + Ibis Bakery** (1624 Grand Blvd., 913/669-9883, www.ibisbakery.com, 7am-6pm daily, $8) is a match brewed and baked in heaven. Ibis puts out delectable breads and pastries, including a raspberry torte, croissants, and an amazing bread pudding. Pair it with one of Messenger's perfectly brewed cups of coffee, and grab a loaf of small-batch bread to take home.

The Roasterie Factory Café (1204 W. 27th St., 816/931-4000, www.theroasterie.com, 7am-6pm Mon.-Fri., 8am-6pm Sat., 9am-3pm Sun., $5) is a local favorite chain of cafés, creating specialty coffees using a unique "air roasted" process. This produces a clean, smooth flavor without the bitterness of traditional drum roasting. The café offers a large menu of coffee drinks, including a cold brew, flavored blends, and espresso, along with CBD additions and baked goods. At this factory location, you can also take a tour (10am and 12:30pm Sun.-Fri., 8am, 10am, 11:30am, and 2:30pm Sat., $5) to see the roasting process, watch a brewing demonstration, and enjoy a complimentary sample.

Shopping
River Market
Planters Seed and Spice Company (513 Walnut St., 816/842-3651, www.plantersseed.com, 7am-6pm Mon.-Fri., 7am-5pm Sat.) is in an 1870s brick building full of modern spices, coffee, and tea. Head home with the perfect herb mix to spice up your fresh veggies.

A fun shop full of Japan-inspired items, **Yoki** (400 Grand Blvd., Suite 426, 816/214-6807, www.yokistore.com, 10am-6pm Mon.-Sat., 10am-5pm Sun.) has Hello Kitty products galore, but also Totoro and other anime characters, beauty items, and tea. Try the Japanese snacks—they make a great gift for anyone back home.

Westport
Take a stroll around the oldest neighborhood in Kansas City for some unique finds. Right across from Pioneer Park is the **Mills Record Company** (4505 Broadway Blvd., 816/960-3175, http://millsrecordcompany.com, 10am-8pm Mon.-Thurs., 10am-9pm Fri.-Sat., 10am-6pm Sun.), a locally owned store with a large selection of new and used vinyl. It also features live local performances, and staff can happily help you track down your favorite tunes.

Find a handmade necklace, artwork, home goods, and more at the colorful **Mid Coast Modern** (314 Westport Rd., 816/599-4574, www.midcoastmodernkc.com, 11am-6pm Mon.-Fri., 10am 6pm Sat., 10am-3pm Sun.). The store's name is a playful nod to its focus of celebrating artists and makers from the middle of the country rather than the coasts.

If you're into running you'll be delighted at **Run 816** (304 Westport Rd., 816/569-0106, www.run816.com, 10am-7pm Tues.-Fri., 10am-4pm Sat., 8am-2pm Sun.), an inclusive runner's utopia of quality gear and events.

For antiques lovers, **Morning Glory Antiques** (313 Westport Rd., 913/484-7425, www.morninggloryantiquesinc.com, 11am-5pm Mon.-Sat.) is a must-stop. It has been offering exquisite items from centuries past for years, and the well-curated store makes finding your treasure a joy.

Country Club Plaza
Country Club Plaza comprises 15 blocks of the best shopping in the city. Over 100 shops and 30 restaurants are within easy walking distance, with plenty of parking options.

Internationally known chains hold court alongside smaller boutiques like luxury jeweler **Tivol** (220 Nicholds Rd., 816/531-5800, www.tivol.com, 10am-5:30pm Mon.-Wed. and Fri.-Sat., 10am-8pm Thurs.); antiques and vintage purveyor **Re: Emporium** (4704 Wyandotte St., 913/274-8321, www.reemporiumkc.com, 10am-7pm daily); trendy mother-and-daughter-owned fashion boutique **Fortuity** (612 W. 48th St., 816/673-1122, www.fortuityusa.com, 10am-8pm daily); and the array of local artists featured at **Made in Kansas City Marketplace** (306 W. 47th St., 816/718-0806, www.madeinkc.co, 8am-10pm daily).

Accommodations
Under $150
Stay near Westport in a room featuring decor conceived by Kansas City venues at the ★ **816 Hotel** (801 Westport Rd., 813/931-1000, www.816hotel.com, $109-250). The specialty rooms have been designed by places like the Boulevard Brewing Co. and The Roasterie. Regular rooms have archival photos of Kansas City. Amenities include Tommy Bahama bath products, a hot breakfast, and a lobby bar offering guests their first drink on the house.

$150-250

Enjoy luxury accommodations with a heavy dose of history downtown at ★ **Hotel Phillips** (106 W. 12th St., 816/221-7000, www.hotelphillips.com, $175-300). Part of the Curio Collection by Hilton, it was built in 1931 and was once the tallest building in town, so stunning and full of art deco stylings that it was named Missouri's most beautiful hotel by *Architectural Digest*. Rooms are spacious and include thoughtful amenities like a Bluetooth clock and USB charging outlets. Treat yourself to the Truman Suite, a 1-bedroom that boasts a canopy bed, claw-foot tub, and corner view. It's an homage to the president, who once owned a haberdashery on the ground where the hotel now stands.

If you want to be close to the shopping, stay at **The Fontaine** (901 W. 48th Ave., 816/753-8800, www.thefontainehotel.com, $160-249). In Country Club Plaza near hundreds of shops, the hotel has 132 luxury rooms and suites at a great price. Its name is a play on Kansas City's nickname, the City of Fountains, and the decor is an elegant dream full of Renaissance artwork, marble floors, damask headboards, and chandeliers.

Between River Market and Country Club Plaza, the centrally located **Hotel Indigo** (101 W. 11th St., 816/283-8000, www.hotelindigo.com, $179-220) has a neighborhood feel in the heart of the city. Recently renovated, the 118 guest rooms feature warm lights with velvet and brass accents and are decorated with giant historical postmarks in a nod to the building's past as a ticket office for the railroad. There's also a train mural evoking the golden age of 1920s travel in the lobby.

Sleep under a brilliant work of art at the **21c Museum Hotel** (219 W. 9th St., 888/511-0078, www.21cmuseumhotels.com, $140-255), a unique contemporary art museum and boutique hotel in one. Each of the 120 rooms and suites is decorated with original artwork and features high ceilings and big windows. The contemporary art collection is spread across the hotel in gallery spaces and hallways and is freely open to the public 365 days a year, with guided tours at 5pm Wednesday and Friday. Guests can enjoy a meal at The Savoy, which still has a booth commemorating President Truman's favorite spot in the lounge.

Southmoreland on the Plaza (116 E. 46th St., 816/531-7979, www.southmoreland.com, $175-225) is a bed-and-breakfast with 12 guest rooms, 1.5 blocks from Country Club Plaza. Each room is named after famous Kansas City residents (such as George Caleb Bingham) and styled after the historical period in which they lived. Enjoy complimentary wine in their beautiful garden upon arrival, and a freshly cooked breakfast each morning.

Over $250

Housed in the former Pabst Brewing Depot, **Crossroads Hotel** (2101 Central St., 816/897-8100, http://crossroadshotelkc.com, $260-289) is in the heart of the Crossroads Arts District. The hotel prides itself on being a community-focused place where stories are told, and the Midwestern spirit of friendliness and artistry in in evidence. The 131 rooms are warm, with exposed brick and wooden accents. Dine at the on-site Italian restaurant Lazia, or enjoy the city from the rooftop bar.

Camping

Just west of downtown in a great location off I-35, **Walnut Grove RV Park** (10218 Johnson Dr., 913/262-3023, http://walnutgroverv.com, $38-48) is a short drive to neighborhoods like Westport and Country Club Plaza. It has 50 full-hookup sites with showers, a dog park, laundry facilities, free coffee, and friendly staff. Book ahead, as it tends to fill up quickly.

Information

The main **Kansas City Visitor Center** (1321 Baltimore Ave., 816/691-3800, www.visitkc.com, 9am-5pm Mon.-Fri., 10am-3pm Sat.) is downtown. If you're driving from St. Louis on I-70, an easy stop is the **Missouri Welcome Center** (4010 Blue Ridge Cutoff, 816/889-3330, 8am-5pm daily spring-fall); heading west on I-70, take exit 9, then turn left onto Blue Ridge Cutoff.

For the most up-to-date information on arts, music, and culture, pick up the free alternative weekly publication *The Pitch* (www.thepitchkc.com).

Along the Trail from Kansas City

Pioneers leaving Missouri were bound for various places—some Oregon, some California, and some Santa Fe, New Mexico. The Three Trails tended to follow the same route for a few days after leaving Missouri before diverging, just south of Kansas City in Gardner, Kansas, when the Oregon- and California-bound headed north and the Santa Fe-bound headed south.

Leaving Kansas City, Missouri, today, you can follow the Three Trails south to two more sites—adding on a net extra 25 miles (40 km) and 45 minutes total to your westward drive to your next stop, Topeka, Kansas's capital city. There are no wagon ruts visible at either location, and no other attractions, so head this way only if you want to follow the true path of the wagons.

Lone Elm Campground

Lone Elm Park (21151 W. 157th St., Olathe, KS, www.olatheks.org, 6am-10pm daily) was once marked by a single elm that's no longer here. It used to be a campground and meeting point for pioneers, recorded in diaries as **Lone Elm Campground**. Today it's a lovely city park with interpretive panels, a picnic shelter, and grassy spaces.

Getting There

From Kansas City, head south on I-35 for 23 miles (37 km) and take exit 214. Turn left onto Lone Elm Road, and drive 1.5 miles (2.4 km) to arrive at the park in 30 minutes.

The Parting of the Trails

The Parting of the Trails is at **Gardner Junction Park** (32499 W. 183rd St., Gardner, KS), which pays tribute to the site where the Oregon and California Trails diverged from the Santa Fe Trail. Interpretive panels offer some information, and you can look out across a field once traversed by wagons. No ruts are visible here, but stone posts mark the path of the Oregon Trail.

Getting There

You can follow NPS signs when leaving Lone Elm; the way is well marked, though it takes you down several bumpy dirt roads. Or you can more easily get to the next stop by heading south 0.6 mile (1 km) on Lone Elm Road and turning right onto West 175th Street, which becomes U.S. 56. Follow it for 7 miles (11.3 km) through Gardner, then turn right onto West 183rd Street. The drive takes 10 minutes.

The Santa Fe Trail

The Santa Fe Trail was a 900-mile (1,450 km) major trade route that predated the Oregon Trail; it was in use 1821-1880. It had several jumping-off points in Missouri, including Independence. The outfitters and general stores that sprang up in the town to serve the Santa Fe-bound wagons were a major reason that Oregon Trail pioneers also set off from Independence. The Santa Fe Trail was primarily commercial, focused on the trade of goods, and didn't see the huge numbers of settler families like the Oregon Trail did. From Gardner, Kansas, the Santa Fe Trail continued southwest across the territory of modern-day Kansas and New Mexico, which were then part of Mexico. Wagons were stocked with cloth (calico, chambray, flannel, linen, and silk), tools, buttons, knives, and clothing for selling and trading. Mexican traders traveled north to Santa Fe along the Camino Real de Tierra Adentro (Royal Road of the Interior Land) from cities like Mexico City, Durango, and Chihuahua. The roads met in Santa Fe, a hub of trading and culture. Mexican traders brought with them silver and gold, as well as mules—popular with the northern traders, as they could be sold for a high profit back in Missouri. In 1880 the Atchison, Topeka, and Santa Fe Railway (ATSF) was completed, connecting Kansas to Santa Fe. The rails effectively ended the trail's use in favor of the faster, safer, more comfortable railroad car.

Topeka, KS

The capital of Kansas, Topeka was once part of the rolling tallgrass prairie that supported herds of bison. Once the wagons started rolling through, pioneers needed a way to cross the Kansas River, a tributary of the Missouri River. Several ferry sites sprang up nearby, many run by members of the Potawatomi Nation. Pappan's Ferry was one of the bigger operations, moving wagons across the river on large wooden platforms steered by long poles. Crossing rivers was dangerous, and many rafts overturned, especially when rivers were swollen with rainfall. Encampments sprouted up near the river fords, as emigrants waited to cross. Many opportunists built trading posts, restaurants, blacksmith shops, and more to serve the pioneers. It wasn't long before those camps got their own post offices, becoming towns in their own right. Topeka was established in 1854 by a group of nine men headed by Cyrus K. Holliday, who would later become mayor and also owner of the Atchison, Topeka, and Santa Fe Railway.

Today, nothing remains of Topeka's ferries, but historians believe Pappan's once operated between Topeka Boulevard Bridge and Kansas Avenue Bridge. The capital of Kansas, Topeka is known for its free-state stance in the years leading up to the Civil War. The town was the scene of violent struggles between anti-abolitionists and anti-slavery forces, which caused the state to be nicknamed "Bleeding Kansas." When an influx of African Americans known as the Exodusters began arriving in the state in 1879, Topeka welcomed them with an organized social welfare and resettlement program. In the 20th century, Topeka was also the site of the famous *Brown* v. *Board of Education,* which ruled that segregation was illegal. Some of this rich history is showcased in museums around town, while the beautiful parks offer visitors a green look at today's Kansas. The Kansas State Capitol is the center of the walkable downtown and is easy to spot above the city.

Getting There and Around

If you're coming **directly from Kansas City,** it's a 63-mile (101-km) drive west to Topeka via I-70, which heads through downtown before turning north and following the Kansas River out of town.

Topeka

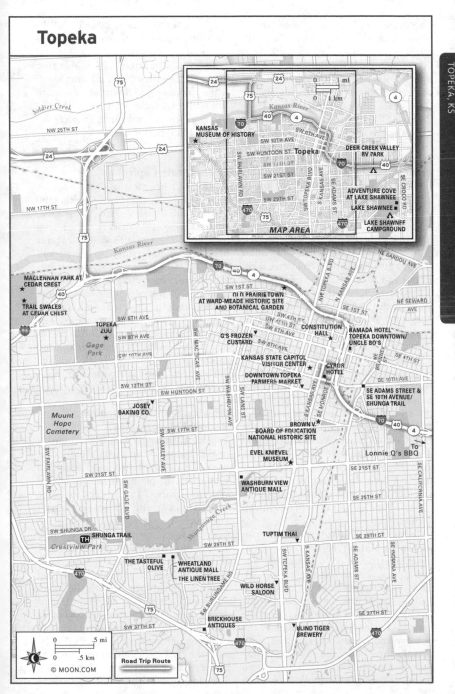

The drive takes about an hour. To get to downtown Topeka from I-70 West, take exit 362C for access to the Kansas State Capitol and the *Brown* v. *Board of Education* National Historic Site. Other attractions are farther west off I-70, like the Kansas Museum of History, Gage Park, or Old Prairie Town. A car is the easiest way to quickly see them all. Note I-70 is a toll road, and the drive from Kansas City costs about $3.50. To avoid the toll, head south from Kansas City via I-35 and continue for 15 miles (24 km) to exit 222B, keeping left to continue onto Highway 10 at exit 1B. Continue for 34 miles (55 km), then use the right lane to take the ramp to Highway 40. Turn left onto Highway 40, and continue 18 miles (29 km) into downtown. This drive takes 1 hour and 20 minutes.

If you came **via the Parting of the Trails on the historic route,** head southwest on U.S. 56 from Gardner Junction Park. In 17.5 miles (28 km), turn right onto U.S. 59 toward Lawrence. Drive 9.7 miles (15.6 km), then turn left onto Highway 10. In 8.5 miles (13.6 km), turn right to take the ramp onto I-70. In 18.4 miles (29 km), take exit 362C for downtown Topeka. The drive takes just under an hour. Expect to pay about $1.25 from Lawrence to Topeka via I-70. To avoid the toll, you can take U.S. 40 instead. From Highway 10 coming from Gardner Junction Park, drive 6.6 miles (10.6 km) and then merge onto U.S. 40, continuing on it for 18 miles (29 km) into downtown Topeka.

Topeka has regular bus services run by **Topeka Metro** (785/783-7000, www.topekametro.org, $2 one-way, $4 24-hour pass, exact change required); find a map online or at the downtown Quincy Street Station (820 SE Quincy St.). Topeka is also known as one of the most bike-friendly communities in the country, and visitors will find a network of paths throughout the city, many away from traffic. The best way to hop on two wheels is through the city's bike-share program, **Topeka Metro Bikes** (785/730-8615, http://topekametrobikes.org, $2.50 per hour). Downtown is walkable and has a few nearby attractions: Old Prairie Town is 1.7 miles (2.7 km) northeast, while the *Brown* v. *Board of Education* site is about 1 mile (1.6 km) south, and the Evel Knievel museum another 0.7 mile (1.1 km) past that.

Sights
Kansas State Capitol
Get a bird's-eye view of the state from the top of the **Kansas State Capitol** (300 W. 10th St., 785/296-3966, www.kshs.org, 8am-5pm Mon.-Fri., 8am-1pm Sat., free). The capitol's stately features have been wonderfully preserved and restored, and visitors can enjoy murals and carvings along with a stunning dome. A 40-minute dome tour allows you to climb the 296 steps up to the top and step outside for sunny views. The tours are free, but reservations are recommended, as they are popular and can fill up fast. You can explore the building during open hours at any time; enter on 8th Avenue.

Brown v. *Board of Education* National Historic Site
Topeka witnessed a watershed moment in U.S. history when the landmark case to end legal segregation was decided in 1954. Both the plaintiffs and the school systems involved in the decision were from Topeka, and the case eventually made its way to the U.S. Supreme Court. You can visit the *Brown* v. *Board of Education* **National Historic Site** (1515 SE Monroe St., www.nps.gov/brvb, 9am-5pm Mon.-Sat., free), located in the old Monroe Elementary School, the once-segregated school that the plaintiff, student Linda Brown, attended. Visitors will find galleries and exhibits in the old classrooms that examine the court decision, the civil rights movement, and the history of segregation and education. The kindergarten room reflects its 1954

One Day in Topeka

Morning

Start off with an early stop at **Josey Baking Co.** for sweet *kolaches*, then head to **MacLennan Park** to hunt for Oregon Trail ruts in the meadow. After that, drive over to the **Kansas Museum of History,** which covers significant events in the state's past, including discussion of the trail. If you have extra time after the museum, you can explore the nature trails on its grounds. Don't delay too long, though, because if it's a weekday, you'll want to head to **Lonnie Q's BBQ** for the city's best lunch—get there early to avoid the line.

Afternoon

After lunch, delve into other histories. The ***Brown v. Board of Education* National Historic Site** is free and examines a seminal moment in the country's civil rights movement. Or explore **Old Prairie Town,** a 19th-century pioneer town where you can peek into an early pioneer log cabin. If you've had enough history for the day, enjoy the daring escapades at the **Evel Knievel Museum,** where you can try a simulated jump yourself.

Evening

Dine at **Blind Tiger Brewery** for a steak and a pint, and if it's a nice evening, walk or bike it off on the paved path around **Lake Shawnee.** Top the day off with some Brown Bread ice cream from **G's Frozen Custard.**

segregated appearance, and a 30-minute video plays in the old auditorium.

Old Prairie Town

The **Old Prairie Town at Ward-Meade Historic Site and Botanical Garden** (124 NW Fillmore St., 785/251-2989, 8am-dusk daily, tours $5 adults, $4 seniors, $3 ages 6-12, free under age 6, grounds free) covers 5.5 acres of beautiful parkland. The "town" is located along the route of the Oregon Trail, and includes a replica 1854 log cabin that pioneer Anthony Ward lived in while constructing the Victorian mansion that now stands on the site. The historical village is an example of the type of town where the pioneers may have lived once they settled into their new lives. The 19th-century buildings, many of which were moved here from their original sites around Kansas, include a train station, a barn, a church, a one-room schoolhouse, and a barbershop.

The gardens are especially gorgeous in spring during Tulip Time, which is celebrated at various places around town,

or the fall Apple Festival. You can wander the site for free, or pay for a $5 tour that affords entrance to many of the old buildings. Tickets can be purchased at the Mulvane General Store. All visitors can visit the **Potwin Drug Store,** a turn-of-the-century soda fountain that serves shakes, malts, and freezes (ice cream and club soda)—be sure to try a taste of the Brown Bread ice cream, made by G's Frozen Custard in Topeka. Can you guess the secret ingredient? It's not actually bread, but Grape-Nuts cereal.

MacLennan Park at Cedar Crest

You can see some excellent trail swales at **MacLennan Park at Cedar Crest** (1 SW Cedar Crest Rd., 785/296-3636, park dawn-dusk daily, mansion tours 1:30pm-3:30pm Mon., free). The French-style governor's mansion, built by a Scotsman, is open once a week for tours. Volunteers show visitors around the 1st floor (the upstairs is the governor's living quarters). The grounds outside are open to the public daily and have miles of trails, making it a popular local spot for running.

You can easily find the swales about 100 yards south of the mansion. Head down the walking path; the swales are to the right, near the trees. In pioneer times, the trees would not have been here, and the path would have continued along the prairie.

Kansas Museum of History

The award-winning **Kansas Museum of History** (6425 SW 6th Ave., 785/272-8681, www.kshs.org/museum, 9am-5pm Tues.-Sat., 1pm-5pm Sun., $10 adults, $5 ages 2-17) showcases significant events in the state's past. Starting with displays covering the varied customs of the people of the plains—including the Osage, Arapaho, and Pawnee peoples—it continues through the modern era. The large museum houses a wagon, a bi-plane, a soda fountain, a log cabin, and even an entire train! The displays are informative, helped by many great artifacts and examples. Visitors will learn about the Oregon and Santa Fe Trails, Bleeding Kansas's role in the Civil War, Amelia Earhart, and the rise of the locomotive. Outside you'll find 2 miles (3.2 km) of nature trails through tallgrass prairie around historic buildings, fences, and bridges. The Oregon Trail passed near here, though no evidence of it remains.

On the grounds of the museum, visitors will also find the **Potawatomi Mission.** While it's not open to the public, it stands as a testament to the country's dark history of Native American boarding schools. Built in 1848 and operated through 1861, the mission was a manual labor boarding school, with attendance required of local families. Their children were given white names, had their hair cut, and were required to speak, read, and write English. This school is a small local example of widespread practices that took place across the nation.

Top to bottom: interpretive panel at Lone Elm Campground; Old Prairie Town; Potwin Drug Store.

The Exodusters

In the post-Civil War era, Kansas was a nearly mythical place for many African Americans, due to its strong history of being antislavery—the state was known as "Bleeding Kansas" because of the violent conflicts that erupted between anti-slavery and anti-abolitionist forces. Leaders such as the formerly enslaved Benjamin "Pap" Singleton spread the word about the state. Over 6,000 black Americans left for Kansas from the South in 1879 in what was called the Great Exodus. Those who moved were known as "Exodusters." By the next decade, Kansas had 27,000 new African American residents.

President Lincoln had rolled out the Homestead Act in 1862, making 160 acres of land available to any citizen age 21 and up who had not borne arms against the U.S. government—including people of color and women. It offered an opportunity for many newly freed people to escape the oppressive racism of the South. While staying on the land and "proving up"—building a home on the land and running a farm for a minimum of five years—was much harder than filing a claim for the land, the act still lit the way for a westward expansion of a diverse range of settlers.

Not all who came stayed. The reality of homesteading was challenging for anyone, and formerly enslaved people faced discrimination from wary neighbors, help from whom was often necessary on the prairie. Just getting to Kansas proved challenging. While many white Oregon Trail pioneers had sold the family farm in order to buy supplies and move west, the formerly enslaved had no farms to sell and no wealth to speak of. Many arrived in Kansas so destitute they couldn't afford to file a claim for land or buy supplies to work and live on it. When crops failed, black settlers who looked elsewhere for work were often turned away.

But there were success stories in many communities that sprang up across the West. Places like Blackdom, New Mexico; DeWitty, Nebraska; and Dearfield, Colorado, grew into vibrant communities of black homesteaders. The most notable was Nicodemus, Kansas, a solely African American community of up to 400 people who thrived for decades until the Dust Bowl of the 1930s.

Evel Knievel Museum

Get a taste of derring-do at the **Evel Knievel Museum** (2047 SW Topeka Blvd., 785/215-6205, www.evelknievelmuseum. com, 10am-6pm Tues.-Fri., 9am-5pm Sat., noon-5pm Sun., $15 adults, $12 seniors, $7 ages 8-16, free under age 8). Topeka's ode to the daredevil motorcycle stuntman is appropriately located next door to a Harley-Davidson dealership. Inside is an incredible collection of dented helmets, costumes, motorcycles, X-rays of broken bones, videos of jumps, and an 18-wheeler. Even those who might not proclaim themselves rabid Evel fans will enjoy the exhibits on his exploits, as well as a virtual reality motorcycle experience.

Constitution Hall

Kansas Territory's delegates took a stand to ban slavery in 1855 at **Constitution Hall** (429 S. Kansas Ave., 785/250-8338, www.oldkansascapitol.org, 10am-noon Sat. Mar.-Nov., free). One of the oldest buildings in the city, it was used as the state capitol 1864-1869. Constitution Hall keeps limited public hours, but visitors can schedule a tour online to find out more about the building, the Underground Railroad, and early Kansas history. Take a peek outside for the bright mural depicting the state legislature.

Recreation
Gage Park

Gage Park (635 SW Gage Blvd., 785/273-6108, http://parks.snco.us, dawn-dusk daily, free) is one of Topeka's oldest parks and full of activity options. Kids will love the mini train ride and the carousel (10:30am-5pm Sat.-Sun. spring and fall,

10:30am-5pm daily summer, $2 each). The train has been a park tradition for over 45 years, following a mile (1.6 km) of track around the green spaces while the conductor recounts historical stories. The 1908 carousel runs to a real band organ—you can sit and listen to the music without riding.

The park is also home to rose gardens and a rock garden, both of which are beautiful much of the year, but particularly so in spring. The crown of Gage Park is the **Topeka Zoo** (635 SW Gage Blvd., 785/368-9180, www.topekazoo. org, 9am-5pm daily, $7.75 adults, $6.75 seniors, $6.25 ages 3-12, free under age 3), home to over 400 animals from all over the world. Talk a walk in Black Bear Woods or the Lion's Pride. The zoo supports a wildlife conservation center.

Lake Shawnee

Built as a Works Progress Administration project in 1935, **Lake Shawnee** regularly attracts Topeka locals to its shores for fun, festivals, fishing, and more. You'll find a disc golf course, boat ramps, softball fields, and an arboretum. For fun on the water, head to **Adventure Cove** (3515 SE Beach Terrace, 785/251-6800, 11am-7pm Mon.-Fri., 8am-7pm Sat.-Sun., $10-12 per half hour), where you can rent paddleboats, paddleboards, canoes, and kayaks, and even giant-wheeled water trikes. It also has snacks, changing rooms, picnic tables, and a sandy beach. A 38-acre garden and arboretum offers great views of the lake—it's especially beautiful during the Tulip Time event that takes place in various spots around town in the spring, or later in June when the roses are in bloom.

A 7-mile (11.3-km) paved walking-biking path encircles the lake, offering great views and a few steep grades up and down. It's easy to join at any point around

Top to bottom: Kansas State Capitol; Gage Park locomotive; *bierocks* at Josey Baking Co.

the lake, and you'll find plenty of water fountains and rest stops along the way.

Biking

Topeka's bike-share system, **Topeka Metro Bikes** (http://topekametrobikes. org, 785/730-8615, $2.50 per hour), has 300 bikes dispersed at 17 stations in key areas around town, including Gage Park, Lake Shawnee, along the Shunga Trail, and downtown. The program is a popular recent addition to the cityscape, with the blue bikes becoming a beloved way to get around for locals and visitors. You'll need an account to ride, but it's easy to sign up online, and one member can check out more than one bike. When you're done, you can drop the bike off at any nearby station; maps are available online, at each station kiosk, or on the mobile app.

A popular bike route that takes you through the heart of the city is the **Shunga Trail,** a 13-mile (21-km) out-and-back trail between Crestview Park (SW 27th St. and SW Fairlawn Rd.) and the intersection of Southeast 10th Avenue and Adams Street. The concrete path follows Shunga Creek through meadows, parks, and woodlands.

Entertainment

Get your kicks in at **Wild Horse Saloon** (3249 SW Topeka Blvd., 785/267-3545, www.wildhorsetopeka.com, 8pm-2am Wed.-Sun.), a cowboy-themed bar and dance club. There's lots of space to move and lots of people to watch, along with good drinks and food. Come at 8pm Thursday for free country dance lessons, or Sunday for karaoke.

The first craft brewery in Kansas, **Blind Tiger Brewery** (417 SE 37th St., 785/267-2739, www.blindtiger.com, 11am-11pm Sun.-Thurs., 11am-midnight Fri.-Sat., $15), has been brewing for over 20 years. The award-winning pub has six flagship beers on tap at all times, like its Tiger Paw Porter or Holy Grail Pale Ale, as well as other special varieties. Pair that with a large menu of steaks, pasta dishes,

burgers, barbecue, and sandwiches, and you've got a delicious meal. Check out the Kansan Burger, made from locally raised Kansas bison.

The local Ramada hotel houses one of Topeka's best music venues, **Uncle Bo's** (620 SE 6th Ave., 785/234-4317, www. unclebos.com, 6pm-midnight Fri.-Sat., $10 cover), which sees local, national, and "soon to be national" acts play weekly. The bar has deep roots in local lore, with design features from historical Topeka, like cobblestone from the streets and stained glass from the governor's mansion. It's a beloved blues institution with good drinks and affordable tickets.

Food

A little bit of barbecue heaven is **Lonnie Q's BBQ** (3150 SE 21st St., 785/233-4227, http://lonnieqsbbq.com, 11am-1pm Mon.-Thurs., 11am-1pm and 5:30pm-7:30pm Fri., $10). With limited hours—they're only open for lunch most days and closed completely on weekends—it might be tricky timing a meal here, but it's worth the effort. The small team crafts delectable pulled pork, beef brisket, and turkey breast—get the "Cup of Heaven" to try all three along with beans and cheesy taters. Arrive early for lunch to ensure your top pick, especially on Thursday-Friday, when ribs are available.

Tuptim Thai (220 SW 29th St., 785/266-2299, www.tuptimthaitopeka.com, noon-8pm Sun., 11am-2:30pm and 5pm-9pm Mon.-Fri., noon-9pm Sat., $12) is a bit farther south of downtown, but it's a great option if you're weary of burgers. It has a solid menu with favorites like drunken noodles, pad thai, and massaman curry, and a few specialties like roasted duck.

It might not be much to look at from the outside, but **G's Frozen Custard** (1301 SW 6th Ave., 785/234-3480, 1pm-8pm Sun., 11:30am-8pm Mon.-Fri., noon-8pm Sat.) serves up some of the best dessert in the city. The homemade custard and ice cream is made daily in flavors like creamy lemon, chocolate chip, and bread pudding. No matter what you order, ask for a taste of the Brown Bread ice cream—it's a local tradition that harks back to the Victorian era. You'll find some covered outdoor seating to enjoy your scoop.

The delicious baked treats at **Josey Baking Co.** (3119 SW Huntoon St., 785/408-1552, 6:30am-3pm Tues.-Fri., 7am-noon Sat., $5) sell out fast. If you're after one of their sweet *kolaches* you'll need to get here early—before 8:30am—or you might miss out. The *kolaches,* a yeasted dough with fruit filling, hails from Eastern Europe and was brought to the area by Bohemian-Czech immigrants as far back as the 1800s. Polish *bierocks,* filled with savory meats, are also available, along with salads and soups. A rotating cast of other baked goods often shows up too, like giant cookies, croissants, cupcakes, and cinnamon rolls.

A staple since the 1930s, the **Downtown Topeka Farmers Market** (12th St. and Harrison St., 785/249-4704, http://topekafarmersmarket.com, 7:30am-noon Sat. mid-Apr.-Nov.) is the place to go in season for colorful food, unique crafts, and friendly folks. You'll find the best of the season out for sale, along with preserves, honey, jerky, woodworking crafts, fiber art, and more.

Shopping

Topeka is an antiques lover's paradise, with dozens of stores offering hidden treasures. Find some of your own at **Washburn View Antique Mall** (1507 SW 21st St., 785/233-3733, www.washburnviewantiquemall.com, 10am-6pm Mon.-Sat., noon-5pm Sun.). It sells collectibles and furniture, and can also polish metal and repair your lamp. **Brickhouse Antiques** (3711 SW Burlingame Rd., 785/266-6000, 11am-5:30pm Mon. and Thurs.-Sat.) has been voted one of the best in town, with 11 showrooms that offer quality heirloom pieces.

Wheatland Antique Mall (2905 SW 29th St., Suite A, 785/272-4222, 11am-5pm Tues.-Sat.) is one of the oldest in town. It's in the Brookwood Shopping Center, an outdoor shopping mall also offering specialty olives oils at **The Tasteful Olive** (2900 SW Oakley Ave., 785/272-7700, www.thetastefulolive.com, 10am-5:30pm Tues.-Fri., 10am-4pm Sat.) and bath and kitchen linens and soap at the **Linen Tree** (2814 SW 29th St., 785/272-9344, www.topekalinentree.com, 10am-6pm Mon.-Fri., 10am-5pm Sat., noon-4pm Sun.).

Accommodations
Under $150
The lobby of the **Ramada Hotel Topeka Downtown** (420 SE 6th Ave., 785/380-8042, www.topekaramada.com, $92-159) opens into a Vegas-style faux streetscape with indoor fountains, streetlights, and a painted-sky ceiling. The seven-floor tower has 213 rooms, and guests will find an indoor waterfall and a seasonal outdoor pool, breakfast in the indoor courtyard, an arcade room, Uncle Bo's blues bar and lounge, and even a museum—the Holley Museum of Military History. It is a five-minute walk from downtown, making it a good base to explore the area.

On the west side of town, a short drive from the Kansas Museum of History or Gage Park, the **Hampton Inn Topeka** (1515 SW Arrowhead Rd., 785/228-0111, http://hamptoninn3.hilton.com, $117-133) provides a convenient stay just off I-70. The 89 rooms all have 37-inch flat-screen TVs, and guests can enjoy a free hot breakfast, an indoor pool, and a fitness center.

$150-250
★ **Cyrus Hotel** (918 S. Kansas Ave., 866/266-3500, http://cyrushotel.com, $94-203) is a boutique hotel that opened in 2018, revitalizing the downtown core. Named for Topeka's founding pioneer Cyrus K. Holliday, the hotel has 109 rooms in a historic building as well as a new eight-story tower behind it. The lobby and rooms feature velvet, marble,

and polished concrete decor, with throwback yet modern flair. A sense of place is present throughout: The attached restaurant and bar serves dishes with local ingredients, and pictures and quotes from Cyrus himself dot the common areas. There's also a fitness center, a 24-hour front desk, and valet parking.

Camping

Pitch your tent or park your RV near the water at **Lake Shawnee Campground** (3425 SE East Edge Rd., 785/251-6834, http://parks.snco.us, tent camping Apr. 15-Oct. 15, RV camping year-round, $17-20). The campground office is staffed April-October, which is also when reservations are accepted. RV campers can use the first-come, first-served sites year-round with a drop-box fee. Electricity is available, as well as showers, laundry, a private natural swimming area, and a playground. Sites 73-95 are the nicest for views over the water, while sites 96-119 are closest to the beach.

Deer Creek Valley RV (3140 SE 21st Ave., 785/357-8555, www.deercreekvalleyrvpark.com, $45) has 54 pull-through full-hookup RV sites. The park has lovely landscaping, showers, laundry, an outdoor pool, and free Wi-Fi.

Information

Located a block from the Kansas State Capitol, the **Topeka Visitor Center** (719 S. Kansas Ave., Suite 100, 785/234-2633, www.visittopeka.com, 8am-5pm Mon.-Fri.) has maps, brochures, and community guides.

Along the Trail from Topeka

A number of Native American nations, including the Pawnee, Osage, Kansa, Arapaho, Cheyenne, Comanche, Kiowa, and Wichita, lived in the Kansas Territory in the early 1800s. The Pawnee people built great earth lodges to live in and in which to hold ceremonies. The Kiowa people migrated seasonally with the bison herds and lived in tepees. The Osage people were descendants of the great Mississippian mound-building cultures. Many nations battled with one another while also negotiating treaties—later broken—with the United States, causing moving borders and territories. On the whole, contact with the settlers passing through their lands was peaceable. Many Native Americans made use of their river knowledge and ingenuity to create ferry crossings, or traded highly coveted fresh produce for pioneer-made goods. Today, there are four federally recognized Native American nations in Kansas, on reservations near this northeastern corner of the state: the Iowa Tribe of Kansas and Nebraska, the Kickapoo Tribe of Kansas, the Prairie Band Potawatomi Nation, and the Sac and Fox Nation.

Leaving Topeka, emigrants continued across the tallgrass prairie. Sometimes they would ford the wide Kansas River in town, while others would continue on the south bank for a later, less crowded crossing. At this point, many wagon trains had settled into a daily rhythm that kept them fed, watered, and moving forward.

The route ahead travels a winding path on state highways through small towns and green prairie farmland. You'll drive west on U.S. 24, where you'll have the choice of continuing on the paved road or following the dirt Oregon Trail Road—on a branch of the historic trail—before heading north on Highway 99. From Topeka to the Hollenburg Pony Express Station, the drive covers 120 miles and takes about 2 hours and 20 minutes. You can zoom through quickly, but give yourself at least half a day to see everything.

Green Memorial Wildlife Area

The **Green Memorial Wildlife Area** (Gilkerson St., Willard, 8am-5pm daily, free) is a pretty place to take in some wildlife and history amid thick oak and hickory trees. The 83-acre area, once called Union Town, was an Oregon Trail village 1848-1859, built up along the Kansas River near a natural rock ford and later a ferry. A few graves of pioneers, victims of cholera, can be found near an interpretive kiosk inside a wooden fence.

Two short trails offer a chance to explore and look for white-tailed deer, red foxes, meadowlarks, great horned owls, and more. The 1-mile (1.6-km) Post Creek Trail heads along the stream. Traces of ruts can be seen on the 0.75-mile (1.2-km) Oregon Trace Hiking Trail—look for the Oregon Trail signpost at marker 12, showing where the ruts are. Keep an eye out for old stone fences as well. Pamphlets for a self-guided interpretive tour can sometimes be found at the kiosk near the parking lot; it's not always stocked, but the trails are well marked with signs. Note that there are no restrooms here.

Getting There
From Topeka, drive west out of town on I-70. In roughly 15 miles (24 km), take exit 346 for Carlson Road. Drive 2.3 miles (3.7 km), then turn right on 2nd Street in Willard. Turn right onto Gilkerson Road after 0.4 mile (0.6 km), and continue for 1 mile (1.6 km). You'll pass a cemetery and soon see the parking area on the right side of the road. The drive takes just over 20 minutes.

St. Marys
This town was once the site of St. Mary's Mission (now St. Mary's Academy & College), a Jesuit mission founded in 1847 to convert the Potawatomi people, who in 1838 were forcibly resettled in the region from the Great Lakes. Their journey is called the Trail of Death: It covered 660 miles (1,060 km), and over the course of 61 days, 40 people died, many of whom were children. The route from Indiana to Kansas now has markers commemorating it.

Early wagon trains passing by St.

Marys didn't find much in the region, but later emigrants used the mission as a stopping point for rest, trade, and social contact, and in the 1860s a town soon sprang up around it.

Getting There
From Green Memorial Wildlife Area, return to Carlson Road and turn right to head north for 4.3 miles (7 km) to U.S. 24 in Rossville, where you'll turn left and drive 7 miles (11.3 km) to St. Marys. The drive takes about 15 minutes.

Indian Pay Station Museum
The oldest surviving building in the town, the **Indian Pay Station Museum** (111 E. Mission St., 785/437-6600, 1pm-6pm daily Memorial Day-Labor Day, or by appointment, free) was built in 1855 for government agents to dole out payments to Potawatomi Nation members who had accepted a forced deal to relocate from the Great Lakes region. The museum tells the story of the early mission years and the Oregon Trail era with well-organized displays and plenty of historical information. In the original pay station you can see the room where payments were made—including a secret hole in the floor where the money was stored. Plan to spend 30-60 minutes, or longer with a staff tour (available during open hours on request or by appointment).

Food
Stock up on road-trip snacks or get a meal at the **Sugar Creek Country Store** (505 W. Bertrand Ave., 785/321-3000, www.sugarcreekcountrystore.com, 6:30am-7pm Mon.-Fri., 7:30am-7pm Sat., $7) on the town's main street. The mom-and-pop store serves up fresh sandwiches without preservatives from its New York-style deli. Try the "almost world famous" Pullman Panini, with roast beef, cream cheese, onions, and jalapeño, a gooey cinnamon roll, or a scoop of ice cream. If you're not hungry for lunch yet, grab

Along the Trail from Topeka

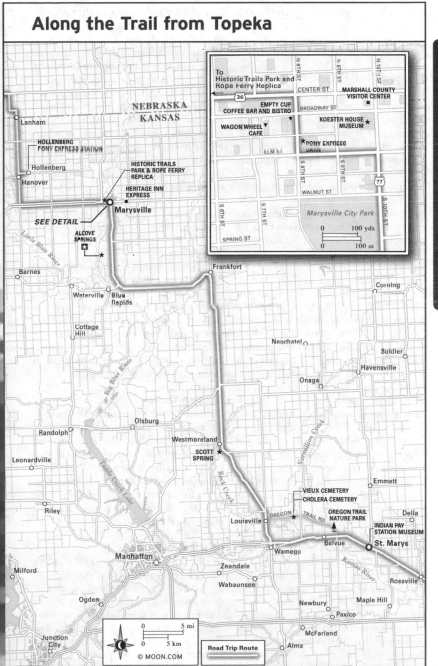

NEBRASKA
KANSAS

Lanham

HOLLENBERG
PONY EXPRESS STATION

Hollenberg

Hanover

HISTORIC TRAILS
PARK & ROPE FERRY
REPLICA

HERITAGE INN
EXPRESS

Marysville

SEE DETAIL

ALCOVE
SPRINGS

Little Blue River

Barnes

Frankfort

Corning

Waterville   Blue
Rapids

Cottage
Hill

Neuchatel

Soldier

Havensville

Onaga

Blue River

Olsburg

Westmoreland

SCOTT
SPRING

Randolph

Emmett

Leonardville

Little Creek Lake

Rock Creek

Vermillion Creek

VIEUX CEMETERY
CHOLERA CEMETERY

OREGON TRAIL
NATURE PARK

Delia

INDIAN PAY
STATION MUSEUM

Riley

OREGON
TRAIL RD

Louisville

St. Marys

Manhattan

Wamego   Belvue

Milford

Zeandale

Kansas River

Rossville

Wabaunsee

Ogden

Newbury   Maple Hill

Paxico

Junction
City

McFarland

Alma

0   5 mi

0   5 km

Road Trip Route

© MOON.COM

Detail inset:

To
Historic Trails Park and
Rope Ferry Replica

CENTER ST

N 8TH ST
N 9TH ST
N 10TH ST

MARSHALL COUNTY
VISITOR CENTER

36

EMPTY CUP
COFFEE BAR AND BISTRO

BROADWAY ST

KOESTER HOUSE
MUSEUM

WAGON WHEEL
CAFE

ELM ST

PONY EXPRESS
BARN

S 8TH ST
S 9TH ST

77

WALNUT ST

S 10TH ST

S 6TH ST
S 7TH ST

Marysville City Park

SPRING ST

0   100 yds

0   100 m

some snacks to go in the general store, which carries a selection of Amish bulk goods like dried fruit, nuts, special jams, and other unique treats.

Oregon Trail Road

The official route follows a dirt road through the farmland outside St. Marys for 15 miles (24 km) and connects with Highway 99 at Louisville. You'll travel along the old wagon route and have the chance to stretch your legs at a park, and see an old cemetery and river crossing. If your vehicle isn't equipped to handle a sometimes bumpy dirt road, or if you're short on time, you can skip this section and save 15 minutes of driving time by taking U.S. 24 directly to Highway 99.

Sights

From St. Marys, head west on Durink Street, which will become the Oregon Trail Road. In 8 miles (12.9 km), a 7-minute drive, you'll arrive at the **Oregon Trail Nature Park,** marked by a silo that rises above the prairie, painted with murals depicting a wagon train, a bison hunt, and Kansas wildlife. Two short loop trails here take about 15 minutes each, winding around a pond, through some woodlands, and up to a few overlooks. Take the longer Sea of Grass trail (30-minute loop) up the hill to get a 360-degree view of the prairie lands, where you can trace the path of the Oregon Trail on the dirt road below. A shelter, restrooms, and a separate picnic area are here.

Continuing west on Oregon Trail Road, in 2.9 miles (4.7 km) the road jogs slightly; turn right on Camp Creek Road then left to remain on the Oregon Trail Road. Continue another 2.8 miles (4.5 km) for the **Vieux Cemetery,** indicated by the tall spire of Louis Vieux's tomb. This is the resting site for the whole family. Louis was the son of a Potawatomi woman and a fur-trading man, and moved to the area near the Vermillion River around 1847. Here he built a toll

bridge over the river and charged pioneers $1 each to cross, earning as much as $300 a day during the busy season.

Another 500 feet (150 m) to the west is the entrance to the **Cholera Cemetery,** marked by a sign before you cross the river. Park and walk north along the access road to find it. There are only a handful of tombstones left to mark the spot where around 50 pioneers were buried in 1849 after cholera ravaged a large wagon train, leaving many of its members dead within a week. Today, you can find the initials of emigrant T. S. Prather on the largest tombstone—others have been lost to time. A plaque tells more about Prather and his wagon train.

Scott Spring

Another emigrant campground was at **Scott Spring** (Hwy. 99, Westmoreland), where wagons would stop to water their livestock and rest. A simple highway pullout marks the site of Scott Spring. You'll find a big wagon wheel marking the entrance, a life-size sculpture of oxen pulling a wagon, and interpretive signs explaining where the springs are.

Getting There

Continue on the Oregon Trail Road for 3.8 miles (6.1 km), then turn right on Highway 99 in Louisville. Drive north on Highway 99 for about 10 miles (16 km) from Louisville, about a 20-minute drive. When nearing Westmoreland, you'll find a sign for a marker on the west side of the highway—Scott Spring is just north of it on a separate pullout.

★ Alcove Springs

Easily the best Oregon Trail sight in Kansas is **Alcove Springs** (off U.S. 77, E. River Rd., 785/363-7721, dawn-dusk daily, free). Well known to Native Americans and then fur trappers of the region, the spring was given its name by Edwin Bryant, a member of the notorious Donner Party; they stopped to rest here in 1846 while waiting to ford the Big Blue

A Pioneer Story: The Donner Party

The Donner Party, or Donner-Reed Party, is notorious today for resorting to cannibalism to survive the deadly cold of the Sierra Nevadas. The party struck out from Independence, Missouri, in May 1846, headed to California. It was a little later in the season—they were the last wagon train to leave that year—and they needed to travel quickly to avoid snow in the mountains of California.

They reached Alcove Springs on May 26, where they were forced to wait for five days for the water in the Big Blue River to go down before they could cross it. Edwin Bryant, who coined the name, wrote of it: "The whole is buried in a variety of shrubbery of the richest verdure.... Altogether it is one of the most romantic spots I ever saw." Though their stop at the spring was a restful one, the party lost its first member: 70-year-old Sarah Keyes, mother of Margret Reed. Keyes had undertaken the trip knowing she had mere months to live with advanced tuberculosis. Her death was the first of a larger tragedy the party faced.

The party pushed on to Fort Bridger, Wyoming, where they made the mistake of taking an untested shortcut: the Hastings Cutoff, through the Utah desert. This choice ended up adding 150 miles (240 km) to their route. After these delays, tragedy struck. On the slopes of the Sierra Nevadas, with only 100 miles (160 km) to go, snow fell on October 28, trapping the party. Research has shown that they ate anything they could think of, including boiled leather and tree bark, but historians believe that at least half the survivors resorted to eating human flesh before rescuers found them. Although the stories have likely been sensationalized, diary entries do mention worried talk of cannibalizing dead members of the party. Of the 81 pioneers who made it to the Sierra Nevadas, only 45 survived.

River. Party member George McKinstry carved the new name, Alcove Springs, into the rocks, and J. R. Reed carved his signature; these and other carvings can still be seen today.

A campsite sprang up at the edge of the Big Blue River near the spring and grew to hundreds as wagons waited to ford what was known as Independence Crossing; this spot became a favorite place for emigrants to rest. For many, this was a peaceful respite before pushing on.

Alcove Springs is productive year-round, its fresh clear water cascading in a small waterfall—best in April-May—over a picturesque ledge of rocks and surrounded by verdant green. Many pioneers were inspired to make note of it in their diaries. It's an easy 0.25-mile (0.4-km) hike to the spring—it's at the top of the waterfall in the streambed, bubbling up a foot away from the ledge; follow the sign near the parking lot kiosk, which also has maps and brochures. Note there are no restrooms at this site.

Hiking

The area has about 4 miles (6.5 km) of trails you can wander on. From the spring are several trail options for easy walks. Head southwest through a meadow for the 1.8-mile (2.9-km) **Independence Crossing Overlook and Emigrant Camp Trail**, about a 45-minute hike. From the overlook, you'll be able to survey the area where the Big Blue River once flowed. You'll continue on to the Emigrant Camp, where there's a headstone for Sarah Keyes—one of the members of the Donner Party, who died here at age 70 from consumption. Deep swales still exist in the prairie; the tracks head straight down the hill, where pioneers forded the Big Blue River, which has since changed course.

You can also head east from the spring on the 2.5-mile (4-km) **Woodland Trail**, which takes about 1.5 hours to hike, toward the old Sehon Homestead, the remains of an abandoned farmhouse. The trail loops around the property to take in the quiet woods. You'll have a chance to spot native animals like deer, songbirds, and rabbits. In 1 mile (1.6 km) there is an option to shorten the loop and turn left to head back to the spring and the parking lot. If you're up for it, continue on to Stella's Meadow, another beautiful spot with swaying prairie grasses surrounded by trees.

Getting There

From Scott Spring, continue north on Highway 99 for 22 miles (36 km) to the community of Frankfort. Turn left onto West 2nd Street/Highway 9 and drive 12.2 miles (20 km), then turn right onto U.S. 77. Drive 1 mile (1.6 km) and turn left on Tumbleweed Road. In 1.2 miles (1.8 km), you'll make a short jog to the left onto 8th Road. Follow it as it curves north and become East River Road. Continue 3.7 miles (6 km) to the parking lot on the right. The route is well marked by signs, and it's on dirt roads that can get muddy in wet weather. The drive takes about 45 minutes.

Marysville

Once called Marshall's Ferry, Marysville was the site of a rope ferry operated by Frank Marshall to serve the wagon trains that came to cross the Big Blue River. Before the ferry started up in 1852, most wagon trains made the crossing at Independence Crossing, south near Alcove Springs. Marshall also ran a trading post with a blacksmith cabin and horse corrals. In 1854 he opened a post office and renamed the town Marysville, after his wife. When the Pony Express opened in 1860, the town served as the first home station—a place where the rider spent the night—west of St. Joseph, Missouri.

Today a small town full of Kansas cheer, Marysville's brick-lined Broadway Street is a good place to grab lunch between Topeka and Beatrice, Nebraska. Marysville is proud of its prominence on the Pony Express Trail—the town

statue pays homage to the riders, the water tower has a rider logo on it, and the museum is beloved. You'll also notice black squirrel statues all around, a tribute to the town's official mascot; grab a map at the **Marshall County Visitors Center** (101 N. 10th St., 785/562-3101, www.visitmarysvilleks.org, 10am-4pm Mon.-Fri.) in the center of town to hunt for them all. The center can also provide maps and other information.

Getting There

From Alcove Springs, head north on East River Road for 3.3 miles (5.3 km), and turn right onto Osage Road. In 0.7 mile (1.1 km), turn left onto U.S. 77. Drive north on the highway for 4 miles (6.4 km) to Marysville.

Sights

Pony Express Barn

The **Pony Express Barn** (106 S. 8th St., 785/562-3825, 9am-5pm Mon.-Sat., 1pm-5pm Sun. Apr.-Oct., $10) was Home Station No. 1 on the 10-day mail delivery route—the first place a rider heading west from St. Joseph would stop to let another rider take over. The original stone barn in Marysville is the oldest surviving building in the county. The original stable was rebuilt in 1991 and turned into a museum covering the tales of the Pony Express, as well as Marysville's role in the Oregon Trail and the railroad. Admission comes with a guided tour, which takes 45-60 minutes.

Historic Trails Park

See how early pioneers crossed the river at **Historic Trails Park** (101 N. 10th St., 785/562-3101, dawn-dusk daily, free), which has a full-size **rope-ferry replica.** The ferry could transport a wagon or a horse and rider across the river using a pulley system. Hundreds of wagons crossed the river via this method until 1864, when the first Marysville bridge was built. Visitors can hop aboard the ferry replica, though it stays on dry land these days.

The Pony Express Trail

The Pony Express was a private mail delivery enterprise that connected the towns of Independence, Missouri, and Sacramento, California, providing a vital communication route to the increasingly populated California. The route began in April 1860 and operated for a mere 18 months until the transcontinental telegraph was connected, in October 1861. The Pony Express operated 24 hours a day and delivered letters in then-record time, before the telegraph took over.

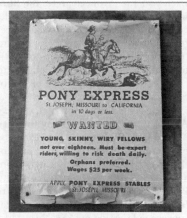

poster for the Pony Express

It was a demanding job to deliver mail over 1,900 miles (3,060 km) in 10 days, operating in all types of weather. The route was dotted with over 180 stations, each ready with fresh horses or new riders: It took 40 riders to get from Independence to Sacramento, and another 40 to get back. Each rider covered 10-15 miles (16-24 km) before changing horses, and 75-100 miles (120-160 km) before being relieved by the next rider. Riders had two minutes to change horses before thundering off again.

Letters were transported in a leather blanket-type bag called a mochila, designed to be easily transferrable to a new horse at each stop. The riders, mostly young men under age 18 and weighing less than 125 pounds, faced daily dangers from weather and exhaustion. Although the entire operation was short-lived, the legends of the Pony Express, popularized by writers like Mark Twain and the memoirs of Buffalo Bill Cody, have grown to become a symbol of the frontier.

Don't be fooled by phone maps, which will tell you the park is right off the main street in town. It is, technically, but there's no access from there. To get here, head south on U.S. 77 out of town. You'll drive over railroad tracks and, after 0.4 mile (0.6 km), turn left to follow a sign for the park. The road will curve and turn left again, going under U.S. 77. You'll see a sign by the train tracks that says "Government Property"; don't be dissuaded—this is the road to take (the sign is directed at hunters). Follow the dirt road around town, along the railroad tracks, for 1.4 miles (2.3 km). Turn left just before the U.S. 36 overpass.

Koester House Museum

A pair of gilded lions welcomes visitors to the **Koester House Museum** (919 Broadway St., 785/562-2417, www.marysvillemuseumsks.org, 10am-4:30pm Mon.-Sat., 1pm-4:30pm Sun. Apr.-Oct., $4 adults, $2 under age 3). The beautiful house offers a glimpse into a wealthy family's daily life before the turn of the 20th century: Charles Koester spared no expense building it in 1876 as a gift to his bride, Sylvia. Outside, the garden is as beautiful today as it was extolled to be 100 years ago—many plants and trees are still in their original places, surrounding 13 white-bronze (made with zinc) statues. A famous visitor was Laura Ingalls Wilder, who wrote about the cast-iron lions in her diary in 1894. The pioneers wouldn't have been treated to such a sight in the days of the trail, but it's a lovely place for today's visitors.

Festivals and Events

Each year the town celebrates **Big Blue River Days** (www.bigbluebbqmarysville. com, Memorial Day), a giant Main Street festival with a barbecue competition (past years have seen up to 40 competitors!) and an auto show. Live music, fun runs, barbecue tastings, and plenty of beer mark the occasion.

The National Pony Express Association sponsors a **Pony Express Re-Ride** (www.nationalponyexpress. org, June) covering the entire route of the original ride. Over 750 riders from all walks of life participate, carrying Pony Express Commemorative Letters in leather mochilas. The letters, official souvenirs of the ride, are $5 each, just like in 1860. Check online for the dates when the riders will pass through Marysville.

Food

The best place in town to eat is at the **Wagon Wheel Cafe** (703 Broadway St., 785/562-3784, www.wagonwheelks.com, 6am-9pm Mon.-Sat., $13). Breakfast classics include biscuits and gravy or fresh-off-the-griddle pancakes. The lunch and dinner menu includes burgers with endless fries, sandwiches, wings, steaks, and hearty salads. Vegetarians will find some good options, and meat lovers will be hard-pressed to choose from options that include whiskey steaks, prime-rib burgers, fried chicken, and even chislic (deep fried tenderloin cubes, a South Dakota specialty), all with friendly service.

Get your caffeine fix at **Empty Cup Coffee Bar and Bistro** (723 Broadway St., 785/562-3354, 7am-7pm Mon.-Fri., 7am-2pm Sat., 10am-2pm Sun., $6), which also serves breakfast and lunch at affordable prices. Pastries in the case are all made in-house each day, and the menu options go a step farther than the standard café, with items like omelets, paninis, and gourmet grilled cheeses—try the sweet options like the Elvis or the caramel apple (with sweetened cream cheese). The wide range of drinks includes soda, chai, tea, drip coffee, lattes, and smoothies.

Accommodations and Camping

The **Heritage Inn Express** (1195 Pony Express Hwy., 785/562-5588, www. marysvilleheritageinn.com, $63-98) makes for a good night's stay. The 41-room motel comes with free breakfast and friendly service, and is just to the east of town along U.S. 36. Upgrade to the King Suite for an in-room whirlpool to melt away the day's travel.

Camp for free at ★ **Marysville City Park** (10th St. and Walnut St., 785/562-5331, free). The four first-come, first-served sites are suitable for tents or RVs, with electricity, a restroom, picnic tables, a large playground, a grassy area, and a nine-disc golf course. Shaded by trees, it's a pleasant spot to stay on a sunny day. It's just three blocks south of the visitors center, walking distance to many of the town's major sights.

Hollenberg Pony Express Station

Just west outside of Marysville, the **Hollenberg Pony Express Station** (2889 23rd Rd., Hanover, 785/337-2635, 10am-5pm daily Mar.-Oct., $6) is the only Pony Express barn still in its original location along the route. The station was originally built in 1857 by Gerat Hollenberg to serve Oregon Trail emigrants. When the Pony Express started in 1860, the station then became a location for riders to switch out their horses for fresh ones; this would have been the first stop for riders after the barn in Marysville. Today you can check out a visitors center and museum, which has artifacts that were uncovered in the old barn, a small display of life on the trail, and other historical items such as a clever wagon mile counter. A short stroll brings you to the station. Inside, learn about Pony Express riders and examine their clothing and a leather mochila that carried letters. The surrounding grounds come alive in spring with wildflowers, and pleasant walks take you to Oregon Trail swales and farmland views. Every year in August the site hosts a Pony Express Festival with riders, letters, and music.

Getting There

From Marysville, head west on U.S. 36 for 11.4 miles (18.3 km), then turn right onto Highway 148. Drive 4 miles (6.4 km), and then turn right on 23rd Road. The station is on the left in 0.8 mile (1.3 km).

◆ Detour: Pawnee Indian Museum, KS

Although slightly out of the way and in a remote location, the **Pawnee Indian Museum State Historic Site** (480 Pawnee Trail, 785/361-2255, 9am-5pm Wed.-Sat. Mar.-Oct., $6 adults, $5 seniors, $3 ages 5-17) is worth a visit for the glimpse it offers into day-to-day Pawnee life. In the 19th century, the Pawnee people were a powerful group who lived throughout Kansas and Nebraska in villages of dome-shaped earth lodges. This site preserves a rare example of an earth lodge from the Kitkahaki band of the Pawnee, who lived in the area. Visitors can step inside the excavated lodge—the museum was built directly over the excavation site, allowing all of the archaeological discoveries to be left where they were found.

Other artifacts on display include Pawnee star charts, a robe made of bison, and the special not-to-be-photographed Sacred Bundle, which contains ceremonial items wrapped in bison hide, that was passed down through families and donated by a member of the Pawnee Nation. Outside, a nature trail guides you past depressions in the earth where other lodges were located in the village. As the great powerhouse of the region, the Pawnee people would certainly have met Oregon Trail emigrants, though the wagons would not have ventured quite as far west as this particular lodge.

This site is notable in that it's the only museum in the entire Kansas and Nebraska region that shows how the Pawnee people lived in its actual setting. In 1875, the Pawnee people ceded their territory in Kansas and Nebraska to the United States, which moved them to reservations in Oklahoma. Today the Pawnee Nation of Oklahoma is a federally recognized government and numbers over 3,200 people who take great pride in their ancestral heritage of rich myths and religious rites, supporting yearly dances and intertribal meetings.

Getting There and Back

The site is located near Republic, Kansas, and this detour takes a net extra two hours of driving time. Drive west from Marysville on U.S. 36 for 65 miles (105 km), then turn right on Highway 266. In 7.6 miles (12.2 km), the highway ends at the museum parking lot.

Rather than driving all the way back to Marysville, you can rejoin the trail at Rock Creek Station in Nebraska. Head back the way you came, heading south via Highway 266 and then east via U.S. 36. After driving 45 miles (72 km), turn left onto Highway 15. Continue on it for 22 miles (35 km). Turn right onto Highway 8, and then make a quick left onto PWF Road. After 4.6 miles (7.4 km), turn right onto 573rd Avenue. In 1 mile (1.6 km), turn left onto 710th Street. Rock Creek Station will be on your right in 1.2 miles (1.9 km).

Nebraska

NEBRASKA

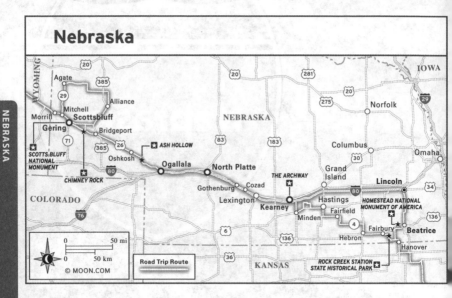

Nebraska

The wide, slow Platte River in Nebraska once defined the area around it, a flow of life to early pioneers that led the way northwest into Wyoming.

Many pioneers remembered the Platte River Valley as one of the most pleasant stretches of the trail, offering plenty of water and grass for livestock. Diaries record amazement at sights such as bison stampedes and the spire of Chimney Rock, and trade relations with the Pawnee people. They also record dangers like death from cholera-laced water, a trail brown from overcrowding, and plenty of human drama. By this point in their journey, emigrants were familiar with hardship, and many had already lost loved ones to disease, accidents, or drownings. While the delicate tallgrass prairie was a beautiful place to travel through, pioneers rushed along to reach the Rocky Mountains and Oregon before the end of summer.

By 1869 the transcontinental railroad was complete—effectively ending the necessity of the trail; the Union Pacific portion stretches across the entire state and is still an integral part of the landscape and economy.

Today's travelers can follow the old trail in style: Detour to Lincoln and you'll find a multicultural and lively college town, while the western cities of Kearney and North Platte promise some of the country's best steaks and a sprinkling of craft breweries. Get a sense of life after the pioneers when the cowboys came to town at Ogallala, or enjoy a rodeo at Buffalo Bill's famous ranch. Scotts Bluff National Monument offers history, great walks and hikes, and geological wonders. It won't take visitors long to see why the state motto is "The Good Life."

Highlights

★ See some of the first wagon ruts in Nebraska at **Rock Creek Station State Historical Park,** a pioneer supply stop turned Pony Express station (page 114).

★ Discover how a landmark act opened the floodgates to westward expansion at the **Homestead National Monument of America.** Then take a hike through the tallgrass prairie (page 119).

★ Learn about how the Great Platte River Road morphed from Native American hunting corridor to the Oregon Trail to an interstate highway at **The Archway** (page 136).

★ Hike along the Oregon Trail at **Ash Hollow,** where you can see deep ruts cut into the hills (page 158).

★ Spot **Chimney Rock,** the most noted landmark on the Oregon Trail (page 161).

★ Mark your progress across the plains at **Scotts Bluff National Monument,** a pioneer landmark that today offers great history and hikes (page 168).

Best Overnight Stops

★ **Lincoln:** It's worth going off-route to stay in the capital city of Nebraska, a college town that offers numerous diversions for road-trippers (page 123).

★ **Kearney:** The fifth-largest city in the state, Kearney is a major stop on I-80 with fun food and nightlife options (page 134).

★ **Lake McConaughy:** A short drive off the main route brings you to Nebraska's watery playground, where you can camp or stay in lodgings on the lake's shore (page 155).

★ **Scottsbluff and Gering:** These neighboring towns sit beside Scotts Bluff National Monument, where Oregon Trail pioneers navigated tricky terrain (page 164).

Planning Your Time

It's about 450 miles (725 km) across Nebraska, arriving from Kansas in the southeast. The drive takes about 6.5 hours. Mileage increases to 500 (800 km) and just over 7 hours total driving time if you detour to Lincoln. Budget about four days in the state, and a little extra if you'd like to spend some time in Lincoln or be more leisurely in exploring the national monuments along the way. On the drive you'll appreciate the endless rolling hills giving way to rocky ledges as you head farther west. If you're not driving in from Kansas, Lincoln or Omaha make good starting points.

Nebraska, like most of the Midwest, has extreme climates: It's cold in winter, averaging 35°F (2°C) and prone to blizzards, and humid and hot in summer, with an average temperature of 85°F (29°C). Spring and fall are likely to have comfortable temperatures, but you'll always run the risk of an early or late snowstorm. Summers see big thunderstorms—a memorable sight across the expansive prairie—and occasional tornados.

Getting There

Starting Points
Oregon Trail Route Notes

In southern Nebraska you'll trace the Oregon Trail, although given the stair-stepping **rural roads** versus the more direct route emigrants would've taken, the route is an approximation. You'll then follow closely in their footsteps once you hit **I-80**, following the Platte River and heading west from Kearney. The river splits near North Platte, where you continue following I-80 along the South Platte River before veering northwest after Ogallala on **U.S. 26**, along the North Platte River as it heads into Wyoming.

Car and RV

If you've been following the route from Missouri and Kansas, you'll enter Nebraska on small rural roads in the southeast corner of the state from Marysville, Kansas, and continue on many more until hitting I-80, either in Kearney or Lincoln.

From Marysville, Kansas, you're within 15 miles (24 km) of the Nebraska

Best Walks and Hikes

★ **Windlass Hill:** On this short hike you'll see deep ruts carved by Oregon Trail wagons at Ash Hollow (page 159).

★ **Daemonelix Trail:** Learn about some of the animals that roamed the land before the pioneers on this easy hike through the fossil-rich hills of the Panhandle (page 164).

★ **Oregon Trail Pathway:** Follow the path of pioneers on this short walk (page 169).

★ **Saddle Rock Trail:** This popular paved path at Scotts Bluff National Monument is easy on the feet but gains some serious elevation, rewarding with sandstone and prairie views (page 170).

border. If you're set on following the original trail as closely as possible, follow the route through southern Nebraska from Rock Creek Station State Historical Park and then continue on to Kearney. Otherwise, the hip city of Lincoln—a university town full of international eats, museums, and nightlife—makes a good detour, along with the town of Beatrice on the way, due north of Marysville.

Another option is to visit Rock Creek Station State Historical Park, then detour to Beatrice and Lincoln. On the way out of Lincoln, you can leave I-80 about 20 miles (32 km) east of Kearney to see Susan Hail's grave site. This allows you to see the main sights without navigating a maze of rural roads.

Rentals

Avis (www.avis.com) has an office in the **Lincoln Airport** (2400 W. Adams St., 402/474-1202, www.avis.com, 9am-11pm Sun., 8am-11pm Mon.-Fri., 8am-6pm Sat.) and decent prices for its rental cars. It also serves the **Omaha Airport** (4501 Abbott Dr., Terminal 3, 402/422-6480, 6am-1am daily). Most of the Avis rentals come with unlimited mileage, but be sure to ask to avoid extra charges.

You can rent an RV at **Leach Camper Sales** (2727 Cornhusker Hwy., Lincoln,

402/466-8581, www.leachrv.com, 8am-6pm Mon.-Thurs., 8am-5pm Fri., 9am-5pm Sat.). Its smaller model sleeps six people ($1,100 per week), and the larger sleeps 8-10 ($1,300 per week). Bookings must be by phone or in person, but pictures, layouts, and more information can be found online. **Cruise America** (www.cruiseamerica.com) is a nationwide company with a location 14 miles (22.5 km) southwest of Omaha Eppley Airfield (4114 S. 90th St., 402/592-1118, 8am-5pm Mon.-Fri., 8am-11am Sat.). For a week, expect to pay around $1,300-1,600 total, depending on mileage.

Fuel and Services

There are plenty of gas stations and amenities along I-80 and U.S. 26, but when heading down the smaller rural roads in the southeastern corner or the Nebraska Panhandle—the area northwest of Ogallala—to Agate Fossil Beds, be sure to fill up your gas tank whenever you can—it may be up to 50 miles (80 km) between stations; cell phone service also drops out in these areas.

Air

Lincoln Airport (LNK, 2400 W. Adams St., 402/458-2480, www.lincolnairport.com) is 5 miles (8 km) northwest of downtown Lincoln. Delta and United serve the small airport with nonstop flights from cities across the Midwest as well as Atlanta and Nashville. From here, you could skip the southern Nebraska route section and head directly west to Kearney on I-80, a two-hour drive.

You may find more flight options and lower fares into the **Omaha Airport,** known as **Eppley Airfield** (OMA, 4501 Abbott Dr., 402/661-8017, www.flyomaha.com), 3 miles (4.8 km) northeast of Omaha. It's served by major airlines including Alaska, Allegiant, American, Delta, Frontier, Southwest, and United Airlines and is the biggest hub in Nebraska. After arriving, you can drive 60 miles (97 km) southwest on I-80 to get to Lincoln, which takes an hour. Factoring in mileage might make the trip more costly: The Lincoln Airport has a handy price comparison tool on its website (www.lincolnairport.com) to help you decide which airport to fly into.

Train and Bus

Amtrak (www.amtrak.com) delivers passengers directly to **Haymarket Station** (277 Pinnacle Arena Dr., 402/476-1295) in downtown Lincoln. The *California Zephyr* runs daily between Chicago and San Francisco, hitting Omaha, Denver, and Salt Lake City on the way. The same line stops at the **Holdrege Ironhorse Station** (100 West Ave., Holdrege), 30 miles (48 km) southwest of Kearney, in the middle of the state.

Lincoln's **Greyhound Bus Depot** (5250 Superior St., 402/474-1071, www.greyhound.com, 9am-1pm and 6pm-10:30pm daily) is 5 miles (8 km) northeast of downtown. Note the strange hours of this depot—it is, in fact, closed 1pm-6pm. Greyhound connects Lincoln to locations across the nation, including Omaha, Kansas City, St. Louis, and Chicago to the east, and North Platte, Ogalalla, and Denver to the west.

Along the Trail from Southern Nebraska to Kearney

The original wagon route through Nebraska cut across the southeastern corner of the state, bumping over the tallgrass prairie on the way to the Platte River. Today, there's not actually a lot to see on the route—it's mostly historical markers next to privately owned fields; the closest route a car can take travels in a stair-step pattern across the plains following **rural roads,** while covered wagons would have taken a more direct path. The route detailed below covers a total of approximately 150 miles (242 km) and takes 2.75 hours to drive point to point from Rock Creek Station to Harold Warp Pioneer Village.

★ Rock Creek Station State Historical Park

Pioneers riding across the plains often stopped at this log cabin station to get a few supplies. Built in 1857, the barn and cabin served as a Pony Express station during the 18 months the service ran in 1860-1861. These old buildings likely would've fallen into the past if it weren't for a shootout that occurred here in the spring of 1859 between the owner, David McCanles, and one James Butler Hickok, who soon became known as "Wild Bill" Hickok. The event left McCanles dead and spurred Hickok's career as a legendary gunfighter—though the fight may not have been fair, as McCanles was likely unarmed. Tales of the incident lent themselves to Wild Bill's legend. An 1867 article in *Harper's Weekly* allows Hickok his own take on the affair: McCanles ran a gang of ruffians who attacked Hickok, in this version of events, and Wild Bill took them on single-handedly, surviving a whopping 11 shot wounds and 13 cuts.

Today the site is the **Rock Creek**

Station State Historical Park (57426 710th Rd., Fairbury, 402/729-5777, www.outdoornebraska.gov/rockcreekstation, 9am-5pm daily, $6 per vehicle Nebraska residents, $8 per vehicle nonresidents), where you can see reconstructed buildings that include the Pony Express station, a barn, a bunkhouse, and a few cabins. Oregon Trail ruts are clearly visible nearby. A few miles of hiking trails offer more views of them; get a map for a self-guided tour from the **visitors center** (1pm-5pm Sat.-Sun. Apr. and Oct., 9am-5pm daily May-Sept., $2 adults, $1 ages 3-13), then hike your way up the hill to wander past the buildings, some covered wagons, and along the ruts. The center has historical information, a short film, and exhibits of artifacts that were excavated on-site. Volunteers can answer your questions or elaborate on the history. Admission to enter the center is per person in addition to the parking fee. Budget 1.5-2 hours for a visit.

For a special experience, visit on the first weekend of June each year for the **Rock Creek Trail Days,** which has living-history demonstrations, shoot-outs, covered-wagon rides, and cookouts.

Camping

Stay overnight at **Rock Creek Station Recreation Area** (57426 710th Rd., Fairbury, 402/729-5777, http://nebraskastateparks.reserveamerica.com, $15-25), which has 25 tent and RV sites, half of which can be reserved ahead online. Full hookups are available, along with showers, restrooms, a playground, and a picnic shelter. The campground is adjacent to Rock Creek Station State Historical Park, a short walk away from the visitors center in a shady wooded area.

Top to bottom: *Rock Creek Station* by William Henry Jackson; covered wagons at Rock Creek Station State Historical Park; *James B."Wild Bill" Hickock* by Jeremiah Gurney.

NEBRASKA

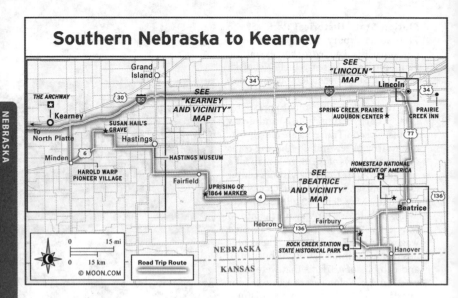

Southern Nebraska to Kearney

Map labels: SEE "LINCOLN" MAP · Lincoln · 34 · 80 · Grand Island · 34 · THE ARCHWAY · 30 · 80 · Kearney · SEE "KEARNEY AND VICINITY" MAP · SPRING CREEK PRAIRIE AUDUBON CENTER · PRAIRIE CREEK INN · 77 · 6 · To North Platte · SUSAN HAIL'S GRAVE · Hastings · Minden · 6 · HAROLD WARP PIONEER VILLAGE · HASTINGS MUSEUM · Fairfield · UPRISING OF 1864 MARKER · SEE "BEATRICE AND VICINITY" MAP · HOMESTEAD NATIONAL MONUMENT OF AMERICA · 136 · Beatrice · 4 · Hebron · 136 · Fairbury · Hanover · ROCK CREEK STATION STATE HISTORICAL PARK · NEBRASKA · KANSAS · 0 15 mi · 0 15 km · Road Trip Route · © MOON.COM

Getting There

Driving from the Hollenberg Pony Express Station, the last stop on the route in Kansas just outside of Marysville, you'll enter Nebraska on Highway 148. After 7 miles (11.3 km), it becomes Highway 112 when you cross the state line. From there, continue north for 3 miles (4.8 km), then head left and west on Highway 8. Follow it for 13 miles (21 km), then turn right onto 573rd Avenue just before the town of Endicott. In 2.8 miles (4.5 km), turn right onto 710th Road to arrive at Rock Creek Station State Historical Park in 1.2 miles (1.9 km), your starting point in Nebraska for the below series of sights. The drive to this first stop takes 30 minutes.

Uprising of 1864 Marker

A **historical marker** (Hwy. 14) in a pullout 9 miles (14.5 km) north of Nelson relates the story of how the Sioux, Cheyenne, and Arapaho peoples attempted to drive settlers out of their lands in 1864. Known as the 1864 Indian Raids, the uprising was part of a broader conflict playing out in the West in the 19th century—collectively known as the Sioux Wars—as

lands were overrun with settlers who indiscriminately killed bison for sport and brought diseases to which indigenous people had no immunity. As more settlers moved into the area to claim farmland and the U.S. government began pushing Native Americans off their ancestral lands and onto reservations, through treaties and threats, the Sioux, Cheyenne, and Arapaho resisted in 1864 by attacking white settlements, ranches, and stagecoach stops. These conflicts gave rise to the myth of the persistent threat of Native American attacks on the Oregon Trail, although many more emigrant deaths occurred from disease or accidents in camp, such as falling off wagons or a gun going off unintentionally.

Getting There

Exit Rock Creek Station State Historical Park at its west end and head north on 574th Avenue. In 1 mile (1.6 km), turn left onto 711th Road/PWF Road to drive 5.6 miles (9 km) into Fairbury. To get through town, turn right on Highway 8 and make an immediate right onto Highway 15, also called K Street. Drive north through town for 1.2 miles (1.9

km), then turn left onto East 14th Street/ Highway 136. Follow it out of Fairbury, continuing west for 21 miles (34 km) before turning right onto U.S. 81 for 11 miles (18 km). Make a left onto Highway 4 and continue west for 26 miles (42 km), before turning right onto Highway 14. A pullout is on the west side of the highway in 1.5 miles (2.4 km). From point to point, this drive takes about 1.25 hours.

Hastings Museum

One of the biggest small-town museums around, the **Hastings Museum** (1330 N. Burlington Ave., Hastings, 402/461-2399, www.hastingsmuseum.org, 10am-4pm Mon.-Thurs., 10am-8pm Fri.-Sat., 9am-6pm Sun., $8), is a great place for a road-trip break. Step inside the natural and cultural museum's galleries for a look at Native American life preceding Western settlement, wildlife dioramas, and a fun collection of rocks and minerals. The "Traveling in Style" exhibit showcases antique vehicles like Oregon Trail wagons, stagecoaches, and horse-drawn buggies. In the firearm exhibit, you'll see over 500 guns and rifles and learn about George Maxwell, the town's one armed sharpshooter. You can also learn about Hastings's pop culture legacy—it was the birthplace of Kool-Aid in 1927. In the planetarium, check out "The Sky Tonight" show (3pm Wed.-Sun.), included in admission, for a glimpse at what constellations and comets can be seen each night.

Getting There

From the 1864 marker, continue north on Highway 14 for 17 miles (27 km) to U.S. 6. Turn left to head west 16 miles (26 km) to Hastings. Turn right onto U.S. 34/North Showboat Boulevard. In 1 mile (1.6 km), turn left onto East 12th Street, then in 1.7 miles (2.8 km) turn right onto North St. Joseph Avenue. At 14th Street, in 0.3 mile (0.5 km), turn left. The parking lot for the museum is in two blocks, on your left. The drive takes 40 minutes.

Susan Hail's Grave

A historical marker for **Susan Hail's Grave** (7000-7938 N. Denman Ave., 44 Rd./Denman Ave. and W. 70th St., Kenesaw) sits on a lonely road outside of Kenesaw, Nebraska, a lone indicator of a site where once many Oregon Trail emigrants were buried, along this Cholera Corridor of central Nebraska. Legend has it that Susan and Richard Hail stopped near here for some water for drinking and cooking. Susan was struck ill and died— some say the water was poisoned on purpose—and Richard buried her with a temporary marker. The story goes that he immediately headed back east to obtain a real marble headstone to honor his wife, leaving his children with their aunt to continue west. Once at either Omaha or St. Joseph, he sold his horses to buy the costly headstone, then set out on foot with a wheelbarrow to push it back to his wife's grave site.

The story has stuck around for years in the area. Many historians think the wheelbarrow part may be somewhat dramatized, since it's also told about two other grave sites in the area. But later records from 1854 confirm that there was a marble headstone here. The original marble marker has since been destroyed, but just east of the historical marker, 0.5 mile (0.8 km) down West 70th Road, a newer marble marker on her grave sits on private property, surrounded by a metal fence. You're allowed to view it, but be respectful.

Getting There

From the Hastings Museum, drive south 2.2 miles (3.5 km) on Burlington Avenue, then turn right to head west on U.S. 34/36 for 14 miles (23 km). Turn right on State Highway 1A Spur/South Smith Avenue and drive 5 miles (8 km) north—you'll pass through Kenesaw—then turn left on West Lochand Road. In 3.4 miles (5.5 km), turn right on 44 Road. The marker is in 1 mile (1.6 km) on the right. The drive takes 30 minutes.

The Longest Graveyard

The Oregon Trail has been called the nation's "longest graveyard." While there are only a handful of grave sites known today, pioneers witnessed death regularly as they traveled, passing an astounding number of single and mass graves. Many people were buried directly in the trail itself—where the weight of wagon wheels over the grave would pack the earth down.

The numbers are staggering: The National Park Service suggests that of an estimated 350,000 who began the journey (some estimates are as high as 500,000), up to 10 percent—or around 35,000 people—didn't make it. Stretching along a 2,000-mile (3,200-km) trail, that's roughly 15 deaths per mile over the years.

Emigrants faced death by drowning from river crossings, gunshot wounds (mostly from misfires), accidents involving wagons and livestock, and malnutrition. By far the biggest danger was disease, and the biggest killer was Asiatic cholera. A bacterial disease often picked up from polluted stagnant water, cholera could kill within 24 hours—emigrants often noted that someone would be healthy in the morning and dead by nightfall. It caused diarrhea, vomiting, and intestinal pain, with brutal effects. The slow-moving Platte River combined with the heavy traffic created the Cholera Corridor across today's Nebraska, with thousands of emigrants succumbing.

If you detoured to Lincoln and want to stop at the grave site on your way to Kearney, drive 105 miles (169 km) west on I-80, then take exit 291. Turn left onto Shelton Road and follow it for 1.8 miles (3.9 km) before turning left as it becomes Cole Chute and then Denman Avenue/44 Road, following it for 3.8 miles (6.1 km). It adds just an extra 10 minutes or so of driving time out-and-back to I-80.

Harold Warp Pioneer Village

The replica town of **Harold Warp Pioneer Village** (138 E. U.S. 6, Minden, 308/832-1181, www.pioneervillage.org, 9am-6pm daily, $14.25 adults, $7.25 ages 6-12, free under age 6) tells the story of U.S. history from pioneer times up to the present. Spread out over a whopping 28 buildings on 20 acres, the village is the brainchild of Harold Warp, a millionaire who bought his failing hometown's oldest buildings and turned them into a museum. The buildings are authentic Nebraska relics from earlier pioneer times, when wagons were making their way across the prairie and settlers beginning to put down roots. Many buildings are original, from the forts to schoolhouses to churches, and were moved to the Pioneer Village.

Opened in 1953, the collection has been added to over the years to reach its now 50,000-strong artifact count. Among the items to see are a sod house, a land office for homestead claims, Warp's own furnished one-room schoolhouse, a steam-powered merry-go-round, antique cars, and much more. The collection can be exhausting, as it's a ton of stuff that isn't always presented in cohesive fashion. The buildings are showing their age in plenty of places, and one can imagine the attraction at its height in the 1950s, but it's still a great place to enjoy pure Americana.

Camping

Allow at least half a day to wander the buildings; some people even stay a few days. Its nearby **RV park and campground** (308/832-2750, $27-35) offers a good resting spot to recuperate before you hit the collection again. The 135 campsites for tents and RVs are shaded and offer full hookups, with showers and restrooms.

Getting There

From Susan Hail's Grave, drive west on West 70th Street, which becomes W Road, for 4.6 miles (7.4 km). Turn left onto 40 Road, and drive 6.2 miles (10 km). Turn right onto U.S. 34/U.S. 6 and follow it 9 miles (14.5 km) into Minden, where you'll find the Harold Warp Pioneer Village on your right.

🐾 Detour: Beatrice

While not directly on the Oregon Trail, Beatrice is a notable detour where you can see the Homestead National Monument, created on the site of the first land claim, filed by Daniel Freeman just after midnight the day the Homestead Act of 1862 took effect. The city of Beatrice—be a local and pronounce the *a* like "at," "be-AT-riss"—was founded in the late 1850s by a band of settlers when Nebraska was still a territory.

Today, travelers can detour from the primary Oregon Trail route to Beatrice quite easily. Then you'll have a choice of heading back to the main route through southeastern Nebraska, or heading farther north to Lincoln, another worthy detour, which Beatrice is on the way to. Both routes take the same amount of driving time, so you can decide if you have time to spend in Lincoln or not. It's also the difference of driving on rural two-lane roads versus a major interstate highway.

Getting There and Around
If you're detouring to Beatrice from **Marysville, Kansas,** head north on U.S. 77 for 34 miles (55 km). The drive takes about 40 minutes. Driving from the Hollenberg Pony Express Station just outside Marysville takes about the same amount of time; head north on Highway 148 for 7 miles (11.3 km), where it becomes Highway 112 as you cross the state line; continue for 3 miles (4.8 km). Turn right to remain on Highway 112 for 6 miles (9.6 km), then turn left to remain on the highway, which merges with U.S. 77 and takes you into Beatrice after 15 miles (24 km).

If you're detouring after stopping first at **Rock Creek Station State Historical Park,** head west on 710th Road. In 1.2 miles (1.9 km), turn right onto 573rd Avenue. Continue for 4.5 miles (7.2 km), then turn right onto U.S. 136. Drive 15 miles (24 km), then make a slight right onto West Locust Road. In 3 miles (4.8 km), turn left onto U.S. 77, which brings you to Beatrice in 3.3 miles (5.3 km). The drive takes just over 30 minutes.

U.S. 136 acts as a Main Street for Beatrice, running east-west, while U.S. 77 cuts through town north-south. The area where they meet is downtown Beatrice, just east of the Big Blue River.

Sights and Recreation
★ Homestead National Monument of America
The Homestead Act of 1862 opened up vast stretches of land (270 million acres, or 10 percent of the area of the United States) to private ownership, distributing land to settlers—including newly arrived immigrants, women, and formerly enslaved people. A forerunner of the act was the Oregon Donation Land Act (1850-1855), under which only white males were able claim land, for themselves and on behalf of their wives. Although the Homestead Act was passed in the later years of the Oregon Trail, which effectively ended with the completion of the railroad in 1869, it was a big impetus for many families to head west. In offering "free" land, the act had far-reaching consequences for the nation, changing the face of the country. A claim cost $18 (about $300 today) but took years of toil—including building a home and farming the land for five years—for any hopeful homesteader, many of whom failed. Over half were successful, though, earning their land and creating a lasting legacy. People such as George Washington Carver, Laura Ingalls Wilder, and Nebraska's beloved author Willa Cather were all homesteaders. The act remained in effect until

1976—the last claim was filed in 1974 in Alaska.

Learn about this history at the **Homestead National Monument of America** (8523 W. Hwy. 4, 402/223-3514, www.nps.gov/home, 8:30am-5pm Mon.-Fri., 9am-5pm Sat.-Sun., free). The monument is spread out over 150 acres, encompassing prairie grass and woodlands, and has two main areas for visitors: the Homestead Heritage Center, which serves as a visitors center and main museum, and the Education Center, situated 1 mile (1.6 km) west.

Start at the **Homestead Heritage Center,** which has exhibits on the impacts of homesteading. The uniquely shaped building is meant to look like a plow cutting through the thick sod, and it points west across the prairie, offering visitors beautiful views of the restored tallgrass ecosystem out of its big glass windows. Don't skip the thoughtful and award-winning film *Land of Dreams—Homesteading America,* which gives voice to Native American nations who were displaced by the act and discusses the continuing reverberations. Visitors can also access digitized records of past homesteaders for free onsite. Historians estimate that 93 million Americans have an ancestor or relative who was a homesteader, and since records were kept for every claim, history hunters have amazing resources here at their disposal.

Just south of the Homestead Heritage Center, you can visit the **Palmer-Epard Cabin,** a restored pioneer building. Built in 1867, the cabin offers a great glimpse into early homesteading life. It sits on the restored prairie, near a heritage fruit orchard and community garden that's tended to by local residents.

If you have a little more time, visit the **Education Center,** 0.9 mile (1.6 km) west on Highway 4, where you can see some examples of farm tools, machines, and living-history demonstrations, and take part in some hands-on crafts.

Homestead National Monument of America

Hiking

A network of 3 miles (4.8 km) of trails winds from the Homestead Heritage Center to the Education Center, crossing the tallgrass prairie and following the edge of the oak woods to the west, offering a look at the types of plants and landscapes pioneers would have seen on their way west. These wide, flat trails make for easy walks, allowing you to enjoy the grassy prairie and cottonwood trees, along with wildflowers, birds, and historical plaques. Maps are available in the Homestead Heritage Center. Trails can be strung together to create a 2.1-mile (3.4-km) loop from the Heritage Center to the Education Center and back, which takes roughly an hour; head out on the **Upper Prairie Loop Trail.** The most direct route between the centers is the 1-mile (1.6-km) **Grain Growers Highway Trail,** which cuts directly west across the prairie. Near the site of the brick house of Daniel Freeman, the first homesteader, you'll

have options for some extra short loops, like the **Woodland Loop Trail** and the **Farm Loop Trail,** which includes a native plants exhibit.

Chief Standing Bear Trail

Chief Standing Bear Trail (trailhead at 577 Perkins St.) is a rails-to-trails line that runs 22.9 miles (37 km) south of Beatrice to the Nebraska-Kansas state line, where it connects to the Blue River Rail Trail, which runs another 12 miles (19 km) south to Marysville, Kansas. Leaving Beatrice, the trail is a well-maintained path that rolls over farmland, under the shade of trees, over bridges, and through prairie grasses. A rest area with picnic shelters, water, and restrooms is located at Holmesville, about 7 miles (11.3 km) down the trail. While there aren't any bike rental options in Beatrice, you can easily walk or run the trail.

The trail is named for Chief Standing Bear of the Ponca Tribe, which owns it today. In 1877 the U.S. Cavalry evicted the Ponca people from their home in northern Nebraska near the Niobrara River. They were forced to walk 200 miles (320 km) to a reservation in Oklahoma, only to find unsuitable conditions when they arrived. One-third of the group died within 18 months from sickness, cold, and poor nutrition. Historical signs and interpretive panels are posted along the trail, allowing visitors to dig deeper into the history of Chief Standing Bear and the Ponca Tribe.

Food

Every serving of baby back ribs, pulled pork, and beef brisket from **Back Alley BBQ & Grill** (2312 N. 6th St., 402/223-5011, www.backalleyeatery.com, 11am-8pm Tues.-Fri., 5pm-8pm Sat., $13) is lightly rubbed with spices and then smoked to perfection over a wood-fired grill. Dinners come with one or two meat options, a cornbread muffin, and classic sides like coleslaw, macaroni salad, green beans, or creamed corn. Lighter options

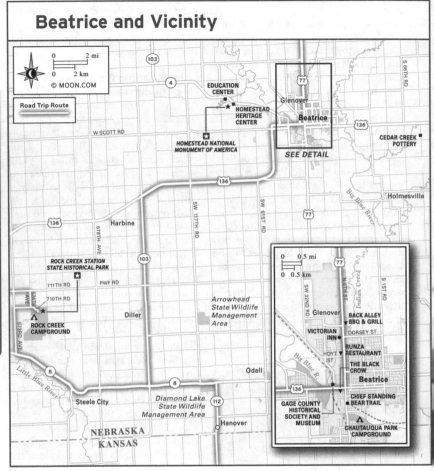

Beatrice and Vicinity

like soups and salads are available too, but come on—you're here for the barbecue. Oh, and the homemade cheesecake and pie.

With a classy menu full of items like oysters rockefeller and roast duck, this restaurant might feel more at home in Kansas City or Omaha than a mid-size Midwestern town. **The Black Crow** (405 Court St., 402/228-7200, www.blackcrowrestaurant.com, 11:30am-2pm and 5:30pm-10pm Tues.-Sun., $20) is here to surprise you, with Nebraska steaks, in-house smoked salmon, and a wine list

that can rival any bigger city's. Lunch has more casual options, including stellar sandwiches.

Shopping

A beautiful white church nestled among the trees in the farmland outside of Beatrice holds a secret. Inside the restored 100-year-old building is a temple of pottery—artist Erv Dixon has been creating his clay pieces since 1976 at **Cedar Creek Pottery** (27639 S. 80 Rd., 402/228-0138, 10am-5pm Mon.-Sat.). The Beatrice local throws pots, plates,

A Ponca Tribe Story: Chief Standing Bear

The Great Plains, encompassing an area including Nebraska as well as Kansas and the Dakotas, was home to many indigenous tribes in the 1800s. One of these was the Ponca Tribe, which the U.S. government relocated to reservations in Oklahoma in 1877, escorted by military guard. Many members of the tribe died along the way, including the daughter and son of a Ponca chief, Standing Bear. When Chief Standing Bear attempted to honor his son's dying wish to be buried in his Nebraska homeland, he was arrested and held for trial. It became a landmark case in 1879 when he argued in Omaha's district court for his right to be recognized as a person under the law, with civil rights. He won the case, garnering newspaper and media attention, and allowing the Ponca people to return back home, where they still live today on ancestral lands near the Niobrara River in Nebraska, about 200 miles north of Lincoln. After the trial, Chief Standing Bear went on to give a lecture tour across the United States and in Europe. He died in 1908. In 2019 his statue was installed in the National Statuary Hall in the United States Capitol in Washington DC.

ornaments, platters, and more, all housed in the old church next to pieces by other artists. It's worth a stop to wander the aisles of the church, even stumbling across the old organ, to admire the myriad pottery pieces on display and for sale at every price point. When you arrive you'll see a sign on the door that invites you in—the lights turn on automatically, and Erv will be over shortly. The shop is about 8 miles (12.9 km) east of Beatrice, off U.S. 136; look for the big blue sign pointing the way.

Accommodations and Camping

Travelers will find a selection of basic hotels in Beatrice. For an affordable stay, the **Victorian Inn** (1903 N. 6th St., 402/228-5955, www.victorianinnhotels.com, $59-129) is a modest hotel with 50 rooms, a heated indoor pool, and complimentary breakfast, located just north of town.

Find a nice place for your tent or RV at **Chautauqua Park** (9th St. and Grable Ave., 402/228-5248, $18). It's just off U.S. 77 and offers access to lots of activities, including horseshoes, tennis courts, a playground, Frisbee golf, walking trails, and river fishing. The 20 campsites have electric hookups, grills, picnic tables, and showers, and all sites are first-come, first-served.

Getting Back on the Trail

Head north on U.S. 77 for 41 miles (65 km), at which point you have the option to stop in Lincoln, or from here continue west 125 miles (201 km) on I-80 to pick up the trail again in Kearney. Exit 272 takes you north to town via Highway 44, the main road through town. The drive there takes 2.75 hours.

Detour: Lincoln

The village that became Lincoln, first called Lancaster, was founded in 1856, well after the Oregon Trail was established. While it's not on the official Oregon National Historic Trail route, the town saw its share of wagon traffic in its early years, as Mormon pioneers traveled through on their way from Illinois to Utah. Before that, Pawnee people made their home along the Platte River Valley that stretches across Nebraska, and the Sioux often came to hunt bison herds. Lincoln quickly grew and became the capital of the new state of Nebraska in 1867. The University of Nebraska (UNL) was established soon after, in 1869. In the early 1900s, German immigrants from Russia brought a wave of Eastern European influence to the area.

One Day in Lincoln

Morning
Start out strong with a breakfast at **The Rabbit Hole Bakery** before wandering or taking a tour of the **Nebraska State Capitol.** From the capitol you can walk about 20 minutes southeast for a stroll through the themed **Sunken Gardens.**

Afternoon
For lunch, head to the quirky **Grateful Bread.** Then continue south for a tour of **Robber's Cave,** a system of caves beneath the city with a storied past. Or stay close to downtown with a visit to the **Great Plains Art Museum.**

Evening
End your day at the **Historic Haymarket District,** where you can browse shops; eat and drink at Lincoln's first brewery, **Lazlo's Brewery & Grill;** and have a delicious dessert at **Ivanna Cone.** Catch a show at the **Bourbon Theatre,** then top the night off at a speakeasy, **The Other Room**—if you can find it!

Historic Haymarket District

Modern pioneers in today's Lincoln come from all over the world—Nebraska has welcomed refugees from Vietnam, Iraq, Afghanistan, Mexico, Bosnia, Bhutan, Sudan, and other countries through a program started in the 1970s, when the State Department identified Nebraska as a "refugee-friendly" state, with a strong economy able to support an influx of newcomers, creating a truly multicultural city; in 2015, Lincoln settled the most refugees per capita in the nation. The University of Nebraska at Lincoln campus is also a major draw for the city, promoting a vibrant arts and culture scene for students and residents.

Getting There and Around
Lincoln is 41 miles (65 km) north of **Beatrice** on U.S. 77, about a 45-minute drive. Exit onto Rosa Parks Way and follow it for 2 miles (3.2 km), turning left onto South 10th Street into town. If you're coming from **Omaha,** drive 50 miles (80 km) southwest on I-80. The drive from Omaha takes about an hour.

Uber (www.uber.com) and **Lyft** (www.lyft.com) operate in Lincoln.

Orientation
Lincoln is laid out in an easily navigable grid of numbers (east-west) and letters (north-south). The numbers get higher as you head east, and the letters are alphabetically organized, beginning with A in the south and ending with Z in the north. O Street is the long main backbone of the city. The **Historic Haymarket District** is near the railroad tracks around 7th and Q Streets, while the **University of Nebraska** campus spreads out north of R Street and west of 16th Street. **Downtown** is conveniently walkable, extending from the Historic Haymarket District to 21st Street, and from the Nebraska State Capitol on H Street to the University of Nebraska campus.

Sights
Nebraska State Capitol
The **Nebraska State Capitol** (1445 K St., 402/471-0448, www.capitol.nebraska.

Lincoln

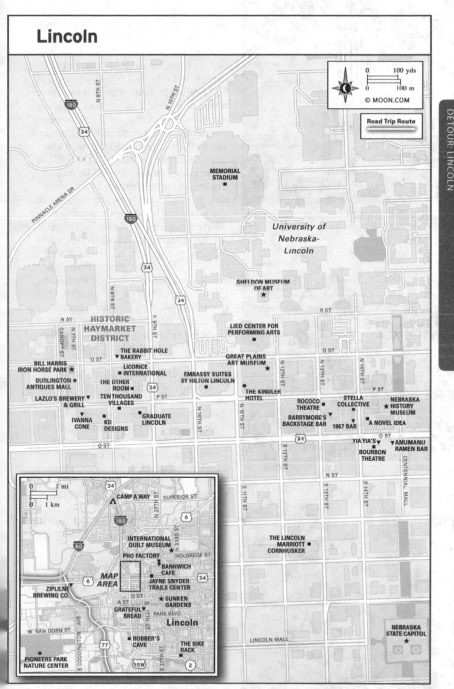

0   100 yds
0   100 m

© MOON.COM

Road Trip Route

N 8TH ST

N 10TH ST

MEMORIAL STADIUM

PINNACLE ARENA DR

University of Nebraska-Lincoln

SHELDON MUSEUM OF ART ★

R ST

HISTORIC HAYMARKET DISTRICT

N 9TH ST

R ST

N 7TH ST

CANOPY ST

LIED CENTER FOR PERFORMING ARTS

Q ST

THE RABBIT HOLE BAKERY ▼

Q ST

BILL HARRIS IRON HORSE PARK ★

N 8TH ST

LICORICE ■ INTERNATIONAL

GREAT PLAINS ART MUSEUM ★

N 12TH ST

N 13TH ST

N 14TH ST

BURLINGTON ■ ANTIQUES MALL

THE OTHER ROOM ■

EMBASSY SUITES BY HILTON LINCOLN ●

P ST

LAZLO'S BREWERY ▼ & GRILL

TEN THOUSAND VILLAGES

P ST

THE KINDLER HOTEL ●

IVANNA CONE ●

KD DESIGNS ■

GRADUATE LINCOLN ●

N 10TH ST

N 18TH ST

ROCOCO THEATRE ●

STELLA COLLECTIVE ●

NEBRASKA ★ HISTORY MUSEUM

BARRYMORE'S BACKSTAGE BAR ●

1867 BAR ●

A NOVEL IDEA ■

Q ST

O ST

YIA YIA'S ● ▼AMUMANU BOURBON RAMEN BAR THEATRE

S 12TH ST

CENTENNIAL MALL

N ST

S 11TH ST

S 13TH ST

S 14TH ST

THE LINCOLN MARRIOTT CORNHUSKER ●

LINCOLN MALL

NEBRASKA STATE CAPITOL ★

Inset map

0   1 mi
0   1 km

34

CAMP A WAY ▲

SUPERIOR ST

N 27TH ST

N 33RD ST

6

180

80

INTERNATIONAL QUILT MUSEUM ★

PHO FACTORY ●

HOLDREGE ST

34

6

MAP AREA

BANHWICH CAFE ●

JAYNE SNYDER TRAILS CENTER ●

ZIPLINE BREWING CO. ▲

S 27TH ST

S 17TH ST

D ST

GRATEFUL ▼ BREAD

A ST

PARK BLVD

★ SUNKEN GARDENS

S CODDINGTON AVE

Lincoln

W VAN DORN ST

77

ROBBER'S ● CAVE

55W

THE BIKE ★ RACK

2

PIONEERS PARK NATURE CENTER ●

LINCOLN MALL

gov, 8am-5pm Mon.-Fri., 10am-5pm Sat., 1pm-5pm Sun., free) was designed by Bertram Grosvenor Goodhue and can be seen for miles as travelers approach the city. It's actually the third building on the site—the first two were much humbler. The current building was constructed 1922-1932 and features a square base, four interior courtyards, and a 400-foot-tall (120-m) domed tower rising from the center. At the top of the dome rises *The Sower,* a tall bronze figure spreading seeds from a sack he carries. Beneath the dome are mosaics of thunderbirds, honoring the legacy of the Native Americans of the plains; the giant mythological bird—considered a giver of life responsible for the sound of thunder—is a prominent figure in many Great Plains communities. Here, it evokes the importance of rain on the prairies, vital to indigenous and modern agriculture alike. The building's exterior features stone carvings that circle the structure in a progression that represents the history of democracy.

It's worth looking inside this stately building. You're free to wander on your own or take a guided tour, available on the hour except at noon. Inside, art deco-style mosaics, murals, and sculptures depict early Nebraska history, featuring Native American and pioneer influences. In the main rotunda, the floor is graced by a marble mosaic of Mother Nature surrounded by representations of the elements: water, air, earth, fire. You can walk inside courtrooms, if court isn't in session, and the legislative offices.

Historic Haymarket District

The **Historic Haymarket District** is the beating heart of this fun city, where history is given new lease in the form of restaurants, shops, nightlife, and galleries. The district is named for the original

Top to bottom: Nebraska State Capitol; *Iron Horse Legacy* by Jay Tschetter in the Historic Haymarket District; Robber's Cave.

market square that sprang up here in 1867 to sell wagons, tools, and hay to local farmers. Spend an afternoon or evening strolling the repurposed warehouses for great dining and shopping options. The district's center is at **Bill Harris Iron Horse Park** (7th St. and Q St.), where visitors can see a three-dimensional brick mural of a locomotive train chugging along; it rises up from the brick wall like a relief, creating the illusion that the train is emerging from the wall. The depicted train is from 1870, the first into Lincoln on Independence Day. The small brick-laid park also has an 1890s water tower, now a fountain, and actual trains in back—see a restored Chicago, Burlington and Quincy Railroad (CB&Q) steam engine beside the old Burlington Northern Railroad depot.

Street parking can be tricky in this area, especially on a Cornhuskers game day. Check the outdoor pay-to-park spots just south of the Burlington Northern Railroad depot, or head to the parking garage at 8th and Q Streets.

Museums

The large collection at the **Nebraska History Museum** (131 Centennial Mall N., 402/471-4782, www.history.nebraska.gov, 10am-5:30pm Mon.-Fri., 1pm-5:30pm Sat., free) holds all sorts of weird, wonderful things that have been resurrected to showcase the past. Visitors can go on a scavenger hunt for items like a furry bison hide coat, a giant tepee, a motorcycle, old clothing, trunks, a mail wagon, and a five-foot-long ceremonial knife that, for reasons unclear, was used to cut a cake celebrating the 10th anniversary of the *Pioneer Zephyr*, a CB&Q streamliner.

Part of the University of Nebraska-Lincoln, the **Great Plains Art Museum** (1155 Q St., 402/472-6220, www.unl.edu, 10am-5pm Tues.-Sat., free) has a permanent collection including bronze sculptures, paintings, and photographs of the West from such monumental figures as well-known Western artists Albert Bierstadt and Frederic Remington. Both men were most productive in the late 1800s after seeing the western prairies and mountains firsthand and contributed greatly to the idea of the American West as a mythic, romantic place, something that still resonates today. The museum also hosts many contemporary artists as well as rotating exhibits.

See American art from the 19th and 20th centuries at the **Sheldon Museum of Art** (12th St. and R St., 402/472-2461, www.sheldonartmuseum.org, 10am-5pm Mon.-Wed. and Sat., 10am-7pm Thurs.-Fri., noon-5pm Sun., free), another gallery space on the UNL campus. The building itself is on the National Register of Historic Places and is surrounded by a pretty sculpture garden. Inside, famous works include paintings by Edward Hopper and Georgia O'Keeffe, and sculptures by Constantin Brâncuşi. The vast collection ranges from Impressionist pieces to contemporary art.

The **International Quilt Museum** (1523 N. 33rd St., 402/472-6549, ww.quiltstudy.org, 10am-4pm Tues.-Sat., 1pm-4pm Sun. Feb.-Nov., $8) began life as part of the Home Economics building at UNL with a huge donation of quilts. In 2008 it moved to its current space, a 37,000-square-foot building to store the growing collection—the biggest in the world! Visitors will learn about the process of caring for the old quilts, including cleaning and re-folding them every year (to ward off harm from creases). Exhibits display gorgeous intricate quilts from all over the world, allowing you to enjoy American works from the 1700s alongside colorful contemporary quilts from India and Kenya. Complimentary docent-led tours (11am Tues.-Fri., 11am and 1pm Sat.) are available. Modern quilters will love the gift shop, full of patterns, tools, and quilting-themed goodies.

Robber's Cave

In the early 1860s, Lincoln's first craft brewery started up in a cave under the city. It went under after a few years, but the cave remained popular, serving a myriad of uses before being closed to the public. It has reopened in recent years for tours. Plenty of folks around town still remember exploring the tunnels or having college parties down here. Many locals who take the tour can locate their own names carved into the soft sandstone walls. The oldest name, Sam Dalton, dates to 1875, when the cave may have seen its most notorious visitor: Jesse James. His possible visit is the reason for the name Robber's Cave.

Robber's Cave Tours (925 Robbers Cave Rd., 402/975-0598, www.robbers cavetours.com, 6pm Wed., 1pm and 2:30pm Sat.-Sun., $10) take you into the 5,600-square-foot cave system. The guided tour lasts 45-60 minutes and is open to all ages. The cave is 3 miles (4.8 km) south of downtown via South 9th Street.

Recreation
Biking
Lincoln is one of the top bike-friendly cities in the Midwest, with over a hundred miles (160 km) of trails as well as on-street bike options. Downtown, the **N Street Cycle Track** is a protected bikeway that runs for 17 blocks along N Street, from 23rd Street to the Haymarket.

The **Jayne Snyder Trails Center** (228 N. 21st St., 402/441-7847, dawn-dusk daily) serves as a bicycling hub, offering trail info and maps, restrooms, and water. It's near the edge of downtown on Union Plaza, a pleasant paved and landscaped space with fountains, a children's play area, outdoor seating, and a giant brick sculpture of a human head called *The Colossus*. Pause here for a moment and you might hear the sound of trickling water emanating from the head, meant to represent the Ogallala Aquifer—a huge underground water source that extends across much of the Great Plains region—and sometimes clanging metal,

representing the effects of humans on the environment.

The center is near the convergence of various bike trails, including the **Billy Wolff Trail,** which cuts southeast across the city and connects the UNL campus to the Sunken Gardens and various city parks, as well as the **Rock Island Trail,** which cuts southwest. Find more information and maps online at **Bike Lincoln** (www.lincoln.ne.gov/city/plan/bike) as well as the **Great Plains Trail Network** (www.gptn.org). The bike trails are open to pedestrians as well.

Bike Rentals
Get a rental at **The Bike Rack** (3321 Pioneers Blvd., 402/488-2101, www.bike-rack.com, 10am-7pm Mon.-Fri., 10am-6pm Sat., noon-5pm Sun., $40 per day, $150 per week), a local company that offers quality bikes. A deposit for the bike's value is necessary for rentals, so come prepared with a credit card. The shop is located south of town, but just a few blocks away from the Rock Island Trail, which heads 4 miles (6.4 km) north to the Jayne Snyder Trails Center.

Sunken Gardens
Find a place of quiet beauty at the **Sunken Gardens** (27th St. and Capitol Pkwy., http://lincoln.ne.gov, 6am-11pm daily, free) southeast of downtown. The small garden has more than 30,000 plants that are redesigned every year based on different themes, like Van Gogh's *The Starry Night* or Sun Salutations, full of fiery colors. Every season has something to offer, from spring tulips to thousands of summer blooms, quieting to a peaceful place of trees and shrubs in fall and winter. The gazebo offers nice views, and brick paths allow for wandering.

Pioneers Park Nature Center
Named in honor of the area's early settlers, **Pioneers Park Nature Center** (3201 S. Coddington Ave., 402/441-7895, http://

lincoln.ne.gov, 8:30am-5pm Mon.-Sat., noon-5pm Sun. summer, free) encompasses 1,100 acres, including rolling hills and trees, with miles of hiking trails that meander past live animal displays. The wildlife refuge is home to creatures including bison, elk, white-tailed deer, and raptors. The visitors center also has displays about the tallgrass prairie and smaller live animals including snakes, turtles, and owls. On the east side of the park, giant sandstone columns, near a pond, make a good place for kids to run around.

From downtown Lincoln, head south on South 9th Street, then turn right onto Rosa Parks Way. In 2.3 miles (3.7 km), continue onto South Coddington Avenue for another 1.4 miles (2.3 km). The entrance to the park is on your right. The drive takes 20 minutes.

Spring Creek Prairie Audubon Center

Find trail ruts on the grounds of the **Spring Creek Prairie Audubon Center** (11700 SW 100th St., Denton, 402/797-2301, www.springcreek.audubon.org, $4), located just southwest of Lincoln. The ruts aren't from the official Oregon Trail but from trails that connected to it from Omaha. The center is focused on the conservation of the tallgrass prairie ecosystem, which native birds like kestrels, owls, terns, geese, and eagles rely on. The prairie here has been preserved much as the landscape would have been in pioneer times, with no crops or farmland. Walking trails wind through the grasslands and near ponds, offering close-ups of birds and other wildlife as well as wildflowers. The **visitors center** (9am-5pm Mon.-Fri., 1pm-5pm Sat.-Sun.) is inside a straw-bale building—the construction technique was developed in Nebraska in the early pioneer era. Inside are interactive exhibits on the prairie ecosystem, where you can see how the hardy plants survived by pushing long roots down into the soil. Some species of prairie flowers, like the dotted gayfeather, can grow up to 15 feet deep!

From downtown Lincoln, head west on O Street, which becomes U.S. 6, then turn left onto Highway 55A. Continue on it for 5.2 miles (8.4 km), then turn right onto West Denton Road. In 0.5 mile (0.8 km), turn left onto Southwest 98th Street. The center is on the left in 3.3 miles (5.3 km).

Spectator Sports

Each fall, the city turns red in support of **Cornhuskers Football** (www.huskers.com, Sept.-Nov., $60-250). The University of Nebraska's football team hosts a series of home games each year that turn Memorial Stadium (1 Memorial Stadium Dr., 402/472-3111) into the state's third-largest city. It hosts 90,000 attendees—all, inevitably, wearing red—and is usually sold out at every game; check for tickets a month or two ahead of time.

Entertainment
Bars and Brewpubs

Named for the year Nebraska became a state, the **1867 Bar** (101 N. 14th St., 531/289-1724, 5pm-2am Mon.-Thurs., 3pm-2am Fri.-Sun.) has 14 taps with Nebraska brews and offers live music covering a variety of genres. Gray walls and brick accents lend a rustic homey feel, and the place attracts the young and old from all over. Plenty of games will keep drinkers busy, including *Jenga,* darts, Nintendo, and pinball. There's also a photo booth.

The Other Room (824 P. St., 402/261-4608, 5pm-1am daily) is unlike any bar around. The speakeasy space is a bit hard to find and a bit hard to get into on weekends, but that's part of the allure. It holds only 25 people at a time, making it a quiet, intimate place to enjoy well-crafted cocktails and good conversation. Pre-Prohibition-style cocktails rotate seasonally, all made with freshly mixed ingredients, including house-made bitters and juices. The bar is hidden in a Haymarket courtyard alley off P Street, with a big brick wall and an iron gate. Locate the big door behind the gate. If the light above is red, it means they're at capacity, and you'll need to wait or come back later. If it's green, you're in luck; knock on the door to enter. Once inside, put down your phone, pay in cash, and sip your masterpiece.

A local brewery that aims to be one of the best of the Midwest, **Zipline Brewing Co.** (2100 Magnum Circle, Suite 1, 402/475-1001, www.ziplinebrewing.com, 3pm-8pm Sun.-Thurs., 1pm-10pm Fri.-Sat.) is on its way, with over a dozen taps including beers like the Daaang! IPA and Post-Hype Pale Ale, as well as seasonal brews, barrel-aged options, and collaborations. Enjoy a pint in the beer garden. Food trucks sometimes visit. Zipline is a zero-waste brewery, meaning it diverts 98 percent of its waste from landfills by sending used grain to farmers and practicing stringent recycling guidelines in-house.

Live Music
Bourbon Theatre (1415 O St., no phone, www.bourbontheatre.com, 11am-6pm Tues.-Fri., $15-60) is located in a renovated 1930s movie theater and offers a variety of live music shows most weekends and many weeknights. Shows are either general admission standing-room-only or seated, depending on the performance. It's a hoppin' place, holding 300-600 people, with multiple bars slinging great cocktails. You can't miss the giant flashing marquee outside, welcoming pedestrians on O Street inside—look for tickets directly at the box office to save a few bucks, or book online ahead of time.

The **Rococo Theatre** (124 N. 13th St., 402/476-6540, www.rococotheatre.com, 10am-5pm Mon.-Fri., $35-70) hosts nationally and internationally known indie, rock, pop, and country acts, as well as a roster of comedians. The large theater has three floors, with standing room in the general admission area and two balconies with seats and tables. Tickets are available online or by phone only. Cash bars are in the lobby for preshow fun, and in the alley behind the stage you can find **Barrymore's Backstage Bar** (124 N. 13th St., www.rococotheatre.com/barrymores, 3pm-1am Mon.-Thurs., 3pm-2am Fri., 5pm-2am Sat.) This is a great place to grab a drink before or after a show. Barrymore's specializes in martinis and cocktails but also has a good beer list. Originally opened in 1974, you can still see the curtain pulley that operated the theater's stage.

The Arts
Part of the UNL campus, the **Lied Center for Performing Arts** (301 N. 12th St., 402/472-4747, wwww.liedcenter.org, $15-70) is a beautiful multitiered venue presenting world-class shows, including Broadway musicals, symphonies, comedic acts, and plays. The red-carpeted Main Stage seats over 2,000, while the Johnny Carson Theater—named after the famous son of Nebraska, who hailed from the nearby town of Norfolk and graduated from UNL—holds 250 for more intimate events. Preperformance talks—providing background and context on the show—take place about 30 minutes before most performances and can really enhance the experience. Some performances make dinner available in the Lied Commons dining area ($35) before the show at 5:30pm, along with a cash bar.

Food
Brewpubs
Lincoln's first brewpub opened in 1991 and has been a solid choice for dinner and a brew ever since. **Lazlo's Brewery & Grill** (210 N. 7th St., 402/434-5356, www.lazlosbreweryandgrill.com, 11am-10pm Sun.-Thurs., 11am-midnight Fri.-Sat., $15) is in a renovated 1880s storefront that has grown to encompass some of the neighboring buildings, including its Empyrean Brewing Co. next door. The fare is American comfort food done well,

Runza, the Sandwich that Powers the Plains

A beloved sandwich that only Nebraskans have heard of, the *runza* is a legacy of immigration across the plains. It's a hoagie-shaped sandwich made of fluffy yeast dough filled with spiced beef, cabbage, and onions. In Kansas it's known as a *bierock* and comes in a bun shape rather than the longer *runza*. The recipes were brought to the area by German-Russian immigrants in the 18th century, passed down to each generation.

Today, the sandwich owes its popularity to a Lincoln-based fast-food chain, also called **Runza** (in fact, the company trademarked the name). The first *runza* was made from family recipes and sold for 15 cents from a food stand in 1949. Runza soon expanded to a second location in 1966 before expanding throughout the state and beyond. The fast-food chain, perhaps the only one to popularize cabbage, makes their sandwiches fresh every day from bread baked in-store, seasoned beef, and freshly chopped kraut. The menu includes burgers, fries, salads, and chicken strips, but there's no reason to go to a Runza and not get a *runza*. If you're in the mood for something a little less fast-food, try a version at **Gering Bakery,** on the west side of the state, where it goes by the name "cabbage burger."

like ribs, hickory-smoked steaks, burgers, big salads, and all the sides, with friendly service to boot. Don't miss the *lahvosh,* a savory cracker bread with various toppings. Pair your meal with one of Empyrean's beers, like the award winning LunaSea ESB or the WatchMan IPA, brewed with Nebraska hops. The restaurant doesn't take reservations, but you can call ahead to get on the waitlist.

Pizza

Find the holy trinity of pizza, beer, and great atmosphere at **Yia Yia's** (1423 O St., 402/477-9166, www.yiayiaspizzaandbeer.com, 11am-11pm Mon.-Thurs., 11am-midnight Fri.-Sat., noon-10pm Sun., $7), a staple on O Street for over 25 years. Find your perfect pizza, which comes fully customizable as a slice or a whole pie. Toppings include the usual pepperoni, garlic, mushrooms, and mozzarella along with more unique offerings like sauerkraut, corn, and cream cheese. Yia Yia's also offers Lincoln's biggest selection of brews, with 24 taps from all over the world supplemented by an even bigger list of 250 bottles and cans. Local Lincoln brews like Zipline nestle next to Belgian and Irish offerings.

Asian

Lincoln might be a college town, but the ramen at **AmuManu Ramen Bar** (1451 O St., 402/261-4619, 11am-3pm and 5pm-9pm Mon.-Sat., 11am-3pm Sun., $10) is light years away from the instant fare that fuels many a late-night study session. Slurp your soup—perhaps in pork belly broth or garlic *shoyu*—and add pork *bao* buns or stir-fried noodles, which you can enjoy in the small but pleasant dining room featuring modern wood paneling and a corrugated tin roof.

Lincoln has had a thriving Vietnamese community since an influx of refugees arrived in the early 1980s. One of the best places to get a taste of the culture is at the Little Saigon Shopping Plaza. The **Pho Factory** (940 N. 26th Ave., 402/261-3213, www.phofactorylincoln.com, 11am-9pm Mon.-Fri., 11am-8pm Sat., 10am-8pm Sun., $11) dishes out stellar soups, clay-pot meals, and noodle dishes, while the nearby **Banhwich Cafe** (940 N. 26th St., 402/261-4655, 10am-9pm Mon.-Sat., 10am-8pm Sun., $8) has over 17 different kinds of sandwiches inspired by Vietnamese, Korean, Chinese, and Thai cuisine. It also offers bubble tea and frozen yogurt.

Local Fast Food

A regional fast-food chain born in Lincoln, **Runza** (1501 N. 56th St. 402/466-1087, www.runza.com, 10:30am-10pm daily, $6) serves traditional Eastern European *bierocks,* a staple food of the plains. The first Runza was a drive-in near Pioneers Park that opened in 1949. It expanded to this location on 56th and Holdrege Streets in 1966, and there are a dozen more locations across the city today.

Cafés and Bakeries

The quirky café at ★ **Grateful Bread** (1625 S. 17th St. 402/474-0101, 11am-6pm Wed.-Sun., $6) is a whimsically decorated place with prayer flags and plastic dinosaurs scattered about. Folks line up at the door for the all-vegetarian homemade soups and cheesy scones. Be sure to sample the classic Moroccan Tomato Soup, so good it remains on the menu every day. Inside, the small space seats 25-30. Note it's cash or check only.

Find **The Rabbit Hole Bakery** (800 Q St., 402/975-2322, http://therabbitholebakery.com, 8am-8pm Mon.-Sat., $7) down an almost-literal rabbit hole beneath a brick building in the Haymarket. Hungry visitors will find plenty to satiate them, all made from scratch. Scones, cakes (carrot, chocolate, and more), fruit tarts, cookies, French macarons, and specialty coffees are all here, along with tea, wine, and special liqueurs.

Ice Cream

You can watch the ice cream being churned right inside the front door at ★ **Ivanna Cone** (701 P St., 402/477-7473, www.ivannacone.com, noon-10pm Sun.-Thurs., noon-10:30pm Fri.-Sat., $5), an old-fashioned ice cream shop that makes small-batch flavors. Up to 17 flavors grace the menu at any time, ranging from classic chocolate and strawberry to esoteric lemongrass ginger, carrot cake, and almond. With sodas, homemade waffle cones, nondairy sorbets, and a kids' play area, there's something for everyone. Note the creamery only takes cash or check, but there's an ATM around the corner, in the building's hallway.

Shopping
Haymarket Historic District

Rejoice, fans of licorice! Whether you prefer black, red, both (or neither), you'll find plenty to sample at **Licorice International** (803 Q St., 402/488-2230, www.licoriceinternational.com, 9:30am-6pm Mon.-Fri., 10am-5pm Sun.). Originally a mail-order business, the space became a popular local place to hunt down favorite candies, and today the store carries over 160 varieties from 12 countries. Find Scottish dogs, Australian black twists, Dutch Salmiak bars, and English wine gums. Samples are happily offered.

One of the oldest fair-trade organizations in the country, **Ten Thousand Villages** (140 N. 8th St., Suite 125, 402/475-4122, www.tenthousandvillages.com, 10am-6pm Mon.-Wed., 10am-9pm Thurs.-Sat., noon-6pm Sun.) arrived in Lincoln over 35 years ago. Through close relationships with artisans worldwide, the retail store offers gorgeous clothing, home goods, jewelry, and more at reasonable prices that still afford makers a living wage for their work.

Now the center of the Haymarket Historic District, inside the Burlington Northern Railroad depot that once served all of Lincoln, **Burlington Antiques Mall** (201 N. 7th St., 402/475-7502, www.burlingtonantiques.com, 10am-6pm Mon.-Thurs. and Sat., 10am-9pm Fri., noon-5pm Sun.) has 5,000 square feet of antiques to browse. Find beautiful jewelry, glass lamps, pottery, and textiles from 20 different dealers, and barely a speck of dust. Each piece is well presented and ready to find a new home.

Build your own charm jewelry at **KD Designs** (151 N. 8th St., Suite 110, 402/304-3039, www.kddesignsjewelry.

com, 10am-6pm Mon.-Wed., 10am-9pm Thurs.-Sat., noon-5pm Sun.), a boutique shop run by a mother and daughter duo. Visit the charming bar inside to choose from themed or colored charms of all kinds, then design your own bracelet or necklace to bring home. The store also sells completed jewelry, made locally, and quirky lawn games like giant handmade wooden dice for "Yardzee."

Downtown

Lincoln's favorite bookstore, **A Novel Idea** (118 N. 14th St., 402/465-8663, www. anovelideabookstore.com, 10am-6pm Tues.-Sat.) has been peddling books since 1991. The shelves contain used books of all genres, in good quality—you might even find a collectible edition signed by the author! You can easily lose an hour browsing the options, with help from the two resident cats.

Filled with plants and soothing colors in an open airy space, the **Stella Collective** (101 N. 14th St., Suite 7, 402/476-0028, www.stella-collective. com, 11am-6:30pm Mon.-Fri., 10am-6pm Sat., noon-5pm Sun.) makes for pleasant browsing. The shop offers several local brands under one roof, including the namesake Stella clothing, alongside vintage furniture and sparkling geodes and accessories. Come away with a stunning new pair of green satin pants, a bold striped skirt, and other trendy pieces.

Accommodations
Under $150

Just east of town, the idyllic ★ **Prairie Creek Inn** (2400 S. 148th St., Walton, 402/488-8822, www.pcibnb.com, $99-269) offers a secluded place to rest and recharge. The main accommodations are in the property's Leavitt House, which has six well-appointed rooms across four levels, with elevator access. The rooms evoke an early pioneer era, but with modern soft beds and large baths. For extra privacy, book the cottage next door, which has a beautiful sunset-view porch. All rooms come with a full breakfast in the Leavitt House dining room. Two suites in the Lake Lodge can be rented separately or as one; the lodge has a private hot tub, two fireplaces, and a view of the adjacent namesake lake.

With a location in walking distance to the UNL campus and Haymarket, **Embassy Suites** (1040 P St., 402/474-1111, http://embassysuites3.hilton.com, $131-220) has 250 convenient guest suites with private bedrooms and separate living areas. Enjoy an evening reception each night with drinks and snacks, then a hot breakfast in the courtyard lobby before a splash in the pool or sauna.

$150-250

The hip **Graduate Lincoln** (141 N. 9th St., 402/475-4011, www.graduatelincoln. com, $155-245) is an ode to students of all ages—a skip away from the UNL campus, the hotel is a laid-back spot that highlights camaraderie and fun. Little nods to Nebraska are everywhere in the 231 guest rooms, from vintage maps to corn curtains. The swimming pool is surrounded by sliding glass doors that open to the outside game area (foosball, Ping-Pong, and more) on the 2nd-floor roof. Local students are welcome to use the lobby to study, and game nights are also offered in the lobby—because you can't study all the time. Guests enjoy complimentary bikes, treats for any pets checking in, and a short walk to plenty of Haymarket attractions.

Stay steps away from Memorial Stadium at **The Kindler Hotel** (216 N. 11th St., 402/261-7800, www.thekindlerhotel. com, $160-195). The modern hotel has 49 rooms in a renovated neoclassical building from Lincoln's early 20th century—it once served as the city's chamber of commerce. After a busy day, relax in your robe and slippers and take a nip from the in-room honor bar.

Promenade down the grand staircase at **The Lincoln Marriott Cornhusker Hotel** (333 S. 13th St., 402/474-7474, www.

marriott.com, $108-325), which has 300 beautiful rooms. Hosting many guests each year for in-house conventions or Husker games, the hotel knows hospitality, and offers shuttle services to and from the airport. It's within walking distance to nearby attractions downtown, just 15 minutes from the Haymarket Historic District and 20 minutes from Memorial Stadium. Hosted on the roof are several honeybee hives; the nearly 100,000 honeybees produce up to 600 pounds of honey, used in the hotel's kitchens. There's no access to see the bees, but you can bring home a jar from the gift shop, labeled "Bee Our Guest."

Camping

At **Camp A Way** (200 Campers Circle, 402/476-2282, www.campaway.com, $25-130), you'll find options for year-round tent and RV camping ($25-58), as well as lodge rooms ($90-100) and cottages ($110-130), along with friendly customer-oriented service. Located a 10-minute drive north of the Haymarket, where I-80 and U.S. 34 meet, the RV park offers fantastic amenities, including cable TV, an indoor spa, a heated pool, and a range of ways to keep kids occupied, from a giant water slide to giant board games in the arcade.

Getting Back on the Trail

To pick up the trail again, head west from Lincoln 125 miles (201 kilometers) on I-80 to Kearney. Exit 272 takes you north to town via Highway 44, the main road through town. The drive takes two hours.

Kearney

The Platte River, which Oregon Trail emigrants first encountered near what's now the town of Kearney, stretched hundreds of miles west to Fort Laramie in Wyoming. The wide, flat river valley was easily traversable, creating something of an early interstate four-lane highway; in many places wagons spread out side to side up to 5 miles (8 km) wide. Oregon Trail traffic traveled along the south bank of the Platte River, while Mormon pioneers, following an alternate path from Illinois to Utah by way of Omaha on what's known as the Mormon Trail, traveled along the north bank, avoiding a river crossing and possible persecution—from which they were fleeing—for their religious beliefs. This thoroughfare became known over the years as the Great Platte River Road. Traffic on both sides of the river became so heavy in some years, such as during the gold rush to California in 1849, that all the grass and livestock feed was decimated on both sides of the river, and the threat of polluted water carrying cholera skyrocketed.

In 1848 Fort Kearny was built to establish a military presence in the area—all the migration was beginning to make neighboring Sioux peoples anxious, which in turn made the U.S. government anxious. The fort served as a resting stop and supply station for wagon trains, and the army stationed here often accompanied parties along the Platte River to offer protection. The Union Pacific Railroad was completed in 1869, making overland travel unnecessary. The town of Kearney was founded in 1871 at a junction of the Union Pacific Railroad to the north of the Platte River, just as Fort Kearny to the south was being abandoned and demolished. Note the different spellings: The fort is named Kearny, but due to an errant post office mistake, the extra "e" in the town's name was added in, and it stuck. Kearney surged to 10,000 residents in the 1880s, rivaling Lincoln, then declined during the Great Depression.

Today Kearney is a fun, surprising city. The University of Nebraska at Kearney keeps an influx of young college students in town, and the downtown is seeing a small revival of businesses on its brick-lined streets. Get out "on the bricks" to enjoy good food and drinks. If you're just

Kearney and Vicinity

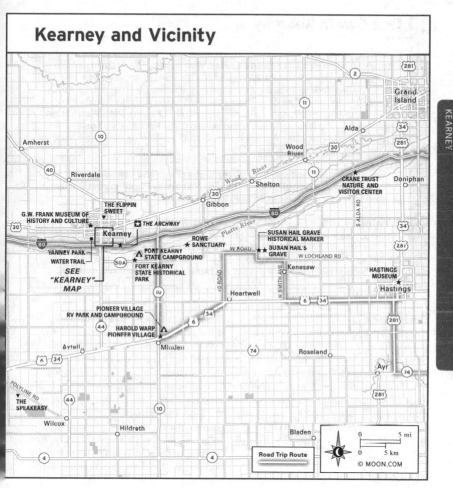

passing through, stop at The Archway, and perhaps grab a pint of popular local brew or some great pizza. If you have an extra day or two, you can enjoy some art, history, biking, and maybe even a kayaking trip along the Platte River.

Getting There and Around

From Minden, location of the Harold Warp Pioneer Village—the last stop on the **southern Nebraska** section of the route—head 10 miles (16 km) north on Highway 10. Turn left onto Highway 50A. After 7 miles (11.3 km), turn right onto Highway 44, which crosses the Platte River and brings you to Kearney in 4 miles (6.4 km). The drive takes 30 minutes.

If you're driving from **Lincoln,** the 125-mile (200-km) drive west to Kearney on I-80 takes about two hours. Exit 275 takes you to The Archway, and exit 272 takes you north to town via Highway 44, the main road through town. If you're coming from **Beatrice,** you'll drive north on U.S. 77 for 41 miles (65 km) to Lincoln, and then hop on I-80; it adds 45 minutes to the drive.

One Day in Kearney

Morning
Grab breakfast at **Kitt's Kitchen and Coffee,** then head to **The Archway,** where you'll learn about the Great Platte River Road and the many journeys along it, including the Oregon Trail. If you want to include some activity, you can get there by bike; rent one in town at **The Bike Shed,** then head to The Archway. If you want to continue along the bike trail, you can keep going to **Fort Kearny State Recreation Area.** If you want to focus on history, head instead to the **Fort Kearny State Historical Park**—site of the first fort built to protect travelers on the Oregon Trail.

Afternoon
For lunch, grab a drink and pub fare at **Cunningham's on the Lake.** Afterward, hop on the **Kearney Water Trail** on a kayak trip with **Kearney Paddle Sports,** or rent a swan paddle boat for the lake at **Yanney Heritage Park.**

Evening
For dinner, enjoy some of the best pizza in Nebraska at **The Flippin Sweet.** It's off the beaten path to the north of town, but it's worth it. Once night falls, head back to the "bricks" of the small but active downtown. Toast your busy day with a local drink at **McCue's Nebraska Taproom** or a pint at **Thunderhead Brewing Company.**

Orientation
Kearney's brick-lined downtown encompasses the area around Central Avenue, between U.S. 30 to the north and the railroad tracks to the south. I-80 cuts through Kearney south of downtown, and it's where you'll find most hotels and traveler amenities. The University of Nebraska at Kearney campus is northwest of downtown, just off U.S. 30 and University Drive.

Sights
★ The Archway
The Archway (I-80 exit 275, 308/237-1000, http://archway.org, 9am-5pm Mon.-Sat., noon-5pm Sun. Labor Day-Memorial Day, 9am-6pm Mon.-Sat., noon-6pm Sun. Memorial Day-Labor Day, $12 adults, $11 seniors, $6 ages 6-12, free under age 6) spans I-80 just before you enter Kearney. You might be tempted to speed on past, but stop for an hour or two to discover a wealth of history. The museum inside is an ode to the history of the Great Platte River Road, a major travel corridor from Omaha, Nebraska, to Fort Laramie, Wyoming, that has been used for centuries—you're still traveling it today! The long, flat river valley route was first used by Native Americans who hunted and traded along the river. Later, the Oregon, California, and Mormon Trails rolled through, followed by military and Pony Express routes, railroads, the Lincoln Highway—one of the earliest transcontinental highways—and finally, today's I-80. Each historical section has its own dedicated room. Giant murals, audio guides, videos, and interactive displays make you feel like you're part of the scene as an emigrant woman pushes her wagon toward Chimney Rock, gold diggers hunt for the mother lode, and a Pony Express rider switches horses.

The Archway's outdoor grounds offer a maze that's fun for kids, a huge bison sculpture, lakeside walking trails, a 1914 truss bridge, and a one-room sod house. A picnic shelter makes a great spot for a snack or lunch. In The Archway's gift shop you'll find the usual sets of souvenirs along with history books, kids' toys, and plenty of unique Nebraska-made goodies like soaps, jewelry, pickles, and pottery. Purchase a bag of mining

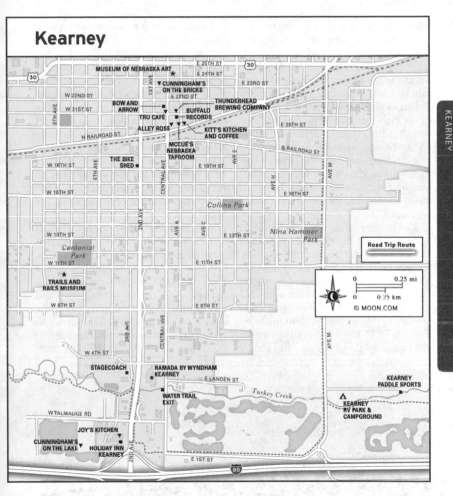

Kearney

rough and take it to the on-site gold-panning sluice, where kids can try their hand at panning. Next to the gift shop, a Nebraska Visitor Center has a wealth of information on local state travel. The grounds, gift shop, and visitors center are free to enter.

Museums

Spend an afternoon at the **Museum of Nebraska Art** (MONA, 2401 Central Ave., 308/865-8559, http://mona.unk.edu, 10am-5pm Tues.-Sat., noon-5pm Sun., free). Its permanent collection includes over 5,000 works by artists of regional, national, and international acclaim, including Jun Kaneko, George Catlin, and *National Geographic* photographer Joel Sartore. Eleven galleries, an outdoor sculpture garden, and a thoughtful museum shop are here. The building itself is a neoclassical stunner from 1911. Find free parking for the museum on its north side.

The **G.W. Frank Museum of History and Culture** (2010 University Dr., 308/865-8284, www.unk.edu, 1pm-5pm Tues.-Fri., noon-5pm Sat.-Sun., free) is in a house built in the unique Richardsonian Romanesque Shingle style, among the first to get electricity and advanced indoor plumbing on the wild frontier. Later the house was used as a sanitarium and housing for the Nebraska State Tuberculosis Hospital staff. Today, tours of the richly decorated interior include a look at the artifacts inside, including a grand piano, hand-carved woodwork, original fireplaces from the 1880s, beautiful stained-glass windows, and hand-blown Italian glass chandeliers. Tours last 45-60 minutes and are free; donations are welcomed.

Run by the Buffalo County Historical Society, a visit to the **Trails and Rails Museum** (710 W. 11th St., 308/243-3041, www.bchs.us, 1pm-5pm Mon.-Fri. Sept.-May, 10am-6pm Mon.-Sat. and 1pm-5pm Sun. June-Aug., $7) includes a guided tour and a look inside a few original 19th-century buildings. The outdoor museum consists of 11 historic buildings and a 1903 steam engine, train car, and yellow caboose. Led by a knowledgeable guide, visitors will get to see Buffalo County's first schoolhouse from 1871 and a one-room log cabin demonstrating how early homesteaders lived. The J. C. Marlatt Blacksmith Shop is especially interesting—it's a fully functioning shop with a roster of blacksmiths who keep the craft alive. Demonstrations are occasionally offered (call ahead to find out when).

Fort Kearny State Historical Park

Fort Kearny once loomed large in emigrants' minds as the only fort along the Platte River and the first fort built to protect travelers on the Oregon Trail. It was an important supply post for military action and passing traffic. By 1849, fort commander Lieutenant Woodbury recorded 4,000 wagons passing by in late spring on their way to Oregon and California. It's worth noting that at the time it was built, there wasn't much to protect the wagons from; the biggest threat to trail travelers in the early years

The Archway

was disease. In the 1860s, as indigenous people resisted the army's presence and white settlements with raids and attacks, the fort became more important as a military staging post.

Today, the historical importance of the fort looms larger than the site itself. The **Fort Kearny State Historical Park** (1020 V Rd., 308/865-5305, http://outdoornebraska.gov/fortkearny, grounds 8am-sunset daily, $8 per vehicle) has a few reconstructed buildings, along with a very small **interpretive center** (9am-5pm daily Mar.-mid-Apr. and May-Sept., by appointment only Oct.-Feb., $2 adults, $1 ages 3-13) with somewhat dusty displays; this also serves as a **visitors center** for the historical park as well as adjoining Fort Kearny State Recreation Area. If you have time you can watch the eight-minute film on fort history before a stroll around the parade grounds to see the reconstructions of the stockade, a blacksmith shop, and a powder magazine; the original fort was decommissioned

and torn down in 1871. If your timing is right, visit the fort around the major summer holidays—Memorial Day or Fourth of July—when it comes alive with living-history demonstrations, including cannon firing and Civil War actors.

The per-vehicle admission fee covers you for both the Fort Kearny State Historical Park and the jointly administered Fort Kearny State Recreation Area just north. To get to the historical park from downtown Kearney, drive south on 2nd Avenue/Highway 44. In 4 miles (6.4 km), turn left onto Highway 50A and drive 4.2 miles (6.7 km). It'll be on your left. The drive takes about 15 minutes.

Recreation
Fort Kearny State Recreation Area
Adjoining the Fort Kearny State Historical Park and jointly administered, **Fort Kearny State Recreation Area** (1020 V. Rd., 308/865-5305, http://outdoornebraska.gov/fortkearnysra, grounds dawn-dusk daily, $8 per vehicle) offers a bevy of outdoor recreation options. It has seven artificial groundwater lakes with sandy shores. Find swimming and a sandy beach at Lake 7 (10am-8:30pm daily Memorial Day-Labor Day), which has restrooms and a picnic shelter. Anglers can cast for bluegill, largemouth bass, and catfish. Get a valid Nebraska fishing license (1-day $10-13) online or at the visitors center in the historical park section.

The Fort Kearny hike-bike trail begins here and heads north over the Platte River for 1.8 miles (2.8 km). It follows an old portion of the Burlington and Missouri River Railroad. A nice destination from here is The Archway, about 4 miles (6.4 km) away.

The recreation area is popular for viewing sandhill cranes during the spring migration season; the cranes spend the night on the shallow Platte River. The interpretive center at Fort Kearny State Historical Park doubles as an information center during this time and is staffed

by knowledgeable, friendly volunteers who are happy to offer directions, tips, and information.

The per-vehicle admission fee covers you for both the Fort Kearny State Historical Park and Recreation Area. From the historical park, head east on Highway 50A. After 0.8 mile (1.3 km), turn left onto 30 Road/Fort Kearny State Recreation Area Road. Follow it 1 mile (1.6 km) into the recreation area.

Walking and Biking

Kearney has an incredible system of walking and biking trails—more than 25 miles (40 km). Paths extend from The Archway's visitors center to Fort Kearny State Recreation Area in the south and Cottonmill Park in the north. Many of the trails were once part of the Burlington and Missouri River Railroad line that crossed the North Platte. Beautiful views of the river abound, and the trail crosses an old railroad bridge and offers covered picnic shelters and wildlife viewing gazebos. Maps are available online (www.cityofkearney.org), at the Nebraska Visitor Center at The Archway, and at Fort Kearny State Historical Park's interpretive center.

Bike Rentals

Rent some wheels at **The Bike Shed** (1800 2nd Ave., 308/234-2453, www.headtotheshed.com, 9am-6pm Mon.-Sat., $15 per day), a local shop full of passionate riders. With a central location in town, you can easily hit the trails right away—The Archway is just a few miles away.

Yanney Heritage Park

To the west of town, **Yanney Heritage Park** (2020 W. 11th St., 308/237-4644, www.yanneypark.org, dawn-11pm daily, free) hosts an 80-foot (24-m) observation

---

Top to bottom: Trails and Rails Museum; *West of Fort Kearny* by William Henry Jackson; McCue's Nebraska Taproom.

tower offering fantastic views, two splash pads (8am-8pm May.-Sept.), flower gardens, playgrounds, a lake with fishing and boating, and more on its 80 green acres. Rent a giant swan-shaped paddleboat, kayak, canoe, or stand-up paddleboard at the **Yanney Swan Shoppe** (2pm-7pm Tues.-Thurs., noon-8pm Fri.-Sun. May-late Aug., $5 per half hour). The Kearney Water Trail runs along the east edge of the park.

Paddling

The **Kearney Water Trail** is a 2.3-mile (3.7-km) route that begins in Yanney Heritage Park and flows to the Platte River. This unique "trail" gets you out onto the water on a tributary channel and artificial canal. Visitors can float around calm river bends and see the city from a different vantage. The floating trip takes about 45 minutes.

Head to **Kearney Paddle Sports** (535 M Ave., 308/708-0792, www.kearneypaddlesports.com, Thurs.-Sun. Apr.-Sept.) to rent a kayak ($10 per hour) for a DIY trip or book a guided paddling tour. The 1.5-hour Turkey Creek Kayak Trip ($25 pp) takes you on the Water Trail and adds on a jaunt to Turkey Creek, the north channel of the Platte River; it runs hourly in season. For a longer trip, you can also head out with the company on the Platte River in tubes or kayaks ($40 pp) for 3-4 hours. Trips run April-early September, but give them a call if you're there later; if the water levels are still good, they'll be happy to accommodate you. The office is at the Kearney RV Park—from M Avenue, head 0.5 mile (0.8 km) east through the park, following the signs. Kayak rentals are also available at the Yanney Swan Shoppe in Yanney Heritage Park.

Entertainment
Bars and Brewpubs

The tagline of **McCue's Nebraska Taproom** (2008 Ave. A., 308/708-7750, http://mccuesnebraskataproom. com, 3pm-10pm Tues.-Wed., 3pm-11pm Thurs., 3pm-midnight Fri., 2pm-midnight Sat., 1pm-6pm Sun.) is "All Nebraska, All the Time." True to its word, all the beer, cider, wine, and spirits on the menu is sourced in the state. The beer selection is strongest, with 30 options on tap. Bourbon, whiskey, vodka, and more are offered from six distilleries, and wine makes an appearance from a handful of Nebraska vineyards. The bar is inside a renovated grocery store that served the town 1925-2003; a sign advertising fruits and vegetables still hangs over the door. The lively taproom has a great sense of community and hosts events like bingo and live music.

Enjoy Kearney's only brewery, **Thunderhead Brewing Company** (18 E. 21st St., 308/237-1558, www.thunderheadbrewing.com, 11am-1am daily), which pumps out beer that's popular across the state. Try the Prairie Peach for a light take on a wheat, or the MacTawisch Scottish Ale for something stronger. If beer isn't your thing, try the signature cocktail, the Thunderpunch, made with homemade grape soda, sweet and sour mix, whiskey, and lime. The kitchen makes great pizzas and calzones in a stone oven. The Thunderpie hits the spot, with chicken, bacon, jalapeño, and pepper jack—beat the heat by dunking it in the accompanying ranch sauce.

Live Music

A great sports bar and live music venue, **Cunningham's Journal** (http://cunninghams-journal.com) has two locations in town: **Cunningham's on the Bricks** (15 W. 23rd St., 308/236-9737, 11am-1am Mon.-Sat., 11am-midnight Sun.), downtown with a big marquee out front and a classic sports bar feel, and **Cunningham's on the Lake** (610 Talmalge St., 308/237-5122, 11am-1am Mon.-Sat., 11am-midnight Sun.), which features modern rustic decor with wood paneling and plenty of TVs to catch a game. Both locations have beautiful outdoor patios

The Speakeasy in Old Sacramento

A small-town steak house boasting big-city sophistication, **The Speakeasy** (72993 S Rd., Holdrege, 308/995-4757, www.thespeakeasyrestaurant.com, 5:30pm-9pm Tues.-Sat., $20) is a hidden treasure in the cornfields, though it's well-known to locals. Run by a Nebraska-raised, Seattle-trained chef who took over his father's popular buffet, the restaurant offers dishes like a tender pork belly served with pickles and stone-ground mustard, and perfect cuts of steak, fried chicken, seafood, and burgers. A range of classic cocktails, including barrel-aged Manhattans and Sazeracs, speak to the restaurant's name, or choose a Nebraska beer. The stretch of rural road where you'll find the steak house was once a town called Sacramento, but The Speakeasy is basically all that's left.

Drive south of Kearney on Highway 44 for 15 miles (24 km), then turn right on U.S. 34/6 for 14 miles (23 km). Make a left on Brewster Road, then another left immediately after onto Polyline Road, following it for 4.2 miles (6.8 km). Turn right onto S Road; The Speakeasy is on the right. The drive takes about 40 minutes.

where live music is hosted on weekends year-round. Over 45 different regional beers are available, and the food menu focuses on burgers, pizzas, and other pub fare.

Festivals and Events

Each spring, as thousands of sandhill cranes descend on the Platte River Valley during their migration to Canada, the Audubon Nebraska and Rowe Sanctuary joins forces with Kearney to celebrate the graceful birds. Over a weekend, usually in late March, the **Sandhill Crane Festival** (http://ne.audubon.org) attracts birdwatchers and ornithologists from the world over for environmental speakers, bird-watching trips, and connecting with other bird lovers. Headquartered at the Holiday Inn Kearney (110 2nd Ave.), the talks take place at the hotel and at Rowe Sanctuary (44450 Elm Island Rd., Gibbon), 20 miles (32 km) east of Kearney. The festival fee is $150, which includes three meals over the weekend and access to all the presentations.

Food
Steak House

Decked out in wood and brass and featuring a tin roof, **The Alley Rose** (2013 Central Ave., 308/234-1261, www.alley rose.com, 11am-10pm Mon.-Sat., $20) has an upscale yet casual dining atmosphere and serves some of the city's best steaks alongside an award-winning wine list. Settle into your road trip with a comforting potato casserole for lunch or dinner, or enjoy a tender osso buco, chardonnay-poached salmon, or a juicy pepper-jack burger from this varied menu.

Italian

Pizzas from ★ **The Flippin Sweet** (3905 2nd Ave., 308/455-4222, http://theflippin sweet.squarespace.com, 11am-9pm Mon.-Thurs., 11am-10pm Fri.-Sat., 11am-8pm Sun., $13) were named best in Nebraska by Zagat. See for yourself by trying a specialty pie, like the Nashville with barbecue sauce and corncob-smoked ham, or the Tenenbaums, featuring fig butter sauce, roasted garlic, arugula, and pistachios. Or build your own, and add into the mix vodka-soaked pears, eggs, or elk sausage, and choose from a range of drizzles. Excellent calzones, pasta, burgers, and sandwiches round out the menu. It's on the far north side of town, about 1.5 miles (2.4 km) from downtown in a suburban area, but it's worth the journey.

Joy's Table (110 S. 2nd Ave., 308/455-8013, www.joystablekearney.com, 11am-2pm and 4pm-10pm Mon.-Sat., $13) is named after the owners' mother and serves comforting pasta dishes, pizzas,

The Sandhill Crane Migrations

The seasonal migration of sandhill cranes along the banks of the Platte River is one of the most popular sights in Nebraska, attracting bird and wildlife lovers from all over the world. Up to 500,000 cranes flock here each year, and this 80-mile (130-km) section of the country along the Platte River in central Nebraska sees 80 percent of the entire world's sandhill crane population.

The birds migrate every spring and fall from Canada to Mexico and back, using the Platte River as a major resting point. Spring (late Feb.-early Apr.) is the biggest event, as the cranes stop for weeks at a time to feed before pushing on; mid-March is the prime season. In fall (mid-Oct.-late Nov.) they stop for only a night or two. During the day the cranes hang out in cow pastures looking for food and roost on the river at night. Morning and evening, you can catch them flocking together, and some days you'll see thousands of them flying, sheets of white specks in the sky.

Other birds, like the endangered whooping cranes, prairie chickens, hawks, and golden eagles, can be spotted too—these species don't migrate, so if you're early or late for the sandhill crane season, you can still enjoy some bird-watching in the area.

Tours

Two organizations near Kearney organize tours ($25-35). Most get you out in the fields before the cranes begin their morning dance in the sky; call for tour schedules. You can also visit the organizations' headquarters, open to the public:

♦ The **Iain Nicolson Audubon Center at Rowe Sanctuary** (44450 Elm Island Rd., Gibbon, 308/468-3282, http://rowe.audubon.org, 8am-5:30pm daily Feb. 15-Apr. 15, 9am-5pm Mon.-Fri., 1pm-4pm Sun. Apr. 16-Feb. 14) is 20 miles (32 km) southeast of Kearney on a beautiful stretch of the Platte River and has some nice walking trails to explore. Inside you'll find small exhibits, a nature store, and information about conservation and birding trips.

♦ The **Crane Trust Nature and Visitor Center** (9325 S. Alda Rd., 308/382-1820, http://cranetrust.org, 9am-5pm Mon.-Sat.), 36 miles (58 km) east of Kearney off I-80, has a live river cam, an art gallery, and educational exhibits. Ask the staff any of your burning birding questions.

DIY Bird-Watching

You can also check out the cranes on your own by driving through fields in the area. The most accessible route is a short loop off I-80 that connects with the **Rowe Sanctuary.** On I-80 from Kearney, take exit 285 and turn right onto Lowell Road to cross the Platte River. In 2 miles (3.2 km), turn right onto Elm Island Road and follow it another 2 miles (3.2 km) to find the Rowe Sanctuary. From there, continue west and then south on Elm Island Road for 3 miles (4.8 km) until you reach a T, turning right onto V Road. In 2 miles (3.2 km) turn right onto Highway 10, which will take you back across the Platte River and I-80 again. The short loop includes some dirt roads, and takes 20-30 minutes to drive. Take your time, and keep an eye out for designated roadside stops to pull over to crane-watch. Remember to be respectful—stay quiet, and don't get too close to the birds.

Closer to Kearney, head to the northeastern corner of **Fort Kearny State Recreation Area.** The bridge over the Platte River makes a perfect spot to spy the cranes. Timed correctly for the early morning or evening, you'll be able to watch them take off from their night's rest, or fly right over you and gracefully land in the water.

salads, and excellent locally sourced steaks cooked to perfection. You'll find authentic Italian dishes alongside more unique options like the Italian Chicken Fried Steak, a Mediterranean twist on a Midwestern favorite. With long tables alongside intimate booths, the place is both family- and date night-friendly.

Cafés

On the bricks downtown, **Tru Café** (2100 Central Ave., 308/236-9422, http://trucafekearney.com, 8am-4pm Tues.-Fri., 9am-4pm Sat., $9) has walls covered in local art and a coffeehouse vibe. The café offers a fresh menu of breakfast and lunch items, including big salads, breakfast wraps, flatbreads, and sandwiches. It specializes in bison—try the meat in a hoagie, on a pizza, barbecued, or braised. Take home roasted coffee or local art after your meal.

Get a fresh cup of coffee and breakfast at **Kitt's Kitchen and Coffee** (2001 A Ave., 308/293-7655, www.kittskitchen.com, 6am-9pm Mon.-Sat., noon-6pm Sun., $5). Watch the trains go by as your sip your latte, snack on a stellar bakery item, or jump into conversation with a university student—this is a popular place to study. You can also purchase house-roasted coffee beans.

Shopping

Deliciously kitschy, from its Western-style facade and boardwalk to the Nebraska T-shirts and souvenirs for sale, **Stagecoach** (310 3rd Ave., 308/234-3313, 8am-10pm daily summer, 9am-6pm Mon.-Sat. and noon-6pm Sun. fall-spring) is just off the highway. Visitors will also find a fantastic selection of jewelry handcrafted by Native American artists with beautiful and complicated inlaid patterns of turquoise, coral, and more. Look for the unique Sonoran Gold turquoise, which has a deep-green color with gold accents. Stock up also on some Nebraska postcards and a mug or two—Stagecoach knows how to choose

high-quality items, having been in the souvenir business for over 40 years. It also has a big variety of Minnetonka moccasins for sale for road-weary feet.

Enjoy the vinyl revival at **Buffalo Records** (19 E. 21st St., 308/224-2290, http://buffalorecords.com, 4pm-7pm Tues.-Wed., noon-8pm Thurs.-Sat., 2pm-4pm Sun.). Dig through the stacks to find your perfect record; staff will happily play you a sample before you purchase. Two whole bookshelves of 45s add to the collection. This is also a place to get your skateboarding supplies—boards line the walls, and tools, wheels, and more are for sale. Occasionally, the shop hosts live music, and new releases every week ensure a wide and ever-changing variety.

Dress yourself in trendy fashions from **Bow and Arrow** (2112 Central Ave., 308/455-1335, www.bowandarrowkearney.com, 10am-6pm Mon.-Fri., 10am-5pm Sun.), a boutique clothing store offering women's dresses, shirts, shoes, and jewelry, with a great girls' section too. Showcase your new-found Nebraska pride with a stylish T-shirt, like the classic boyfriend cut or a baseball tee.

Accommodations

Hotel options in Kearney are mostly of the chain variety—the two most reasonable are listed below. Both are near I-80 and have great pools to cool off in.

Under $150

Holiday Inn Kearney (110 2nd Ave., 308/237-5971, www.ihg.com, $80-120) has 163 rooms across two floors. It serves as one of the main event centers in town, hosting events like the Sandhill Crane Festival. Kids especially will love staying here, with the fantastic Captain's Lagoon indoor recreation pool with its 30-foot slides, and a video game room. Customer service is top-notch: A free shuttle will take you anywhere within 10 miles (16 km), and Joy's Table is next door, so you can begin or end your day with a good meal.

It's a tropical paradise on the plains inside the **Ramada by Wyndham Kearney** (301 2nd Ave., 308/237-3141, www.wyndhamhotels.com, $97-139). The Thai-inspired Elephant's Eye Bar overlooks an indoor pool, where you can enjoy drinks on the veranda after a dip. In the morning, enjoy custom-made omelets made by friendly staff. Rooms near the pool and lobby area can get noisy on a busy night, so request a quieter hallway if you need to be in bed early.

Camping
Fort Kearny State Recreation Area (1020 V Rd., 308/865-5305, http://nebraskastateparks.reserveamerica.com, $10-35) has a campground with 120 sites, 94 of which have electricity. Shaded sites under giant cottonwood trees, showers, restrooms, and easy access to the lakes dotting the park make it a beautiful place to stay. In addition to camping fees, there is a vehicle fee to enter the recreation area ($6 per vehicle Nebraska residents, $8 per vehicle nonresidents).

Enjoy a full-service RV stop at **Kearney RV Park & Campground** (1140 E. 1st St., 308/237-7275, www.kearneyrv.com, $25-45). It offers pleasant views across nearby Getaway Bay Lake, where you can also enjoy fishing and swimming at two sandy beaches.

Along the Trail from Kearney

Fort Kearny marked the emigrants' first glimpse of what was to be their traveling companion for the next 535 miles (860 km): the Platte River. The Great Platte River Road stretched across the plains to the next supply stop and "safe haven" at Fort Laramie, in eastern Wyoming. Life along the river took on familiar rhythms for emigrants: waking at dawn, cooking, herding animals, and breaking

camp. Throughout the day, the children's task was to look for buffalo chips on the treeless plains; they'd walk along with a stick to poke into chips and check for dryness—if dry, the chips would provide fuel for a fire that evening. Lunch was often a quick affair as the wagons tried to keep to a pace of 15-20 miles (24-32 km) a day. On hotter days, they might take a break in the heat of the day to rest and sleep, waiting for the coolness of evening to continue; this was called "nooning" and is depicted in paintings like Albert Bierstadt's *Nooning on the Platte* (1859). At night, wagon parties would make camp and settle in, eating a larger meal and passing the time with songs or games after camp chores. Then it was off to sleep, only to start again the next morning.

Gothenberg Pony Express Station
A sleepy farming community just north of the Platte River, Gothenburg boasts of being the "Pony Express Capital of Nebraska." It's tree-lined streets and parks make a nice break from driving for an afternoon picnic or stop to stretch your legs. Its **Pony Express Station** (1500 Lake Ave., 308/537-9876, www.ponyexpressstation.org, 9am-3pm daily Apr. and Oct., 9am-7pm daily May-Sept., free) has seen a lot of action over the years. The old building was originally built in 1854 for use as a trading post for Oregon Trail travelers. When the Pony Express started up in 1860, the station converted into an overnight rider post. After the Pony Express ended in 1861, it was still used as a trail stop and bunkhouse for folks traveling west. It was moved to its current location in Gothenburg from its original site just outside the city in 1931. Today visitors can stop by and take a look inside the small log cabin-turned-museum to see Pony Express artifacts, including guns and the leather mochila used to carry letters, and learn about the riders. It won't take long to visit but it's a

Roadside Refueling Surprise

Heading out of Kearney, on the way to Gothenburg, you'll find a surprisingly stellar road stop in the form of **Jay's Taste of India** (74975 Rd. 44, I-80 exit 248, Overton, 308/987-2111, 6am-11:30pm daily, $8), 26 miles (41 km) west of town. Stop to fill your gas tank at the seemingly middle-of-nowhere Jay Bros. station, where—inside the gas station, connected to the convenience store—you'll find a small dining room serving some of the best Indian food along I-80. Cuisine is Punjabi-style and includes meat and vegetarian dishes like *chana masala* (chickpeas in tomato sauce), *aloo tikki* (spiced potato and pea fritters), naan, and the popular butter chicken. It's all made fresh to order—there's no buffet food sitting around here. In the restaurant you'll also find a small selection of dried goods and Indian snacks, perfect to grab for the road.

pleasant place to stop, set in a park location with a nearby playground.

Getting There

From Kearney, head west on I-80 for 63 miles (101 km). Take exit 211 and turn right onto Highway 47. Continue north for 1 mile (1.6 km) to Gothenburg. The drive takes about an hour.

Fort McPherson National Cemetery

Fort McPherson once stood along the Great Platte River Road, protecting emigrants on the trail and escorting wagon traffic for hundreds of miles. Built in 1863, it played an important role in the so-called Indian Wars of the 1860s, until its closure in 1880. Buffalo Bill served here, and George Custer stayed here. Today, the only thing left is the **Fort McPherson National Cemetery** (12004 S. Spur 56A, Maxwell, 308/582-4433, www.nps.gov, dawn-dusk daily). Visitors are welcome to pay their respects to the more than 10,000 soldiers buried here from the Vietnam War, both World Wars, the Civil War, and conflicts across the plains. Notable soldiers buried here include several Medal of Honor recipients and 63 Buffalo Soldiers of the 9th and 10th Cavalry—the regiments of black soldiers who often served in the Great Plains region after the Civil War. Nothing remains of the old fort, but the site is marked by a

monument about 1 mile (1.6 km) southeast of the cemetery.

Getting There

From Gothenburg, head west on I-80 for 22 miles (35 km). Take exit 190 and turn left onto Highway 56A Spur, continuing on it for 2 miles (3.2 km). The drive takes 25 minutes.

North Platte

The town of North Platte didn't exist during the days of the Oregon Trail. At the time, there wasn't even a notable trail stop or station nearby, just the Platte River winding west to Wyoming, with scores of wagons trundling along on either side. It was here that the wide Platte River split into its north and south paths. Oregon and California emigrants followed the South Platte River, while Mormon emigrants continued along the North Platte River.

The region was notorious for rain, especially in late spring, right as the wagons were traveling through. Massive thunderstorms brewed regularly and soaked the emigrants, some recording up to 12 inches an hour. Hailstones fell too, as big as goose eggs, and lightning lit the sky. A Midwestern thunderstorm today is an impressive marvel, but to view it while huddling inside a rain-soaked wagon must have caused its share of misery.

Mosquitoes were also a huge nuisance, as many travelers noted in their diaries.

In 1868, the Union Pacific Railroad spurred the growth of North Platte, which served as a railhead as the tracks pushed west, and it became a boomtown. Some such towns died when the work was done, but as construction pushed on and the railroad continued west, North Platte remained. Later, Buffalo Bill Cody bought a ranch outside town, contributing a Wild West sensibility to the place. Today, visitors can enjoy some of this Western heritage. The city still considers itself a railroad town, with the world's biggest railyard in its backyard.

Getting There

North Platte is 100 miles (161 km) west of Kearney, a 1.5-hour drive. From Fort McPherson National Cemetery, just continue west on I-80 for 12.5 miles (20 km). From I-80, take exit 177 onto U.S. 83, which takes you into town.

Downtown North Platte is a walkable area near East 4th Street and U.S. 83. Most of the attractions are dispersed, requiring drives of 5-10 minutes, so a car is a good idea for getting around.

Sights
Buffalo Bill Ranch State Historical Park

One of the West's most famous personalities, Buffalo Bill Cody owned a ranch outside North Platte for years. He called it Scout's Rest Ranch and used it as a place to rest and relax between touring with his Wild West Show. Today, his home is preserved as the 250-acre **Buffalo Bill Ranch State Historical Park** (2921 Scouts Rest Ranch Rd., 308/535-8035, www.outdoornebraska.gov/buffalobillranch, 9am-5pm daily Memorial Day Labor Day, 9am-5pm Wed.-Sun. Labor Day-Sept. 30, 9am-5pm Thurs.-Sun. mid-Mar.-Memorial Day, $8 state park entry,

Top to bottom: tanking on the river; Golden Spike Tower; Grain Bin Antique Town.

NEBRASKA

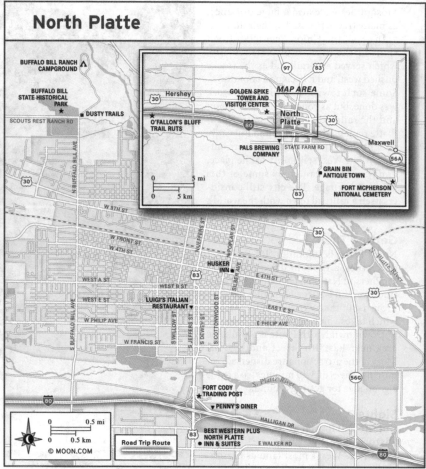

North Platte

BUFFALO BILL RANCH CAMPGROUND

BUFFALO BILL STATE HISTORICAL PARK

DUSTY TRAILS

SCOUTS REST RANCH RD

Hershey

GOLDEN SPIKE TOWER AND VISITOR CENTER

MAP AREA

North Platte

O'FALLON'S BLUFF TRAIL RUTS

PALS BREWING COMPANY

STATE FARM RD

Maxwell

GRAIN BIN ANTIQUE TOWN

FORT MCPHERSON NATIONAL CEMETERY

0   5 mi
0   5 km

W 8TH ST

W FRONT ST

W 4TH ST

WEST A ST

HUSKER INN

E 4TH ST

WEST B ST

LUIGI'S ITALIAN RESTAURANT

WEST E ST

EAST E ST

W PHILIP AVE

E PHILIP AVE

W FRANCIS ST

S. Platte River

FORT CODY TRADING POST

PENNY'S DINER

HALLIGAN DR

BEST WESTERN PLUS NORTH PLATTE INN & SUITES

E WALKER RD

0   0.5 mi
0   0.5 km

Road Trip Route

© MOON.COM

$2 mansion tour), which encompasses several sites just northwest of town.

At the mansion you can tour Bill's old house, built in 1886 at the height of the show's popularity. A barn has memorabilia displays and exhibits on ranching life. Outside are a few resident bison. Take a look at the peak of the barn's roof, where you can see Annie Oakley's lucky Ace of Hearts symbol with a bullet hole in the middle; Oakley was one of the best sharpshooters of all time, who performed with Buffalo Bill's rodeo 1885-1901, and she regularly demonstrated her great aim

by shooting a bullet through an Ace of Hearts card from a distance.

Golden Spike Tower

If you're into trains, you'll love visiting the **Golden Spike Tower** (1249 N. Homestead Rd., 308/532-9920, www. goldenspiketower.com, 9am-7pm daily May-Sept., 10am-5pm daily Oct.-Apr., $7). The eight-story-tall tower, built to look like a railroad spike, offers amazing views from its 7th-floor outdoor platform at the world's largest railroad classification yard, Union Pacific's Bailey Yard,

A Pioneer Story: Buffalo Bill Cody

The life of William "Buffalo Bill" Cody has come to symbolize the Wild West. As one of its most mythic figures, along with Kit Carson and Davy Crockett, Cody's exploits have been embellished and romanticized.

Born in 1846 in Iowa, Cody started his career riding horses at age nine for the Russell, Majors and Waddell freight company. Later he claimed he joined the Pony Express and supposedly rode an impressive 322 miles (518 km) in one day; in reality, the tall tale may never have happened, but it didn't really matter—people wanted to believe it. Cody made his name by becoming intimately familiar with life in the American West. He was a civilian scout and guide in Kansas, Nebraska, and farther west, and in high demand, being an excellent marksman. He had large stores of knowledge about the terrain and local Native Americans. He regularly jumped at the chance to lead dangerous scouting missions in the U.S. Army's skirmishes with the Sioux, Cheyenne, and other indigenous nations. In 1867 he earned his name by hunting buffalo in order to feed the crews laying the Union Pacific Railroad lines.

Dime store novels spun tales of his daring, and the charismatic Cody soon organized a revue showcasing the most exciting bits of frontier life: *Buffalo Bill's Wild West*. It was a circus, a rodeo, a pageant. It hugely influenced conceptions of the West that continue to this day. Staged Pony Express rides, shooting tricks, and faux dramatic episodes influenced books and movies of the early 1900s, and gave rise to the country's sense of how it would like to believe it settled the West—heroically. Even Mark Twain was impressed with the rodeo antics, and wrote letters to Buffalo Bill complimenting how "painfully real" the bucking horses were.

Often considered the first Western rodeo, the show ran 1883-1916, traveling throughout North America and to Europe, with a whopping 650 staff in its biggest years. The troupe comprised cowboys, sharpshooters like Annie Oakley, trick riders, and Native Americans who played themselves—for instance, Chief Sitting Bull, the Lakota chief who had united the various Sioux tribes of the area and led the resistance against the U.S. Army. Notably, Cody was an early advocate of women's suffrage and the rights of indigenous people—even as his show supported some negative stereotypes.

where 150 trains go by each day; each car gets sorted onto the right tracks here, depending on its final destination. The sorting is helped along by the "hump," a gentle mound that uses gravity to roll the cars onto their new tracks. Watch the action as the hump sorts onto an astounding 301 sets of rails. Workers train with NASCAR to process the cars as fast as they can. A volunteer is stationed at the indoor 8th-floor viewing platform; volunteers are usually former employees of the train yards and more than happy to answer your questions. The railyard operates 24 hours daily, seven days a week. If your visit coincides with the third Saturday of the month, visit the tower for a Twilight Tour, when it stays open later (until 10pm May-Sept., until 7pm Oct.-Apr.), and you can enjoy views of the train tracks all lit up after dark.

From downtown, head west on Front Street for 3.5 miles (5.6 km), then turn right onto North Homestead Road. The tower is on your right in 0.2 mile (0.3 km).

Fort Cody Trading Post

Find the kitschiest of all roadside shops at **Fort Cody Trading Post** (221 Halligan Dr., 308/532-8081, www.fortcody.com, 9am-9pm daily summer, 9am-6pm Mon.-Sat., noon-6pm Sun. spring and fall, 9am-5:30pm Mon.-Sat., noon-5:30pm Sun. winter, free), a heavily advertised venture featuring an enormous faux fort with a free museum and gift shop. The museum has a miniature (and animated!) version of Buffalo Bill's show, a two-headed calf, and animatronic fortune tellers. Outside is a frontier village with a jail, a stockade, a log cabin, and covered wagons scattered about. On Thursday nights in summer, stop by for live music. This is a fun and quirky step back in time, more like roadside America circa 1960 than covered wagons circa 1860.

From downtown, drive south on Jeffers Street/U.S. 83 for about 2 miles (3.2 km), and turn left onto Halligan Drive.

Recreation

Dusty Trails (2617 N. Buffalo Bill Ave., 308/530-0048, www.dustytrails.biz), an adventure company that also has a petting zoo, offers trail rides on horses ($10-20 pp) in and around the Buffalo Bill Ranch State Historical Park. It also offers the unique Nebraska activity of tanking. What's that, you ask? Imagine floating down the river with your friends and family in a giant stock feed tank. It's crazy and quirky and has become a favorite local way to float alongside the plains. The company takes care of all the transportation and shuttling; you just sit back and relax. Your flotation device is a circular buoyant livestock watering tank, with benches—bring a cooler for a picnic, there's room in the middle! It holds 3-8 people, and you get a paddle to help with steering. This affords a slow, calm ride, great for all ages. Tanking costs a flat $100 for the tank rental, then $25 per person for a 1.5-2-hour trip, or $50 per person for a full-day trip. Dusty Trails also offers kayak, canoe, and tube rentals ($25 pp per hour).

Entertainment and Events

Enjoy offerings like pizza and baked cheese curds as well as local beer at **Pals Brewing Company** (4520 S. Buffalo Bill Ave., 308/221-6715, www.palsbrewingcompany.com, 4pm-9pm Tues.-Wed., 4pm-10pm Thurs., 11am-11pm Fri.-Sat., 11am-6pm Sun., $12). The restaurant-brewery also happens to encompass four acres of fun, with indoor and outdoor seating. You'll also find volleyball courts, cornhole, and other lawn games, as well as weekly live music and a great front-row seat to Nebraska's sunset shows. Plan to spend a whole evening here.

An arrow shot away from Buffalo Bill Cody's mansion, the state's biggest celebration is held at the ranch's Wild West Arena in the third week of June. **NEBRASKAland Days** (308/532-7939, www.nebraskalanddays.com) includes four nights of rodeo fun, live country music featuring top performers, and parades. The Buffalo Bill Rodeo is the main event—started in 1882 by the man himself, it's the oldest spectator rodeo in the country. While Annie Oakley doesn't shoot out the arena anymore, the men and women who show up to ride the bucking broncos and wrangle the steers still make it a darn good show. Admission is charged for the rodeo ($12), the concerts ($40), and parking ($9), but many other events are free and family-friendly.

Food

Harking back to the days of the Lincoln Highway, when roadside diners were the place to go, **Penny's Diner** (473 Halligan Dr., 308/535-9900, 24 hours daily, $10) is a 1950s time machine. Continuously open and proudly serving truckers, bikers, and everyone in between, this is a friendly place with classic diner fare like burgers, omelets, steak, and mashed potatoes. No matter when you visit, you'll get good food, fast, from friendly waitresses.

Luigi's Italian Restaurant (520 S. Jeffers St., 308/221-2961, www.luigisnp.com, 11am-9:30pm Tues.-Thurs., 11am-10pm Fri.-Sat., 11am-9pm Sun.-Mon., $12) serves up fresh Italian food, including gluten-free options. The small place has an old diner feel, with booths and big windows. The menu is full of all your favorites, like fettucine alfredo, chicken marsala, tortellini, and pizza. Don't skip the cannoli for dessert!

Shopping

The **Grain Bin Antique Town** (10641 S. Old Hwy. 82 Rd., 308/539-7401, www. grainbinantiquetown.com, 10:30am-5pm Mon.-Sat. Memorial Day-Labor Day, 10:30am-5pm Tues.-Sat. Labor Day-Oct., 10:30am-5pm Wed.-Sat. Nov.-Apr., free) is a unique spot to do some treasure hunting. The "town," down the highway 3 miles (4.8 km) south of North Platte and off a dirt road, has 13 repurposed circular grain bins and one giant red barn, all holding secret treasures. Each bin is roughly themed so you know where to look for teacups or vintage signs, while the barn has high-quality vintage crystal, furniture, and stone crock ware. Antiques lovers and casual browsers will enjoy hunting through each bin for the perfect souvenir.

Accommodations and Camping

Accommodations in the area are clustered near the interstate and are mostly of the chain variety. Most notable among these is the **Best Western Plus North Platte Inn & Suites** (3201 S. Jeffers St., 308/534-3120, www.bestwestern.com, $136-180), a pet-friendly hotel with 146 rooms and 25 suites, offering an indoor heated pool and hot breakfast. It's also RV friendly: Check in with the front desk or call first, and if it's a slow night, they'll let you park your rig in their giant lot at no cost, and you can treat yourself to the hot tub.

In a central location downtown, the ★ **Husker Inn** (721 E. 4th St., 308/534-6860, $60-75) is a budget motel that's big on friendliness. Harking back to an earlier time of automobile travel, the family-owned motel is a quaint and homey place with service that outstrips the larger chains closer to the freeway.

The 21 modern rooms surround a lovely landscaped courtyard. If you're lucky, you might even get to try some of the owners' homemade food!

Stay right near Buffalo Bill's ranch at the **Buffalo Bill Ranch State Recreation Area Campground** (2921 Scouts Rest Ranch Rd., 308/535-8035, www.outdoornebraska.gov/buffalobillsra, $10-35), along the Platte River. It has 23 RV sites with concrete pads and electricity, and 8 tent sites. Hiking and fishing are available.

Along the Trail from North Platte

Emigrants on the Oregon and California Trails continued west, following the South Platte River. Days went by as usual as they slowly knocked out the miles.

O'Fallon's Bluff Trail Ruts

Some of the best trail ruts in Nebraska are at a highway rest area along I-80. **O'Fallon's Bluff** is a 20-mile (32-km) stretch of hilly terrain that starts west of North Platte. Near Sutherland, the bluffs come close to the South Platte River, which forced the pioneers to traverse a narrow route between the South Platte River to the north and the bluffs to their south. Tracks and swales can still be seen, preserved even as the interstate cut through the prairie. At the rest area of I-80, interpretive panels provide information, and visitors can see iron wheels set into the prairie along the rut lines, echoing the wheels of wagons that once drove by.

Getting There

To see these ruts, you have to do a little backtracking, as they can only be seen from the eastbound direction. From North Platte, head west on I-80 for about 20 miles (32 km) to exit 158, near Sutherland (you can also take U.S. 30, then catch I-80 eastbound at Sutherland).

Do a quick turn-around to get back on the highway headed east, where you can follow signs for the eastbound rest area, in just over 1 mile (1.6 km). To get back on the interstate heading west, you have to continue east for 5 miles (8 km) to Hershey, where you can turn around at exit 164.

Ogallala

For centuries, the Oglala band of Lakota Sioux lived on the plains in villages near what's now the town of Ogallala. In the trail's early years, they traded with emigrants up and down the banks of the South Platte River. Wagons mostly passed by this spot without noting anything about it—they were gearing up to tackle California Hill, one of bigger ascents they had yet to see.

The town of Ogallala sprang up as the Union Pacific Railroad pushed west; it was named after the Oglala band. In 1873, the Oglala and the Brule Sioux peoples were forced out of the Platte River Valley to northern Nebraska.

Ogallala found its fame after the Oregon Trail had largely ended and the railroad was in full swing, in the late 1800s. It served as the northern end of the Texas Cattle Trail, which started in deep Texas, headed through the rough-and-tumble Dodge City in Kansas, and ended at the Union Pacific Railroad line in Ogallala. From Ogallala, cattle were boarded onto train cars and shipped to Chicago—some for slaughter there, some to continue farther east. During the active years of the cattle trail, 1875-1885, cowboys drifted into the boomtown in droves looking for saloons, gambling, and fortunes. The gunfights that broke out killed many a cowboy and contributed to the town's Wild West reputation. Today, the "Cowboy Capital of Nebraska" is full of old-fashioned kitsch. It's also a good jumping-off point for nearby Lake McConaughy.

Getting There

Ogallala is 50 miles (80 km) west of North Platte on I-80. Take exit 126 for U.S. 26 to cross the South Platte River into town. A giant cowboy sign welcomes you.

Sights
Front Street

Ogallala's **Front Street** (519 E. 1st St./U.S. 30, 308/284-6000, www. ogallalafrontstreet.com, 11am-8pm Mon.-Wed., 6:30am-9pm Thurs.-Sat., 8am-2pm Sun., free) was once a place where cowboys ran wild and shootouts happened daily. The "street" today isn't a real one, but a block-long replica town that evokes the Wild West but gone kitsch. The whole thing is like a movie set, and run by the same folks. First opened in 1963, it still evokes the roadside attractions of earlier times. Behind the storefronts, visitors will find a fun museum, a jail, a general store, a barber shop ("tonsorial" is an old word for barber), and more. Each shop connects inside, so the whole thing is like one large building. Park in the lot out front and spend 30 minutes wandering for some great photo ops and goofy fun. Inside the Crystal Palace Saloon, you can stay for dinner and a wild show.

Petrified Wood Gallery

A labor of love from twin brothers who began collecting in the 1950s, the **Petrified Wood Gallery** (418 E. 1st St., 308/284-9996, www. petrifiedwoodgallery.com, 8am-4pm Mon.-Sat., free) is an amazing showcase of arrowheads, rocks, gems, fossils, and plenty of petrified wood, much of it found within 25 miles (40 km) of Ogallala. Visitors can see huge slabs of tree trunks turned to stone alongside intricate artwork made by brothers Harvey and Howard Kenfield, including small houses and music boxes made from petrified wood. You might even see them hard at work, or hear stories from the volunteers who run the place. More artwork

Ogallala and Lake McConaughy

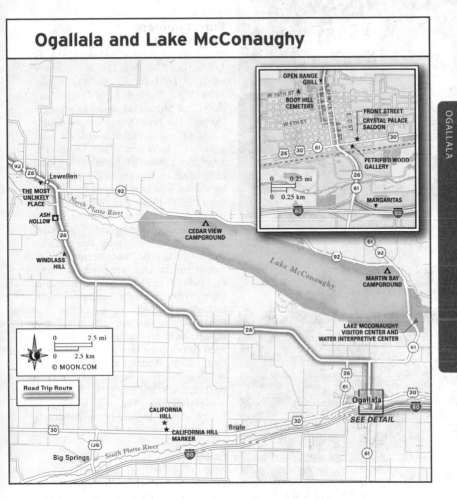

is on loan from visiting artists, such as a collection of pewter figurines and Native American art.

Boot Hill Cemetery

Many of the cowboys and ruffians who spent time in Ogallala never left—the town had a reputation for being a wild place, and saw more violent deaths during a 10-year span than the notorious Dodge City, Kansas, renowned for its frontier lawlessness. Many were buried on a hill near town, most with their boots still on, as was the tradition,

earning the cemetery the name Boot Hill. Today you can take a walk on **Boot Hill** (Rd. 113 and Elm St., 308/254-5395) and see old grave sites. Many of the markers are modern additions, but some original ones still remain near the statue of *The Trail Boss,* a horseback rider who looks back over the cattle trail to Texas, mirroring an identical statue in Dallas. The most famous tale buried here involves Rattlesnake Ed, who was shot over a $9 bet in 1884. Find information on the grave sites and burials on the kiosk at the bottom of the hill.

Entertainment

Enjoy a meal in the dining room at the **Crystal Palace Saloon** (519 E. 1st St./U.S. 30, 308/284-6000, www.ogallalafrontstreet.com, 11am-8pm Mon.-Wed., 6:30am-9pm Thurs.-Sat., 8am-2pm Sun., $12). You can swagger through the Front Street venue's double doors, sidle up to the bar, and down a sarsaparilla. The saloon, of course, also has a range of harder drinks, including local beer, wine, and cocktails. If you're brave, try some Rocky Mountain oysters—deep-fried bull testicles, a common specialty in restaurants across the West. Other menu items include great sandwiches and Nebraska beef steaks. You can also stay for the **Crystal Palace Revue** (Thurs.-Sat. Memorial Day-July, Wed.-Sat. July-mid-Aug., $14), a fun dip into Americana with a Western shootout and some high-kicking cancan. It's maybe a little silly, but if you can suspend your disbelief, it makes for a fun evening. The show has been running for over 50 years, starring local college students and depicting the rough-and-tumble life of a real Old West cattle town. While this palace is a rebuilt modern version, the original Crystal Palace was a real place in early Ogallala history that cowboys often visited.

Food

A local favorite is **Margaritas** (401 Stagecoach Trail, 308/284-9879, http://3margaritasmex.com, 11am-9pm daily, $15). Fresh warm tortilla chips come right away, along with salsa with just the right level of spice. Enchiladas, tacos, burritos, and more are on the menu. Beware—portions are large; you won't go home hungry.

The **Open Range Grill** (1108 N. Spruce Dr., Ogallala, 308/284-0899, 11am-8pm Sun.-Thurs., 11am-1am Fri.-Sat., $12) is a great family-run place with solid

Top to bottom: Front Street welcome sign; Boot Hill Cemetery; camping on the beach at Lake McConaughy.

burgers—try the El Patron Burger, with grilled jalapeños, bacon, and pepper jack cheese, served with perfectly crisp french fries. Salads are good as well. In the back, patrons can enjoy a pool table and video games, and there's also a great kids' play area with a few toys—just right to work out the wiggles.

◆ Side Trip: Lake McConaughy

You may not think of white-sand beaches when you think of Nebraska, but the state's largest reservoir, Lake McConaughy—called "Big Mac"—has miles of just that. **Lake McConaughy State Recreation Area** (1475 Hwy. 61 N., 308/284-8800, www.outdoornebraska. gov/lakemcconaughy, $8 per car day-use) is a great outdoor playground. At 22 miles (35 km) long and four miles (6.5 km) wide, the lake stretches across 30,500 surface acres with over 100 miles (160 km) of shoreline. Fish grow to trophy sizes, with many state records won on these shores. Just east and adjacent to Lake McConaughy is Lake Ogallala, a smaller recreational area with about 5 miles (8 km) of shoreline and great fishing.

The **Lake McConaughy Visitor Center and Water Interpretive Center** (1475 Hwy. 61 N., 308/284-8800, www. outdoornebraska.gov/lakemcconaughy, 8am-5pm daily Memorial Day-Labor Day, 8am-4pm daily Labor Day-Memorial Day, free) has exhibits on the Platte River, the local watershed, and Kingsley Dam. Public restrooms, fishing licenses, and camping information are here as well.

Getting There

Head north out of Ogallala via Spruce Street and Highway 61. In 9 miles (14.5 km), about a 10-minute drive, you'll find yourself at Lake McConaughy. To return to the trail simply backtrack and continue west out of Ogallala via U.S. 30

Recreation

Swimming

Every inch of the shoreline at the lake is open to swimming, but the only designated beach is at **Martin Bay,** on the northeastern side of the lake at Martin Bay Campground. It's the easiest to get to—it's just off Highway 61—and has a great wide beach area.

Fishing

Get a valid Nebraska fishing license (1-day $10 residents, $13 nonresidents; 3-day $31 residents, $37 nonresidents) at the visitors center or online at www. outdoornebraska.gov. You'll need a license whether you're headed out on your own or joining a guided trip.

Lake McConaughy Guide Services (308/289-1904 or 402/690-3393, http:// lakemcconaughywalleyeguide.weebly. com, May-Nov., $350-700) offers guided fishing excursions for beginners as well as experienced anglers. The company provides expert instruction on various casting methods, depending on the season and the fish. Walleye is the primary species of note here—the fish can reach lengths of up to 20 inches—but there are also wiper, white bass, and catfish. The full-day trips include all the bait and tackle you'll need. Rates are $350 for two people, $450 for three people, and $700 for four people (in two boats). Book ahead by phone during the busy summer months of May-July.

Fish the Plains (308/289-6499, www. fishtheplains.com, $250-450) offers walleye fishing trips as well. Led by a fishing tournament winner, the five-hour trip (3pm-8pm) costs $250 for one person, plus $50 for each additional person, up to four. A longer eight-hour option starts at $300 for one person, adding $50 per additional person, up to four. In the winter, ice-fishing trips are available ($150 pp).

Boating

Rent a boat from **Beach Bumz** (308/289-3376, www.beachbumzrentals.com), a mobile business that will bring it straight to your campsite. Call or book online to reserve Jet Skis ($60 per hour), a pontoon boat with optional tubes ($90 per hour), or the unique Sonic Jet ($80 per hour), a boat that maneuvers like a Jet Ski. Each of these rentals has a four-hour minimum.

At **Big Mac Marina** (302 Hwy. 92, 308/355-5555, www.bigmacmarina. com, 9am-6pm Memorial Day-Labor Day), you'll find a variety of rental options, including kayaks ($25 for 2 hours), Jet Skis ($85 for 1 hour), ski boats ($115 for 1 hour), and pontoon boats ($90 for 1 hour). Life jackets are included, but prices don't include fuel (as relevant). The small store also operates as a fuel dock and store, with ice and ice cream. Find it in Arthur Bay, about 2 miles (3.2 km) west of Martin Bay Campground.

Note that for all boats and personal watercraft, Nebraska law requires anyone born after 1985 to carry proof of having completed a boating safety course, either from Nebraska or their own home state; rental companies won't rent to you without it.

Bird-Watching

Due to its location along the Central Flyway, the route through the United States that millions of birds take on their migration from Latin America to Canada, Lake McConaughy is an excellent spot for bird-watching. Kestrels, cardinals, woodpeckers, and bald eagles are regular visitors to the area. The renowned sandhill cranes come through in early spring.

Food and Camping

In the small town of Lewellen on the west side of the lake is **The Most Unlikely Place** (205 Main St., Lewellen, 308/778-9557, www.themostunlikelyplace.com, 9am-2pm Wed.-Sat. mid-Mar.-mid-Nov., $9). The brightly colored building that the restaurant occupies also serves as a local artists gallery, so you can enjoy beautiful artworks while you eat. Try a breakfast of french toast with fruit, plus a specialty coffee, or a lunch of homemade soup and a sandwich. End the meal with a slice of raspberry pecan chocolate cake, straight or à la mode.

The most popular camping spot at Lake McConaughy State Recreation Area is the year-round ★ **Martin Bay Campground** ($12), on the lake's northeastern shore off Highway 61, which has fine sand that makes for a great swimming beach as well as trees for shade. A boat ramp is here, and it's popular with fishing enthusiasts, water-skiers, and sailors. Be sure you have a vehicle that can handle sand—the campground is literally on the beach. You'll find mostly tents here; there are no showers, but restrooms are available. RVs and trailers are welcome to drive and park on the beach as well, but be smart so you don't get stuck! A 4WD vehicle is recommended. If you do get stuck, **Beachside Towing** (303/898-6893) can help.

Cedar View Campground ($15-35) is on the northwest side of the lake and has a sandy beach and 85 sites with electricity and water as well as 17 basic sites for tent camping. RV pads, a dump station, and showers are also here. All campsites are open year-round, but October-May sees more limited facilities and camping may be dependent on weather conditions.

Along the Trail from Ogallala

Just past the modern-day city of Ogallala, the South Platte River takes a southwest turn. Emigrants on the south bank needed to cross to the north to stay on the path to Fort Laramie; this meant a dangerous river crossing. Although various sites were used to cross the South Platte, the primary one was here near California Hill—the path led directly to Ash Hollow, the most strategic approach to entering the North Platte River Valley. For this crossing, one brave swimmer

Ogallala to Scottsbluff and Gering

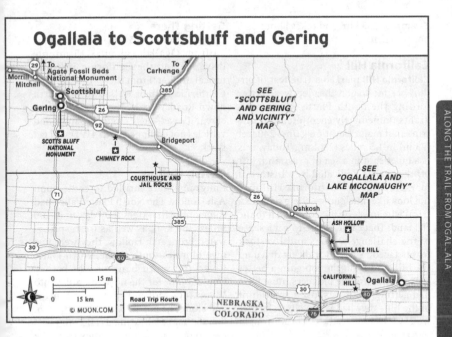

headed out across the rushing water carrying a rope, often between his teeth. The river here was about 0.75-mile (1.2-km) wide, but he would often need to swim farther to find solid enough footing in the sandy bank to pull himself out. Inevitably, he would swallow the dirty water, which could later cause fever, chills, or something more serious such as cholera. Once across, the rope would be secured to a tree and used to pull wagons across in improvised ferries. Oxen, mules, and any other animals needed to be guided individually. For a large wagon train, this ordeal could take up to six days. Sioux men often helped the wagons by guiding emigrants and swimming animals across.

Once safely on the north side, wagon parties could continue west. Emigrants would notice, as travelers will today, that the flat plains here give way to hills; these are the Sand Hills of middle and eastern Nebraska, grass-covered sand dunes. Unlike the vast acres of farmland covering the state today, most of the Sand Hills

have never been plowed—early attempts at farming failed, mostly because the soil was far too sandy for crops. The hills stretch west across what is now known as the Nebraska Panhandle, the western part of the state that juts out north of Colorado before meeting Wyoming.

The Sand Hills are dotted with lakes and ponds that come from the massive Ogallala Aquifer right beneath them, creating a unique wetland ecosystem that is home to many plants, animals, and migrating birds. Oregon Trail emigrants often recorded in their journals the profusion of wildlife they encountered here—antelopes, rabbits, turkeys, bison, and more. As they left the plains of eastern Nebraska behind, they began to encounter larger bluffs and steeper inclines.

From Ogallala, I-80 continues into Colorado, but you'll follow the wagon trail northwest along the North Platte River, primarily on **U.S. 26.** Between Ogallala and Scottsbluff, including point-to-point stops (but not including stopping time), this section totals about

145 miles (233 km) and takes about 2.75 hours to drive.

California Hill

California Hill marked a true test of endurance for wagons headed west. After fording the South Platte River, emigrants immediately encountered it, the trip's first major elevation gain—240 feet (73 m) in 1.5 miles (2.4 km). Today, this is a quiet spot in a sea of grassland, just off the prairie, indicated by a historical marker. Although California Hill may not look like much now—there's an electrical wire tower on it—compare it to the flat lands that came before to get a sense of the challenge wagons and livestock teams faced. You can walk or drive up the hill, and from the top gain a better sense of the trouble pioneers must have had getting up; it was just a small hint of the hills they had yet to climb farther west. Visible ruts on the hill head straight to Ash Hollow.

Getting There

Drive 14 miles (23 km) west on U.S. 30 from Ogallala, about a 15-minute drive, to find the California Hill historical marker. From there, you can spot California Hill, or walk or drive north down Road West M N to the top. Take care if it's wet—it's extremely sandy, and vehicles not equipped with 4WD will get stuck.

★ Ash Hollow

Emigrants were thrilled to come upon Ash Hollow. The North Platte Valley had some of the first trees they'd seen in 100 miles (160 km), as well as fresh springwater. From Ash Hollow, they were just several miles south of the North Platte River, the south bank of which they would follow for the next 250 miles into Wyoming. Mormon pioneers continued along the north bank. First, though, Oregon and California Trail emigrants had to descend into the valley from the

Courthouse and Jail Rocks

hills—Windlass Hill, relatively free of jagged rocks, was deemed the best place.

Today, **Ash Hollow State Historical Park** (4055 U.S. 26, Lewellen, www. outdoornebraska.gov/ashhollow, 8am-sunset daily, $5 parking) is split into two sections. You'll come across the **Windlass Hill** site first, where you'll find a sod house, a giant metal wagon with informational kiosks, and a paved trail that takes you up the hill to see ruts. The 0.5-mile (0.8-km) loop takes 30 minutes to hike and offers excellent views of the hilly terrain that wagons conquered on their way down into the valley—deep ruts and gorges are visible along the trail, and a stone monument at the top marks where the Oregon Trail passes.

The rest of the Ash Hollow site is 2.5 miles (4 km) north of Windlass Hill on U.S. 26. Turn right into the gate to find the **visitors center** (9am-4pm Tues.-Sun. Memorial Day-Labor Day, $2) at the top of the hill. It has historical displays as well as fossils from prehistoric creatures

like mammoths and mastodons. From the center, a short walk takes you to a prehistoric cave and archaeological dig site; the "cave" is more of a rocky overhang, but is worth a visit to see the dig site and prehistoric tools displayed there, proof of early Americans as long ago as 9,000 years. Some trails wander through the park and along the Oregon Trail—ask for a map in the visitors center or follow the posted signs.

Just down the road, farther north on U.S. 26, is **Ash Hollow Cemetery,** where you can find Rachel Pattison's grave. An 1849 Oregon Trail emigrant, 18-year-old Rachel was traveling from Illinois with her new husband, Nathan, whom she had married only three months prior. She fell ill on a June morning near Ash Hollow and died by nightfall. Her stricken husband made it all the way to Oregon, but never remarried.

Each year the community puts on the **Ash County Historical Pageant** (www. visitgardencounty.com, mid-June), a stellar show incorporating real pioneer diaries performed on the ruts of the Oregon Trail itself. The popular show is free; bring a chair or blanket to sit on. Other events take place the same weekend, including a fun run, a chuck wagon dinner, and more.

Getting There
From California Hill, continue west on U.S. 30. In 4.7 miles (7.5 km), turn right on Road 207 and drive north for 10 miles (16 km). Turn left onto U.S. 26. In 3.1 miles (4.9 km), you'll arrive at the Windlass Hill section of the Ash Hollow State Historical Park. Entrance to the visitors center is another 2.5 miles (4 km) along U.S. 26 on the right. The drive takes about 30 minutes on rural roads.

Courthouse and Jail Rocks
As you continue west on U.S. 26 and approach the town of Bridgeport, keep an eye on the south side of the highway for the massive **Courthouse and Jail Rocks,**

Pioneer Quotes, on Seeing Chimney Rocks

"At ten o'clock we came in sight of the celebrated 'Chimney Rock....' one of the greatest curiosities—perhaps the greatest—in the whole valley of the Mississippi...."

Chimney Rock

J. Henry Carleton, 1845, *The Prairie Logbooks: Dragoon Campaign to the Pawnee Villages in 1844, and to the Rocky Mountains in 1845*. Carlton was an officer in the U.S. Army whose Kansas-based regiment often joined wagon trains to offer protection. In 1845 he joined a scouting expedition to South Pass, Wyoming, noting the landmarks in his journal along the way.

"June 9. Started very early this morning and went 18 miles we passed chimney rock at ten o'clock this is the most remarkable object that I ever saw and if situated in the states it would be visited by pearsons from all parts of the world...."

William G. Johnston, 1849, *Experiences of a 49er*. Johnston was from Ohio and traveled in the first wagon train to enter California in the famous gold rush year of 1849. Later in life he started a printing business back home in Pittsburgh, and in 1892 he published an account of his journey.

"June 10 . . . We came in sight of Chimney Rock, at a distance of thirty miles, it had the appearance of a tall post seen a mile off.... June 11 ... On the left, the square bluffs were like the Hudson Palisades, with here and there a pilaster of silvery white, right in front, stood the lofty white Chimney Rock, like the pharos of a prairie sea...."

Philip St. George Cooke, 1845, *Scenes and Adventures in the Army: Or, Romance of Military Life*. U.S. Cavalry officer Cooke went on regular expeditions west and later served as a Union general in the Civil War.

"Starting early this morning we came some 15 miles and encamped for noon opposite Chimney Rock on the south side of the Platte River.... I saw hundreds of names out in the rock some at a dizzy height while others less ambitious had been content to subscribe their names lower down. I wrote mine above all except two and theirs were about 8 feet higher than mine but I should have written mine as high if not higher than theirs if I had not left my knife on the other side of the river."

Charles M. Tuttle, 1859, *California Diary of Charles M. Tuttle, 1859*. Tuttle was a young farmer from Wisconsin who traveled the California Trail in 1859, keeping notes along the way about the landscape, plants, animals, and other wagon trains.

rising 240 feet (73 m) above the grasslands. These were some of the first monoliths that pioneers saw and were often noted in diaries, by a variety of names; sometimes they were referred to as castles. If you'd like to get close to them, you can drive up, park, and follow a couple unofficial hiking paths up to the rocks.

Getting There

From Ash Hollow, drive west on U.S. 26 for 46 miles (74 km), then turn left onto Highway 92 in the town of Broadwater. In 13.6 miles (21.8 km), turn left onto South Railroad Avenue, and in 1.1 miles (1.7 km) turn left again onto Highway 88, heading south. In 3.3 miles (5.3 km), turn right onto Road 81, which leads to the base of the rocks. The drive takes 1.25 hours. If you're content to see the giant rocks from a distance, continue driving northwest on Highway 92 into Bridgeport rather than turning onto Railroad Avenue.

TOP EXPERIENCE

★ Chimney Rock

As you continue west on U.S. 26, you'll soon spot the spire of **Chimney Rock,** standing tall over the prairie. A remnant of volcanic ash and clay left from ancient floods and weathering, it's the most mentioned landmark of the Oregon, California, and Mormon Trails, capturing the imagination of pioneers year after year and recorded in hundreds of diaries. Travelers were in awe of it, some sure that it was about to topple or decompose at any moment. In reality, the rock is pretty tough, and most geologists believe the height then was about the same as it is now. The spire is 325 feet (99 m) tall from its base, which made it visible for several days before and after reaching it—for the pioneers, that is; modern travelers will see it and leave it behind in an hour or so as they continue their westward journey. With a spring near its base, the rock offered a nice spot to camp,

and emigrants made sure to mark their names here, as they did in so many other places along the trail. Modern travelers who have played the classic Oregon Trail computer game will recognize Chimney Rock as a famous stop for their pixelated wagon party.

Today, you can only see Chimney Rock from a distance; in order to preserve it, there is no access or trail to its base. Road-trippers can easily identify it from the highway, so if you need to continue on, the sight of it may be enough. If you'd like to get slightly closer, you can get a good view from the **Chimney Rock Visitor Center** (9822 County Rd. 75, www.nps.gov, 9am-5pm daily, $3), which has telescopes pointed right at the rock. Inside there's also a good introductory film and historical exhibits on the Oregon and Mormon Trails. The center showcases a great collection of historical drawings and paintings of Chimney Rock, from pioneer times up through today, and visitors have a chance to sketch their own version to add to the wall. A few kids' activities round out the museum, as well as a gift shop and an outdoor theater space with a stellar view of the spire for presentations and ranger talks.

Getting There

From Bridgeport, head west on U.S. 26, which becomes Highway 92, for 13 miles (21 km), then turn left onto Chimney Rock Recreation Road and drive 1.5 miles (2.4 km); the visitors center is on the right. The drive takes about 20 minutes.

⚑ Detour: Carhenge and Agate Fossil Beds

If you have some spare time, you can detour from Bridgeport to catch two interesting sights. The route is about 170 miles (275 km) and takes about three hours of driving time. It'll take you in a counterclockwise loop from U.S. 26, and deposit you back on U.S. 26 farther northwest, near Scottsbluff. Note this detour from Scottsbluff to Agate Fossil Beds National Monument and Carhenge is an almost 100-mile (161-km) stretch with no gas, so top off before heading out.

If you opt for the loop detour, you'll skip the section of the trail route between Bridgeport and Scottsbluff, which is where Chimney Rock lies. Although you can just make out Chimney Rock from Bridgeport, it's a distant view. If you're set on seeing it all, Chimney Rock is a simple 30-minute backtrack (one-way) along Highway 92 from Scottsbluff.

You could also opt to make individual side trips to each of these. From Bridgeport, Carhenge is a 40-mile (64-km) drive one-way, a 45-minute ride in each direction. From Scottsbluff, Agate Fossil Beds National Monument is a 45-mile (72-km) drive one-way, a 50-minute ride in each direction.

Carhenge

Carhenge (Hwy. 87, 308/762-3569, www.carhenge.com, 24 hours daily, free) may be one of the weirdest sights in Nebraska: a circle of cars rising high in the sky like a surrealistic Paleolithic monument. This remote site—dreamed up by Jim Reinders, who was inspired by Stonehenge while living in England—manages to attract around 60,000 visitors each year. After Reinders's father died, the idea of a memorial was brought up, and Jim had a wild idea; the family agreed, and came together in the summer of 1987 to build it. They placed 39 vehicles in the exact dimensions of the original Stonehenge. It's a strange experience to wander around the gray cars on the remote prairie. Nearby, the **Car Art Preserve** outdoor gallery holds additional car sculptures, like a Conestoga wagon and a spawning salmon. The **Pit Stop Gift Shop** (10am-5pm Mon.-Sat.) offers plenty of postcards and other souvenirs.

Carhenge by sculptor Jim Reinders

Getting There

To begin the loop from **Bridgeport,** follow the signs directing you to Carhenge, heading northward to U.S. 385. In 35 miles (56 km), just past Alliance, turn right onto Nance Road, then in 2.2 miles (3.5 km), turn left onto Highway 87. Carhenge is on the east side of the highway in 1.5 miles (2.4 km).

Agate Fossil Beds National Monument

One of the remotest national park sites is in the Panhandle of eastern Nebraska. **Agate Fossil Beds National Monument** (308/665-4113, www.nps.gov/agfo, 9am-5pm daily mid-May-Sept., 8am-4pm daily Oct.-mid-May, free) is small but packs a big punch for those interested in fossils, prehistoric mammals, or big prairie views. This site, encompassing massive deathbeds of prehistoric creatures, was a rich land for fossil hunters of the 1880s, when the study of paleontology was booming. Many of the larger fossil

specimens are now preserved at institutions such as Harvard University and the Smithsonian. A small but excellent museum is at the national monument, and two interpretive trails allow you to see fossils in situ and enjoy beautiful views.

Getting There

From Carhenge, head north on Highway 87 for 0.5 mile (0.8 km), then turn left onto Logan Road. In 3.3 miles (5.3 km), turn right onto U.S. 385. In 4 miles (6.4 km), turn right to get onto Highway 2, continuing on it for 22 miles (34 km), at which point it becomes Highway 71. Continue for another 19.6 miles (32 km). Turn right on Pink School House Road—keep an eye out, as the dirt road isn't well marked. After 0.6 mile (0.9 km), turn left onto Cut Across Road. In 6 miles (9.6 km), turn right onto Highway 29. After 10 miles (16 km), follow signs for the monument, turning right onto River Road. The visitors center is in 3 miles (4.8 km). The drive from Carhenge takes 1 hour and 20 minutes.

If you're opting to do this as a side trip from Scottsbluff, drive west of town on U.S. 26 for 9 miles (14.5 km), then turn right onto Highway 29. In 34 miles (55 km), turn right onto River Road; you'll arrive at the visitors center in another 3 miles (4.8 km).

Note there aren't many services in the area. At the monument, you'll find water fountains and a vending machine. Cell phone service is limited.

Visitors Center

The **visitors center and museum** shows a 12-minute introductory movie, *The Fossil Hills,* upon request, and friendly rangers are available to answer your questions. Exhibits showcase life-size replica skeletons of prehistoric mammals that once roamed the plains; these creatures seem almost imaginary in their weirdness—from a prehistoric beaver that created corkscrew-shaped burrows to a huge horse-rhino cross called *Moropus.*

The museum also has an excellent collection of over 500 Sioux artifacts and artwork, most of it gifted by tribe members to James Cook, a fossil-hunter who lived on a nearby ranch and spent his free time searching for fossils. Cook had solid relationships with Oglala Lakota members, including Red Cloud, the famous chief who resisted government efforts to move the Oglala Lakota people from their lands across what is today Nebraska. Red Cloud often brought his entire family to visit the Cook ranch; the friendship between the families of a white rancher and a Lakota chief was notable in a time when relations were often strained and conflict was the norm.

Hiking

The easy, paved 2.6-mile (4.2-km) **Fossil Hills Trail** starts at the visitors center and heads south to explore the area where fossils were first discovered here in the 1880s. You'll cross the Niobrara River and see the two hills that had the most digs—University Hill and Carnegie Hill. No active digs are taking place anymore—most major excavations ended by 1923—but along the trail are plenty of interpretive signs identifying features of the natural environment and history of the area. From the top of the small hill, you'll catch great views of the monument. The walk takes about an hour.

Walk the easy, 1-mile (1.6-km) **Daemonelix Trail** for a look at one of the most unique sites in Nebraska: corkscrew-shaped burrows made by a prehistoric beaver known as *Palaeocastor*. The word *daemonelix* translates to "devil's corkscrew" and demonstrates how confounded early paleontologists were by these formations. It took years to figure out that the casts—sand-filled tubes of fossilized plant material—were created by the rodents. On the trail today you can see a protected view of one of the burrows in situ. Great views of the surrounding hills can also be seen along the way, and if you're here in spring or early summer, wildflowers are plentiful. The trailhead

for the 30-minute walk is near the entrance of Agate Fossil Beds National Monument, on River Road, just east of Highway 29.

Camping

The nearest lodging is in Scottsbluff, but you can camp 1.5 miles (2.4 km) east of the visitors center, at **Pavement Ends Campground** (435 River Rd., 308/665-5524, $25), which has space for tent camping and eight drive-through full-hookup RV sites.

Getting Back on the Trail

From the monument, drive south on Highway 29 for 34 miles (55 km). Turn left onto U.S. 26 and continue for 9 miles (14.5 km). Turn right onto Avenue B, which leads into central Scottsbluff in just under 1 mile (1.6 km).

Scottsbluff and Gering

The sister cities of Scottsbluff and Gering—separated by only a few miles—are cuddled close to each other just east of Scotts Bluff National Monument, sandstone bluffs that threw up another barrier to the pioneers' path. Founded after the Oregon Trail's time, the relatively small towns are now also surrounded by industrial agricultural farmland. Together they form the largest urban area in western Nebraska, and are an excellent base for exploring the nearby monument.

Scottsbluff is slightly larger and has a charming main street, Broadway, while Gering claims the honor of being right on the path of the Oregon Trail, which cuts through it as M Road/Old Highway 92, becoming County Road K/Old Oregon Trail Road as it enters Scotts Bluff National Monument.

Getting There

If you drive here **directly from Ogallala,** the roughly 122-mi (196-km) drive via U.S. 26 takes about 2.25 hours. From

Scottsbluff and Gering and Vicinity

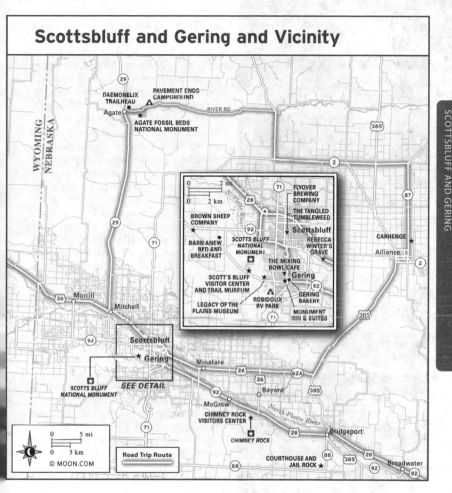

Chimney Rock, continue west on U.S. 26/Highway 92. In 11 miles (17 km), turn right onto Highway 79. In 2 miles (3.2 km), turn left back onto U.S. 26. Drive 7.5 miles (12 km), then turn left onto East 20th Street to head into Scottsbluff. The drive takes 30 minutes.

From Scottsbluff, Gering is 3 miles (4.8 km) south via 10th Street or Five Rocks Road.

Sights
Rebecca Winters's Grave
Thousands of pioneers died from cholera on the way to Oregon and California. Most of them were buried in unmarked graves, often in the middle of the trail itself, so that the heavy wagon wheels would pack down the earth—in hopes the site would be undisturbed. A handful of grave sites along the trail are known today, one of which belongs to Rebecca Winters. She was a Mormon pioneer traveling with her husband, Hiram, when she became sick and died of cholera near the monument of Scotts Bluff on August 15, 1852. Hiram and a friend, William Reynolds, buried her with great

care. They dug a deep grave for Rebecca and lined it with wooden wagon planks, wrapping her in blankets before laying her to rest. William chiseled her name on a metal wagon rim that they pounded over the grave; this rim later allowed surveyors for the Burlington Northern Railroad to discover the site in 1899. Rebecca's remains were carefully moved in 1995, farther away from the railroad, and today a plaque marks the spot, along with a historical marker telling her story. The metal rim still guards her grave site all these years later.

From central Scottsbluff, drive south on Broadway. In 0.9 mile (1.4 km), turn left onto South Beltline Highway. In 2.6 miles (4.1 km), you'll cross the railroad tracks—turn right here into the entrance to the site. The grave is located just north of the historical marker.

Legacy of the Plains Museum
The **Legacy of the Plains Museum** (2930 Old Oregon Trail, Gering, 308/436-1989, www.legacyoftheplains.org, 9am-5pm Tues.-Sat., $10) is on an 80-acre working farm, with a sod house, a blacksmith shop, and plenty of farm equipment, all within view of Scotts Bluff National Monument. Snap a goofy pic next to huge potato and corn statues, or test your horsepower, milk a cow, or try out one of the other 37 hands-on activities. While the museum highlights agriculture and historical farm implements, it contains a wide variety of artifacts covering thousands of years of High Plains history, from discoveries of early inhabitants to stories of westward expansion and early settlers. In the Prairie Trails exhibit, learn how folks got around on the trails, from fur trappers and traders on foot to emigrants in wagons to industrialized society in trains, and, finally, automobiles.

Top to bottom: Legacy of the Plains Museum; *Scotts Bluff* by William Henry Jackson; Flyover Brewing Company taster tray.

Brown Sheep Company

About a 10-minute drive east of Scottsbluff, off Highway 92, you can visit a family-owned and operated yarn mill at **Brown Sheep Company** (100662 County Rd., 308/635-2198, www. brownsheep.com, 8am-5pm Mon.-Fri., tours 10am Tues. and Thurs., free). Even if you're not a knitter, it's interesting to get a glimpse into the industry. Brown Sheep dyes over 100 colorways and has 24 product lines distributed throughout the country. It prides itself on green practices—each skein is dyed using recycled water. Take a tour of the mill (10am Tues. and Thurs.) to see the spinning, dyeing, and packaging process, then shop for goodies at the outlet store, where you can find seconds of the hand-dyed lots along with knitting needles, books, and accessories.

Just down the road is the company's Brown Sheep Fiber Schoolhouse, which offers classes in fiber arts out of its renovated 1930s schoolhouse. Check online for the calendar—many classes are quick one-day options, while some are week-long intensives that allow for a deeper dive into a topic like weaving, felting, and, of course, knitting.

Food

★ **The Mixing Bowl** (1945 10th St., Gering, 308/633-1288, www.mixing bowlgering.com, 7am-3pm Mon. and Wed.-Sat., 9am-2pm Sun., $12) serves the best breakfast and brunch around, with a menu including eggs Benedict, breakfast burritos, Swedish pancakes, and a *chile relleno* grilled cheese. Each Sunday a special brunch is offered, with a rotating menu of seasonal goodies. Check out the bakery case for doughnuts, cookies, giant cinnamon rolls, and plenty of German specialties like *grebel*, a doughnut-like fried pastry, and *dinna kuga*, breakfast bread similar to coffee cake. The eatery also serves a huge variety of specialty coffees, Italian sodas, and seasonal lemonades. If you're in a rush,

head to the drive-through on your way to the monument.

Flyover Brewing Company (1824 Broadway, Scottsbluff, 308/575-0335, www.flyoverbrewingcompany.com, 3pm-11pm Wed.-Fri., 11am-11pm Sat.-Sun., $13) makes great beers and tasty wood-fired pizzas in a modern brewery environment. As the only craft brewery in the Nebraska Panhandle, Flyover takes its role seriously, sourcing ingredients from the state to create tasty lagers and ales.

Dine in a transformed gas station or on the quaint patio at **The Tangled Tumbleweed** (1823 Ave. A, Scottsbluff, 308/633-3867, 11am-10pm Wed.-Sat., $12), a tapas and wine bar. Small plates include pulled pork sliders, bacon mac and cheese, and lots of seasonal vegetable-forward and vegan options. The wine is some of the best served in town, and beer comes from Nebraska breweries like Zipline in Lincoln. Save room for house made desserts.

Try a *runza*, Nebraska's iconic state sandwich at the humble and delicious **Gering Bakery** (1446 10th St., Gering, 308/436-5500, www.geringbakery.com, 5:30am-5:30pm daily, $5). It's called a "cabbage burger" here since *runza* is trademarked by fast-food chain Runza. They're homemade with love and plenty of beef and cabbage in a fresh bun. People with a sweet tooth are quite happy here as well, with chocolate doughnuts, peanut butter pretzels, maple bacon bars, and a wide range of cakes and cupcakes to choose from. Gering Bakery's master bakers are trained in-house to make everything from scratch. Their goods are delivered all over the region. There isn't much seating in the bakery, so squeeze into a small table or order to go.

Accommodations and Camping

A renovated homestead on the prairie just west of Scottsbluff, ★ **Barn Anew Bed and Breakfast** (170549 County Rd. L, Mitchell, 308/632-8647, www.barnanew. com, $140-150) offers travelers fine accommodations served with a side of Oregon Trail history. Watch the sunrise over the sandstone cliffs of Scottsbluff from your Pony Express or Fur Trapper room, furnished with Western antiques—like maybe a player piano. Or spring for an adventurous stay in the sheep wagons outdoors, historical wagons where sheepherders once slept while tending flocks. Owners Char and Allan Maybee offer a passionate and expert look at the region's Oregon Trail history—both have ridden the entire trail on horseback, and offer guided tours of the local sights and stories.

You'll know you're at the right place by the covered wagon in front of **Monument Inn & Suites** (1130 M St., Gering, 308/436-1950, www.monumentinnsuites.com, $99-208). Inside, murals and Nebraska-themed quilts carry the pioneer theme through. Guest rooms are comfortable and have flat-screen TVs, and a hot breakfast is served. A 3-mile (4.8-km) drive west down M Street—the Old Oregon Trail Road—follows the path of the wagons and brings you to Scotts Bluff National Monument.

For breathtaking views of Scotts Bluff National Monument, park your RV at **Robidoux RV Park** (585 Five Rocks Rd., Gering, 308/436-2046, www.gering.org/robidoux-rv-park, $12-33). Each of the 42 sites offers a concrete pad for parking, with patios, picnic tables, cable TV, and electricity, some with full hookups. Tent sites are also available, along with on-site shower and laundry facilities. Best of all, you're a five-minute drive to the monument.

★ Scotts Bluff National Monument

TOP EXPERIENCE

Up until this point, emigrants had been closely following the North Platte River. But this region's landscape of bluffs, rising hundreds of feet from the river so

Scotts Bluff National Monument

close to the sandy banks, made it impossible for them to continue in the river valley. They were forced to find a route through the rocky formations. Early travelers found one via Robidoux Pass, a few miles south, but by the 1850s pioneers created an easier road through Mitchell Pass. By this point, pioneers would have been on the road for months, and the imposing bluffs were a striking sight; they became a well-known landmark along the trail.

Today, **Scotts Bluff National Monument** (308/436-9700, www.nps.gov/scbl, visitors center 8am-6pm daily Memorial Day-Labor Day, 8am-4:30pm daily Labor Day-Memorial Day, grounds sunrise-sunset, free) encompasses Scotts Bluff and South Bluff, bisected by Mitchell Pass. The road through the monument takes you through Mitchell Pass, following the path of the Oregon Trail. This is a fantastic place to get out and enjoy some history, hikes, and great views. The monument has an active event

program, with guest speakers, teachers, and living-history demonstrations. Rangers lead group hikes and spin tales of the history of the region. Call or ask at the visitors center, or check online for the latest happenings.

Getting There
From Gering, follow the same path as the pioneers to get to the monument. Driving west for a few miles on M Street/Old Highway 92 brings you to the monument, at which point the road becomes County Road K/Old Oregon Trail Road.

Sights and Recreation
Oregon Trail Museum and Visitor Center
Renovated in 2019, Scotts Bluff National Monument's **Oregon Trail Museum and Visitor Center** holds a collection of artifacts from Oregon Trail pioneers, including diaries, weapons, and children's toys. An introductory film explains more about the geological importance of the area and its role in westward expansion. Most notably, the museum holds the largest collection of paintings, photographs, and drawings in the world by William Henry Jackson, an artist famed for his depictions celebrating the West. Although his first trip west was in 1866, just as the Oregon Trail was diminishing, Jackson later in life painted dozens of Oregon Trail scenes set in popular locations like Chimney Rock or Independence Rock in Wyoming. His artwork depicts pioneers crossing rivers and wagons streaming across the prairies.

Outside you'll find a handcart, which Mormon pioneers used instead of wagons, and examples of different wagons; emigrants used the smaller Studebaker and Murphy wagons, while the larger Conestoga was later used for hauling larger freight.

Oregon Trail Pathway
Just outside the visitors center are wagons that look ready to roll away to

Scenic Drive: Robidoux Pass

Until Mitchell Pass opened in 1851, pioneers used Robidoux Pass to get through the hills around what's now Scotts Bluff National Monument. Robidoux's route was named for a Frenchman who opened a trading post along the way; many emigrant diaries mention the post and the blacksmith services offered there. Today, you can drive out to **Robidoux's Trading Post,** just south of Scotts Bluff National Monument. It's a beautiful scenic drive; you'll leave the plains and enter the foothills, with grassy bluffs flecked by pine trees surrounding you. There isn't much to do at the post, but you'll find some trail ruts with historical markers, reconstructions of the trade buildings, and possibly some rattlesnakes.

From Scotts Bluff National Monument, head back toward Gering on K Road, the Old Oregon Trail. In 1 mile (1.6 km), turn right onto Five Rocks Road. Follow this road, which becomes County Road 21 and then Highway 71, for 2.5 miles (4 km). Turn right onto Carter Canyon Road, continuing on it away from town and into hills for 8 miles (12.9 km)—you'll see the trading post on your right. The last 2 miles (3.2 km) of the route is on dirt roads, which can get muddy and treacherous after a rainstorm, so use caution. The drive takes about 20 minutes one-way.

Oregon—these restored beauties are on the old Oregon Trail itself. From here you can take a short 1-mile (1.6-km) round-trip walk; it takes 30 minutes. Once the paved path transitions to dirt, you're hiking on the actual Oregon Trail. There are no ruts here due to erosion, but there are big swales where the roadbed can be seen. Wagons would travel single file through the bluffs at this point, where it was called Mitchell Pass. Soon you'll be back on asphalt, and the old trail will be marked by wooden posts. The trail ends at a campsite where William Henry Jackson (see his paintings and sketches in the visitors center museum) stayed in 1866. The path has very little shade, so be prepared with sunscreen and a hat on a sunny day.

Scotts Bluff Summit

From the visitors center you can drive 1.6 miles (2.6 km) up **Summit Road** to the top, which takes about 10 minutes. The beautiful winding road was built in the 1930s, and you'll pass through three tunnels on the way up. Note that trailers and RVs aren't allowed, but a free **Summit Shuttle** operates seasonally from the visitors center, depending on staffing availability, an option for those driving larger vehicles or travelers who want to hike

one-way to the top; inquire at the visitors center. All cars must be down from the summit 30 minutes before closing time at the visitors center.

Hiking

Rising 800 feet (245 m) above the plains, the summit of Scotts Bluff offers striking views. A small network of trails from the summit parking lot offers access to several overlooks. The 0.5-mile (0.8-km) **North Overlook Trail** takes you to the highest point on the bluff, 4,658 feet (1,420 m) above sea level, while the 0.4-mile (0.6-km) **South Overlook Trail** offers excellent views of Mitchell Pass and the South Bluff beyond it.

Saddle Rock Trail is Scotts Bluff's most popular trail, beloved by locals as a great place for a jog. From the visitors center, the trail takes you to the bluff's summit, 1.6 miles (2.6 km) one-way. Going up, the paved path is easy on the feet, but you'll gain some elevation—about 435 feet (133 m). Scotts Bluff looms before you, and you'll pass Scott's Spring before arriving at a foot tunnel in the hill. Look up as you walk through—the tunnel was dug by hand, and you can still see pickax swipes on the soft stone roof. The Civilian Conservation Corps dug it as a test tunnel in the 1930s, before they created the three larger vehicle tunnels on the Summit Road. After the tunnel, you'll head up on a steeper incline, coming across the namesake Saddle Rock formation before reaching the summit. On the way you'll catch extensive views of the surrounding sandstone landscape and prairie, dotted by the occasional kestrel, hawk, or maybe some golden eagles. At the top, a few interpretive signs offer geological lessons, and you'll find the parking lot for the Summit Road. If you don't want to return down the way you came, you're in luck—you can catch the Summit Shuttle. Budget 1.25 hours for the hike up, or 2 hours for the total up-and-down hike.

Wyoming

Wyoming

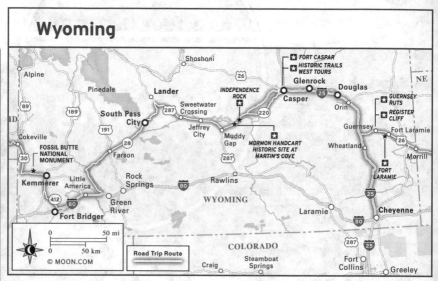

Wyoming was the mid-point for emigrants on the Oregon Trail, here a rocky path full of rough sagebrush. Days were hot and grueling.

Wagon parties had left Missouri when the spring grass was bright green in May and considered themselves on track if they made it to Independence Rock in Wyoming by the Fourth of July—if they didn't, they might face early snowstorms and wet conditions in October or November in Oregon.

This land then was nowhere, technically: Wyoming didn't become a territory until 1868, and before that, these parts were variously a section of the Louisiana Purchase and a small part of Mexico, ceded to the United States in 1848. Of course, before that it was the land of the Plains peoples and their ancestors, nomadic nations that include the Sioux, Shoshone, Arapaho, Cheyenne, Crow, and Ute peoples.

In Wyoming, emigrants continued following the North Platte River and then the Sweetwater River. From there, they made their way to the crucial South Pass over the Continental Divide—without the gentle slope of the pass, which climbs gradually to a high elevation, the trail to Oregon may never have existed. Crossing the Continental Divide meant you were truly in the West. Mormon pioneers followed the same path to Fort Bridger in southwest Wyoming, where they split off to Utah.

Today, Wyoming promises a rugged taste of the Old West for curious road-trippers, with sagebrush-filled valleys and the dramatic backdrop of the Rocky Mountains. Explorers can visit forts and see the deepest ruts on the trail, as well as visit the home of the mythical jackalope, dig for fossils, eat bison steaks, drink locally brewed beer, and maybe see a rodeo.

Highlights

★ Explore **Fort Laramie**, where emigrants once resupplied and rested along the trail (page 179).

★ Walk alongside the **Guernsey Ruts,** the most striking on the trail—cut over four feet deep into rock from the bite of wagon wheels (page 180).

★ Pore over hundreds of pioneers' names carved into

the sandstone at **Register Cliff** (page 183).

★ Check out a replica ferry and bridge at **Fort Caspar**, where emigrants crossed the North Platte River (page 204)

★ Ride a covered wagon to a Dutch oven cookout with **Historic Trails West Tours** (page 205).

★ Gaze at **Independence Rock,** a landmark that was cause for celebration if emigrants made it there before the Fourth of July (page 211).

★ Try pulling a handcart like Mormon pioneers used along the trail at the **Mormon Handcart Historic Site at Martin's Cove** (page 213).

Best Overnight Stops

★ **Cheyenne:** It's off the Oregon Trail, but the biggest city in Wyoming is worth a side trip, offering a taste of the Wild West that reaches a crescendo during its Frontier Days festival (page 184).

★ **Casper:** The city of Casper offers history, food, and fun to last a few days (page 202).

★ **Lander:** A short way off the route, this outdoorsy town near the Wind River Mountains is a great place to spend a night, with excellent food and good camping and lodging options (page 215).

Planning Your Time

Wyoming is big. You'll cover about 550 miles (885 km) across the state, and much of it will be on two-lane highways through beautiful and rural rugged country. There's plenty to keep you busy, so you'll need at least three days, but plan on five if possible to make your way from the Nebraska state line through Casper, South Pass, Fort Bridger, and Kemmerer to Idaho.

At the U.S. 26 and I-25 junction, 61 miles (98 km) west of the Nebraska border, those with more time can opt to head south on I-25 to take a side trip to Wyoming's capital city of Cheyenne, or continue following the trail north. Farther west, outdoor enthusiasts may want to save time for a trip to Lander, near the Wind River Mountains.

Wyoming weather can be fickle, with snow falling as early as October and as late as June. I-25 heading north-south between Cheyenne and Casper can be relied on to be relatively clear of snow, but the rest of the Oregon Trail route is on smaller highways that often close. Stay attentive to weather reports and check for road closures before heading out. Find a map and information on conditions via the **Wyoming Department of Transportation** (WYDOT, http://wyoroad.info). You can also download its smartphone app, Wyoming 511.

Getting There

Starting Points
Oregon Trail Route Notes

In Wyoming you'll follow a close approximation of the old trail, sometimes driving right on it, sometimes paralleling it on modern highways. You'll start on **U.S. 26** along the North Platte River, as the emigrants traveled; U.S. 26 is on the north bank, as the Mormon emigrants were, while Oregon and California Trail emigrants were on the south bank. At the junction with **I-25**, past Guernsey, you trace the trail via the interstate all the way to Casper. From there, the route is more faithful, leaving town on **Highway 220** through the Sweetwater River Valley. Modern highways cut north to Lander then south to South Pass—the emigrants would have followed the river due west, taking the shortest way possible. After South Pass, **Highway 28** follows the trail closely, and then you veer off on other highways to reach Fort Bridger. Leaving Fort Bridger, you follow a loose approximation of the trail until you find the actual path again closer to the state line, at the junction of U.S. 30 and Highway 89.

Car and RV

If any state typifies the vast expanses of the West, it's Wyoming. It's the country's least populated state and the 10th largest by area. Its biggest city, Cheyenne, has a

Best Walks and Hikes

★ **Guernsey Ruts:** A short walk of less than half a mile leads you to the best wagon ruts of the Oregon Trail, cut deep into the rock (page 180).

★ **Garden Creek Waterfall:** Get splashed by a waterfall on this short hike at Casper Mountain (page 206).

★ **Historic Quarry Trail:** Fossil beds in a prehistoric lake are the main feature of this heartier hike (page 231).

population just a fraction of neighboring state capitals like Denver. Full of rural roads, cattle, ranchers, and friendly people, a car is all but required to get around.

If you've been following the route, you enter Nebraska via U.S. 26. From Scottsbluff, the Wyoming border is 24 miles (38 km) west, a 30-minute drive. Fort Laramie in Wyoming is 50 miles (80 km) away, about an hour's drive from Scottsbluff.

Rentals
Enterprise (www.enterprise.com) has an office at the **Cheyenne Regional Airport** (2200 Missile Dr., 307/632-1907, 7:30am-6pm Mon.-Fri., 9am-2pm Sat., 9am-1pm Sun.), one in east **Casper** (2200 E. 2nd St., 307/234-8122, 7:30am-6pm Mon.-Fri., 9am-noon Sat.), and one at **Denver International Airport** (24530 E. 78th Ave., 303/342-7350, 24 hours daily).

In Cheyenne, rent an RV from **Rich Carter's Adventure RV** (9310 Hutchins Dr., 307/638-3800, www.greatrvdeals.com, 8am-5pm Mon.-Fri., 8am-3pm Sat.), which offers RVs and trailers for $137 per night. It rents primarily April-October, depending on weather; off-season rentals are winterized—meaning no running water.

Near Denver, rent a van from **Native Campervans** (2919 E. 42nd Ave., 877/550-5335, 9am-4pm daily by appointment), 20 miles (32 km) west of Denver International Airport. Choose from the Biggie van ($1,800 per week June-Sept., $1,250 per week Oct.-May) or the Smalls

van ($1,100 per week June-Sept., $800 per week Oct.-May). Most models sleep two adults comfortably and come with a kitchen, bedding, chairs, a cooler, and propane tanks. You'll get 100 free miles (161 km) per day, and dogs are allowed with a $100 fee per animal. Vans come with basic insurance and roadside assistance. Native Campervans also has a location in Salt Lake City, Utah (3010 W. 500 S., Suite 2, 877/550-5335, www.nativecampervans.com, 9am-4pm daily by appointment), with a one-time $300 fee for a one-way trip. There's also an outpost of **Cruise America** (www.cruiseamerica.com), a nationwide company, 28 miles (45 km) west of Denver International Airport (8950 Federal Blvd., 877/784-3733, 8:30am-5pm Mon.-Fri., 9am-4pm Sat.). For a week, expect to pay around $1,300-1,600 total, depending on mileage.

Fuel and Services
Gas stations, restaurants, and hotels are sparse between cities, so make sure to fill up on gas before you head out, and always carry some water, food, and emergency supplies. Cell phone service is also sparse, so keep paper maps on hand, or download Google Maps for offline use. The state's small highways are often closed in inclement weather—the most reliable roads are I-25 and I-80, which have rest stops or amenities every 40 miles (64 km) or so. From Casper on, fill up when you have the opportunity since stretches without stations can far exceed that.

Air

If you plan to fly into Wyoming and rent a car, the easiest starting point is Cheyenne. You can fly into Cheyenne or the larger hub of Denver, 100 miles (160 km) south via I-25, a 1.75-hour drive. As you continue north on I-25 from Cheyenne, you can easily head east on U.S. 26 to see one or all of the eastern Wyoming section's sights, some of the state's Oregon Trail highlights (Fort Laramie is the farthest east, about 30 miles (50 km) from the I-25/U.S. 26 junction), before backtracking slightly and continuing west along the Oregon Trail.

Several daily flights from Dallas fly into small **Cheyenne Regional Airport** (CYS, 4020 Airport Pkwy. W., 307/634-7071, www.cheyenneairport.com). It's just 2 miles (3.2 km) north of downtown Cheyenne. Travelers pay $50-100 more to fly into Cheyenne rather than Denver, but you save 1.5 hours of driving time.

Denver International Airport (DEN, 8500 Pena Blvd., 303/342-2000, www.flydenver.com) has nonstop flights to 200 destinations on 20 airlines. It's one of the busiest airports in the country due to its central location. The airport serves as a hub for Southwest, Frontier, and United, which make up most of the traffic.

Bus

You can get from Cheyenne to Casper by bus. The **Greyhound station** (601 N. Center St., 307/266-2353, www.greyhound.com, 8:30am-12:30pm and 4:30pm-7:30pm Mon.-Fri.) is near downtown. The bus leaves Cheyenne once daily in the afternoon and takes 3.5 hours ($60 one-way). From Casper, you need a car to head farther west.

Along the Trail in Eastern Wyoming

After passing through Mitchell Pass in Nebraska, wagons continued northwest along the North Platte River, entering rougher sandstone hills on the way to Wyoming. From the pass, it was roughly 50 miles (80 km), or 3-4 days, to the next supply stop at Fort Laramie, 535 miles (860 km) from the last one at Fort Kearny; today it only takes an hour by car. For most it would be late June or even July at this point in their journey. Fort Laramie was a last-chance point: the last reasonable place to turn around and go back home. For many, the journey so far had been hard enough. They'd lost loved ones, gone hungry, been soaked by rain, and were disillusioned with the promise of the trail. They called it "seeing the elephant," a term that once conveyed seeing something amazing (like a circus elephant), and over the years on the trail it came to mean experiencing hardship. For those who had seen the elephant and no longer wanted to continue, the last leg of the Platte River Valley, with its thunderstorms and mosquitoes, was nothing but the last straw.

For those continuing on, it was time

to say farewell to the Great Platte River Road, one of the easier sections of the trail, with its plentiful water and grass. After Fort Laramie, wagons would still follow the North Platte River on its south side, but it would no longer be the wide, slow companion they had known for the last month.

The below sequence of sights is just off **U.S. 26** and covers about 20 miles (32 km) total, and 30 minutes of driving.

★ Fort Laramie

The trading post that would become **Fort Laramie** (965 Gray Rocks Rd., 307/837-2221, www.nps.gov/fola, grounds sunrise-sunset, free) was founded by fur traders in 1834. When it fell into disrepair, the American Fur Company built an adobe replacement in 1842—it's this structure that most emigrants saw on their westward journey when they stopped for supplies. The small outpost was the only permanent trading place for 800 miles (1,300 km) in the 1840s.

At an average of 15 miles (24 km) per day, it was about 20 days travel from Fort Kearny in central Nebraska, and well over a month from Fort Bridger in southwest Wyoming. In 1849, the U.S. Army purchased Fort Laramie, deciding it needed a larger presence on the overland routes.

Fort Laramie and the earlier trading post sat on a small spit of land between the Laramie River and the North Platte River. To get to the fort, wagons needed to cross the Laramie River. Strong swimmers would go first with ropes, which they would use to pull wagons and livestock across. Once at the trading post, emigrants could relax for a time, with grass for livestock and fresh water, as well as a chance to bathe, repair wagon wheels, reshoe horses, and buy provisions (though often at an egregiously inflated price).

The Commissary Storehouse (follow the signs up the road from the parking lot) serves as the headquarters and

barracks at Fort Laramie

visitors center (307/837-2221, 8am-4:30pm daily Labor Day-Memorial Day, 9am-7pm daily Memorial Day-Labor Day). Here you can find maps, a bookstore, daily event information, and a museum. An 18-minute film offers historical information, and exhibits cover army life and include uniforms and weapons. Visitors will learn about the influence of the fort on 19th-century life, as an important trading post for emigrant wagons and a base for U.S. soldiers in the Sioux War campaigns. Then take a self-guided tour of the structures that make up the National Historic Site, which includes 11 restored army buildings that were in use 1849-1890, and ruins or foundations of 9 more.

In summer there are daily living-history programs, when park staff dress in period clothing and share stories and facts about fort life, and on weekends a weapons demonstration (12:30pm) is offered near the visitors center. Ask in the center about the daily schedule, which varies July-September.

Getting There

From Scottsbluff, you're not far from the Nebraska-Wyoming border. Continue west on U.S. 26 for 51 miles (82 km) until you reach the town of Fort Laramie in Wyoming—note that this is distinct from the city of Laramie, as well as from the Fort Laramie National Historic Site. In the town, turn left onto Merriam Street. Following signs for the fort, drive 2.5 miles (4 km) to the entrance of the site. The drive takes just over an hour.

★ Guernsey Ruts

The **Guernsey Ruts** (dawn-dusk daily, free) are, hands down, the most striking of the entire trail, the result of thousands of wagons forced to roll through a section of soft sandstone, creating deeper and deeper ruts that are up to

Top to bottom: *Fort Laramie* by William Henry Jackson; Guernsey Ruts; Register Cliff.

The Stray Cow and the Sioux Wars

Maffet Ledger drawing by Southern and Northern Cheyenne artists

Eastern Wyoming was once the land of the Great Sioux Nation and neighboring Cheyenne, among other peoples. In the early years of the Oregon Trail, they viewed emigrants as a novelty, and helped them ford rivers and traded for food. As wagon traffic increased through their home, they grew concerned about the incoming tide, about resource depletion as emigrant livestock ate all the grass, and about the overhunting of bison, which they relied on for food and furs. While relations between the Sioux and the emigrants were neutral overall, individual prejudices on both sides contributed to a growing sense of unease. By 1849, the U.S. Army decided it needed a larger presence along the overland trails to protect emigrants from the perceived threat of attack, and purchased Fort Laramie to serve as a military outpost. Relations became especially strained during that year due to the California gold rush, as thousands of emigrants poured through the fort.

Tensions erupted near Fort Laramie on August 18, 1854, in what became known as the Grattan Fight, or Grattan Massacre. On that day, members of a nearby Sioux camp found a sick cow that had strayed from a wagon train, and innocently ate it for dinner. The loss was reported to Fort Laramie. Chief Conquering Bear apologized for the mistake, and offered a horse or mule as repayment—a pretty good deal for the time. Although he wasn't the fort commander, Lieutenant John Grattan thought force was needed. Grattan was young, impulsive, and a known antagonist of the Sioux and other nations. With permission, he led 29 armed men and two howitzer cannons to the camp where Brule, Miniconjou, and Oglala Lakota Sioux waited. His interpreter was reportedly drunk on whiskey and shouting insults. Grattan demanded the cow thief. Chief Conquering Bear tried to defuse the situation, but the lieutenant refused to back down. The standoff ended with the death of all 29 soldiers, as well as Grattan and Conquering Bear.

Retaliation by the U.S. Army was swift and disastrous for both sides; the Grattan Fight sparked an entire generation of battles, known as the Sioux Wars. Despite several successes, the Sioux were outnumbered. Chief Crazy Horse surrendered in 1877, and the Sioux Wars effectively ended with the devastating Wounded Knee Massacre in 1890, in which the U.S. Army lost about 30 men and killed 250-300 Lakota Sioux men, women, and children.

Eastern Wyoming to Douglas

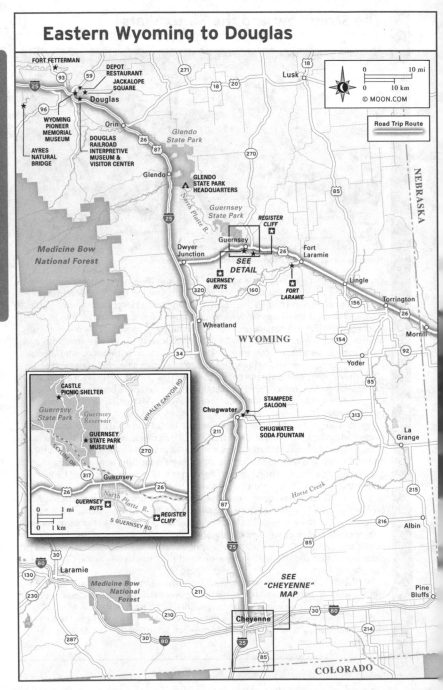

four feet deep in places; the sandstone was worn down by earlier wagon parties, and it was too difficult to pull wagon wheels out of the ruts—so emigrants continued following the same grooves. From the parking lot, head up the paved trail to see the ruts; you'll know them when you see them. The easy, 0.4-mile (0.6-km) loop continues past more ruts and back to the parking lot. The site also offers a picnic shelter, restrooms, and informational kiosks that describe the history of the area.

Getting There

From the town of Fort Laramie, drive 12.5 miles (20 km) west on U.S. 26. Turn left in the small town of Guernsey onto West Wyoming Avenue, which becomes South Guernsey Road, following signs for the site and crossing the North Platte River. Turn right after 0.8 mile (1.3 km), heading west on the dirt road. Continue 0.5 mile (0.8 km) then turn left into the site area, where there is a small parking lot. The drive takes 20 minutes from Fort Laramie.

★ Register Cliff

Just a short drive away from the Guernsey Ruts is another stunning glimpse into the past at **Register Cliff** (dawn-dusk daily, free), where hundreds of emigrants carved their names into the sandstone just before their wagons carved their wheels into the earth. As you park and approach the cliff, you can see numerous names; most of these are actually modern graffiti from wannabe pioneers. Turn left and head to the cliff's east end to find a section protected by a fence—these are the historical signatures. Some of the earliest date to the 1820s, when fur trappers passed through. Swallows use the cliffs above the signatures for nests—you can see whole condominiums built out of mud, and maybe even spy them swooping in the air. As you approach the cliff, to the right is a small pioneer cemetery with a few graves.

Getting There

From the Guernsey Ruts, head east, back in the direction you came down the dirt road, and turn right to continue south on South Guernsey Road. In 1.8 miles (2.8 km), turn left at the sign for Register Cliff. The parking lot is in front of the cliff in 0.5 mile (0.8 km). The drive takes less than 10 minutes.

◈ Side Trip: Guernsey State Park

If you have time, head 2 miles (3.2 km) north of **Guernsey,** via Highway 317, off U.S. 26, for a recreational break. From 1934 to 1937 the Civilian Conservation Corps (CCC) built the many picturesque bridges, hiking trails, overlooks, and buildings that now grace **Guernsey State Park** (2187 Lakeside Shore Dr., Guernsey, 307/836-2334, http://wyoparks.wyo.gov, day-use Wyoming residents $6 per vehicle, nonresidents $9 per vehicle), a shining example of their artistic stonework. Be sure to stop by the **Castle,** a beautiful picnic shelter, to walk its winding steps for great views of the park. Another CCC-built treasure is the **Guernsey Museum** (9am-5pm daily May-Sept., free), which has historical and geological information about the park. Also in the park is excellent **camping** ($10 Wyoming residents, $17 nonresidents); it has 13 campgrounds surrounding the Guernsey Reservoir. Stop by the park headquarters, just after the main entrance, for maps, camping permits, and other information. The trailhead near Brimmer Outlook, an overlook offering views of the reservoir's stunning geology, has an extensive map of all the trails in the region.

◈ Side Trip: Chugwater

The little town of Chugwater was historically a trading post between Fort Laramie and Cheyenne. Today the town, population 212, is known for being the home of Chugwater Chili, and the once home of Steamboat the Horse, whose likeness bucks on the Wyoming license plate. Travelers will find a modern and well-kept rest-stop area with a gas station and two restaurants to try the eponymous chili.

Getting There

Driving west on U.S. 26 from Guernsey, I-25 is in 16 miles (26 km). From the **U.S. 26/I-25 junction,** head north toward Douglas and Casper to continue on the Oregon Trail route; or, if you have more time, head south on I-25 for a visit to Wyoming's biggest city and state capital, Cheyenne, stopping in the town of Chugwater along the way. From the junction—the point to which you'll need to backtrack, north, to pick up the Oregon Trail route again—it's 35 miles (56 km) to Chugwater, a 30-minute drive.

Food

The ★ **Chugwater Soda Fountain** (314 1st St., 307/422-3222, www.chugwater sodafountain.com, 8am-9pm Mon.-Fri., 8am-7pm Sat., 9am-7pm Sun., $6) prides itself on being Wyoming's oldest-running soda fountain, at over 100 years old. Part vintage museum, part souvenir shop, part dining room, it's a great stop for breakfast, lunch, or dinner. It offers homemade soups, burgers, pies, sandwiches, and more—enjoy a bowl of the famous Chugwater Chili, then wash it down with a traditional chocolate malt or shake. A small beer garden is outside with plastic tables under a shady tree.

For a hearty meal, hurry to **The Stampede Saloon and Eatery** (417 1st St., 307/422-3200, www.thestampedesaloon. com, 11am-9pm Wed.-Thurs., 11am-midnight Fri.-Sat., noon-3pm Sun., $15), where you'll find big servings and bigger hearts, with a buffet on Friday-Saturday nights and Sunday afternoon. The dining room is full of wooden booths and tables with ranch branding and Hollywood Wild West posters, while a mural of horses watches over the buffet. Friday-Saturday nights are for live music, when the local community turns out for the crooners, filling the small dance floor. Don't be shy; join in!

⬥ Side Trip: Cheyenne

Cheyenne started when the railroad arrived in Wyoming. In 1867 it was where the tracks of the Union Pacific Railroad stopped—for six months, until the crew moved on. The tracks would connect with the Central Pacific in 1869 at Promontory Point, Utah, creating the first transcontinental railroad. Cheyenne boomed during this time and established itself as a lasting city; since most other end-of-the-tracks towns died away, Cheyenne became known as the "Magic City of the Plains." It attracted a growing population with the wild character of the West, but also businesses, industry, the U.S. Army, and other stabilizing forces. In 1869 it was named the territory's temporary capital, a title that became permanent when Wyoming became a state in 1890.

Today, Wyoming's biggest city still feels more like a town, with charming Western storefronts, a few dilapidated buildings, and lots of heart. Visitors will find plenty of fun as they encounter trains, cowboys and cowgirls, bison, and some of the country's best steaks. If you're visiting at the end of July, hopefully you booked your hotel ahead of time and grabbed your Stetson—the town's biggest party is Frontier Days, a giant rodeo, country music concert, and cultural event.

Getting There and Around

From **Chugwater,** it's about 47 miles (76 km) south on I-25 to Cheyenne. This makes it 82 miles (132 km) from the I-25 junction with U.S. 26—the point to which you'll need to backtrack, north, to pick up the Oregon Trail route toward Douglas

One Day in Cheyenne

Morning
Start the morning with a big plate of steak, eggs, or french toast at **Luxury Diner.** Then head to a museum; dive into Cheyenne's railroad past at the **Cheyenne Depot Museum,** or learn more about frontier women at the **Cowgirls of the West Museum.**

Afternoon
Get a burger for lunch at **2 Doors Down,** then head south of town to the **Terry Bison Ranch** for an afternoon of Wild West adventure. Take a train ride to see the bison herd and feed them by hand. You can also go horseback riding or hop on an ATV tour.

Evening
Stick around the Terry Bison Ranch for a steak dinner at the **Senator's Steakhouse,** or head back into town for a nice night out at **Poor Richard's Restaurant.** End the night with drinks at **Accomplice Beer Company** near Depot Plaza.

and Casper. It's a 1.25-hour drive one-way—at that distance, Cheyenne is worth at least an overnight stay.

If you're coming north from **Denver, Colorado,** Cheyenne is 100 miles (160 km) north via I-25, a 1.75-hour drive. Most of Cheyenne's attractions are within a mile or two (1.6 3.2 km) of downtown around the **Cheyenne Depot Plaza,** along the main thoroughfare of **Lincolnway** and the cross street of **Warren Avenue.**

Uber (www.uber.com) and **Lyft** (www.lyft.com) operate in Cheyenne.

Sights
Wyoming State Capitol
Originally built in 1888 to serve the Wyoming territory, the **Wyoming State Capitol** (200 W. 24th St., 307/777-7881, http://capitolcomplex.wyo.gov, 8am-5pm Mon.-Fri., free) was, and is, the center of Cheyenne. Take a self-guided tour of the complex beginning at the visitors center; enter from 26th Street through the underground Capitol Extension. The complex comprises three parts: the main capitol building with legislative offices and Senate and House chambers; the Herschler Building, which holds state employee offices; and the Capitol Extension, an underground tunnel that

connects the two buildings and contains a student learning center, an auditorium, and the visitors center.

In 2019 the capitol finished a massive project that restored historical details, including wall paintings, original fireplaces, stained glass, and the golden dome. While you're here, look for statues of Esther Hobart Morris, the first woman elected justice of the peace in the United States, and Chief Washakie, a prominent and outspoken Shoshone leader in Wyoming in the mid-19th century.

Wyoming State Museum
See the story of the entire state at the **Wyoming State Museum** (2301 Central Ave., 307/777-7220, www.wyomuseum.state.wy.us, 9am-4:30pm Mon.-Sat., free). Spread over two floors, exhibits cover cultural and natural history of Wyoming, from dinosaurs to bison, coal mining to ranching, original inhabitants to new settlers. An exhibit on transportation methods has an emigrant wagon that helps tell the story of the Oregon and California Trails in Wyoming. The interactive kids' area keeps the little ones busy while older learners can find displays on paleontology or geology. With free admission, it's an easy place to spend an hour or so.

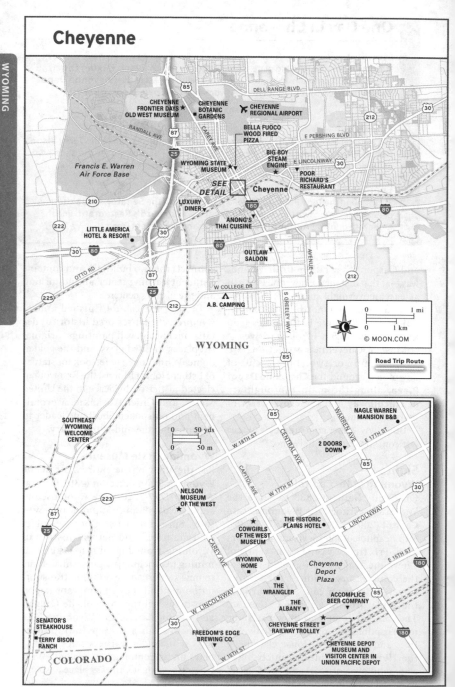

Cheyenne

DELL RANGE BLVD.

CHEYENNE FRONTIER DAYS ★ OLD WEST MUSEUM

CHEYENNE BOTANIC GARDENS

CHEYENNE REGIONAL AIRPORT

RANDALL AVE.

E PERSHING BLVD.

BELLA FUOCO WOOD FIRED PIZZA

Francis E. Warren Air Force Base

WYOMING STATE MUSEUM

BIG BOY STEAM ENGINE

E LINCOLNWAY

POOR RICHARD'S RESTAURANT

SEE DETAIL   Cheyenne

LUXURY DINER

ANONG'S THAI CUISINE

AVENUE C.

LITTLE AMERICA HOTEL & RESORT

OTTO RD.

OUTLAW SALOON

W COLLEGE DR

S GREELEY HWY

A.B. CAMPING

WYOMING

0   1 mi
0   1 km
© MOON.COM

Road Trip Route

SOUTHEAST WYOMING WELCOME CENTER

SENATOR'S STEAKHOUSE

TERRY BISON RANCH

COLORADO

---

0   50 yds
0   50 m

NAGLE WARREN MANSION B&B

W. 18TH ST.

CENTRAL AVE.

WARREN AVE.

E 17TH ST.

2 DOORS DOWN

CAPITOL AVE.

W. 17TH ST.

NELSON MUSEUM OF THE WEST

THE HISTORIC PLAINS HOTEL

E LINCOLNWAY

COWGIRLS OF THE WEST MUSEUM

CAREY AVE.

E 15TH ST.

WYOMING HOME

Cheyenne Depot Plaza

THE WRANGLER

W LINCOLNWAY

THE ALBANY

ACCOMPLICE BEER COMPANY

FREEDOM'S EDGE BREWING CO.

CHEYENNE STREET RAILWAY TROLLEY

W. 15TH ST.

CHEYENNE DEPOT MUSEUM AND VISITOR CENTER IN UNION PACIFIC DEPOT

A Shoshone Story: Chief Washakie

In Wyoming, you may come upon many reminders of Chief Washakie, a highly regarded leader of the Shoshone people, active in the mid- to late 1800s. Statues of him grace the Wyoming State Capitol, as well as Washington DC's National Statuary Hall; along with the country's first elected female justice of the peace, Esther Hobart Morris, the two represent the best of the state to the country. Hot springs, visitors centers, a county, and even a small town in Wyoming are named for him. Washakie earned the respect of his people; local settlers, traders, and "Indian agents"; as well as the U.S. military for being a noted warrior but also a peacemaker. He was amicable to incoming emigrants and settlers and skillful in negotiations, acting as a spokesperson for the Shoshone in treaty negotiations such as the Treaty of Fort Laramie in 1851 and Fort Bridger Treaty of 1868; he upheld the dictates of the various treaties, keeping the peace and working to provide the best lives possible for his people in a changing world. Upon his death in 1900, he became the only known Native American to be given a full military funeral.

Cheyenne Depot

The **Cheyenne Depot** (121 W. 15th St.) is a former Union Pacific Depot from 1886 that served as a key stop along the transcontinental rail line. Today it's a gorgeous example of 19th-century architecture. Outside the station stands a statue of a 19th-century pioneer woman, a testament to Wyoming's history as a leader of women's suffrage. Inside is a **visitors center** (307/778-3133), a good stop for any questions, maps, or information. Grab a map for a self-guided tour of downtown. The large lobby has a beautiful inlaid mural on the floor that details the route of the Union Pacific train tracks across the West. The Cheyenne Depot Museum makes its home inside, and at the other end of the depot is a brewery.

Many summer events are held here and on the adjoining **Cheyenne Depot Plaza**, including concerts, Frontier Days, brewfests, and more. Check the website for the latest happenings.

Cheyenne Depot Museum

The main event inside the former Union Pacific Depot is the **Cheyenne Depot Museum** (121 W. 15th St., Suite 300, 307/632-3905, www. cheyennedepotmuseum.org, 9am-6:30pm Mon.-Fri., 9am-5pm Sat., and 11am-3pm Sun. June-Aug., 9am-5pm Mon.-Fri., 9am-3pm Sat., and 11am-3pm Sun. Sept.-Apr., $8 adults, $7 seniors and military, free under age 13). It offers a deep look into the history of Cheyenne, which is tied to the transcontinental railroad. Exhibits recall how folks used to travel west (wagons, clipper ships, the many westbound trails) before the arrival of the railroad. The small space packs in a lot; upstairs is an amazing model train that chugs along through landscapes of the West. The model is of the Union Central and Northern lines—nearby, the real train plies its route outside the depot, viewable from an indoor platform.

Cheyenne Street Railway Trolley

Get oriented in the city with a tour via the **Cheyenne Street Railway Trolley** (121 W. 15th St., 307/778-3133, www. cheyennetrolley.com, 10am-5:30pm daily May-Sept., $12). Its Wild West tour runs daily in summer and stops at seven sights in 1.5 hours—hop off for more time at any of them, then jump back on the next trolley. Tours depart from the Cheyenne Depot and take riders by the Nelson Museum of the West, Wyoming State Museum, Wyoming State Capitol, Cheyenne Frontier Days Old West Museum, and more. If you're planning on going inside the museums, upgrade

Pioneering Women of Wyoming: First to Vote

Women gained the right to vote in the United States with the passage of the 19th Amendment in 1920. In the Wild West of Wyoming, though, they had it 50 years earlier, in 1869. When the Wyoming territory became a state in 1890, it was asked to rescind women's rights, but the territorial legislature refused: "We will remain out of the Union one hundred years rather than come in without the women."

Some historians believe the move to afford women voting rights in Wyoming was politically motivated—to garner more support for the Democratic Party, which had proposed the bill—and attract more women to the state (men outnumbered women 6 to 1). No matter the reason, the bill passed, and women could vote and hold political office for the first time.

A New Beginning by Veryl Goodnight outside the Cheyenne Depot

Other early feminist victories that took place in Wyoming included Esther Hobart Morris becoming the United States' first woman justice of the peace in the mining boomtown of South Pass City in 1870, Estelle Reed becoming one of the first women elected to state office as the superintendent of public education in 1894, and Nellie Taylor Ross becoming the first female governor in the country in 1924.

to the Trolley Plus Pass, which gets you free entry for each stop for only $7 more. On weekends, the daily tour includes free entrance to the Cheyenne Frontier Days Old West Museum.

Cowgirls of the West Museum

Celebrate the contributions of the Equality State's frontier women at the **Cowgirls of the West Museum** (205 W. 17th St., 307/638-4994, www.cowgirlsofthewestmuseum.com, 11am-4pm Tues.-Fri., 11am-3pm Sat., free). The main event here is a series of monthly summer luncheons ($20 pp) during which guests are regaled with remarkable stories of women's contributions to the history of the West. While the genre is broad, topics cover everything from pioneering women in aviation to early cowgirl participation in rodeos to the role of Native American women in frontier times. Luncheons are on the second

Monday of each month—call ahead to reserve.

In the museum, volunteers curate a small but informative selection of antique homesteading equipment, saddles, rodeo memorabilia, and more, all focused on the women of the Old West. One interesting exhibit tells the story of single homesteaders, another the tale of Sacagawea. There are also stories of rodeo queens: These crowned "royalty" from around the country are skilled and knowledgeable horse riders who serve a year-long tour as a rodeo queen, representing their region at public events and rodeos. A great documentary film introduces even more stories, and the museum store has fun memorabilia to take home.

Nelson Museum of the West

A huge number of items are on display in the 11,000-square-foot **Nelson Museum of the West** (1714 Carey Ave.,

307/635-7670, www.nelsonmuseum.com, 9am-4:30pm Mon.-Fri. May and Sept.-Oct., 9am-4:30pm Mon.-Sat., June-Aug., $5 adults, $4 seniors, free under age 13). This private collection offers a fascinating look at Western artifacts, including saddles, stirrups, beaded vests and moccasins, 19th-century firearms, taxidermy, military uniforms, and outlaw displays. Everything is well organized and explained for an engaging experience, and a variety of rotating exhibits add to the story.

Cheyenne Frontier Days Old West Museum

Cheyenne's biggest annual event by far is Frontier Days, which attracts crowds of up to 200,000 for rodeo and Wild West fun. If you can't visit during the festival, get a historical taste of it at the **Cheyenne Frontier Days Old West Museum** (4610 Carey Ave., 307/778-7290, www.cfdrodeo.com, 9am-5pm daily, extended hours during Frontier Days, $10 adults, $9 seniors and military, $5 ages 6-12, free under age 6). The museum traces the history of Frontier Days, the world's largest and one of the oldest rodeos—it started back in 1897. Stories of the rodeo are told through interactive displays in the museum. In addition to a plethora of Western artifacts, memorabilia, and artwork, it has a large collection of carriages, evoking a romantic era of transportation.

Trains

A few trains can be spotted around the city, including **Locomotive 1242,** the oldest in Wyoming, at the Cheyenne Botanic Gardens (Carey Ave. and Lions Park Dr.). The most impressive is the powerful **Big Boy Steam Engine** (Holliday Park, 17th St. and Morrie Ave.)—the world's biggest steam locomotive. This huge machine

Top to bottom: one of the *Cheyenne Big Boots* sculptures painted by local artists in Cheyenne Depot Plaza; Terry Bison Ranch; The Wrangler.

could pull 3,600 tons over the steep hills of Wyoming—it's an imposing sight.

Recreation
Terry Bison Ranch
Named after its first owner Charles Terry, who bought the ranch in 1881, the **Terry Bison Ranch** (51 I-25 Frontage Rd., 307/634-4171, www.terrybisonranch. com) was owned by F. E. Warren, the state's first governor, and was visited by President Theodore Roosevelt. More recently, the 27,500 acres have become a working bison ranch and a premier place to see the giant beasts roaming the land. It's not often you get to see a bison up close, so the ranch's **Bison Train Tours** (9am, noon, 2:30pm, and 4pm daily, $14 adults, $7 ages 4-12, free under age 4) offer a nice opportunity. The train was entirely built by hand and moves slowly along the track: The real experience is feeding the bison, with their long tongues, by hand. For a ride in the old-fashioned dining car and a meal, enjoy the **Sunday Lunch Train** (noon Sun. mid-May-Sept., $14 plus cost of meal); reservations are required.

The ranch offers other activities, including one-hour **guided horseback rides** ($48). The gentle horses are great for anyone, though riders must be age eight and older and able to mount without assistance. For the littler folks down to age two, they've got smaller pony rides ($10) and other cowpoke activities like roping practice. For a thrill, tour the spacious ranch on one of the daily **ATV tours** ($69-79). Or spend a relaxing afternoon **fishing** ($22 pp) in the ranch's pond, stocked with rainbow trout. No license is needed, and you get to keep what you catch. Bring your catch to the on-site Senator's Steakhouse restaurant to have them clean and cook it for you!

Cheyenne Botanic Gardens
Cheyenne Botanic Gardens (710 S. Lions Park Dr., 307/637-6458, www.botanic. org, 10am-5pm Tues.-Sat., noon-5pm Sun., grounds dawn-dusk Tues.-Sun., free) is a beautifully curated green space just 2 miles (3.2 km) north of downtown. With free admission, it's a perfect place to bring a picnic lunch or just wander for a few hours. Twenty different gardens showcase all manner of plants. Be sure to visit the three Rotary Plazas, which tell the stories of early Cheyenne residents through native plants of the 1700s to plants that settlers of the 1800s were familiar with. If you have kids, a must-visit is the Paul Smith Children's Village, a 0.75-acre site full of fun for all ages, with interactive water pumps, a colorful geodesic dome, a historic sheep wagon, and plenty of space to run wild.

Entertainment
Bars and Brewpubs
Built in 1905, **The Albany** (1506 Capitol Ave., 307/638-3507, www. albanycheyenne.com, bar 11am-late daily, liquor store 10am-10pm daily) was originally a hotel, but it has operated under its current family name since the early 1940s. Across the street from Cheyenne Depot Plaza, it's a great place to quench your thirst after a museum or a day downtown. On tap are 15 beers and stiff drinks, and the dining room serves burgers, steaks, and sandwiches until 9pm. Visit the liquor mart to find a drink to bring back to your hotel room; it offers chilled beer, an extensive domestic and imported wine selection, and plenty of spirits—many in smaller travel bottles.

Located in the Cheyenne Depot, **Accomplice Beer Company** (115 W. 15th St., 307/632-2337, www.accomplicebeer. com, 11am-10pm Sun.-Thurs., 11am-midnight Fri.-Sat.) is in the heart of the action. A wall of 14 self-serve taps and a charge-by-the-ounce concept allows patrons to create their own flights. Accomplice offers 10 of its own beers, 3 seasonal taps, and 4 guest taps. The food menu has solid sandwiches and pizzas, and snacks like pretzels or fried pickles. All meals come with a hearty kale salad

The American Bison

For centuries, bison herds roamed the West, 20-30 million strong. Indigenous people from the plains to the Rocky Mountains relied on their meat for food, bones for tools, and hides and furs for shelter and warmth. So important were bison to their daily lives that the animals were revered as sacred, an intrinsic part of indigenous spiritual and cultural traditions.

American bison

The first European emigrants were astounded at the bounty of bison as they passed through. One emigrant recorded waiting two hours for a stampede to pass by. Europeans called them "buffalo," thinking they were related to the water buffalo of South Asia and the Cape buffalo of Africa. In reality, the North American animals are not related to buffalo. Bison have thick wiry beards and smaller horns. The name stuck, however, and today bison are commonly known as "buffalo" throughout the West.

Upon coming upon a herd, emigrants on the trail would rush out to hunt them, and the whole wagon train would get swept up in excitement. While bison were relatively easy for emigrants to kill with guns, a dead bison was not very useful to them, and the enterprise overall was wasteful. Most didn't have the time, knowledge, or skills to properly skin and utilize the meat, which they found very tough anyway, and bison required many bullets to kill. Most emigrants simply cut out the tongue—which they ate as a delicacy—and left the rest, an offense to the indigenous people.

In the late 1800s, during the Indian Wars—the name given to various conflicts between the U.S. military and the Lakota Sioux, Cheyenne, Arapaho, and other indigenous groups—General William Tecumseh Sherman was sent west to command U.S. troops and help protect the railroad expansion. As the railroad stretched west, encountering thundering buffalo herds, some discovered a new sport: "hunting by rail." Hunters shot from railcar windows or from the roofs, leaving animals dead where they lay—thousands at a time in a matter of hours. While some raised concerns at the slaughter, General Sherman supported it, claiming the destruction of the buffalo would weaken the army's enemy nations and support the U.S. military's cause. By 1889, bison numbers were estimated to be under 1,000 in the entire country.

Nineteen federally recognized Native American tribes, including the Eastern Shoshone Tribe and Blackfeet Nation in Wyoming, came together in 1991 to create the InterTribal Buffalo Council to encourage the restoration of bison on Native American lands, and to preserve their cultural and spiritual heritage for future generations. Today the council includes over 60 tribes from 20 states, and manages a collective herd of more than 20,000 bison. They work closely with various nonprofits and government entities, including the National Bison Association, National Park Service, and U.S. Fish and Wildlife Service.

Across the nation, almost 400,000 bison are in Native American, public, and private herds. In 2016 Congress passed the National Bison Legacy Act, making the bison our national mammal, on par with the bald eagle. This doesn't offer any protections, but it helps elevate the importance of the creature to the past, present, and future people of the continent.

to offset all the beer. Outdoor seating offers a great view of the plaza.

A relaxed, family-friendly venue, **Freedom's Edge Brewing Co.** (1509 Pioneer Ave., 307/514-5314, www. freedomsedgebrewing.com, 3pm-10pm Mon.-Thurs., 3pm-11pm Fri., 1pm-11pm Sat., 1pm-7pm Sun.) features a rotating selection of brews just down the street from Depot Plaza in the heart of downtown. It flings its garage door open on nice days to let the sun in, and is a great place to spend the afternoon playing games or chatting with locals.

Live Music

Catch a live show at the **Outlaw Saloon** (312 S. Greeley Hwy., 307/635-7552, www. cheyenneoutlawsaloon.com, shows $10-20), which has bands seven nights a week, with plenty of big-name acts. It's a giant place, with three levels, a stage inside and outside, and a whopping five bars to order from.

Depot Plaza is the place to be for **Fridays on the Plaza** (1 Depot Square, www.cheyenneevents.org, 5:30pm-8:30pm Fri. June-Aug., free), a fun series of live music concerts held during summer. Each night sees different bands play on a big stage, alongside food vendors, beer, outdoor games like giant *Jenga,* and more. The opener starts at 5:30pm, with the headliner at 7pm. The best part? It's totally free.

Cheyenne Frontier Days

A wild trip to the West isn't complete without catching the action at **Cheyenne Frontier Days** (307/778-7222, www. cfrodeo.com, July). This festival and professional rodeo draws up to 200,000 people annually and is by far the biggest party Cheyenne throws every year, for 10 days near the end of July. All the action happens at Frontier Park (1230 W. 8th Ave.), about 2 miles (3.2 km) northwest of downtown, where admission is $5. Rodeos, carnival, and concerts are all ticketed separately ($17-55), but there are

a multitude of packages and daily deals that allow visitors to pick and choose. All rodeos begin at 1pm, but plan on getting there early for preshow fun from the rodeo clown at 12:15pm. Then it's a wild ride as you watch cowboys and cowgirls wrestle steers, rope calves, ride bulls, and racehorses.

Take the free hour-long Behind the Chutes Tour, offered a few times daily, to get a look at what happens on the other side of the rodeo arena. Afterward, head to the carnival midway for over 50 rides, activities, games, and—the best part— food stands. During Frontier Nights, Frontier Park's bandstand transforms into country music central, with top names like Rascal Flatts and Miranda Lambert. Every day there's something to explore, including pancake breakfasts, chuck wagon cook-offs, a cattle drive, opening day celebrations, a Frontier Village, and an Indian Village. Indigenous people have been invited to the rodeo to participate as performers since 1898 and, in recent years, members of the Wind River Reservation dance troupe have performed traditional dances from across North American cultures and history; visitors can enjoy these authentic dances along with costumes, storytelling, and handicrafts.

Food
Steak House
★ **Poor Richard's Restaurant** (2233 E. Lincolnway, 307/635-5114, www. poorrichardscheyenne.com, 11am-2:30pm and 5pm-close Mon.-Sat., $16) has been serving great food for over 40 years. This romantic restaurant balances old-school sophistication with casual ambience, perfect for everything from a first date to a 50th wedding anniversary. The name is a nod to the almanac published by Benjamin Franklin, whose quotes adorn the walls. The restaurant has won awards for serving the best bison steak in Wyoming, and the menu also features top cuts of prime rib and

The World's Largest Outdoor Rodeo

Cowboys have been bucking and roping at Cheyenne's Frontier Days for a long time. It started back in 1897 as a chance for cowboys and cowgirls to show off their roping and riding skills. The first Frontier Day included pony races, bronco busting, and steer roping. The next year, a parade and an extra day were added. From there, the event grew into an annual 10-day happening that attracts hundreds of thousands to the biggest rodeo in the West. Harking back to the past, each year kicks off with a cattle drive that runs over 500 cattle through the streets of the city, a unique sight in modern times.

at Cheyenne Frontier Days

In the rodeo, professional cowboys and cowgirls come to compete for more than $1 million in prizes. The three types of events are rough stock events, like bareback or bull riding, where a rider must stay on a bucking animal for eight seconds using only one hand; timed events, like barrel racing, steer wrestling, and tie-down roping; and the favorite Wild Horse Race, an all-out race around the track.

sirloin steak, along with chicken, pasta, and seafood.

Get a bison steak or award-winning bison short ribs right on a working bison ranch! **Senator's Steakhouse at Terry Bison Ranch** (51 I-25 Frontage Rd., 307/634-4171, www.terrybisonranch. com, 11am-9pm daily, $15) has a large menu of steaks, burgers, pastas, and appetizers. Every weekend in summer, there's a prime rib buffet.

Burgers
With a location downtown just blocks away from Depot Plaza, **2 Doors Down** (118 E. 17th St., 307/634-6008, www.2doorsdown.net, 11am-9pm Mon.-Sat., $12) is easy to find and easy to enjoy. A casual café, it serves a large variety of unique burgers like teriyaki, tuna, or Italian, alongside the classics, all with bottomless fries and the option to add a frosty milk shake.

Pizza
Bella Fuoco Wood Fired Pizza (2115 Warren Ave., 307/514-2855, http:// bellafuocopizza.com, 11am-2pm and 5pm-9pm Tues.-Fri., 5pm-9pm Sat., $11) began with a wood-fired oven inside a roaming food truck and today is a friendly and delicious neighborhood joint. Its oven still fires the pizza perfectly, creating a crisp crust, and the pizzas come with a variety of toppings. For a kick, try the jalapeño popper pizza with cream cheese, jalapeños, and a sweet chili sauce, or the lasagna pizza with sausage and ricotta. The menu also includes paninis, salads, soups, and even an appetizer of duck wings.

Thai
The exterior of **Anong's Thai Cuisine** (620 Central Ave., 307/638-8597, www. anong-thai.com, 11am-3pm and 5pm-9pm Mon.-Sat., 11am-3pm and 5pm-8pm Sun., $10) might not look like much, but inside the walls are adorned with Thai artwork, and the menu is full of delights that include perfectly spiced curry, noodles, and rice dishes. Try the *larb* (a meat

or tofu salad finished with fresh lime juice and green onion) and *rad nha* (rice noodles and veggies in a creamy gravy sauce).

Breakfast and Lunch
Hidden beneath a motel sign, you might miss the classic ★ **Luxury Diner** (1401 W. Lincolnway, 307/638-8971, www. luxurydiner.com, 6am-2pm Mon.-Thurs., 6am-3pm Fri.-Sun., $10), but that would be a shame. It's a classic hole-in-the-wall with a dash of the West thrown in. Half of the small restaurant is in an actual trolley car that clanged down the streets of Cheyenne 1894-1912, and the other half is stuffed with small tables and a bar, creating a very cozy dining room. Breakfast is the main attraction—omelets, french toast, and breakfast burritos—though the eatery also offers a range of burgers and sandwiches for lunch.

Farmers Markets
The **Cheyenne Farmer's Market** (Depot Plaza, Lincolnway and Capitol Ave., 307/635-9291, www.calc.net, 7am-1pm Sat. Aug.-Oct.) runs later in the summer and into fall to better take advantage of Cheyenne's warmest season. Stroll through the market to get a taste of local goodies, including fresh fruits and veggies, honey, bread, and pastries. It's especially hard to resist the roasted chilies or tamales—why even try? Find free parking in the Jack Spiker parking garage on the corner of Lincolnway and Pioneer Avenue.

Shopping
One of the granddaddies of Western wear stores is **The Wrangler** (1518 Capitol Ave., 307/634-3048, www.bootbarn.com, 9am-8pm Mon.-Sat., 10am-6pm Sun.), in a building right off Depot Plaza, crowned by a giant unmissable sign. Inside are thousands of options to outfit your rodeo or Wild West adventures—visit the hat room for Stetsons, the jean racks for Levi's, or the boot room for every color

and style of cowboy and cowgirl boot you can imagine.

True to its name, **Wyoming Home** (216 W. Lincolnway, 307/638-2222, 9am-6pm Mon.-Fri., 9am-5pm Sat., noon-5pm Sun. Memorial Day-Labor Day, 10am-6pm Mon.-Fri., 10am-5pm Sat. Labor Day-Memorial Day) offers a bit of Wyoming to bring home. Find beautiful intricate rugs, bronze statues, and wonderfully moody paintings. The shop also has a selection of gorgeous jewelry studded with turquoise, red coral, and silver, some featuring beaded patterns.

Accommodations
Under $150
Built in 1911, ★ **The Historic Plains Hotel** (1600 Central Ave., 307/638-3311, www.theplainshotel.com, $100-160) has turn-of-the-20th-century charm that has been lovingly restored. Start your visit in the grand lobby, featuring a beautiful stained-glass ceiling and tiled floors. Head up in the tiny elevator (small in size to discourage cowboys from bringing up their horses) and exit into hallways decked with tasteful Western decor. The 131 rooms and suites have antique fixtures and soft beds. The on-site restaurant and lounge serves breakfast (included), lunch, dinner, and cocktails in wooden booths with leather accents. The hotel is located in downtown Cheyenne, a block from Depot Plaza.

$150-250
Part of a small regional chain of grand hotels, the **Little America Hotel & Resort** (2800 W. Lincolnway, 307/775-8400, http://cheyenne.littleamerica.com, $140-239) is 3.5 miles (5.6 km) southwest of downtown. The hotel is a popular event center and has 188 large rooms, with 47-inch flat-screen TVs and sitting areas. The grounds of the resort include a nine-hole seasonal golf course and a driving range, with a clubhouse that rents clubs and carts. Horseshoes, cornhole, volleyball, and an outdoor swimming pool keep

families busy, and the on-site restaurant is an easy way to end the day.

Over $250

For luxury and elegance blocks from Depot Plaza, stay at the **Nagle Warren Mansion Bed & Breakfast** (222 E. 17th St., 307/637-3333, http://naglewarrenmansion.com, $230-290). Built in 1886 by the wealthy businessman Erasmus Nagle, the mansion was sold in 1910 to F. E. Warren, Wyoming's first governor and longtime U.S. senator. The opulent mansion has turn-of-the-20th-century decor and furniture, including a grand piano in the sitting room. The 12 lovely rooms also have modern amenities, including a television, Wi-Fi, and air-conditioning for those hot summer nights. Each room is named for historical members of the Nagle and Warren families (except the Teddy Roosevelt room), and are spread out across the mansion and adjoining carriage house. Shared spaces include a dining room, a garden hot tub, a library, and a modern exercise room.

Camping

The **Terry Bison Ranch Resort** (51 I-25 Frontage Rd., 307/634-4171, www.terrybisonranch.com) is 11 miles (18 km) south of Cheyenne along I-25 and open year-round. The resort and working bison ranch have plenty of activities to keep families busy, and it's a great place to camp. For an RV or trailer, the ranch has 86 full-hookup pull-through spaces ($30-60). Or stake your claim on a grassy tent site ($23). There are also seven one-room cabins that sleep four ($115). Large crowds can descend on the ranch in summer, so reserving ahead of time is a good idea. Note that prices easily double during Cheyenne's Frontier Days in late July.

Closer to town, **A. B. Camping** (1503 W. College Dr., 307/634-7035, www.campcheyenne.com, Apr.-Oct.) is 3 miles (4.8 km) south of downtown. With 82 full-hookup sites ($30-46) under a canopy of trees, it's a pleasant place to stay. Tent sites ($23) are also available. You'll be tempted to stay in for the night at the on-site restaurant, AB BBQ, serving hot ribs, sides, and pies nightly.

Information and Services

The **Southeast Wyoming Welcome Center** (5611 High Plains Rd., 800/225-5996, www.travelwyoming.com, 7am-6pm daily), about 7 miles (11.3 km) south of Cheyenne on I-25, offers more than pamphlets and restrooms; it's a full information center with the state's travel bureau in-house. The beautiful space has museum-quality exhibits that make a fun stop for kids. Marvel at the giant mammoth, send your kids to jail (there's a slide to escape), and discover some of the state's adventures in the great outdoors. You can stock up on maps, which is strongly recommended, as many stretches of the state aren't covered by cell phone service.

◆ Side Trip: Glendo State Park

Less than a 15-minute drive off the route, just 4.5 miles (7.2 km) off I-25 on the way to Douglas, **Glendo State Park** (park headquarters 397 Glendo Park Rd., Glendo, 307/735-4433, http://wyoparks.wyo.gov, 7:30am-5pm daily Memorial Day-Labor Day, 7:30am-4pm daily Labor Day-Memorial Day, day-use Wyoming residents $6 per vehicle, nonresidents $9 per vehicle) surrounds the Glendo Reservoir and offers camping, hiking, and water access for boating, fishing, and swimming.

Getting There

From the **U.S. 26/I-25 junction,** 16 miles (26 km) west of Guernsey, head north on I-25 for 19 miles (31 km), take exit 111 for Glendo, and follow signs to the park, turning—in quick succession—right on A Street, right again on Highway 319, left on C Street, and then right onto South Lincoln Avenue, which becomes Glendo Park Road, following it 4.4 miles (7.1 km) east.

Recreation

Rent a boat in the state park at **Rooch's Marina** (383 Glendo State Park Rd., 307/735-4216, www.roochsmarina.com, 8am-9pm daily). It offers pontoons and fishing boats ($175 half-day, $350 full-day), kayaks and paddleboards ($15 per hour, $40 half-day, $75 full-day), and inner tubes (single $35 per day, double $75 per day). Stock up on ice, snacks, fishing tackle, and firewood at the general store. An on-site café offers delicious down-home breakfast, lunch, and dinner ($9-20).

There's also an **archery range** (free), open year-round, with bows available to borrow at no extra charge from the park headquarters. During summer, the course becomes 3-D, with moving targets like dinosaurs and wolverines.

Camping

There are over 20 **campgrounds** around the park with 500 spots for tents and RVs. On top of the entrance fee, expect to pay the overnight fee (Wyoming residents $10 per vehicle, nonresidents $17 per vehicle). RV sites with electricity are an extra $10 per night. Find more info at the park headquarters.

Douglas

After leaving Fort Laramie, the trail was less clear for the wagon trains. Some continued cleaving close to the North Platte River on its south bank, winding around the curves as best they could in a route that roughly follows today's I-25. They were headed to the North Fork of the North Platte near present-day Casper. Others took a more direct route due west from Fort Laramie, finding freshwater from tributary streams and passing

nearer Ayres Natural Bridge. The journey was rocky, and there was no sign of settlement anywhere until the army built Fort Fetterman, late in 1867, near the end of the trail's popularity. Early emigrants had to rely on their own resources and guides to make it through the area near what is now Douglas.

Douglas grew into a city when the Wyoming Central Railway came through town in 1886, connecting Chadron, Nebraska, to Casper. It's still a railroad town today, with a depot, now a railroad museum, at the center. The town's other claim to fame is as the origin point of the mythical jackalope.

Getting There

If you're following the route straight from **eastern Wyoming,** head north 46 miles (90 km) to Douglas on I-25 from the U.S. 26/I-25 junction 16 miles (26 km) west of Guernsey. If you took a side trip to **Cheyenne,** drive north on I-25 for 124 miles (200 km). Take exit 135 for I-25 Business, turning left to remain on it for 2.4 miles (3.9 km) before turning right onto South 4th Street. The center of town, near Jackalope Square, is in 0.8 mile (1.3 km). The drive from Guernsey takes about an hour, and the drive from Cheyenne takes just under two hours.

Sights
Jackalope Square

Find the eight-foot-tall statue of Douglas's favorite beast in **Jackalope Square** (100 S. 3rd Ave., 307/358-3462, 5am-11pm daily, free). In addition to the statue, the square has a gazebo and hosts plenty of town events throughout the summer, like the popular Jackalope Days in early June each year.

Douglas Railroad Interpretive Museum & Visitor Center

Douglas Railroad Interpretive Museum & Visitor Center (121 Brownfield Rd., 307/358-2950, 9am-8pm Mon.-Fri.,

Douglas, Home of the Mythical Jackalope

The Douglas tourism board states that the first jackalope sighting in Wyoming was in 1834 by Roy Ball, "an occasionally sober trapper." Many stories are told about jackalopes—their voices are a beautiful tenor, often heard singing along to cowboy's campfire songs; their milk is tasty, but notoriously hard to come by; their favorite drink is whiskey; they tend to mate only during lightning flashes. Wagons trains were often attacked by its more vicious cousin—the saber-tooth jackalope, with foot-long fangs.

Jackalope Square

In fact, the jackalope—essentially a jackrabbit with antler horns—is Wyoming's favorite mythical creature. It was created in 1934 by hunters and taxidermist brothers Douglas and Ralph Herrick. By the 1970s Ralph Herrick was churning out 400 mounted jackalopes a year (after creating the creature, his brother Douglas decided against pursuing the jackalope trade). Douglas died in 2003 and Ralph in 2013, but other taxidermists took up the cause; the beasts still adorn hotels and restaurants across the West.

Home of the jackalope, Douglas boasts a statue of the horned rabbit in Jackalope Square and another one near the Douglas Railroad Interpretive Museum & Visitor Center. Souvenirs and jackalope-themed logos are all over town. You can also get a bona fide hunting license for the jackalope from the visitors center; it states that holders have the right to take home one jackalope between sunrise and sunset on one day only: June 31.

10am-5pm Sat.-Sun., free) is the lively center of town and town history. Once serving the Wyoming Central Railway, today you can explore trains and railcars surrounding the little red depot, like a steam locomotive, a dining car, a sleeping car, and a caboose, many of which you can enter to explore. Inside the depot, built in 1886, are historical displays and railroad artifacts, along with mounted jackalopes. Memorabilia like women's hats, trunks, and tickets bring the railroad era to life, along with the volunteers' tireless willingness to answer questions.

The museum doubles as a visitors center and chamber of commerce; get your souvenir jackalope hunting license here. Outside the museum is a jackalope statue.

Wyoming Pioneer Memorial Museum

There's a lot to see at the **Wyoming Pioneer Memorial Museum** (400 W. Center St., 307/358-9288, 8am-5pm Mon.-Sat. Memorial Day-Labor Day, 8am-4pm Tues.-Sat. Sept.-mid-Nov., 8am-4pm Fri.-Sat. mid-Nov.-Mar., free). While you can breeze through, you could also as easily spend a couple of hours enjoying the artifact displays, which range from the Oregon Trail era up to World War II. Artifacts include emigrant wagons, plenty of guns and early weapons, dolls, tools used for homesteading, a wooden wheelchair, and most famously, a tepee from the movie *Dances with Wolves*. The scope of the collection makes it hard to dig into any one era, but the sheer volume is impressive, and friendly staff is happy to help with questions.

Fort Fetterman

Fort Fetterman State Historic Site (752 Hwy. 93, www.wyostateparks.state. wy.us, 9am-5pm Tues.-Sat. Memorial Day-Labor Day, $3 adults, free under age 18) is the site of an early wooden fort, built in 1867, that served as a base for several campaigns against the Sioux and Cheyenne peoples in the 1870s, during the Sioux Wars. Tensions were high as the Sioux attempted to protect their territory named in the 1868 Treaty of Fort Laramie from emigrants, settlers, and gold-rushers. Over the years, each side broke the treaty at various time, sparking years of warfare; the U.S. military eventually succeeded in pushing the Sioux onto reservations in the late 1870s

The military abandoned Fort Fetterman in 1882, and it fell into disrepair as nearby Douglas grew. Not much is left today: the restored officers' quarters, which now houses a museum with historical displays and a handful of artifacts, and the ordnance warehouse, which once stored weapons. Ask questions of the helpful staff, and they'll gladly paint a picture describing what life was like in the early days of the fort, often featuring drudgery and hardship: a snowy, windy plain with only a canvas tent to protect the soldiers, no fresh produce from the failed gardens, and a posting that caused many to desert.

Today, especially in the summer, this is a nice spot for a picnic and a break from the car. You can take pleasant walks on the grounds, and there's a gazebo near the river. A cemetery of mostly civilian settlers' graves from the late 1800s is about a 1-mile (1.6-km) walk from the museum along a signposted route.

From downtown Douglas, drive west on Center Street over the train tracks and across the North Platte River. In 1.4 miles (2.2 km), turn right onto Highway 59, then make a quick left onto Highway 93.

In 7.7 miles (12.4 km), turn right for the site. Watch closely for the signs—they're easy to miss. The drive takes about 15 minutes.

Ayres Natural Bridge

> "Rode off in advance of the camp to visit a remarkable mountain gorge... a natural bridge of solid rock over a rapid torrent... wild cliffs, 300 feet perpendicular beetled above us, and the noisey current swept along among huge fragments of rock at our feet."
>
> Matthew C. Field, July 13, 1843, *Prairie and Mountain Sketches.* Field was a reporter for the New Orleans *Picayune,* traveling with an expedition of the British army officer and adventurer Sir William Drummond Stewart to the Rocky Mountains.

While some wagon trains closely followed the south bank of the North Platte River, others cut a more direct westward

route across the land, aiming for present-day Casper. They had to navigate tougher terrain, including steep ravines, but this route saved a few days of travel along the wider but meandering Platte River route. A couple of miles downstream of this route is **Ayres Natural Bridge** (208 Natural Bridge Rd., 307/358-3532, 8am-8pm daily Apr. 15-Oct. 15, free). The limestone bridge arches over pretty La Prele Creek, named for the French word for the horsetail plants that grow along its banks. Emigrants on the more direct route found water in tributary streams such as this one. This natural bridge was once a fascinating tourist attraction to emigrants, who would've gone out of their way to see it.

The road to Ayres today is a beautiful drive through red-walled canyons and sagebrush, but for the emigrants, it was likely a tough 2 miles (3.2 km), involving scrabbling down the canyon wall. Plenty still stopped to marvel at the natural wonder, and those who did were duly impressed. Modern travelers can also enjoy gazing at the bridge at what's now a beautiful public park, with hiking paths, water to splash in, and space to enjoy a picnic lunch. If you have a tent or small RV, there's a handful of basic **campsites** at the park at no charge.

To get here, head 11 miles (18 km) west of Douglas on I-25, take exit 151, and drive 5 miles (8 km) south down Natural Bridge Road. The drive takes just over 20 minutes.

Festivals and Events

An annual four-day event on the first weekend in June, **Jackalope Days** (307/358-2950, www. seewhatconversecando.com, early June, free, some events by admission) has been going strong for over 50 years. Most of the fun is centered around Jackalope Square, where visitors can enjoy vendors, chalk art competitions, a street dance with live entertainment, and a brew-fest ($15 pp). The fun continues at the

Ayres Natural Bridge

Douglas Railroad Interpretive Museum & Visitor Center, with a free hot dog lunch, free mini train rides, and a steak dinner ($25 pp).

Food

Douglas isn't a city with a lot of restaurant options, but a great choice if you're hungry is the **Depot Restaurant** (100 E. Walnut St., 307/358-9999, 11am-9pm Mon.-Thurs., 11am-10pm Fri.-Sat., $15), inside the early 1900s train depot. It serves steak, burgers, pastas, flatbread, and Rocky Mountain oysters. It's a casual, family-friendly place with a few outdoor tables and good service.

Glenrock

Glenrock began as a trading post, Deer Creek Station, along the Oregon Trail route in 1857. The nearby Rock in the Glen, where pioneers carved their names, was a popular camping spot for emigrants. Deer Creek Station later served as a stop along the Pony Express in 1860-1861, and was soon connected to the telegraph system that expanded coast to coast. Today, Glenrock is a small town of under 3,000 people on the pretty North Platte River. With historic buildings and a trace of the Oregon Trail, it's a pleasant stop to see some history or dig deeper into the past on fossil tours.

Getting There

From Douglas, head 27 miles (43 km) west via I-25 and take exit 160 for Glenrock. The drive takes 30 minutes.

Sights
Oregon Trail Park Ruts and Playground

Glenrock has some ruts right in the middle of town at the tiny **Oregon Trail Park** (E. Oregon Trail and Pioneer Pl.). On the west side of the triangular park you can see shallow ruts running past an interpretive marker, in ground that has been preserved in its natural state—no development mars the sagebrush or topsoil around the ruts. It's not the biggest stretch of ruts by any means, but it's notable to see them in the middle of a neighborhood. On the east side of the park is a playground, complete with a covered-wagon play structure.

Paleon Museum

Wyoming is one of the best places in the world to see dinosaur fossils and is renowned for discoveries of prehistoric artifacts such as stegosauruses, *Tyrannosaurus rex,* mammoths, and more. The state has multiple dig sites, and dinosaur discoveries made here have found homes in major museums. Play paleontologist for a day at the **Paleon Museum** (506 W. Birch St., 307/436-2667 www.dinosaurswyoming.com, 10am-5pm Wed.-Sat., June-Aug., 11am-4pm Thurs.-Sat. Sept.-May, $5 adults, free under age 13). Every visit comes with a tour by the Bone Biddies—knowledgeable volunteers who clean and prep fossils for display—and the museum showcases cool fossils, many of which were found nearby, like Stephanie the Triceratops, discovered on a ranch near Glenrock two decades ago; the triceratops is also Wyoming's State Dinosaur. The museum also creates casts of its own fossils in-house, which are for sale in its gift shop.

For a more in-depth paleontological exploration, join the staff for a dig out in the Wyoming countryside. You can head out for a day ($140), two days ($300), or a week ($750). You'll see working paleontologists dig, learn their techniques, and get a hands-on look at history. It's a great activity for kids in grade school. Book ahead online or by phone.

Deer Creek Museum

A visit to **Deer Creek Museum** (935 W. Birch St., 307/436-2810, 10am-4pm Tues.-Sat. Memorial Day-Labor Day, free) is a deep dive into local history, complete with old maps and stories of local

Glenrock to Casper

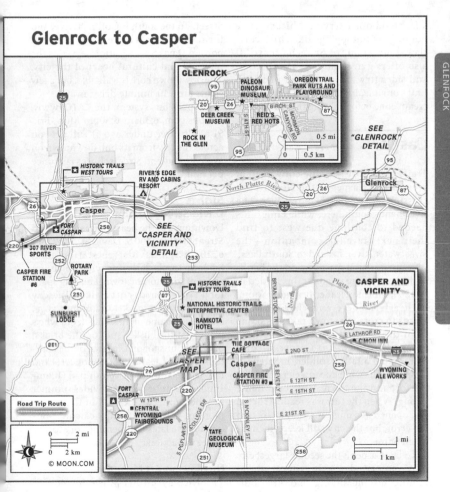

events. Glenrock saw plenty of Oregon, California, and Mormon Trail emigrant traffic, then later the Pony Express, and later still the first telegraph wires. Exhibits at this small museum also showcase artifacts of life from the early 1800s, including arrowheads, spears, rifles, an early laundry machine, and an old-fashioned dentist chair.

Rock in the Glen

Pioneers headed west tended to scribble their names on anything they could find along their path, and the **Rock in the Glen**

is no exception. The large rock just west of town has a few emigrant signatures on its south side. You can walk around the rock, which later contributed its name to the town, to see the signatures. Find the highway pullout about 500 feet (150 m) west of the Deer Creek Museum on U.S. 20/26. From here, a short trail leads to the rock.

Food

If you're hungry for lunch or dinner, grab a bite at **Reid's Red Hots** (206 S. 4th St., 307/436-7120, 11am-8pm Mon.-Sat., $7), a fast-food diner serving Chicago-style hot dogs with toppings like chili, coleslaw, sauerkraut, or Sriracha mayo. It also offers gyros, burgers, sandwiches, and sides (try the spicy fried pickles!). End your meal with a hand-dipped ice cream cone before hitting the trail again.

Casper

Trails from Fort Laramie converged at present-day Casper at the North Fork crossing of the North Platte River. The river bends south here, while emigrants needed to continue due west to find their next traveling companion—the Sweetwater River, headed to South Pass.

A campground sprang up on the banks of the river where wagon trains forded it. In 1849, Mormon leader Brigham Young built a ferry here and charged emigrants to cross. The town takes its name from the fort, but notice the spelling: Originally named Fort Casper, it commemorated a fallen solider, Lieutenant Caspar Collins, but due to a clerical error, the fort and the town spelled his name wrong. When the fort was reconstructed and opened as a museum, they corrected the error, but the city still keeps its mistaken name.

Today, Casper is the second-largest city in Wyoming and relies heavily on oil and mining. Fishing, hiking, and other outdoor pursuits are popular, with the North Platte River and nearby Casper Mountain prominent playgrounds. Downtown has a lively, still developing core with a public events space, shops, and restaurants.

Getting There and Around

From Glenrock, head 24 miles (39 km) west on U.S. 26. I-25 cuts right through town. Most of the area's hotels and gas stations are in the east, near neighboring Evansville.

Downtown is bordered by the North Platte River to the west, stretching roughly a mile (1.6 km) east to Kimball Street. To the south is Collins Drive, and the railroad tracks serve as the northern border. Davis Street Station serves as the physical and cultural heart of the city. The downtown core is walkable, but a few sights are a 10-minute drive away.

Casper's bus system, the **CATC** (www. catcbus.com, 6:30am-6:30pm Mon.-Fri., $1 adults, free under age 6) will get you across the city from its hub downtown on Wolcott and 2nd Streets. Buses run once per hour.

Sights
David Street Station

Downtown, at the heart of Casper, **David Street Station** (200 S. David St., 307/235-6710, http://davidstreetstation.com, 8:30am-10pm daily) provides a living room of sorts for the town, creating space for a First Thursday art walk, a Tuesday evening farmers market in summer, yoga, and family game nights. Check out who's playing at the busker spot on the bricks, or grab your spot on the lawn of the community stage, featuring free concerts and movies in summer. A splash pad (10am-10pm daily June-Sept.) provides summer fun, becoming an ice rink in the winter months. Check the events calendar online for the latest happenings, or stop by to see the action.

Nicolayson Art Museum

The **Nicolayson Art Museum** (400 E. Collins St., 307/235-5247, www.thenic. org, 10am-5pm Wed.-Sat., noon-4pm Sun., $5), nicknamed "the NIC," features art from the Rockies and High Plains. A busy event calendar keeps the community involved, and kids will have a blast at the Discovery Center, a hands-on art activity area allowing them to experiment with finger paint, crayon rubbings, blocks, magnets, and more. More mature guests can enjoy permanent works by Matisse and Picasso, along with contemporary art in the rotating galleries. It's a small space that's worth a short stop. Admission is free on Sunday.

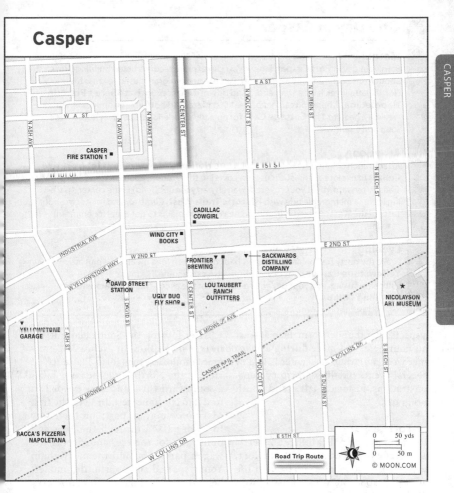

Casper

Map labels:
- E A ST
- W A ST
- N ASH AVE
- N DAVID ST
- N MARKET ST
- N CENTER ST
- N WOLCOTT ST
- N DURBIN ST
- CASPER FIRE STATION 1
- E 1ST ST
- W 1ST ST
- N BEECH ST
- CADILLAC COWGIRL
- WIND CITY BOOKS
- INDUSTRIAL AVE
- W 2ND ST
- E 2ND ST
- W YELLOWSTONE HWY
- FRONTIER BREWING
- BACKWARDS DISTILLING COMPANY
- DAVID STREET STATION
- S CENTER ST
- LOU TAUBERT RANCH OUTFITTERS
- NICOLAYSEN ART MUSEUM
- UGLY BUG FLY SHOP
- S DAVID ST
- YELLOWSTONE GARAGE
- E MIDWEST AVE
- E ASH ST
- CASPER RAIL TRAIL
- S WOLCOTT ST
- E COLLINS DR
- S BEECH ST
- S DURBIN ST
- W MIDWEST AVE
- RACCA'S PIZZERIA NAPOLETANA
- E 5TH ST
- W COLLINS DR
- Road Trip Route
- 0 50 yds
- 0 50 m
- © MOON.COM

National Historic Trails Interpretive Center

Try pulling a handcart like Mormon pioneers used or fording a virtual river in your wagon at the **National Historic Trails Interpretive Center** (1502 N. Poplar St., 307/261-7700, http://nhtcf.org, 8am-5pm Tues.-Sun., free), just north of downtown on a hilltop overlooking Casper. The museum focuses on the historic trails that once passed through Casper—the Oregon Trail as well as the California Trail, the Mormon Trail, the Pony Express, and the Wyoming Central Railway. A 15-minute presentation in the amphitheater kicks off the experience. Exhibits are modern, well designed, and interactive. The Bureau of Land Management (BLM) runs this site, and rangers are on hand to answer your questions and offer maps of the area.

From the parking lot, you can also follow interpretive panels about the Oregon, California, and Mormon Trails to a beautiful viewpoint of the city and mountains beyond, as well as a covered wagon and small cabin. Watch the clouds—if you're lucky, you might have a front-row seat to

One Day in Casper

Morning

Start your day at **Fort Caspar,** where you can explore reconstructed buildings, learn about frontier life, and see a replica ferry of the one emigrants used to cross the North Platte River. If it's a weekend, head downtown for brunch at **Racca's Pizzeria Napoletana,** where you can get a breakfast pizza (and bottomless mimosas!). If it's a weekday, head to **The Cottage Café** for an early and delicious lunch of homemade soup and a sandwich.

Afternoon

After brunch or lunch, head up the hill to the **National Historic Trails Interpretive Center** to explore a fantastic museum covering the Oregon, California, and Mormon Trails. Afterward, meet your covered-wagon party (book ahead) in the center's parking lot for a memorable ride with **Historic Trails West.** Climb aboard for its two-hour Taste of the West tour and ride across the Wyoming plains to get a feel for emigrant road life.

Evening

Leave the dusty trail behind and head back downtown for a meal and a pint at **Yellowstone Garage,** where you might also catch some live music. If you're still going strong, end your day with a cocktail at the circus-themed **Backwards Distilling Company.**

a spectacular thunderstorm. Plan at least an hour here, and more during a summer weekend, when the center is full of special events like living-history demonstrations, historical talks, and youth programs.

★ Fort Caspar

With a museum, replica bridge and ferry, and reconstructed emigrant-era fort, you can get a good look into frontier life at **Fort Caspar** (4001 Fort Caspar Rd., 307/235-8462, www.fortcasparwyoming. com, buildings 8am-4:30pm daily, museum 8am-5pm daily May-Sept., museum 8am-5pm Tues.-Sat. Oct.-Apr., $4 adults, $3 seniors and ages 13-18, free under age 13). The reconstructed fort is laid out just like the original, which was established as the Platte Bridge Station in 1862. Built as a U.S. Army post, the original station was meant to safeguard the new telegraph line. Today it consists of a dozen wooden buildings with period artifacts and decor. You can peek inside the officers' quarters, the mess hall, the store, and the laundry room.

After fording the South Platte River near Ash Hollow in Nebraska, emigrants followed the North Platte River. Here at the North Fork, the river takes a southward turn, and they needed to ford it to continue west. In 1847, the first Mormon emigrant party on their way to Utah passed through the area and built rafts for the crossing. Seeing the wagon parties behind them, Brigham Young spotted an opportunity, and left behind some volunteers to run a ferry and charge non-Mormon emigrants up to $3 to cross; they operated it for a few years until 1850, when rival ferries and alternate crossings put them out of business. In 1859, trader Louis Guinard built a trading post on the site and replaced the old ferry system with a bridge that wagons could cross much more quickly. A **replica of Guinard's bridge** can be found at the fort today and, next to it, a **replica of the Mormon-run ferry** has a wagon lashed to it.

Also on the grounds is the **Fort Caspar Museum,** a small but thoughtful gallery of exhibits on local history beginning with the prehistoric and running through the present day, including a portion on the experience of ferrying the river in a pioneer wagon. If you've got kids, ask for an activity book at the museum's front desk—children earn a certificate if they finish the scavenger hunt. There's also a playground near the parking lot.

Tate Geological Museum

You are welcomed by a huge *Tyrannosaurus rex* skeleton outside the **Tate Geological Museum** (125 College Dr., 307/268-2447, www.caspercollege. edu, 9am-5pm Mon.-Fri., 10am-4pm Sat. and holidays, free). Part of Casper College, this small museum packs a big punch—it's bursting with fossils, skeletons, minerals, and gemstones, many from Wyoming. Take a selfie with 11,600-year-old Dee the Mammoth, put your foot in a dinosaur footprint, watch staff prep fossils in the lab, and see prehistoric wonders of the land and sea. Kids will have a great time, with loads of things to touch and play with. Staff can answer any paleontological question, like which dinosaur was the scariest, or what did mammoths eat, anyway?

Recreation

TOP EXPERIENCE

★ Historic Trails West Tours

Stepping into a wagon and bumping along a hill in the Wyoming wild will drive home the experience of the Oregon Trail like nothing else. Try it with **Historic Trails West** (307/266-4868, www.historictrailswest.com). Owner Morris Carter has actually taken a wagon on a six-month journey along the Oregon Trail, and has a keen understanding of the struggles of the emigrants and their place in the world. He or a colleague guides the trips, and you'll hear a wealth

Top to bottom: David Street Station; Fort Caspar; Tate Geological Museum.

of historical stories as you ride in a large canvas-covered wagon pulled by horses; with a capacity of about 20, the wagons are a bit larger than what a pioneer would have taken on the trail.

Tour options include a 2-hour Taste of the West ($65), a 3-4-hour lunch or Dutch oven dinner tour ($115-125), and a full-day tour ($165) that brings you to a few grave sites and landmarks on the trail. There are also multiday tours ($1,095-1,495); these longer overnight treks head out from Casper and visit locations along the trail. On the way, travelers ford rivers in wagons, ride horses, and learn camp skills, including Dutch oven cooking, similar to how the pioneers would have cooked along the trail.

Book online or by phone, and meet your wagon party at the parking lot of the National Historic Trails Interpretive Center. From there, you follow in your car to the trailhead for your excursion, about 10 minutes away.

Floating and Paddling

On a hot summer day, join the locals and cool off with a float along the North Platte River. A great trip starts at **Morad Park** (2800 SW Wyoming Blvd.) in the southwest of town, and floats about 4 miles (6.4 km) to an easy pullout at the **Platte River Whitewater Park** (1007 W. 1st St.), 1.4 miles (2.2 km) west of downtown. If you have your own tube, you can get right in—but be safe and wear a life jacket. If you need one, borrow it from the **Casper Fire Department** (Fire Station 1, 200 W. 1st St.; Fire Station 3, 1240 E. 12th St.; Fire Station 6, 185 Valley Dr.)—every fire station has them stocked and will let you borrow one for free. For rentals, shuttle services, and more, contact **307 River Sports** (5625 Cy Ave., 307/267-0170, http://307riversports.com, 8am-5pm daily). The outfitter will get you out on the river for a lazy float with a personal tube ($18 per day). It also rents canoes ($50 per day), kayaks ($45 per day), stand-up paddleboards ($45 half-day, $70

full-day), and rafts ($100 per day), and offers rafting tours lasting 1-3 hours ($40-60) out on the rapids.

Fishing

The North Platte River is one of the best in the world for fly-fishing. Unless you're an experienced angler, a great way to get on the water is with a guide. **Crazy Rainbow Fly Fishing** (307/266-0701, http://crazyrainbow.net) offers half- or full-day trips ($395-525 per boat for 2 guests) to the company's private river access site, where you might be the only ones out on the water. You can opt for an instructional tour, or just get fishing for those trophy-size trout. Each trip includes lunch, drinks for the day, and all fishing tackle—just bring appropriate clothes, a fishing license, and a tip for the guide. Overnight trips with private cabin accommodations are also available at $250 per night for up to five people, or book the whole eight-person lodge for $600 per night.

Hiking

Casper's epic playground, **Casper Mountain,** is just south of town. Head here for a day of hiking, picnicking, or waterfall hunting. The best place to start is the beautiful **Rotary Park.** It has trail options as well as grills and fire pits for post-hike celebrations. One of these is the **Garden Creek Waterfall trail.** Part of the larger 5-mile (8-km) **Bridle Trail**—which rises over 1,200 feet (360 m) and can be challenging—this shorter 1.3-mile (2-km) loop option is spectacular, and takes you to a waterfall, with several platforms offering great views. The hike is generally easy, with a few steep sections, and takes about an hour.

From downtown Casper, drive south on Wolcott Street, which becomes Highway 251/Casper Mountain Road, for 4.8 miles (7.7 km). Turn right onto Highway 252/Garden Creek Road, and in 0.4 mile (0.6 km), make a slight left onto Highway 511/Rotary Park Road. Follow this for about 0.5 mile (0.8 km) into the parking lot.

Entertainment
Brewpubs and Distilleries

Backwards Distilling Company (214 S. Wolcott St., 307/472-1275, http://backwardsdistilling.com, 3pm-9pm Mon.-Thurs., 3pm-10pm Fri., noon-10pm Sat., noon-5pm Sun.) makes strong spirits and has the vibe of a speakeasy. The locally produced line is bottled in small batches and named for circus tent characters: Strongman Gin, Ringleader Vodka, and Sword Swallower Rum. The downtown tasting room slings cocktails in the same theme, with drinks called the Big Top and Veiled Prophet, amid quirky circus decor. For a look behind the curtain, head to the production facility 2.5 miles (4 km) west for a one-hour **Backstage Tour** (158 Progress Circle, 2pm Sat.-Sun., $10) of the shiny distillery barrels and tools before you head to the tasting room for 30 minutes of guided sampling. Reservations are recommended; book online.

Casper's only local beer is brewed and served downtown at **Frontier Brewing Company and Taproom** (117 E. 2nd St., 307/337-1000, 3pm-10pm Wed.-Fri., 11am-10pm Sat.). A self-serve system allows folks to pour their own beers and pay by the ounce, so you're not locked into a flight. Choose from four flagship brews along with a variety of seasonal beers. Board games are available, kids are welcome inside, and live music is regularly on tap. No food is served here, but patrons are welcome to bring outside food in—food trucks are often parked around.

Festivals and Events

The skies above Casper come alive with vibrant colors every year with dozens of hot-air balloons launching on the 4th weekend in July during the **Casper Balloon Roundup** (www.visitcasper.com). The free festival attracts balloonists from all over the country and includes launches at 6am each day Friday-Sunday. If that's too early for you, head to the Downtown Balloon Fest on Saturday evening at David Street Station instead, where you can see the balloons up close, meet pilots, and enjoy live music, food vendors, and a beer garden. The balloons launch from the Wyoming Central Fairgrounds (1700 Fairgrounds Rd, 307/235-5775), but you can also get great views from Casper Mountain or on the hilltop of the National Historic Trails Interpretive Center.

The **College National Finals Rodeo** (CNFR, www.cnfr.com, Events Center, 1 Events Dr., 509/529-4402, $8-25) is a weeklong event each June that sees over 400 of the country's best college and university rodeo athletes compete in one of the city's biggest events. Daily performances showcase the riders' skills at saddle bronc riding, tie-down roping, steer wrestling, barrel racing, bareback riding, and more. The week culminates in a championship round with awards. Be sure to stop by the trade show—included in the cost of admission—to peruse clothing, saddles, jewelry, hats, and more.

Combining a wild rodeo with fairground fun, the **Central Wyoming Fair and Rodeo** (1700 Fairgrounds Rd., 307/235-5775, www.centralwyomingfair.com, early June, gate admission $5, free under age 9, rodeo $10-22, carnival day-pass $36) is a nine-day event with an amusement carnival, monster trucks, rodeo wrangling, a parade, and a singing competition, the Voice of Casper. Purchase rodeo tickets in advance to save on gate admission, and look online for bundles that save on carnival passes.

Food

Once a gas station and auto body shop, ★ **Yellowstone Garage** (355 W. Yellowstone Hwy., 307/215-7266, www.yellowstonegarage.com, 11am-9pm Tues.-Wed., 11am-10pm Thurs.-Fri.,

7am-10pm Sat., 7am-2pm Sun., $15) is a rollicking place to enjoy a meal, grab a drink, and hear some live music. The family-friendly space serves up a wide range of classics made from scratch, including burgers, fish tacos, mac and cheese, and rib eye, along with beer and wine. Grab a table outside near the eatery's outdoor stage for the best seat in downtown Casper.

Racca's Pizzeria Napoletana (430 S. Ash St., 307/337-2444, www.raccaspizzeria.com, 11am-10pm Sun.-Thurs., 11am-11pm Fri.-Sat., $15) imported its wood-fired pizza ovens directly from Italy; in fact, it's the only certified Neapolitan pizzeria in the state. The thin crusts are blazed to perfection and topped with ingredients like Parma ham, buffalo mozzarella, pine nuts, and porchetta. Plan your visit so you're there on the weekend for brunch, where you can get a personal breakfast pizza. Check out the pancetta, fresh mozzarella, arugula, and cracked egg pizza to go along with bottomless mimosas.

On the eastern side of town, **Wyoming Ale Works** (5900 E. 2nd St., 307/472-5900, www.wyomingaleworks.com, 11am-11pm Mon.-Thurs., 11am-midnight Fri.-Sat., 11am-9pm Sun., $18) is a casually upscale spot with a menu sure to please, with all the usual burgers and salads along with some surprises like a Nashville hot chicken and shepherd's pie. Also on tap are a whopping 40 craft beers. The outdoor patio makes a nice spot for lunch or dinner.

A sweet and homey cottage house with blue trim and a green patio, **The Cottage Café** (116 S. Lincoln St., 307/234-1157, www.cottagecafecasper.com, 11am-1:30pm Mon.-Fri., $9) is only open for lunch weekdays, so plan ahead to make sure you can enjoy its homemade soups and sandwiches on freshly baked bread. Each sandwich and wrap is served alongside a salad of your choice, with options like chickpea, dill and cucumber, and feta and spinach.

Shopping

You can't miss the giant neon sign welcoming you to **Lou Taubert Ranch Outfitters** (125 E. 2nd St., 800/447-9378, http://loutaubert.com, 9am-5:30pm Mon.-Sat., noon-4pm Sun.). The store takes up a whopping nine floors and carries all manner of Western wear, including clothing, hats, and belts, not to mention 10,000 pairs of boots from top brands for all genders and all ages.

Cadillac Cowgirl (147 S. Casper St., 307/473-5858, 10am-5:30pm Mon.-Sat.) has a fun selection of women's fashion, including clothing, kooky socks, shoes, beeswax lip balms, and Western-studded purses. You can easily walk away with a whole new outfit.

Wind City Books (152 S. Center St., 307/315-6003, www.windcitybooks.com, 10am-6pm Mon.-Fri., 10am-5pm Sat.) has over 17,000 books covering local and regional topics, fiction, nonfiction, kids' books, and more. Stop in to peruse the well-curated selection of titles, and be sure to ask the staff for recommendations.

With everything an angler might need to get out on the river, from top brands like Orvis and Patagonia, **Ugly Bug Fly Shop** (240 S. Center St., 307/234-6905, http://crazyrainbow.net, 9am-5:30pm Mon.-Fri., 8am-4pm Sat.) has new bobbins, waders, rods, and solid hats. It also offers guided fishing tours via its Crazy Rainbow Fly Fishing.

Accommodations

Enjoy the crisp air at ★ **Sunburst Lodge** (2700 Micro Rd., Casper Mountain, 307/235-9086, http://sunburst-lodge.com, $135-165), perched on Casper Mountain and offering stunning views. The lodge is a beautiful and rustic dream, and only a 20-minute drive south of downtown. Its six rooms come with TVs and private baths with heated floors. Some rooms can access a large shared main deck overlooking the mountain, and all guests enjoy a tasty breakfast spread each morning.

Local art evoking Wyoming and the West adds a special touch.

Right off I-25 and U.S. 26, about a 10-minute drive east of downtown, **C'mon Inn Casper** (301 E. Lathrop Rd., 307/472-6300, www.cmoninn.com/casper, $110-180) is more than a typical roadside motel. The regional chain hotel has a Western lodge atmosphere, including big stone columns outside and a giant fireplace inside. Its 125 rooms have stone walls and wooden accents. Inside the atrium, where the included breakfast is served, a waterfall cascades into koi ponds, and guests have a choice of five hot tubs. A larger heated pool allows kids to splash off their road-trip energy.

For lodging closer to downtown and the National Historic Trails Interpretive Center, a good choice is **Ramkota Hotel** (800 N. Poplar St., 307/266-6000, http://ramkotacasper.com, $122-170). Its 230 rooms include suite and adjoining options, and the whole place is pet-friendly. Kids will especially love the water play land, a swimming pool with water cannons and kiddie slides.

Camping

Just east of Casper, **River's Edge RV and Cabins Resort** (6820 Santa Fe Circle, Evansville, 307/234-0042, www.riversedgervresort.net) is a good place for a few nights' stay, with full RV hookups ($45-52) and tent spaces ($22-28). Five cabins ($60) are also available. It's not a campground with a lot of grass or trees in the main area, but there are shadier spots near the North Platte River. The lodge has a recreation room with games and ice cream; a playground, horseshoe pits, and a basketball court offer outdoor fun.

Along the Trail from Casper

At this point, emigrants had to bid farewell to the North Platte River, their traveling companion of 400 miles (640 km). This marked a turning point on the trail, when water was no longer guaranteed, and the danger of dehydration was real. The next stretch entailed a hard road, full of alkaline pools not fit for drinking. Dust storms blinded and choked people and livestock, and desperate thirsty animals would drink the salty water and collapse. A few springs provided welcome relief, but all were relieved when they encountered the aptly named Sweetwater River near Independence Rock.

The Sweetwater Valley, though rocky and higher in elevation, generally made a pleasant journey for wagon trains, with green grass and decent water access—although they would have to cross the Sweetwater River nine times. Some years were good for hunting. In the distance to the northwest, the snowcapped Wind River Mountains—part of the Rocky Mountains—were a beautiful and menacing sight to the travelers. It would take 10-20 days from here to cross the 100 miles (160 km) to the strategic Continental Divide crossing at South Pass.

As in so many other places, the trail had varying paths. Some chose to cross the North Platte River earlier than others to avoid the sandy banks farther south, opting instead to make their way across more arid land before finding the Sweetwater River. Today you can trace the main route via **Highway 220** from Casper—your first stop is **Independence Rock**—and then eventually connect to **U.S. 287** at the **Muddy Gap Junction,** 73 miles (118 km) west, or 1.25 hours of driving without stops.

You can also leave Casper via **backcountry roads**—County Road 319, also called the **Oregon Trail Road**—that more closely follow the old trail, and connect with Highway 220 just before Independence Rock, so you won't miss any sights along the main route, and you can catch Emigrant Gap, Avenue of Rocks, Willow Springs, and Prospect

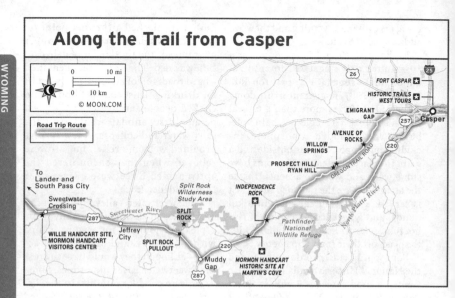

Along the Trail from Casper

Hill. This route to Independence Rock takes 1.5 hours, adding 30 minutes more than the direct route via Highway 220. Heading out of Casper, the roads are paved, but from Poison Spider Road on are packed dirt. Use caution if conditions are wet, as the roads can become muddy and impassable.

Emigrant Gap

After the North Platte River crossing, one of the trail's paths headed west through a gap in the hills, climbing up out of the Platte Valley. The road here involved a steep ascent up a sandy hill, followed by a hard-packed dirt path. Today **Emigrant Gap** is marked by a BLM interpretive sign in a roadside pullout and offers expansive views of the surrounding valley and bluffs. This was only the start of a 40 hard miles (64 km) for the pioneers, who had to cross an alkaline desert full of deadly pools of water and little grass for livestock. Many diarists recorded seeing dead livestock left along the road under the hot sun. Along the drive today, watch for swales and white posts marking the original route of the wagons, which crosses the modern road.

Getting There

From downtown Casper, head west on U.S. 26 for 4.5 miles (7.2 km), then turn left onto Zero Road. After 5.5 miles (8.8 km), turn left again onto 10 Mile Road. Drive 0.5 mile (0.8 km) and turn right on Poison Spider Road. In 1.6 miles (2.6 km) is a sign for Emigrant Gap. The drive takes 20 minutes.

Avenue of Rocks

Avenue of Rocks, also known as **Devil's Backbone,** was another popular place for emigrants to sign their names. Here, rocks jut out of the rolling prairie. Look for "W. H. Stephens, July 5, '49" by walking along the northeast ridge for about 40 yards (40 m); at Independence Rock, look for the same name, dated the next day, July 6. Watch for rattlesnakes here.

Getting There

From Emigrant Gap, continue southwest on Poison Spider Road for 1.4 miles (2.2 km), then turn right for a quick jog on County Road 306, making a quick left again back onto Poison Spider Road/County Road 201. In 1.8 miles (2.8 km), turn left onto Oregon Trail Road/County

Road 319. Follow it for 6.9 miles (11.1 km) to Avenue of Rocks on the west side of the road. The drive takes 20 minutes.

Willow Springs

The freshwater at **Willow Springs** became a life-giving place for many a thirsty emigrant and their livestock along this route. The area was also a campground—so popular that in some busy years conditions deteriorated to a miry bog and many began avoiding it. Today, you can drive past and look; the springs are on private land—and you're more likely to see the dry landscape that pioneers had to slog through.

Getting There

Continue southwest on Oregon Trail Road/County Road 319. After Avenue of Rocks, you pass by Clayton's Slough in 2 miles (3.2 km), named for an emigrant who complained fiercely about the nauseating water and swampy soil, then the north end of Willow Springs in another 3 miles (4.8 km). The south end of Willow Springs is another 2.9 miles (4.6 km) down the road.

Prospect Hill

Prospect Hill, today called **Ryan Hill,** involved a steep 400-foot (120-m) ascent for pioneers, but at the top they were welcomed with beautiful views (or "prospect") of the Sweetwater Valley and mountains beyond, such as Laramie Peak. Today you can find distinct ruts at the top. Views here feel straight from the pioneer era, with no modern changes; from the ruts, you can imagine you're looking out across the same landscape that an 1843 emigrant saw.

Getting There

The south end of Willow Springs is at the base of Prospect Hill-Ryan Hill. Drive southwest, heading uphill on County Road 319—in about 0.8 mile (1.3 km), halfway up the hill, there's a pullout with a good view of some

swales. In another 0.6 mile (1 km), at the top, turn right onto the gravel road—it leads to a circular parking lot with BLM signs. A short footpath takes you to the excellent wagon ruts, marked by white BLM posts.

TOP EXPERIENCE

★ Independence Rock

"After breakfast, myself, with some other young men, had the pleasure of waiting on five or six young ladies to pay a visit to Independence Rock.... Facing the road, in all splendor of gun powder, tar and buffalo greese, may be seen the name of J. W. Nesmith, from Maine, with an anchor."

J. W. Nesmith, July 1843, *Diary of the Emigration of 1843*. James Willis Nesmith grew up in New England and traveled the trail to Oregon when he was 23. There, he studied law and served as the Supreme Judge of the Provisional Government of Oregon, before the territory became a state. He was later elected to the U.S. Senate in 1860 as a Democrat, and to the House of Representatives in 1873.

Striking, dome-shaped **Independence Rock** stands 136 feet (41.5 m) high and measures about a mile (1.6 km) around. Before the time of the trail, Cheyenne, Kiowa, Shoshone, Lakota, and Arapaho peoples hunted and traded in the area and used the rock as a meeting spot as well as a place to carve and paint, features now washed or worn away. For emigrants, the monolithic rock evoked many images: a loaf of bread, a whale, half an apple, a backbone. Wagon trains knew they were on schedule if they reached Independence Rock by the Fourth of July—to which the rock owes its name; if they did, they would likely make it to Oregon before the risk of snow. Many emigrants celebrated timely arrivals with celebrations of gunfire, drinking, and songs. Many also

paused to make their mark in the granite. While many signatures were written in axle grease or tar and have faded with time, numerous carved signatures remain.

Here, as with other places along the entire route, emigrants used the rock as a sort of bulletin board to pass messages along. They noted where to find good water or campsites, or warned travelers about a perilous location ahead, or perhaps advertised someone's skills as a guide for hire. At Independence Rock, these messages might've been carved in the rock, though no such vestiges remain today. At other locations an inventive system of cloth strips, wood posts, and most popularly, bones, were used.

Today Independence Rock makes a nice rest stop. It has an interpretive area, and you can follow a trail around the rock, viewing signatures near the base. While it's possible to climb to the top and see a few other emigrant signatures, be aware there are no hand bars or safety features on the rock, and it can get quite slippery when wet.

Getting There

From **Prospect Hill,** continue driving southwest on Oregon Trail Road/County Road 319. In 0.6 mile (1 km), turn right to continue on the road. In 9.9 miles (16 km), continue straight on County Road 319. In 2.9 miles (4.6 km), turn right onto Highway 220, the main route. From here, it's 10.3 miles (17 km) southwest to Independence Rock.

If you're driving **directly from Casper,** head southwest on Highway 220 for 55 miles (89 km). Independence Rock is accessible from a rest area off the highway to the left. The drive takes about an hour.

Top to bottom: *Independence Rock* by William Henry Jackson; Devil's Gate; Mormon Handcart Historic Site at Martin's Cove.

Devil's Gate

"The chasm is one of the wonders of the world. The water rushes roaring and raving into the gorge, and the noise it makes as it comes in contact with the huge fragments of rock lying in its course is almost deafening."

Charles E. Boyle, 1849, *The Gold Rush Diary of Charles E. Boyle*. Dr. Charles E. Boyle was a physician from Columbus, Ohio, who traveled the California Trail during the gold rush years.

Visible from Independence Rock, a few miles west is **Devil's Gate,** another unique rock formation that served as a memorable landmark for pioneers. The "gate" is a gorge on the Sweetwater River. Due to the unique effects of water erosion, the river looks as if it bored straight through a rock wall, which baffled the pioneers. On the west side of Devil's Gate is a BLM pullout with great views of the cleft. From the parking lot, short walking paths lead to several interpretive panels detailing pioneer stories.

Getting There
From Independence Rock, head 6.7 miles (10.7 km) southwest on Highway 220. Turn right into the parking lot.

★ Mormon Handcart Historic Site at Martin's Cove

The year 1856 was especially tragic for two groups of Mormon emigrants. The Willie and Martin companies set out on the trail late that year, with the Willie company traveling slightly faster than the Martin company. On October 20, both parties were in the Sweetwater Valley when a snowstorm struck, piling up 18 inches. Over the next six days they struggled through the icy snow. The Martin company was forced to find shelter in a cove just past Devil's Gate, now called Martin's Cove, while the Willie company continued on, fording the freezing Sweetwater River several times. Dozens died each night from the cold or starvation. Eventually rescue parties reached both companies, although altogether up to 250 of the 1,000 members died, and many others lost limbs or extremities to frostbite. It's a tragedy that dramatically outstrips the Donner Party—which lost 42 members—yet remains relatively little known in U.S. history.

Today, the Mormon Church leases the land near Devil's Gate and Martin's Cove from the state, and the **Mormon Handcart Historic Site at Martin's Cove** (47600 Hwy. 220, 307/328-2953, 9am-9pm daily Memorial Day-Labor Day, 9am-7pm daily Labor Day-Oct., 9am-4pm daily Nov.-Memorial Day, free) tells the stories of the Willie and Martin companies, as well as the larger story of the Mormon migration west to Utah. Don't be shy if you're not a member of the Mormon Church—the staff is welcoming and happy to answer any questions you might have.

Many Mormon emigrants pulled handcarts rather than used wagons, and the site has numerous handcarts you can try. Kids can ride in them as you test your strength around the gravel Prairie Park at the site, which offers beautiful views of Devil's Gate. Trail options include a 5-mile (8-km) round-trip hike out to Martin's Cove or 2-mile (3.2 km) round-trip hike to Devil's Gate. Visitors are welcome to take the handcarts on sections of these trails as well. Ask staff before setting out, and they'll get you set up. Along the trail to Martin's Cove is a monument to the rescuers of the handcart company and some traces of the original wagon trail—at the cove itself, nothing marks the spot but memories.

Getting There
From the BLM pullout for Devil's Gate, drive west on Highway 220 a short 0.7 mile (1.1 km), then turn right on Martin Cove Road for the Mormon Handcart Historic Site; you'll be welcomed by a sign stretching over the road. It's 0.6 mile

The Mormon Trail

The Church of Jesus Christ of Latter-Day Saints (LDS) was founded in 1821 in New York by Joseph Smith. The religion grew quickly and expanded to Ohio and Missouri, attracting both avid devotees and enemies. Tenets of the LDS faith are based on Christian concepts and include a deep emphasis on family, missionary work, a connection between church and state, and in the early days, the practice of polygamy, which officially ended in 1890. The tight-knit communities outside the mainstream were often pushed out of regions where they tried to settle.

Mormon Party Near Fort Bridger by William Henry Jackson

Mormons, or the "Saints," as they called themselves, settled in Nauvoo, Illinois, in 1839. But it was made clear the religion was not welcome when a mob murdered Joseph Smith and his brother, Hyrum, in 1844. In 1845, Smith's successor, Brigham Young, chose a new home he thought no one else would want: the Great Salt Lake Basin in Utah, a desert land thought to be unfit for farming.

In the 1850s, the poor, mostly European immigrants were able to move west supported by church funds. Given poor harvests and empty treasuries, Young supplied them with cheaper wooden handcarts rather than full wagons. He expected them to be able to move quickly and easily, getting to Utah faster. Each handcart carried about 500 pounds of supplies: clothing, bedding, food, and tents. Each person was allowed about 17 pounds, with five people per handcart. The handcarts looked like large, flat wheelbarrows: a flatbed over two large wheels, with two pull shafts and a crossbar that allowed one person to pull it. Traveling in groups, about 3,000 people moved west in this fashion over the decade, or around 10 percent of all Mormon emigrants.

The 1,200-mile (1,930-km) trail from Illinois that Mormons followed to find their new home was active 1846-1868, and generally mirrors the Oregon Trail starting from Kearney, Nebraska, where the routes converged. Mormon emigrants traveled along the north bank of the North Platte River, coming from Illinois via Omaha, Nebraska. This allowed them to skip a river crossing, as well as kept them on the opposite riverbank from Oregon and California Trail emigrants, many of whom were the same people who had persecuted them back east. Although they traveled much of the way on opposite sides of the river, the emigrants shared similar experiences: Mormon pioneers recorded seeing Chimney and Courthouse Rocks, and all parties struggled with cholera, rainstorms, lack of fresh food, and the rigors of daily travel. At Fort Laramie, Mormon emigrants crossed the river and joined the main flow of traffic. All three trails crossed the Continental Divide and then headed to Fort Bridger in southwestern Wyoming, and from there, Mormon emigrants broke off to head south into Utah.

In the 1860s, the Mormon Trail became a two-way route, as wagon companies headed back east in the spring to pick up emigrants bound for Utah. This worked well until the railroad was completed and effectively ended the need for large wagon movements.

(0.9 km) from here to the visitors center parking lot.

Split Rock

Made of the same granite as Independence Rock and Devil's Gate, **Split Rock** was another notable landmark for pioneers, as well as for today's travelers; true to its name, it's defined by a perfect V-shaped split at the top, pointing the way west toward South Pass. The notched rock creates a triangular cutout that was known as a perfect gunsight, which could be seen for a day or two on either side. In 1860 a Pony Express station was established here, known as Sweetwater Station, but nothing remains of it today.

Getting There

From Martin's Cove, continue west on Highway 220 for 16 miles (26 km) to the Muddy Gap Junction, where you turn right onto U.S. 287 to head north—but before you do, check your gas tank; the junction is a great place to fill up if needed (the next gas station is 25 miles (40 km) away in Jeffrey City). A pleasant rest stop for Split Rock is about 8 miles (12.9 km) past the Muddy Gap Junction, but oddly, the rock itself can't be seen well from here. Down the road 3.2 miles (5.1 km) is another pullout with a historical marble monument that has a much better view. The drive from Martin's Cove takes 20 minutes. Or catch glimpses through your rearview window after the rest stop.

Willie Handcart Site

Another Mormon missionary center, the **Willie Handcart Site** (4181 Hwy. 789, 307/544-2215, 9am-9pm daily Memorial Day-Labor Day, 9am-7pm daily Labor Day-Oct., 9am-4pm daily Nov.-Apr., free) has a smaller museum than the one at Martin's Cove, and offers additional information on the Willie and Martin companies that were trapped nearby in a blizzard in 1856. It features an introductory video and interactive exhibits. You can also borrow handcarts here, and hike with or without them to the **sixth crossing of the Sweetwater River,** 3 miles (4.8 km) one-way, heading southwest. Oregon, California, and Mormon Trail emigrants needed to cross the Sweetwater River nine times in total on their way to South Pass. Normally a comparatively easy crossing, the Willie company was forced to cross during a fierce October snowstorm in 1856, and many members suffered frostbite or died before the party was rescued. Today the river is a memorial location for the Mormon Church, and the destination of many short pilgrimages by modern LDS members—especially Mormon kids and teenagers in summer—who visit this site as well as the Mormon Handcart Historic Site at Martin's Cove as a way to honor their heritage.

Getting There

From Muddy Gap Junction, Willie's Handcart Site is 43 miles (69 km) west on U.S. 287, or 30 miles (48 km) west if you're coming from the marble monument near Split Rock. Turn left at the sign for the Mormon visitors center. The drive from Split Rock takes 30 minutes.

⬥ Detour: Lander

Lander remained hunting grounds for the Shoshone people during the time of the Oregon Trail, a sidestep away from the path. Today it's a busy outdoorsy town on the way to Yellowstone National Park and a destination for climbing, with beautiful views of the Wind River Mountains, the Popo Agie River running through it, great local museums focused on the area's settlers and indigenous people, and some good food. The **Coalter Block** on Main Street is a coalition of several local businesses, and serves as the hub of town nightlife.

For Oregon Trail travelers, Lander makes a great place to spend the night after Casper—it's about 2.5 hours' drive west—and might even tempt you to stay

Beaded Necklace

Scream Shack

Scream Shack

"world famous"
chokecherry

an extra day or two. The town is just 10 miles (16 km) off the route, and in the summer affords the option to do a great loop drive that connects with South Pass City, where you can get back on the historic route.

Getting There

Following the route from Casper via Highway 220 and U.S. 287, the drive takes about 2.5 hours, without stops. From the Willie Handcart Site, continue west on U.S. 287 for 30 miles (48 km). At the junction with Highway 28, turn right to continue on U.S. 287 for 8.5 miles (13.7 km) to Lander. The drive takes 40 minutes.

It's easy to make a stop in Lander a side trip and then simply backtrack, adding 20 minutes total additional driving time, to the U.S. 287/Highway 28 junction, continuing straight on the latter into South Pass City. Or you can take the Loop Road for a scenic detour to South Pass City.

Fuel and Services

Make sure to fill up on gas before you head out; the next gas station is in Farson, past South Pass City, about 85 miles (137 km) southwest of Lander.

Sights
Museums

Lander has two great museums next door to each other. The **Museum of the American West** (1445 W. Main St., 307/335-8778, www.museumofthe americanwest.com, 9am-4pm Mon.-Fri. May-Oct., free) is an outdoor pioneer village with buildings from the 1880s to the 1930s, including a church, a schoolhouse, a cabin, and a barn full of wagons and farm equipment; for example, step inside a pioneer-era "RV"—an early camper van that sheepherders slept in while following their flocks. Entering most of the buildings activates a video that offers

Top to bottom: Lander landscape; Fremont County Pioneer Museum; ice cream from The Scream Shack.

historical information and background details. The museum also partners with the Eagle Spirit Dancers from the nearby Wind River Reservation; weekly dance performances take place in summer (7pm, free), and the event ends with a Friendship dance, in which visitors are invited to participate.

Nearby is the **Fremont County Pioneer Museum** (1443 W. Main St., 307/332-3339, www.fremontcountymuseum. com, 9am-5pm daily, $6 adults, $5 seniors, students, and military, free under age 13), which has a well-presented gallery of settler artifacts as well as an especially great collection of pieces from Sioux and Shoshone artists, including a turn-of-the-century buffalo hide by Shoshone artist Cotsiogo and numerous beaded moccasins, bags, and gloves.

Two striking Sioux war bonnets are on display, as is a rare collection of Sioux ledger art. Ledger art was popular among Plains peoples such as the Oglala Sioux, Kiowa, Cheyenne, and Arapaho, who traditionally painted on buffalo hide but utilized other materials that became available—often in the form of settlers' ledger books—creating rich scenes of battles, dances, and dreams. The artwork was most prevalent during the 1860s-1920s and has seen a resurgence among modern Plains artists today. The museum's collection contains work by early artists such as Chief Yellow Bear, Red Dog, and Nadya Loomis, one of the few female ledger artists.

Recreation

Lander and the nearby areas of Wild Iris and Sinks Canyon are world-famous for climbing. For a guided climbing tour, book a trip with **Wind River Climbing Guides** (307/335-3439, www. windriverclimbing.com, Apr.-Oct., $110-475), who expertly plan a trip for your skill level, whether you're a beginner or advanced, and take you to the peaks of Wild Iris, Sinks Canyon, Lankin Dome, and Cranner Rock. For a quick thrill, take a 2.5-hour rappelling course to find out how fun lowering yourself down a cliff can be. A bigger challenge is the half- or full-day climbing course, where you learn to scale a cliff in a safe, guided, and fun environment. More advanced climbers can book the Sport Climbing Course or Trad Climbing Course, both two-day workshops where you learn advanced techniques for belaying and crack climbing.

Advanced climbers looking for gear can head to **Wild Iris Mountain Sports** (166 Main St., 307/332-4541, www. wildirisclimbing.com, 9:30am-6:30pm Mon.-Sat., 10am-5pm Sun.), an outdoors store whose primary passion is climbing. It stocks ropes, shoes, harnesses, and carabiners, and the employees take advice-giving seriously and can offer suggestions for the best climbing experience for you. The store also carries tents, shoes, backpacking guides, and clothes.

Food

★ **The Middle Fork** (351 Main St., 307/335-5035, www.themiddleforklander. com, 7am-2pm Mon.-Sat., 9am-2pm Sun., $10) easily has the best breakfast in town. Try the luscious eggs Benedict, served with local bacon and a tarragon béarnaise sauce, or a perfectly crispy Monte Cristo sandwich with turkey, ham, and swiss cheese on sourdough. Those with a sweet tooth can enjoy the blueberry corn bread french toast or almond crunch pancakes (sourdough cakes topped with candied nuts and a white chocolate crumble). Vegetarian and gluten-free options are available, and the eatery has a beautiful garden patio to enjoy your meal.

Widely known as the best place to get a burger in town, **Gannett Grill** (126 Main St., 307/332-8228, www.landerbar.com, 11am-9pm daily, $12), which uses locally raised grass-fed beef from Wyoming Custom Meats, is also the best place to enjoy a summer evening, with its shady patio. Also on the menu are big salads and sourdough pizzas featuring produce

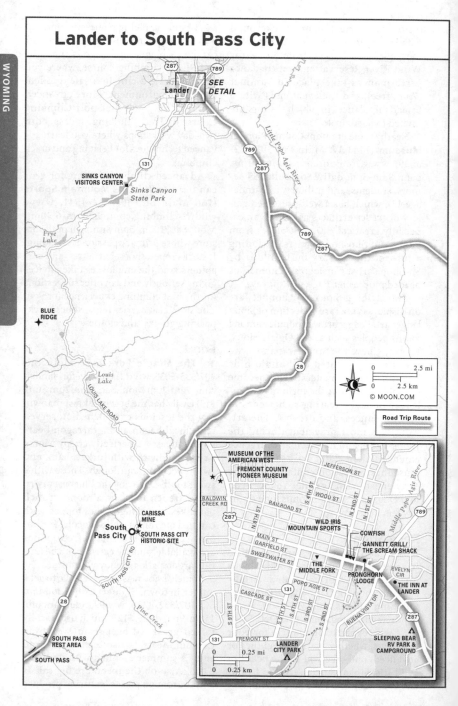

Lander to South Pass City

from the restaurant's organic garden. Order at the counter before you take a seat—the casual dining room displays old fishing lures, mining photos, and Western wear. The adjoining **Lander Bar** (11am-2am Mon.-Sat., 11am 10pm Sun.) is a saloon that originally opened in 1908 and serves a wide selection of whiskey, locally brewed beer, and tall tales of the Wild West.

For something more upscale, have a night out at **Cowfish** (148 Main St., 307/332-8227, www.cowfishlander.com, 8am-2pm and 5pm-10pm daily, $25). With a menu covering all manner of land and sea options, you can enjoy everything from a veggie-focused fresh mushroom pasta to a perfectly grilled steak covered in chimichurri and topped with battered shrimp. While here, enjoy a pint from **Lander Brewing,** which first started nearby in the 1800s. It fell to Prohibition but has been reignited in recent years and is proud to be Lander's first and only local brewery. The brewery is inside Cowfish and serves its product at the restaurant and at the Lander Bar next door.

The Scream Shack (126 Main St., 307/332-8228, www.landerbar.com, 11am-10pm daily June-Aug., $4) is a ramshackle place built from recycled materials that dishes out ice cream, shakes, smoothies, and more. Its specialty, as advertised on a sign of a giant tongue licking a cone, is its "world famous" chokecherry shake. A small stone fruit that packs a sour punch but sweetens when ripe, chokecherries are a popular traditional Native American food. Shoshone and Paiute peoples would often enjoy the vitamin- and mineral-rich berry in a pudding.

Accommodations and Camping

The Inn at Lander (260 Grandview Dr., 307/332-2847, www.innatlander. com, $93-158) has 101 rooms, wooden mountain-lodge stylings, and an on-site restaurant that serves breakfast, lunch, and dinner. Queen or king bed and suite options are available, and some rooms overlook a seasonal heated outdoor pool. There's an outdoor hot tub and fitness equipment. The inn is on the east end of town, a 10-minute walk to the central Main Street area.

The wooden-beamed **Pronghorn Lodge** (150 E. Main St., 307/332-3940, www.pronghornlodge.com, $80-100) may be a Rodeway Inn, but it has an old-cabin-meets-highway-motel feel. Right on the river downtown, the lodge is a short walk from restaurants and bars on Main Street. The 56 rooms are basic and have free Wi-Fi, air-conditioning, and access to a 24-hour front desk and a hot tub.

Wake up to a magnificent view of the Wind River Mountains at **Sleeping Bear RV Park & Campground** (715 E. Main St., 307/332-5159, www.sleepingbearrvpark. com), just a short walk to downtown Lander and open year-round. It has sites for tents and RVs ($25-46), as well as three cabins ($48-58). Most sites have fire pits and picnic tables, and on a hot summer day, nothing beats the splash pad.

Camp for free at **Lander City Park** (405 Fremont St., 307/332-4647, free), where there are 20 spots to park your RV or tent. The park is shady, the Popo Agie River runs through it, and there are restrooms and plenty of grass to spread out on, as well as a great playground for kids. You can stay up to three nights for free. This is popular spot on a summer evening, so don't dally to claim a spot. Be wary of GPS directions to get here; the correct entry is from 3rd Street.

Loop Road Scenic Drive to South Pass City

If you're traveling in summer and have some spare time, consider driving half of the **Loop Road route** (typically open late June-Sept.) to connect back to the Oregon Trail near South Pass City instead of backtracking. The drive south from Lander to South Pass City is only 40 miles (64 km) via **Highway 131,** which becomes **Louis Lake Road/Road 300,** a

1.75-hour drive without stops—versus 40 minutes on the 32-mile (52-km) direct route to South Pass City via U.S. 287 and Highway 28. On this detour, you avoid retracing your steps and catch beautiful scenery of mountains, alpine lakes, and red-streaked canyon walls, and you won't miss any notable Oregon Trail sites. It's a backcountry drive on dirt roads: A 4WD vehicle is recommended, as is a full tank of gas. There is no cell phone service.

From Lander, head south on Highway 131 for 5 miles (8 km) from its junction with Mortimer Lane. You'll soon have views of Table Mountain to your left, and the road will enter **Sinks Canyon State Park** (free) among tall sandstone cliffs. The park is known for its unique "disappearing" river; the Popo Agie flows underground for a short stretch here, descending in a pool called **The Sinks** and reemerging later at another pool called **The Rise.** On this drive, you're following the river upstream, so you'll come upon the pools in reverse, catching sight of The Rise first, 1 mile (1.6 km) from the park's entrance, then The Sinks after another 0.5 mile (0.8 km). Both pools have parking lots and short footpaths to them. At The Sinks' parking lot is the **Sinks Canyon visitors center** (3079 Sinks Canyon Rd./Hwy. 131, 307/332-6333, www.sinkscanyonstatepark.org, 9am-6pm daily Memorial Day-Labor Day), which has natural history displays, videos on the canyon's flora and fauna, and information on the unique geology that leads to the disappearing river.

After The Sinks, continue on Highway 131, where you'll start climbing up an unnamed peak along some hairpin curves and steep drop-offs, during which there are sweeping views of the forested valley. Beyond are the snowcapped Wind River Mountains above Lander. On the way up, the road becomes Louis Lake Road/Road 300. Continue on to pass pretty **Frye Lake,** actually a reservoir; **Blue Ridge,** the highest point of the road, at 9,500 feet

(2,900 m); and the alpine **Louis Lake** area, which gives the road its name.

From here, continue down the last leg of the road. At the junction with Highway 28, turn right to head south and rejoin the Oregon Trail route (turning left and heading north, back to Lander on Highway 28, would complete the loop). After 2.3 miles (3.7 km), turn left onto South Pass City Road. In 1.6 miles (2.6 km), veer right to remain on the road, and continue 0.6 mile (1 km) to South Pass City.

South Pass City and Vicinity

South Pass was the key to the entire overland trek. Without its gentle slope, which allowed wagons to gradually climb and cross the Continental Divide, it's entirely possible that mass migration to Oregon wouldn't have happened. While emigrants knew it as a landmark place, many

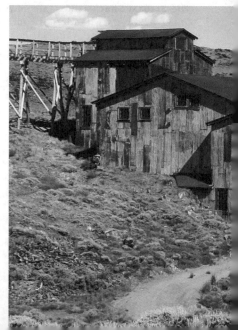

may not have grasped the importance of the pass as they rolled through.

Nearby, the mining town of South Pass City boomed in the mid-1800s—near the end of the Oregon and California Trails' popularity—when gold and coal were discovered in the hills. The South Pass gold rush in 1867 was Wyoming's largest, and the town sprang up to serve the Carissa Mine, which pumped out the precious metal. By the mid-1870s the gold had been thoroughly depleted, and the city shrank. The Carissa Mine closed for good in 1949. Today, South Pass City is a ghost town with a year-round population of 4—plus some cats and dogs, according to the town sign—which keeps up the historic site. The city is on the National Register of Historic Places.

Getting There

The drive from **Casper** takes about 2.75 hours total if you head out of town on Highway 220; add on 30 minutes if you head out on the Old Oregon Trail Road

From the Willie Handcart Site, continue west on U.S. 287 for 30 miles (48 km). At the U.S. 287/Highway 28 junction, turn left to head south on Highway 28. After 23 miles (37 km), turn left onto South Pass City Road. In 1.6 miles (2.6 km), veer right to remain on the road, and continue 0.6 mile (1 km) into South Pass City. The point-to-point drive takes 30 minutes.

If you made a side trip to **Lander,** drive south on U.S. 287 and continue straight on as it becomes Highway 28. After 32 miles (52 km), turn left onto South Pass City Road. The drive takes 40 minutes.

South Pass City

Start your visit to the ghost town of **South Pass City** (125 South Pass Main St., 307/332-3684, www.southpasscity. com, 9am-6pm daily May 15-Sept., last ticket sold 5pm, $3 adults Wyoming residents, $5 adults nonresidents, free under age 19) at the first building near the gated entrance, where you'll receive a map for a self-guided tour around the

Carissa Mine

23 abandoned buildings. They've been set up with period decor and artifacts, providing a sense of what town life may have been like in the 1860s-1870s gold-mining heyday. Visit the butcher shop, see the old saloon, and buy a souvenir in the general store turned gift shop. You'll also see the house of South Pass City's Esther Hobart Morris, who became the first female justice of the peace in the United States in 1870.

Carissa Mine

It's generally a bad idea to enter old mine shafts, but the **Carissa Mine,** which processed gold off and on 1867-1949, has been fully restored and is open for **tours** (125 South Pass Main St., 307/332-3684, www.southpasscity.com, 2pm Thurs.-Sun., $5). Visitors enter the mine and head up steep stairs and past loud rock-pulverizing machines. You'll learn how gold is separated from ore and see processing facilities as well as a mine cart, and then enter the old shaft. This is a popular tour, so reservations are recommended. Visitors must be at least eight years old. The guided tours last two hours—sign up online or in South Pass City, where the tour begins. From town, the mine is a 20-minute walk north, or a short drive along the main road.

Hiking

The easy 1.7-mile (2.7-km) **Flood and Hindle Trail** meanders along Willow Creek through a pine forest and past willow trees. Along the way you'll get a tour of the mining era—the loop trail passes by a reconstruction of an arrasta (an old ore-crushing machine), as well as a homestead, a stamp mill, and brick kilns. Find the trailhead at the South Pass City parking lot. Budget an hour for a round-trip walk.

South Pass

Highway 28 passes through one of the key sites on the Oregon Trail: **South Pass.** Without this gently sloping pass that crosses the Continental Divide, wagons would have had to tackle the Rocky Mountains in much rougher areas, and it's likely many emigrants wouldn't have been able to continue as far west as they did. This pass marked the crucial midpoint of the trip, the flip from the eastern watershed to the western, as emigrants made their way into what was then Oregon Territory; many pioneers never even noticed they'd made it over because the pass was so gradual.

A **rest area** 9.3 miles (14.9 km) south of the Highway 28/South Pass City Road junction has an interpretive center with information about the historic pass. Another 5.3 miles (8.5 km) south of the rest area is the **South Pass Overlook,** a BLM site, on the east side of Highway 28. The pullout has signage with information about the legendary pass, as well as great views.

If you want to go to South Pass itself, you'll need to follow 3 miles (4.8 km) of dirt road. Be sure your vehicle has high clearance; don't drive the route after heavy rains; and note that it's closed in winter. At the pass, you can walk on the actual Oregon Trail and find two monuments. From the South Pass rest area, drive south on Highway 28 for 0.9 mile (1.4 km) and turn left onto Oregon Buttes Road. Drive down the dirt road, crossing two cattle guards along the way. At the 2.8-mile (4.5-km) mark, the road starts to curve south; keep an eye out for the old wagon road that crosses your path here—this is the actual Oregon Trail, a two-track wagon road with marks of modern traffic. You can drive on this section, so turn right onto the un-signposted road, heading west.

Or, if it looks too rough, you can park here and walk the short way down the road instead. Along the way, you'll see parallel wagon tracks along the road; parties often fanned out to avoid eating other people's dust. These alternative ruts are unmarred by modern traffic, so keep your vehicle off them, but feel free

A Pioneer Story: Ezra Meeker

As you follow the path of the Oregon Trail today and appreciate the monuments, museums, and signs denoting the route, take a moment to give thanks to Ezra Meeker. An emigrant born in 1834 in Ohio, he and his wife, Eliza Jane, took their seven-week-old son and hit the trail in 1852—five months later they made it to Oregon with no mishaps. Out west, he built a hop farm empire, founded the town of Puyallup in Washington, became its first mayor, served as a bank president, and found himself a wealthy man. By 1900 he was in his 70s and became devoted to the cause of preserving the Oregon Trail and the legacies of his fellow emigrants, something he continued until his death in 1928.

Oregon Trail Marker ink drawing by William Henry Jackson

At age 76 he struck out on the trail a second time in a covered wagon, headed east this time, to raise awareness of the old route. It was 1906, and the nation was charging into the new century, rapidly forgetting the old frontier ways; Meeker refused to let anyone forget. Along the way, he marked the old trail with granite columns—the BLM markers you can see along the route today are a nod to his efforts. He traveled the route again by wagon in 1910, then again in 1916 by car. By then he had gained support from President Theodore Roosevelt and had interested the nation in preserving the trail's history. In 1924, the then 90-year-old Meeker traveled the Oregon Trail once more, this time in a biplane. Just before he died, the 98-year-old was planning yet another journey, this time in a Model A Ford with a covered-wagon-style back.

Due to his extraordinary efforts in marking the trail's history on the ground and in Congress, he's known as the first preservationist of the Oregon Trail. He was the founder of the Oregon Trail Memorial Association, a forerunner of today's Oregon-California Trail Association (OCTA), which works to further Meeker's cause of preserving and protecting the overland route for future generations.

to walk around. After 0.8 mile (1.2 km), you'll arrive at the **South Pass Summit,** at about 8,000 feet (2,440 m) elevation, where you'll find BLM interpretive signs. You'll also find a stone marker emblazoned "Old Oregon Trail, 1845-57"; this stone was erected in 1906 by Ezra Meeker, an 1852 emigrant who later traveled back across the Oregon Trail several times to spearhead its preservation. To the right of it is a monument to Narcissa Whitman and Eliza Spalding: These two missionaries crossed South Pass with their husbands in 1836, becoming the first European-American women to do

so. Narcissa and Marcus Whitman would go on to found the Whitman Mission in Walla Walla, Washington, and Eliza and Henry Spalding would found the Lapwai Mission near Lewiston, Idaho.

Return to Highway 28 the way you came, and turn left to continue west 4.5 miles (7.2 km) to the South Pass Overlook pullout.

Food

Stop at the **Farson Mercantile** (4048 U.S. 191, Farson, 307/273-9511, www.farsonmerc.com, 10am-7pm daily fall-spring, 10am-9pm daily summer, $6). It's famous as the "Home of the Big Cone," and they're not kidding: It's big. One scoop stacks a hand span tall—if that's too much, go for the baby scoop, which is a bit more reasonable. There's also coffee, pizza, and deli sandwiches as well as a general mercantile inside with the usual travel center finds and souvenirs. Locally made Wyoming goodies like honey can be taken home, and there's a nice stash of toys and road games. From the South Pass Overlook, Farson is about 30 miles (48 km) west on Highway 28, at the junction with U.S. 191. The drive takes 30 minutes.

Fort Bridger

"I have established a small fort, with a blacksmith shop and a supply of iron in the road of the emigrants on Black Fork of Green River, which promises fairly . . . "

Jim Bridger, 1843, from a letter Bridger sent to Pierre Choteau Jr., requesting supplies.

Established in 1843 by mountain man Jim Bridger and his partner, Louis Vasquez, Fort Bridger was one of the westernmost stops for wagons to resupply on their journey. It became an important stop for wagons that had just made it over the South Pass and through the arid high desert.

In the early days of the trail, this was also where some California-bound emigrants, such as the Donner Party in 1846, took the ill-fated Hastings Cutoff. Advertised and encouraged by the spurious guide Lansford Hastings, the route went southwest from Fort Bridger toward the Great Salt Lake, and from there straight across the desert, supposedly saving over 300 miles (482 km). Hastings wrote *The Emigrants's Guide to Oregon and California* in 1845, but the author had never actually taken the cutoff himself. In the guide, he blithely wrote that travelers

would pass the Great Salt Lake "and from there continue down to the Bay of St. Francisco." He neatly forgot to mention the desert and subsequent rugged peaks of the Sierra Nevada Mountains, where the Donner Party would be trapped by early snowstorms and reduced to cannibalism to survive.

Mormon emigrants split from the Oregon and California Trails at Fort Bridger, heading to the Salt Lake Valley. Many Mormon also decided to settle in the area around Fort Bridger, causing some problems for Jim Bridger. He and Vasquez ran their post for about a decade, 1843-1853, when Bridger had a few run-ins with Brigham Young and Mormon settlers. They claimed he was out of legal bounds by selling alcohol locally, and sent a militia to arrest him, but he fled Fort Bridger. The fort ended up in Mormon hands for a few years, though it's unclear if Bridger sold it to them or not. After that, the U.S. Army occupied the fort from 1858 until it was abandoned in 1890.

Getting There

From South Pass City, head west via Highway 28. In 46 miles (74 km), you'll reach a junction with U.S. 191 at Farson; continue straight and west on Highway 28. In 29 miles (47 km), turn left onto Highway 372 toward Green River. After 27 miles (43 km) turn right to merge onto I-80 headed west and continue for 46 miles (74 km). If you need to fill up, stop for gas on the way at Little America at exit 68. For Fort Bridger, take exit 39, turning left onto Highway 414. In 2.9 miles (4.6 km), turn right onto I-80 Business Loop; you'll arrive in 2.5 miles (4 km). The drive takes an hour and 40 minutes.

Fuel and Services

Be aware that there are few amenities near Fort Bridger. The historic site sits in a town named Fort Bridger, but there is no gas station here and few choices for

A Pioneer Story: Mountain Man Jim Bridger

One of the largest legends of the West is mountain man Jim Bridger, a fur trapper, trader, U.S. Army guide, and adventurer. Born in 1822 in Virginia, Bridger headed west at age 17 to be a fur trapper, quickly rising in the ranks to become a partner in the Rocky Mountain Fur Company. Beaver pelts were in high demand, and the fur trade thrived in the 1820s-1830s.

Bridger gained vast knowledge of the West, mostly unsettled by Europeans at the time, and was described as a big gregarious man who stood over six feet tall. He had good relationships with local indigenous people, and married a Flathead woman and then a Ute woman, both of whom died in childbirth. He counted the Shoshone Chief Washakie as a close friend and married his daughter as well. When the fur trade began to wane—as fashions changed and less expensive pelts became available—Bridger focused on the increasing traffic on the new Oregon Trail. In 1843 he and Louis Vasquez established a trading post along the route, which quickly became a key supply stop for emigrants.

In his old age he left the frontier and headed east to settle in Westport, Missouri, today the oldest neighborhood of Kansas City, where he died in 1881. A monument in Independence, Missouri, facing west, today celebrates the old mountain man.

accommodations and convenience stores. Plan to fill your gas tank on the way here in **Little America** (I-80, exit 68). Little America is also a good place to stop for restrooms or ice cream, and it also has accommodations at the **Little America Hotel** (I-80, exit 68, 888/652-9042, http://wyoming.littleamerica.com, $80-160), with 140 rooms, a sparkling outdoor pool, and restaurants. No camping or hookups are available, but RVers are welcome to park in the lot. If you miss Little America, there is a small **Gas'n'Go** (2787 County Rd. 321, 307/786-2264, 24 hours daily) about 10 miles (16 km) northeast of Fort Bridger State Historic Site, near the Lyman junction at I-80, exit 41. Fill up on gas before heading out; once you leave I-80 on the way to Kemmerer, you'll only encounter gas stations every 30-60 miles (48-96 km).

Sights
Fort Bridger State Historic Site
Fort Bridger State Historic Site (37000 I-80 Bus., http://wyoparks.wyo.gov, visitors center 9am-5pm daily May-Sept., 9am-5pm Fri.-Sun. Oct.-Apr., grounds dawn-dusk daily, $3 pp Wyoming residents, $5 pp nonresidents, free under age 18) is home to 37 buildings and charts the course of history as it passed through this site. The grounds house structures representative of the main eras of the fort, from 1843 to the present.

A reconstruction of Jim Bridger's original wooden trading post, which served emigrants along the Oregon Trail, today houses a gift shop. An active archaeological dig on view behind the visitors center is uncovering fortifications built by Mormons during their occupation of the fort. Many of the existing buildings are from the U.S. Army era; structures include a schoolhouse, an ice house, a Pony Express barn, and a carriage house. The Milk Barn-Motel era covers the period when the fort was used for dairy cattle and as a stop for travelers along the 1930s Lincoln Highway, one of the country's first coast-to-coast roads. The museum exhibit showcases the efforts of today's preservationists and archaeologists in researching and exhibiting the fort's history.

During summer, period actors from throughout the fort's history, including mountain men and military officers, wander the site in costume, ready to chat. Depending on your level of interest, plan to spend 1-3 hours here. Guided tours are available daily in summer.

Festivals and Events

The tradition of the Mountain Man Rendezvous goes back to 1825, when a fur-trading company left a cache of supplies near the Green River in southern Wyoming and declared they'd meet there in July the next year. Word traveled along the trade routes, and the event became a huge gathering of trappers and traders, a time to share tall tales, show off skills, trade goods, and shore up trading relationships. It was a brilliant move—instead of hauling furs all the way back to St. Louis to sell, they could trade and restock their supplies right there. Hundreds came every year, a cultural mashup including English, Sioux, Shoshone, German, Spanish, Nez Perce, Iroquois, Delaware, and French people, among others.

Today, the spirit of the Mountain Man meetup continues during the **Fort Bridger Rendezvous** (www. fortbridgerrendezvous.net, 8am-6pm daily Labor Day weekend, $5). If you're up for it, you can dress in pre-1840s garb, all the way down to your shoes (no sunglasses), and skip the entrance fee. Activities include knife-throwing and other skill demonstrations, dances, a Dutch oven cook-off, historical talks, and children's games. Over 100 traders keep the tradition of the early 1800s alive, selling items like jewelry, tools, leather, clothing, blankets, and more. The event is on the grounds of the fort, a great way to experience the historic site.

Camping

Fort Bridger RV Camp (64 Groshon Rd., 307/782-3150, fbrv@bvea.net, $40) has 37 green and grassy spaces for RVs and trailers of all sizes, with full hookups. Restrooms, laundry, and friendly staff are on-site. It's a short walk to the historic site from the camp.

Kemmerer

The main Oregon Trail route from Fort Bridger passed south of what is today Kemmerer. No modern road follows the route, so the closest approximation is U.S. 30. Emigrants who chose to follow Sublette's Cutoff, a path that branched off the main Oregon Trail route just after South Pass, would have passed just north of Kemmerer, heading due west to Fort Hall in Idaho after skipping Fort Bridger. The cutoff could save wagons a few days' travel, but it was a dangerous route across 45 miles (72 km) with little water or grass for livestock. Emigrants encountered a landscape of rocky buttes and sagebrush valleys that wagons would've struggled through; the tall sagebrush often grew to hip height. The area remains remote even today, so modern visitors can still get a sense of what the pioneers saw.

The town of Kemmerer sprang up in 1897, long after the Oregon Trail diminished, with the discovery of coal, which the expanding railroad lines desperately needed. Today this small rural town is best known as "The Fossil Fish Capital of the World" for the millions of fossils found here. Some excellent fossil shops are in town, and some can take you on fossil-hunting digs. Great summer festivals happen at **Triangle Park,** the center of town. Kemmerer's other claim to fame is that J. C. Penney opened his first department store here, which is still standing, in 1902.

Getting There

From Fort Bridger, drive north on Highway 414 and continue as it crosses I-80 to become Highway 412. After 22 miles (35 km), turn right on U.S. 189. Continue north for 13.9 miles (22 km), then turn left to continue on U.S. 189 for 1.7 miles (2.7 km) through Diamondville, which has some hotel options, to Kemmerer. The drive takes 45 minutes.

Kemmerer and Vicinity

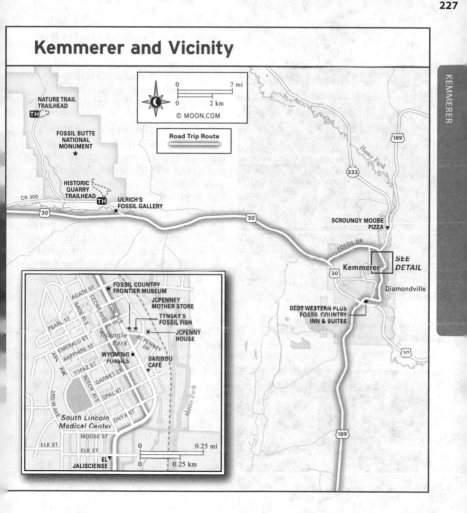

Fuel and Services

Be sure to fill up on gas in Kemmerer before you leave. The next gas station is in Cokeville, near the Idaho border, 45 miles (72 km) west, or Garden City, Utah, 55 miles (89 km) west.

Sights and Recreation
Triangle Park

At the cultural center of town is tiny **Triangle Park,** surrounded by 100-year-old buildings; it's just off Pine Avenue, across from the JCPenney mother store. It's a locals' meeting place and hosts a variety of town events, from vintage car shows to farmers markets and the summertime bonanzas that are the area's most popular events: Fossil Fest and the Oyster Ridge Music Fest.

Fossil Country Frontier Museum

A fun small-town museum, **Fossil Country Frontier Museum** (400 Pine Ave., 307/877-6551, www.hamsfork.net, 9am-5pm Mon.-Sat. Memorial Day-Labor Day, 10am-4pm Mon.-Fri. Labor Day-Memorial Day, free) has a little bit of everything. Visitors can enjoy an

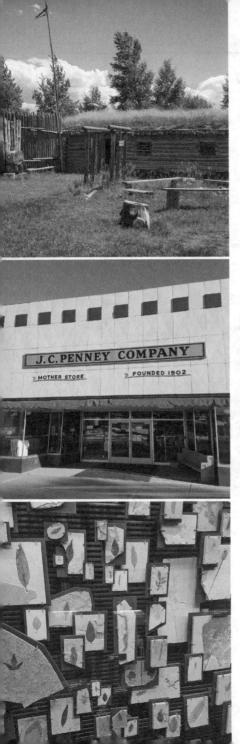

interactive coal mine experience, learn about the town's bootlegging history, and find lots of fossils and dinosaur footprints. Kids might especially enjoy the two-bodied lamb or the set of clothes from a lightning strike victim.

JCPenney Mother Store and House

Kemmerer's claim to fame, other than fossils, is that it's the hometown of Mr. James Cash Penney, the department store mogul who created an empire. The Penney's brand found huge success across the nation as one of the world's largest department stores, growing to a peak of 2,053 stores in 1973. Find the original store, opened in 1902, still operating today. The **JCPenney Mother Store** (722 JC Penney Dr., 307/877-3164, http://stores.jcpenney.com, 10am-6pm Mon.-Sat.) is a retail store, and visitors can also see the original cash register near a display of period merchandise. Friendly staff are happy to tell you more about the store's history and offer handouts with more details.

A block down the street is the **JCPenney House** (307/877-3164, 10am-4:30pm Mon.-Sat., 11am-4pm Sun. Memorial Day-Labor Day, free) where Penney lived 1902-1909. He was born in Hamilton, Missouri, but headed west hoping that the dry climate would be better for his health. In 1902 he lived in Kemmerer with his wife and infant son, moving there from Colorado to start his own store. Volunteers give tours of the small house.

Fossil Shops and Digs

Fossil Country offers plenty of ways to delve deeper into paleontology, with fossil stores and galleries, as well as companies that can take you on digs. Dig up your own discoveries at **American Fossil** (801/836-7269, www.americanfossil.com,

Top to bottom: Fort Bridger State Historic Site; JCPenney Mother Store; Fossil Butte National Monument.

The Rich Record of Fossils in Wyoming

Wyoming is one of the best states to learn more about paleontology. With a rich deposit of fossils throughout the state, many local discoveries have found their way into national and international museums. The Green River Formation is an ancient lakebed that runs along the present-day Green River near Kemmerer in central Wyoming, and into Utah and Colorado. It lies directly atop the Wasatch Formation, and together they're one of the most important sites for understanding the Eocene and Early Eocene era, which came after the extinction of dinosaurs, when the land was covered in large inland lakes, with subtropical palms and sycamores. In this remote location of the country, the land has been left relatively undisturbed, so more complete fossils can be unearthed. The oldest discovered mammal, a bat, was discovered in the formation at Fossil Butte National Monument.

$35 per hour, $85 half-day, $120 full-day). With no storefront, you have to go online or call to book a dig. Its private quarry is 12.4 miles (20 km) northwest of Kemmerer, a 30-minute drive, in the Green River Formation—world-famous for the millions of fossil fish found, and a prolific site where hunters can easily find dozens of specimens in a day. You get to keep anything you find up to $100,000—quite a promise in a place that contains fossils of crocodiles, turtles, bats, stingrays, paddlefish, and even raptors and three-toed horses. Prices are half for ages 7-14 and free under age 7.

Tynsky's Fossil Fish (206 Beryl St., 307/877-6885, 8am-4pm Mon.-Fri.) has a gift shop with a collection of ancient fish such as the *Knightia eocaena,* Wyoming's state fossil. On the wall is a plaster cast of an enormous six-foot-tall soft-shell turtle that shop owner Jim Tynsky and team discovered. You can join day digs (3 hours, $50-65 pp, free under age 8) in Tynsky's private quarry—all equipment is provided, and visitors get to take home up to 10 of the fossil fish they find.

On the road into Fossil Butte National Monument, **Ulrich's Fossil Gallery** (4400 Fossil Butte County Rd., 307/877-6466, www.ulrichsfossilgallery.com, 8:30am-5pm daily Memorial Day-Labor Day, 9am-4pm Mon.-Fri. Labor Day-Memorial Day) shows off some gorgeous specimens. Large wall mounts display hundreds of fish fossils. Purchase a unique kit to take home ($35-85): a split rock from Ulrich's quarry containing a fossil that you can prepare yourself (tools included), or book a day of fossil hunting (3 hours, $125) that allows each digger to collect 6-8 fish. Call ahead to reserve a space.

Skip the dig and browse prior discoveries at **Wyoming Fossils** (921 Pine Ave., 245/223-3204, http://wyomingfossils.com, 9am-6pm daily). The place has the name "Sawaya's" on its storefront, a leftover sign from the building's previous life as a long-running shoe store. Inside is a wonderful shop full of fossils, rocks, gemstones, and minerals, at every price point and in every size. Visitors will find everything from fossilized fish gracing four-foot-tall plaques to tiny button size fish that will slip into your pocket. The shop digs up many of its fossils, specializing in local Green River Formation fossils, and carries others from around the world.

Festivals and Events

Ever see a parade of fossilized fish march down the road? You'll get your chance at Kemmerer's annual **Fossil Fest** (www.fossilfest.org, June), a family-friendly festival for which the whole town turns out. Fun includes a 5K run, a water fight, live music, a tiny rodeo, food and craft vendors, games, and other activities.

For some great tunes, head to the **Oyster Ridge Music Fest** (www.oysterridgemusicfestival.com, July), Wyoming's top free music fest, featuring three days full of live bluegrass and country music. Nationally recognized artists have included multiple Grammy winners, attracting up to 5,000 spectators to Triangle Park on the last weekend in July every year. Get there early to stake out your place on the lawn—bring blankets, coolers, cash for food trucks, and your own instrument for casual jams.

Food and Accommodations

★ **Scroungy Moose Pizza** (179 Hwy. 233, 307/877-4233, 4pm-9pm Mon.-Sat., $16) makes Kemmerer's best pizza. Just north of town, it's nearly hidden behind two big trees along the highway. You can't go wrong with the Frontier Bar pie, featuring pepperoni and Italian sausage. For a bigger adventure, try the Scroungy Cousteau with shrimp and smoked oysters. Build-your-own and gluten-free crust options are available. This place is takeout only—call ahead to avoid a wait.

Find a casual and hearty meal at **Caribou Café** (1012 Pine Ave., 307/224-9949, 8am-9pm Mon.-Sat., 8am-4pm Sun., $12), serving generous portions for breakfast, lunch, and dinner. It's a tasty place to chow down before or after a day of fossil hunting on breakfast burritos, fried chicken, large salads, and burgers in a diner-style atmosphere.

The burritos and carne asada at **El Jalisciense** (1433 Central Ave., 307/877-2948, 9am-8:30pm Mon.-Sat., $13) could rival any spot closer to the border. The fresh salsa has a kick, the guacamole is laid on thick, portions are generous, and the space is small but inviting, with wooden booths.

There aren't a lot of accommodations options in town, but the **Best Western Plus Fossil Country Inn & Suites** (760 U.S. 30, 844/705-6419, www.bestwestern.com, $117-159) is the most comfortable and reliable, located just off the highway before you pass Diamondville, 2 miles (3.2 km) south of downtown Kemmerer. It's a pleasant place to stay, with a pool, a hot tub, and free breakfast.

Fossil Butte National Monument

Fossil Butte National Monument encompasses a rolling landscape of rocky buttes and sagebrush valleys that sit on an ancient lakebed; the 50-million-year-old Fossil Lake was once a subtropical ecosystem. Conditions in the area were perfect for the preservation of fossils: calm waters and no scavenger animals meant that dying creatures were left alone and slowly got covered in the fine silt of the lake. The quality of fossils found here continues to impress scientists. Fish skin, eyes, delicate plants, and even flowers are perfectly preserved in stone. Given the huge numbers of fossils that have been pulled from the area, it's been called an "aquarium in stone." Running through the monument are the Wasatch Formation and Green River Formation, two horizontal geological beds. The Wasatch Formation is characterized by streaks of red and purple, and holds teeth and bones from mammals in the early Eocene era. The Green River Formation lies atop it, and is less colorful, but is the source of some of the more famous fish fossils, from the later Eocene.

This remote area—the national monument is one of the least visited in the West—is full of fragrant sagebrush bushes and short grass; take a look around on your visit to conjure what it was like for a wagon train passing through—the landscape is much the same as that emigrants encountered.

Getting There and Around

From Kemmerer, head west on U.S. 30. In 8 miles (12.9 km), turn right on County Road 300, following signs for Fossil Butte National Monument. In 2.3 miles (3.7 km), turn right onto Chicken Creek Road. The visitors center is to your right in 1.2 miles (1.9 km). The drive takes 20 minutes. The parking lot can accommodate RVs, and there are two hiking trailheads.

Sights

You can see the fossilized remains of entire schools of fish at Fossil Butte National Monument. It's open year-round, though seasonal snow may impact many of the roads and trails. Start at the **visitors center** (864 Chicken Creek Rd., 307/877-4455, www.nps.gov/fobu, 8am-4:30pm daily Mar.-late May and early Oct.-Nov., 8am-6pm daily late May-early Sept., 8am-5pm daily early Sept.-early Oct., 8am-4:30pm Mon.-Sat. Dec.-Feb., free), which has a beautiful gallery and interpretive space showcasing over 300 fossils discovered in the buttes; many are casts, or replicas, but there are plenty of real ones too. Fish feature prominently, and you'll also see a giant 13-foot crocodile, a huge turtle, mammals, birds, plants, and flowers. There are a few great examples of "mass mortality" fossils—with many overlapping fossils in one panel—when an event occurred that caused many fish to die at once.

Outside, on the patio surrounding the center, stroll around the **Journey through Time** exhibit, a walk through a series of interpretive panels describing a prehistoric timeline starting 4.54 billion years ago. The timeline is set to scale, so each step you take corresponds to a set number of years. Follow the panels around the visitors center and enjoy great views. Note the end of the massive timeline—on such a large scale, recorded human history is barely a blip.

A **scenic drive** (late May-Nov.) takes you from the visitors center to the top of a mesa. It's a 10-mile (16-km) out-and-back trip on gravel roads, a 30-minute drive in total. From the visitors center, continue north on Chicken Creek Road for 2 miles (3.2 km) to the Nature Trailhead and picnic area; the road is paved to this point, and afterward gets narrower, steeper, and turns to gravel—it's not recommended for RVs or trailers. (You're welcome to unhook your trailer in the parking lot here or at the visitors center to continue.) Continue another 3 miles (4.8 km) up the steep road to the top of the mesa. From here, a few unpaved trails allow access to surrounding BLM land. The most expansive views of the landscape are from Rubey Point—turn left on the second unpaved road and drive 1 mile (1.6 km) on the mesa to reach it, or park and walk.

Hiking

From the visitors center, head 2 miles (3.2 km) north on Chicken Creek Road to find the **Nature Trail,** an easy 1.5-mile (2.4-km) loop that takes you through wildflowers, sagebrush, and aspen forests, and past a pond. It offers plenty of opportunities to see wildlife such as deer and birds. The path winds up a gentle hill, from the top of which you'll get some great views overlooking the sagebrush-dotted landscape of buttes topped by rocky outcrops. Plan on about an hour for the hike.

For a longer, more strenuous hike, go for the **Historic Quarry Trail.** The 2.5-mile (4-km) loop hike gains 600 feet (180 m) in elevation and can be hot, with little shade. Along the way you'll head up some buttes, and can see the Wasatch and Green River Formations, as well as visit a historical fossil quarry. Budget 1.5-2 hours for this hike.

For both hikes, make sure to apply sunscreen before heading out, and bring water.

IDAHO

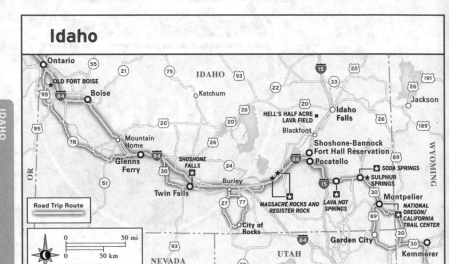

Idaho

The romance of the road may have been thinning for pioneers once they reached Idaho, but modern travelers are in for some of the richest rugged landscape on the route.

After struggling across the vast Wyoming desert, emigrants and their livestock arrived in Idaho in midsummer, tired and thirsty. Most wagon trains reached this point in 2-4 months, and still had more months to go. Wagon traffic didn't extend across the state until a trail was blazed in 1840—before that, fur trappers and early emigrants left their wagons at Fort Hall near Pocatello and continued on foot.

But the first days in Idaho were full of luxuries for the pioneers; at Soda Springs, they found drinkable mineral water, and at Lava Hot Springs they could soak. After that, the road was a rough one over dry wasteland, jagged volcanic fields, and dusty roads until—if they made a treacherous Snake River crossing—they reached the green and lush Boise River Valley, also known as Treasure Valley. The roaring "accursed mad" Snake River was always within view but not often within reach of the thirsty travelers, rushing far below in the inaccessible canyon.

Modern visitors today can enjoy the same delights as the pioneers, such as the hot springs, and are likelier to appreciate the harsh but scenic landscapes: volcanic fields, high deserts swept by fragrant sagebrush, toothy jagged mountains, and the Snake River. At the western edge of the state, the capital, Boise, which grew out of Fort Boise, an emigrant waystation, is an up-and-coming destination offering restaurants, nightlife, and access to outdoor fun.

Highlights

★ Stock up on provisions and take a wagon ride in a simulated journey across the plains at the **National Oregon/California Trail Center** (page 245).

★ Sip bubbling mineral water like emigrants did at **Soda Springs** (page 248).

★ Soak in the same waters as the pioneers at **Lava Hot Springs** (page 252).

★ Take a break at **Massacre Rocks** (page 269), then check out emigrant signatures nearby at **Register Rock** (page 271).

★ Admire **Shoshone Falls,** which dazzled emigrants with its rush of water and sound (page 280).

Best Overnight Stops

★ **Garden City, Utah:** Near the turquoise waters of Bear Lake, a short detour off the route, Garden City is a summer dream of a town, with beaches, vacation rentals, and local raspberries (page 238).

★ **Lava Hot Springs:** Soak your troubles away in this small town that offers a developed hot springs complex, eateries, and hotels—many with their own private hot springs (page 251).

★ **Twin Falls:** With a historic downtown, good restaurants, nearby sights like Shoshone Falls, and easy access to the Thousand Springs Scenic Byway, this town is a good stopping point before Boise (page 276).

★ **Boise:** The capital of Idaho is a fun and vibrant place full of great restaurants, nightlife, outdoor activities, and lodgings (page 299).

Planning Your Time

The Oregon Trail covered 400 miles (645 km) of ground in Idaho. Plan on at least four days to hit the main attractions along the route in this lava-scarred state. With extra time, you can do more hiking or hot springs soaking, and add on trips to Idaho Falls, City of Rocks, or Bruneau Dunes. You might also want an extra day or two in Twin Falls or Boise.

Campsite reservations should be made 4-5 months in advance for the state parks.

The weather in Idaho is hot and dry in the summer; be prepared for hot days in July-August, with average temperatures reaching up to 90°F (32°C). It can be quite cold and snowy in winter and into early spring, with temperatures dropping below 30°F (-1°C). Late spring into early fall is the best time to explore.

Getting There

Starting Points
Oregon Trail Route Notes
From Wyoming, you follow two-lane **U.S. 30** into Idaho to follow the Oregon Trail into Pocatello, before heading west via **I-86/I-84,** on which you'll spend most of the drive through Idaho; the wagons

followed the south bank of the Snake River across the state to Boise, and these interstate highways trace an approximation of this route, sometimes jumping to the north side of the river. In between, for a stretch you'll be back on U.S. 30, which is closer to the wagon route. From Twin Falls, U.S. 30 is part of the **Thousand Springs Scenic Byway.** At Three Island Crossing, emigrants made a choice either to continue following the Snake River as it bent south through a dry wasteland, or to cross to the north side and continue to Fort Boise via the lusher Boise River. You can also make this choice, speeding to the modern city of Boise via I-84 or taking the **South Alternate Route** through Bruneau Dunes via **Highway 78.**

Car and RV
Following the Oregon Trail route from Wyoming, you head west on U.S. 30 before arriving at the Highway 89 junction, 10 miles (16 km) west of Fossil Butte National Monument, and 25 miles (40 km) west of Kemmerer. To continue on the main Oregon Trail route, turn right to head north and then west on U.S. 30 for 30 miles (48 km) to reach the Idaho state line.

You can also opt to take a far more scenic detour around Bear Lake. Turn left and head south and then west at the **U.S.**

Best Walks and Hikes

★ **Canyon Rim Trail:** Hop onto this paved route along the Snake River for a quick stretch, or walk to the eastern end for Shoshone Falls (page 281).

★ **Box Canyon Trail:** This hike leads you to a stunning blue pool deep in a canyon (page 287).

★ **Emigrant Trail:** Walk in the dusty path of the pioneers alongside impressive ruts (page 289).

★ **Bruneau Dunes Loop:** Challenge yourself with a sandy walk up this state park's highest dune (page 294).

★ **Table Rock Trail 15:** Hike up a mountain for great views of Boise (page 304).

GETTING THERE

30/Highway 89 junction in Wyoming, and follow Highway 89 for several miles into Utah, at which point it becomes Highway 30, before looping back up north alongside Bear Lake to rejoin the Oregon Trail route in 60 miles (97 km) at Montpelier, Idaho, a 1.25-hour drive that requires only about 10 miles (16 km) and 20 minutes more driving than taking the Oregon Trail route.

Rentals

Rent a car in Boise at the airport from **Enterprise** (3201 Airport Way, 208/381-0650, www.enterprise.com, 6am-11:30pm daily), which offers a large variety of cars.

From the Salt Lake City International Airport, **Alamo** (776 N. Terminal Dr., 801/575-2211, 6am-midnight daily) or **Hertz** (775 N. Terminal Dr., 801/531-3563, www.hertz.com, 5am-2am daily) are good options.

Rent a camper from **Wandervans** (888/861-6776, www.wandervans.com) in Boise (277 S. 27th St.) or Salt Lake City, Utah (971 W. Margret Ave.); each location is about a 10-minute drive from its respective airport. Campers are $100-140 per day and include a kitchen, sheets, a two-burner stove, a table, camp chairs, and 150 miles (240 km) per day. The small and medium sizes sleep two, while the largest sleeps up to five in a bunk-bed-style arrangement. One-way rentals

are offered between locations, but it's a steep $750 transfer fee to account for the mileage back.

Cruise America (www.cruiseamerica. com) is a nationwide company with a location 25 miles (40 km) west of Boise Airport (117 N, 21st Ave., 800/671 8012, 9am-5pm Mon.-Fri., 9am-noon Sat.) and 14 miles (23 km) south of Salt Lake City International Airport (4125 S. State St., 800/983-3184, 8:30am-5pm Mon.-Sat.). It has four styles, from a truck camper that sleeps three up to a large RV motorhome that sleeps seven. For a week, expect to pay $1,300-1,600 total, depending on mileage.

For a fun experience, rent a van from **Native Campervans** (3010 W. 500 S., Suite 2, 877/550-5335, www.nativecampervans. com, 9am-4pm daily by appointment only), just 6 miles (9.6 km) from Salt Lake City International Airport. Choose from the Biggie van ($1,800 per week June-Sept., $1,250 per week Oct.-May) or the Smalls van ($1,100 per week June-Sept., $800 per week Oct.-May). Most models sleep two adults comfortably and come with a kitchen, bedding, chairs, a cooler, and propane tanks. You'll get 100 free miles (160 km) per day, and dogs are allowed with a $100 fee per animal. Vans come with basic insurance and roadside assistance. Native Campervans also has a location in Denver (2919 E. 42nd Ave.,

877/550-5335, 9am-4pm daily by appointment only), with a one-time $300 fee for a one-way trip.

Fuel and Services

Boise is the biggest city and the state capital. On the eastern side of the state, cities are smaller, with fewer amenities. You'll find gas stations every 30 miles (48 km) or so, but hotels and restaurants will be limited to chains, truck stops, and older diners in Montpelier and Soda Springs.

Air

The **Boise Airport** (BOI, 3201 W. Airport Way, 208/383-3110, www.iflyboise.com) is small but offers daily flights on Alaska, Allegiant, American, Delta, Frontier, Southwest, and United. The airport is 4 miles (6.5 km) south of downtown. Airport transportation options to downtown include bus lines 2, 3, and 4 on **Valley Regional Transit** (http://valleyregionaltransit.org, 6:15am-9:30pm Mon.-Fri., 8:15am-6:30pm Sat., $1)., which runs every half hour on weekdays and every hour on Saturdays; the ride takes 15-30 minutes depending on the line (3 is the fastest, 2 is the slowest). You can also get from the airport to town via **Uber** and **Lyft** (about $15) or **taxi** (about $13).

Salt Lake City International Airport (SLC, 776 N. Terminal Dr., 801/575-2400, www.slcairport.com) offers nonstop flights to over 75 cities. Air Canada, Alaska, American, SkyWest, Delta, Frontier, JetBlue, KLM, Southwest, and United offer daily flights all over North America. Heading north 125 miles (200 km) via I-15 and U.S. 89, you'll reach Garden City, Utah, in 2.25 hours. From here you can connect with the Oregon Trail at Montpelier in eastern Idaho, another 30 miles (48 km) north via U.S. 89, an additional 40 minutes' drive.

Bus

Boise's **Greyhound station** (1212 W. Bannock St., www.greyhound.com,

5:30am-9pm and 10pm-2:30am Mon.-Fri., 5:30am-10am, 3pm-9pm, and 11pm-midnight Sat.-Sun.) has buses between Boise and Portland ($58-120) departing once daily at midday; the bus ride takes 9 hours. Boise to Pocatello ($80-140) buses leave once daily in the evening, a 13-hour overnight trip with an extended 8-hour stop in Twin Falls for the day.

In Pocatello, Greyhound operates at the **Pocatello Regional Transit station** (5815 S. 5th Ave., 208/234-2287, 8am-7pm Mon.-Fri., 9am-5:30pm Sat.), 5 miles (8 km) from downtown. There's no direct return service from Pocatello to Boise, but you can create your own itinerary with two tickets and an overnight layover: Pocatello to Twin Falls ($39), a 2.5-hour trip that leaves twice daily, and Twin Falls to Boise ($30-53), a 2.25-hour trip that departs early in the morning. From the Pocatello Regional Transit station, you can also hop on or off the **Salt Lake Express** (208/656-8824, http://saltlakeexpress.com), a charter shuttle and bus service that operates to and from Salt Lake City, Utah, and Pocatello (from $40 one-way).

⚑ Detour: Bear Lake

Bear Lake (http://stateparks.utah.gov, http://parksandrecreation.idaho.gov) is a turquoise jewel that sparkles in the summer sun beneath mountain peaks. Suspended limestone deposits create its bright color, so bold that it's often called the "Caribbean of the Rockies." The lake straddles Idaho and Utah.

Emigrants didn't typically travel south to see the lake, continuing north from Kemmerer through Cokeville in Wyoming, but in later years of the trail, large numbers of Mormon emigrants settled in this area. They founded most of the towns nearby, including Paris and Montpelier in Idaho, and **Garden City, Utah,** which is the largest town along the lakefront. Today, the area is a popular summer vacation spot. And while you could opt just to take the pretty drive around the lake and then reconnect with the Oregon Trail, you may want to budget some extra time to stop and enjoy the lake and its environs—and get a raspberry shake.

Getting There

From the U.S. 30/Highway 89 junction in Wyoming, west of Kemmerer and the Fossil Butte National Monument, follow Highway 89 for 4 miles (6.4 km) into Utah, at which point it becomes Highway 30. Follow the highway west and then north for 26 miles (42 km) to reach Garden City, the largest town on Bear Lake. On its western shore, it offers the most amenities if you're planning on spending some time here.

The 1.25-hour drive from the U.S. 30/Highway 89 junction in Wyoming only requires about 10 miles (16 km) and 20 minutes more driving than taking the Oregon Trail route, and it's far more scenic. The only sight you'll miss if you opt for this detour is Big Hill, about 7 miles (11.3 km) south of Montpelier on U.S. 30—which you could easily backtrack to.

Sights and Recreation
Minnetonka Cave

Just west of Bear Lake is the beautiful limestone **Minnetonka Cave** (west of St. Charles, ID, 208/540-0266, www.fs.usda. gov, tours daily mid-June-Labor Day, $8 adults, $6 ages 6-15, free under age 6), one of the larger cave systems in Idaho, with nine rooms full of stalactites and stalagmites.

Descend underground on a 1.5-hour guided tour to wander amid fantastical shapes—like stalagmites over 10 feet (3 m) tall!—and learn about the limestone deposits and ancient sea fossils found here. You'll also get a good workout, taking 880 steps as you loop through the cave system. Five different species of bat live in the caves; help protect them from white-nose syndrome by not bringing

clothing or items you've brought into other caves—even if you've washed them, spores that spread the devastating fungal growth can stick around for over a decade.

Tickets are available on a first-come, first-served basis on the same day. It's a good idea to send one person early in the day to get tickets for your party at a later time—otherwise, be prepared to wait around a few hours for your tour time. If you have a group larger than 15, you can call ahead to make reservations; time slots for reserved tours are limited to 9:30am, 5:40pm, and 6pm. Otherwise, tours run regularly throughout the day. Dellene Rigby has worked at the cave for over 20 years and is passionate about giving people the best time possible—for any questions, call (or better, text) her at 208/540 0266. Dress warmly, as the cave maintains a steady temperature of 40°F (4°C)—and don't forget gloves for the chilly railings.

From Garden City, drive 13 miles (21 km) north on U.S. 89, through the small town of St. Charles on the Idaho side, and then turn left onto Minnetonka Cave Road, following it west for 10 miles (16 km). The drive takes about 45 minutes; the scenic canyon road to the cave is slow going. Note there's very limited cell phone service here.

Bloomington Lake

Just northwest of Bear Lake, a short and easy 0.5-mile (0.8-km) walk brings you to **Bloomington Lake,** a beautiful glacier lake in shades of turquoise and green set against a backdrop of jagged cliffs. Lined with wildflowers in spring and summer, it makes a nice picnic spot. It's also perfect for kids: The highlight of a visit to the lake is a rope swing they can use to fling themselves into the glacial lake; just be ready—it's cold!

From Garden City, drive 18 miles (29 km) north on U.S. 89. Turn left at the small town of Bloomington, on the Idaho side, onto Canyon Street, which becomes

Bloomington Canyon Road. Continue for 8 miles (12.9 km), then turn left onto Forest Road 409 and remain on it for 3.2 miles (5.1 km) to the Bloomington Lake parking lot. The drive takes 30 minutes.

Beaches

Bear Lake rules are that any exposed beach below the high-water mark is public land and free to enjoy. However, summer often sees a full lake that goes above the high-water mark, so available beaches can be limited. Consider staying in a resort that includes beach access, or spending your day out on the water instead of the sand. Otherwise, you can find an open beach by driving along the lake's western shore on U.S. 89 and watching for turnouts.

Boating

Bear Lake Rentals (2126 S. Bear Lake Blvd., Garden City, UT, 435/946-8611, www.bearlakerentals.com) offers reservable Sea-Doos, pontoon boats for 10-18 people, and boats for 8-14 people (1 hour $79-189, 8 hours $299-719), as well as a range of nonmotorized equipment (1 hour $15-20, 8 hours $60-80) like paddleboards, tubes, and sea kayaks. Life jackets are included with every rental. The outfitter is located on the private beach at the Blue Water Resort, making it convenient for guests staying there. If you're not staying at the resort, note that use of the beach is only for guests, so plan to stay out on the water or motor your craft to another location.

Epic Recreation (Adventure Center: 201 N. Bear Lake Blvd., Garden City, UT, 435/946-3742, www.epicrecreation. net, 9am-7pm Mon.-Fri., 8am-7pm Sat.; RV Park and Marina: 2410 S. Bear Lake Blvd., Garden City, UT, 435/946-2910, 9am-7pm Mon.-Fri., 8am-7pm Sat., 1pm-7pm Sun.) offers equipment rentals at two locations on the lake. Choose from motorized boats (1 hour $135-430, 8 hours $325-715) or nonmotorized options (1 hour $10-59, 8 hours $49-199)

Bear Lake

like kayaks, paddleboards, and even a water trampoline.

Off-Roading
Epic Recreation (Adventure Center: 201 N. Bear Lake Blvd., Garden City, UT, 435/946-3742, www.epicrecreation.net, 9am-7pm Mon.-Fri., 8am-7pm Sat.; RV Park and Marina: 2410 S. Bear Lake Blvd., Garden City, UT, 435/946-2910, 9am-7pm Mon. Fri., 8am-7pm Sat., 1pm-7pm Sun.) also rents off-road UTVs (4 hours $199-309, 8 hours $255-395) for two or four people, along with advice on where to go.

Entertainment and Events
Enjoy a live performance at the **Pickleville Playhouse** (2049 S. Bear Lake Blvd., Garden City, UT, 435/946-2918, www.picklevilleplayhouse.com, 7:30pm Thurs.-Fri., 2pm and 7:30pm Sat. May-June and Sept., 7:30pm Mon.-Fri, 2pm and 7:30pm Sat. July-Aug., $22-30), offering hilarious family entertainment every summer since 1977. Each season

offers a popular Broadway musical like *Hairspray* or *Beauty and the Beast* as well as the long-running "Juanito Bandito" shows, Wild West adventure tales starring a recurring Spanish villain known as Juanito. Dinner at The Pickleville Grill ($15) is offered on-site at 6:30pm every evening, open to all whether you're attending a show or not.

Bear Lake Raspberry Days is held the first weekend in August and celebrates the region's star fruit. Three days of fun mark the occasion, with parades, live concerts, a craft fair, dances, and a rodeo with bull roping and goat chasing. The festival wraps up with a boat light parade and a burst of fireworks over the lake. The majority of events, including concerts, are free, though the rodeo charges entry ($8 adults, $5 ages 4-11, free under age 4).

Food
At **Campfire Grill** (427 N. Paradise Pkwy,, Garden City, UT, 844/464-5267, www.campfiregrillrestaurant.com, 8am-11am and 5pm-9pm Sun.-Fri., 8am-2pm and 5pm-9pm Sat., $18), at the Conestoga Ranch, you can find a great meal every night. Start with truffle french fries or a fresh salad, then move on to a wood-fired pizza or hearty grilled or roasted meats, like a Wagyu beef burger or barbecue pork chops. You'll dine in view of Conestoga wagons, and on nice nights the tent-like panels of the dining room are pulled back to let the evening air in.

The **Bear Trapper Restaurant** (216 S. Bear Lake Blvd., Garden City, UT, 435/946-8484, www.beartrapperrestaurant.com, 8am-8:30pm Mon.-Sat., $15) is a rustic steak house serving up diner-style food for breakfast, lunch, and dinner. Friendly waitstaff bustle around booths in the homey interior, slinging mashed potatoes, steaks, burgers, fries, and chicken. Watch for the hot fresh rolls that come out first—they're served with fresh raspberry jam.

Enjoy breakfast or lunch at **Ruca's**

Bear Lake Raspberry Shakes

Bear Lake's high elevation helps keep raspberry plants cool in the hot summer sun, a perfect climate for growing delicious raspberries. Farmers here grow older varieties that don't keep or travel as well as conventional berries, and these raspberries are small but oh so sweet, with bright flavors. You can grab a raspberry shake at almost any restaurant in town during harvest season in July-August, but these are some of the best options.

♦ **Chevron on U.S. 89** (604 Logan Rd., Garden City, UT, 435/946-3604, 6am-11pm daily, $3) surprisingly serves some of the best shakes in town, made with hand-scooped ice cream (instead of soft serve) and raspberries well mixed in. Bonus: Check your tire's air pressure while you wait.

♦ **LaBeau's Drive-In** (69 N. Bear Lake Blvd., Garden City, UT, 435/946-8821, 9am-5pm daily summer, $5) is known as the home of the "original" raspberry shake. Its shake isn't too thick or too thin and has good raspberry flavor. Burgers and fries are also available.

♦ **Hometown Drive In** (105 N. Bear Lake Blvd., Garden City, UT, 435/946-2727, 10am-9pm Mon.-Thurs., 10am-10pm Fri.-Sat., 10am-8pm Sun. summer, $4) offers shakes made with soft-serve ice cream made thick with a big hit of raspberry. Pair your shake with a double cheeseburger for the full experience.

(284 S. Bear Lake Blvd., Garden City, UT, 435/946-3691, 8am-7pm Mon.-Sat., 8am-3pm Sun., $9). Run by a descendant of Bear Lake's early settlers, the small highway café serves homemade dishes with care, like big salads and fresh sandwiches. It shines for breakfast, though: don't miss their *aebelskivers,* a Danish pancake ball served with various toppings like fresh raspberry preserves, Nutella, or powdered sugar. You can also get eggs, bacon, and sausages. Coffee and espresso are available, along with outdoor seating in view of the lake.

Get a casual meal at **Cody's Gastro Garage** (88 S. Bear Lake Blvd., 435/946-3644, www.codysgastrogarage.com, 8am-9pm Sun.-Thurs., 8am-10pm Fri.-Sat., $12), a hip place with classics including burgers, rib eye, and fried chicken, along with snazzier updates like loaded quesadillas. The place is permeated with an automobile theme, like a retro 1950s diner.

Accommodations and Camping

Book up to four months in advance for summer to get the best hotels or houses in the Bear Lake area, which is a popular vacation spot.

Stay in a hotel right on the lake at **Blue Water Resort** (2126 S. Bear Lake Blvd., Garden City, UT, 435/946-3333, http://bluewaterresort.net, $99-289). Its Park Hotel is 100 yards (90 m) from the beach and has 16 rooms, most with kitchenettes, while its 20-room Beach Hotel is great for families, with full kitchens, connecting-room options, and more beds, as well as direct beach access. It also has two log cabins and a 10-person beach house with a deck. All guests can enjoy the beautiful private beach, an outdoor pool, and indoor hot tub. On-site watercraft rentals (guests get 15 percent off) are available. The resort has camping and RV sites, but they're only for members.

Glamp at ★ **Conestoga Ranch** (427 Paradise Pkwy., Garden City, UT, 385/626-7395, http://conestogaranch.com, $160-270), where you can spend the night in a swanky tent with authentic 1800s furnishings, soft beds, and electricity. Or upgrade and stay in a Conestoga wagon, complete with king beds and

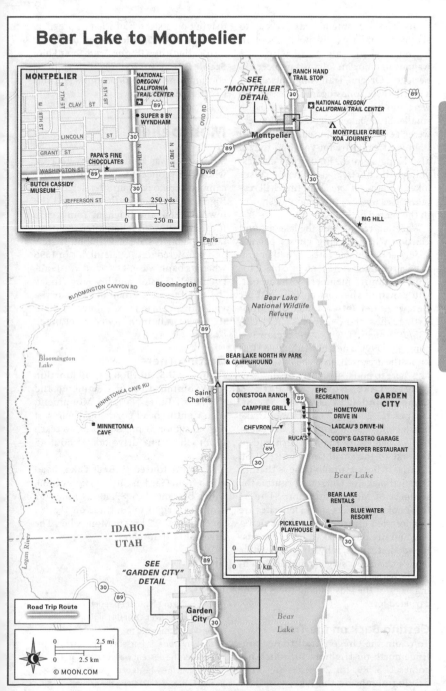

Bear Lake to Montpelier

MONTPELIER

N 7TH ST
CLAY ST
N 5TH ST
N 6TH ST
8TH ST
LINCOLN ST
GRANT ST
WASHINGTON ST
JEFFERSON ST
N 4TH ST
N 3RD ST
30
89

NATIONAL OREGON/CALIFORNIA TRAIL CENTER
★ SUPER 8 BY WYNDHAM
PAPA'S FINE CHOCOLATES
★ BUTCH CASSIDY MUSEUM

0 250 yds
0 250 m

SEE "MONTPELIER" DETAIL

RANCH HAND TRAIL STOP
NATIONAL OREGON/CALIFORNIA TRAIL CENTER
MONTPELIER CREEK KOA JOURNEY
Montpelier
OVID RD
Ovid
Paris
Bloomington
BLOOMINGTON CANYON RD
Bear Lake National Wildlife Refuge
Bear River
BIG HILL

Bloomington Lake
MINNETONKA CAVE RD
MINNETONKA CAVE
Saint Charles
BEAR LAKE NORTH RV PARK & CAMPGROUND

GARDEN CITY
CONESTOGA RANCH
CAMPFIRE GRILL
CHEVRON
RUCA'S
EPIC RECREATION
HOMETOWN DRIVE IN
LADEAU'S DRIVE-IN
CODY'S GASTRO GARAGE
BEAR TRAPPER RESTAURANT
Bear Lake
BEAR LAKE RENTALS
BLUE WATER RESORT
PICKLEVILLE PLAYHOUSE

0 1 mi
0 1 km

IDAHO
UTAH
Logan River

SEE "GARDEN CITY" DETAIL
Garden City
Bear Lake

Road Trip Route

0 2.5 mi
0 2.5 km
© MOON.COM

baths. The wide wagon beds sleep up to six people and are fully mobile; book in a group and you can literally circle the wagons to enjoy an (almost) pioneer experience. Oregon Trail emigrants didn't actually use Conestoga wagons, which were too big and heavy, instead using smaller Studebaker wagons; the pioneers weren't exactly glamping either. Staff will light your campfire for you, and they'll also bring s'mores. Enjoy yoga classes, volleyball courts, a game tent, cruiser bikes, and the on-site Campfire Grill restaurant, as well as a warm rainfall shower in the shared bathhouse.

Vacation rentals rule the lake around Garden City, offering guests private spaces at affordable rates. Whether you need a romantic suite for 2 or a place for your 35 family members to hang out, you can find the best options at **Epic Getaways and Retreats** (865 N. Harbor Village East Dr., Garden City, UT, 435/799-4645, www.myepicgetaways. com, $89-399). The knowledgeable staff know the area well, so if you're stumped on where to book, give them a call.

Bear Lake North RV Park & Campground (220 N. Main St., St. Charles, ID, 208/945-2941, www.bearlake north.com, $23-26 campsites, $110 cabins) is located on the northern end of the lake in the small community of St. Charles, whose claim to fame is that it's the birthplace of Gutzon Borglum, the sculptor of Mount Rushmore. The 34 full-hookup RV sites and 15 tent sites are in a forested grassy area, with picnic tables and fire pits. Also available are rustic wooden cabins, fully furnished with a double bed and a single bunkbed, kitchenette, bath, shower, and TV. Bring sleeping bags for the kids and put them in the carpeted loft.

Getting Back on the Trail

To rejoin the Oregon Trail route, continue north on Highway 30, which becomes U.S. 89, for 24 miles (39 km), driving alongside the lake; you'll be driving on a stretch of what's known as the **Bear Lake Scenic Byway** (in Utah), also called the **Oregon Trail-Bear Lake Scenic Byway** (in Idaho). Turn right to continue on U.S. 89 for 5.7 miles (9.2 km) to Montpelier, Idaho.

Montpelier

Montpelier was known as Clover Creek when the pioneers came through and camped here to regroup after descending Big Hill. Mormon settlers founded the town in 1864, and Brigham Young gave it the name Montpelier, after the capital of his birth state of Vermont. It grew and prospered until a fateful day in 1896 when its bank was hit by Wild West outlaw Butch Cassidy and his gang. Today the small town is proud of its history—you can experience a pioneer wagon train and walk in the footsteps of Butch Cassidy, all in a day.

Getting There

From the **U.S. 30/Highway 89 junction** in Wyoming, west of Kemmerer and the Fossil Butte National Monument, turn right to head north and then west on U.S. 30 for 51 miles (97 km) to reach Montpelier. The drive takes about 45 minutes.

If you detoured to **Bear Lake,** head north from Garden City on Highway 30, which becomes U.S. 89, for 24 miles (39 km). Turn right to continue on U.S. 89 for 5.7 miles (9.2 km) to Montpelier. The drive takes 40 minutes.

Sights
Big Hill

"We came to a high steep spur that extends to the river. Over this high spur we were compelled to climb. . . . Part of the way I rode on horseback, the rest I walked. The descent was very long and steep. All the wheels of the wagon were tied fast, and it slid along the ground.

At one place the men held it back with ropes, and let it down slowly."

Margaret A. Frink, July 6, 1850, *Journal of the Adventures of a Party of California Gold-Seekers*. Frink traveled the trail with her husband Ledyard and kept a diary that offers an excellent account of the journey. The Frinks settled in California near Sacramento and then Oakland.

One of the steepest descents of the entire Oregon Trail, and certainly the longest, rivaled only by California Hill or Ash Hollow in Nebraska, and Laurel Hill in Oregon, was at **Big Hill**, about 7 miles (11.3 km) southeast of Montpelier. Emigrants tied their wagon wheels together to lock them in place and keep them from running into their livestock, then used ropes to slowly lower the wagons down the hill. Making it more challenging, emigrants often hit the area in late July, at the hot peak of summer.

Today you can view the hill from roadside pullouts along west-bound U.S. 30: Look for mileposts 440.1, 441.7, and 454.5. As you come around the hill near milepost 440.1, looking back, you can see the wagon ruts winding down the hill. Historical signs are in a pullout near milepost 441.7, which is easy to see from either direction—look for two tall wooden signs along the road.

If you arrived via the Bear Lake Scenic Byway, you'll have to head back southeast 9 miles (14.5 km) to find Big Hill. If you haven't seen other hills or wagon ruts along the trail yet, this makes a notable stop, but there's not much to do except marvel at the steep hillside.

TOP EXPERIENCE

★ National Oregon/ California Trail Center

The **National Oregon/California Trail Center** (320 N. 4th St., 208/847-3800, http://oregontrailcenter.org, 9am-5pm Mon.-Sat., 9am-3pm Sun. May-Sept.,

$12 adults, $11 seniors, $9 ages 8-17, $5 ages 4-7, free under age 4) is one of the best museums on the trail today, especially for kids. Visitors get to experience the 2,000-mile (3,200-km) journey via guided living history tours. Your party will be greeted by live actors in character as, for instance, a storefront owner or wagon guide. These characters will help your family stock up in the general store, guide you on a bumpy simulated ride in a wagon, and tell stories around a "campfire" about life on a wagon train. The six-month trip will be condensed into about an hour, but you'll come away with a sense of the daily life of pioneers: how they traveled, cooked, cleaned, and befriended each other in wagon camps. Call for reservations if you'd like to lock in a tour time, or just stop by; you'll be included in the next available tour, which runs about every hour.

After the tour, take some time to peruse 44 paintings that depict landmarks along the Oregon Trail by artist Gary Stone (look for him in each work!). The center was built on the site of the Clover Creek Encampment, where pioneers rested and regrouped after tackling Big Hill. Outside the center are a series of statues depicting settlers holding back a wagon heading down the hill.

Summer sees large crowds as tour buses stop at the museum on their way between Yellowstone National Park and Salt Lake City—plan your visit before 10am or after 2pm to avoid the rush.

Butch Cassidy Museum

Wild West train and bank robber Butch Cassidy was the leader of a criminal gang known as the Wild Bunch, known for roaming across the West and eluding the law for years around the turn of the 20th century. Their robbery of the Bank of Montpelier kicked off a years-long spree during which they hit banks in Wyoming, Nevada, South Dakota, and New Mexico. They were depicted in the Oscar-winning *Butch Cassidy and the*

Sundance Kid (1969), starring Robert Redford and Paul Newman.

Today the Bank of Montpelier is the only one still standing that was robbed by Cassidy and the gang, on August 13, 1896. It's now home to the **Butch Cassidy Museum** (833 Washington St., 801/706-4004, www.butchcassidymuseum.com, 10am-4pm daily Memorial Day-Labor Day, free). See the original vault from which the gang stole, and walk on the same floor as the robbers—it's even marked with boot straps! Estimates vary, but Cassidy and his men probably made off with $5,000-15,000. The museum's exhibit pays homage to the number 13, the day on which it was robbed, and a number that was eerily important in Cassidy's life—he was born on April 13, was the oldest of 13 children, and robbed the Bank of Montpelier at 3:13 after making a $13 deposit, the story goes.

The museum has limited hours, but the passionate owner is often willing to show it even during off-hours, so call to arrange a tour. A reenactment of the robbery is held every year on the Saturday nearest the August 13 anniversary, along with a cook-off. Watch the gang rob the bank and make out with the cash. Will they be caught this year?

Food and Accommodations

Get a taste of the sweet life at ★ **Papa's Fine Chocolates** (484 Washington St., 208/847-0117, 10am-9pm Mon.-Thurs., 10am-10pm Fri.-Sat., $6), a family-owned business since 1922. With five generations of experience, the shop scores big on flavor and friendliness. You'll find truffles, bars, and almonds coated with dark or milk chocolate. The best part: The staff cheerfully provides samples until you find your perfect match. Be sure to try the Bavarian mint and dark chocolate chunks with orange. If you have room, have a scoop of ice cream in a homemade waffle cone.

The **Ranch Hand Trail Stop** (23200 U.S. 30, 208/847-1180, www. ranchhandtrailstop.com, 24 hours daily, $9) has been a favorite stop of truckers for years. Yes, this is a greasy diner at a truck stop, but don't be deterred—the food is homemade and delicious. Pancakes come bigger than the plate, cinnamon rolls are gooey, and the biscuits are hand-size. And for dinner, you can get an entire platter of chicken fried steak. Hungry at 2am? No problem—they're open 24 hours a day.

Of the handful of hotels in town, the standout is **Super 8 by Wyndham** (276 N. 4th St., 208/847-8888, www. wyndhamhotels.com, $83-105), next door to the National Oregon/California Trail Center. It has 50 rooms with queen or king beds, some suites, and amenities that include an indoor pool, hot breakfast, and staff ready to give area advice. If you're traveling in a group, it also has a large four-bed suite in a separate annex (from $450).

The extensive grounds of **Montpelier Creek KOA Journey** (28501 U.S. 89, 208/847-0863, www.koa.com, Apr. 15-Sept., $49-58 campsites, $136 cabins) include plenty of RV and tent sites, along with five cabins, as well as numerous amenities like showers, an outdoor pool, a forested nature trail along the creek, and a dog run. Enjoy your downtime fishing in the creek or playing boccie ball, horseshoes, or basketball. The campground is a few miles east of town.

Soda Springs

"Traveled about 22 miles along the bank of the Bear River and are encamped at Soda Springs. This is indeed a curiosity. The water tastes like soda water, especially artificially prepared. The water is bubbling and foaming like boiling water."

Sarah White Smith, July 24, 1838, *Diary of Sarah White Smith*. Smith was one of four newlywed couples who traveled the trail as part of a wagon train of missionaries heading to the Whitman Mission. She didn't stay long, eventually heading farther west—to Hawaii.

Soda Springs was a treat for the pioneers. Water from the hundreds of natural springs in the area bubbled from the earth, reminding them of soda or beer. They eagerly tried it, flavoring it with syrup, using it to bake bread, or just drinking it straight, and many recorded their experience in diary entries, eager to note such a unique event. Camping at Soda Springs was pleasant; there was plenty of water, trout to fish, animals to hunt, wood for fires, and grass for the livestock. After the dry hardscrabble lands of Wyoming, Soda Springs provided a wonderful place to rest before the emigrants hurried north toward Fort Hall. Today, travelers can drink from the same sparkling springs that pioneers dipped their cups into, as well as see a sky-high geyser that was the result of an ill-planned attempt to create a hot spring.

Getting There
From Montpelier, drive 30 miles (48 km) northwest on U.S. 30. The drive takes 30 minutes.

Top to bottom: Soda Springs geyser; Hooper Springs; Wagon Box Grave.

Sights and Recreation
Sulphur Springs

Sulphur Springs, which still casts its distinct aroma, can be found on the way to the town of Soda Springs, just southeast of town on U.S. 30. It was often noted in diaries and was one of the first springs that emigrants came across in the area. Today you can find it with information panels describing its geology. Depending on recent rainfall, it might be a shallow lake or a muddy puddle, but see if you can spot bubbles formed by the escaping gas (which you might also smell).

From Montpelier, head 25 miles (40 km) west on U.S. 30. Instead of continuing the 4.5 miles (7.2 km) to Soda Springs, take a right on the gravel Sulphur Canyon Road. Drive 1.3 miles (2.1 km) to the first road junction; park at the fork, and follow on foot the two-track dirt road on the left that heads north. In 75-100 yards (70-90 m) you'll find the signs and spring on the right.

TOP EXPERIENCE

★ Soda Springs

There are two springs in town today where you can taste the same carbonated mineral water that the pioneers did when they passed through. They're slightly different, and worth comparing. If it's a nice day, consider strolling the 2-mile (3.2-km) path between them.

Start at **Octagon Springs Park** (50 N. Main St.), a nice city green with some informational panels and a picnic area. Look for the octagonal wooden gazebo—redone in 1995, replacing a kiosk built in 1890—in the corner to find the springs. A boardwalk from the gazebo takes you alongside the creek fed by the spring. Dip a cup or your hand into it for a taste.

From Octagon Springs Park, you can walk the **Hooper Trail walkway,** a pleasant 2 miles (3.2 km) to Hooper Springs along Soda Creek. Head north from the park on Main Street. It becomes a dirt path as it leaves the neighborhood, closely following Soda Creek as it winds around Chester Hill to Hooper Springs Park.

The spring at **Hooper Springs Park** (1805 Government Dam Rd.) feeds a small pool under a covered pavilion, built in 1882. Around it you can find picnic tables, benches, and a playground. After the railroad arrived in Soda Springs, the town tried to sell itself as a resort, and the sparkling waters from this spring were marketed nationally. Dip your cup into the water to compare it to the other spring.

To drive between the springs, head east from Octagon Springs Park on Hooper Avenue for 0.4 mile (0.6 km), then turn left onto North 3rd Street East. Continue driving as the road becomes Government Dam Road. In 0.8 mile (1.2 km), turn left to stay on the road. Hooper Springs Park is on the left in 0.5 mile (0.8 km).

Geyser Park

Geyser Park (39 W. 1st St.) is home to the only "captive geyser" in the world—meaning it is controlled by the city. In 1937, the town dug 315 feet (96 m) into the earth hoping to create a natural mineral hot springs pool. Instead, they struck a geyser that quickly flooded the town and took two weeks to plug! Today the geyser remains plugged, building pressure, which is released once an hour on the hour to reach a height of 100 feet (30 m). The eruptions last 4-5 minutes, so you'll have plenty of time for some photos. There's a platform to walk up above it, and a boardwalk around it, offering good views. A kiosk-like visitors center features interpretive signs and restrooms, open seasonally (May-Sept.). Find the park off Main Street behind a row of businesses.

Wagon Box Grave

Learn the sad story of the **Wagon Box Grave** in Fairview Cemetery (165 S. 1st St. W.). A family of seven traveling in 1861 stayed behind their wagon train to look for their stray horses, but were killed during the night in a raid

Soda Springs

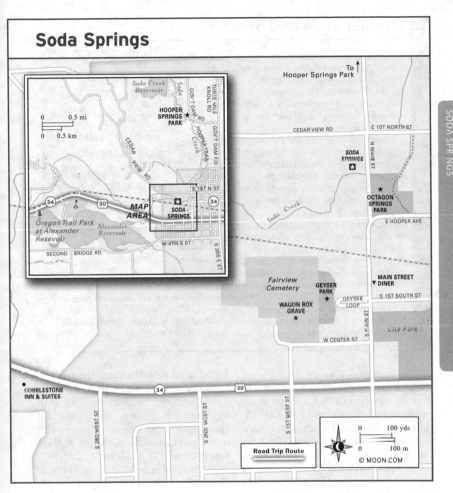

by Native Americans. They were found later and buried in their wagon box, covered in quilts. The grave site was later moved to the cemetery. Today visitors can find a headstone commemorating the event off the main road entering the cemetery, to the east in between two trees, by a bench.

Formation Springs and Cave

About 5 miles (8 km) outside Soda Springs, you'll find a 195-acre Bureau of Land Management (BLM) preserve that's home to **Formation Springs and Cave**

(2942 Trail Canyon Rd., 208/776-5221, sunrise-sunset daily, free). While it's not recorded in any Oregon Trail diaries, it's a good guess that emigrants knew about and visited the pools and springs along with the more popular Soda Springs. Today the area is a refuge for local birds and wildlife such as deer and elk, and visitors can see spring-fed pools and unique geological formations—by-products of the calcium carbonate deposits from the springs—as well as a cave. From the parking lot, a short trail, less than 1 mile (1.6 km), loops around the pools and preserve.

Pioneer Soda and Bread

Finding the water supply at Soda Springs was a unique treat for the pioneers, and they noted several ways of enjoying it. Some found the taste disagreeable, and they mixed it with syrup to make flavored sodas, which were popular back east at early soda fountain shops.

The spring water contained saleratus, or sodium bicarbonate—the white, chalk-like substance that gathers near geysers and looks somewhat like baking soda. In fact, pioneers brought store-bought saleratus with them, carefully packaged in paper, in order to bake soda bread in cast-iron pans over outdoor fires. By Soda Springs, their supplies might have been running low, so many supplemented their stash with the naturally occurring saleratus, to mixed reactions. Some, like

mineral deposits from Soda Springs

Sarah White Smith, enjoyed it: "We find it excellent for baking bread, no preparation of water is necessary. Take it from the fountain and the bread is as light as any prepared with yeast." Others were not as impressed, and thought it imparted a bitter taste; Elizabeth Smith thought the soda water was "far from being equal to artificial saleratus although looks as good . . . it will not foam buter milk one bit."

You can explore the cave on your own. It's a bit steep as you enter, but easy to explore once inside, with three short passageways to choose from. Bring a flashlight or headlamp, and watch out for sharp rocks and low-hanging ceilings. Find the cave from the parking area by heading across the small bridge and continuing until the trail splits—take the right fork for about 20 yards (18 m) and look for the depression of the cave entrance.

Head east via U.S. 30 from Soda Springs, turning left onto South 3rd Street East, followed by a right onto Hooper Avenue in 0.3 mile (0.4 km). Follow Hooper Avenue for 2.8 miles (4.5 km) as it curves north and becomes Highway 34. Near milepost 60.8, turn right onto Trail Canyon Road and drive 1 mile (1.6 km) before turning left onto a dirt road for the parking lot.

Food and Accommodations

Soda Springs is a small town with few dining options. Consider stocking up in Montpelier or pushing on to Lava Hot Springs for more choices. But you can find a good breakfast or lunch at **Main Street Diner** (71 S. Main St., 208/547-3928, 7am-2:15pm Mon.-Sat., $9) near Geyser Park. An easygoing place, the neighborhood joint serves up sandwiches and big burgers and has a salad bar. Start the day with a breakfast burrito, short stack of pancakes, or a Tex-Mex omelet.

There aren't a lot of accommodations options in town, but **Cobblestone Inn & Suites** (341 W. 2nd St., 208/547-1920, www.staycobblestone.com, $115-130) is a good bet for an overnight stay. The hotel offers simple but comfortable rooms with hot breakfast included and a wine and beer bar.

Along the Trail from Soda Springs

Oregon Trail Park

See the ruts heading away from town as you leave Soda Springs. The Alexander Reservoir covers most of the trail that came through this area, but there are a few ruts left to see at **Oregon Trail Park** at the edge of the reservoir. This is also a great place to picnic, enjoy fresh air, and do some bird-watching to see pelicans, hawks, and seagulls.

Getting There

The ruts are visible on the left as you enter the park, 1.8 miles (2.8 km) west of Soda Springs on U.S. 30.

Hudspeth Cutoff Marker

The **Hudspeth Cutoff** is where many emigrants broke off the main trail either for a shortcut or an alternate route to California. The Oregon Trail wasn't one main route, but a series of routes and paths, cutoffs, and shortcuts, as wagons tried their best to find the shortest and safest way west. On any given path, wagons might veer off the main trail to find better grazing for their oxen or mules, or just to get out of the dusty wake of the trail. Many times a wagon train leader would decide that there was a shorter or better way to get somewhere, and would blaze a new trail, sometimes successfully, sometimes not. The most famous shortcut mistake was the Hastings Cutoff, which left the trail in Wyoming and resulted in the Donner Party tragedy.

Leaving Soda Springs, the main Oregon-California Trail for years went northwest in a direct attempt to reach Fort Hall, navigating between mountain peaks. In the summer of 1849, Benoni M. Hudspeth instead went south, leading his wagon train through a small gap in the mountains and creating a rough, but more direct, route to California.

His shortcut rejoined the main trail just north of City of Rocks, bypassing Fort Hall and the Snake River completely. While Hudspeth hoped it would save a huge amount of time, in reality it shaved off about 25 miles (40 km), and added several rough, difficult sections. But as gold rush fever swept the country, many forty-niners headed to California followed Hudspeth, and his new route became a well-traveled part of both the California and the Oregon Trails. There's not much to see here along the highway other than a marker, but it marks a significant junction on the trail.

Getting There

Heading west from Soda Springs on U.S. 30, find the historical marker in a highway pullout to your left after 16 miles (25 km).

Lava Hot Springs

The town of Lava Hot Springs is a small community built around two mineral hot springs tucked near the Portneuf River in a pretty valley. The steaming mineral springs were well known to Shoshone and Bannock tribes, who roamed the area and used the springs—which they called Poha-Ba—as a gathering place and for spiritual and physical healing. Ute, Paiute, and Cheyenne peoples were also frequent visitors.

By the 1820s, fur trappers were familiar with the hot springs. It remained somewhat unknown to early trail emigrants; from Soda Springs, the main trail for years headed directly northwest to Fort Hall, but in 1849, after the discovery of the Hudspeth Cutoff, which headed directly west, traffic shifted. From Lava Hot Springs, California-bound travelers would continue west, while the Oregon-bound would follow the Portneuf River north to Fort Hall. Emigrants found the springs a fortuitous place to bathe and do laundry.

IDAHO

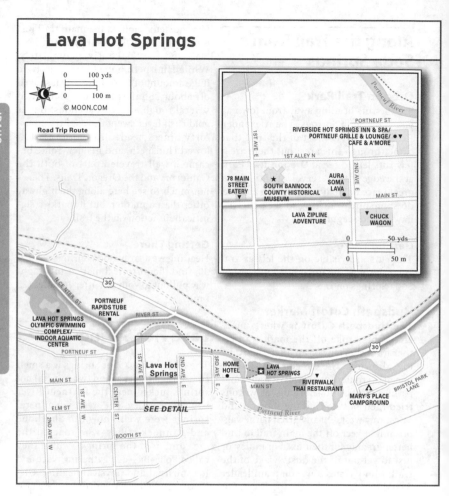

Lava Hot Springs

0 100 yds
0 100 m
© MOON.COM

Road Trip Route

Detail map labels:
PORTNEUF ST
1ST AVE E
RIVERSIDE HOT SPRINGS INN & SPA/
PORTNEUF GRILLE & LOUNGE/ ● ▼
CAFE & A'MORE
1ST ALLEY N
2ND AVE E
78 MAIN STREET EATERY ▼
SOUTH BANNOCK COUNTY HISTORICAL MUSEUM ★
AURA SOMA LAVA ●
MAIN ST
LAVA ZIPLINE ADVENTURE ■
CHUCK WAGON ▼
0 50 yds
0 50 m

Main map labels:
30
N CENTER ST
PORTNEUF RAPIDS TUBE RENTAL ■
RIVER ST
LAVA HOT SPRINGS OLYMPIC SWIMMING COMPLEX/ INDOOR AQUATIC CENTER ■
PORTNEUF ST
1ST AVE E
Lava Hot Springs
2ND AVE E
3RD AVE E
HOME HOTEL ●
LAVA HOT SPRINGS ★
30
MAIN ST
1ST AVE W
CENTER ST
ELM ST
1ST AVE W
2ND AVE W
BOOTH ST
SEE DETAIL
Portneuf River
RIVERWALK THAI RESTAURANT ●
MARY'S PLACE CAMPGROUND ⋀
BRISTOL PARK LANE
Portneuf River

Today, Lava Hot Springs offers an excellent respite for the long-distance roadtripper—soak in the mineral hot springs, tube the spring-fed Portneuf River that cuts through town, or ride a zip line. If you have time, you can easily spend a few days in the small town, but plan ahead—everyone else has the same idea in the high season between Memorial Day and Labor Day. You'll want to book your accommodations in advance, but don't worry about the hot springs, as no reservations are required (though it might be a good idea to arrive early on the day of your visit).

Getting There

From Soda Springs, drive west on U.S. 30 for 22 miles (35 km). Turn left onto Main Street to head into the town of Lava Hot Springs, less than a 30-minute drive.

Sights

TOP EXPERIENCE

★ Lava Hot Springs

Lava Hot Springs today is developed and comprises two parts: the hot springs area, and about 0.5 mile (0.8 km) west, a water

The California Trail

It wasn't only Oregon Fever that was sweeping the nation, but California Fever, even before gold was discovered there. Descriptions in guidebooks told of a lush land that seemed like paradise to burdened Easterners in the grip of an economic depression. After gold was discovered at Sutter's Mill near present-day Sacramento, people poured onto the trail, hoping to strike it rich. Estimates are that up to 250,000 people packed up and headed to California between 1841 and 1869, about equal to the number of Oregon emigrants. The California Trail was arguably the hardest of the overland routes as it traversed the Great Salt Lake Desert and the peaks of the Sierra Nevada.

California Trail sign

"It was awful coming up those mountains. There were great rocks, waist high, that the wheels had to bump over, and it was all the poor oxen could do to drag the lightened loads."

Frances Anne Cooper, recalling her 1848 trip to California along with her family, *San Francisco Chronicle*, September 9, 1900. She was the first white woman to be married in California.

Wagons headed to California following the same trail as their Oregon-bound neighbors through the Rockies at South Pass, Wyoming, after which they spread out on various paths. The trail from this point forward has been described as a "rope with frayed ends," ending up all across Northern California—usually closest to the nearest gold strike. One trail, the Hastings Cutoff, broke off from the main route near Fort Bridger, Wyoming, while most others waited until the Hudspeth Cutoff near Soda Springs. Still others continued with their Oregon-bound companions until the last offshoot in the middle of Idaho, where they could bypass the Great Salt Lake Desert in Utah by going south through the City of Rocks into Nevada.

The first wagon train to make it through to California was the Bidwell-Bartleson party in 1841. They left Missouri with 69 people and reached Fort Hall in Idaho relatively easily. There, some of the party balked at the road to California, since the group had no guide and no map. They decided to take the road to Oregon, while the majority continued on to California. The California group headed into Nevada, where they were forced to abandon their wagons in the rocky Sierra Nevada foothills and continue on foot with pack animals. One member was the first woman to cross overland to California: Nancy Kelsey, 19 at the time, who carried her baby with her.

park-like complex with indoor and outdoor features. A discounted combination pass is available to visit both in one day ($12.50 summer, $9.50 winter).

In emigrant times the hot springs were another in a long line of fabulous springs they had come across in recent days. Most diaries are more concerned with the earlier Soda Springs, where they could taste the water, bake with it, and marvel at it. By the time they reached Lava Hot Springs, emigrants may have been feeling less amazed and ready to hurry on toward Fort Hall, where they could restock. But the hot water was still welcome for bathing and washing clothes.

Today you can soak in mineral water in five outdoor pools fed by the underground spring at **Lava Hot Springs** (430 E. Main St., 208/776-5221, http://lavahotsprings.com, 8am-11pm daily May-Sept., 9am-10pm Sun.-Thurs., 9am-11pm Fri.-Sat. Oct.-Apr., $6-8). The pools range in temperature 102-112°F (39-44°C), have ledges to sit on, gravel bottoms, and umbrellas and shades covering them. You can peek into a split rock in the wall to see the spring—which has no sulfur (so no odor!)—bubbling and steaming. Soak near the Sunken Gardens, which has native plants and flowers in the rock wall next to the flowing Portneuf River. Cool off under a cold-water deck shower, then hop in another pool for more soaking. Towels and lockers are available to rent, and there are dressing rooms and showers.

If you've got more active water play in mind, or if you have kids, head to the **Olympic Swimming Complex** (195 N. Center Ave., 208/776-5221, http://lavahotsprings.com, noon-8pm late May-mid-June, 11am-8pm mid-June-early Sept., $7.50-10). It's a large outdoor pool that's naturally heated and has numerous slides, like a speed slide with a 60-foot vertical drop and some twisty tube slides. It's open only in the summer, so for off-season fun there's also the **Indoor Aquatic Center**, featuring a warm swimming pool with a diving board and even a climbing wall right in the water, a 10-person natural hot pool, and the Portneuf Kiddie Cove, a shallow wading pool with fountains, geysers, buckets, and slides. Hours vary by day and season, so call ahead or check online.

South Bannock County Historical Museum

Learn a little more about the area at the **South Bannock County Historical Museum** (10 E. Main St., 208/776-5254, www.lavahistoricmuseum.weebly.com, noon-5pm Thurs.-Sun., $2). Housed in a former bank on Main Street, the

Lava Hot Springs

museum has permanent and rotating exhibits that explore the region's past and present. Start with "Poha-Ba, Land of Healing Water," to discover how Native Americans used the waters for hundreds of years; the exhibit was curated with input from Shoshone-Bannock Tribe members, using recorded interviews from grown children who once lived in the area. Other exhibits are a bit of a hodge-podge but include Oregon and California Trail pioneer artifacts like wagon wheels and photos from early in Lava Hot Springs's history.

Recreation
Tubing
Float down the river via **Portneuf Rapids Tube Rental** (195 N. Center St., 208/317-2097, http://lavatuberental.com, 10am-dark Mon.-Sat. Memorial Day-Labor Day), which has single ($5-10), double ($10-20), triple ($15-30), and quad tube ($20-40) options. Your rental comes with a map showing a few options for where to

put in—head up to higher ground for a waterfall and more rapids, or lower for a gentler experience. From end to end, the float run takes under an hour, but you can walk back 3.5 blocks to the start and do it again. Rentals come in increments of two hours, half-day, or full-day. A shuttle is available as well ($5-15). Every rental comes with a life jacket. Note that although the Portneuf River is fed by the hot springs, it can be chilly!

Zip-Lining
If you're in search of more thrills, get in touch with **Lava Zipline Adventure** (155 E. Main St., 208/589-1734, www.lavazipline.com, daily summer, Sat.-Sun. fall-spring, $46). Its 3.5-hour zip-line trip includes transportation to a private canyon outside Lava Hot Springs, where you'll glide high over lava flows at heights of 800-1,500 feet (240-450 m). Also at the site are a high ropes course, climbing wall, and geodesic dome. Wear closed-toed, comfortable shoes, and be prepared for a short hike up the canyon through remarkable scenery. Time slots vary seasonally; reserve ahead of time.

Food
The welcoming **Chuck Wagon** (211 E. Main St., 208/776-5141, 6:30am-9pm Sun.-Thurs., 6:30am-10pm Fri.-Sat., $9) offers big portions and friendly service. The burgers are towering and the fries crispy, and the breakfast menu features great omelets and pancakes with homemade raspberry jam (buy a small jar to take home with you).

Offering good food in a casual environment, **78 Main Street Eatery** (78 Main St., 208/776-5106, 8am-9pm Sun.-Thurs., 8am-10pm Fri.-Sat., $15) has a bar area and large dining room, as well as a patio for dining in nice weather. Try the bison burger, Reuben with homemade sauerkraut, or prime rib. Kids' meals come in a cardboard car.

One of the more upscale places in town, the **Portneuf Grille & Lounge** (255

E. Portneuf St., 208/776-5504, www. riversideinnhotsprings.com, 5pm-9pm Sun.-Tues., 5pm-11pm Wed.-Sat., $18) is at the Riverside Hot Springs Inn & Spa. It's the place to go for fine-dining on fresh seafood, steaks, and pastas as well as vegetarian options. Each entrée has a suggested wine pairing, or try a lovingly crafted cocktail. On Friday night, go for the popular cioppino. Also in the Riverside Hot Springs Inn & Spa is **Café & A'more** (255 E. Portneuf St., 208/776-5504, www.riversideinnhotsprings.com, 7am-11am daily), good for a light breakfast with a coffee or mimosa. Don't miss the big cinnamon roll.

At the edge of town is a gas station with "Thai Food" emblazoned in red; **Riverwalk Thai Restaurant** (695 E. Main St., 208/776-5872, 1pm-9pm Tues.-Sun., $13) has repurposed the old station. It's a busy family-run place with a familiar menu of curries, noodles, and fried rice, offering a nice alternative to burgers and steaks.

Accommodations and Camping

Enjoy the hot springs in the privacy of your own room at ★ **Home Hotel** (306 Main St., 208/776-5050, www.homehotel. com, $79-139), where most of the 27 rooms include a natural hot springs bath, some on a private patio. Each room is named after an artist, such as Frida Kahlo and Pablo Picasso, and showcases replicas of their work. The restored building is over 100 years old and right on Main Street, within easy walking distance to everything.

A peaceful place to stay for the night

is **Aura Soma Lava** (196 E. Main St., 208/776-5800, www.aurasomalava.com, $85-250), downtown. In addition to 20 well-appointed rooms, five tiny houses and five cottages have kitchens. A private outdoor mineral hot spring for the hotel is a block away, where guests can relax after walking a rock labyrinth on a nearby riverfront meadow. Many rooms have their own jetted tubs, and massage services can be booked for a truly relaxing stay.

The **Riverside Hot Springs Inn & Spa** (255 E. Portneuf St., 208/776-5504, www. riversideinnhotsprings.com, $90-125) is a romantic destination for travelers wishing to wash their cares away. Built in 1914 and listed on the National Register of Historic Places, the hotel has 18 classically decorated rooms for adults and children age 16 and over. A full-service spa offers its own hot springs, also open to nonguests, and a wide range of massage services. After your treatment, enjoy dinner at the on-site Portneuf Grille & Lounge. Hotel guests also receive a voucher for breakfast at Café & A'more in the lobby. It's an easy walk to the Lava Hot Springs pools, restaurants, and other activities.

Park your RV or trailer at **Mary's Place Campground** (300 Bristol Park Lane, 208/776-5026, http://marysrvcamp.com, mid-May-early Sept., $50-60). It has full hookups, Wi-Fi, showers, and secluded sites near the river. Tent camping is also available. The park is just across the Portneuf River from town, far enough to feel away from it all but within easy walking distance.

Pocatello

Chief Pocatello (Tondzaosha, in the Shoshoni language) was the leader of the Shoshone people in the mid-1800s. Faced with waves of settlers as the United States expanded, he led the resistance with attacks against the newcomers in the 1850s. Once the U.S. Army stepped in, he sued for peace to save his people, and was one of the signers of the Fort Bridger Treaty of 1868, which assigned the Shoshone-Bannock people the Fort Hall Reservation. He died in 1884, and when the railroad extended north, spurring development of a settlement in the area, it was named Pocatello in his honor. The town of Pocatello today is home to Idaho State University and has an active small-town college feel, with interesting museums, great restaurants, and some lively bars.

Old Town Pocatello, the heart of the city, lines both sides of the railroad tracks. The Historic Warehouse District, part of Old Town, is where much of the action is today, on the west side of the tracks along Main Street, from Benton Street to East Gould Street.

Getting There

From Lava Hot Springs, drive 12 miles (19 km) west on U.S. 30, then merge with I-15 and U.S. 91, heading north. Continue for 19 miles (31 km), then take exit 67. Turn left to follow 5th Avenue into town. After 2.3 miles (3.7 km), turn left onto Benton Street and then right in about five blocks for Main Street. The drive takes about 40 minutes.

Sights

Bannock County Historical Museum and Fort Hall Replica

The **Bannock County Historical Museum** (3000 Ave. of the Chiefs, 208/233-0434, www.bchm-id.org, 10am-6pm Mon.-Sat., 1pm-5pm Sun. Memorial Day-Labor Day, 10am-4pm Tues.-Sat. Labor Day-Memorial Day, $5) is a large one-room museum focused on local Pocatello and Bannock County history. Visitors will find a riot of diverse artifacts, ranging from an antique dentist chair to model railroad tracks and a stagecoach that once saw a shootout, not to mention an entire frontier general store. Staff are friendly and helpful, happy to dig deeper into any historical questions.

The best reason to visit, though, is the **Fort Hall Replica** on the museum's grounds. Built in 1834 by Nathaniel Wyeth, Fort Hall was a fur trading post soon bought by England's Hudson's Bay Company, which made extensive improvements. It quickly became a major supply stop for emigrants on their way west. It was somewhat ironic that the fort was owned by England, which had zero interest in helping the United States strengthen their claims on western land.

The actual location of the fort is on the Shoshone-Bannock reservation just north of town—it fell into disuse and disrepair in the 1860s, and this replica was built in 1962. The replica's picturesque white walls are built to the exact specifications as the old Hudson's Bay Company's plan. Inside the huge log doors are replica living quarters, clothing, pioneer wagons, and blacksmith tools, as well as old recipes, letters, and maps. Staff are delighted to give visitors guided tours on request. Budget about an hour to visit both the museum and fort replica.

Zoo Idaho

Zoo Idaho (2900 S. 2nd Ave., 208/234-6264, http://zooidaho.org, 10am-5pm daily May-Aug., 10am-4pm Sat.-Sun. Apr. and Sept.-Oct., $6) is a small but lovingly tended ode to Idaho's spectacular local wildlife. Rather than showcase animals from exotic places, the zoo features wildlife from the Intermountain region right in its backyard, up close. Animals include bison, mountain lions, birds of prey, elk, and wolves. The Grizzly Bear Exhibit encompasses a half acre of lava

IDAHO

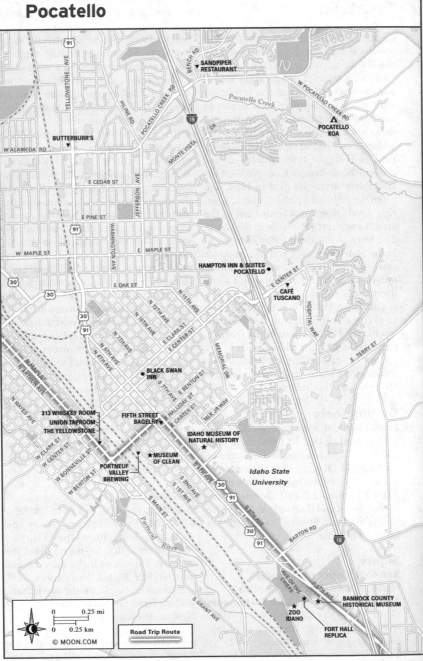

Pocatello

YELLOWSTONE AVE
91
BENCH RD
▼ SANDPIPER RESTAURANT
W POCATELLO CREEK RD
Pocatello Creek
HILINE RD
POCATELLO CREEK RD
15
▲ POCATELLO KOA
BUTTERBURR'S
W ALAMEDA RD
MONTE VISTA
DR
E CEDAR ST
JEFFERSON AVE
E PINE ST
91
WASHINGTON AVE
W MAPLE ST
E MAPLE ST
30
HAMPTON INN & SUITES POCATELLO •
E OAK ST
E CENTER ST
CAFÉ TUSCANO
30
91
N 15TH AVE
HOSPITAL WAY
N 12TH AVE
N 10TH AVE
E CLARK ST
E CENTER ST
N 7TH AVE
MEMORIAL DR
E TERRY ST
N 5TH AVE
N 4TH AVE
N MAIN ST
N ARTHUR AVE
• BLACK SWAN INN
S 7TH AVE
E BENTON ST
E BENTON ST
E HALLIDAY ST
E CARTER ST
MLK JR WAY
N HAYES AVE
313 WHISKEY ROOM
UNION TAPROOM
THE YELLOWSTONE
FIFTH STREET BAGELRY ▼★
W CLARK ST
W CENTER ST
IDAHO MUSEUM OF NATURAL HISTORY
★
W BONNEVILLE ST
★ MUSEUM OF CLEAN
Idaho State University
W BENTON ST
PORTNEUF VALLEY BREWING
S 3RD AVE
S 2ND AVE
S 1ST AVE
S 4TH AVE
30
91
S 5TH AVE
S MAIN ST
Portneuf River
30
91
BARTON RD
15
AVE OF THE CHIEFS
S 5TH AVE
S GRANT AVE
★ ZOO IDAHO
★
FORT HALL REPLICA
BANNOCK COUNTY HISTORICAL MUSEUM

0   0.25 mi
0   0.25 km
Road Trip Route
© MOON.COM

rocks, trees, and a pool that the two resident bears can frolic in. Kids can check out a discovery backpack with themed activities, and enjoy discovery stations around the zoo.

Museum of Clean

Enjoy some clean fun at the quirky **Museum of Clean** (711 S. 2nd Ave., 208/236-6906, www.museumofclean. com, 10am-5pm Tues.-Sat., $6), dedicated to the notion that cleaning makes for a better world. This isn't some dusty collection of old vacuums, but a giant complex of hands-on fun and cleaning history that spans 2,000 years. It's especially great for kids, who will love a three-story playground that'll help get them excited about recycling and sweeping. They can try doing laundry pioneer-style by spinning a metal drum by hand, act out the part of a chimney sweep in the Old English Village (and learn why the olden times had rampant health problems), and use antique cleaning tools like pre-electric vacuums. Depending on time and interest, you can see the exhibits with or without the included guided tour, which can take an hour or more. Either way, plan some time to explore on your own and take photos next to the giant garbage can or inside an old-fashioned washtub. The whole place, as you might expect, is spotless.

Idaho Museum of Natural History

On the Idaho State University campus, the **Idaho Museum of Natural History** (698 E. Dillon St., 208/282-3168, www. isu.edu/imnh, noon-6pm Tues.-Fri., 9am-5pm Sat., noon-5pm Sun., $7) offers a short, fun tour through Idaho history, rooted in science. Roam Pocatello's most recent ice age with prehistoric animals like saber-toothed cats and giant ground sloths. There's a 150 million-year-old local shark species, *Helicoprion*. Then take in one of the traveling exhibits focusing on areas like paleontology, earth science, and anthropology. Volcanic activity, stone-age weapons, and monster snakes await.

Entertainment

You'll feel like a local at **Portneuf Valley Brewing** (615 S. 1st Ave., 208/232-1644, www.portneufvalleybrewing.com, 11:30am-9:30pm Mon.-Thurs., 11:30am-11pm Fri.-Sat., $12), a neighborhood favorite. Artwork adorns the brick-lined walls, and weekends offer live music and comedy shows in the intimate dining room. Look for the easy-drinking Twisted Stick Amber Ale or the hoppy Grog, a session IPA. In addition to craft beer, the brewery also offers wine and handcrafted sodas. The food menu is an international tour of flavors, with jambalaya, teriyaki chicken, a smothered burrito, and a giant salty pretzel among the offerings. Tip: Show your room key for any local hotel and get 10 percent off your order.

The **313 Whiskey Room** (230 W. Bonneville St., 208/234-7000, www. theyellowstonerestaurant.com, 4pm-10pm Mon.-Sat.) is located inside the former Hotel Yellowstone, at the entrance to Old Town. The bar features original interiors of the century-old hotel, such as wallpaper and intricate woodwork. Whiskey, rye, scotch, and bourbon lovers will find over 170 varieties from the United States, Canada, Japan, Ireland, and more. On Wednesday, there's a discounted Whiskey Flight Night, where a themed selection of tastings is 20 percent off. In the same building, sister bar **Union Taproom** (4pm-10pm Mon.-Sat.) offers a casual pub atmosphere with craft beer on tap, as well as a food menu of burgers, soups, fish-and-chips, and fried appetizers. It also has an outdoor patio with heaters and fire pits.

Food

Everything at ★ **Café Tuscano** (2231 E. Center St. 208/233-7702, www. cafetuscano.com, 11am-10pm daily, $14) is inviting, from the interior decorated

with Tuscan murals and hanging plants to the racks of international wine. The menu features decadent pastas like a tri-tip fettucine with blue cheese, crispy pizzas, charcuterie and cheese boards, and classic desserts like tiramisu. You'll enjoy your meal so much you'll forget about the quirky location—the restaurant is inside a gas station!

Steaks and seafood rule the dining room at **Sandpiper Restaurant** (1400 Bench Rd., 208/233-1000, http://idahosandpiper.com, 4:30pm-10pm Mon.-Thurs., 4:30pm-10:30pm Fri.-Sat., $25). One of the top dishes is the Steak Sandpiper, a filet wrapped in bacon then finished with a mushroom cap and béarnaise sauce. Or opt for scallops, a stuffed halibut, a fresh Idaho trout, or a spicy Cajun shrimp pasta.

At the entrance to Old Town, a green neon sign lights up a building's roof, welcoming visitors with a bright "Hotel Yellowstone." The hotel opened in 1915 across from the railroad tracks, still a hopping part of the city. While it no longer operates as a hotel, a fine-dining restaurant opened inside in 2018 to much acclaim. **The Yellowstone** (230 W. Bonneville St., 208/234-7000, www.theyellowstonerestaurant.com, 11am-10pm Mon.-Sat., $17) crafts farm-to-table dishes with items like locally fished ruby red trout. Creative touches add to the elegance of the meal, and a solid menu of cocktails is offered.

A family-owned shop, **Fifth Street Bagelry** (559 S. 5th Ave., 208/235-1311, www.5thstreetbagelry.net, 6:30am-5pm Mon.-Fri., 7am-4pm Sat.-Sun., $6), serves up fresh bagels and coffee with friendly service. Peruse the extensive menu, and if you can't decide, ask the staff, who readily suggest their favorites. Daily specialty bagels like a spinach florentine or cheddar jalapeño are on offer, along with

Top to bottom: cleaning supplies at the Museum of Clean; inside the Fort Hall Replica; Shoshone-Bannock Fort Hall Reservation.

plenty of breakfast and lunch sandwiches. Top things off with a gourmet mocha or latte to start your day right.

Named after an inn-owning hobbit in Tolkien's *Lord of the Rings* trilogy, **Butterburr's** (917 Yellowstone Ave., 208/232-3296, www.butterburrs.net, 6am-10pm Mon.-Thurs., 6am-11pm Fri., 7am-11pm Sat., 7am-9pm Sun., $9) has been a Pocatello mainstay for decades. The focus is on homemade baked goods like bread, maple twists, cinnamon rolls, and an oatmeal pie. Breakfast is served all day and includes traditional diner favorites done right (eggs, potatoes, bacon, toast, pancakes). For lunch, try the SST (soup, sandwich, treat) and get your choice of a sandwich on homemade bread, a delicious soup, and a slice of freshly made pie.

Accommodations and Camping

Stay in the Wild West, Atlantis, or a Mayan rainforest at the ★ **Black Swan Inn** (746 E. Center St., 208/233-3051, www.blackswaninn.com, $189-239). The English Tudor-style house was originally built in 1933, and each of its 15 themed rooms is decorated in unique decor, so visitors can lounge on a bed inside a giant clam or dip into an Egyptian oasis pool. Every room comes with a king bed, a kitchenette, a steam sauna, and a large TV you can see from the bathtub.

Many accommodations in Pocatello are of the standard hotel and motel chain options; the best of these is the **Hampton Inn & Suites Pocatello** (151 Vista Dr., 208/233-8200, http://hamptoninn3. hilton.com, $167-205). It has 89 rooms and suites with king or queen beds and top-notch service. Enjoy the indoor pool and hot breakfast before taking off on your adventures for the day. The hotel is a quick eight-minute drive from Zoo Idaho, Fort Hall, or Old Town.

A short drive east of town, **Pocatello KOA** (9815 W. Pocatello Creek Rd., www. koa.com, $37-47) has over 30 green spaces for RVs or tents. Amenities include picnic tables, showers, laundry facilities, and full hookups.

Shoshone-Bannock Fort Hall Reservation

Just north of Pocatello is the current home of the area's indigenous residents, the Shoshone-Bannock Tribes. Comprising two bands of the Northern Shoshone and Bannock peoples, or Northern Paiute, as they're collectively called, their ancestral lands covered a vast area that extends from today's Idaho, Oregon, Nevada, Utah, Wyoming, and Montana into Canada. Although the tribes are distinct, they're culturally related and have a long history of traveling and hunting together. In 1868 they both agreed to a peace treaty with the United States, the Fort Bridger Treaty, which assigned them 1.8 million acres in eastern Idaho. Some of their ancestors are the Agaidika, or Salmon Eaters, sometimes called the Lemhi Shoshone, of which Sacagawea was a member.

Today, the Shoshone-Bannock Tribes (Sho-Ban for short) are a federally recognized, self-governing sovereign nation, with elected leaders and about 6,000 members. The languages of the Shoshone and Bannock are mutually intelligible and are being revived and taught both at the reservation and at Idaho State University. Over time the boundaries of the reservation changed, reduced to its current 544,000 acres.

The original Fort Hall was built nearby in 1834, and became a major destination for wagon trains along the Oregon and California Trails. Today nothing remains of the original building, but a replica of the fort is in Pocatello. While you won't find a pioneer-era trading post, travelers today should make the time to stop by for a visit to the museum here, which tells the history of the Shoshone-Bannock Tribes. During the time of the trail, Shoshone lived, fished, and hunted up and down the Snake River, and often encountered emigrants following the river west, offering salmon and trout for trade.

Getting There

From Pocatello, drive north 12 miles (19 km) on I-15, and take exit 80 for the Shoshone-Bannock Fort Hall Reservation. The drive from town takes 20 minutes.

Sights

Shoshone Bannock Tribal Museum

On a trail that's dominated by stories from white settlers, the **Shoshone Bannock Tribal Museum** (I-15 Exit 80, Simplot Rd., 208/327-9791, www2.sb-tribes.com, 9:30am-5pm daily June-Aug., 9:30am-5pm Mon.-Fri. Sept.-May, $3.50) offers a significant look from an indigenous perspective, lending insight into how ancestors of the Shoshone-Bannock peoples moved across the land, what they hunted, and with whom they traded. Visitors can read stories about the Fort Bridger Treaty of 1868, which created the Wind River Reservation in Wyoming, where the majority of Eastern Shoshone people live today, and the era of Native American boarding schools in the 20th century, during which the United States attempted to assimilate indigenous children by discouraging them from practicing their traditions. Exhibits showcasing the beautiful crafts and artwork for which Shoshone artists are internationally renowned are also on display, including excellent beadwork and porcupine quill work. A staff member is on hand inside to answer your questions and elaborate on tribal history and traditions. In summer, a visitor from the tribes' extensive buffalo herd lives just outside the museum in the field.

Festivals and Events

The **Shoshone-Bannock Indian Festival** (www.shobanfestival.com, Aug.) is held the second weekend of August every year. The powwow is a weeklong event attracting members of various indigenous tribes as well as the general public. It features traditional dancing, a buffalo and salmon feast, traditional gaming, art shows, parades, a rodeo, drum competitions, arts and crafts booths, and plenty of food. One competition is the Indian Relay Race, which began on the Fort Hall Indian Reservation over 100 years ago; the horse race features one bareback rider who must complete a lap on three horses, switching without losing control at any time. The festival also includes the Miss Shoshone-Bannock pageant, where a young woman is crowned tribal ambassador. Contestants wear their finest handmade deer skin and beadwork and compete in areas such as public speaking and dancing.

Shopping

The **Donzia Gift Shop** (I-15 Exit 80, Simplot Rd., 208/237-8778, www.shobangaming.com, 9am-7pm Mon.-Sat., 9am-6pm Sun.), inside the reservation's casino, carries many authentic pieces of work from local artists, including fine beadwork on jewelry, purses, a wide range of moccasins, handmade knives, and buffalo robes. You'll also find some kids' toys and snacks.

Food and Accommodations

The **Shoshone Bannock Casino Hotel** (I-15 Exit 80, Simplot Rd., 208/237-8778, www.shobangaming.com, $169-325) encompasses over 80,000 square feet. The casino features high-stakes gaming and video gaming. The hotel offers 156 guest rooms (with 11 suites) richly decorated in Shoshone-Bannock artwork. Guests can also enjoy a fitness center, an indoor pool, a hot tub, a spa, and a cedar wood sauna. Restaurants on-site include a coffee bar, a sports grill, a deli, a buffet, and a night lounge for those 21 and over. Note that smoking is allowed only in designated areas—most of the establishment is smoke-free.

For a relaxing stay on beautiful green grounds, the **Buffalo Meadows RV Park** (208/237-8774, www.shobangaming.com, $27) has 27 year-round spots available. Full hookups with electricity, showers, and laundry facilities are offered, along with horseshoe pits, barbecue grills, and picnic tables, within walking distance of the casino and restaurants. Tent sites ($12.50) are also available.

◈ Side Trip: Idaho Falls

While the Oregon Trail pioneers didn't venture as far north as Idaho Falls, the area did see some early emigrant traffic on the lesser known Montana Trail, as hopeful gold-seekers headed there during the 1860s and 1870s. The Montana gold rush attracted miners to the north from Salt Lake City, which by then was one of the major metropolises in the West, via Idaho. By the time of the gold discovery in the 1860s, the Oregon Trail wasn't in heavy use, but those later emigrants would likely have met plenty of hopeful miners.

Idaho Falls today is a fun, outdoorsy city with an active greenbelt lining the river that cuts through it. With some great museums and breweries and a couple of quirky attractions, it's worth a stop for a night or two. Downtown Idaho Falls is bisected by the Snake River, and West Broadway Street is a primary thoroughfare running through it. Shops and restaurants line the river on either side. The older section of town is on the east, stretching to Yellowstone Avenue.

Getting There and Back

From Pocatello, drive north on I-15 for 52 miles (84 km), or 40 miles (64 km) from the Shoshone-Bannock Fort Hall Reservation, 50- and 35-minute drives, respectively. Take exit 118 for downtown. Idaho Falls is about an hour one-way off the route. You'll backtrack to Pocatello to continue westward along the Oregon Trail route.

Sights
Museum of Idaho

Over 25,000 historical and scientific artifacts await your inspection at the grand **Museum of Idaho** (200 N. Eastern Ave., 208/522-1400, http://museumofidaho. org, 10am-8pm Mon., 10am-6pm Tues.-Sat., 1pm-5pm Sun., $12), which attracts world-class international exhibits to the small town. In 2019 a major expansion opened a new exhibit hall, practically doubling the museum's space and allowing for a new permanent exhibit about Idaho history called "The Way Out West." The updated space takes a balanced look at the social, cultural, and political history of the state, from mammoths roaming the riverbanks to an emigrant-era settler town complete with a barbershop.

The museum also tells the indigenous history of the state, with input from the Shoshone-Bannock Tribes. Visitors can walk through a partial re-creation of a Shoshone-Bannock village, learn about the Lewis and Clark expedition, and visit an early one-room schoolhouse. One of the most surprising exhibits chronicles Idaho's leading role in the history of atomic power. The museum also hosts a vibrant schedule of events, like the monthly Museum After Dark ($20) for adults, with trivia and "irreverent" tours.

Art Museum of Eastern Idaho

The city's premier spot for visual culture, **The Art Museum of Eastern Idaho** (300 S. Capital Ave., 208/524-7777, www. theartmuseum.org, 10am-5pm Tues.-Wed. and Fri.-Sat., 10am-8pm Thurs., $4) hosts rotating exhibits and regular community workshops. Exhibits change every few months; past exhibits have covered cowboys, scientific art, and local artist retrospectives. While small, the museum's location on the river is

Idaho Falls

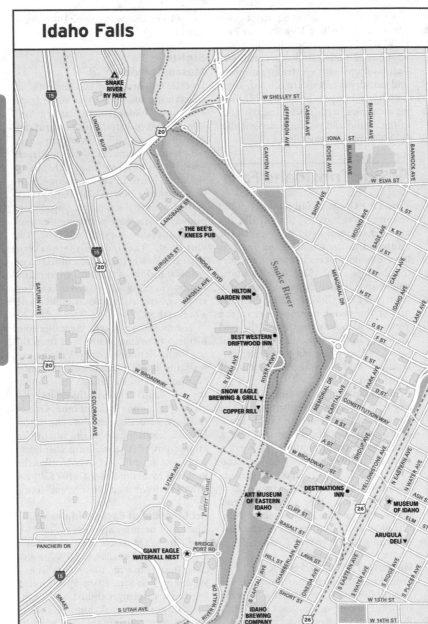

SNAKE RIVER RV PARK

THE BEE'S KNEES PUB

HILTON GARDEN INN

BEST WESTERN DRIFTWOOD INN

SNOW EAGLE BREWING & GRILL

COPPER RILL

ART MUSEUM OF EASTERN IDAHO

DESTINATIONS INN

MUSEUM OF IDAHO

ARUGULA DELI

GIANT EAGLE WATERFALL NEST

IDAHO BREWING COMPANY

TAP-N-FILL

Snake River

© MOON.COM

beautiful, and it's got a great hands-on kids' area.

Collectors Corner Museum

Collectors Corner Museum (900 John Adams Pkwy., 208/528-9900, 10am-5pm Tues.-Sat., $2) is the result of lifetimes spent hunting down precious items to curate the perfect collection. The museum is the passion of Jim and Nida Gyorfy, who have been collecting all manner of things their whole lives. Now, they show it all off in a small museum storefront in an Idaho Falls neighborhood. Model planes, a Barbie collection, trains, Precious Moments figurines, coins—this museum has it all. Many items are extremely rare and can't be purchased anymore. The main room features a special collection that changes seasonally. Feel free to open drawers to discover even more collections.

Giant Eagle Waterfall Nest

Take the short trip to a traffic circle to see the massive, impressive sculpture in the middle. Commonly referred to as the **"Giant Eagle Waterfall Nest,"** the official name of this sculpture is *The Protector.* Two giant eagles, each with a wingspan of 21 feet, circle a nest with baby eagles. Waterfalls flow down boulders and logs on which the nest perches. In winter, the water freezes mid-flow, making a striking sight. Circle the rotary by car or on the sidewalk on foot. To find the sculpture, head west across the Snake River on Broadway Street, then turn left on the first street past the river, Utah Avenue. The traffic circle is in 0.7 mile (1.1 km).

Idaho Potato Museum

Idaho has its share of quirky museums, so of course there's an **Idaho Potato Museum** (130 NW Main St., Blackfoot, 208/785-2517, www.idahopotatomuseum. com, 9:30am-7pm daily June-Aug., 9:30am-5pm Mon.-Sat. Sept.-May, $6). Located 29 miles (47 km) south of town in Blackfoot—a 30-minute drive via

I-15—the museum details everything about the surprisingly interesting world of Idaho's most famous export. Take your photo by the giant spud out front, then head inside the stone building, once a railroad depot. You'll learn more about potatoes and potato history than you ever thought possible; for instance, did you know Marilyn Monroe once posed for a fashion magazine in an Idaho potato sack? And of course, you can enjoy a real Idaho baked potato from the café before you leave.

Recreation

Idaho Falls Greenbelt

The **Idaho Falls Greenbelt** is an easy, scenic paved path that loops 11 miles (18 km) total along both sides of the Snake River in town, passing gardens, waterfalls, and memorials. The central portion of the walking and biking trail is in downtown Idaho Falls near West Broadway.

Bike Rentals

Rent some wheels at **Bill's Bike & Run** (930 Pier View Dr., 208/522-3341, www. billsbikeandrun.com, 10am-6pm Mon.-Sat.), located 1 mile (1.6 km) south of West Broadway Street on the west side of the Snake River, just off the greenbelt. It offers a variety of bicycles available from four hours up to a week, including cruisers and youth bikes (4 hours $19, $29 per day) and tandem bikes (4 hours $29, $39 per day), as well as helmets (4 hours $3, $5 per day).

Hell's Half Acre Lava Field

Most of Idaho was once a massive lava flow, now broken up into canyons and leftover chunks. The **Hell's Half Acre Lava Field** south of Idaho Falls is a great example of a more recent lava flow from the stretching of the earth's crust; this lava pushed the path of the Snake River to where it is today. Two interpretive trails—accessed at a highway rest stop— take you through some of the hardened black lava landscape, as well as past the hearty plants and spring wildflowers that make their home here. The trails are paved and well marked. Each 0.8-mile (1.3-km) loop only takes about 30 minutes to walk.

From I-15 northbound or southbound, take the Blackfoot Rest Area exit. The exit is about 18 miles (29 km) south of Idaho Falls.

Entertainment

One of the biggest craft brewers in the eastern part of the state, **Idaho Brewing Company** (775 S. Capital Ave., 208/534-7232, www.idahobrewing.com, 3pm-7pm Mon., 3pm-9pm Tues.-Wed., 3pm-10pm Thurs.-Fri., 3pm-8pm Sat.) has a tasting room with a view of the Snake River. It's a comfortable neighborhood joint with friendly staff. The beers, found throughout Idaho, are award-winning. Try a Deep Creek Ale, Black Lager, or the juiced-up What a Pear. Enjoy your pint on the outside patio while you catch sunset over the river, or warm up near the indoor fireplace. It can be tricky to find, but head to the corner of Trask and Chamberlain Streets, or access it via the parking lot near the Mini Bazaar off South Capital Avenue.

To find a wide selection of local and national brews, head to **Tap-N-Fill** (1494 Milligan Rd., 208/524-4577, noon-10pm Mon.-Sat.). Get a growler or try a sampler of four beers—it has 40 taps, organized by type, from IPAs to sours, including a wide range of harder-to-find dark beers. Mead, kombucha, cider, and wine round out the offerings, and the knowledgeable staff are happy to help you make a choice. It's in a great location along the Snake River, 1 mile (1.6 km) south of downtown, just off the greenbelt on the west side of the river.

Food

Have a wonderful night out at the upscale ★ **Copper Rill** (415 River Pkwy., 208/529-5800, www.copperrill.com, 4pm-8:45pm Mon.-Sat., $20). The menu features

Idaho Potato Museum

succulent chicken Wellington, filet mignon, and golden crab cakes, as well as fresh salads. Choose from an extensive wine list; staff are happy to help with recommendations. If it's a nice evening, enjoy the outdoor seating near the lawn, where views take in the Snake River.

Snow Eagle Brewing & Grill (455 River Pkwy., 208/557-0455, www.snow eaglebrewing.com, 11am-10pm Mon.-Sat., $13) has partnered with Wasabi Sushi Bar to bring patrons two great experiences at one place, with excellent sushi alongside beer. At least eight varieties of beer are always on tap, ranging from an award-winning cream ale to milk stout. Also available are a variety of Japanese entrées, as well as burgers, steak, and sandwiches. The big hall is right downtown near the greenbelt.

Find a hearty Bolivian-inspired gourmet sandwich at **Arugula Deli** (261 Walnut St., 208/656-7784, www. aruguladeli.com, 11am-9pm Mon.-Sat. $14), where everything is made from scratch with the freshest of ingredients. Cubanos, smoked pork shoulder, *pão de queijo* (cheesy bread), and chorizo with homemade chimichurri sauce are among the offerings. For a less meat-centric meal, go for the quinoa beet salad or a fried plantain wrap with cilantro-jalapeño dressing. There are so many flavors to choose from, you might have to take a few sandwiches to go! Find them inside the O. E. Bell Building a few blocks southeast of the Museum of Idaho—the main entrance is on the south side.

The Bee's Knees Pub (850 Lindsay Blvd., 208/524-1669, www.beeskneespub. com, 11am-11pm daily, $12) is a great hole-in-the-wall: small, unassuming, and delicious. It serves the usual pub menu but has a knack for flavor combinations; try the jalapeño burger with cream cheese, or the bourbon barbecue burger. Try the namesake Bee's Knees cocktail (vodka, milk, and honey) if you feel adventurous.

Grab a hearty breakfast at **Abracadabra's** (2040 Channing Way, 208/881-9024, 8am-3pm Sun.-Fri., 7:30am-3pm Sat., $11), serving up great-tasting and generous portions. Go sweet with the Captain Crunch French Toast or savory with a Mediterranean omelet. For lunch, burgers, sandwiches, and salads are on the menu.

Accommodations and Camping

Destinations Inn (295 W. Broadway St., 208/528-8444, www.destinationsinn. com, $139-199) is a sister property to the equally unique Black Swan Inn in Pocatello. It offers 14 guest rooms whose decor whisks you to Egypt, Thailand, Rome, or Hawaii. Rooms have king beds and giant jetted bathtubs, and many also have fireplaces, steam showers, or water fountains. You'll be greeted with complimentary sparkling cider and cheesecake upon arrival.

Visitors to Idaho Falls will largely need to rely on chain hotels and motels. Steps away from the greenbelt and a

quick walk into town, the **Best Western Driftwood Inn** (575 River Pkwy., 208/523-2242, www.bestwestern.com, $85-95) is a friendly, convenient place to rest. The outdoor pool is heated and within view of the Snake River, and a few king suites have overlooking balconies. Breakfast is a freshly made omelet or breakfast sandwich. Also close to the greenbelt and offering easy access to town is the **Hilton Garden Inn** (700 Lindsey Blvd., 208/522-9500, http://hiltongardeninn3.hilton.com, $95-130). It takes advantage of its setting along the river with huge windows that line the hallways, deluxe rooms with views, and a seasonal outdoor patio near the water.

With a great location just 2 miles (3.2 km) from downtown and open year-round, the **Snake River RV Park** (1440 Lindsey Blvd., 208/523-3362, www.snakeriverrvpark.com, $37-52) is a great place to stay the night. Campsites accommodate tents, trailers, and RVs, and four cabins are also available. With Wi-Fi, showers, a pool, and a playground, it's great for families. You can order an all-you-can-eat pancake breakfast for $3 in summer.

Along the Trail from Pocatello

"Most of the country is a barren waste."

Loren B. Hastings, September 22, 1847, referring to this stretch of the Snake River, *Diary of Loren B. Hastings.* Hastings was born in Vermont, and as a young man was so excited to move west he named his son Oregon. He finally traveled the Oregon Trail with his family in 1847, settling in Portland, then soon traveled farther north to settle for good in Port Townsend, Washington, where he was elected justice of the peace and a representative of the county in the territorial legislature.

By the time emigrants reached Fort Hall, many believed the hardest roads were behind them; they were wrong. The route began following the south bank of the Snake River through a sagebrush-spiked landscape that was hot in midsummer, when emigrants would've been traveling through the area, and it was dry, dusty, and full of volcanic rock. Soon after departing the area, the river descended into a canyon that was easy to see but maddeningly hard to access. From Fort Hall, emigrants aimed west 270 miles (434 km) to Fort Boise. At a rate of roughly 15 miles (24 km) on a good day, they faced a minimum of 18 days along the Snake River.

In the early years of the trail, wagons stopped at Fort Hall, at which point pioneers would abandon their wheels and continue west on foot with their animals. The first wagons wouldn't make it through until 1836, after mountain men had found passes through the surrounding mountain ranges. In 1843 the first large wagon train, called "The Great Migration," pulled their wheeled loads all the way to Oregon. The train was led by Marcus Whitman, who had established a mission out west and came back to guide more emigrants. At his urging, they continued with their wagons, clearing the trail where needed, successfully reaching The Dalles in Oregon by October. It was this year, and this trip, that established the viability of the western reaches of the trail.

Today, the fields around the Snake River are served by massive irrigation works that create a fertile farm economy. Leaving Pocatello, you'll follow the actual wagon route via **I-86** through Register Rock, after which you'll continue on the interstate highway, although it diverges slightly from the wagon route, which follows a parallel track just south.

Snake River Overlook

Just south of the town of American Falls, a rest stop along westbound I-86 has a nice place to stop, view the river, and see some deep wagon ruts—you can also

The Relocation of American Falls

"We passed the great American falls. The fall must be 40 to 50 feet in about 70 or 80 yards.... The roaring of the waters can be heard for many miles. They rush with great velocity over and through the vast lumps that lay in massive piles in the channel."

James Pritchard, July 5, 1849, *The Overland Diary*. Pritchard was headed to California to seek his fortune.

American Falls was once a major landmark on the Oregon Trail. But the American Falls Dam, built in 1925, with an addition down the river in 1978, submerged the waterfall and any trail marks, so there's not much to see here now. The nearby city of American Falls has a unique history due to the dam, however. The city of American Falls, 25 miles (40 km) west of Pocatello via I-86, was founded in the early 1880s and named after the waterfall, then just downstream. As the area became more settled and farmers moved in, the Snake River was eyed as a useful water source for dry fields, as well as a potential power source for the electricity springing up across the West. In 1925, construction began on a dam—it would provide power, and the resulting reservoir could be used for irrigation. But there was one problem: The town of American Falls was in the way. Once the dam was installed, the town would be flooded and submerged under the lake. For the government, that seemed like a fair price to pay for progress, so they decided to simply move the town. They lifted and relocated 344 residents along with their homes, churches, schools, over 40 local businesses, even grain elevators and a flour mill. The new city was on higher ground farther east, away from the impending lake—planners set it at an angle, with diagonal streets, so that "the sun shines in every window" (which is still the town's motto today).

One structure was left behind: the 106-foot-tall (32-m) Oneida Milling and Elevator Company's grain elevator, which was too difficult to move because of its deep foundation. Today its top rises above the water from the old town site. And every so often, when the lake level is low enough, other aspects of the abandoned city are revealed, such as old sidewalks and concrete foundations. You can view the grain elevator from the town of American Falls by driving along Highway 39 today.

If you're here when it's open, or make an appointment, you can swing by the **Power County Museum** (500 Pocatello Ave., 208/226-2325, www.co.power.id.us, 10am-2pm Thurs. May-Labor Day, or by appointment, free). It's a very small local museum with a handful of exhibits—the most interesting of which are photos and information on how the town of American Falls was moved to make way for the dam.

access these from Massacre Rocks State Park. From the rest area there's a walking path, interpretive signs detailing pioneers' experience at this point in the trail, and a view of the Snake River to gaze over sagebrush-flecked hills. From the overlook, you can head left and follow the tunnel under both lanes of the highway—the wagon ruts are just beyond, along with more interpretive panels. Altogether it's a roughly 1-mile (1.6-km) walk.

Getting There
The rest area is at milepost 31 from westbound I-86. From Pocatello, drive 33 miles (53 km) west on I-86, about a 30-minute drive. Enter the rest area and continue driving past the restrooms and through the loop until you find a kiosk with interpretive signs.

★ Massacre Rocks
Wagons had a tough time getting to Massacre Rocks. **Devil's Gate,** a leftover volcanic wonder, was once a narrow gorge through which wagons had to pass single file, slowing down large wagon trains considerably. Today, the

gate is still here but much wider—U.S. 30/I-86 cuts through it; you'll see the stacks of rocks on either side of the highway just before entering Massacre Rocks State Park.

The area now encompassed by **Massacre Rocks State Park** (3592 Park Lane, 208/548-2672, http://parksandrecreation.idaho.gov, day-use $5 per vehicle) once offered Native Americans and emigrants excellent Snake River access and a place to rest. It retains those features today, offering picnic sites, camping, and river access and views. The park is popular with birders, rock climbers, hikers, history buffs, and disc golfers.

The **visitors center** (10am-7pm Sun.-Tues., 7:30am-9pm Wed.-Sat. May-mid-Oct.) acts as a mini museum, with exhibits inside and out, and plenty of interpretive information explaining the natural and historical significance of the area. It's great for an overview of the area's history and has a covered-wagon exhibit.

Recreation

The park's **disc golf course** is considered unique, as it uses the area's natural geography for extra challenges; you'll be throwing Frisbees over canyons and cliffs, and it's easy enough that kids can enjoy it.

Over 8 miles (12.9 km) of trails are open to hiking and biking so you can explore the juniper and sagebrush landscape. Wagon ruts can be seen in the eastern park area; take the 0.8-mile (1.2 km) **Wagon Rut/Old Oregon Trail** from the North Pole parking lot—signs point the way. You'll go under both highway lanes to find the ruts, which can also be accessed along westbound I-86 from the Snake River Overlook, 2 miles (3.2 km) before the exit for the state park.

Get disc golf supplies or trail maps at the visitors center, where you can also

City of Rocks

rent **canoes and kayaks** (1 hour $5-8, 4 hours $15-20, 8 hours $25-30).

Camping

Massacre Rocks State Park has a beautiful **campground** (888/922-6743, http://idahostateparks.reserveamerica.com) along the Snake River, with green and shaded tent and RV sites ($12-29). It also has cabins ($50-65).

Getting There

From Pocatello, drive west on I-86 for 35 miles (56 km) to exit 28 for Massacre Rocks State Park. Turn right onto Register Road, and then make another right immediately after onto Park Lane, which leads into the park. The drive takes about 40 minutes.

★ Register Rock

Two miles (3.2 km) southwest of the Massacre Rocks site, you'll find **Register Rock** (Register Rd., 208/548-2672, http://parksandrecreation.idaho.gov, $5 per

vehicle day-use), where pioneers once carved their names into a giant boulder while resting; some of the names are still visible today. You can also rest at this great picnic spot, but leave your name off the boulder. Enjoy the green lawn, horseshoe pits, barbecue grills, and restrooms. Register Rock is also part of **Massacre Rocks State Park**, but not accessible by foot from the first section; the day-use pass covers both the Massacre Rocks and Register Rock sites.

Getting There

From the Massacre Rocks site, drive south on Park Lane for 1 mile (1.6 km), then turn left onto Register Road. Continue 2.4 miles (3.8 km), crossing over the highway twice before turning left into the site. The drive takes about seven minutes.

🔷 Detour: City of Rocks

"Another 2 miles enter a rocky dell some 4 miles long by a winding road running among the most grotesque rocks standing out singly in the valley, or grouped fantastically together. There were sphynxes and statues of every size, and haystacks and wigwams and castles, and towers, and pyramids and cones and projecting turrets and canopies, and leaving columns, and so on throughout a thousand varieties of fantastic shapes."

Bernard J. Reid, August 11, 1849, *The Gold Rush Diary of Bernard J. Reid*. Originally from Ohio, Reid traveled to California and worked in mining and trading and as a professor at Santa Clara College. In 1852 he traveled back east to study law, and later served as a Union major in the Civil War.

The California Trail had numerous paths and cutoffs that splintered off from the Oregon Trail, and the farthest west of these diverged south toward California after Register Rock—cutting

right through the City of Rocks, which is worth a day trip to enjoy a scenic drive amid the strange rock formations known to pioneers as "The City." Hard granite rock in various states of erosion offered landmarks begging to be named. Some emigrants even thought they were seeing the last of the rocks, convinced they would soon erode away completely in a few more years, due to their sometimes precarious-seeming natures. They're still here, and visitors today can see signatures inscribed in the stone or written in axle grease.

Getting There and Around

This detour takes you on an 89-mile (143-km) loop that encompasses part of the **City of Rocks Scenic Byway.** The route heads south from the town of **Burley,** west of Massacre Rocks State Park. You won't miss any sights along the main Oregon Trail route, and you'll see some stunning rock formations and emigrant signatures, and have a chance to stretch your legs on some hikes.

From Register Rock in Massacre Rocks State Park, continue west on Register Road, which becomes Osborn Loop and parallels the highway. After 6 miles (9.6 km), turn right to cross over I-86, and then left onto the ramp for I-86 west-bound, which eventually becomes I-84. In 34 miles (55 km), or 40 miles (64 km) if you're coming straight from the Massacre Rocks site rather than the Register Rock site, take exit 208 toward Burley. Turn left onto Highway 27 and drive for 2.5 miles (4 km) to cross the Snake River into Burley. The drive from Massacre Rocks State Park to Burley, from which you'll begin the detour loop, takes about 45 minutes.

From Burley, begin the loop by driving south on Highway 27 for 5.2 miles (8.3 km), then turn left onto East 500 South. Continue for 8.5 miles (13.6 km), then turn right onto Highway 77. In 4 miles (6.4 km) you'll pass the small town of

Albion, which is the official start of the City of Rocks Scenic Byway.

Planning Tips

While you can zoom through the City of Rocks in two hours, you may want to budget an entire day to enjoy the opportunity to stop at your leisure. Drive in a **clockwise loop** so you can stop at the visitors center for maps and information in **Almo**—3 miles (4.8 km) from the park entrance—before heading in. Almo also has gas, food, and lodging, as does **Oakley,** which you'll pass after you leave the park and begin to loop back north. You might want to pause in the town, which was founded by Mormons and ranchers in 1878 and is on the National Register of Historic Places. It's dotted with stone and brick buildings that date to its early days.

The drive through the national reserve itself is only about 9 miles (14.6 km) via the main **City of Rocks Loop Road,** but it's on a twisty dirt road that's narrow at times. Drive slowly to allow for plenty of rock-gazing, and watch for numerous pullouts for interpretive signs and trailheads. If you're pulling an RV or trailer, be aware that the dirt roads on this loop can be quite bumpy and narrow, and may be unpassable in heavy rains or in winter.

Sights
Visitors Center

You'll find the **City of Rocks National Reserve Visitor Center** (3035 S. Elba Almo Rd., 208/824-5519, www.nps.gov/ciro, 8am-4:30pm daily mid-Apr.-mid-Oct., 8am-4:30pm Tues.-Sat. mid-Oct.-mid-Apr.) before you enter the reserve, in Almo, if you drive the loop clockwise. Stop here for maps, to check weather updates (the roads in the reserve can be closed during wet or snowy weather), and to watch an introductory film about the area.

From Albion, drive 11 miles (18 km) farther south on Highway 77, and then

City of Rocks

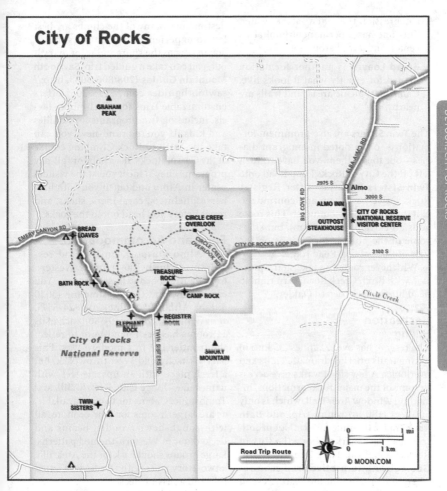

turn right onto Elba Almo Road, following it for 16 miles (26 km) to arrive at the visitors center.

Landmarks

The primary and best route through the **City of Rocks National Reserve** (208/824-5901, www.nps.gov/ciro, 24 hours daily, free) is via the City of Rocks Loop Road. Turn right onto it 0.4 mile (0.6 km) south of the visitors center on South Elba Almo Road/South 85 East. City of Rocks Loop Road passes the landmarks below in this order:

- **Camp Rock** has pioneer signatures that you can view on a walk around the formation.

- **Treasure Rock** offers another chance to see emigrant inscriptions and a few interpretive panels.

- **Register Rock** has still more signatures, some in axle grease.

- **Elephant Rock** is pretty unmistakable; you'll quickly see why it bears its name. It's a popular climbing rock today.

- **Bath Rock** is the most notable example of a pan hole, a rock formation with a depression that often catches water. This one has a permanent pool at its center, and a trail around it.

- **Bread Loaves** is another formation named for exactly what it looks like. Campsites, picnic areas, and trails are nearby.

The **Twin Sisters** are also prominent formations—often noted in emigrant diaries—but to see them, you have to turn left off the City of Rocks Loop Road onto **Twin Sisters Road** just after Register Rock. Drive past them and continue to exit the park in the southwest. This route adds an extra 5 miles (8 km), but skips some of the notable formations on the City of Rocks Loop Road route.

Whichever route you take, at the junction with Birch Creek Road, turn right to head north, back toward Oakley.

Recreation
Hiking
The reserve has over 22 miles (35 km) of hiking trails offering dramatic views and overlooks. A few short walks give access to some of the major rock formations, including **Window Arch Trail,** which is only 600 feet (180 m) round-trip, and **Bath Rock Trail,** a 0.3-mile (0.5 km) loop; both trailheads are marked along the City of Rocks Loop Road. The 1.2-mile (1.9-km) **Geological Interpretive Trail** features 12 stations that point out features such as pan holes and pinnacles, and you'll also enjoy some great views of the City of Rocks, taking in the rock formations called Twin Sisters to the south. This trail begins from Circle Creek Overlook Road; turn right off City of Rocks Loop Road about a mile after entering the park to find the trailhead. Pick up a trail map in the visitors center before you head out for the day.

Climbing
With its challenging jumble of rocks, boulders, walls, and pinnacles, the City of Rocks is a nationally known climbing destination. Many of the climbs are best left to experienced adventurers, but if you're new to the sport and want to try it out, you can take a guided trip. **Sawtooth Mountain Guides** (208/806-3063, http://sawtoothguides.com, $125-205) offers customizable trips for all climbing levels, including fun programs for families and kids. If you're brand-new, you can take the Intro to Rock Climbing course at the City of Rocks. It's a half- or full-day program. They'll meet you at the visitors center in Almo and outfit you with harnesses, helmets, carabiners, shoes, and ropes before you head out to the rocks.

Food and Accommodations
The Almo Outpost, an inn and restaurant, is built like a small Western town, with boardwalk storefronts. You can stay here at the ★ **Almo Inn** (3020 S. Elba Almo Rd., Almo, 208/824-5577, www.almoinn.com, $110-180); each of its 11 rooms has been hand-built to reflect the frontier life in a modern way. This isn't a kitschy Old West throwback, but a fresh place with an upscale feel, with names like Dodge City, Buffalo Bill, and Tombstone. Cabins for two are available, as are larger rooms for four or more, all with rough-hewn wooden beams and decked out in Western-themed patterns. Large groups should ask for the Amarillo, a two-story suite with five beds, a jetted tub, and a private deck.

The hotel's **Outpost Steakhouse** (11:30am-8pm Mon.-Thurs., 11:30am-9pm Fri.-Sat., 11:30am-6pm Sun. May-Oct., $17) is a great place to get a charbroiled steak with potatoes cooked in a Dutch oven, fried chicken or fish, or homemade pie. Don't miss the "pioneer pudding" (bread pudding with ice cream).

Camping
Spend the night in the ancient "city." ★ **City of Rocks National Reserve** (http://idahostateparks.reserveamerica.com, $10-13) offers tent camping in designated

areas, tucked between and behind giant rocks and arches, mostly spread out between Elephant Rock and the Bread Loaves. Each of the 64 sites has a fire ring and picnic table. Some are accessible from the road and some are walk-in sites, located farther back. Vault toilets are available, and drinking water can be found at the centrally located Bath Rock April-October. Campsites are very popular here during the April-October season, so reserve ahead, especially for weekends and holidays. If you didn't reserve ahead of time, pay fees at the Bath Rock.

Getting Back on the Trail

Follow the City of Rocks Loop Road, or Twin Sisters Road, to the junction with Birch Creek Road, where you turn right and head north for 12 miles (19 km) or 17 miles (27 km), respectively, into Oakley, where the road becomes Main Street. Turn right onto South Center 450 West street, continuing north as it becomes Highway 27 for 21 miles (33 km), back into Burley.

Along the Trail in Mid-Idaho

Much of the Snake River runs far below deep in a gorge, offering tortuous views of fresh water that's often inaccessible. At this point in their journey alongside the river, emigrants were exhausted. They were forced to climb down cliffs to get water, using up precious time and energy. The south bank they traveled along was mostly sharp obsidian lava rocks that cut their livestock's feet, with thorny weeds poking through and little green grass. Wagons passed dead cattle daily. Maddeningly, the inaccessible north bank was often lush with grass.

From **Burley,** travelers can follow **U.S. 30** west along the old route of the wagon trains again. You can also skip these sights and stay on the parallel I-84 to

Twin Falls instead, which will save about 30 minutes of drive time from the I-84/Highway 27 junction just north of Burley.

Milner Ruts

You can explore a few sets of well-preserved ruts at **Milner Historic Recreation Area** (15 E. 200 S., Burley, 208/677-6600, www.blm.gov/visit/milner-historic-recreation-area, $3 per vehicle day-use). Bureau of Land Management markers are posted along a trail, where deep depressions cut across the landscape. This area was a challenge to navigate for emigrants, who had to wend their wagons and livestock over rough lava rocks and hardscrabble grazing land. Near today's Milner Ruts, wagons camped next to a section of the river that was gentle and accessible. Interpretive panels and a recently updated 1.3-mile (2.1-km) ADA-accessible path lead to the ruts.

Getting There

From Register Rock in **Massacre Rocks State Park,** continue west on Register Road, which becomes Osborn Loop and parallels the highway. After 6 miles (9.6 km), turn right to cross over I-86, and then left onto the ramp for I-86 westbound, which eventually becomes I-84. In 34 miles (55 km)—or 40 miles (64 km) if you're coming straight from the Massacre Rocks site rather than the Register Rock site, take exit 208 toward Burley. Turn left onto Highway 27 and drive for 2.5 miles (4 km) to cross the Snake River into Burley. The drive from Massacre Rocks State Park to Burley takes about 45 minutes.

If you detoured to **City of Rocks,** drive west on U.S. 30 for 5 miles (8 km) from Burley. Turn right onto the South 500 West road, then make an immediate left onto Milner Road. Follow signs on Milner Road for 5.7 miles (9 km), then turn right into the recreation area. The drive takes 20 minutes.

Rock Creek Station and Stricker Homesite

Lush grass along the waters of Rock Creek made a pleasant campsite for early pioneers, and it became a popular stop over the years. In 1865 a trading post was built on the site, and in 1876 Herman Stricker, a German immigrant, bought the station and built a house, living and working there until 1897. The **Rock Creek Station and Stricker Homesite** (3715 E. 3200 N., 208/423-4000, http://history.idaho.gov/stricker, 1pm-5pm Sun. Apr.-Sept., free) is open for viewing today, and you can still see the trading post, as well as walk through underground rooms that once stored goods. The station was at the junction of two important trails—the Oregon Trail and Kelton Road, which was a trail for stagecoach traffic from Salt Lake City, Utah, to Boise, Idaho. An interpretive center on-site offers information and exhibits about the trails and how the station served them.

Getting There

From Milner Historic Recreation Area, head west on Milner Road. In 0.7 mile (1.1 km), turn left onto the South 1100 West road, and in 2 miles (3.2 km) turn right onto U.S. 30. Follow it for 8.8 miles (14.1 km) west, then turn left onto North 4475 East. In 1 mile (1.6 km), turn right onto East 3200 North. Continue on it for 7.5 miles (12 km); the site is on the left. The drive takes about 30 minutes.

Twin Falls

The area around the Snake River Canyon was once a popular place for Shoshone bands to gather and fish during spawning season. Fish pooled in the base of the massive Shoshone Falls, making for easy fishing. The Oregon Trail route passed by the area a few miles to the south—but many emigrants made special trips to see the impressive sight.

The modern city of Twin Falls, named after another waterfall in the area of the same name, is worth a night or two to stop and explore the area, slowing down along the Snake River to enjoy scenic views and outdoor activities.

Getting There and Around

From the Rock Creek Station and Stricker Homesite **along the trail in mid-Idaho,** continue west on East 3200 North for 2.1 miles (3.3 km), then turn right onto 3500 East. In 3 miles (3.8 km), turn left onto East 3500 North. In 1.9 miles (3 km), turn right onto North 3300 East/Champlin Road. After 3 miles (4.8 km), turn left onto U.S. 30, which brings you to Twin Falls in another 3 miles (4.8 km). The drive takes 25 minutes.

For those coming via **I-84,** from the junction with Highway 27 just north of Burley, continue 25 miles (40 km) west on the interstate to exit 182. Turn left onto Highway 50 toward Kimberly/Twin Falls, which becomes U.S. 30 and takes you into

Twin Falls in 10 miles (16 km). The drive takes about 40 minutes.

The lively and walkable **Downtown Historic District** area has recently undergone a major renovation of the five blocks between Jerome and Fairfield Streets, where you'll find restaurants and other businesses lining the welcoming streets. Shoshone Falls and Twin Falls are just outside of town, with drives of 15-20 minutes.

Sights
Buzz Langdon Visitor Center
Start your visit to the area at the **Buzz Langdon Visitor Center** (3591 Blue Lakes Blvd. N., 208/733-9458, 8am-5pm daily, free), on the edge of the Snake River Canyon. Inside you'll find all the regional information you need, including a local trail map, along with some exhibits on area attractions. Look for the Owyhee candy bars for sale in the center—the Idaho Spud Bar, Old Faithful Bar, and Cherry Cocktail Bar have been made by the Idaho Candy Company since the 1920s; the visitors center is staffed by senior volunteers, many of whom will recount to you their favorite memories of the candy bars.

Outside, take a stroll to the viewing platform and see if you can spot any BASE jumpers at Perrine Bridge. The bridge, 1,500 feet (460 m) long and 486 feet (148 m) above the river, is one of the only built structures worldwide where BASE jumping is legal. If you want to have your own adventure, plan far, far ahead—you'll need to log at least 150 skydives to even begin training!

You'll find a plaque near the viewing platform commemorating Evel Knievel's attempted jump over the canyon in 1974 with a rocket motorcycle. Knievel's parachute malfunctioned on takeoff and jettisoned him out; he landed safely on the riverbank below. Looking east from the visitors center, you might be able to spot the big dirt ramp from which he took off. You can't drive there, but a 2.6-mile

the Perrine Bridge over the Snake River Canyon

IDAHO

Twin Falls to Glenns Ferry

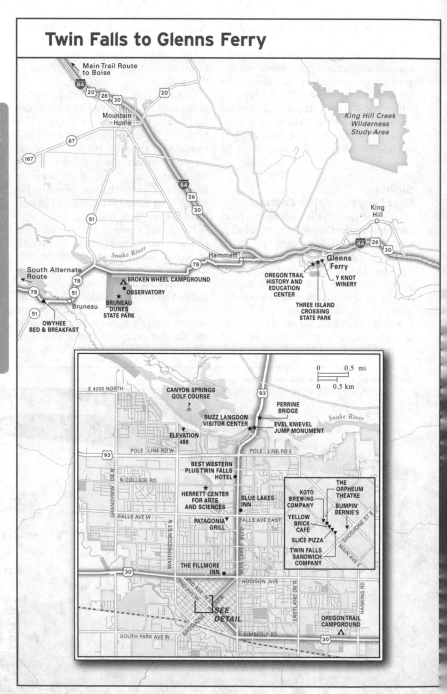

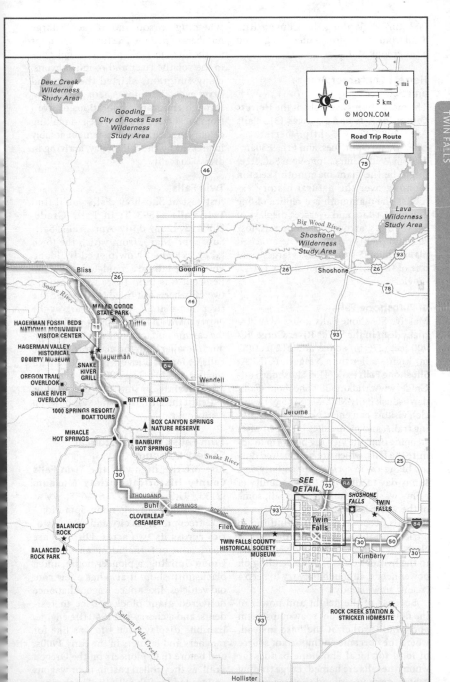

(4.2-km) walk along the Canyon Rim Trail from the visitors center will get you a closer look at it.

Herrett Center for Arts and Sciences

The most impressive sight at the **Herrett Center for Arts and Sciences** (315 Falls Ave., 208/732-6655, http://herrett.csi.edu, 9:30am-9pm Tues. and Fri., 9:30am-4:30pm Wed.-Thurs., 1pm-9pm Sat., free) might be the giant mammoth skeleton looming over the natural history exhibits. The mammoth is a replica of one dug up in Utah, and oversees displays of spear points, arrowheads, minerals, fossils, and prehistoric tools. The attached **planetarium** ($4-6) is Idaho's largest, and one of the only ones that shows IMAX movies.

★ Shoshone Falls

Massive Shoshone Falls pours over lava rocks deep in the Snake River Gorge. It's 900 feet (275 m) across and 212 feet (65 m) high—taller than Niagara Falls! At **Shoshone Falls Park** (4155 Shoshone Falls Grade, www.tfid.org/309/Shoshone-Falls, dawn-dusk daily Mar.-Sept., $5 per vehicle), visitors can enjoy playgrounds, hiking trails, and picnic sites before or after stepping onto the viewing platform to admire the falls, which are best viewed during high flow in spring, particularly on a sunny day to allow for the possibility of rainbows. In the summer and fall, some of the water is diverted for irrigation so the falls become smaller, dwindling to a trickle in the winter when the park is closed. A nearby dam often diverts water to the hydroelectric plant depending on power needs, although they try to keep a "scenic flow" steady.

Because of the height and power of the falls, fish could not spawn upstream and would gather at the base instead, where they became an important source of food for local Shoshone bands, for whom the falls are named. Large trading centers grew up around the area during spawning season and attracted large numbers of people. The first explorations for the Oregon Trail missed the falls; due to the volatile river and rough canyons, many emigrants skirted the area and never even knew it was here. Eventually, through emigrant explorations or word from local trappers, they began making detours to see it. Travelers remain notably impressed by the falls today, arriving in droves to see it.

Twin Falls

Just east of Shoshone Falls you'll find **Twin Falls** (3593 Twin Falls Grade, 208/423-4233, daily Apr.-Aug., Sat.-Sun. Sept.-Mar.), from which the town takes its name. Now owned by Idaho Power, the falls are regulated by a dam. Before it was built there were actually two falls here, but the dam diverted the river into a single waterfall. Park by the power plant and take a short walk along the canyon rim to view the falls. Though much smaller than the massive Shoshone Falls, it makes a lovely alternative with smaller crowds. The 200-foot-high (61-m) waterfall crashes down a narrow outlet in the cliff, throwing rainbows on sunny days.

Twin Falls County Historical Society Museum

Just off the highway, the **Twin Falls County Historical Society Museum** (21337 U.S. 30, 208/736-4675, www.twinfallsmuseum.org, noon-5pm Mon.-Sat., free) preserves city and county stories across its two acres. Displays are inside and out, including an old 1914 Union Building, a pioneer house, and a blacksmith shop. It also has a few cool old vehicles, like an ice wagon that once delivered giant blocks of ice to residents, and a cherry-red 1940 fire engine. Exhibits display what life was like for ranchers and farmers in the early 1900s, and before that, pioneers on the Oregon Trail, as they rolled past in their wagons and traded for fish with the Shoshone.

Recreation
Canyon Rim Trail
Offering stunning views along the Snake River and popular with locals as well as visitors, the paved 6-mile (9.7-km) **Canyon Rim Trail** (www.tfid.org) offers a scenic and easy walk, run, or bike ride. Its western trailhead is at Washington Street and East 4150 Road, and its eastern trailhead is at Shoshone Falls, but various access points make it easy to break up the stretch into shorter segments. The Buzz Langdon Visitor Center is a convenient entry point that offers great views of Perrine Bridge, where you can watch BASE jumpers, and walk 4 miles (6.4 km) east to Shoshone Falls. Or take a shorter walk from the western trailhead; head 0.2 mile (0.3 km) east to Elevation 486, a great place for drinks on an outdoor patio with stellar river views. Continue east another 0.3 mile (0.5 km) to catch views of the 190-foot-tall (58-m) **Perrine Coulee Falls,** which crash through a narrow cliff onto the rocks below with impressive strength.

Paddling
The Snake River is a welcoming playmate, so don't hesitate to get out on the water. **Centennial Waterfront Park** (Canyon Springs Rd.) is the perfect launchpad, just west of the visitors center and in view of the Perrine Bridge. A lovely riverside park, it has boat launches, picnic tables, barbecue grills, and short trails. You can rent a kayak on-site with the helpful **AWOL Adventure Sports** (208/735-5344, www.paddlethesnake. com, 9am-dusk daily Memorial Day-Labor Day). Solo kayaks (2 hours $15, 4 hours $25, 8 hours $35) and tandem kayaks (2 hours $25, 4 hours $40, 8 hours $55) are available, as are stand-up paddleboards (2 hours $20, 4 hours $30, 8 hours $40). All rentals include life jackets, paddles, and whistles. Reservations aren't required, but these are popular activities in the area, so booking ahead is recommended.

From Centennial Park, you can do a 2-mile (3.2-km) round-trip paddle to Perrine Bridge, which will take about an hour. For a longer trip, head farther east to **Pillar Falls,** a 4-mile (6.4-km) round-trip, which takes about 2-3 hours. The falls here crash through several tall basalt columns. For a challenging paddle to Shoshone Falls—7.5 miles (12 km) round-trip—plan to take 4-6 hours. Note you'll need to portage, or carry, your kayaks along a path from Pillar Falls, then get back in the water to continue to Shoshone Falls. This trip offers unique views of the massive falls from water level. Use caution and don't get too close.

BASE Jumping
The **Perrine Bridge** is famous for being one of the only built structures worldwide that allows BASE jumping. The acronym BASE stands for the things one can jump off: building, antenna, span (bridges), and earth. It's an extreme sport that many view as a step up from parachuting, thrill-wise, as adrenaline junkies fling themselves off standing structures. Because BASE jumpers don't start from as high an elevation as skydivers, this sport is far more dangerous. For a casual traveler, it's enough of a rush just to watch.

If you're set on learning *and* have completed the required 150 skydives (seriously), sign up for a four-day intensive course ($1,200) at **Apex Base** (951/719-3941, http://legacy.apexbase. com), a respected outfitter and teaching center. You'll learn how to pack your own parachute and how to safely jump, with lessons covering canopy control, landing, and weather conditions. An advanced course ($400), for those who are already practiced and want to extend their skills, is also available. Reserve online or by phone—the company doesn't have a storefront in town so holds much of the course at a local hotel; detailed information will be provided once you're booked.

Golfing

Swing the clubs for a day at one of the prettiest courses in the state, **Canyon Springs Golf Course** (199 Canyon Springs Rd., 208/734-7609, www.canyonspringsgolf.com, $15-34). Since the weather down in the Snake River Canyon is warmer, the course can be played most of the year. The 18 holes are along gentle terrain by the river, with views of the Perrine Bridge.

Entertainment and Events

In an old brick building in the center of downtown, built by Japanese immigrant Torijo Koto in 1920, you'll find **Koto Brewing Company** (156 Main Ave. W., 208/933-2570, http://koto.beer, 11am-10pm Mon.-Thurs., 11:30am-midnight Fri.-Sat., 10am-4pm Sun.). The brewery is super local, with a hometown head brewer and the local high school gym floor repurposed as tables. Visitors can choose from a small but strong selection of craft brews, including double IPAs, pale ales, blonds, and seasonals. If you're hungry, there's a menu of burgers, tacos, and salads.

Swing by **Bumpin Bernie's** (139 Shoshone St. N., 208/329-1575, http://bumpin-bernies-lounge-bar.business.site, 6pm-1:30am Wed.-Thurs., 8pm-1:30am Fri.-Sat., 5pm-midnight Sun.), where there's bound to be a crowd. The lively spot has DJ music, a big dance floor, hookahs, and drinks.

The Orpheum Theatre (146 Main Ave. W., 208/595-2600, www.orpheumtwinfalls.com, $5-50) is a charming 1920s venue on Main Street. The renovated venue shows classic movies like *Casablanca*, but primarily focuses on live theater and musical performances, as well as comedy. Beer and wine is available for live shows.

The biggest show at the biggest falls

Top to bottom: Shoshone Falls; along the Thousand Springs Scenic Byway; CloverLeaf Creamery in Buhl.

around, **Lights and Lasers at Shoshone Falls** (May, $12-50) takes place over four days in May, drawing 1,500 people a night, and features a laser show projected directly onto Shoshone Falls. Come early for family-friendly activities, live music, and food vendors. Check the website (http://visitidaho.com) in March to keep an eye out for tickets—they sell fast. And don't forget to bring a flashlight to navigate the dark paths after the show.

Food

For the best night out in town, head to ★ **Elevation 486** (195 River Vista Pl., 208/737-0486, http://elevation486.com, 11am-close daily, $20), a fine-dining restaurant whose outdoor patio offers stunning views of the Snake River Canyon. It's a perfect place to sit with a glass of wine on a warm summer evening to watch the setting sun. On the menu are a signature burger with grilled apple, butternut squash ravioli with pistachio sauce, Kobe beef meatloaf, and a perfectly prepared Idaho ruby red trout straight from the river below—pan-broiled with roasted red pepper butter.

The spacious **Yellow Brick Café** (136 Main Ave., 208/731-9827, 9am-8pm Mon.-Thurs., 9am-9pm Fri.-Sat., 9am-2pm Sun., $15) serves fresh flavors, with items like a Thai steak salad, a bison and beef burger, and veggie-packed bowls. Breakfast and weekend brunch offerings include a signature brioche french toast and a killer smoked trout Benedict.

Patagonia Grill (772 Falls Ave., Turf Plaza, 208/324-2073, 11am-9pm Mon.-Sat., $12) is a small café hidden in a suburban shopping department that dishes out amazing food. Everything is made with care and bursts with flavor. You can get a traditional Argentinian steak with homemade chimichurri, but the real stars are the empanadas, stuffed full of cheese, meat, onions, or maybe eggs, and browned to perfection. Or try the *milanesa* (a fried breaded beef cut) sandwich or the *choripán* (sausage sandwich)

served with chimichurri; all sandwiches come on homemade bread. Top off your meal with a sweet treat of *tres leches* cake, made with three types of milk, or flan.

Slice Pizza (132 Main Ave., 208/595-2777, 11am-8pm Mon.-Sat., $15) offers a variety of pizzas, along with calzones, pastas, big salads, and beer and wine. You might also catch some live music or a movie screening here.

A well-known and lively neighborhood joint, **Twin Falls Sandwich Company** (128 Main Ave. N., 208/734-8372, www.twinfallssandwich.com, 7am-8pm Mon.-Sat., $8) is serious about its sandwiches, with numerous hot and cold options, including classics like a grilled cheese as well as paninis and burgers. They're all hits, whether you opt for a homemade pastrami or barbecue pork. Pair it with a local beer or cider.

Accommodations and Camping

A renovated old motel located just a couple of miles north of downtown, the ★ **Blue Lakes Inn** (952 Blue Lakes Blvd., 208/933-2123, www.bluelakesinn.com, Apr.-Sept., $125-169) now offers travelers a modern boutique experience, an unexpected delight for road-trippers. Each of its 23 rooms has individually designed decor and furniture. Local art adorns the spacious rooms, available in a variety of sizes, from standard to suite; there are also rooms with kitchenettes and a bunk-bed room that holds up to six people. The outdoor pool is surrounded by a pleasant fenced patio, and the breakfast nook offers locally produced yogurt, bread, and meat. The inn even has electric vehicle charging stations.

The Fillmore Inn (102 Fillmore St., 702/580-3310, www.thefillmoreinn.com, $160-235) is in a beautiful brick Tudor house near the center of town, a short walk to restaurants and the movie theater. Three luxurious rooms, and one additional loft room that can be booked alongside, have jetted bathtubs, walk-in showers, and fluffy beds. The house is full of hand-carved touches and antiques that evoke a Victorian turn-of-the-century abode, and a delicious breakfast is served in the dining room each morning. Note that children under 10 aren't allowed at the inn.

If you've got kids, they'll love staying at the **Best Western Plus Twin Falls Hotel** (1377 Blue Lakes Blvd., 208/736-8000, www.bestwestern.com, $98-130). Start your visit with a freshly baked chocolate-chip cookie upon check-in. Kids can splash the afternoon away in a large heated indoor pool with a hot tub nearby. Rooms are comfortable and spacious and come with a great hot breakfast. Located right along the main highway, it's a mere mile (1.6 km) from the canyon rim.

The **Oregon Trail Campground** (2733 Kimberly Rd., 208/733-0853, http://oregontrailcampground.com, $38) is just a 5-minute drive from downtown and a 10-minute drive from Shoshone Falls, and includes sites for tents and full hookups, Wi-Fi, and laundry. Staff happily provides maps and tips on local sights and activities.

Thousand Springs Scenic Byway

Road-trippers who rattle through southern Idaho on I-84 at breakneck speed might think the state a flat, brown, dusty land, with not much to write home about. But a short way off the highway, one can find rushing springs, waterfalls, and fascinating geology.

This stretch follows part of the **Thousand Springs Scenic Byway** from Twin Falls to Bliss, which connects some of the units that make up the **Thousand Springs State Park** (http://parksandrecreation.idaho.gov), as well as some small towns and private hot springs. Along the way you'll have great views of the Snake River Canyon. The area doesn't quite have a thousand springs, but there are a lot of them, usually at their fullest

in spring; the unique limestone geology of the region leaches water away from the Snake River, which resurfaces as springs. Part of the route also closely tracks with the Oregon Trail, and you can see impressive ruts at Hagerman Fossil Beds National Monument.

Getting Around

On this stretch, you'll follow part of the Thousand Springs Scenic Byway along **U.S. 30.** The itinerary assumes you're continuing on your Oregon Trail journey westward and so outlines a one-way trip covering 45 miles (72 km) west from **Twin Falls** to **Bliss.**

Planning Tips

Just driving U.S. 30 between Twin Falls and Bliss takes an hour—adding only about 15 minutes' driving time over taking I-84 point to point. But many of the sights along the scenic byway require a bit of a drive off the highway, so if you have time, plan for a full day to make spur trips and stops to explore the area. If you're going to hike or get out on the water, consider making this a day trip from Twin Falls so that you have nearby accommodations you can return to at the end of the day; from Malad Gorge, you can loop back 38 miles (61 km) to Twin Falls via I-84, which takes 45 minutes. For those planning to explore the area in more depth, **Buhl** serves as a base point; from here, you can continue west along U.S. 30 for the scenic drive and hit the hot springs, Hagerman Fossil Beds, and Malad Gorge, or you can head south for a spur to Balanced Rock or north across the Snake River for trips to Ritter Island and Box Canyon.

Beginning from Buhl, you'll pass through farmland and fields before catching up with the Snake River, when the views begin. Keep an eye on the river for sneaky waterfalls and springs pouring forth along the canyon. It's this stretch of the road that gives the state park and byway its name. As you drive north on

U.S. 30, look east across the river to see some of the "thousand" springs, cataracts of flowing water that cascade down the cliff in white rivulets.

Buhl

The small town of Buhl is along the old Oregon Trail route, although it doesn't have much to show for it now. Today it focuses on trout fisheries and dairy farming.

CloverLeaf Creamery

The best reason to stop in Buhl is for a bottle of fresh and creamy chocolate milk or an ice cream scoop at **CloverLeaf Creamery** (205 S. Broadway, 208/543-4272, 9am-6pm daily). In an old downtown dairy from the 1930s, the creamery has been nationally recognized for its humane and healthy treatment of its herd of Holstein cows. The award-winning animals live up to four times as long as an average dairy cow and produce delicious milk. The product is bottled as milk, yogurt, and cream, and used to make over 20 varieties of ice cream, all sold here from this retail storefront.

Getting There

From Twin Falls, drive 15 miles (24 km) west on U.S. 30 to Buhl; the creamery is on the left. The drive takes 20 minutes.

Balanced Rock

On this fun spur trip just southwest of town in Buhl, you might think you're driving to the middle of nowhere, past farms and rural houses. But you'll eventually descend into a rocky canyon marked by red sandstone. At the bottom of the canyon is Salmon Falls Creek, and there's a nice park alongside it for picnics and rest breaks. **Balanced Rock** is another mile (1.6 km) up the road, clearly visible on the right. It might be considered one of the mascots of Twin Falls. The impressive, precarious-looking formation was created by years of wind erosion. It weighs over 40 tons and is 48 feet (15 m)

tall, and it makes a fun spot to snap a few goofy "holding it up" photos.

Getting There

From Buhl, drive southwest on Main Street for 0.5 mile (0.8 km), then turn right onto 4100 North Road/Burley Avenue. In 0.2 mile (0.3 km), turn left onto 1400 East/Castleford Road South. Veer right in 4 miles (6.4 km) for East 3700 North and continue on the road for 8 miles (12.8 km) until you descend into the canyon. Balanced Rock is just across the river in 1 mile (1.6 km). The drive from Buhl takes 20 minutes.

Miracle and Banbury Hot Springs

Miracle Hot Springs (19073A U.S. 30, 208/543-6002, http://miraclehotspring. com, 8am-11pm Mon.-Sat., $10 adults, $8 seniors, $4 ages 4-13, $1 under age 4) is near a tributary of the Snake River and has four outdoor pools. It also has 15 private pools for an additional fee (1 hour $4, 2 hours $12) and 6 larger VIP pools (1 hour $8, 2 hours $24). The pools' design evokes a kind of Southwest adobe feel and has rich wood accents. This is a relaxing place with nice touches like a chessboard near seats in the water.

Owned by the same folks as Miracle Hot Springs, **Banbury Hot Springs** (1128 Banbury Rd., 208/543-4098, http://miraclehotspring.com, 8am-10pm Mon.-Sat., $10 adults, $8 seniors, $4 ages 4-13, $1 under age 4) is on the Snake River and has one large outdoor geothermal swimming pool, as well as private mineral hot tubs and jetted tubs. You can also find **kayak rentals** ($15-40) from Banbury Hot Springs if you want to get on the river. Also on offer is a huge "Megladon" six-person paddleboard, a lightweight but very stable giant board that can actually fit your whole family, renting for $40-60. From here, it's just a 1-mile (1.6-km) paddle north to find the stunning Blue Heart Springs near Box Canyon, accessible only by boat. The cove is surrounded by black lava rocks and has sapphire-clear water.

For slightly upscale camping, Miracle Hot Springs has **camp domes** ($89-94) with electricity and heat or air-conditioning. Banbury Hot Springs has **condos** ($140-220) that include a full kitchen and bath. Domes and condos also include soaking fees for your whole stay. RV sites ($20) and tent sites ($10) are also available at both.

Getting There

From Buhl, follow U.S 30 west for 11 miles (17 km). At the junction with East 4800 North, you'll see signs for Miracle and Banbury Hot Springs; turn left for Miracle Hot Springs, which is just off the highway, and right for Banbury Hot Springs, 1.8 miles (2.8 km) east down the road. The drive takes about 15 minutes from Buhl.

1000 Springs Resort

The **1000 Springs Resort** (18734 U.S. 30, 208/837-4987, www.1000springsresort. com, 11am-8:30pm Tues.-Thurs., 11am-9:30pm Fri.-Sat., noon-6pm Sun., $7 adults, $6 ages 6-17, $3 seniors and under age 6) has the only indoor spring-fed pool in the area. Its heated mineral waters are a perfect place to spend the day. The large pool has diving boards, a water slide, and lifeguards on duty. There's also a separate kiddie pool and 15 private indoor hot tubs.

The best place to see the **Thousand Springs** itself—waterfalls cascading down the cliffs—is across the river from the resort, where the falls trace lacy patterns on the green cliff sides.

Also at 1000 Springs Resort is **1000 Springs Tours** (18696 U.S. 30, 208/888-6611, www.1000springs.com), which offers river cruises on its catamaran. The 1.5-hour **Scenic River Cruise** ($35) takes you up close to bubbling springs and careening waterfalls along the Snake River Canyon. The cruise runs year-round (an enclosed area is available on the boat) up

to four times daily, but spring and fall are typically the most spectacular times to go, with the gush of snow-fed springs and brilliant wildflowers or fall colors lining the canyon. Summer is high season for bird-watching or simply beating the heat under the canopy with a cool cocktail. Choose a two-hour lunch or dinner cruise ($50-60) and enjoy a full meal along with your cruise. Reserve ahead to guarantee your spot.

To explore the river on your own, 1000 Springs Tours also offers **kayak, canoe, and paddleboard rentals** (9am-6pm Fri.-Sun., half-day $35, full-day $50-70). The launch spot is directly across the river from Ritter Island, a beautiful place to explore the springs, see wildlife, and stop for a picnic lunch. For a longer trip, head south on the river 5 miles (8 km) one-way to see the beautiful Blue Heart Springs near Box Canyon. Reservations are recommended, especially during the busy June-August season.

The resort's year-round **campground**

has 18 full-hookup RV sites ($35) and 40 tent sites ($25). The grassy grounds are located right next to the river within view of cascading waterfalls and green canyons. Picnic tables line the water's edge.

Getting There

From the U.S. 30/East 4800 North junction near Miracle and Banbury Hot Springs, head north 3.4 miles (5.5 km) for the 1000 Springs Resort, to the right between the highway and the river. Signage is prominent. The drive takes five minutes.

Box Canyon

The **Box Canyon Springs Nature Preserve** (Thousand Springs State Park, $5 per vehicle day-use) is a great place to stretch your legs while enjoying the nation's 11th largest spring. On the 4 mile (6.4-km) round-trip **Box Canyon Trail** (trailhead at the pullout on S. 1500 E. St.), you may be unimpressed by the early stretch, but have your camera at the ready once you reach the gorge—you'll come upon grand views of a beautiful blue spring-fed pool and the river below. You can turn back now if you're satisfied, or continue along the rim.

Soon, the trail descends into the canyon, eventually arriving at a small platform and waterfall. The falls bubble over rocks and streams through the canyon—they're not the tallest falls, but they're wide and have an impressive frenzied flow. The wet climate down here creates a green oasis that's markedly different than the clifftops above. The climb back up the canyon can be a challenge on the rocky trail—but it's worth it. You'll gain 620 feet (189 m) of elevation overall. Budget two hours for the hike. Watch for poison oak lining the path.

Getting There

Be wary of using phone GPS directions to get here, as they might send you down the wrong road; if you do, make sure to input "Box Canyon State Park" for

Box Canyon

directions (not "Box Canyon Springs Preserve"). From **Buhl,** drive northeast on Main Street, then turn left on North 1500 East/Clear Lakes Road and continue on as it becomes South 1700 East. Drive 6.8 miles (11 km), then turn left on 3500 South. After 2.1 miles (3.4 km), turn right onto South 1500 East. A small parking lot will be on your left in 0.9 mile (1.4 km). The drive takes 15 minutes.

From **1000 Springs Resort** on the other side of the Snake River, drive north on U.S. 30 for 4 miles (6.4 km), then turn right onto East 2900 South/Vader Grade. In 3.7 miles (5.9 km), keep right to follow Hagerman Highway. In 1.6 miles (2.5 km), turn right onto South 1500 East. You'll see the small parking lot for Box Canyon on your right in 4.6 miles (7.4 km). The drive takes just under 20 minutes.

From **Ritter Island,** exit the island parking lot on Thousand Springs Grade, then turn right onto South 1300 East. In 0.5 mile (0.8 km), continue straight when the road forks, becoming East 3300 South after 0.8 mile (1.2 km). Continue on it for 1.2 miles (1.9 km), then turn right onto South 1500 East. The parking lot will be on your right in 1 mile (1.6 km). The drive takes 10 minutes.

Ritter Island

Tiny **Ritter Island** (Thousand Springs State Park, 208/837-4505, 10am-3pm Thurs.-Mon. May-Sept., free) is a bit of a hidden treasure, offering history, springs, and beautiful strolls. No cars are allowed on the island—to visit, you park nearby and walk across a small footbridge, or you can access the island via watercraft; rent kayaks or canoes across the river at 1000 Springs Resort. On the island is a dairy barn built by Minnie Miller, an enterprising businesswoman who raised Guernsey cattle on the island in the early 1900s; from the barn, located right across the footbridge, you can follow a short 0.25-mile (0.4-km) trail to the natural springs named after Miller, who

lived here 1918-1954. The spring gushes forth from rock and runs crystal clear into the river below, which maintains a cool 55°F (13°C) year-round. Volunteers are usually on-site during open hours to show visitors around the barn and talk about the local history of the area and Minnie herself. Another easy 2-mile (3.2 km) path circles the island, offering nice river views.

Getting There

You can paddle to Box Canyon from 1000 Springs Resort, as well as get here by vehicle via 1000 Springs Resort and Buhl.

From **Buhl,** drive northeast on Main Street, then turn left on North 1500 East/Clear Lakes Road and continue on as it becomes South 1700 East. Drive 6.8 miles (11 km), then turn left on 3500 South. After 2.1 miles (3.4 km), turn right onto South 1500 East. Box Canyon is on the left in 0.9 mile (1.5 km); continue north on South 1500 East for another 1.1 miles (1.7 km), then turn left on 3300 South. In 2.1 miles (3.3 km), veer right at the fork for South 1300 East. After 0.5 mile (0.8 km), turn left onto Thousand Springs Grade. Follow the winding road for 1 mile (1.6 km) to get to the Ritter Island parking lot. The drive from Buhl takes 25 minutes total, or 10 minutes from Box Canyon. The footbridge to the island is easy to spot from the parking lot.

From **1000 Springs Resort** on the other side of the Snake River, drive north on U.S. 30 for 3.6 miles (5.7 km), then turn right on East 2925 South. In 0.5 mile (0.8 km), turn right on South 1050 East, heading south. Continue for 1.1 miles (1.7 km), and veer left when the road forks to continue onto East 3000 South for 0.7 mile (1.1 km), when the road curves right and becomes South 1200 East. Drive 1.8 miles (2.8 km), then make a slight right on South 1300 East. In 0.8 mile (1.2 km), make another right onto Thousand Springs Grade, where you'll find the parking lot in 1 mile (1.6 km). The drive from 1000 Springs Resort takes just over 15 minutes.

Hagerman Fossil Beds National Monument

The land encompassed by **Hagerman Fossil Beds National Monument** (www. nps.gov/hafo, free) was first excavated in 1929, turning up fossils that became world-renowned for their quality and completeness. Today you won't find any archaeological digs going on, and there aren't many fossils left to see in the area, but you will find a set of well-preserved wagon ruts. Hagerman Fossils Beds is near the site of the former Salmon Falls, which is no longer visible due to dams. Salmon Falls was historically a popular spot for Shoshone fishers, and they often traded with emigrants in the area. From Salmon Falls, the wagon trains broke a trail due west across the hills, leaving the Snake River for a spell and meeting back up with it at Three Island Crossing near today's Glenns Ferry. Here you can see the ruts left behind by the wagons striking out west on their slight shortcut across the sagebrush.

Getting There

From 1000 Springs Resort, drive 1.7 miles (2.7 km) northwest on U.S. 30. Just before the Snake River crossing, turn left on **Bell Rapids Road,** which leads you to the monument's two overlooks.

Sights and Recreation

There are two overlooks in the park. You'll come across the first, the **Snake River Overlook,** 2.8 miles (4.5 km) from the left turn onto Bell Rapids Road. Here you can take a short walk on a boardwalk to views of the Snake River and the gentle surrounding hills. You might catch a glimpse of hawks or falcons circling above the water here. The second is the **Oregon Trail Overlook,** 3 miles (4.8 km) west from the Snake River Overlook along Bell Rapids Road. From atop the bluff where the perch is, you can walk 0.5

mile (0.8 km) of interpretive trails, which provide views of the pioneers' wagon ruts and the landscape. On the drive to this overlook, you'll see some ruts to the left of the road, and at the overlook you can follow the ruts with your eyes as they continue to the right. You can also keep driving past the overlook parking lot to see a few more visible rut sections. Once the road hits gravel, you're on private land, so turn around here.

If you have 3-4 hours, you can also hike between the two overlooks via the **Emigrant Trail** to walk alongside the impressive wagon ruts. Hiking past the empty hills might give you a sense of what the pioneers may have experienced; many emigrants walked alongside their wagons. You can hike in either direction, but if you start from the Snake River Overlook, you'll gain 900 feet (274 m) in elevation as you scale the big hill to the Oregon Trail Overlook; from the other direction, the elevation gain is 600 feet (183 m). Note that this hike can be hot and dusty. Bring lots of water and be on the lookout for rattlesnakes and scorpions.

If you have two cars and don't want to tackle the 6-mile (9.6-km) round-trip hike, use one for a shuttle at either overlook parking lot. Otherwise, the short trails atop the Oregon Trail Overlook give you a nice sample without as much work.

Hagerman

The town of Hagerman shares its name with the nearby fossil beds monument and the most famous fossils found there: the Hagerman Horse. Here you'll find the Hagerman Fossil Beds National Monument's interpretive center. This is also a good place to stop for a break, gas, or a meal.

Getting There

To get to the town of Hagerman, continue north past the Bell Rapids Road turnoff into Hagerman Fossil Beds National

Monument, just before the Snake River crossing, on U.S. 30 for 4.5 miles (7.2 km). The drive takes five minutes.

While driving between the monument and the town of Hagerman, watch for **Melon Gravel,** big boulders in the fields left over from the Bonneville Flood during the most recent ice age. The massive flood carried giant boulders of basalt in the flood waters, rounding out their edges and depositing them all across southern Idaho. They got their name after a humorous sign went up along the highway in the 1950s that said "Petrified Watermelons: Take one home to your mother-in-law."

Sights
The **Hagerman Visitor Center** (221 N. State St., 208/933-4105, 9am-5pm daily Memorial Day-Labor Day, 9am-5pm Thurs.-Mon. Labor Day-Memorial Day, free) is in town on the east side of U.S. 30. Inside you'll find a variety of fossils and some exhibits on how they were excavated in the Hagerman Fossil Beds; this is the place to dig into that history. Of particular interest is the huge skeleton of the Hagerman Horse, the single-toed *Equus simplicidens,* Idaho's official state fossil. It was found here in the fossil beds in the 1930s. Other fossils discovered in the area include a giant otter, a giant badger, and many species of swans and voles.

For more on the cultural history of the area, including indigenous peoples, explorers, and settlers, pause at the small **Hagerman Valley Historical Society Museum** (100 S. State St., 208/837-6288, www.hagermanmuseum.org, 9am-5pm Thurs.-Sun., free). Along the Oregon Trail, many emigrants would cast off items that they no longer needed or wanted to carry, and the museum has a few of these that were found in the area, such as pioneer shoes with holes in them and engraved powder flasks. You can also see prehistoric fossils, arrowheads, geodes, and more in the museum, which is housed in a turn-of-the-20th-century

Oregon Trail ruts in the Hagerman Fossil Beds National Monument

bank. Be sure to chat with the passionate volunteers who run it.

Food

The **Snake River Grill** (611 Frogs Landing, 208/837-6227, www.snakeriver-grill.com, 7am-2pm Mon., 7am-9pm Tues.-Sun., $17) serves meals made with classic French techniques. Diners enjoy seafood, steak, Idaho potatoes, and special sturgeon nuggets. The head cook is an avid hunter and fisher, and offers weekly wild game dinners. The trout is fresh, pulled from the nearby Snake River.

Malad Gorge

Semis and cars zooming by on I-84 have no idea that they're driving over a gorgeous 60-foot (18-m) waterfall, the **Devil's Washbowl,** in **Malad Gorge State Park** (Thousand Springs State Park, 8am-4pm daily, $5 per vehicle). From the park's parking lot, walk over the metal bridge and follow the path 0.3 mile (0.5 km) to an overlook for great views of the falls gushing into the "washbowl," or pool, encased in the striking rocks of the gorge. Note that there are no railings here, so watch your kids and don't get too close to the edge.

Getting There

From Hagerman, drive north 1.8 miles (2.8 km) on U.S. 30 and turn right on Justice Grade. Follow the street for 2.6 miles (4.1 km), then turn left on Ritchie Road. In 1.6 miles (2.5 km), turn left into the park entrance, following signs for the Devil's Washbowl. The drive takes just over 10 minutes.

From I-84 westbound, take exit 147 for Tuttle. Turn left on East 2350 South and after 0.4 mile (0.6 km) turn right on Ritchie Road, following it for 0.3 mile (0.5 km) into the park.

Glenns Ferry

"Husband had considerable difficulty in crossing the cart. Both cart and mules were turned upside down in the river and entangled in the harness. The mules would have drowned but for a desperate struggle to get them ashore. Then after putting two men swimming behind to steady it, they succeeded in getting it across."

Narcissa Whitman, August 13, 1836, *The Letters and Journals of Narcissa Whitman.* Whitman was one of the first European-American women to cross South Pass into the West. She and her husband, Marcus, traveled to Oregon Territory and established the Whitman Mission.

From Fort Hall, emigrants had been traveling along the south bank of the Snake River, often peering down into rapids far below. But from this point on, the river flowed west into an even drier and more desolate landscape, and pioneers had a crucial decision to make: Continue on, or risk a dangerous crossing to the north

side—where there was easier access to water, better grazing for livestock, and a shorter route to Oregon.

Three Island Crossing, as the pioneers called it, was at a wide and shallow part of the Snake River dotted by three small islands. Emigrants stood on both banks and used ropes to pull the wagons across, sometimes three wagons at a time for sturdiness against the current. They pulled wagons to each of the three islands along the way, one by one—island hopping, pioneer-style. Because of the time and effort involved and the size of large wagon trains, it could often take days to get everyone across, and they couldn't rush—the danger of getting tangled in the ropes and drowning, or a wagon capsizing, was very real. Pioneer diaries record many drownings at the crossing; this was one of the most dangerous junctions along the whole trail.

Three Island Crossing was used until 1869, when a ferry was constructed by Gus Glenn, from whom the town takes its name. Today the sleepy community of Glenns Ferry sits on the north bank of the river, and a state park commemorates where pioneers once risked their wagons in the waters.

Getting There

From Malad Gorge, you can complete the **Thousand Springs Scenic Byway** by continuing from the U.S. 30/Justice Grade junction north on U.S. 30 for another 6.8 miles (10.9 km) to Bliss, and then turning right and then left to merge onto I-84 westbound. But it makes more sense to head out directly via I-84 and skip the last section of the byway—you won't miss any sights and will save about 10 minutes of driving time. From the Devil's Washbowl, head south on Ritchie Road for 0.3 mile (0.5 km), then turn left onto East 2350 South, which takes you to the on-ramp for I-84 westbound. In 25 miles (40 km), take exit 121. Turn left onto Old U.S. 30 and continue straight onto East 1st Avenue, which takes you into

downtown Glenns Ferry. The drive takes 25 minutes.

If you have less time and want to skip the Thousand Springs Scenic Byway—although note that simply driving straight through via **U.S. 30** only adds 15 minutes—you can make it to Glenns Ferry in an hour from Twin Falls. Head north out of town via U.S. 93, then merge onto I-84 for 51 miles (82 km).

Sights
Three Island Crossing

At **Three Island Crossing State Park** (1083 S. Three Island Park Dr., 208/366-2394, http://parksandrecreation.idaho.gov, 9am-5pm Sun.-Wed., 9am-6pm Thurs.-Sat., $5 per vehicle) you'll find the **Oregon Trail History and Education Center.** It has some dusty dioramas, as well as some interactive exhibits that make it worth looking around. Outside is a wagon and a few monuments to the early pioneers. But what you're really here for are the views; the shady park is in view of the three islands the pioneers used to cross the Snake River. You can walk a short trail from the museum down to the river, where you can see ample evidence of the wagons' crossing: wide swales head into the river from the banks. The Snake River looks particularly lovely flowing around the islands and against the rolling hills. Stay overnight to catch sunset here.

Y Knot Winery

Find award-winning vintages at **Y Knot Winery** (1289 W. Madison Ave., 208/366-2313, www.yknotwinery.com, 10am-11pm daily, tasting and tour $7-13), where you can taste reds and whites, then take a tour to see the winery and the barrel room. The on-site restaurant, **Y Knot Restaurant & Tavern** (hours same as winery, $15) serves lunch and dinner, offering a fine-dining experience in the Snake River Valley. Enjoy Idaho red trout, shrimp, and steak along with house wines. The restaurant has live music at 7pm most Fridays-Saturdays.

Camping

Three Island Crossing (1083 S. Three Island Park Dr., http://idahostateparks. reserveamerica.com) has 82 campsites for tents and RVs ($22-45), with electricity and water. There are also eight cabins ($50-65) mere feet from the river. They can sleep up to five people and are comfortable, with heating and air-conditioning, fire pits, and grills—but bring your own bedding.

South Alternate Route

The South Alternate Route was not for the faint of heart. Rather than risking a river crossing at Three Island, many wagon trains chose to continue on the south side of the Snake River into southwestern Idaho, in what today is Owyhee County. It was dusty and arduous for both pioneers and their livestock. Today this route, traced by **Highway 78**, is still a long haul, from the highway's start in **Hammett**, east of Glenns Ferry, to its northwest end in **Marsing**, it's nearly 100 miles (160 km), about 1.75 hours of driving without stops. There aren't many notable stops along the way, but if you have a lot of time and want to explore some quirky Idaho backcountry, go for it. Otherwise, you might just check out Bruneau Dunes and then head back to the main trail route.

Fuel and Services

Note that cell phone service is spotty on this route, and there are few places to get gas or food, so stock up before heading out. It's a good idea to fill up on gas at **Grand View,** 49 miles (79 km) west of Glenns Ferry; it's the last station for 40 miles (64 km). Keep an eye out for livestock on the roads, as the area is open range. If you drive the whole route,

Top to bottom: old wagon at Three Island Crossing; Owyhee Mountains in Owyhee County; rippling sands at Bruneau Dunes.

you'll end up near Parma, west of Boise. Consider staying the night in Boise or heading on to Ontario in Oregon.

Bruneau Dunes

Secrets and amazing sights await you at **Bruneau Dunes State Park** (27608 Sand Dunes Rd., 208/366-7919, http://parksandrecreation.idaho.gov, $5 per vehicle), full of giant sand dunes left by the ancient Bonneville Flood. Because the dunes sit in a valley, they don't drift much. The visitors center has a few exhibits on the local flora and fauna, and the unique geological features of the dunes, and you can find information, maps, sandboard rentals, and friendly rangers here. The rangers lead guided tours on summer weekends explaining the unique geology. Don't miss the nighttime scorpion tour, during which a guide leads you on a blacklight hunt for the creatures, or borrow a blacklight from the observatory to hunt on your own—it's an otherworldly experience. And while you should be careful around all wildlife, don't worry—these scorpions aren't venomous!

Getting There and Around

From Glenns Ferry, begin the route by driving west on I-84 for 9 miles (14.5 km). Turn left on Highway 78 and continue for 14 miles (22.5 km), then turn left onto Bruneau Sand Dunes Road, following signs. Find the visitors center just past the park entrance to the right. The drive takes just over 30 minutes.

From the visitors center, continue down the paved Park Road to find the Broken Wheel Campground on the right, and the Bruneau Dunes Observatory on the left. The road ends at a picnic area near the Big Dune and Big Lake.

Sights and Recreation
Sandboarding
Sled in the summer sun on the dunes! Bring your own board—any sled meant for snow will work—or rent a sandboard

($15 per day) at the visitors center. Head up either **Small Dune** or **Big Dune**—the tallest in the park at 470 feet (143 m); it takes about 30 or 40 minutes, respectively. Going down is much faster, of course.

Hiking
The strenuous **Bruneau Dunes Loop** is a 6-mile (9.7-km) round-trip hike. It takes in the Big Dune and Small Dune, as well as Big Lake and Small Lake. The trail is on shifting sands for much of the way, so there's no path to follow. Pick up a map in the visitors center and follow the series of white marker posts. Along the way, you may see coyotes, jackrabbits, lizards, frogs, and waterfowl, as well as wildflowers in late spring. Budget 4-5 hours for the entire trail, although you can also opt for shorter segments. Start at the visitors center for the whole loop, or for shorter versions, start at the observatory or parking lot near Big Lake. It's hot here in summer, as you can imagine, with no shade, so hike in the morning or late evening and bring plenty of water (1-2 quarts pp).

Stargazing
The remoteness of the Bruneau Dunes makes it an excellent spot for stargazing. You can see the Milky Way and plenty of shooting stars with the naked eye, but for a closer look, go to the **Bruneau Dunes Observatory,** open only Friday-Saturday evenings late March-mid-October, weather permitting. The observatory is one of the largest in the region, with state-of-the-art equipment offering great glimpses of the night sky; you might spot Jupiter, the Owl Nebula, and the Hercules Cluster. Stop by an hour before sunset for an **observatory tour** (from 6:30pm Fri.-Sat. late Mar.-May and Aug.-mid-Oct., from 7:30pm Fri.-Sat. June-July), followed by a short orientation. Afterward, you can look through telescopes (until 11:30pm Fri.-Sat. late Mar.-May and Aug.-mid-Oct., until 12:30am Fri.-Sat.

Rockhounding in Idaho

Rockhounding, the hobby of looking for gems and minerals, is popular in Idaho, called the Gem State both for its natural beauty and for its gem and mineral riches. The numerous gems and semiprecious stones found across the state include star garnet, amethyst, and sapphire.

Owyhee County is home to many special rocks. Bruneau Jasper and Owyhee Jasper are types of a gemstone known as picture jasper, which features naturally occurring patterns, or "scenes," that look like landscapes. Opals are often found deep in the canyons near Givens Hot Springs. Petrified wood, fossils, and agates are common in the area as well. A casual rock hunter might keep an eye out for interesting finds.

June-July). There's a viewing fee ($5 pp), but it's free for children under age six.

Accommodations and Camping

For a soft bed and hot breakfast, stay at **Owyhee Bed & Breakfast** (31063 T Ranch Rd., 208/908-2615, $100-120), about 10 miles (16 km) west of the state park outside the town of Bruneau, with gorgeous views overlooking the Bruneau Valley. It also offers a rotating schedule of workshops and events you can join in on, such as cheese-making, watercolor painting, or rope-making.

Broken Wheel Campground (Bruneau Dunes State Park, 27608 Sand Dunes Rd., $12-29) is inside the state park near the observatory and has more than 80 tent and RV sites in a grassy area with shady trees. Sites also have fire pits and covered shelters for shade, and there are shower facilities.

Emu-Z-Um

The **Emu-Z-Um** (22142 River Rd., Grand View, 208/834-2397, http://emuzum. com, 9am-5pm Fri.-Sun. Mar.-Sept., $10) is one of the strangest things you'll see in the middle of the western Idaho desert. If you're into antiques and history, make time for a stop. The main attraction is a reconstructed pioneer village that showcases what life was like for early Owyhee settlers. But there's so much more: This museum is huge, made up of over 15 buildings filled with room upon room of dense, massive collections of all sorts,

arranged around rough themes—for example, you'll find a whole wall of salt and pepper shakers and dozens upon dozens of baseballs, bats, and mitts. Stop by for a quick visit and you'll end up spending hours trying to see everything. The owners offer tours themselves. Oh, and the name? The ranch was once home to 100 emus; now there are only a handful left, but you might catch a glimpse of them.

Getting There

From Bruneau Dunes, head west on Highway 78. Follow it for 25 miles (40 km)—at which point you'll pass the small town of Grand View, where you might want to fill up on gas; you won't see another station for 40 miles (64 km). Continue another 7 miles (11.3 km) west on Highway 78, then turn right onto River Road. Follow the quirky signs 1 mile (1.6 km) to the museum. The drive takes 40 minutes.

Murphy

Murphy is the Owyhee County seat but has a population of just 50 people, one of the smallest county seats in the country. It sprang up around mining, like other towns in the area, and when nearby Silver City declined, it became the central county town.

A great local museum, bigger than you might expect, is the **Owyhee County Museum** (17085 Basey St., 208/495-2319, www.owyheemuseum.org, 10am-4pm

Tues.-Sat., $5), tucked just off the highway. Exhibits cover local history, such as the area's rich mining heritage, and there are displays that include antique furniture, sheepherding wagons, and cowboy brands. Huge collections of arrowheads, horseshoes, driving bits, and spurs line the road.

Food

Stop in for a bite to eat and to shake off the trail dust at the **Murphy General Store** (20449 Hwy. 78, 208/495-1144, 8am-5pm Wed.-Sun., $7), serving classic omelets, burgers, sandwiches, fries, and tots, mostly homemade and always satisfying. While you eat, you can watch the occasional small planes take off and land at the private airstrip just across the highway.

Getting There

From Grand View, continue northwest on Highway 78 for 28 miles (45 km). The drive to Murphy takes 30 minutes.

Givens Hot Springs

Many weary emigrants stopped at these hot springs, including Oregon Trail pioneers Milford and Mattie Givens. Charmed by the restorative waters, the couple stayed and established a hotel and bathhouse in 1881. Today, weary road-trippers can still stop at **Givens Hot Springs** (11309 Hwy. 78, 208/495-2000, www.givenshotsprings.com, noon-9pm daily) to soak and relax in a large indoor pool ($5-8 pp) or private soaking tub ($10 pp per hour). The aging grounds are in the midst of needed upgrades but are open.

A shady, grassy **campground** ($25-35) offers sites for tents and RVs, and prices include swimming for two. Because the property is located directly on hot springs, it's recommended you bring your own drinking water—all the water here is hot!

Getting There

From Murphy, continue northwest on

Bonneville Point

Highway 78 for 18 miles (29 km). The drive takes 20 minutes.

Getting Back on the Main Trail

To rejoin the main trail, continue northwest on Highway 78 from Givens Hot Springs for 11.4 miles (18 km) to Marsing. Turn right onto Highway 55 and continue east for 14.4 miles (23 km), then head right to merge onto I-84. Continue for 15.5 miles (25 km) and then, keeping left, take exit 49 for I-184, following it as it becomes U.S. 26 for 5 miles (8 km) into downtown. The drive takes one hour.

You could also continue north to Parma and then onward into Ontario, Oregon. In Marsing, turn left on Highway 55, which will become U.S. 95. Continue on it for 21 miles (34 km), then follow the road right as it curves to get onto U.S. 26 west, continuing for 1.8 miles (2.8 km) into Parma. The drive takes 40 minutes. If you want to continue into Oregon from Parma, head west out of town via Grove Street, which becomes U.S. 26/U.S. 95.

Continue for 13.6 miles (22 km), merging left onto I-84 westbound. In 3.8 miles (6 km), take exit 376A, and turn right onto U.S. 30 to follow it 0.8 mile (1.2 km) into town. The drive takes 20 minutes.

Main Trail Route to Boise

Pioneers who crossed the Snake River at Three Island Crossing soon reached the lush green of the Boise Valley, a welcome relief from the lava rocks they'd been traversing since Fort Hall. Their destination was Fort Boise, where they could resupply and rest before tackling the last legs of their journey. Today **I-84** from Glenns Ferry traces this route. At this point it was usually late August, or later—it would take another month or more to cover the last 500 miles (800 km) to Oregon City.

Bonneville Point

Overlooking the Boise Valley, **Bonneville Point** is named for Captain Benjamin Bonneville, an explorer who led a party of French fur trappers to the region in 1833. The story goes that as the group left the sagebrush-crusted desert of Idaho, their eyes fell on the valley's trees and they exclaimed in excitement, *"Les bois! Les bois!"* (Trees! Trees!), which became the name for the river feeding the valley, and the city that later grew there.

Today a nice shelter sits at the top of the point, and there are some interpretive panels along with the same tree-lined views seen by the early explorers (with the addition of a few power lines). You can hike along Oregon Trail wagon ruts here, though some have been run over by modern ATV traffic. Short trails lead from the shelter to and along the ruts.

The point is a nice place for a picnic or to stretch your legs, but if you're at the tail end of a long drive into Boise, it's skippable, especially if you've seen other ruts, as it's a 20-minute drive one-way off I-84.

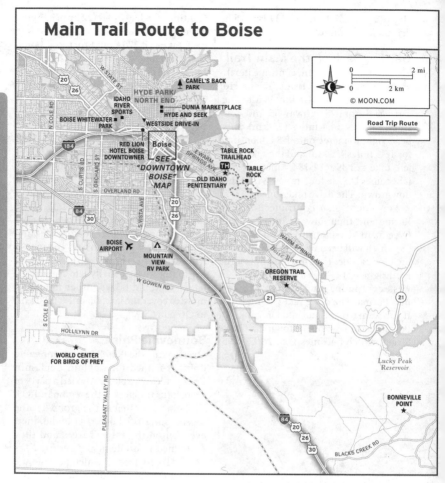

Main Trail Route to Boise

Getting There

From Glenns Ferry, drive west on I-84 for 57 miles (92 km). Take exit 64, turning left onto Blacks Creek Road. In 3.6 miles (5.8 km), turn left and follow the signs 2.6 miles (4.2 km) to Bonneville Point. The drive takes just over an hour.

Oregon Trail Reserve

Stop at the **Oregon Trail Reserve** (5000 Lake Forest Dr., www.cityofboise.org, sunrise-sunset daily, free) for a look at the **Kelton Ramp,** where you can see impressive ruts cut into the cliff side. Pioneers needed a way to make their way from the high canyons down into the Boise River Valley, now called Treasure Valley, and so they cut the Kelton Ramp directly into the rocky canyon wall in the early 1860s. It later became part of the Kelton Road, a stagecoach path from Salt Lake City, Utah, to Boise that was heavily traveled in the 1870s and 1880s.

History doesn't record exactly how the ramp was cut into the rocks, but before it was built, early emigrants used the rope method to get down the steep cliff sides—they'd tie ropes, lock the wheels, and slowly lower a wagon down the hill. Today you can walk on the same ramp—which has been wonderfully preserved—and touch the lichen-covered rocks, once scraped by wagons as they came through.

There's also 1.5 miles (2.4 km) of preserved Oregon Trail ruts. The grounds are located behind a suburban housing development, but the ruts are circled by well-kept walking trails that provide wonderful views of Boise and the surrounding mountains. Walking paths range 0.8-2.6 miles (1.3-4.2 km). Maps are at the kiosks at each parking lot, and the Kelton Ramp and ruts are easy to find, with signs posted throughout the park.

Getting There

From I-84 westbound, take exit 57 for Highway 21, and turn right. In 2.3 miles (3.7 km), turn left on Lake Forest Drive to find two parking lots that both access the reserve; the first lot is the best for seeing the Kelton Ramp and ruts.

Boise

Named by French fur traders for the forested *bois* (woods) around the area, Boise grew from a namesake fort—it was home to the second Fort Boise after the first one, near today's Parma, flooded in the late 1850s. Today nothing remains of either fort. The Oregon Trail passed through here while the second Fort Boise was active, and travelers during the 1860s later enjoyed the amenities of one of the largest cities along the route. Pioneers traveled along the Boise River, entering a green, wooded basin that was a welcome relief after 270 miles (434 km) of grueling travel along the dusty and dry Idaho lava. At the fort, they had another chance to stock up on much needed provisions or make repairs.

The capital of Idaho, Boise is one of the largest cities along the route—it's a young, vibrant spot that's experiencing a huge population growth. More restaurants, shops, and nightlife options pop up each year, though beyond the downtown core it still has a small-town feel. Boise State University, south of downtown, also adds to the city's youthful, artsy vibe.

Getting There and Around

From I-84 westbound, take exit 54 for Highway 20 and follow it downtown. Boise is 9 miles (14.5 km) northwest of the Oregon Trail Reserve, and 70 miles (113 km) west of Glenns Ferry, just over an hour's drive via I-84. If you took the South Alternate Route, head east from Marsing via Highway 55 for 14.4 miles (23 km), then head right to merge onto I-84. Continue for 15.5 miles (25 km), and then, keeping left, take exit 49 for I-184, following it as it becomes U.S. 26 for 5 miles (8 km) into downtown. The drive takes 45 minutes.

Uber (www.uber.com) and **Lyft** (www.lyft.com) operate in Boise.

Orientation

The Boise River cuts through the city, with downtown on the north bank and Boise State University on the south bank.

Downtown

Boise Downtown (BoDo to the locals) is the happening spot, with dozens of shops and restaurants opening every year as the city grows. The center is bordered roughly by State Street to the north and the Boise River to the south. The most walkable section is the 10 blocks surrounding the Basque Block. The western border is 15th Street, and the eastern is 1st Street and Broadway Street. Old Boise is on the east end of the downtown commercial district—though it's part of the downtown core, it has a unique heritage and style that differentiates it. You'll find shops, bars, and brick buildings showcasing the city's history.

IDAHO

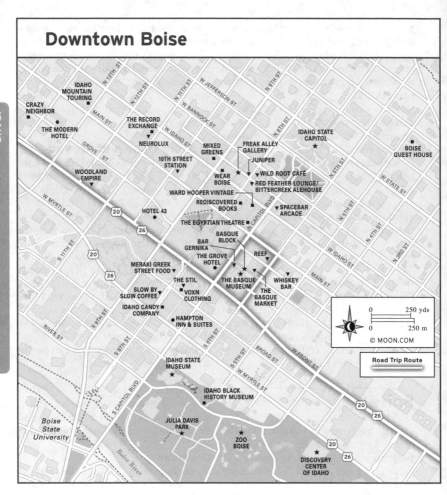

Downtown Boise

CRAZY NEIGHBOR

IDAHO MOUNTAIN TOURING

THE MODERN HOTEL

THE RECORD EXCHANGE

NEUROLUX

WOODLAND EMPIRE

10TH STREET STATION

MIXED GREENS

FREAK ALLEY GALLERY

JUNIPER

WEAR BOISE

WILD ROOT CAFE

RED FEATHER LOUNGE/ BITTERCREEK ALEHOUSE

WARD HOOPER VINTAGE

REDISCOVERED BOOKS

SPACEBAR ARCADE

HOTEL 43

THE EGYPTIAN THEATRE

IDAHO STATE CAPITOL

BOISE GUEST HOUSE

BASQUE BLOCK

BAR GERNIKA

THE GROVE HOTEL

REEF

MERAKI GREEK STREET FOOD

THE STIL

VOXN CLOTHING

THE BASQUE MUSEUM

WHISKEY BAR

SLOW BY SLOW COFFEE

IDAHO CANDY COMPANY

THE BASQUE MARKET

HAMPTON INN & SUITES

IDAHO STATE MUSEUM

IDAHO BLACK HISTORY MUSEUM

JULIA DAVIS PARK

ZOO BOISE

DISCOVERY CENTER OF IDAHO

Boise State University

Boise River

0   250 yds
0   250 m
© MOON.COM

Road Trip Route

Hyde Park

Also called North End, the Hyde Park neighborhood is on the National Register of Historic Places for its distinctive architecture and heritage dating back to 1900. It's a couple of miles northwest of downtown Boise, bordered by the diagonal Fort Street on its southern end and Camel's Back Park hill on its northern end. The pleasant old neighborhood has wide streets and active retail businesses and restaurants.

Sights

Idaho State Capitol

Step inside for a self-guided tour of the **Idaho State Capitol** (700 W. Jefferson Blvd., 208/332-1012, http://capitolcommission. idaho.gov, 7am-7pm Mon.-Fri., 9am-5pm Sat.-Sun., free) to explore its stonework, dome, and indoor murals and art. The rotunda at the entrance has informational panels about the state and the building. Check out the 4th-floor public galleries to see the House and Senate chambers.

Two Days in Boise

Day 1

Start with a coffee and pastry at **Slow by Slow** before heading to **Julia Davis Park** to wander the green and learn about the state's history, including its Oregon Trail history, at the **Idaho State Museum,** inside the park. For lunch, make your way to the **Basque Block** to try some of the regional cuisine, and if you still have room to spare, get some ice cream at **The STIL.** Burn it off with a bike ride on the **Boise River Greenbelt.** Finish the day off with dinner at the **Bittercreek Alehouse,** and if you still have energy catch a show at **The Egyptian Theatre.**

Day 2

Hopefully it's a weekend so you can get brunch at **Juniper.** On a weekday, head to **Bacon** for the namesake, which comes in many varieties. Then drive out to the **World Center for Birds of Prey** to spend the morning with the raptors. For lunch, go to **Westside Drive-In,** and be sure to get the Idaho Ice Cream Potato! In the afternoon, head out again for a hike on the **Table Rock Trail 15** after touring the **Old Idaho Penitentiary,** where the trailhead is located. Then relax with a pint at **Woodland Empire**—pairing it with food from **Manfred's food cart**—and game the night away at **Spacebar Arcade.**

Freak Alley Gallery

Take a walk outside and enjoy the murals at **Freak Alley Gallery,** containing a few blocks of fantastical artwork. Murals changes every few years, so there's always something fresh to see. It's the largest outdoor art gallery in the Northwest, located in the alleys off 8th Street between Bannock and Idaho Streets.

Basque Block

Making up an entire block of downtown, on Grove Street between South Capitol Boulevard and 6th Street, the **Basque Block** (www.thebasqueblock.com) is lined with Basque businesses and restaurants, and is the heart of Basque culture in Boise. Check out Grove Street itself: It's painted with a red and green *lauburu* symbol—a traditional Basque cross. On the sidewalks you can also see lyrics to Basque songs and poems.

The Basque Museum

The Basque Museum (611 W. Grove St., 208/343-2681, http://basquemuseum.eus, 10am-4pm Tues.-Fri., 11am-3pm Sat., $5) is a tidy center that has exhibits on the history of the Basque people in the region, along with rotating exhibits that dive deeper into topics such as Basque food and dance. There's a fun area where you can see a sheepherder's wagon, and kids can prepare a make-believe camp breakfast like Basque sheepherders would. At the museum you'll hear the interesting Basque language, Euskara, being spoken and see pictures of arborglyphs—carvings in aspen trees left by lonely Basque sheepherders. The museum is on the Basque Block, across the street from the Basque Market.

Julia Davis Park

Set along the river's north bank, **Julia Davis Park** is the city's oldest green space and the home of most of its major museums as well as the zoo. The park has roots in the Oregon Trail, if only by association: It's named for an early Boise philanthropist, Julia Davis, who would welcome Oregon Trail travelers and offer them assistance, a place to rest, and supplies. The large park has gardens, walking and biking paths, pavilions, ponds, and playgrounds.

Basque Culture in Boise

In the late 1800s and early 1900s, Basque immigrants came from northern Spain, leaving the limited economic opportunities there to follow the silver mines to Idaho. Soon, the first immigrants discovered that sheepherding was a more lucrative business, providing a booming industry with meat and wool. Word spread back to their families at home, and more Basque people came to the area. In the 20th century, another wave of immigrants fled Spain during the persecution of the Basque people by the Franco regime, including the bombing of the city of Guernica in 1937. Today Boise has the largest and most active concentration of Basque people in the Americas: nearly 15,000. They are fiercely proud of their roots and work hard to keep their culture

The Basque Museum in Boise

alive by sharing it. In the **Basque Block** in downtown Boise there are numerous restaurants, markets, a museum, and a community center that offers language and dance lessons.

Every five years Boise celebrates **Jaialdi** (www.jaialdi.com), which means "festival." This massive celebration of all things Basque includes food, music, and games, and attracts around 35,000 people. The next one is set for summer 2020 and then 2025. Hotels and tickets for special events book up fast, but many events are free and open to all.

Idaho State Museum

The **Idaho State Museum** (610 Julia Davis Dr., 208/334-2120, http://history.idaho.gov, 10am-5pm Mon.-Sat., noon-5pm Sun., $10) is an interactive, hands-on space that everyone in the family can enjoy. With multimedia elements that include touchscreens, games, videos, and touchable displays, the museum celebrates the state and its people. In the theater, a film plays on a loop to allow members of the state's five indigenous tribes to tell their stories; don't miss it. You can see a life-size Oregon Trail wagon and try guiding your own pixel-wagon raft across the Snake River. Kids will love the exhibits in Boomtown, where they can use dynamite to mine gems, blow a train whistle, and play architect for a block city. Allow at least 45 minutes

for a quick tour, up to a few hours to explore and play.

Idaho Black History Museum

A small church, built in 1921 by Reverend William R. Hardy for his predominantly African American St. Paul Baptist Church congregation, sits in Julia Davis Park. It was moved here in 1998 to serve as home to the **Idaho Black History Museum** (508 E. Julia Davis Dr., 208/433-0017, www.ibhm.org, 10am-3pm Tues., 10am-4pm Wed.-Thurs., 11am-4pm Sat., free), which has displays on local and national black history. Highlights include two massive murals by Idaho artist Pablo Rodriguez Jr; one depicts Martin Luther King Jr., and the other, titled *From Slave to President*, illustrates 400 years of black American history leading up to the election of Barack Obama.

Zoo Boise
Zoo Boise (355 Julia Davis Dr., 208/608-7760, http://zooboise.org, 10am-5pm daily, $10) lets you get up close to animals from around the world, from giraffes to sloth bears (you can feed these furry beasts mealworms for only $3!). Other special creatures to see are the llamas, red pandas, and a Gila monster. Then hop on a solar-powered boat (10am-4pm daily May-Sept., $1) and cruise around the zoo's lagoon while looking inside exhibits such as the white-backed vultures or patas monkeys.

Discovery Center of Idaho
All exhibits at the science-based **Discovery Center of Idaho** (131 Myrtle St., 208/343-9895, www.dcidaho.org, 10am-5pm Mon.-Sat., noon-5pm Sun., $12) encourage interactive participation, ensuring kids and adults have a great time. It has a permanent installation of experiments, as well as rotating displays that cover topics from astronomy to lasers.

World Center for Birds of Prey
The **World Center for Birds of Prey** (5668 W. Flying Hawk Lane, 208/362-8687, www.peregrinefund.org, 10am-5pm Tues.-Sun. Mar.-Nov., 10am-4pm Tues.-Sun. Dec.-Feb., $10) allows visitors an up-close look at a variety of live raptors, including hawks, falcons, vultures, eagles, ospreys, and kites, with daily presentations and outdoor aviaries. The California condors are a special treat to see—once critically endangered, they're now making a comeback thanks to the conservation efforts of the center and a handful of others along the West Coast. There's also a museum component and falconry archives that contain artifacts from around the world involving ancient traditions of keeping falcons and hawks. The center is especially worth a visit in the fall, when you can watch an outdoor flying demonstration (3pm Fri.-Sun. Sept.-Nov.) in the scenic amphitheater;

the popular events fill up quickly, so arrive an hour early if possible.

The center is located 12 miles south of downtown via I-84 and South Cole Road, a 25-minute drive.

Old Idaho Penitentiary
Opened as a territorial prison in 1870, the **Old Idaho Penitentiary** (2445 Old Penitentiary Rd., 208/334-2844, http://history.idaho.gov, 10am-5pm daily, $6) was established two decades before Idaho was a state. Stones for subsequent buildings were quarried by the prisoners themselves (as well as for the state capitol), and they remain attractive buildings today. Inside, however, the small cells convey an ugly, crowded reality. The prison was in use until 1972 and held more than 13,000 inmates: desperadoes, murderers, train robbers, and bandits. The youngest inmates were 10 and 11 years old!

Your entry ticket allows you to wander the buildings at your own pace, but the prison's stories of murders, escapes, and executions are best experienced on one of the daily guided tours (hours vary seasonally)—note they're not very appropriate for kids under 10. Look for bored prisoners' graffiti inside the cells, and a display of contraband confiscated from the prisoners. A collection of swords, guns, and other weapons is also on display. The penitentiary is 2 miles (3.2 km) east of downtown via East Warm Springs Avenue and Old Penitentiary Road, a 10-minute drive.

Recreation
Boise River Greenbelt
The **Boise River Greenbelt** (www.cityofboise.org) is the green heart of the city, lining the river on its north bank and connecting neighborhoods, parks, and sights via a paved 25-mile (40-km) path. Its eastern trailhead is Lucky Peak Dam, and its western trailhead is the small town of Eagle, 10 miles (16 km) west of downtown Boise. The greenbelt is heavily used by walkers, joggers, cyclists, and

everybody in between, and hits over 10 city parks. Some of the highlights along the way are Julia Davis Park, with its rose gardens and museums; the Anne Frank Human Rights Memorial, just west of Julia Davis Park; and the waves at Boise Whitewater Park.

Hiking

A few trails can be explored from the **Old Idaho Penitentiary parking lot** (2445 Old Penitentiary Rd.). Look for the trail kiosk, which has a map. Follow signs for **Table Rock Trail 15.** The 3.7-mile (6-km) round-trip hike winds up the mountain behind the penitentiary to a viewpoint that encompasses the city and Treasure Valley, green and wooded in its basin and surround by hills dotted with sagebrush and taller peaks often dusted with snow. It's a popular, busy trail and easy enough for kids, though there are some sections that are moderately steep; it gains about 900 feet (275 m) of elevation. Allow about 1.5 hours to hike it. From the Old State Penitentiary parking lot, you can also do the shorter 1.5-mile (2.4-km) **Shoshone-Paiute Tribes Loop** for good views with less effort.

   Camel's Back Park (1200 W. Heron St., http://parks.cityofboise.org, sunrise-sunset daily) encompasses a beloved hill with an extensive trail system; it also serves as a wildlife refuge, with ongoing restoration efforts—stay on the trails! The winding, well-marked **Camel's Back Trail** heads up the sagebrush-dotted hillside and offers a great view of Boise and the surrounding valley from the top of the "camel's hump"; hiking here is easy and kid-friendly, except for this last steep push. The 1.6-mile (2.5-km) loop takes about an hour to hike.

Biking

Boise is nestled in the foothills of Treasure Valley's mountains, offering amazing access to some of the best mountain-biking terrain in the country. For a great introductory ride, head just north of downtown through Hyde Park to **Camel's Back Park** (1200 W. Heron St., http://parks.cityofboise.org, sunrise-sunset daily). In the park's main parking lot you'll find restrooms, water, and a bike tool station. Hop on the **Red Fox Trail,** an artery that feeds into many other trails such as the **Lower Hull's Gulch Trail,** a popular trail offering moderate technical riding through the hills.

Bike Rentals

For road bikes, mountain bikes, or even electric cruiser bikes, head to downtown's **Idaho Mountain Touring** (1310 W. Main St., 208/336-3854, 9:30am-7pm Mon.-Fri., 9am-6pm Sat., 11am-5pm Sun., from $40), where you can walk away with everything you need for the day. The friendly staff are happy to help find the best fit for what you want to do and point you to some great places to go. You can also find kids' bikes and trailers for rent. Rentals start at $40 for four hours and include options up to a week. Helmets are included in the rentals. From the store, it's an easy ride to either the greenbelt or Camel's Back Park.

Water Sports

Find white waves right in the city at **Boise Whitewater Park** (www.boisewhitewaterpark.com, sunrise-sunset daily, free), a section of the Boise River engineered to create waves via artificial concrete structures under the water, which interact with the river's flow. It offers 0.5 mile (0.8 km) of easygoing flows offering fun for beginner kayakers and boogie-boarders as well as more challenging sections for advanced surfers and kayakers. Multiple access points are along the whitewater park, located next to Esther Simplot Park (3206 W. Pleasanton Ave.).

   Idaho River Sports (601 N. Whitewater Park Blvd., 208/336-4844, http://idahoriversports.com, 9:30am-7pm Mon.-Fri., 9am-6pm Sat.-Sun., $20-40) offers hourly rentals of stand-up paddleboards, surfboards, canoes, and kayaks; the first hour is $20, with $5 every additional half hour past that. More serious paddlers can rent whitewater kayaks or recreational kayaks by the day ($40). The Boise Whitewater Park is a short 0.5 mile (0.8 km) walk through Esther Simplot Park. If you're interested in more placid waters, the outfitter is located close to calm Quinn's Pond.

Entertainment
Bars

Located in the basement of the Idanha Hotel, **10th Street Station** (104 N. 10th St., 208/344-2677, www.tenthstreetstation. com, 2pm-2am daily) is the oldest bar in Boise; it served time as a speakeasy during Prohibition. Today it's a not quite a dive bar and not quite a sports bar, but it's a casual spot that pours stiff drinks and encourages conversation; you might make some new drinking buddies.

Red Feather Lounge (246 N. 8th St., 208/429-6340, www.bcrfl.com, 11am-midnight Mon.-Thurs., 8am-1:30am Fri.-Sat., 8am-11pm Sun.) is a swanky place that serves craft cocktails ranging from the classic, such as the beautiful boulevardier, to the modern, as in the newfangled bourbon and berry-habanero syrup blend. The food menu includes shareable small plates and large portions. If you have too much to drink and it's a weekend, come back for brunch "cure" (gravy on biscuits, gravy on fried chicken, or gravy on pizza). The lounge is a sister property of Bittercreek Alehouse.

In Old Boise, the **Whiskey Bar** (509 Main St., 208/429-5755, www. whiskeybarboise.com, 3pm-2am Wed.-Sat., 7pm-2am Sun.) serves up a good night full of its namesake spirit, with over 200 whiskeys. The dark bar has aging barrels for tables and a pool table in back.

Beat your highest score at **Spacebar**

Top to bottom: along the trail to Table Rock; *croquetas* at Bar Gernika; Westside Drive-In's Idaho Ice Cream Potato.

Arcade (200 N. Capitol Blvd., www. spacebararcade.com, 4pm-midnight Sun.-Thurs., noon-2am Fri.-Sat.). The basement gaming bar-arcade has dozens of modern and vintage games, including pinball, and offers beer, wine, and regular trivia nights.

Get a taste of the tropics at Reef (105 S. 6th St., 208/287-9200, www.reefboise. com, 11am-10pm Mon.-Thurs., 11am-2am Fri., 3pm-2am Sat.), Boise's only tiki bar. Munch on pupu platters or sushi while sipping your choice of cocktail. All the classics are here, including mai tais and rum-pineapple combos, made with fresh-squeezed juices.

Brewpubs

It's hard to resist the bright-yellow building that houses Woodland Empire (1114 W. Front St., 208/426-0510, http:// woodlandempire.com, 2pm-10pm Mon.-Thurs., noon-11pm Fri.-Sun.): Order the brewery's classic City of Trees IPA or try one of the other dozen choices on tap as you attempt your highest pinball score or play a game of Battleship. If you're hungry, you can pop into the alley to find Manfred's food cart (208/343-7202, http://manfredscatering.com, 11am-10pm Tues.-Fri., 1pm-10pm Sat., 2pm-8pm Sun., $7), serving a roster of items that go great with beer: solid sandwiches, a garlic soup, and one really great salad.

Just south of downtown near the Boise River, Payette Brewing Co. (733 S. Pioneer St., 208/344-0011, www. payettebrewing.com, 11am-10pm daily) has a taproom and beer garden next to its brewery. The taproom is a large, friendly space that welcomes all ages (and your pup!). Named for the French Canadian trapper François Payette, who left his mark and name in many Idaho locales, the brewery churns out eight year-round brews with a long line of rotating small-batch varieties. Take a self-guided tour anytime by heading up the stairs to the mezzanine to look over the production area. For a more in-depth look, hop on

the 30-minute Group Brewery Tour (1pm, 1:45pm, and 2:30pm Sat., $10 pp), which includes a pint of beer plus the glass to take home. Local food trucks can be found outside the brewery on a rotating schedule.

Live Music

The best place for the hottest shows in town is Neurolux (111 N. 11th St., 208/343-0886, www.neurolux.com, noon-2am daily, $5-20), a trendy spot that attracts indie and rock bands from all over. The narrow, intimate space hosts shows several times a week. If you're not here for a show, you can just enjoy a well-mixed drink on the small patio or shoot some pool.

The Arts

The Egyptian Theatre (700 W. Main St., 208/387-1273, http://egyptiantheatre.net, box office 11am-4pm Tues.-Fri., 11am-2pm Sat., $15-80) opened in 1927 and has been entertaining Boise ever since. The lovingly restored building has beautiful architecture, top-notch acoustics, and hosts classic and modern film screenings as well as live performances; you might catch anything from a comedian to a jazz band on any given night. The decor evokes ancient Egypt, with papyrus scroll figures on the walls and pillars, and a winged scarab beetle above the stage.

Festivals and Events

Boise's Treefort Music Fest (www. treefortmusicfestival.com, festival pass $125-385) is held every year in late March. A major festival in the region, it attracts big-name national bands, with more than 400 booked in venues across the city over five days. The festival blankets over 10 alternative "forts": Alefort, Yogafort, Comedyfort, Filmfort, and more. While connected to the festival, these are largely independent events put on by community organizers, but a Treefort pass will get you into the other forts. The small size of Boise means that visitors rarely have to walk very far to get to any of the shows, and the event inspires an intense sense of community. A festival pass gets you into as many events as you can handle (the higher-priced Zipline pass lets you skip to the front of any music venue line), and individual tickets to events are also sold.

Food
Creative Contemporary

★ **Bittercreek Alehouse** (246 N. 8th St., 208/429-6360, www.bittercreekalehouse. com, 11am-midnight Sun.-Thurs., 11am-2am Fri.-Sat., $13) is right downtown and deservedly popular. It gets busy on weekend nights, but it's worth the possible wait to sample the great food and beer. The menu capitalizes on Idaho's favorite root vegetable with crispy fries and poutine. Try the smoked trout salad, or a deliciously juicy burger. The tap list is extensive and ranges from nearby Woodland Empire beers to California crafts. All leftovers are composted on-site by worms in the basement—this is the only restaurant using worm composting in the continental United States; the rich compost is distributed back to the farms that provide the veggies and meat.

Hark back to the golden days of Boise at ★ **Westside Drive-In** (1929 W. State St., 208/342-2957, www.westsidedrivein.com, 11am-10pm Mon.-Sat., 11am-9pm Sun., $8), sort of. The eatery has been around for over 60 years, and in the last few decades has been run by a fine-dining chef. The same culinary level of care is imbued in the drive-in's menu, with scratch-made sauces and items like prime rib and focaccia sandwiches. The cheeseburger is still tops and served with "gems" (that's a tater tot to non-Idahoans), or some of the best crispy fries ever. Don't miss the famous Idaho Ice Cream Potato for dessert—vanilla ice cream rolled in cocoa dust in the shape of a potato and topped with whipped cream.

Juniper (211 N. 8th St., 208/342-1142, http://juniperon8th.com, 11:30am-close Mon.-Fri., 9:30am-close Sat.-Sun., $14)

has fresh, brick-wall, woodsy decor and a dash of Prohibition-era style. Local fare is king, from Idaho potatoes to the wine and beer. Come for any meal and enjoy impeccable grilled kale and eggs with crispy prosciutto, pear-fig grilled cheese, or red curry Idaho trout. Cozy up to the bar for a killer cocktail, or reserve the namesake juniper-wood chef's table for an exclusive five-course meal made just for you ($50 pp, optional wine pairing $26, call to reserve).

Basque

★ **The Basque Market** (608 W. Grove St., 208/433-1208, www.thebasquemarket. com, 10am-6pm Mon.-Wed. and Sat., 10am-8pm Thurs.-Fri.) sells olives, paprika, and seafood on its tidy shelves, and the educated staff are either Basque or have visited the region and can answer any questions. The market offers dine-in options, such as *pintxos* (Basque tapas) for lunch and happy hour. The real treat is the market's paella parties, where you can enjoy a paella demonstration and meal on the patio for lunch (noon Wed. and Fri., $10). This is a popular event, so arrive before 11:30am to make sure you get a plate. Vegetarians might want to wait until the first Friday of the month, when the veggie paella is served for lunch. On Thursday, enjoy a paella dinner inside the market (6pm Thurs., $17). The meal comes with a tapa and salad, and the full tapas menu is available if you want more.

For a taste of Basque cuisine, try **Bar Gernika** (202 S. Capitol Blvd., 208/344-2175, www.bargernika.com, 11am-11pm Mon.-Thurs., 11am-midnight Fri., 11:30am-midnight Sat., $9). The Spanish-style pub serves sandwiches and *pintxos*. Order a local pint or the traditional *kalimoxto*—red wine and cola—and the fried crust of *croquetas* (breaded and fried meat ragù) while you wait for the *tortilla de patatas* (egg, potatoes, and onions with bread) to arrive. If you visit on a Saturday, order the famous beef tongue, served in a tomato-garlic sauce with a hunk of bread—it's served from opening until they run out, so go early!

Greek

For fresh vegetables and sizzling flavors, head to vegetarian-friendly **Meraki Greek Street Food** (345 S. 8th St., 208/639-1693, www.merakigsf.com, 11am-9pm daily, $8). Gyros, salads, rice bowls, dolmas, and falafel are all flavorful. Unique local sodas, like a black cherry tarragon, are on fountain tap. The dining room seems like a combination between a chain lunch restaurant and a neighborhood café that you might find in a Greek alley. A big garage door opens onto a patio on nice days.

Breakfast

Boise loves bacon, and **Bacon** (121 N. 9th St., 208/387-3553, www.baconboise. com, 7am-3pm daily, $10) sells over eight tons of it every year via its breakfast and brunch menu. Order the goods by the strip in five different flavors, or include them with a breakfast plate, lunch sandwich, or much lauded combo with cheesy lasagna. Bacon also serves fresh coffee and espresso and has a full bar; the Bloody Mary comes with bacon, of course. And don't worry, vegetarians: The eatery also serves plenty of nonbacon options, like veggie-forward egg scrambles, soups, biscuits, and salads.

Find colorful dishes chock-full of fresh veggies at **Wild Root Café** (276 N. 8th St., 208/856-8956, www.wildrootcafe. com, 8am-3:30pm Tues.-Sat., $12), which serves breakfast and lunch. Dishes are largely plant-based, but this spot isn't only for vegetarians—chicken, pork, and Wagyu beef show up as well. The food served is nourishing and made with care, and the big outdoor patio is a perfect downtown people-watching spot in nice weather.

Coffee and Desserts

Find an elevated ice cream experience

Westside Drive-In

at **The STIL** (786 W. Broad St., 208/953-7007, www.ilovethestil.com, noon-10pm Sun.-Thurs., noon-11pm Fri.-Sat., $6), where you can pair ice cream with beer or wine flights, order a beer float, or get a scoop sandwiched between giant cookies. Some ice cream options also incorporate alcoholic beverages, such as the honey bourbon ice cream and rose wine sorbet. Check out the category called "The Lab" for even wilder options. Even though the shop caters to the over-21 crowd, it's still super kid-friendly.

Find gourmet third-wave coffee at **Slow by Slow** (403 S. 8th St., www.slowbyslow.com, 7am-5pm Mon.-Sat., 9am-2pm Sun., $5), serving pour-overs, lattes, mochas, and more from house-roasted beans. The baristas love their coffee and their customers, and show careful attention to both. Specialty pastries are paired with unique drinks like an espresso and ginger beer with fresh lime. Grab a bag of beans to take home on your way out.

Shopping
Downtown
Clothing and Accessories

Locally designed with a distinct Boise point of view, **Voxn Clothing** (778 W. Broad St., 208/392-1112, www.voxnclothing.com, 11am-8pm Mon.-Sat., 10am-3pm Sun.) started out as an online shop before gaining a following and opening a brick-and-mortar store. The women's clothing line has modern pieces that are outdoors-ready but fit for strolling downtown in style. The store also carries other brands that round out the options with bright jumpers, floral skirts, plaid button-ups, and soft sweaters.

Show off your love for your new favorite city with a shirt from **Wear Boise** (828 W. Idaho St., 208/680-6017, http://wearboise.com, 11am-6pm Mon.-Thurs., 11am-5pm Fri., 10am-5pm Sat.-Sun.). Its popular line of Boise-themed clothing and housewares is imprinted with beards, beer, and goats, among other designs. You'll also be reminded how to pronounce the city's name: Boy-see.

Housed in a bright-blue brick building with a rich interior, **Crazy Neighbor** (415 W. Grove St., 208/957-6480, www.crazyneighbor.biz, 10am-6pm Mon.-Sat., 10am-3pm Sun.) is a fun, colorful shop. Its offerings trend toward the performative, with wigs, stage makeup, feather boas, gloves, and parasols. If you're not appearing on stage anytime soon, the sunglass and hat collections offer items that can fit into everyday life quite easily, while jazzing up your appearance.

Gifts and Home

Find local and handmade goods at **Mixed Greens** (213 N. 9th St., 208/344-1605, http://ilikemixedgreens.com, 10am-6pm Mon.-Sat., 11am-4pm Sun.), with an ever-changing inventory of gifts, accessories, bath products, homewares, and garden goodies. You may find a beautiful new necklace, a sweet little succulent, or a handmade stuffed animal.

Both an artist's gallery and a well-curated vintage shop, **Ward Hooper Vintage** (745 W. Idaho St., 208/287-8150, www.wardhooper.com, 10am-5pm Mon.-Sat.) is run by local Boisean Hooper, whose style is classic vintage Americana mixed with a pop modern sense. His series of Idaho travel posters captures iconic images of the state, and his portraits depict everyone from Thomas Edison to Janis Joplin. The gallery showcases his big canvases, while the store has posters, prints, vintage Pendleton clothes, homewares, and more.

Music and Books

Rediscovered Books (180 N. 8th St., 208/376-4229, www.rdbooks.org, 10am-8pm Mon.-Sat., 10am-6pm Sun.) is deceptively small on the outside but offers a big selection of popular books in a variety of genres, including fiction, history, and cooking. A giant blue whale looms over the kids' section, and big comfy chairs dot the space, inviting visitors to stay and relax.

Plug into the local music scene at **The Record Exchange** (1105 W. Idaho St., 208/344-8010, www.therecordexchange.com, 10am-9pm Mon.-Thurs., 9am-9pm Fri.-Sat., 9am-7pm Sun.), Idaho's biggest independent music store. It has up to 17,000 records at any given time, neatly arranged. If you're road-tripping in your old beater and can only listen to cassettes, stock up from the store's giant wall of selections.

Gourmet Goodies

For a sweet taste of history, find the **Idaho Candy Company** (412 S. 8th St., 208/342-5505, http://idahospud.com, 7am-4pm Mon.-Fri.). In 1901, T. O. Smith started selling his homemade candy door-to-door out of shoeboxes, and by 1909 he'd built a state-of-the-art factory. It still churns out the popular candy bars today, including the famous chocolate-covered marshmallow that is the Idaho Spud Bar, as well as the Cherry Cocktail Bar and Owyhee Butter Toffee. Stop by the retail store to stock up, or look for the bars in many stores across Idaho.

Hyde Park

You'll feel good about shopping at **Dunia Marketplace** (1609 N. 13th St., 208/333-0535, www.duniamarketplace.com, 10am-6pm Mon.-Sat., 11am-4pm Sun.), Idaho's only nonprofit fair-trade store. Here you'll find mostly handmade items from around the world, including intricate woven baskets, textiles, and clay housewares, as well as a selection of spices and pantry goods.

Hyde and Seek (1521 N. 13th St., 208/914-6146, 10am-8pm Mon.-Wed., 10am-9pm Thurs.-Sat., 10am-7pm Sun.) is an appropriately named shop full of goodies to hunt for; you could spend a long time gazing through all its nooks and crannies. The store carries paper products, gifts, home decor, textiles, and more in a riotous jumble of colors and styles.

Accommodations
Under $150

Stay out of the hubbub of the city yet close by at the **Boise Hillside Suites** (4480 N. Kitsap Way, 208/336-6502, www.boisehillsidesuites.com, $129-159), a beautiful lodge-like house aptly set into a hillside. Its three rooms offer a range of amenities that might include a private bathtub, a fireplace, or views of the city skyline. All of that and you're only a 15-minute drive from the downtown action.

Many of the downtown hotels are chains; if you're going that route, you have some good options. The **Hampton Inn & Suites Boise-Downtown** (495 S. Capitol Blvd., 208/331-1900, http://hamptoninn3.hilton.com, $109-122) is in the thick of the action and offers everything the weary traveler needs: comfortable beds, views of the city from its 186 rooms, a hot breakfast, a kid-friendly indoor saltwater pool, and an airport shuttle. Step out the door to find restaurants, bars, shops, and parks.

Red Lion Boise Downtowner (1800 W. Fairview Ave., 208/344-7691, www. redlion.com $86-109) offers a comfortable stay at a low cost. The full-service hotel offers a hot breakfast, an outdoor pool, a fitness center, an airport shuttle, and an on-site restaurant and bar. It also offers complimentary bike rentals, which you can take to the greenbelt. The hotel is a block outside downtown's western edge.

$150-250

Take an old Travelodge, renovate its 39 rooms to incorporate bright copper accents, bold yellow and blue tufted headboards, and mid-century modern decor that pays homage to the building's roots, and you've got ★ **The Modern Hotel** (1314 W. Grove St., 208/424-8244, http:// themodernhotel.com, $141-329). Guests can also enjoy a courtyard with year-round fire pits and the on-site restaurant headed by a James Beard-nominated chef with some of the best cocktails in the city. If you ever want to leave, grab a free bike—the hotel is on the west end of downtown, just a few blocks from the greenbelt.

★ **The Grove Hotel** (245 S. Capitol Blvd., 208/333-8000, www.grovehotel boise.com, $179-309) welcomes all visitors with an iconic river sculpture on its exterior. Each of its 250 rooms is beautifully furnished with cloud-soft beds and thick towels, and suites come with private terraces and jetted tubs. Guests enjoy top-notch services and amenities like valet parking and an extensive fitness center with a pool, a spa, and a sauna. Bicycles are available to borrow. The downtown location means great bars and restaurants are only steps away.

Nine suites and a bungalow in three locations around downtown and Hyde Park make up the **Boise Guest House** (614 N. 5th St., 208/761-6798, http:// boiseguesthouse.com, $179-229). Suite sizes include studio and one-bedroom

options, and each is in an inviting lodge-style house that comes with a kitchen, a lounge area, and a bath. Decor features local art and bright colors, and the guest house sets you up for exploration with cruiser bikes.

Taking its name from its location on the 43rd parallel in the country's 43rd state, **Hotel 43** (981 W. Grove St., 208/342-4622, http://hotel43.com, $144-320) is centrally located downtown and has a range of rooms and suites, some offering plush robes and downtown views. The on-site Chandlers Steakhouse serves a delicious dinner, and you can start the next day off right in the Metro Café.

Camping

With a great location just 5 miles (8 km) south of downtown, right off I-84, **Mountain View RV Park** (2040 W. Airport Way, 208/345-4141, www.boiservpark. com, $38) makes a great home base for road-trippers to explore Boise. The 60 grassy, shaded lots are for full-hookup RVs or trailers. Showers, laundry machines, a dog run, and Wi-Fi round out the offerings. Reservations are strongly recommended—call to reserve your spot.

Parma

The small town of Parma is notable for being the site of the original Fort Boise, built in 1834. Before buying out the competing Fort Hall, the Hudson's Bay Company built this fort to establish itself in the region's fur trade. It soon began serving emigrants heading west, until it was abandoned due to flooding in the 1850s, as well as threats of attack from local Shoshone bands and land claims by the United States. Another fort was built closer to present-day Boise.

Today Parma is surrounded by hop farms. Pioneers probably brought hops to the West, just as they did apple trees and rosebushes, which would be carefully transported and planted in hopes of

An Iowa Tribe Story: Marie Dorion

Marie Dorion isn't well-known, but her epic story is one of great courage and determination. A member of the Iowa Tribe, Marie was the only woman on a fur expedition from Missouri to the Pacific Northwest on an early version of the Oregon Trail sponsored by John Jacob Astor in 1811-1812. Her husband, fur trapper Pierre Dorion, joined the expedition, along with Marie and their two sons, ages 5 and 2.

The group left Missouri in April 1811 and made decent progress until Idaho, when expedition leader Wilson Price Hunt decided they should ditch their horses in favor of dugout canoes—he inaccurately believed they could travel the Snake River to the Columbia River. When the rapids became too rough, they had to leave the canoes behind and continue on foot. At this point, Marie was about eight months pregnant, and likely carrying her younger son much of the way. Through hardships that included dwindling food, the group pressed on and reached eastern Oregon. On December 30, 1811, in the Blue Mountains, Marie gave birth to her third child—and the next day she was on the move again. The baby died of malnourishment, but the rest of the group reached their destination on the Oregon coast safely.

Two years later, her family joined a party led by John Reed on a beaver-trapping trip, camping at the trading post, an early version of Parma's Fort Boise. Marie and her children were the only woman and children in the party. Some of the local Shoshone people were resentful of their presence; in January 1814 Marie found out about an upcoming attack. She took off on a horse with her two children to warn her husband, and discovered him dead. When Marie returned to the main camp, all the other men had also been killed. She was now alone with her sons in the winter wilderness.

She headed back west on horseback, aiming for the Native American communities along the Columbia River, but was forced to stop by heavy snows in the Blue Mountains. She built a rough hut and lived in it with her sons until spring, surviving off horse meat. The family then attempted the walk again, through snows so deep that Marie was forced to leave her children behind in a fur-lined hole so she could go in search of help. Starving and snow-blind, she found the Walla Walla people, who gave her food and assisted her in saving her sons.

Marie went on to remarry, have more children, and live a long life in Oregon. She died in 1850, as thousands of settlers were pouring in on a trail she helped blaze.

---

cultivating familiar tastes and smells in their new homes. Idaho is second only to Washington in terms of the country's hop production. The crop likes long hot summers but also cold winters—most hops are grown between the 35th and 55th parallels worldwide. Hops grown on the farms in this region are used by many of the state's craft brewers, such as Portneuf Valley Brewing, Woodland Empire, and Payette Brewing Co.

Getting There

From **Boise,** head west out of town on Front Street, continuing onto I-84. In 3 miles (4.8 km), stay in one of the left two lanes to merge onto I-84. In 23 miles (37 km), take exit 26 for U.S. 20/U.S. 26 and follow it for 13 miles (21 km) to Parma. The drive takes 45 minutes.

If you took the **Southern Alternate Route** and skipped Boise, you'll come up through Parma from the south. From Givens Hot Springs, continue 11.4 miles (18 km) northwest to Marsing, then turn left on Highway 55, which will become U.S. 95. Continue on it for 21 miles (34 km), then follow the road right as it curves to get onto U.S. 26 west, continuing for 1.8 miles (2.8 km) into Parma. The drive takes 40 minutes.

Sights

Parma's **Old Fort Boise Park** is home to the **Fort Boise Replica** (1008 Stockton Rd., 208/722-5138, 1pm-3pm Fri.-Sun.

June-Aug., donation), a few miles from where the original once stood, near the river, from 1834 until it flooded and was abandoned in 1853. A new Fort Boise was built in 1863, over in present-day Boise, away from the prone-to-flooding river. The replica here in Parma is built on a slightly larger scale than the original fort. Inside, visitors can see a log cabin, a schoolroom, a kitchen, farm equipment, and Native American artifacts and clothing. Outside the fort is a statue of a woman with a young child—she is Marie Dorion, a woman of astonishing strength and perseverance who made an impressive snowy trek in this area in 1814.

Old Fort Boise Park also has a picnic area, restrooms, a playground, and a basic campground with a few RV spots ($13) and tent sites ($7). There's a fee box to pay for them in the park.

Although nothing is left of the original fort today, a small monument marks the site of **Old Fort Boise,** at the confluence of the Snake and Boise Rivers. It's located in a Wildlife Management Area (30845 Old Fort Boise Rd., 208/722-5888, 5am-10pm daily Apr.-Sept., 6am-8pm daily Oct.-Mar., free), where fishing and hunting birds is popular. From town, head north on U.S. 26/U.S. 95 for 3.4 miles (5.4 km), then turn left onto Old Fort Boise Road and drive another 3 miles (4.8 km) until you reach the Snake River. Turn right onto the gravel road and continue past two parking areas; the monument is on the left amid the trees. The drive takes about 15 minutes.

Food

Right across the street from the fort is the teensy-tiny **Apple Lucy's** (203 N. 9th St., 208/722-5511, 11am-8pm Mon.-Sat., $7), a welcoming diner. The menu features classic comfort food, with burgers, fries, and chicken salad, but the biggest draw is the homemade pie. You can even try a pie shake—a slice blended with a scoop of ice cream! Top flavors include Dutch apple and marionberry.

South of town 4.5 miles (7.2 km), the **Parma Ridge Winery** (24509 Rudd Rd., 208/946-5187, www.parmaridge.wine, noon-7pm Wed.-Thurs., noon-9pm Fri.-Sat., 11am-5pm Sun., $5 tasting fee) shows off another local crop: grapes. The vineyards are near the Snake River, and the tasting room offers stunning views as well as tastes of award-winning blends and varieties including chardonnay, zinfandel, merlot, and cabernet. Small bites are available on Wednesday-Thursday, with a full menu ($14) on weekends. Enjoy rosemary garlic truffle fries, filet mignon, flatbread pizzas, salmon, and more. Due to the small size of the dining room, reservations are required Friday-Saturday evenings.

Oregon

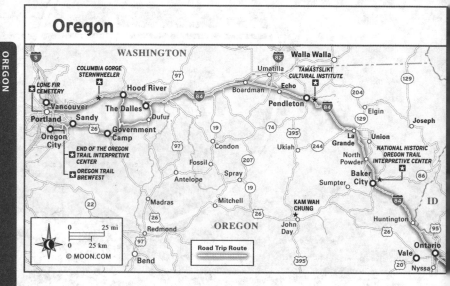

Oregon

Oregon! The Promised Land!

"I am thinking while I write, Oh Oregon you must be a lovely country."

Amelia Stewart Knight, 1853, *Diary of Mrs. Amelia Stewart Knight*. Knight traveled the Oregon Trail from Iowa in 1853 with her husband and seven children. When they departed, Knight was in the first trimester of pregnancy with their eighth child, whom she gave birth to in Oregon at their journey's end. Though she kept a detailed diary, it rarely mentions complaints of her condition.

For emigrants, leaving the Snake River just past Idaho meant the beginning of the end of the ordeal. However, they were still over a month away from their destination in the Willamette Valley. Most pioneers wouldn't call the rugged desert of eastern Oregon the paradise they were seeking; days were full of dusty drives down rough roads, hoping for water at every bend. They likely sat at night and dreamed of the fertile soil they'd encounter at their journey's end, so tantalizingly close now.

Paradise called, and they pushed more than 500 miles (800 km) over deserts scarce with water, sagebrush hills, and heavily forested mountain passes. Confronted by the Columbia River Gorge, many emigrants traded their wagons for a raft to continue west down the rushing river. Others risked dangerous roads around Mount Hood and the deadly Laurel Hill. Evidence of their progress remains in the myriad of ruts travelers can still see today, pressed deep into the prairie or along mountain slopes. Along the way, emigrants traded for salmon and fresh supplies with Native Americans, including the Cayuse, Walla Walla, and Chinook peoples.

Today, the risk of choosing a route is lower—both offer stunning views and beautiful hikes. Visitors can buy a cowboy hat in the Old West town of Pendleton and surf the wind at Hood River. The official end of the trail in Oregon City is a short jump from fabled Portland, full of craft breweries, green spaces, restaurants, and live music to ease the burdens of weary travelers.

Highlights

★ Find perfectly preserved trail ruts in the desert sage at the **National Historic Oregon Trail Interpretive Center** (page 326).

★ Dive into 10,000 years of history at the **Tamástslikt Cultural Institute,** which offers an indigenous perspective on the Oregon Trail, along with exhibits on present and future plans (page 344).

★ Ply the waters that pioneers once floated on the *Columbia Gorge Sternwheeler* (page 371).

★ Celebrate your journey's success with a visit to the **End of the Oregon Trail Interpretive Center** (page 386).

★ Time it right and toast the end of the road at Oregon City's **Oregon Trail Brewfest,** which celebrates beer from each state along the way (page 389).

★ Honor the memories of pioneers with a stroll through **Lone Fir Cemetery,** where many are buried (page 398).

Best Overnight Stops

★ **Baker City:** This Victorian town in the high desert has one of the best hotels on the route, a renowned brewery, and a fantastic Oregon Trail museum nearby (page 324).

★ **Pendleton:** Steeped in the Old West, this town celebrates its heritage with an annual rodeo, food, and drink (page 343).

★ **The Dalles:** This growing destination, where eastern Oregon meets the Columbia River Gorge, was a critical junction on the Oregon Trail and offers today's travelers all the services they need (page 357).

★ **Hood River:** This charming town on the Columbia River Gorge is a small hive for water recreation, breweries, and great restaurants (page 364).

★ **Portland:** Close to the official end of the trail, Portland is a fantastic place to celebrate your journey's end, with all the attractions, amusements, and amenities you could want (page 392).

Planning Your Time

You'll want 4-5 days to see the main sights along the trail in Oregon—though note you could conceivably make the entire 375-mile (604-km) drive from Ontario, just across the Idaho border in Oregon, to Portland in about six hours. If you have more time, add on some side trips to Joseph or Walla Walla, Washington, or spend more time in the Columbia River Gorge and Portland at the end. Summer is the most popular time for touring in the state, and you'll want to make reservations 2-3 months ahead for accommodations and camping.

The entrance to the scenic Columbia River Gorge at The Dalles marks the change from eastern to western Oregon; the former is often sunny and dry, while the western side stays rainy and temperate much of the year. Summer is typically dry across the state, and eastern Oregon can be particularly hot and dusty. In winter—and often spring and fall—eastern Oregon and Mount Hood see heavy snow, which you'll likely encounter on the Blue Mountain pass between La Grande and Pendleton, and on the Barlow Road route (Hwy. 35 and U.S. 26) around Mount Hood. Carry snow chains in the area in winter; they're sometimes required. In summer, use caution on the inclines and twists, and be aware of thunderstorms.

Getting There

Starting Points
Oregon Trail Route Notes
The route largely remains on **I-84** from Idaho, though it sometimes veers off onto smaller parallel highways like **U.S. 30** from Baker City to La Grande and along the Columbia River Gorge. At Hood River, you'll have a choice: Continue along the **Columbia River Gorge** and then take **I-205** or **I-5** south to Oregon City, or take the **Mount Hood Scenic Byway** along the **old Barlow Road** route via **Highway 35** and **U.S. 26** to Sandy, then west to Oregon City.

Car and RV
On your way out of Idaho, you can head north from Parma to follow the old Oregon Trail via U.S. 26 for 18 miles (29 km) to Ontario, just over the Oregon border, or I-84 west for 55 miles (89 km) from Boise, Idaho.

Best Walks and Hikes

★ **Hoffer Lakes Trail:** Hike in view of craggy peaks and crystal-clear water that offers places to swim in summer (page 333).

★ **Hurricane Creek Trail to Slick Rock Falls:** Enjoy the beauty of the Wallowa Mountains on this hike to cascading falls (page 340).

★ **Multnomah Falls:** Hike up some steep switchbacks to the top of the state's most famous, most photographed waterfall (page 371).

★ **Angel's Rest:** A tough ascent affords stunning views of the Columbia River Gorge (page 372).

★ **Barlow Road Trail:** Walk along the old wagon route to place a rock on the grave of an unknown pioneer woman (page 378).

★ **Trillium Lake Loop Trail:** Stroll boardwalks around this jewel of a lake and gaze at the majesty of white-capped Mount Hood (page 380).

Rentals

Portland International Airport has the best options for car rentals. Find **Enterprise** (7105 NE Airport Way, 844/366-0498, www.enterprise.com, 4:30am-1:30am daily) for a wide selection, or **National Car Rental** (7105 NE Airport Way, 844/366-0499, 4:30am-1:30am daily) for slightly lower prices.

Located 20 miles (32 km) west of Portland International Airport, **RV Northwest** (11655 SW Pacific Hwy., 503/641-9140, www.rvnorthwest.com, 9am-4pm Mon.-Fri., 10am-5pm Sat.) has friendly service and a wide variety of sizes, classes, and options (from $250 per night); you'll be sure to find something for your trip. **ROAMERICA** (906 NW Corporate Dr., Troutdale, 503/473-9907, www.roamerica.com, 9am-5pm Mon.-Sat. by appointment), 10 miles (16 km) east of Portland International Airport at the western end of the Columbia River Gorge, offers campervan rentals. Each van is stocked with two beds that sleep 4-5, with camp gear such as headlamps and a lantern, cooking equipment, and bedding. You'll get 125 miles (200 km) per day included, and the van is car-seat friendly. Choose from two-wheel drive

($200-250 per night) or four-wheel drive ($250-275 per night). **Cruise America** (www.cruiseamerica.com) is a nation-wide company with a location in Portland (8400 SE 82nd Ave., 503/777-9833, 9am-5pm Mon.-Fri., 9am-2pm Sat.). It offers options from a truck camper that sleeps three to a large motorhome sleeping seven. For a week, expect to pay $1,300-1,600 total, depending on mileage.

Fuel and Services

On the western side of the state, you won't have problems finding services, but eastern Oregon is known for its wide empty spaces; you'll find gas stations in Baker City, La Grande, and Pendleton, with about 40-50 miles (64-80 km) between. If you head off I-84 on any side trips in this part of the state, between Baker City and Pendleton, be sure to keep your tank above half.

Air

Portland International Airport (PDX, 7000 NE Airport Way, 503/460-4234, www.flypdx.com) is regularly voted one of the best airports in the country and is served by daily international flights from major airlines. It is 12 miles (19.3 km) north of the city center. Airport transportation to downtown Portland includes MAX Light Rail service on the Red Line run by **TriMet** (http://trimet. org, 4:45am-11:50pm daily, $2.50 one-way), which takes about 40 minutes and runs approximately every 15 minutes. From the airport you can also hail ride-sharing companies **Uber** and **Lyft** (about $30) or a **taxi** (about $40).

Boise Airport (BOI, 3201 W. Airport Way, 208/383-3110, www.iflyboise.com) is small but offers daily flights on Alaska, American, Delta, Southwest, and United. This is a more convenient entry point to the eastern side of the state; Ontario, Oregon, is 55 miles (89 km) northwest of Boise, Idaho, less than an hour's drive.

Train

Amtrak (www.amtrak.com) runs the *Empire Builder* line, departing every evening from Portland's **Union Station** (800 NW 6th Ave., 5:30am-1:30pm and 3pm-12:30am daily) and stopping in the Columbia River Gorge at the **Bingen-White Salmon station** (Hwy. 14 and Walnut St.) in Washington before heading north to Spokane. Trains return from Spokane to Portland every morning. It takes 10 minutes by car to get from the Bingen-White Salmon station across the Hood River Bridge (toll $3) to Hood River on the Oregon side.

Bus

Greyhound (www.greyhound.com, 800/231-2222) runs buses between many cities in Oregon. It has a ticket counter in Portland's **Union Station** (800 NW 6th Ave., 503/243-2361, 5:30am-1:30pm and 3pm-12:30am daily). Greyhound stops in Hood River (Mount Hood Railroad, 110 Cascade Ave., 24 hours daily), The Dalles (802 Chenoweth Loop Rd., 24 hours daily), Pendleton (The Pendleton Market, 2101 SE Court Ave., 9am-5:30pm daily), and Baker City (Baker Truck Corral, 515 Campbell St., 24 hours daily). Outside Portland, tickets aren't sold at the bus stations; purchase online or by phone.

Ontario

Just over the Idaho state line, sunny Ontario is Oregon's easternmost city— it's actually in the mountain time zone instead of Pacific. Surrounding it are some of Oregon's loneliest regions. The pioneers rode through here, continuing on their rough route along the Snake River, through landscape that was barely producing enough grass for the livestock to eat.

Ontario's later claim to fame has been as the home of the Ore-Ida potato company, which invented tater tots in 1953. Today, this is a conservative town in the high desert. Travelers mostly use it as a jumping-off point to explore some of the most rural reaches of the state and Idaho. It's full of standard chain restaurants and hotels.

Getting There

From **Boise, Idaho,** drive 55 miles (89 km) northwest on I-84, then take exit 376A for Ontario. The drive takes just under an hour.

From **Parma, Idaho,** head west out of town via Grove Street, which becomes U.S. 26/U.S. 95. Continue for 13.6 miles (21.8 km), merging left onto I-84 westbound. In 3.8 miles (6 km) take exit 376A, and turn right onto U.S. 30 to follow it 0.8 mile (1.2 km) into town. The drive takes 20 minutes.

Sights

The **Four Rivers Cultural Center** (676 SW 5th Ave., 541/889-8191, http://4rcc.com, 9am-5pm Mon.-Fri., 10am-5pm Sat., free) is the main attraction and cultural hub of the area. It's named for the four waterways that wind along the Idaho-Oregon border: the Snake, Malheur, Owyhee, and Payette Rivers. The name also represents the flow of communities who have called this place home, including Native American, Japanese, Mexican, and Basque people. The

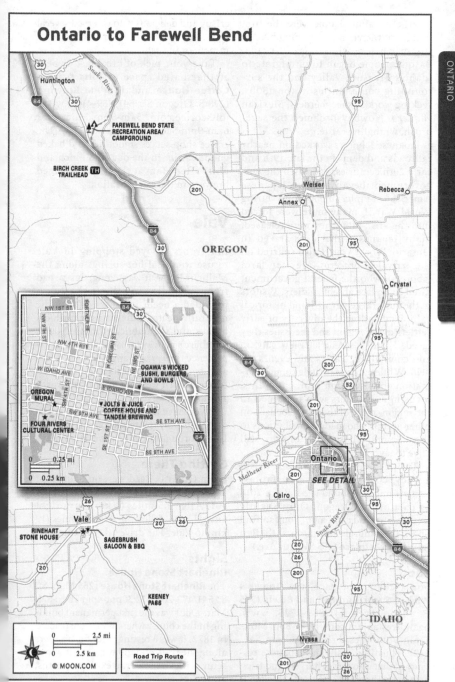

Ontario to Farewell Bend

- Huntington
- Snake River
- FAREWELL BEND STATE RECREATION AREA/ CAMPGROUND
- BIRCH CREEK TRAILHEAD
- OREGON
- Weiser
- Annex
- Rebecca
- Crystal

Detail inset:
- NW 1ST ST
- FORTNER ST
- NW 4TH AVE
- N OREGON ST
- SW 3RD ST
- OGAWA'S WICKED SUSHI, BURGERS, AND BOWLS
- W IDAHO AVE
- E IDAHO AVE
- OREGON MURAL
- SW 4TH AVE
- JOLTS & JUICE COFFEE HOUSE AND TANDEM BREWING
- FOUR RIVERS CULTURAL CENTER
- SW 5TH AVE
- SE 5TH AVE
- SE 1ST ST
- SE 9TH AVE
- 0   0.25 mi
- 0   0.25 km

- Malheur River
- Ontario
- SEE DETAIL
- Cairo
- Snake River
- Vale
- RINEHART STONE HOUSE
- SAGEBRUSH SALOON & BBQ
- KEENEY PASS
- Nyssa
- IDAHO

- 0   2.5 mi
- 0   2.5 km
- © MOON.COM
- Road Trip Route

Northern Paiute people were the first to inhabit the vicinity, camping here in summer before wintering in Nevada. Basque people began to immigrate to Idaho's Treasure Valley and the surrounding communities in the 1800s, seeking work as sheepherders. Mexican *vaqueros* (cowboys) roamed the sagebrush, wrangling cattle.

Japanese laborers worked on nearby railroads and dams in the late 19th and early 20th centuries, and when the U.S. government began sending Japanese Americans to internment camps during World War II, many more were forced into the area; after they were released, many Japanese Americans stayed in Ontario. World War II also spurred on the arrival of *braceros* (Mexican farm laborers), who the federal government hired to replace absent soldiers. Visitors to the cultural center will find historical exhibits detailing the diversity of early settlers in the region and the issues they faced. There's a serene Japanese garden, and community classes and events are held. While exhibits include some information about Oregon Trail emigrants, focusing on settlers who remained in the region, more of the space focuses on other groups who made contributions to the area and whose traditions are still alive today.

Travel Oregon, the state's tourism agency, commissioned seven fantastic new murals around the state in 2018 as part of its "Oregon, Only Slightly Exaggerated" ad campaign. You can find one of these murals in Ontario, at the **Red Apple Marketplace** (555 SW 4th Ave.).

Food

For a change of pace, try **Ogawa's Wicked Sushi, Burgers, and Bowls** (375 E. Idaho Ave., 541/889-2725, www.ogawasrestaurant.com, 11am-8pm Mon., 11am-9pm Tues.-Fri., noon-9pm Sat., $12), a bustling sushi and Japanese restaurant that also serves burgers and fries. The *mafa* (breaded and fried) chicken is crispy and delicious, and is served several ways: in a bento box, in a rice bowl, with ramen, or in sushi.

Take your pick of breakfast or beer at the shared space of **Jolts & Juice Coffee House** and **Tandem Brewing** (298 S. Oregon St., 541/889-4166, www.joltscoffee.com, 5am-9pm Mon.-Fri., 6am-9pm Sat., 6am-6pm Sun., $7). The coffee shop serves smoothies and baked goods earlier in the day, and lunch and pints after 11am at the bicycle-themed brewery in the same location.

Vale

Emigrants enjoyed stopping in Vale to use the local hot springs along the Malheur River. It was a long, dusty road from Fort Boise, so a dip in the waters provided a needed reprieve. Today the naturally heated water is used for local homes and the public swimming pool, but there's no way for tired visitors to experience the springs anymore. The town also has notable murals and preserved trail ruts; just west of Ontario, it's worth a quick stop.

If you have less time, you may want to skip this spur, as it takes you off the main I-84 thoroughfare for a short stretch.

Getting There

From Ontario, head west on Southwest 4th Avenue, then turn left onto Highway 201. After 2.5 miles (4 km), turn right onto U.S. 26, following it for 12 miles (19 km) to Vale. The drive takes 20 minutes.

Sights
Rinehart Stone House

The **Rinehart Stone House** (255 Main St. S., 541/473-2070, 12:30pm-4pm Tues.-Sat. Mar.-Oct.) was the first permanent building in the county when it was constructed in 1872. It was a resting place for travelers along the trail, and today serves as a museum with Oregon Trail exhibits, photos, and relics.

Outdoor Art Gallery

Take a walk around town to find Vale's many murals, more than 25 and counting. Each year, Vale's **Outdoor Art Gallery** adds a new mural and works to preserve the old ones. Each depicts historical moments, and many describe scenes related to the Oregon Trail, such as *The Hot Springs,* which depicts emigrants taking a dip in the local waters. Others pay tribute to local history and community, such as the area's early Japanese American farmers and Basque sheepherders. Many murals are along the parallel A Street and Washington Street, between Clark Street and Glenn Street.

Keeney Pass

While some wagons followed the twists of the Snake River as best they could, others took different routes into Oregon. You can see some of the first trail ruts in the state at **Keeney Pass** (Lytle Blvd., dawn-dusk daily, free), just south of Vale. Brown posts mark the path of the trail ruts through the sagebrush. In spring, the area is abloom in red, blue, and yellow wildflowers. Don't miss the 0.3-mile (0.5-km) trail to an overlook: From the top you can see all the way to Boise, a distance that took the emigrants an entire day to travel.

The pass is named for pioneer Jonathan Keeney, who made several treks west from his home in Missouri. He first traveled with Jim Bridger's fur-trapping expedition in 1834. In the 1840s he brought his family along to settle down near Vale, running a ferry across the Snake River just north of Old Fort Boise.

Follow Glenn Street, which becomes Lytle Boulevard, south for 6 miles (9.7 km). You'll see a large parking lot on the right, marked by a small kiosk.

Top to bottom: trail marker at Keeney Pass; Farewell Bend sign; trail ruts near Baker City.

Food

Get your burger or barbecue fix at the **Sagebrush Saloon & BBQ** (197 A St. E., 541/473-3377, www.sagebrushsaloon. com, 11am-close Sun.-Thurs., 11am-2:30am Fri.-Sat., $8). It's a kid-friendly dining option with an outdoor patio, pool table, and karaoke on Friday nights.

Farewell Bend

The Snake River marks the border of Idaho and Oregon. The old wagon trail, which had followed the Snake River through Idaho, broke off from the river's path near Old Fort Boise in today's Parma, but here in Farewell Bend, the trail meets the river again. At this bend in the Snake River, pioneers had a chance to rest and regroup before bidding farewell to their dependable water source for the last 330 miles (530 km) and heading west into harsher land.

Today, **Farewell Bend State Recreation Area** (http://oregonstateparks.org, dawn-dusk daily, free) welcomes visitors with restored covered wagons, picnicking areas, and informational kiosks about the emigrants' experiences. Trail ruts are just down the road from the campground, off a small parking lot marking the Birch Creek Trail Site. The ruts here aren't as deep as at Keeney Pass, but it's striking to see the Bureau of Land Management posts marking the winding path through the hills. You can explore on foot, but after about 1 mile (1.6 km), the ruts pass onto private land.

The park's **campground** (800/452-5687, http://oregonstateparks.reserve america.com, Mar.-Nov.) offers 91 electrical RV sites ($26), 30 tent sites ($18), and two log cabins ($46-56). Reservations are available and recommended May-early October.

Getting There

From Ontario, drive 25 miles (40 km) northwest on I-84. Take exit 353 for Farewell Bend.

Baker City

Bookended by the Elkhorn Mountains, a small section of the Blue Mountains to the west, and the Wallowa Mountains to the east, Baker City is a picturesque town with an Old West feel. Thousands of wagons passed through the area on their way west, rolling over Flagstaff Hill, but it wasn't until gold was discovered in the hills in the 1860s that anyone thought of staying.

The town soon became a bustling hub for the county, and once the railroad connected it to the rest of the state, the city boomed. Miners who struck it rich attracted bankers, builders, prostitutes, and businesspeople, and by 1900 Baker City was the third-largest city in Oregon. It hosted a happening cultural scene that drew traveling theater companies, and Victorian architecture sprang up, creating the Main Street we see today. The town was also home to a thriving Chinatown; Chinese workers built the railroad and worked in the nearby mines.

Today, Baker City is a small but flourishing town. You'll find ranchers, fishers, and young families strolling the quaint streets. Barley Brown's brewery is a big draw, with its award-winning beer, and hints of a burgeoning artisanal food movement are in the air.

Getting There

From Farewell Bend, drive 46 miles (74 km) northwest on I-84. Take exit 306 to continue for 2 miles (3.2 km) into town via U.S. 30. The drive takes 50 minutes. Baker City is about 130 miles (210 km) from Boise, a two-hour drive.

Sights

Baker City's **Historic District** is worth an afternoon stroll. A walking tour brochure is available from the **Baker County Visitors Bureau** (490 Campbell St., 541/523-3356, www.visitbaker.com, 8am-5pm Mon.-Fri.) or your hotel. The town

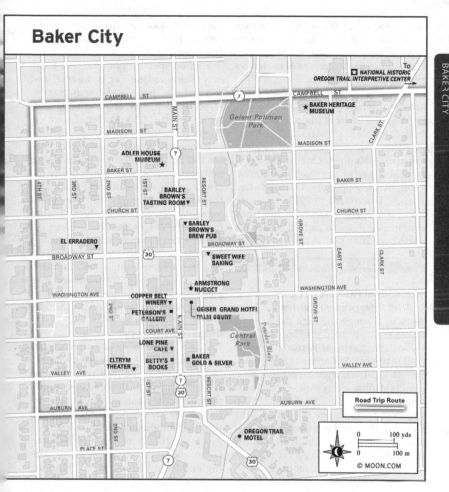

Baker City

(Map labels:)

To NATIONAL HISTORIC OREGON TRAIL INTERPRETIVE CENTER

CAMPBELL ST

★ BAKER HERITAGE MUSEUM

Geiser Pollman Park

MADISON ST

CLARK ST

ADLER HOUSE MUSEUM ★

BAKER ST

BARLEY BROWN'S TASTING ROOM ▼

CHURCH ST

RESORT ST

GROVE ST

EAST ST

▼ BARLEY BROWN'S BREW PUB

BROADWAY ST

EL ERRADERO ▼

BROADWAY ST

▼ SWEET WIFE BAKING

★ ARMSTRONG NUGGET

WASHINGTON AVE

COPPER BELT WINERY ▼

PETERSON'S GALLERY ■

GEISER GRAND HOTEL PALM COURT

COURT AVE

Central Park

Powder River

LONE PINE CAFE ▼

ELTRYM THEATER ▼

BETTY'S BOOKS ■

■ BAKER GOLD & SILVER

VALLEY AVE

VALLEY AVE

AUBURN AVE

AUBURN AVE

OREGON TRAIL MOTEL ●

PLACE ST

Road Trip Route

0   100 yds
0   100 m

© MOON.COM

---

has more than 100 historically significant buildings, and the self-guided tour leads you to some of the best in about two hours.

Baker Heritage Museum

Get a sense of Baker County in the 19th century at the **Baker Heritage Museum** (2480 Grove St., 541/523-9308, www.bakerheritagemuseum.com, 9am-4pm daily mid-Mar.-Oct., $6 adults, $5 seniors and ages 13-17, free for children 12 and under), where you can dive into the stories of miners, saloon owners, showgirls, and more from its gold-mining heyday. Exhibits on early Baker City life and Chinese culture are notable, and the collection of rocks, fossils, and minerals is exceptional; established by two sisters in the 1930s, the agates, jaspers, and crystals are stunning examples of what's hidden in the hills.

Adler House Museum

The **Adler House Museum** (2305 Main St., 10am-2pm Fri.-Mon. Memorial Day-Labor Day, $7 adults, free under age 13) is in a lovely Victorian house with original decor—including the wallpaper! Get a sense of what life was like for the people of Baker City 100 years ago at the former home of Leo Adler, one of the town's greatest philanthropists.

Armstrong Nugget Display

Step into the lobby of Main Street's **U.S. Bank** (2000 Main St., 541/523-7791, 9am-5pm Mon.-Fri.) for a glimpse of the giant **Armstrong Nugget.** One of the largest gold nuggets discovered in the area, it weighs a whopping 80.4 ounces—five pounds! Discovered in 1913, it's a rare example of a large nugget, as most finds were melted down to cash in. Today it's worth over $100,000.

TOP EXPERIENCE

★ National Historic Oregon Trail Interpretive Center

Heading through the high desert sage, wagon trains headed up Flagstaff Hill. Today, the **National Historic Oregon Trail Interpretive Center** (22267 Hwy. 86, 541/523-1843, www.oregontrail.blm.gov, 9am-6pm daily Apr.-Oct., 9am-4pm daily Nov.-Mar., $5-8 adults, $4-6 seniors, free under age 16) sits atop the Flagstaff Hill, and is possibly the best museum on the Oregon Trail. Follow the pioneers' long journey via the center's life-size display of wagons, artifacts, maps, and more. Kids can get a bingo sheet to hunt the displays for items like a horseshoe or a butter churn (find them all for a prize from the ranger).

Outdoors you'll find a wagon train encampment, interactive reenactments in summer, and 4 miles (6.4 km) of hiking trails to explore the sagebrush landscape and wagon ruts carved into the prairie, as well as remnants of an old gold mine. Hike the 0.75-mile (1.2-km) trail to Panorama Point atop Flagstaff Hill to look over the valley on the same perch where pioneers once stood, taking in views of the imposing Blue Mountains and Wallowa Mountains. Continue on over the hill to access the striking wagon ruts marking the prairie, traveling from east to west.

Plan on spending at least half a day here. Summer heat can be intense, and there's little shade, so bring hats, sunscreen, and plenty of water. The center is 9 miles (14.5 km) east of town via Highway 86; follow the signs.

If you want to see the wagon ruts without visiting the center or going on a hike, pull over on Highway 86 just before the center; you'll see a historical marker on the side of the highway with a few parking spots. You can walk a short distance to view the deep ruts. Also keep an eye out for a small granite marker erected by Ezra Meeker in 1906. Meeker first traveled the Oregon Trail in 1852, and over his lifetime repeatedly traversed it to place markers documenting the route, spearheading efforts to preserve the trail.

Chinese Cemetery

Just outside town in a rather forgotten corner lies the **Chinese Cemetery** (Windmill Rd., behind the Chevron station), an ode to the hard and largely forgotten contributions of Chinese settlers in the area. Baker City once had a thriving Chinese population, with many people working as merchants, physicians, tailors, cooks, and miners, as well as helping build the Union Pacific Railroad. This small city even had a Chinatown with gates that closed at night. The community was often the target of rampant racism. Today at the site of this cemetery, used exclusively by the Chinese population, a memorial pavilion, built in Suzhou, China, honors the memories of those who lived, worked, and died here. The remains of the 67 people once buried here have been returned to China, but a plaque records 17 of the known names, and small depressions in the earth mark the onetime grave sites.

From town, head north on 4th Street and turn right on Campbell Road. Continue for 1.5 miles (2.4 km), crossing

I-84, then turn right onto Windmill Road just after the Chevron station. The cemetery is 0.2 mile (0.3 km) up the road on the left.

Recreation

Stretch your legs along the **Leo Adler Memorial Parkway,** a pleasant 3-mile (4.8-km) paved path that runs from Bridge Street on the south end of downtown north to Hughes Lane. Much of the trail follows the tree-lined Powder River, and it passes through residential neighborhoods and the city park, **Geiser-Pollman Park** (5:30am-10pm daily), which has a covered wagon-themed playground, horseshoe pits, and picnic areas.

Rent a bike to ride along the parkway at **The Trailhead** (1828 Main St., 541/523-1668, www.thetrailheadbakercity.com, 9am-6pm Mon.-Sat., noon-4pm Sun.). The shop rents casual cruiser bikes ($5 per hour, $20 per day), as well as mountain bikes ($45 per day). It's also a full-service repair shop and has maps for purchase and trail information, and even some local brews on tap. The friendly space is staffed by folks enthusiastic about outdoor fun.

Entertainment and Events

The town is pretty quiet at night, but stop by the **Barley Brown's Tasting Room** (2200 Main St., 541/523-2337, www.barleybrownsbeer.com, 2pm-close daily) for a taste of some of Oregon's best beer. They don't often bottle it, so try it while you can. This venue has a full bar with 22 taps and occasional live music. The beer runs the gamut from light pale ales to toasty porters and stouts; it's hard to go wrong. A limited food menu is served from its restaurant, Barley Brown's Brew Pub, directly across the street, but the tap house has a larger selection of beers.

What's better than cheese and wine? **Copper Belt Winery** (1937 Main St., 541/519-0949, http://copperbeltwinery.com, 1pm-6pm daily) has vineyards about 25 miles (40 km) outside town, but you can try everything at the Main Street tasting room. As you sip the Ranchers Red blend, take a gander at the cheese case from **The Cheese Fairy,** which partners with the winery to offer cheese inside the shop.

Catch a first-run movie at the **Eltrym Theater** (1809 1st St., 541/523-2522, www.eltrym.com, $9), a restored 1940s theater just off Main Street. On Tightwad Tuesdays, tickets are $3 off.

On the first Friday of each month, the city sponsors the **First Friday Art Walk** (5pm-8pm), showcasing participating galleries and shops. Visitors can enjoy a rotating cast of local and regional artists, with refreshments often offered.

Food

When the local watering hole offers award-winning beer—it has won over 100 medals so far—it's bound to be popular. At **Barley Brown's Brew Pub** (2190 Main St., 541/523-4266, www.barleybrownsbeer.com, 4pm-10pm Mon.-Sat., $15), you'll find young families chatting about recent fishing trips alongside adventure-seekers and brew nuts. Dine on elevated pub grub like fish-and-chips, a Kobe beef burger, lobster mac and cheese, or deep-fried green beans and pickles.

On Friday nights, enjoy live music in the restored **Palm Court lobby restaurant** (1996 Main St., 541/523-1889, www.geisergrand.com, 5pm-9pm daily, $30) while enjoying a meal or just a slice of pie beneath the space's huge skylight. The elegant room has a romantic vibe and serves items like steak, smoked prime rib, salmon, and local wild mushrooms in cream sauce. It all evokes the turn of the 20th century, while never feeling stuffy.

When you wander into the hip **Lone Pine Cafe** (1825 Main St., 541/523-1805, 8am-3pm daily, $11) you might think you've already made it to Portland. It has comfy seating, friendly service, and a record player in the corner; wander over and put on an LP while you wait for your

OREGON

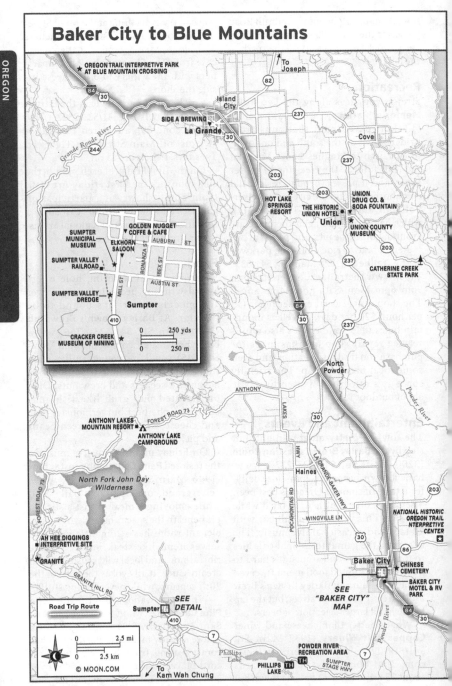

Baker City to Blue Mountains

★ OREGON TRAIL INTERPRETIVE PARK
AT BLUE MOUNTAIN CROSSING

84 30

To Joseph

82

Island City

237

SIDE A BREWING
La Grande

30

Cove

Grande Ronde River

244

203

237

203

237

HOT LAKE
SPRINGS
RESORT

THE HISTORIC
UNION HOTEL
Union

UNION
DRUG CO. &
SODA FOUNTAIN

UNION COUNTY
MUSEUM

203

237

CATHERINE CREEK
STATE PARK

Sumpter detail:

GOLDEN NUGGET
COFFE & CAFE

SUMPTER
MUNICIPAL
MUSEUM

ELKHORN
SALOON

AUBURN ST

BONANZA ST

IBEX ST

SUMPTER VALLEY
RAILROAD

MILL ST

AUSTIN ST

SUMPTER VALLEY
DREDGE

Sumpter

410

CRACKER CREEK
MUSEUM OF MINING

0   250 yds
0   250 m

84 30

237

North
Powder

ANTHONY

30

Powder River

ANTHONY LAKES
MOUNTAIN RESORT

FOREST ROAD 73

ANTHONY LAKE
CAMPGROUND

LAKES

FOREST ROAD 73

North Fork John Day
Wilderness

Haines

LA GRANDE-BAKER HWY

POCAHONTAS RD

30

203

WINGVILLE LN

NATIONAL HISTORIC
OREGON TRAIL
INTERPRETIVE
CENTER

AH HEE DIGGINGS
INTERPRETIVE SITE

★ GRANITE

GRANITE HILL RD

30

86

Baker City

CHINESE
CEMETERY

BAKER CITY
MOTEL & RV
PARK

Road Trip Route

Sumpter

SEE
DETAIL

SEE
"BAKER CITY"
MAP

84 30

Powder River

0   2.5 mi
0   2.5 km

410

7

Phillips
Lake

POWDER RIVER
RECREATION AREA

PHILLIPS
LAKE

SUMPTER STAGE HWY

7

© MOON.COM

To Kam Wah Chung

food. The eatery uses fresh ingredients, offers breakfast and lunch, and serves most meals with a big slice of homemade German rye.

Locals love the tacos, enchiladas, and burritos served at **El Erradero** (2100 Broadway St., 541/523-2327, 11am-9pm daily, $9). Colorful murals adorn the walls and booths; find the one of a man harvesting the heart of an agave plant to make mescal and tequila, and then order one of the restaurant's strong (and affordable) margaritas.

For an all-star roster of baked goods made from scratch, head to **Sweet Wife Baking** (2080 Resort St., 541/403-6028, www.sweetwifebaking.com, 7:30am-3pm Wed.-Sun., $7). Run by a former professional Women's National Basketball Association player who taught herself how to bake when she moved to Baker City, the café offers delicious options for breakfast and lunch. Try the house-made shrubs, a fruit- and vinegar-based nonalcoholic drink, and order some macarons or a gooey cinnamon roll.

Shopping

Betty's Books (1813 Main St., 541/523-7551, 9:30am-5:30pm Mon.-Sat.) has a nice selection of new and used books, including a whole wall dedicated to local and Oregon Trail history, along with a great children's reading nook. Be sure to ask staff about the displays of salt licks along the shelves, from the town's annual salt lick auction!

In addition to showcasing gorgeous artwork from regional artists, **Peterson's Gallery** (1925 Main St., 541/523-1022, 10am-6pm Tues.-Sun.) holds a secret: It also offers gourmet chocolates at a shop in the back. Daughter Alyssa Peterson is the on-hand certified chocolatier who whips up truffles and ganache. Visit on the first Friday of the month, when the shop stays open until 10pm, to introduce the new month's featured artist.

Baker Gold & Silver (1812 Main St., 541/523-2133, 9am-4pm daily) holds a mishmash of antiques, coins, and other collectables. If you've been lucky enough to strike gold in the mountains, this is where you can sell it—the store still buys gold and silver.

Accommodations and Camping

Stay in restored jewel ★ **Geiser Grand Hotel** (1996 Main St., 541/523-1889, www.geisergrand.com, $170-250), once known as the finest hotel between Salt Lake City and Seattle. Built in 1889 at the height of the gold boom, the Geiser served a rotating cast of bankers, cattle barons, opera singers, and even Teddy Roosevelt in its rooms and in the Palm Court restaurant. The property brought elegant sophistication to the Old West town and was one of the first hotels in the state with electricity and an elevator. After the gold boom ended, in the 20th century the hotel closed and fell into disrepair. Today it has been painstakingly restored to match old photographs and is back on the roster of the finest hotels in the West. Enjoy excellent service and luxurious amenities in one of 50 guest rooms, some with balconies overlooking Main Street.

Welcoming travelers with a retro sign sporting an iconic wagon wheel, the **Oregon Trail Motel** (211 Bridge St., 541/523-5844, $60-80) is a good budget stop. Rooms aren't fancy, but they're clean, comfortable, and come with friendly service and breakfast.

Baker City Motel & RV Park (880 Elm St., 541/523-6381) is 1 mile (1.6 km) from Main Street on the south side of town. Its small motel offers clean rooms ($53) with TVs and Wi-Fi, and behind them are 20 full-size RV spots ($33) outfitted for water, sewage, cable TV, and Wi-Fi.

◈ Side Trip: Sumpter and Vicinity

Not far from Baker City is the mining ghost town of Sumpter. The short out-and-back trip offers a change from the dusty prairie scenery: cows grazing in the sagebrush hills, bubbling creeks, thick forests, nearby peaks of the Elkhorn Mountains, and far-off Wallowa Mountains in the distance. Get there via **Highway 7,** part of the **Elkhorn Scenic Byway;** there are hiking opportunities along the way. Travelers with more time can opt to continue from Sumpter and drive the entire byway, which makes a clockwise loop back to Baker City.

Phillips Lake and Powder River Recreation Area

As you drive southwest of Baker City, notice the change of scenery as you enter the hills: The sagebrush and wide ranches of the high desert give way to rocky red canyons and cottonwood trees. The Powder River is your traveling companion; the road follows it into the hills, dotted with pine trees as you enter the Wallowa-Whitman National Forest, to Phillips Lake.

Getting There

From Baker City, head southwest for about 15 miles (24 km) on Highway 7 for the Powder River Recreation Area. The drive takes 20 minutes.

Hiking

From a lower parking area just off Highway 7, marked by a sign that says "Powder River Recreation Area," you can access the **Powder River Interpretive Trail.** Take a flat, easy 1.2-mile (1.9-km) out-and-back walk on either side of the Powder River; on its north side is an asphalt path, and on its south side a narrower dirt trail. Both offer beautiful river views, bird-watching opportunities, fishing access points, and a few picnic sites, and end at an upper parking lot where you'll find restrooms.

Drive 0.5 mile (0.8 km) past the Powder River Recreation Area's parking lot and turn left on Forest Road 1145 to find the **Phillips Lake South Shore Trail.**

Park on the left side of the road near the dam and hike down. This hike heads west along Phillips Lake through ponderosa forest to Millers Lane Campground, offering scenic views of the lake and surrounding Elkhorn Mountains as well as plenty of inlets to access the lake for swimming. Watch for birds, deer, and elk. Mountain bikers and horseback riders also use this trail. It's a flat, easy walk, 10 miles (16 km) total out-and-back—you can turn around at any point.

Sumpter

One of the many ghost towns that are relics of the gold boom, **Sumpter** (www.historicsumpter.com) got its start when five men discovered gold in nearby Cracker Creek in 1862. The isolated campsite grew gradually over the next decades, fueled by the promise of riches. Eventually, the narrow-gauge Sumpter Valley Railroad reached it, and by 1900 there were around 4,000 people living in the bustling town. With 35 mining camps and gold flowing through the coffers, the city earned the nickname Queen City of the Mines. At one point it had 16 saloons, seven hotels, three newspapers, and an opera house. A fire in 1917 burned most of the town. It recovered, but with dwindling gold, in the 20th century Sumpter was gradually abandoned. Today it's mostly a tourist destination. There's still gold deep in the rocks of the valley, tempting visitors.

Getting There

From Baker City, drive southwest on Highway 7 for 25 miles (40 km). Turn right onto Highway 410 and continue for 3 miles (4.8 km) to Sumpter. The drive takes 30 minutes. Sumpter is less than 10 miles (16 km) west of Phillips Lake. After you pass the lake, look on the left to see mine tailings—piles of rock and gravel—left by the Sumpter Valley Dredge.

Sights

The town mostly comprises dilapidated

buildings now housing antiques stores and tourist shops. Get your bearings in the oddly busy ghost town by grabbing a walking tour brochure in the **Sumpter Municipal Museum** (245 Mill St., 3pm-6pm Wed., 11am-3pm Thurs.-Sun. May-Oct., 3pm-6pm Wed., 11am-3pm Thurs.-Sat. Nov.-Apr., free), which also has a dusty exhibit on local history, including some great mining equipment, a collection of rocks for geology nuts, and a horse-drawn fire engine. In the back you'll find a small community library.

Don't miss the **Sumpter Valley Dredge State Heritage Area** (211 Austin St., 541/894-2486, park 7am-7pm daily May-Oct., dredge access 8am-5pm daily May-Oct., free), which details the history of the five-story, 1,240-ton dredge that churned up the valley looking for gold; it stirred up an amazing 1,600 acres during its operation. While dredges are typically used to excavate bodies of water, this one ended up miles from water, in the mountains, searching for gold. About 1935-1954, the dredge operated 24 hours daily and extracted $4.5 million in gold. You can visit the restored behemoth right where it stopped operating, in a pond it created, with either a self-guided tour or, on the weekend, a ranger-led tour from the **visitors center** (10am-5pm Mon.-Thurs., 9am-5pm Fri.-Sat. May-Oct.). In a testament to nature's tenacity, surprisingly vibrant wetlands full of willows and cattails have sprung up around the dredge, drawing cranes, ospreys, and kingfishers in search of fish. Take a stroll along 1.5 miles (2.4 km) of trail around the area.

Take a ride on the **Sumpter Valley Railroad** (211 Austin St., 541/894-2268, www.sumptervalleyrailroad.org, round-trip $24 adults, $20 seniors, $14 ages 5-15, family pass $60). The narrow-gauge railroad that brought hopeful prospectors to the area has been revived and now runs regular trips on a 5-mile (8-km) stretch between the town of McEwen, just east, and Sumpter. Visitors can take a trip on a steam engine straight from 1918, run and maintained by passionate volunteers. The train runs on weekends in summer, with extra trips added on some holidays and special events like staged train robberies. The entrance to the Sumpter station is inside the Sumpter Dredge Park.

You'll see hulking mining equipment on the north side of the highway as you drive into town; this is the **Cracker Creek Museum of Mining,** still in development. There are hopes for a full visitors center in the future, but for now it's free to wander and a good place to stretch your legs while you look around. Interpretive signs offer hints of what the behemoths were used for.

Festivals and Events

One of the biggest bazaars in the state, the **Sumpter Flea Market** (541/894-2314) is a huge event for the area. It happens every year on the weekends of Memorial Day, July 4th, and Labor Day. Over 150 vendors, from families to large businesses, sell new and used items, including Western gear, artwork, and handicrafts, in tents all over the town. It's a great event for browsers and antiques lovers.

Food

Step back into the Old West at the **Elkhorn Saloon** (180 Mill St., 541/894-2244, noon-8pm Tues.-Wed., 7am-11am and noon-8pm Thurs.-Sun., $13); you might feel as if you'll run into a gold miner in the dark corners of the 1920s-era building. Find a huge variety of hamburger options: 42, in fact! The saloon also has Taco Tuesdays and Pizza Thursdays.

For a quick snack, pop into the old Western storefront of the **Nugget Coffee & Cafe** (160 N. Mill St., 541/894-2400, 9am-2pm daily, $6). It serves a good variety of breakfast, lunch, and grab-and-go items. Don't miss the homemade pudding. The café also sells CBD-infused goods.

Elkhorn Scenic Byway

If you have more time, get some great views of alpine lakes and mountain peaks by continuing along the Elkhorn Scenic Byway. From Sumpter, the byway heads northwest to Granite, then loops around back to Baker City. The entire drive takes 2.5 hours without stops—primarily via **Highways 7 and 410, Forest Road 73,** and **U.S. 30**—but you could easily fill a whole day with diversions along the way, such as the recommendations below, which are listed in clockwise order from Sumpter.

Be sure to fill up on gas in Sumpter or Granite, as there are no services beyond. The road is RV-friendly. Note that if you embark on the drive October-June, you might encounter snow along the route.

Granite

The wee town of **Granite**—only 24 people call it home now—is categorized as a "near ghost town." Another old mining town, Granite's story is similar to Sumpter's; it was active during the area's gold rush in the 1860s, then died down when the mines closed in the early 20th century. Today it's a great place to see dilapidated old buildings such as the Granite Town Hall and the old dance hall.

From Sumpter, drive northwest on Highway 410, which becomes Granite Hill Road and Bull Run to Baker Road, for 16 miles (26 km), then turn right onto Center Street for Granite.

Ah Hee Diggings Interpretive Site

Chinese miners in the area were often barred from owning claims—so they worked extra hard to squeeze what gold they could out of the streambeds. The **Ah Hee Diggings Interpretive Site** (www.fs.usda.gov) tells the story of an industrious band of miners who created huge rock piles as they exposed the streambed,

Top to bottom: Sumpter Valley Dredge State Heritage Area; Anthony Lake; Kam Wah Chung.

catching gold that bigger operations had missed. This highway pullout area has a small display with interpretive information about the diggings; the 1870 census documents 337 Chinese miners working in the area, many of whom may have looked for gold in these rocks.

Turn right in Granite on Forest Road 73 to continue the byway. In 1.5 miles (2.4 km) is the Ah Hee Diggings Interpretive Site parking lot, on the side of the road.

Anthony Lake and Hoffer Lakes

Continue on Forest Road 73, heading north. The road climbs from here—in winter it's covered in snow. After about 20 miles (32 km), you'll reach the **Elkhorn Summit,** at an elevation of 7,395 feet (2,254 m). From here, you can reach several different sapphire-colored lakes by following signs for the Anthony Lake Campground. The namesake Anthony Lake is the biggest, but there are a few smaller lakes in this area, often referred to as Anthony Lakes. Anthony Lakes Mountain Resort is just west of the campground.

Anthony Lakes Mountain Resort

Situated near the lakes and peaks of the Elkhorn Scenic Byway, **Anthony Lakes Mountain Resort** (47500 Anthony Lakes Hwy., 541/856-3277, www.anthonylakes. com, 9am-4pm Thurs.-Sun. Dec.-Mar., daily during spring break, lift tickets $40 adults, $29 ages 13-18, $21 ages 7-12, free under age 7 and over age 70) is a small winter paradise in eastern Oregon. The mountain has an average annual snowfall of 300 inches, making for powdery fun in season. The resort has one chairlift that accesses 21 runs, the longest of which is 1.5 miles (2.4 km), and cross-country skiers can enjoy groomed Nordic tracks nearby. The lodge has a rental shop (skis and snowboards $28 adults, $21 ages 6-12; snowshoes $17; cross-country skis $18 adults, $12 ages 6-12), a café and bar, and a retail shop, but no overnight lodging. Discounts tickets are available after

1pm each day, and every Thursday is half price.

In summer, the trails become a hot spot for single-track mountain biking. Snow usually melts by late June. At the Anthony Lakes Mountain Resort, you'll find kiosks with communal bike tools and maps of the area's trails. There are no rental providers on the mountain, so come prepared—grab a bike in Baker City before you head out. **The Trailhead** (1828 Main St., Baker City, 541/523-1668, www.thetrailheadbakercity.com, 9am-6pm Mon.-Sat., noon-4pm Sun.) rents out mountain bikes ($45 per day).

At the lodge, the **Starbottle Saloon** (9am-4pm Thurs.-Sun. Dec.-Mar., 11am-6pm Fri.-Sun. July 5-Labor Day, $13) serves breakfast, homemade soups and chili, and pizza by the slice. Ingredients are locally sourced from Baker City and Haines, and you'll find draft beers, cider, and liquor from Baker City; this is one of the few places outside town that you'll find Barley Brown's beers on tap. While most of the lodge closes in summer, the saloon stays open on weekends with a small pizza and burger menu to serve hiker and bikers.

Hiking

The easy 2.5-mile (4-km) **Hoffer Lakes Trail** is a lollipop loop, making a circle around Anthony Lake, with a spur to the twin Hoffer Lakes. The trail takes about 1.25 hours to hike and runs beneath craggy Gunsight Mountain and alongside the lakes and bubbling Parker Creek. In summer the area blooms with wildflowers, including the brilliant paintbrush, and the lakes provide a cool place to wade or swim. Start at the Anthony Lake Trailhead, near the Anthony Lake Campground.

Camping

The popular **Anthony Lake Campground** (47500 Anthony Lakes Hwy., 541/894-2332, www.recreation.gov, July-Sept., $10-14) is 7,000 feet (2,130 m) above sea level next to a subalpine lake amid evergreen forests, wildflowers in summer, and resident mountain goats. The campground offers easy access to trails and swimming, as well as stunning views of the surrounding peaks. RVs are welcome, but note that there are no hookups. The limited summer season fills up fast—make reservations.

Getting Back to Baker City

From Anthony Lake Campground, proceed on Forest Road 73, heading east and continuing as it becomes Anthony Lakes Highway and Pocahontas Road, veering left after 22 miles (35 km) for Haines, where you turn right onto U.S. 30 to return to Baker City.

⬥ Side Trip: Kam Wah Chung

While this side trip may take extra time—three hours total for the out-and-back drive alone—it's worth it for the scenic drive and to visit an impeccably preserved site commemorating the area's Chinese community. Plan to take a day to enjoy the site.

Getting There

From Baker City, drive southwest on Highway 7. Soon after passing Phillips Lake, veer left to continue on the highway, driving through the Strawberry Mountains and beautiful John Day River Valley. After 51 miles (82 km) on Highway 7, turn right onto U.S. 26 and continue 28 miles (45 km) into John Day. The drive takes 1.5 hours.

If you're visiting Sumpter, you could also tack this trip on. From the Highway 7 and Highway 410 junction, instead of continuing east to return to Baker City on Highway 7, you can follow it southwest and then continue as described above.

Kam Wah Chung

After gold was discovered nearby at Canyon City in 1862, miners, many of whom were Chinese, streamed into the area. At the height of the era in the 1880s, nearby John Day's Chinatown had a population of as many as 2,000 people, making it the third largest in the United States—only slightly smaller than San Francisco and Portland. Although the mines eventually closed, the Chinese population continued to thrive due to the efforts of two men: Ing "Doc" Hay and Lung On went into business together in the early 1870s, Lung On as the store proprietor and the Doc as a traditional herbal medicine practitioner. For the next 50 years they became the social, medical, and cultural hub of the entire state's Chinese population. Their storefront served as a residence as well as a clinic, community center, general store, and boardinghouse. The businesses thrived well into the mid-20th century; the mercantile closed when Lung On died in 1940, while Doc continued to run the clinic until 1948, when he closed it for health reasons.

The **Kam Wah Chung State Heritage Site** (541/575-2800, http://oregon stateparks.org, 8am-noon and 1pm-5pm daily May-Oct., by guided tour only, free) offers an incomparable look into the life of the two Chinese men who made a huge impact on the community. The interior of the building is stunning; it's easy to forget you're in eastern Oregon when you step inside. All items inside the shop are original and beautifully preserved, from packages of Chinese tea and herbs stacked high to the men's dining room dishes, still on the table. Rooms include Doc's clinic and apothecary, a storeroom, a bedroom, a kitchen, and a tiny boarding area that was rented out to visitors.

Start your visit at the nearby **interpretive center** (9am-5pm daily May-Oct.), where you can pick up free tickets for the guided tour. Tours start at the top of each hour and last about 45 minutes. The interpretive center has extensive exhibits with more information about Doc Hay, Lung On, and their community.

Food

Little Canyon Food Cart (234 S. Canyon Blvd., 541/620-2911, 7am-2pm Tues.-Fri. Apr.-Oct., $7) makes great on-the-go meals for breakfast or lunch. Grab a breakfast burrito with creamy goat cheese and a cup of Portland-roasted Stumptown coffee, or try the signature Thai curry for a lunch. Find the cart in John Day, one block south of the stoplight—the only one in Grant County.

For an all-you-can-eat prime-rib dinner or a delicious home-cooked meal, visit **Grubsteak Mining Company Bar & Grill** (149 E. Main St., 541/575-1970, 11am-9pm daily, $12). The friendly family-owned place is known for great service and delicious dishes, including burgers, steaks, and a mean meatloaf. Visit on Thursday for its ode to the region's ethnic heritage with a special Chinese American menu of items like kung pao chicken and Szechuan beef.

Along the Trail from Baker City

Union

Union was first settled in 1862 by pioneers who planted pear and apple trees they brought from the East. Main Street, with its stately Victorian houses, is on the National Register of Historic Places. See if you can spot some of the old fruit trees while rolling through town.

Getting There

From Baker City (keep an eye out along the freeway for the "45th Parallel" sign, marking the spot where you're halfway between the north pole and the equator), drive 18 miles (29 km) north on I-84. Take exit 285 for Highway 237 and continue for 16 miles (26 km). The drive takes 45 minutes.

Sights and Recreation

Stop by the **Union County Museum** (333 S. Main St., 541/562-6003, www.ucmuseumoregon.com, 10am-4pm Mon.-Sat. mid-May-mid-Oct., $5), which has small exhibits on the cultural and natural history of the region. You'll find pioneer cabins, a replica blacksmith shop, and a great exhibit on the area's cowboy culture, covering cattle barons and rodeos.

Catherine Creek State Park (http://oregonstateparks.org, mid-Apr.-mid-Oct., day-use free) is 8 miles (12.8 km) southeast of Union off Highway 203. The creek runs through a canyon here, and the park has trails tucked in the stately ponderosa pines. This makes a great place for a picnic, a dip in the cool water, or a short hike. The park also has campsites ($10) that can accommodate tents and self-contained RVs.

Food and Accommodations

The old-fashioned "Rexall Drugs" sign marks the **Union Drug Co. & Soda Fountain** (105 N. Main St., 541/562-5441, 9:30am-5:30pm Mon.-Fri., $7). Serving the local community as a pharmacy since 1903, the newest owner has also added a restored 1940s soda fountain. The café serves old-fashioned sundaes, banana splits, and homemade sandwiches and soup. Fresh bread is baked every morning.

The Historic Union Hotel (326 N. Main St., 541/562-1200, http://thehistoricunionhotel.com, $97-155) dates to the 1920s and has been restored. It offers 15 uniquely decorated rooms, all with views of the outdoor gazebo and nearby Catherine Creek.

Hot Lake Springs Resort

Tucked away in the hills, the once-epic **Hot Lake Springs Resort** (66172 Hwy. 203, 541/963-4685, www.hotlakesprings.com, $100) is now a curious roadside attraction. The site has natural hot springs used by local Native Americans for thousands of years. Oregon Trail pioneers used the spot as a place to rest and recoup, and the first proto-hotel was built here in 1864. The resort saw its heyday in the early 1900s as a sanitarium. After a fire destroyed most of it, its various uses included a nursing school, a retirement home, and an insane asylum before it was abandoned for some decades. Rumors of hauntings abound, and the labyrinthine hallways and mist rising off the lake lend the requisite atmosphere.

The current owners, deep in restoration work, understandably downplay its murky past and rent out 12 guest rooms as they continue to renovate. The upper floors hold a series of odd exhibits covering military and Native American artifacts, surgery, and bronze casting. Visitors can soak in the mineral hot springs; water from the adjacent spring-fed lake is cooled from 208°F (98°C). Stay overnight for unlimited access, or just visit for the day and enjoy the hot springs ($25 per hour).

Getting There

From Union, drive 6 miles (9.7 km) northwest on Highway 203. The drive takes less than 10 minutes.

La Grande

In the Grande Ronde Valley, along the path of the Oregon Trail, La Grande was settled in the 1860s, mainly by emigrants bound for Oregon City. Perhaps tired of their travels and seeing a decent place, they simply stayed. Today, it's a small town that serves mainly as a jumping-off point to explore Joseph and the Wallowa Mountains.

Food

Pause for a meal or a pint at **Side A Brewing** (1219 Washington Ave., 541/605-0163, www.sideabeer.com, 11am-9pm Sun.-Thurs., 11am-10pm Fri.-Sat., $13), which serves thoughtful food sourced from local partners, including a peanut butter bacon burger, along with its own crafts, such as the Oregon Fog Hazy

Hot Lake Springs Resort

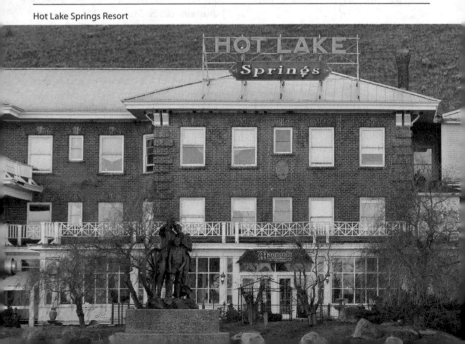

IPA. Decor is inspired by the adjacent fire museum: Knots made of hoses adorn the walls, and a convivial long table makes it feel like you're one of the fire crew.

Getting There
It's 8 miles (12.9 km) northwest from Hot Lake Springs Resort, or 14 miles (23 km) from Union, to La Grande via Highway 203. Driving directly from Baker City, La Grande is 45 miles (72 km) north via I-84. You can continue west from here on I-84 for Pendleton, or take a side trip east to Joseph on Highway 82.

◈ Side Trip: Joseph

The town of Joseph has only about 1,000 residents, but it's a bustling tourism destination nestled at the base of the Wallowa Mountains. Named for Nez Perce leaders Old Chief Joseph and his son Chief Joseph, it boasts beautiful mountain views, a charming Main Street dotted with bronze sculptures, and outdoor recreation options. Summer is high season for hiking, riding a gondola to epic views, and playing in Wallowa Lake, just south of town. You can visit Joseph in a day, but consider spending the night to take advantage of all it has to offer.

Getting There
From **La Grande,** drive east on Highway 82 for 70 miles (113 km) to Joseph. The drive takes 1.5 hours and runs through fields and ranches as you wind closer to the Wallowa Mountains.

Sights
Valley Bronze of Oregon
Start your tour of town by walking along Main Street for the **Joseph Art Walk,** a collection of seven monumental bronze statues set against the backdrop of the Wallowa peaks. The bronze artworks hail from the 1982 founding of the **Valley Bronze of Oregon** (307 W. Alder St., 541/432-7551, www.valleybronze.com, 6:45am-4pm Mon.-Thurs., 6:45am-11pm Fri.). Take a fascinating tour ($15) of the foundry for a look at what it takes to cast a giant sculpture. Hint: It involves wax, rubber, silicone, plaster, air tubes, and a plasma torch. Tours last about 1.5 hours.

Wallowology
Learn all about regional geology and woolly mammoths at **Wallowology** (508 N. Main St., 541/263-1663, www.wallowology.org, 10am-3pm Tues.-Sun. May-Sept., free). The museum is especially great for children—with a hands-on kids' area featuring animal skulls, rocks, and bugs to touch and feel—but interesting to anyone with an interest in natural history.

Iwetemlaykin State Heritage Site
Just north of Wallowa Lake, **Iwetemlaykin State Heritage Site** (off Hwy. 351, 541/432-4185, http://oregonstateparks.org, free) is a sacred spot for the indigenous Nez Perce people, a peaceful place

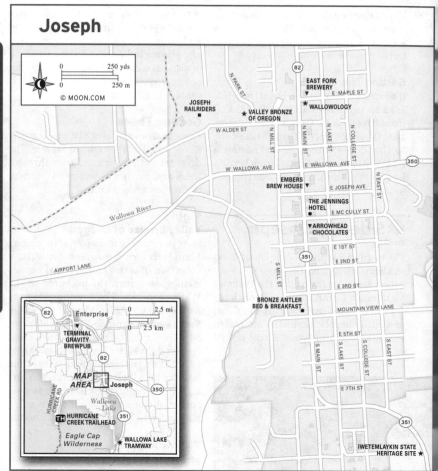

Joseph

to honor their history in their homelands. Pronounced ee-weh-TEMM-lye-kinn, the site's name translates as "at the edge of the lake." A 2.3-mile (3.7-km) trail at the site winds around a pond, grasslands, and forests, all against the stunning backdrop of the Wallowas. From here you can also walk to the **Old Chief Joseph Gravesite** (www.nps.gov/nepe), which honors one of the Nez Perce leaders for whom the town is named. From the parking lot for the heritage site, the grave site is 0.4 mile (0.6 km) southeast, either by foot or by car on Highway 351.

Recreation
Wallowa Lake

Wallowa Lake is a beautiful sapphire jewel nestled beneath the wild peaks of the Wallowa Mountains. It's a perfect summer playground for swimming, boating, and fishing. The north shore, 1 mile (1.6 km) south of Joseph, has a day-use area with a protected swimming area and a boat ramp, while the busier south shore at Wallowa Lake State Park includes a marina and campground.

The **Wallowa Lake Marina** (Wallowa Lake State Park, 541/432-9115, www.

wallowalakemarina.com, 8am-8pm Memorial Day-Labor Day, 10am-6pm mid-May-Memorial Day and Labor Day-mid-Sept.) offers watercraft rentals. You'll find paddleboards ($20 per hour, $100 per day), paddleboats for three people ($20 per hour), kayaks and canoes ($20 per hour), and motorboats for four people ($30 per hour, $150 per day). Call to reserve motorized boats in summer; everything else is first-come, first-served. The marina also offers fishing licenses, bait, tackle, and other supplies for anglers. Fishing is popular here: The lake holds eight state records and one world record for the local kokanee trout.

Wallowa Lake Tramway

View the Wallowas from on high with a ride in a gondola via the **Wallowa Lake Tramway** (59919 Wallowa Lake Hwy., 541/432-5331, www.wallowalaketramway. com, 10am-4pm daily June and Sept., 9am-5pm daily July-Aug., $35). This summertime treat takes visitors up to the peaks in a 3,700-foot (1,128-m) vertical climb to the top of Mount Howard. Each gondola carries up to four people and takes 15 minutes to reach the summit. Once there, you'll have views of sapphire Wallowa Lake below, nestled among the towering peaks. On a clear day you can see into Washington and Idaho. Take a short hike on 2 miles (3.2 km) of trails accessible at the top, or settle on the outdoor Alpine Patio at the **Summit Grill** (541/432-5331, 10am-3:30pm daily June-Labor Day, $13), serving a casual bistro lunch along with microbrews.

Joseph Railriders

Pedal along a former railroad track through wildflower meadows and green pastures on a railrider, a recumbent unit with four wheels. This unique form of transportation is found at **Joseph**

Top to bottom: Side A Brewing in La Grande; a barn and the Wallowa Mountains in Joseph; the Old Chief Joseph Gravesite.

A Nez Perce Story:
Old Chief Joseph and Chief Joseph

Tuekakas, or Old Chief Joseph, was a Nez Perce leader from the 1840s until his death in 1871. He was a Christian convert and worked hard to support peace between the Nez Perce people and incoming settlers, helping to broker a deal with the U.S. government for a reservation in Oregon and Idaho in exchange for the promise that the federal government wouldn't intrude on their sacred Wallowa Valley homeland. That promise was broken, however, when gold was discovered in the valley, motivating the government to draw up a new treaty that rescinded almost six million acres. Old Chief Joseph was incensed; his nation never agreed to the second treaty, and he refused to leave for the new reservation in Idaho, now one-tenth of its original size. He died in 1871 while negotiations were still ongoing.

photo of Chief Joseph by Charles Milton Bell

His son, Chief Joseph, inherited his name and his people's struggle. He oversaw the forced evacuation of the Nez Perce from the Wallowas, planning to eventually retreat to Canada to join the Sioux people. Instead, winter and fighting took their toll. His people were starving and his warriors were dying. He surrendered in November of 1877 with the words, "from where the sun now stands, I will fight no more forever."

The town of Joseph is named for both chiefs. At the edge of Main Street you can see a large bronze sculpture of the younger Joseph, and you can visit the **Old Chief Joseph Gravesite** (www.nps.gov/nepe), a sacred place for the Nez Perce people, near Wallowa Lake just outside the Iwetemlaykin State Heritage Site.

Railriders (501 W. Alder St., 541/786-6149, www.jbrailriders.com, Thurs.-Mon. May-Oct.), and makes for a fun way to spend an afternoon. Rides on the popular Joseph-to-Enterprise tour ($30 over age 15, $15 under age 16) last two hours round-trip, or take a longer six-hour tour to the Wallowas ($60), leaving from the town of Minam, 37 miles (60 km) west of Joseph. Kids are welcome—you can even strap a car seat into the railriders for kids under three. Advance reservations are recommended, especially June-August.

Hiking

The Wallowas offer plenty of hiking options. Some basic information is posted on kiosks at each trailhead.

One long, spectacular hike departs from **Hurricane Creek Trailhead,** 6 miles (9.7 km) southwest of town via Hurricane Creek Road. Hurricane Creek Trail heads 19 miles (31 km) into the Wallowas—you're welcome to tackle the entire thing, but there's plenty to see within the first few miles. On this early moderate section, you'll hike through thick forest along the creek, eventually trading trees for alpine meadows. After gently ascending—you'll gain 1,000 feet (305 m) of elevation—you arrive at **Slick Rock Falls,** tumbling over rocks into the river. This makes a nice turnaround point for a 5.7-mile (9.2-km) round-trip hike; budget three hours.

Many other options depart from the

popular **Wallowa Lake Trailhead,** near the southern end of Wallowa Lake—7 miles (11.3 km) south of Joseph via Highway 82/Highway 351.

Food

Follow Highway 82 north from Joseph for 6 miles (9.7 km) to neighboring Enterprise—a seeming road to nowhere—to find the delightful ★ **Terminal Gravity Brewpub** (803 E. 4th St., Enterprise, 541/426-0158, www. terminalgravitybrewing.com, 11am-9pm Wed.-Sat., $12). With a cozy interior and large outdoor patio near a creek, it's a perfect setting to relax and enjoy the eastern Oregon sun. It has award-winning beer and great food. Vegetarians will love the twist on the Reuben sandwich, made with beets. The Joseph outpost of Terminal Gravity, **East Fork Brewery** (600 N. Main St., Joseph, 541/432-1500, 11am-9pm Wed.-Mon., $12) provides more experimental small-batch beers alongside a solid choice of pub fare. It's a perfect community watering hole, with nice outdoor seating and historical photos inside. The small dining room and staff means waits can be long in summer.

Boasting the largest selection of microbrews in eastern Oregon, according to its sign, **Embers Brew House** (204 Main St., 541/432-2739, 11am-9pm Mon.-Sat., noon-8pm Sun., $12) is a popular spot—be prepared to wait—that also has really good pizza and offers a chance to mingle with the locals or catch a game on TV.

Arrowhead Chocolates (100 N. Main St., 541/432-2871, www. arrowheadchocolates.com, $5) is a great place for a midday pick-me-up. Sit in the café and watch the production behind the counter while sipping a Stumptown coffee or hot chocolate. It won the national Good Food Award for its huckleberry truffle—try it for yourself, and taste a few others while you're at it, like the hot chili or the cherry amaretto. And bring home a molded chocolate cowboy hat for your friends.

Accommodations and Camping

Find ★ **The Jennings Hotel** (100 N. Main St., www.jenningshotel.com, $95-160) on the south end of town. Known as the hotel that Kickstarter built—per the social media campaign that funded its renovation—this hip place hosts artist residencies along with nine rooms. Each room has been designed by local Portland artists. Guests can enjoy a dry sauna, a community kitchen, and great views down Main Street. All check-ins are run through Airbnb, and there is no staff on-site, but the communal dining area and library encourage mingling.

Located on the edge of town, the thoughtfully decorated **Bronze Antler Bed & Breakfast** (209 S. Main St., 541/432-0230, www.bronzeantler.com, $156-255) has six sumptuous rooms and serves a delicious breakfast. The Wallowas will bid you good day from your window, while closer in, you might spy deer in the garden on any given day.

The year-round **Wallowa Lake Campground** (800/452-5687, http:// oregonstateparks.reserveamerica.com), in Wallowa Lake State Park on the south shore of Wallowa Lake, has 121 full-hookup sites ($32), 89 tent sites ($20), and yurts ($45). It's extremely popular in summer, so book 4-5 months ahead, though some sites are held on a first-come, first-served basis.

Blue Mountains

Blue Mountain Crossing

"Commenced the ascent of the Blue Mountains. It is a lovely morning. . . . all seem to be delighted with the prospect of being so near the timber again, after the weary months of travel on the dry, dusty sage plains, with nothing to relieve the eye. . . . a most beautiful country."

Amelia Stewart Knight, August 18, 1853, *Diary of Mrs. Amelia Stewart Knight.*

Driving the pass over the Blue Mountains, often snowcapped in summer and with its steep inclines, can make for a tricky drive even today. Imagine being part of a wagon party. Emigrants had to cut down some of the ponderosa pines in the heavily forested area to make room for wagons to pass through. You can still see evidence of their passage through the region at the **Oregon Trail Interpretive Park at Blue Mountain Crossing** (9am-7pm Tues.-Sun. Memorial Day-Labor Day, $5 per vehicle or Northwest Forest Pass), which has some of the best-preserved trail ruts in the state. The interpretive park tells the tale of wagons struggling up and down the peaks over multiple short hiking trails with interpretive panels. On the 0.25-mile (0.4-km) Independence Loop, an ADA-accessible paved path, you'll pass wagon ruts as well as trees scarred by the wheels of hundreds of wagons that rubbed up against them as they passed. During some summer weekends and holidays, visitors can enjoy living-history reenactments.

Getting There
From La Grande, drive 13 miles (21 km) northwest on I-84. Take exit 248 and continue on Old Emigrant Hill Scenic Frontage Road for 0.7 mile (1.1 km). Turn right onto Forest Road 1843 and continue for 2.5 miles (4 km). The drive takes 30 minutes.

Emigrant Springs
A spring was discovered here in 1834 by Jason Lee, an Oregon-bound missionary, and the excellent water source made the area a favorite spot for pioneers to camp. While the springs no longer exist, the area—situated near the summit of the Blue Mountains—is now the **Emigrant Springs State Heritage Area** (541/983-2277, http://oregonstateparks.org, free). An interpretive kiosk and trail tell the history of the wagon route through the

Blue Mountains

Blue Mountains, and in summer actors offer historical reenactments.

Emigrant Springs also hosts a full-service, year-round **campground** (800/452-5687, http://oregonstateparks. reserveamerica.com), with tent sites ($17) and full-hookup sites ($26). There's also a horse camp and six log cabins ($43). Reservations are recommended, and can be made up to nine months in advance online or by phone. A few campsites remain open to walk-ins if you're swinging by.

Getting There

From the Blue Mountain Crossing, drive 18 miles (29 km) northwest via I-84, and take exit 234. The drive takes 25 minutes.

Pendleton

In the early years of the trail, emigrants crossed the Blue Mountains and then headed farther north into the Walla Walla Valley to seek shelter and supplies at the prominent Whitman Mission. After the mission closed down in 1847, emigrants had no reason to make the trek, and by 1851 a trading post had sprung up at present-day Pendleton. From here, wagon parties continued westward to find the Columbia River Gorge and then on to Oregon City. By the 1860s, the trading post grew into a settlement. Pendleton's excellent agriculture along with the Union Pacific Railroad's route through it by the 1880s made it a hub for commerce, and by 1900 there were 5,000 residents, making it the fourth-biggest city in the state.

The region's original inhabitants were the Cayuse, Walla Walla, and Umatilla peoples. In 1855, they ceded a territory the size of Maryland to the U.S. government in a treaty. Today, the Umatilla Indian Reservation, comprising 172,000 acres, is right outside of Pendleton and operates a fantastic cultural center on its land.

Pendleton today is a year-round hub of cultural activity in the region, and comes even more alive every summer for the town's wildly popular Round-Up rodeo. The town still holds on tight to its Old West history: Take a tour and hear tales of its past in underground tunnels, buy a cowboy hat, or stop for a whiskey in a saloon while walking the Western storefronts.

Note that lodging rates in the city go up dramatically during the Pendleton Round-Up in September; book 4-6 months in advance.

Getting There and Around

From La Grande, drive northwest 48 miles (77 km) on I-84. Use caution on this stretch of road, as you'll be driving over the Blue Mountains; as you descend into Pendleton you'll tackle some switchbacks—take it easy and stay mindful. Take exit 213 and continue 3 miles (4.8 km) into town on U.S. 30.

The small historic downtown is

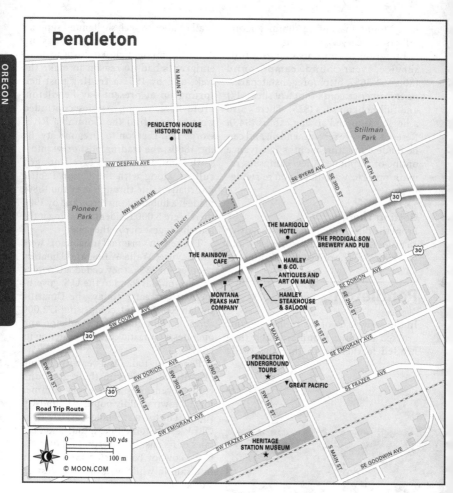

Pendleton

bounded by the Umatilla River to the north and Emigrant Avenue to the south, and SE 6th Street to the east and SW 3rd Street to the west.

Sights
★ Tamástslikt Cultural Institute
Run by the Confederated Tribes of the Umatilla Indian Reservation—a union of Cayuse, Umatilla, and Walla Walla peoples—the **Tamástslikt Cultural Institute** (47105 Wildhorse Blvd., 541/429-7700, www.tamastslikt.org, 10am-5pm Mon.-Sat., $9 adults, $7 ages 6-17, free under

age 6) provides a vital glimpse into the perspective of the tribes, who have called these lands home for more than 10,000 years; it's also the only Native American-run museum along the route that offers an indigenous perspective on the Oregon Trail. Exhibits are split into three sections: We Were, We Are, and We Will Be, which detail the history of the tribes, their current efforts in areas such as salmon recovery, and their future plans.

Take a seat around a simulated fire and learn the story of Spilyáy, the trickster coyote god, and how he vanquished the forces of darkness—as told through shadow puppetry. Learn about the tribes' vast trade networks and interactions with arriving pioneers, as well as the impact of forced U.S. boarding schools on indigenous communities. In summer, step outside to enjoy the Living Culture Village, which features full-size replicas of the houses, lodges, and tepees that Plateau cultures have called home. And stop in the **Kinship Café** (541/429-7702, 11am-2pm Mon.-Sat.) for a lunch of fresh salmon and other indigenous-inspired foods; its specialty, Indian Fry Bread, is served once a month (call ahead for details).

The museum is just outside town. Head east on I-84 and take exit 216, turning left onto Highway 331. Drive 0.9 mile (1.4 km), then turn right onto Wildhorse Boulevard, continuing for 1.3 miles (2.1 km).

Pendleton Woolen Mills

Pendleton Woolen Mills (1307 SE Court Pl., 541/276-6911, www.pendleton-usa. com, 8am-6pm Mon.-Sat., 9am-5pm Sun., free) has been weaving its iconic blankets since 1909. Early settlers found this region ideal for growing cotton and raising sheep; by 1900 there were over three million of the wooly creatures roaming the hills in eastern Oregon. Pendleton's prominence as a railroad center made it the perfect location for a mill, and so Pendleton was born. Today, Pendleton products are nationally recognized and known for their excellent quality and distinctive designs.

The original mill stands in the same location and weaves the same designs, with the addition of an attached retail store. Stop by Monday-Friday for a free 45 minute mill tour (9am, 11am, 1:30pm, 3pm) to see how raw wool is processed, from dyeing and carding to spinning and weaving. You can also check out a historical exhibit adjacent to the showroom. Plan on spending some time in the retail store before choosing your favorite blanket to help you stay warm on the road.

Pendleton Underground Tours

Learn about some of the history of this Wild West town with the nonprofit **Pendleton Underground Tours** (31 SW Emigrant Ave., 541/276-0730, www. pendletonundergroundtours.org, 10am-5pm Mon. and Wed.-Sat., $15). Running since 1989, tours are led by knowledgeable and passionate locals who walk you through Pendleton's underground tunnels, which were originally built by the area's Chinese population so that they would be able to move about without the fear of persecution that accompanied them aboveground—discrimination against Chinese people was pronounced enough in the late 1800s that it was unsafe for them to be out past sunset. Evidence of the Chinese community's daily life remains in a Chinese bathhouse, a bunkhouse, and more.

Eventually, businesses both legal and illegal operated in this underground city, which grew to include speakeasies and brothels. Aboveground, you'll have a chance to look into what was one of the longest-running brothels in the town's history; at one point Pendleton had 18 brothels, which were shut down in 1933—but Madame Stella managed to hold on until the 1960s. Open to ages 6 and up, tours run 1.5 hours and are available regularly Monday and Wednesday-Saturday.

Heritage Station Museum

The **Heritage Station Museum** (108 Frazer Ave., 541/276-0012, www. heritagestationmuseum.org, 10am-4pm Tues.-Sat., $5) is a historical train depot that now holds galleries on the region's history, including exhibits on local agriculture history, the impact of the railroad, and the Oregon Trail. There are also re-created Old West storefronts. Outside, you'll find more to explore: Check out the homestead, get a lesson in the one-room Byrd Schoolhouse, or jump aboard

a bright-yellow caboose. You could easily spend a few hours getting lost in the stories here, and train-loving kids and adults will enjoy the railroad tracks and trains inside and out.

Pendleton Round-Up and Happy Canyon Hall of Fame

The **Pendleton Round-Up and Happy Canyon Hall of Fame** (1114 SW Court Ave., 541/278-0815, www.pendletonhalloffame.com, 10am-4pm Mon.-Sat., $5) is a museum that commemorates the town's annual rodeo and biggest event. Each year a new honoree is inducted into the Hall of Fame from the Round-Up. In addition you can see historical saddles, clothing, and guns used in past Round-Ups and Happy Canyon Pageants, and lots of rodeo memorabilia. If you can't see the Round-Up itself, this is the next best thing.

Festivals and Events
Pendleton Round-Up

Established in 1910, the **Pendleton Round-Up** (www.pendletonroundup.com, mid-Sept., from $15) is the biggest event in town, drawing 50,000 people to Pendleton for 12 days in the second week in September. Professional cowboys and cowgirls from all over North America flaunt their skills in 10 events, including saddle bronc riding, calf roping, and steer wrestling. While the rodeo is the heart of the festivities, the Round-Up is also an all-around raucous time to let loose and have fun; in the early days of the event, drinking was such an essential feature that during Oregon's Prohibition (the state voted to ban all alcohol in 1915, four years before national Prohibition) the county allowed liquor just for the week of the rodeo. Today the Round-Up is a family-friendly event that adds on parades, costume contests, live music,

Top to bottom: Tamástslikt Cultural Institute; The Rainbow Café; The Prodigal Son Brewery and Pub.

games, and more. Pendleton's Main Street is closed to traffic during the event and becomes a carnival and parade ground.

The Confederated Tribes of the Umatilla Indian Reservation work closely with festival organizers to participate, and many families have been attending the event to showcase their heritage for 100 years, setting up traditional tepees on the grounds and performing in the acts. One of these is the **Happy Canyon Pageant,** which is not to be missed. It's a riot of a show that tells the story of the settling of the West—beginning with Native Americans, portrayed by members of the Confederated Tribes of the Umatilla Indian Reservation—then moving on to Lewis and Clark, the wagon trains of the Oregon Trail, and then life in a frontier town. It's a larger-than-life, rollicking depiction—though it still includes some outdated stereotypes that could be left in the past.

Tickets for the Round-Up go on sale 10 months in advance, and are ticketed by day and event. If you're traveling with kids, the best deals are the Family Tickets, which offer admission to events and dinner.

Annual Kidz Pow Wow

The **Annual Kidz Pow Wow** (Sept.) at the Tamástslikt Cultural Institute (47105 Wildhorse Blvd., 541/429-7700, www. tamastslikt.org) is for the 12 and under set. Tribal and nontribal kids are invited to join in a day of dancing, singing, drumming, games, and races. The event closes out the museum's outdoor Living Culture Village season with a bang, offering local and visiting children the chance to perform and compete for giveaways and prizes. The event is free with standard museum admission and takes place a week before the Pendleton Round-Up.

Food

If you're in the mood for a nice steak dinner, **Hamley Steakhouse** (8 SE Court Ave., 541/278-1100, www.hamleysteakhouse. com, 5pm-8:30pm Sun.-Thurs., 5pm-9pm Fri.-Sat., $20) won't disappoint. It also gets extra points for its authentic Old West feel; its **saloon** (4pm-9:30pm Sun.-Tues., 4pm-10:30pm Wed.-Thurs., 4pm-midnight Fri.-Sat.) boasts tin ceilings and an 18th-century wooden bar, and the restaurant is littered with Western artifacts. Get a taste of Pendleton or Hamley Whiskey at the saloon's daily happy hour (4pm-6pm Sun.-Tues., 4pm-6pm and 10pm-close Wed.-Sat.), and end your meal with a Mile High Mud Pie—to share or not!

The Rainbow Cafe (209 S. Main St., 541/276-4120, 6am-2am Mon.-Sat., 6am-midnight Sun., $10) is one of Oregon's oldest restaurants, open since 1883. The old saloon is now a modern diner serving big portions of breakfast, lunch, and dinner. The walls are a veritable museum of Western memorabilia, including a giant buffalo head and photographs of past Round-Up rodeo winners. Order a filet mignon or the special pressure-cooked chicken, and raise a glass to the Wild West.

A delicious and family-friendly dining option is **The Prodigal Son Brewery and Pub** (230 SE Court Ave., 541/276-6090, www.prodigalsonbrewery.com, 11am-10pm Tues.-Sat., noon-9pm Sun., $13). It has big tables in the main room, a long bar in back, and a separate kids playroom to let parents eat in peace. The menu features burgers and sandwiches but also pushes past the usual pub fare with items like oysters and fried cauliflower. Happy hour is daily (3pm-6pm).

Great Pacific (403 Main St., 541/276-1350, www.greatpacific.biz, 10am-9pm Mon.-Thurs., 10am-10pm Fri.-Sat., $12) offers pizzas, sandwiches, wine, beer, and coffee, served in a building from the 1880s. Brick walls line two distinct spaces, giving the impression of a daytime coffee café and evening wine bar—and both have spot-on menus. Live music in the evening contributes to the ambience (find the event calendar online).

OREGON

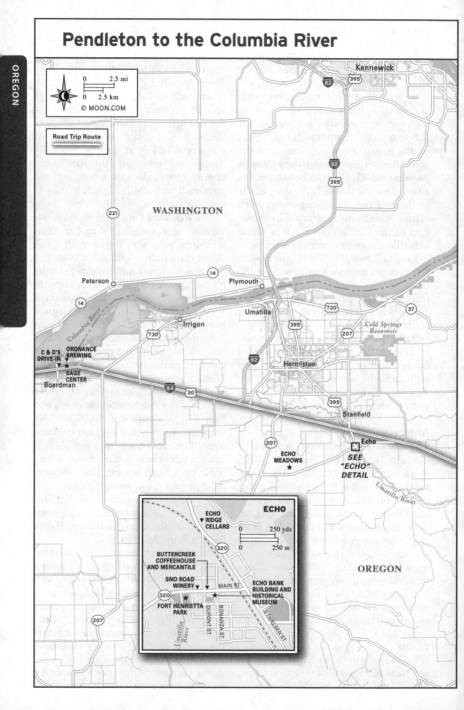

Pendleton to the Columbia River

0   2.5 mi
0   2.5 km
© MOON.COM

Road Trip Route

WASHINGTON

Paterson

Plymouth

Columbia River

Irrigon

Umatilla

Cold Springs Reservoir

C & D'S DRIVE-IN

ORDNANCE BREWING

SAGE CENTER

Boardman

Hermiston

Stanfield

Echo

SEE "ECHO" DETAIL

ECHO MEADOWS

Umatilla River

ECHO

ECHO RIDGE CELLARS

0   250 yds
0   250 m

BUTTERCREEK COFFEEHOUSE AND MERCANTILE

SNO ROAD WINERY

MAIN ST

ECHO BANK BUILDING AND HISTORICAL MUSEUM

FORT HENRIETTA PARK

DUPONT ST

BONANZA ST

S THIELSEN ST

Umatilla River

OREGON

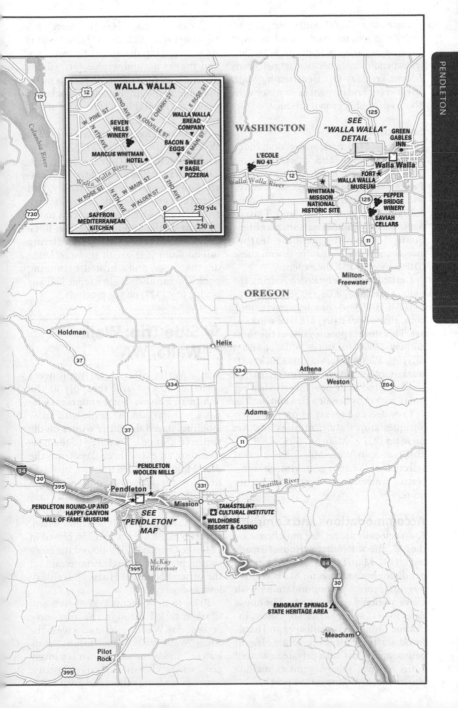

Taste the region's bounty and get groceries and special handcrafted items at **Pendleton Farmers Market** (Main St., www.pendletonfarmersmarket.net, 4pm-7:30pm Fri. May-Oct.), enlivening Main Street every Friday night in summer with booths of freshly grown produce.

Shopping

Hundreds of ranchers, professional rodeo riders, cowboys, and cowgirls know and love the quality hats at **Montana Peaks Hat Company** (24 SW Court Ave., 541/215-1400, www.montanapeaks.com, 8:30am-6pm Mon.-Tues. and Thurs.-Sat.). Made with materials such as high-quality beaver fur, genuine leather sweatbands, and soft satin liners, these hats are well worth the expense.

Crafted with care by Pedro Pedrini, the saddles at **Hamley & Co.** (30 SE Court Ave., 541/278-1100, www.hamleywesternstore.com, 10am-6pm daily) are true works of art. This store is possibly one of the most authentic Western stores in the country, offering Western wear, horse tack, artwork, vintage silver, and finely crafted jewelry. Find your new favorite leather boots, a cowboy hat, or a fine belt buckle.

Crowded and messy as only the best antiques stores are, **Antiques and Art on Main** (221 S. Main St., 509/953-8746, 10:30am-5pm Wed.-Mon.) has a great selection of Western gear, vintage signs, Native American artifacts, and plenty more.

Accommodations and Camping

Known locally as the "big pink house on the hill," the ★ **Pendleton House Historic Inn** (311 N. Main St., 541/276-8581, www.pendletonhousebnb.com, $135-225) offers sumptuous accommodations with views overlooking downtown. The house dates to 1917 and retains its opulence, including Chinese silk wallpaper and hardwood staircases leading to an elegant ballroom. Rooms with private or shared baths are available. Amenities include plush robes and wine on the porch.

The cheery yellow **Marigold Hotel** (105 SE Court Ave., 541/276-3231, $50-90) is within spitting distance of downtown and makes a comfortable, affordable place to spend the night. It's more a motel than the name implies, and parking, a basic continental breakfast, and attentive staff are all offered.

Wildhorse Resort & Casino (46510 Wildhorse Blvd., 541/278-2274, www.wildhorseresort.com) offers rooms ($150-230) with sweeping views of the high desert. Some rooms are dog-friendly, and guests can enjoy the indoor pool, sauna, and hot tub, as well as easy access to the 24-hour casino and in-house Hot Rock Café. Also here is an RV park offering full hookups ($47), with showers, laundry machines, and a heated swimming pool. You can also stay in a tepee ($40) or pitch a tent ($27) on the grounds.

⮞ Side Trip: Walla Walla, WA

Walla Walla offered early pioneers a chance to rest and resupply at the Whitman Mission. Some emigrants who got a late start on the trail, with snow looming, stayed the entire winter on the sheltered grounds. Traveling to the mission took an extra three days from the Blue Mountains, then another two days to follow the Walla Walla River west to the Columbia River, a distance that may have been a reasonable trade-off for fresh produce, supplies to fix a wagon wheel, or medicine. After the mission closed in 1847, the Oregon Trail followed the more southerly route through Pendleton that the official National Historic Trail follows today.

Prior to the Oregon Trail, Lewis and Clark traveled through the area, now present-day Washington, and gave it the name "Walla Walla," which means "many waters." Today the small town is a lovely gem, where visitors can enjoy history, wineries, a scenic valley, and great food.

Getting There

From Pendleton, head northeast on Highway 11, which becomes Highway 125 as you cross the state line into Washington, for 39 miles (63 km). Turn right onto Rose Street, which takes you through downtown. The drive takes 50 minutes.

Sights

Whitman Mission

The **Whitman Mission National Historic Site** (328 Whitman Mission Rd., www.nps.gov/whmi, visitors center 9am-4pm daily Memorial Day-Labor Day, 9am-4pm Wed.-Sun. Labor Day-Nov. and Feb.-Memorial Day, grounds dawn-dusk daily, free) offers a thoughtful look at the history between the indigenous Cayuse people and the missionaries who came to convert them to Methodist Christianity. The National Park Service works with the Confederated Tribes of the Umatilla Indian Reservation to tell the complicated story of this tragic interaction between Native Americans and early settlers.

In 1836, Marcus and Narcissa Whitman established the mission, which became an important stop along the Oregon Trail as a place for emigrants to rest their animals, trade, and find water and supplies. When a measles epidemic broke out in the area, the Cayuse people lost children and other loved ones to the disease while witnessing white settlers—who had some immunity—recover under the Whitmans' care. Tensions that had been building for some time erupted violently in 1847, when a group of Cayuse killed Marcus and Narcissa Whitman along with 12 others, an event that became known around the country as the Whitman Massacre. News of it reached Washington DC and led to the creation of the Oregon Territory in 1848. It also led to the Cayuse War, ultimately resulting in the tribe's removal to the Umatilla Reservation.

The park contains the mass grave where the victims were buried, a memorial obelisk atop a hill, and reconstructed trail ruts along with a replica wagon. Visitors can find trails that lead to the original mission site, though no buildings remain. Instead, the pleasant walk passes by the marked foundations of a few buildings, a pond, and a pioneer-era apple orchard. The visitors center has a small museum inside that showcases items from both the Cayuse people and the Whitmans, side by side, as well as more displays about the event's circumstances and consequences.

Fort Walla Walla Museum

Fort Walla Walla Museum (755 NE Myra Rd., 509/525-7798, www.fwwm.org, 10am-5pm daily Mar.-Oct., 10am-4pm daily Nov.-Feb., $9) is a surprisingly big museum for a small town—you could easily spend a half-day here. With five exhibit halls and a re-created Pioneer Village, the museum dives deep into the history of the Walla Walla region, showcasing Native American artifacts, period furnishings, textiles that include fashionable hats and military outfits, and a life-size replica of 33 mules pulling a wheat combine! There's also plenty to keep kids interested, including living-history performances on summer weekends.

The museum doesn't have much to do with the original Fort Walla Walla, which was established in 1818 by the Hudson's Bay Company about 25 miles (40 km) west of this location, and active until just after the Whitman Mission period. Most Oregon Trail emigrants would have skipped the British fort—today under the waters of the Columbia River—in favor of the U.S. mission. Another incarnation of Fort Walla Walla was built at this location in 1856, about 7 miles (11.3 km) east of the modern city's downtown. It was active until 1910, and some of the original structures are still in use by the local VA hospital.

A Pioneer Story: Narcissa Whitman

Narcissa Whitman was an early pioneer and the first European woman to make the wagon journey west, along with Eliza Spaulding, also traveling in her party, in 1836. A passionate Protestant missionary, Narcissa married the accomplished doctor Marcus Whitman in February 1836, when she was 28 years old. The next month, in March, they set out from New York for Missouri, then headed out on the relatively new Oregon Trail to build a mission.

sketch of Narcissa Whitman by Drury Haight

Narcissa found the Oregon Trail to be a place to push past the gender norms of the time and find a degree of freedom. An accomplished rider, she rode sidesaddle the whole trail—at a time when women were not thought capable of traveling such a distance riding in a wagon train or walking beside one, she rode ahead of them, even losing sight of the caravan at times. Letters she sent back home to her family were shared widely and published in national newspapers, catapulting her and the Oregon Trail to fame. She was an evangelist for the trail, offering tantalizing glimpses into the beauty and opportunities the West offered. Thousands found inspiration in her words and succumbed to "Oregon fever."

> "I wish I could describe to you how we live so that you can realize it. Our manner of living is far preferable to any in the States. I never was so contented and happy before neither have I enjoyed such health for years. ...Do not think I regret coming. No, far from it; I would not go back for a world."
>
> Narcissa Whitman, 1836, *The Letters and Journal of Narcissa Whitman.*

The happiness and freedom she felt on the trail was tempered somewhat after the Whitmans established their mission. Without any fellow females or friends, it was a lonely existence, and Narcissa sank into depression when her only child, a two-year-old daughter, drowned.

Like many pioneers, extending cultural sensitivity and understanding to the region's indigenous peoples wasn't part of Narcissa's aim; she didn't try to learn the local language or mix with the Cayuse people she sought to convert. Although she and her husband became martyrs of their time when they were killed in the sensationalized event that came to be known as the Whitman Massacre, today Narcissa Whitman illustrates something more complicated: the hopes and failings of the evangelical pioneers.

Wineries

Right in downtown Walla Walla you can get a taste of the valley's excellence at **Seven Hills Winery** (212 N. 3rd Ave., 509/529-7198, www.sevenhillswinery.com, 10am-5pm daily, $10 tasting fee, $25 tour and tasting). The tasting room is in a wood mill from 1904, which has been lovingly restored to house the winery, which focuses on merlots and cabernet sauvignons. You can also take a 45-minute winery tour (10am daily, $25), which includes a tasting.

Just south of town, **Saviah Cellars**

(1979 J. B. George Rd., 509/522-2181, www.saviahcellars.com, 10am-5pm daily, $10 tasting fee) produces balanced wines that show off the unique terroir of the Walla Walla Valley. You can sample its wines while browsing the art on display in its gallery. Relax on the dog-friendly patio, or take an hour-long tour with your tasting (11am, 1pm, and 3pm Fri.-Sun., $25). Nearby is **Pepper Bridge Winery** (1704 J. B. George Rd., 509/525-6502, www.pepperbridge.com, 10am-4pm daily, $15 tasting fee), which offers spectacular views of the vineyards and the Blue Mountains from its outdoor deck. The winery is a leader in sustainable viticulture, using processes such as composting, drip irrigation, and strategic planting to attract beneficial insects. Enjoy tastes of the excellent merlot, cabernet sauvignon, and sauvignon blanc, or go for an hour-long winery tour with tasting (on request, $20).

About 12 miles (19 km) west of town is one of the oldest wineries in the Walla Walla Valley and winner of numerous awards, **L'Ecole No 41** (41 Lowden School Rd., 509/525-0940, www.lecole.com, 10am-5pm daily, $15 tasting fee). Taste its Bordeaux blends and more at the tasting room set in a 1915 schoolhouse. You can also enjoy a 1.5-hour walking tour and private tasting of eight wines (3pm Fri. Apr.-Nov., $40).

Food

Start your day off in the best way possible at farm-to-table ★ **Bacon & Eggs** (57 E. Main St., 509/876-4553, www.baconandeggswallawalla.com, 8am-2pm Thurs.-Tues., $11). Choose from eclectic options that include shrimp and grits, a tofu stir fry, and huevos rancheros.

Finely crafted Mediterranean dishes are served at **Saffron Mediterranean Kitchen** (330 W. Main St., 509/525-2112, 2pm-9pm Mon.-Fri., noon-9pm Sat.-Sun., $25), including wood-grilled octopus, house-made linguini with wild mushrooms, and Spanish-inspired rib-eye

steak. If you can't settle on a dish, don't worry; the attentive servers are happy to make recommendations.

Find more than just café fare at bakery-restaurant **Walla Walla Bread Company** (201 E. Main St., 509/522 8422, www.w2breadco.com, 8am-4pm Tues.-Sun., $17), which serves dishes like steak and eggs, wood-fired pizzas, and hot sandwiches on signature crusty loaves. The bakery rolls out sourdough, rye, and French baguettes along with a daily special.

Sweet Basil Pizzeria (5 S. 1st Ave., 509/529-1950, www.sweetbasilpizzeria. com, 11am-9pm daily, $9) is a casual dining room slinging New York pies with local ingredients, including sweet Walla Walla onions. Get it by the slice or order a whole pie, along with a stromboli or calzone. Local beer and wine top off the experience.

Accommodations

Rising above the city skyline in all its 1920s grandeur, the ★ **Marcus Whitman Hotel** (6 W. Rose St., 509/525-2200, http://marcuswhitmanhotel.com, $130-180) combines history, comfort, and hospitality. A 1928 ordinance states that nothing can rise higher than the Marcus Whitman Hotel—and that remains true today. The hotel originally opened in 1928 before falling into disrepair. Today it's back to its former glory, with plenty of original features like key cubbies behind the front desk and old phone booths.

Downtown and refurbished to full mid-century modern glory, **The Finch** (325 E. Main St., 509/956-4994, www.finchwallawalla.com, $120-280), formerly a motel, is full of Pacific Northwest touches like warm wood accents and wool blankets. Its 80 rooms offer everything from bunk beds for four to queen and king beds to two-room suites. A fleet of bikes is on hand to explore the region.

The **Green Gables Inn** (922 Bonsella St., 509/876-4373, www.greengablesinn. com, $170-235) is in a beautiful house close to downtown. Originally built in 1909, it has been lovingly restored and offers five guest rooms and two adjacent guest houses. A hot gourmet breakfast is served in the morning.

Along the Trail from Pendleton

Echo

In the area that's now the small town of Echo (founded in 1880), emigrants stopped to rest, water their livestock, and camp along the Umatilla River before fording it at the Lower Crossing. Today the town has seen a resurgence of interest and is something of a local secret. Much of it has been remodeled and brought back to life by local winery owners.

Getting There

From Pendleton, head 17 miles (27 km) west on I-84. Take exit 193, turning left onto Echo Road. Continue for 4 miles (6.4 km), then turn right onto Thielsen Street into town. The drive takes just under 30 minutes.

Alternately, you can get to Echo by following the old trail route, a closer approximation of what the Oregon Trail pioneers would have taken, along Reith Road, which winds along the Umatilla River, under some pretty cliff formations and rolling hills, and past farmhouses and sheep pastures. It has better views than the I-84 corridor, though it takes a little longer. Leave Pendleton via U.S. 30 and continue on as it becomes County Road 1300, Reith Road, and eventually Thielsen Street, for 22 miles (35 km). The drive takes 45 minutes.

Sights
Fort Henrietta Park

See the Lower Crossing where pioneers forded the Umatilla River at **Fort Henrietta Park** (10 W. Main St., 541/571-3597, www.echo-oregon.com, dawn-dusk daily, free), on the western edge of Echo. Fort Henrietta was built in 1851 out of logs, a notable fact recorded in numerous diaries—many emigrants hadn't seen a wooden building along the trail since Wyoming. It served as a base for the local "Indian agent," a federal employee authorized to interact with Native American nations—in this case, the Umatilla, Cayuse, and Walla Walla peoples. The post wasn't successful—the Umatilla burned the fort down in 1855 when they joined with the Yakima people in an uprising known as the Yakima War.

Today, the park has a rebuilt replica of the blockhouse, a freestanding fortification near the fort's original location. Archaeological digs around the old fort foundations have turned up items from the original fort and agency; informational panels explain more. Visitors will also find a display of covered wagons, including a vintage fire wagon, and the first county jail. Tent and RV campsites ($20-26) are also available here.

Wineries

Sno Road Winery (111 W. Main St., 541/376-0421, http://piercyfamily vineyards.com, 11am-6:30pm Wed.-Thurs., 11am-8:30pm Fri., noon-6:30pm Sat. summer, $5 tasting fee) is housed in a renovated historical space that encompasses a tasting room, a beautiful patio, and a large ballroom and event space. Wines include earthy and rich tempranillo, pinot noir, and cabernet sauvignon. Regular events and live music add to the fun.

Just north of downtown in a restored grain elevator, **Echo Ridge Cellars** (551 N. Thielsen St., 541/376-8100, www.echoridgecellars.com, 2pm-8pm Wed.-Fri., noon-8pm Sat., 1pm-4pm Sun. summer, 2pm-6pm Wed.-Fri., noon-6pm Sat. winter, $5 tasting fee) is an impressive architectural sight, and the winery offers beautiful seating indoors or outdoors to enjoy its wines. Enjoy a range of reds, including merlot, syrah, and cabs. Live music and regular events are also held here.

Food

Buttercreek Coffeehouse and Mercantile (201 W. Main St., 541/376-5540, 7am-2pm Mon.-Fri., 8am-2pm Sat., $8) is the place to go for coffee and baked goods. It also includes a small grocery shop offering grab-and-go treats. There are plenty of tables at which to relax.

Echo Meadows

After leaving their campsites at the Lower Crossing near the Umatilla River, emigrants faced a dry and dusty route through sagebrush, and here you can see some evidence of their hard travels in the deep ruts cut into the prairie. **Echo Meadows** (off Hwy. 320, 541/376-8411, dawn-dusk daily, free) has a 0.5-mile (0.8-km) paved path to the preserved trail ruts; they stretch for another mile (1.6 km). On the way to the ruts you'll also see an offshoot from the main path, a narrower dirt trail that leads up a hill. Follow it for some great prairie views similar to what emigrants would have seen.

trail ruts in Echo Meadows

Getting There

Be aware that GPS navigation may misdirect you here. Leave Echo on Oregon Trail Road/Lexington-Echo Highway heading southwest. Drive about 6 miles (9.7 km), then turn right onto the gravel road; you'll see a highway sign noting an Oregon Trail site is here. About 1.2 miles (1.9 km) up the gravel road, pull over to the parking lot on the right for an informational kiosk and entrance to the meadows.

Biggs Junction

At **Biggs Junction,** wagons topped the rolling hills and came across their first views of the mighty Columbia River. After the dry stretches and hardships of eastern Oregon, the landscape was showing hints of the promised beauty and majesty pioneers had envisioned and worked so hard to reach. Some preserved trail ruts can be found here off the highway. Stand here and take in the river's vista, and imagine the welcome sight it must have been.

Getting There

From Echo, head west on I-84 for 84 miles (135 km). Take exit 104 for U.S. 97, then turn right onto Biggs-Rufus Highway. The ruts are 2.1 miles (3.4 km) down the road; keep going past the historical marker on the right. You'll see an Oregon Trail signpost on the left, with ruts visible in the cliff behind it. You can walk up the hill a ways to get a good view of the gorge: Remember to tread lightly on the historical ruts, and don't drive on them. A popular geocache can be found here. The drive takes an hour and 20 minutes.

Columbia River Gorge

TOP EXPERIENCE

The stunning Columbia River Gorge spans 73 miles (117 km) from The Dalles to Troutdale, and separates Oregon from Washington. For more than 13,000 years, Native Americans flourished along the rushing river, fishing plentiful salmon and creating vast trading communities—in fact, goods from as far away as the Midwest and Southwest have been uncovered here. French Canadian fur trappers were some of the first European-Americans to explore the waters, followed by Lewis and Clark in their 1804-1806 expedition. Missionaries including the Whitmans came by in the 1830s, followed by Oregon Trail emigrants who, until Sam Barlow forged an alternate route inland around Mount Hood, were forced to navigate the area's tricky terrain by floating down the then-wild Columbia River. Eventually dams and locks calmed the rapids of the river to make way for steamboats, and a highway was carved into the riverside.

Today, this National Scenic Area is a big draw in the region. It boasts the largest concentration of waterfalls in North America, including renowned Multnomah Falls. Hiking trails wind through the area to help you explore the lush abundance.

Getting Around

Highways line both sides of the gorge, following the path of the Columbia River. The main thoroughfare through the gorge is **I-84.** Following the interstate, you can drive from The Dalles to Portland in 1.5 hours. I-84 is well suited to RVs, and just driving through without stops affords plenty of beautiful views.

Alternatively, you can meander west through the gorge on the **Historic Columbia River Highway (U.S. 30),** a scenic byway and one of the wonders of the 1920s. It was built 1913-1922 and is a beautiful example of that era's elegant craftsmanship. Hand-cut stone and masonry grace the tunnels and walls of the gently curving road, which has been designed to offer both stunning river views and waterfall glimpses. It's also a popular cycling route, so proceed cautiously and allow plenty of room when passing.

The Lewis and Clark Trail

Although the Oregon Trail began to take off more than 30 years after William Clark and Meriwether Lewis made their famous trek to the Pacific, the pioneers owed much to the explorers. Theirs was the first venture west, the United States' first contact with the area's indigenous peoples, and the first attempt at mapping many rivers, including the Snake and Columbia. In many ways the 1804-1806 expedition could be called the beginning of the Oregon Trail story.

The route Lewis and Clark took differed greatly from the pioneers in that they traveled by river, as wagons couldn't traverse much of the mountainous terrain at that time. But they had similar starting and ending points; the Lewis and Clark expedition began in St. Louis and also traveled through Independence, Missouri—where the Oregon Trail pioneers set off—before heading north via the Missouri River through Nebraska and the Dakotas, and west through Montana and Idaho. The routes converge at the Columbia River Gorge; both included floating the river, until the Barlow Road opened as an overland trail in 1846. Lewis and Clark pushed farther west to reach the Pacific Ocean, while pioneers generally stopped once reaching fertile land in the Willamette Valley.

The narrow highway is not well-suited for RVs.

Just west of The Dalles, you can follow a section of the highway to Mosier, and then you'll need to hop onto I-84—parts of the old highway have been closed to traffic and transformed into walking-biking thoroughfares, and are now part of the Historic Columbia River Highway State Trail. You can get back on U.S. 30 at Dodson, just west of Bonneville, where you can continue on the historic highway to Troutdale; this section has the most waterfalls, though it's also packed with visitors in summer and has limited parking. Taking the scenic route from The Dalles adds about 40 more minutes than taking just I-84. The Eagle Creek Fire raged through here in 2017, burning 48,000 acres of and forcing many portions of the historic highway to close, but they are open once again. Even so, watch for burned sections, which are more prone to rockslides.

Across the Columbia River, **Washington's Highway 14** offers a smaller, slower route, with scenic finds of its own.

Consider exploring the region car-free via **Columbia Gorge Express,** which runs buses five times daily to and from Portland, Troutdale, Multnomah Falls, Cascade Locks, Hood River, and The Dalles. If you have time to make a base in The Dalles or Hood River, the service provides an easy way to explore the area on day trips. The bus drops off in the downtown center of each city—except for Portland, where it goes to Gateway Transit Center on the east side of town, from where you can jump on the MAX Light Rail to get downtown. A trip from Portland and Cascade Locks, Hood River, or The Dalles is $10, which you can pay in cash when you board.

The Dalles

"Nov 2 we took off our wagon wheels layed them on the raft placed the wagon beds on them and started ... on 12 logs 18 inches through and 40 ft long the water runs 3 inches over our raft. Nov 3 we are floating down the Columbia cold and disagreeable weather."

Elizabeth Dixon Smith, 1847, *Diary of Elizabeth Dixon Smith*. Smith left Indiana with her husband and seven children to travel the Oregon Trail in 1847. Her husband died after their arrival. She remarried, then died in 1855.

Upon arriving at The Dalles, Oregon Trail emigrants encountered a new challenge: The only way to navigate the area's tricky terrain in the early days—until an alternate route was forged around Mount Hood—was to raft down the Columbia River.

The Dalles—note that leaving "The" off the name will instantly mark you as a tourist—is French for "flagstone," derived from French-Canadian fur trappers speaking about the basalt rocks in the once-rushing narrows of the Columbia River. Before the construction of dams along the waterway, the Columbia was a wild river with rapids and waterfalls. Fur traders passed by the spot as early as 1810—in that time, and for thousands of years prior, the area just east of The Dalles, Celilo Village, was a vital trading center, drawing Native Americans from miles around. In 1838 a Methodist mission was established here, and by the 1840s Oregon Trail wagons were rolling through in order to put in at the river just after Celilo Falls.

Getting There

From I-84 westbound, take exit 85, turning left onto Brewery Overpass Road. After 0.2 mile (0.3 km), turn right onto 2nd Street, the town's main thoroughfare. From Biggs Junction, The Dalles is a 20-mile (32-km), 20-minute drive west. From Pendleton, the 125-mile (201-km) drive west takes 1.75 hours. The downtown core is along 2nd and 3rd Streets, between Lincoln and Taylor Streets.

Sights

Murals

Visitors will enjoy a series of **murals** (www.thedallesmuralsociety.com) dotting downtown, all depicting famous moments in local history. Several offer audio boxes that tell the mural's story. *Decision at The Dalles*, on Federal Street between 2nd and 3rd Streets, depicts a key Oregon Trail moment: choosing whether to float

Horsethief Butte in Columbia Hills Historical State Park

the Columbia River or take the Barlow Road around Mount Hood.

Museums

The **Columbia Gorge Discovery Center & Museum** (5000 Discovery Dr., 541/296-8600, www.gorgediscovery.org, 9am-5pm daily, $9 adults, $7 seniors, $5 ages 6-16, free under age 6) is a surprisingly great museum along the cliffs of the river, with exhibits on local history, regional geology, and natural history. One exhibit depicts a fast track from the most recent ice age through the pioneers to today. Kids will find plenty to enjoy, with secret tunnels, a giant woolly mammoth, and an Explorer Room with hands-on activities. Special raptor presentations offer a chance to see live falcons and hawks up close—times change daily, so call ahead. Outside, take a stroll along one of the trails for stunning views, native plants, and historical panels.

One of the oldest museums in Oregon, the **Fort Dalles Museum** (500 W. 15th St.,

541/296-4527, www.fortdallesmuseum. org, 10am-5pm daily Mar.-Oct., $8 adults, $5 seniors, $1 ages 7-17, free under age 7), opened in 1905. Local history exhibits cover the Columbia River before European settlement and early missionaries to the area. Across the street is the Anderson Homestead, a Swedish log home that you can tour with museum admission.

The **National Neon Sign Museum** (200 E. 3rd St., 541/370-2242, www. nationalneonsignmuseum.org, 10am-5pm Thurs.-Sun., $10) opened in 2018 inside the 1910 Elks Temple. The collection is entirely owned by a Washington local and contains thousands of neon-related items, including signs for old barbershops, jewelry stores, and ice cream parlors.

Recreation

Riverfront Trail

The 10-mile (16-km) **Riverfront Trail** (www.nwprd.org) is a wide paved path that follows the winding course of the Columbia River. Starting at the Columbia Gorge Discovery Center & Museum, the trail meanders southeast along the river, offering windy overlooks and opportunities to spot eagles or hawks. It's a great path for walking or biking—if you have your own (the closest place to rent a bicycle is in Hood River, an hour away).

Columbia Hills Historical State Park

One of the best scenic hikes in the area is over the river in Washington at **Columbia Hills Historical State Park** (85 Hwy. 14, 509/767-1159, http://parks.state.wa.us, 6:30am-dusk daily Mar.-Oct., day-use $10 or Washington Discover Pass). A free 1.5-hour guided tour (9am Fri.-Sat. Apr.-Oct.) leads you 0.75 mile (1.2 km) to one of the most famous pictographs in North America, *Tsagaglalal,* or *She Who Watches.* The legend goes that a trickster coyote betrayed the chief of a local Native American nation and turned her into stone. She has been here on the cliff

The Dalles to Hood River

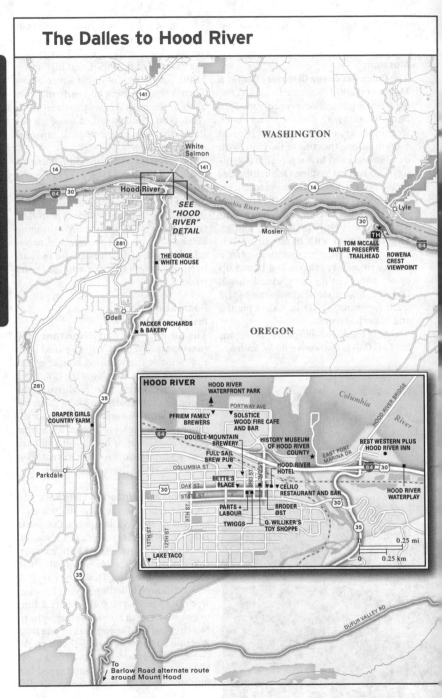

WASHINGTON

White Salmon

141

Hood River

Columbia River

Lyle

SEE "HOOD RIVER" DETAIL

Mosier

14

30

TOM MCCALL NATURE PRESERVE TRAILHEAD

ROWENA CREST VIEWPOINT

THE GORGE WHITE HOUSE

281

Odell

PACKER ORCHARDS & BAKERY

OREGON

281

35

DRAPER GIRLS COUNTRY FARM

84

Parkdale

30

35

To Barlow Road alternate route around Mount Hood

HOOD RIVER

HOOD RIVER WATERFRONT PARK

Columbia River

PORTWAY AVE

PFRIEM FAMILY BREWERS

SOLSTICE WOOD FIRE CAFE AND BAR

HOOD RIVER BRIDGE

DOUBLE-MOUNTAIN BREWERY

HISTORY MUSEUM OF HOOD RIVER COUNTY

EAST PORT MARINA DR

BEST WESTERN PLUS HOOD RIVER INN

FULL SAIL BREW PUB

HOOD RIVER HOTEL

84

30

COLUMBIA ST

HOOD RIVER WATERPLAY

BETTE'S PLACE

CELILO RESTAURANT AND BAR

OAK ST

STATE ST

30

PARTS + LABOUR

BRODER ØST

35

TWIGGS

G. WILLIKER'S TOY SHOPPE

13TH ST

12TH ST

9TH ST

3RD ST

2ND ST

LAKE TACO

DUFUR VALLEY RD

0   0.25 mi

0   0.25 km

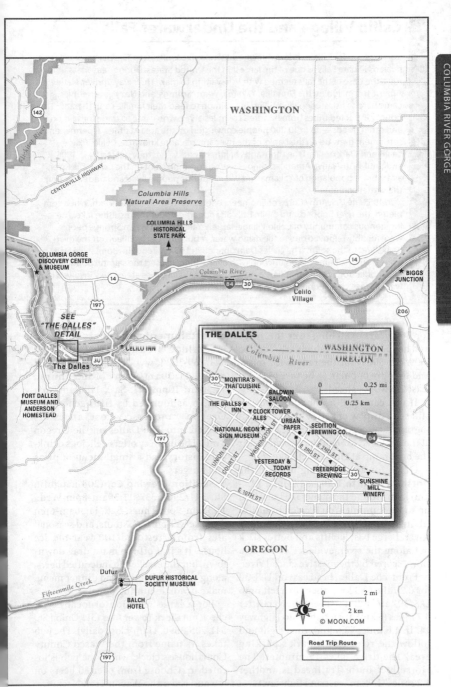

Celilo Village and the Underwater Falls

Celilo (se-LIE-lo) Falls, previously located 13 miles (21 km) east of The Dalles, once rivaled Niagara Falls as one of the largest in the United States. During seasonal salmon runs, the base of the falls teemed with fish waiting to make their way upriver. Native Americans, including the Umatilla, Yakama, Warm Springs, and Nez Perce peoples, came here to fish seasonally, pulling out salmon to feed their families and to trade. The bounty attracted tribes from hundreds of miles away, who came to trade for salmon and other goods—up to 10,000 people converged on the area at times. A permanent settlement grew up on the banks of the river and became known as Celilo Village. Lewis and Clark noticed the thousands of inhabitants when they passed by in 1805, and until 1910, Native American canoes were a common sight on the Columbia River, as a vibrant population of Yakama and Warm Springs people lived and traded among the settler community.

In 1953 the U.S. Army Corps of Engineers began work on the Dalles Dam. When completed, the river flooded, and Celilo Falls disappeared under the resulting lake. The indigenous community of Celilo Village, largely Yakama and Warm Springs people, were forcibly removed due to the rising water, rebuilding Celilo Village off the riverbanks and to the south. The Dalles Dam opened in 1957, joining the Bonneville Dam from 1938. The dams, in conjunction with overfishing, caused the salmon population to dwindle. Today, the Umatilla, Cayuse, and Walla Walla tribes are heavily involved in work to restore and bring back salmon along the river.

for 300 years, watching over the gorge and her people. Reservations are required (509/773-5007) for the ranger-led tours, and they are popular, so be sure to call at least 2-3 weeks ahead.

If you can't get on the tour, you can still see a display of petroglyphs and pictographs, rescued from the area's dams, at the trailhead to *She Who Watches*, near the boat ramp at Horsethief Lake.

Or go for an hour-long hike on the **Horsethief Butte Trail,** a 1.7-mile (2.7-km) loop around the namesake butte and up to the summit. You'll catch beautiful (though windy!) views of the Columbia River. Large basalt cliffs and buttes stick out along the river, evidence of old lava flows scored by the massive glacial river.

From The Dalles, head east on U.S. 30 for 0.2 mile (0.3 km), then turn left onto U.S. 197 and follow it over the river. After 3.7 miles (6 km), turn right onto Highway 14. In 1.6 miles (2.6 km), turn right and follow the road to the park's parking area. The drive takes 15 minutes. The Horsethief Butte Trailhead is another 1.2 miles (1.9 km) east on Highway 14.

Entertainment and Events
Freebridge Brewing (710 E. 2nd St., 541/769-1234, www.freebridgebrewing.com, 11:30am-9pm Mon.-Thurs., 11:30am-10pm Fri.-Sat., 11:30am-8pm Sun.) was founded by fifth-generation Oregon ranchers, whose ancestors walked into The Dalles on the Oregon Trail. The brewery offers delicious drinkable history and a small menu of pizza and burgers.

Sedition Brewing Co. (208 Laughlin St., 541/296-2337, 11:30am-8pm Wed., 11:30am-9pm Thurs.-Sat., 11:30am-6pm Sun.) serves porters, stouts, and seasonal ales from a restored 100-year-old ice house. It's just off the main drag downtown, but the excellent handcrafted beers, along with a full lunch and dinner menu, make it worth hunting down.

For a large selection of local beers, check out **Clock Tower Ales** (311 Union St., 541/705-3590, 11am-close daily). The pub takes its name from the Wasco County Courthouse's clock, which the pub is located in. Choose from over 30 beers on tap and order the Wagon Trail Nachos.

A Pioneer Story: George Washington Bush

Many early pioneers who traveled to the fabled land of Oregon discovered that their destination wasn't welcoming to all settlers. In 1844 George Washington Bush, a well-to-do farmer of African and Irish descent, traveled the Oregon Trail from Missouri with his wife, of German descent, and five sons.

Born in Pennsylvania, Bush had worked as a trader and fur trapper for the Hudson's Bay Company, which led him all over the West on numerous expeditions. Having heard of his knowledge and experience, Irish immigrant Michael T. Simmons requested Bush lead a wagon party on the Oregon Trail. Bush decided to emigrate with his family. Arriving in The Dalles by the fall of 1844, the Bush-Simmons party discovered that the newly established Oregon Territory had enacted discriminatory laws banning black people. Appreciative of his generosity and selflessness, the rest of the wagon party abandoned their plans to settle in Oregon and joined Bush in heading north instead. By 1845, they were settled south of Puget Sound, near the lands of the Nisqually people. Bush's family made long-lasting friendships with their neighbors, learning their language and welcoming them into their home. The Bush family also helped treat local tribes when epidemics swept the region.

The community formed by the five families of the Bush-Simmons wagon party, now Tumwater, was the first U.S. settlement in what became Washington state. Bush and Simmons set up a flour mill, a sawmill, and a successful farm in the area, planting fruit trees from seeds carried over the Oregon Trail. To incoming settlers, Bush was well-known for his magnanimous nature, sharing his crops even in leaner years. When Oregon's exclusion laws began encroaching on Washington, the territorial legislature voted unanimously to grant Bush a special act to allow him to remain in the state.

Pioneers have been celebrated for their rugged individualism, but Bush is a reminder that pioneering also required collaboration and community.

The Dalles' favorite annual festival is the **Northwest Cherry Festival** (http://thedalleschamber.com), which runs for three days in April to celebrate the region's agricultural heritage. Sample your favorite sweet juicy jewel from the Oregon Cherry Growers, then enjoy a range of events like a parade, a 10K race, a classic car show, and a carnival.

Food

The towering old mill at ★ **Sunshine Mill Winery** (901 E. 2nd St., 541/298-8900, www.sunshinemill.com, noon-6pm daily, $8) is hard to miss. Give in to your curiosity and stop for lunch or a glass of wine. The sun splashed edifice is the only designated skyscraper in the Columbia River Gorge! Wheat was once milled here, and today it's home to Quenett and Copa Di Vino wineries, which showcase their wines along with a short menu of gourmet lunch items and a rotating cast of events. Take some time to explore the grounds, which has original milling machinery, an outdoor amphitheater, and more. This is a popular local spot for weddings and events.

One the best French restaurants and bakeries in the area is **Petite Provence** (408 E. 2nd St., 541/506-0037, www.provencepdx.com, 7am-3pm daily, $12). With a few locations in Portland, this outpost in The Dalles is their farthest afield. Breakfast is the stunner, with savory omelets and Benedicts (try the Wild Salmon Hash), or grab a pastry to go, like the macarons, tarts, brioches, or flaky croissants.

Baldwin Saloon (205 Court St., 541/296-5666, 11am-9pm Mon.-Thurs., 11am-10pm Fri.-Sat., $16) has been around since 1876 in numerous iterations—including a brothel. Today the bar still has a rich, elegant interior with original 19th-century oil paintings, chandeliers, a mahogany bar, and a piano from 1894 whose keys are tickled on the weekends. The menu includes items from a simple but great burger to scallops in a cream and sherry sauce, and the bar serves Pacific Northwest wines and a full cocktail menu.

Montira's Thai Cuisine (302 W. 2nd St., 541/769-0550, 11am-9pm Tues.-Sun., $12) serves traditional Thai favorites made with care. Curries are balanced and tasty, while the black jasmine rice gives the plates a punch.

Shopping
Yesterday & Today Records (414 E. 2nd St., 541/296-1441, 10am-5:30pm Mon.-Sat.) specializes in 1960s and 1970s rock, but you'll find good choices in every category at this small store. Prices are lower than in Portland, so snap up your favorites!

All your crafting needs will be fulfilled at **Urban Paper** (415 E. 2nd St., 541/298-2767, 10am-6pm daily), which has racks and racks of beautiful stock for any paper fanatic, and lots of other gifts and craft supplies to go with it.

Accommodations
Settle in for the night on the bluffs just east of town at the ★ **Celilo Inn** (3550 E. 2nd St., 541/769-0001, www.celiloinn. com, $90-150), a renovated retro motel in full view of Mount Hood. Each of the 46 rooms has comfortable beds featuring sweeping views of the Columbia River above the Dalles Dam. In summer, enjoy the outdoor mineral pool—great for cooling off on hot dry days—and live music on the outdoor patio. You'll receive a free pour of wine on check-in, and a Columbia Gorge Wine Passport that confers discounts to six area wineries and 2-for-1 deals at three local museums.

Stay in one of the 64 comfortable rooms at **The Dalles Inn** (112 W. 2nd St., 541/296-9107, www.thedallesinn.com, $80-130). On the main drag within walking distance of plenty of restaurants, bars,

and attractions, the inn has a fitness center and heated outdoor pool on-site, and rooms are dog-friendly.

Rowena Crest Viewpoint and Tom McCall Nature Preserve
Breathtaking **Rowena Crest Viewpoint** is high on a bluff. At the height of the plateau, look east toward The Dalles for a stunning view of the Columbia River. Any time of year is lovely here, and don't discount a rainy day—the mist and fog only add to the view's poetic moodiness. Spring offers a wildflower profusion of balsamroot and lupine, peaking March-April, and fall showcases a blaze of colors.

Accessible from the viewpoint are hiking trails at **Tom McCall Nature Preserve.** The moderate **Tom McCall Point Trail** (May-Oct.) follows parts of an old road that was likely an 1870s wagon road from The Dalles to Hood River. You'll get amazing views in all directions on this 3.25-mile (5.2-km) hike, gaining 1,070 feet (326 m) of elevation, and in summer the area is abloom with wildflowers. Mount Adams can be seen to the north, and to the west are Mount Defiance and an elegantly arched bridge. From the summit are views of Mount Hood. Stay mindful as you hike that the area can be full of poison oak. Note that there are no restrooms and dogs are not allowed in the park. Budget 2.5 hours for the hike.

Getting There
From The Dalles, drive 13 miles (21 km) west on I-84, and take exit 76 from I-84 to get on the historic highway. Or take the historic highway directly there, driving 12 miles (19 km) west on U.S. 30. The drive up to the view loops past elegant cherry orchards.

Hood River
Emigrants rode the rapids of the Columbia River past today's Hood River, but a few pioneers pushed into the area by land and found a nice place to settle.

Traveler's Choice:
Columbia River Gorge or Mount Hood?

When emigrants arrived at The Dalles, the trail before them required a different sort of navigation. No more driving mules and oxen overland, as the route transitioned to the rocky impassable gorge, with the mighty Columbia River tearing through. The only way forward was to make a raft, buy one from local Native Americans, or rent a boat from the Hudson's Bay Company for the exorbitant cost of $80 (roughly $1,500 today). Emigrants rode the river to Fort Vancouver, where they were encouraged by the resident British officers to continue south to Oregon City; Britain's Hudson's Bay Company occupied lands north of the Columbia in today's Washington, and weren't thrilled to see emigrants arriving to strengthen the United States' claims to the area. Floating the river was a final, often deadly, hurdle to overcome. Many rafts overturned on the rapids; supplies were lost, and pioneers drowned. If emigrants chose not to rent or buy a boat, they needed to turn their wagons into rafts—the wooden vessels were unloaded, disassembled, and rebuilt to create a raft to float on, with people and supplies placed on top.

In 1845 Sam Barlow ran out of patience while waiting for a raft and forged a path around Mount Hood with his wagon party, later returning with financial backing to carve out the rough Barlow Road. It officially opened in 1846, offering pioneers an alternative to floating the river. But the route was treacherous in its own way, with one of the steepest and most dangerous descents of the entire trail at Laurel Hill. What was perhaps most offensive to pioneers was that Barlow charged a toll for his road—$5 per wagon (about $160 today). After traveling for five months and over 1,000 miles (1,060 km), they balked at being charged a toll for this final, possibly deadly, section. Perhaps given this, almost one in four emigrants still chose to float the river even after the Barlow Road opened.

Today's travelers also have a choice: Drive along the Columbia River Gorge or around Mount Hood to arrive in Oregon City. While the emigrants made this choice at The Dalles, modern travelers typically decide just west of the town, at **Hood River.** Both routes from here offer spectacular scenery and recreational options. If you have time, both scenic areas are easy to backtrack to if you'd like to choose one and return from Portland to experience the other later.

♦ Continuing along the **Columbia River Gorge route,** you'll come upon **Cascade Locks** with its sternwheeler, great **hiking** opportunities, and multiple waterfalls, including the stunning **Multnomah Falls.** Since the pioneers traveled this section by river raft, there isn't much evidence of their journey along the way. For this route, you can choose to drive primarily on **I-84,** or hop on the slower but more scenic **Historic Columbia River Highway (U.S. 30)**—itself something of an attraction—which adds about 30 minutes of driving to this stretch.

♦ The **Barlow Road route** (page 377) follows the **Mount Hood Scenic Byway** via **Highway 35 and U.S. 26,** which takes 15 or 45 minutes longer to drive than taking either the Historic Columbia River Highway (U.S. 30) or I-84 along the gorge, respectively, but you'll have a chance to stop at iconic **Timberline Lodge,** discover **hiking** options in summer and **skiing and snowboarding** options in winter, and find more **trail-related evidence,** including more ruts and grave sites.

In the 1850s, Nathaniel Coe was one of the first to plant fruit trees in the valley, and by the early 1900s Hood River became famous for its apples. Today, the region's orchards produce bushels of delicious treats—the area is particularly known for Anjou pears—and the charming small town is a hot spot of windsurfing and kiteboarding activity. Hood River is also known for its burgeoning food scene, and for making some of the state's best brews.

Getting There
From The Dalles, head west on I-84 for 23 miles (37 km). Take exit 63 for downtown Hood River; the drive takes 30 minutes. From the I-84/U.S. 30 junction for Rowena Crest, Hood River is just 13 miles (21 km) west via I-84.

Downtown Hood River is on a small bluff, along the main thoroughfare of Oak Street. You can access the waterfront by heading north on 2nd Street.

Sights
Fruit Loop
Spend an afternoon tooling around the **Fruit Loop** (www.hoodriverfruitloop. com). The roughly 30-mile (48-km) loop passes farms, orchards, vineyards, and lavender fields set against the backdrop of white-peaked Mount Hood, for a scenic drive or bike ride. March-May, the fruit trees and flower fields blossom in profusion, while September-November brings stunning fall colors and pumpkin festivals. Depending on the season, you'll find U-pick options that include peaches, cherries, blueberries, and more—you can find over 80 varieties of apples and pears in the area. Notable stops along the way include:

- **The Gorge White House** (2265 Hwy. 35, 541/386-2828, www.thegorge whitehouse.com, 10am-6pm Fri.- Mon. Apr.-May and Oct., 10am-6pm Tues.-Thurs., 10am-7pm Fri.-Mon. June-Sept., 11am-5pm Fri.-Mon. Nov.,

noon-5pm Sat.-Sun. Dec.) lets you taste expertly crafted wine, beer, and cider from the region.

- **Packer Orchards & Bakery** (3900 Hwy. 35, 541/234-4481, http://packer orchards.com, 11am-5pm Fri.-Sun. Apr., 11am-5pm Wed.-Sun. May, 10am-5pm daily June-Oct., 11am-4pm Fri.-Sun. Nov.-mid-Dec.) serves yummy apple pies, cookies, and more. Get a huckleberry cinnamon roll and peach milk shake to melt all your troubles away.

- **Draper Girls Country Farm** (6200 Hwy. 35, 541/490-8113, www.draper girlscountryfarm.com, 10am-6pm daily June-Nov.) has seasonal U-pick dahlias, fresh-pressed apple cider, and plenty of fruit like apples, pears, peaches, cherries, raspberries, blueberries, and more.

To embark on the loop, head south from Hood River on Highway 35 to Parkdale, then back north on Highway 281. You can pick up a detailed map at the **Hood Rivers Visitors Center** (720 E. Port Marina Dr., 541/386-2000, http://visithoodriver.com, 9am-5pm Mon.-Fri., 10am-4pm Sat.-Sun.), or at most stops along the way.

History Museum of Hood River County
The **History Museum of Hood River County** (300 E. Port Marina Dr., 541/386-6772, http://hoodriverhistorymuseum. org, 11am-4pm Mon.-Sat., $5) is in a cheery yellow building near the river. A giant red waterwheel outside celebrates the region's river-focused heritage. Inside, a range of artifacts delves deeper into the region's indigenous history as well as early settler life. Kids will enjoy the hands-on activities of the Children's Exploration Space.

Recreation
Windsurfing and Kiteboarding
The winds that whip through the canyon of the gorge create some blustery days, but fans of windsurfing and

kiteboarding wouldn't have it any other way. Whether you're new to the sports or an old pro, you'll find plenty of fun out on the water. The best access is at the marina and public beachfront, reached by heading north from downtown on 2nd Street. Public access stretches west to **Hood River Waterfront Park,** a relatively new community park with a sandy beachfront, an excellent kids' playground, and a small rock-climbing wall. This is a great jumping-off spot for water adventures, and even if you'd like to stay dry, it's still a fun place to hang out and watch the windsurfers and kiteboarders in action.

For lessons and rentals, head over to **Hood River WaterPlay** (100 Port Marina Way, 541/386-9463, http://hoodriverwaterplay.com, 9am-5pm daily), where friendly staff will get you set up on their private beach near the Best Western. You can try out windsurfing (rentals $68 per day, lessons from $89) or Hobie Cat sailing (rentals $119-159 per day, lessons from $139). For an easier water outing, you can also rent stand up paddleboards (rentals and lessons $20 per hour), kayaks ($20-25 per hour), or Jet Skis (rentals $89 per hour, $249 for 4 hours).

Historic Columbia River Highway State Trail

The **Historic Columbia River Highway State Trail** (http://oregonstateparks.org) has repurposed old stretches of U.S. 30 into walking-biking trails, closed to car traffic. The easternmost of these runs 4.5 miles (7.2 km) from Hood River east to Mosier, and heads through the lovely Mosier Twin Tunnels. Covered in rubble until the 1950s, they have been lovingly restored for access again.

From Hood River, drive east via State Street, then veer left onto Old Columbia River Drive. You'll find the parking lot

Top to bottom: apples on the Hood River Fruit Loop; windsurfing in Hood River; waterfall along the Historic Columbia River Highway State Trail.

($5 per vehicle) for the western Mark O. Hatfield Trailhead in 1.3 miles (2.1 km). The drive from town takes less than 10 minutes. For the eastern trailhead and parking lot ($5 per vehicle), head east out of town via I-84. After 5.5 miles (8.9 km), take exit 69 for Mosier, turn right on U.S. 30, and then make a quick left onto Rock Creek Road. You'll arrive in 0.7 mile (1.1 km). The drive from Hood River takes just over 10 minutes.

Biking

Beautiful bicycling options abound in every direction in Hood River. Hop on the Fruit Loop or bike the car-free section of the Historic Columbia River Highway to Mosier. Head to **Discover Bicycles** (201 State St., 541/386-4820, www.discoverbicycles.com, 10am-6pm Mon.-Fri., 10am-5pm Sat.-Sun.) for cruisers ($40 per day) and road bikes ($60 per day), or **Hood River Bicycles** (208 4th St., 541/387-3276, http://hoodriverbicycles. com, 9am-5pm Wed.-Sun.) for full-suspension bikes ($100-150 per day), mountain bikes ($80 per day), or kids' bikes ($35 per day).

Entertainment
Brewpubs

Full Sail Brew Pub (506 Columbia St., 541/386-2247, www.fullsailbrewing. com, 11am-11pm daily) is the largest of the town's breweries and has been churning out beer since 1987. Its amber, pilsner, and IPAs have won 40 awards over the years. The brewpub has a scenic setting overlooking the Columbia River and also offers tasty pub grub. You can join a 30-minute brewery tour (4pm Mon.-Fri., 1pm and 3pm Sat.-Sun., free).

Named for the two big volcanos you can see from Hood River—Mount Hood and Mount Adams—**Double Mountain Brewery** (8 4th St., 541/387-0042, www. doublemountainbrewery.com, 11am-close daily) was founded by a Full Sail brewer and whips up an award-winning India Red Ale, an easy drinking Kolsch,

and other fantastic beers, along with artisanal pizzas and sandwiches. The taproom is cozy and offers regular live music. On nice days you can spread out to the sidewalk. Kids are welcome until 9pm.

pFriem Family Brewers (707 Portway Ave., 541/321-0490, www.pfriembeer. com, 11:30am-9pm daily) finds its place in the beer-saturated town by focusing on Belgian-style and sour beers. The kid-friendly tasting room is big and modern, with large tables and outdoor seating. Even so, you might find yourself waiting for a spot. The menu is based on seasonal local goods and features a smoky mac and cheese, Belgian mussels and *frites,* and the gravy goodness of poutine.

Festivals and Events

Hood River's most popular events (www. visithoodriver.com) tend to focus on the region's bounty. In April, celebrate **Blossom Time,** a monthlong celebration throughout the Fruit Loop marked by various farm events, craft shows, and wine and cider tastings. At the end of summer, turn your sights to downtown's **Hood River Hops Fest** ($10 adults, $20 beer tasting, free under age 21), with over 40 local breweries showcasing their skills. Late fall brings the **Harvest Fest** ($8 adults, free under age 12), a three-day event on the Hood River waterfront that sees over 120 booths overflowing with harvest bounty, with all the fun of an old-fashioned fall festival—including giant pumpkins!

Food

Find excellent Scandinavian fare at ★ **Broder Øst** (102 Oak St., 541/436-3444, www.brodereast.com, 7am-2pm Mon.-Fri., 7am-3pm Sat.-Sun., $13), tucked into the bottom floor of the Hood River Hotel. The fourth outpost of the Portland-based Swedish café offers breakfast and lunch. Try the Danish *æbleskivers* (spherical pancakes served with lingonberry jam and lemon curd),

Swedish meatballs, or smoked trout hash. Wash it down with an aquavit-laced cocktail like the Danish Mary or a *spanska* (Spanish coffee, Swedish-style).

Just steps away from the windsurfers, ★ **Solstice Wood Fire Cafe & Bar** (501 Portway Ave., 541/436-0800, www.solsticewoodfirecafe.com, 11am-8pm Sun.-Mon. and Wed.-Thurs., 11am-9pm Fri.-Sat., $15) is a beloved local spot for its wood-fired pizzas and regional craft beer selection. Pizzas are topped with ingredients inspired by the gorge, such as the award-winning Country Girl Cherry with fruit from down the road and housemade chorizo sausage. Finish off with a wood-fired s'more—a broiled homemade marshmallow and graham cracker topped with chocolate ganache. The restaurant is kid-friendly and has gluten-free and vegan options.

With a deep knowledge of where their food comes from, **Celilo Restaurant and Bar** (16 Oak St., 541/386-5710, www.celilorestaurant.com, 5pm-10pm Mon.-Thurs., 11:30am-3pm and 5pm-10pm Fri.-Sun. May-Oct., 5pm-10pm daily Nov.-Apr., $23) is a mainstay that offers a taste of the Columbia River Gorge in every season, with locally foraged mushrooms, locally grown vegetables, and locally fished salmon. The dining room has a warm mountain lodge feel, and the fantastic food and award-winning wine list elevate it to an upscale experience.

Lake Taco (1213 June St., 541/386-2276, 11am-8pm Mon.-Sat., $6) is a hidden gem that serves fresh Mexican food. *Tortas,* carne asada, burritos, Baja-style fish tacos, and posole grace the small menu, which is full of hits. Made-to-order handmade corn tortillas come warm. It's hidden off 13th Street; coming from downtown, you turn left into what looks like an alleyway, but you will soon find the restaurant—it's a riot of color.

Bette's Place (416 Oak St., 541/386-1880, www.bettesplace.com, 5:30am-3pm daily, $12) is a comfortable diner that serves a killer breakfast and lunch—like the giant plate-size cinnamon rolls, the Dungeness crab omelet, and homemade soups, sandwiches, and burgers. The family-friendly space has been operating for four decades from its central downtown location.

Shopping

Women's clothing boutique **Parts + Labour** (311 Oak St., 541/387-2787, www.parts-labour.com, 10am-6pm Mon.-Sat., 11am-5pm Sun.) has brands like Prairie Underground and Wildfox. Find warm sweaters, cool tank tops, glittering nail polish, and a selection of Portland's Betsy and Iya jewelry.

Stop in **Twiggs** (305 Oak St., 541/386-6188, www.twiggshoodriver.com, 10am-6pm Mon.-Sat., 11am-4pm Sun.) for a great selection of earrings, candles, and home goods. Find beautiful hammered brass earrings or beaded bracelets inspired by Native American designs. The shop is bright and airy and has price points for everyone.

If you have kids with you, they'll want to visit **G. Williker's Toy Shoppe** (202 Oak St., 541/387-2229, www.gwtoyshoppe.com, 10am-6pm Mon.-Sat., 10am-5pm Sun.). Find a wacky puppet or a noisy thingamabob on the 1st floor, or head downstairs to find a new game. Be sure to check out the shop's wall of stuffed animals.

Accommodations

★ **Hood River Hotel** (102 Oak St., 541/386-1900, http://hoodriverhotel.com, $110-250) is a 1912 throwback with hip modern vibes. Everything from the deer's bust in the lobby to the giant black-and-white vintage photos in the guest rooms is styled to perfection. It's right downtown for easy access to all the good stuff, though you might get too cozy indoors and spend the whole day in the sauna, by the lobby's fireplace, or in the adjoining restaurant, Broder Øst. Book a family suite that sleeps up to five and has a full kitchen, or ask for one of the ground-level, pet-friendly rooms if you're bringing the pooch.

The **Best Western Plus Hood River Inn** (1108 E. Marina Way, 541/386-2200, www.hoodriverinn.com, $113-200) has 194 guest rooms, many with balconies overlooking the Columbia River. The location is one of the best in town, with expansive views from its heated riverside pool. Get a massage after a long day of windsurfing, or ask about the free wine-tasting package at 13 local wineries. On the east side of town, the hotel has easy access to the waterfront and water-sports rentals, and is a 20-minute walk to downtown.

Cascade Locks

Thousands of years ago, a natural stone bridge crossed the mighty river at this spot. Native American legends tell of Tamanawas, the Bridge of the Gods, cared for by the Great Spirit, Sahale. Each legend differs slightly, but they all say that in time, a fight broke out between the spirit's sons over the pretty Loowit and, in the process, the stone bridge was destroyed. It tumbled into the river below, causing huge rapids to form. The sons and their love interest were turned into the region's three mountains: Mount Hood, Mount Adams, and Mount St. Helens.

In the pioneers' time, the Cascade Rapids near here posed great danger, dropping 20 feet (6 m) in 400 yards (366 m) through the narrowing canyon. Many pioneers lost their rafts or lives trying to conquer them instead of taking the extra time to portage around.

Cascade Locks today is a small community mostly known as the main connection point between Oregon and Washington via a constructed bridge that spans the river—also named the Bridge of the Gods—as well as for its location along the Pacific Crest Trail.

Getting There
From Hood River, continue west on I-84

for 17 miles (27 km), and take exit 44 for Cascade Locks. The drive takes just over 20 minutes.

Sights
Bonneville Dam
The **Bonneville Dam complex** has several areas of interest for visitors, including the dam and visitors center, the navigation locks, and the fish hatchery. You can easily spend an afternoon in the area.

The massive Bonneville Dam was completed in 1938, the first federal locks and dam on the Columbia or Snake Rivers. It remains an active hydroelectric power plant today, and has been designated a National Historic Landmark, spanning both sides of the river. On the Oregon side, head to the **Bradford Island Visitor Center** (I-84 westbound exit 40, 541/374-8820, www.nwp.usace.army.mil/bonneville, 9am-5pm daily, free), just west of Cascade Locks. Here you'll learn about the history of the river, including the dam's construction, as well as how dams affect fish migration, particularly salmon spawning. You can also view a fish ladder, which adult salmon swim through on their way upstream to spawn in September-October.

On the south bank of the river, along Bonneville Way, the **Navigation Lock Visitor Center** (1pm-4pm daily Memorial Day-Labor Day, free) has videos and small exhibits on the locks. The original locks and canal were built a few miles upstream in 1896 to allow ships to pass the dangerous Cascade Rapids. When the dam was constructed, the old locks were submerged, and a new set was built near the dam. Today these locks allow ships to pass through the Bonneville Dam; you can watch from the banks, or experience it yourself aboard the *Columbia Gorge Sternwheeler*.

Be sure to visit the **Fish Hatchery** (70543 NE Herman Loop, 541/374-8393, 7am-8pm daily Mar.-Oct., 7am-5pm daily Nov.-Feb., free), administered separately from the dam by the Oregon Department of Fish and Wildlife. The hatchery has numerous open-air ponds with chinook and coho salmon. It also hosts other types of fish for viewing, including rainbow trout that you can feed for a quarter, and sturgeon. This is a great place for kids of all ages—make sure to introduce them to Herman the Sturgeon, a 10-foot-long fish that's over 60 years old. From exit 40 off I-84, turn right on Bonneville Way. In 0.3 mile (0.5 km), take a left, following signs to the fish hatchery, onto Sturgeon Lane.

★ Columbia Gorge Sternwheeler

Ply the waters on the **Columbia Gorge Sternwheeler** (299 NW Portage Rd., 503/224-2900, www.portlandspirit. com), a paddlewheel riverboat. Choose from a one- or two-hour sightseeing cruise (Thurs.-Tues. May-Oct., $28-32) to see some of the area's wonders from the water, from old Native American fishing platforms to the Bonneville Lock and Dam. For a special night, book a dinner cruise (daily June-Oct., $55-60) to enjoy seasonal Pacific Northwest fare during twilight. You won't have to construct your own raft, but you'll cruise the waters that emigrants once floated, navigating rapids now smoothed by the dams, and the sights are much the same, from the tall basalt cliffs studded with waterfalls to the forested mountains beyond. Cruises depart from the Cascade Locks visitors center and dock.

Food

The **Eastwind Drive-In** (395 Wa Na Pa St., 541/374-8380, 6:30am-8pm daily, $10) is a favorite stop for hungry adventurers in Cascade Locks. The small shop and drive-through serves egg croissants for breakfast and cheeseburgers for lunch, but the real draws are the shakes, floats, and ice cream cones. Order a soft serve and prepare yourself—the "small" towers six inches tall!

Bridgeside (745 Wa Na Pa St., 541/374-8477, www.bridgesidedining.com, 6:30am-8pm daily, $12) has been serving burgers and other diner fare since 1963. Order at the counter, then take your food to the dining room, outside or in, for great views of the Bridge of the Gods. Make sure to try the marionberry pie!

Multnomah Falls

The most famous waterfall in the state, **Multnomah Falls** drops 620 feet (189 m), its two-tiered torrents gracing postcards and snapshots. You can see the falls from the road as you drive by, or pull into the parking area to pause and admire them. It's a short uphill walk on a paved path to Benson Bridge, a great vantage to take in the falls. For a longer hike and more views, continue uphill on the well-maintained and signed path via 11 switchbacks to the top of the falls; you'll gain 870 feet (265 m) in elevation. It's just over 1 mile (1.6 km) up to the first viewpoint, and another 0.2 mile (0.3 km) to a second viewpoint. Budget 1.5 hours for the full 2.4-mile (3.9-km) round-trip hike. Note that there are steep drops and no rails along the path.

Afterward, refuel at the **Multnomah Falls Lodge** (53000 E. Historic Columbia River Hwy., 503/695-2376, www. multnomahfallslodge.com, 9am-6pm Mon.-Thurs., 8am-8pm Fri.-Sun.), serving ice cream, coffee, and snacks since 1925 at its outdoor kiosk. Inside is a restaurant serving Pacific Northwest cuisine with views of the falls, a U.S. Forest Service information center, and a gift shop.

Getting There

From I-84, take exit 31 for Multnomah Falls. To drive the scenic Historic Columbia River Highway, take exit 35 from I-84 west of Bonneville Dam, and continue for 4 miles (6.4 km). The drive from Cascade Locks is about 13.5 miles (22 km) and takes 20 minutes either way.

Angel's Rest

The moderate 4.8-mile (7.2-km) **Angel's Rest trail** heads up a rocky bluff in the gorge and offers hikers spectacular views from the top. On the way up you'll gain 1,475 feet (450 m) in elevation and get intermittent views of some waterfalls. The trail was badly scorched by the Eagle Creek Fire in 2017 but is back in good shape after maintenance; you'll still see burned trees, especially as you climb higher, but from Angel's Rest Landing at the top are views up and down the gorge. Budget 3.5 hours for the hike. There are no handrails on the steep cliff sides, so be cautious. While most of the trail is packed dirt, some is on loose basalt rocks that are tough to get traction on. This trail is popular and can get quite busy, especially on summer weekends.

Getting There

Angel's Rest is along the Historic Columbia River Highway. From Multnomah Falls, the 3.1-mile (5-km) drive west takes 7 minutes. There's no direct access from I-84 westbound, so you have to take exit 31 for the Historic Columbia River Highway before Multnomah Falls and drive 7.7 miles (12.4 km), an 18-minute drive. From I-84 eastbound, take exit 28.

Bridal Veil Falls

Bridal Veil Falls is one of the prettiest in the gorge, gracefully falling two levels before making its way to the Columbia River. An easy 30-minute walk of just over 0.5 mile (0.8 km) takes you to it; it's great for families with young children. The path to the falls has some stairs that wind down to a creek, then head up to a wooden viewing platform in front of Bridal Veil Falls. Back near the parking lot, you can also find a paved 0.5-mile (0.8-km) loop that takes you to a gorge overlook. Along the loop, interpretive panels explain some of the geological and natural history of the area.

Getting There

Bridal Veil Falls is along the Historic Columbia River Highway. From Angel's Rest, the 0.5-mile (0.8-km) drive west on the highway takes three minutes. There's no direct access from I-84 westbound, so take exit 31 for the Historic Columbia River Highway before Multnomah Falls. From I-84 eastbound, take exit 28.

Vista House at Crown Point

The **Vista House at Crown Point** (40700 Historic Columbia River Hwy., 503/695-2230, www.vistahouse.com, 10am-4pm daily mid-Mar.-Oct.) is a fantastic spot to take in epic views of the Columbia River Gorge. Built in 1918 as a rest stop for folks traveling the old highway, it was also intended as a memorial to the pioneers who made their way down the river. It's a beautiful old building of marble and bronze in an equally beautiful location high above the river. While the main attraction is the outdoor views, visitors can step inside for a small historical exhibit. A gift shop and espresso cart are also here.

Getting There

Vista House at Crown Point is along the Historic Columbia River Highway. From Bridal Veil Falls, the 4.5-mile (7.2-km) drive west takes 13 minutes.

Troutdale

After making it through the rapids in one piece, many pioneers got off the river as soon as they could find a sandy bank, which was near present-day Troutdale. The small community is located at the gateway to the Columbia River Gorge and its convergence with the Sandy River. Most emigrants reassembled their rafts into wagons here to head south in their final push to Oregon City and the Willamette Valley. In the 1850s, some emigrants chose to settle nearby in the grassy treeless meadows—their location was lucky, as later emigrants who decided

Cascade Locks to Troutdale

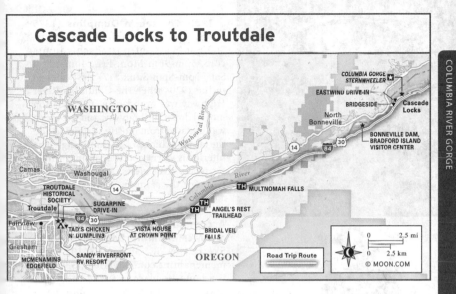

to stay had to clear the land of old-growth firs before they could farm.

Getting There

Troutdale is along the Historic Columbia River Highway. From Vista House at Crown Point, the 9-mile (14.5-km) drive west on the highway takes 20 minutes. From I-84 westbound, take exit 18 and turn left onto Jordan Road/Crown Point Highway, which winds around and follows the Sandy River south. In 0.7 mile (1.1 km), turn right to head over the bridge, returning to the Historic Columbia River Highway and following it into town.

Sights and Recreation

The **Troutdale Historical Society** (726 E. Historic Columbia River Hwy., 503/661-2164, www.troutdalehistory.org) runs a few nearby museums, including the stately **Harlow House** (1pm-3pm Sun., free) built in 1900, the **Depot Rail Museum** (10am-2pm Fri., free), with its cheery yellow Union Pacific caboose, and the bright red **Barn Exhibit Hall** (10am-3pm Wed.-Sat., 1pm-3pm Sun., $5 adults, free under age 13), which has rotating exhibits. Behind the Harlow House, faint ruts are still visible in the hill, from pioneers who reassembled their wagons to head south to Oregon City.

Enjoy the river from Troutdale's sandy banks at **Glenn Otto Community Park** (1102 E. Historic Columbia River Hwy.), a popular summertime swimming hole. The mile-long (1.6-km) beach is a prime spot for sunshine, with plenty of sand and shallow spots for splashing about, but be warned that it gets crowded, and the current is strong; weak swimmers should use caution.

Food

The Instagrammable aesthetics of ★ **Sugarpine Drive-In** (1208 E. Historic Columbia River Hwy., 503/665-6558, www.sugarpinedrivein.com, 11am-6pm Wed.-Thurs. and Sun., 11am-9pm Fri.-Sat., $7) are expertly curated, but the food is worth enjoying after that selfie. Crisp salads, piled-high sandwiches, and grilled cheese waffles with kimchi go head-to-head with soft-serve ice cream and frosé (that is, frozen rosé). Enjoy them all on the banks of the Sandy River at this hip retro-style eatery.

Tad's Chicken 'n Dumplins (1325 E. Historic Columbia River Hwy., 503/666-5337, http://tadschicdump. com, 5pm-9pm Mon.-Fri., 4pm-10pm Sat., 3pm-8pm Sun., $17) first opened in the 1920s when the Columbia River Highway was brand-new. The location moved down the highway, and the menu was updated from mostly seafood to add the famous chicken and dumplings. The interior is warm and welcoming, with a fireplace, river views, and a lodge-like feel. Try the salmon, smoked on local alder wood.

Accommodations and Camping

★ **McMenamins Edgefield** (2126 SW Halsey St., 503/669-8610, www. mcmenamins.com/edgefield, $80-170) is a fantastic place to spend the night. Owned by the local McMenamins company, masters in restoring and transforming historical properties into quirky resorts, the site was a farm in the early 1900s. On 74 acres of old farmland, Edgefield has 100 rooms—with both private and shared bath options—and is a world unto itself, with restaurants, bars, a first-run movie theater, two par-3 golf courses, an on-site glassblower, and a soaking pool. It's also home to a popular live music venue. The property is just a 20-minute drive from Portland. Some rooms are pet-friendly.

If you're road-tripping in an RV, a good option is the **Sandy Riverfront RV Resort** (1097 E. Historic Columbia River Hwy., 503/665-6722, www.sandyrv.com, $48). Bordered by the Sandy River and a creek behind it, the property features plenty of sites with water views. It's also within walking distance to Troutdale's main street and river access. Portland is about a 20-minute drive, making this a good base.

Top to bottom: Multnomah Falls; soft serve at Sugarpine Drive-In in Troutdale; Fort Vancouver.

Vancouver, WA

Vancouver, Washington, shares its name with the Canadian city, but the U.S. city is actually older. It owes its existence to the Hudson's Bay Company's Fort Vancouver, an economic and political hub in the region for decades. Before that, Lewis and Clark visited the area in 1805, with Meriwether Lewis noting its superior location for settlement. The British kept their foothold in the Pacific Northwest via Fort Vancouver in the beginning of the 19th century, but Oregon Trail settlers soon overwhelmed the area, and the United States eventually gained control.

Vancouver was separated from Portland, just across the Columbia River, until 1917, when the Interstate Bridge was built. Today the bridge is a major traffic artery between the cities. Vancouver, or "the 'Couve," as it's sometimes called, is always in the shadow of the bigger and more bustling Portland. The smaller but thriving city shines with some pioneer history, beautiful riverfront views, and craft beer, of course.

Getting There

To get to Vancouver, you have to cross the Columbia River, which can be a commuting nightmare given its proximity to Portland; try to avoid rush hour (8am-10am and 3pm-6pm Mon.-Fri.) if possible. During these times, I-205 is a better option than I-5. Depending on your level of interest in the historic fort—the primary attraction—you may choose to skip this stop on the way to Oregon City, or make it a side trip from Portland later.

From **Troutdale,** head west on Halsey Street for 1.2 miles (1.9 km), then turn right onto NE 238th Drive, using one of the left two lanes to merge onto I-84 westbound. In 6 miles (9.7 km), take exit 9 for I-205 north to cross the Columbia River. Take exit 27 in 4.2 miles (6.8 km), and keep left to merge onto Highway 14.

Continue 5.7 miles (9.2 km), then use the middle lane to exit to "City Center." The total drive covers 20 miles (32 km) and take 25 minutes.

From **Portland,** head north via I-5 for 7 miles (11.3 km), and take exit 1B toward the city center. Without traffic, the drive takes 15 minutes.

Sights and Recreation
Fort Vancouver

Fort Vancouver was built in 1825 as the headquarters of the British Hudson's Bay Company, a thriving fur-trading business. Over the years, and especially under the leadership of John McLoughlin, the fort grew to be the center of the region's political, cultural, and commercial activities. Employees of the company lived with their families in cabins just outside the fort, which acted as a storehouse for goods and trading operations. Many emigrants aimed their rafts here as they floated down the Columbia River in the 1830s and 1840s. McLoughlin offered them hospitality and supplies for their final push south to Oregon City. He provided hundreds of loans to penniless emigrants, many of which were never repaid. Because of his generosity and kindness toward American emigrants, he fell out of favor with the Hudson's Bay Company and later moved to Oregon City, becoming known as the "Father of Oregon."

In 1866, Fort Vancouver burned down, and in the 20th century the National Park Service built a reconstruction on the fort's original footprint. **Fort Vancouver National Historic Site** (1501 E. Evergreen Blvd., 360/816-6230, www.nps.gov/fova, visitors center and fort 9am-4pm Tues.-Sat., grounds dawn-dusk daily, fort $10 adults, free under age 16, grounds free) comprises the reconstructed fort, a series of barracks buildings now occupied by government offices, and the long-running Pearson Airfield and adjacent aviation museum. The grounds require a bit of walking, but the trails are ADA-friendly. Start at the **visitors center** for maps and to see a short introductory film and an exhibit featuring Native American artifacts.

If you're short on time, head straight to the **reconstructed fort,** where you can wander on your own. A counting house and trade warehouse give a sense of the massive trading operations that took place here—it was the West's largest trading fort in the 19th century. You can also visit the home of the head trader, called the chief factor; the impressive house acted as a cultural hub and center of political strategy, with a large hall for hosting regular parties. If a visiting wagon train included prominent people, they might have enjoyed tea with McLoughlin during their visit. The garden outside the fort flourishes in summer, growing historically accurate produce such as beets, carrots, cabbage, peas, and many flowers, including roses and dahlias.

Living-history demonstrations allow visitors to watch a master blacksmith create weapons at his forge, or a baker pull a batch of sea biscuits from a giant brick oven. These demonstrations are volunteer-based and not always on a regular schedule, though summer weekends are the best time to catch them. If you're visiting in winter (Nov.-Mar.), sign up for a guided nighttime Lantern Tour for a look at the fort by candlelight.

Also on the grounds is the **Pearson Air Museum** (9am-4pm Tues.-Sat., free), which tells the story of Vancouver's surprisingly rich aviation history. During World War I this was a renowned spruce mill site, producing lumber for airplanes 24 hours a day. The adjacent Pearson Field is one of the oldest continuously operating airfields in the country. The museum is well organized, and visitors will come away with a sense of aviation history. The museum showcases biplanes that performed acrobatics in the early 20th century, and plenty of World War II-era items.

Alongside the fort's grounds, you'll find **Officer's Row,** stately Victorian houses where British officers and their families used to live. A few houses are open to the public, including the **Marshall House** (1301 Officers Row, 360/693-3103, www.cchmuseum.org, 9am-5pm Mon.-Sat., $3-5), with its beautiful stained-glass windows. Admission includes a guided tour of the house. Or enjoy a glass of wine with dinner at the **Grant House Restaurant** (1101 Officers Row, 360/906-1101, http://eateryatthegranthouse.com, 11am-9pm Tues.-Fri., 10am-9pm Sat., 10pm-3pm Sun., $20).

Vancouver Waterfront

Vancouver Waterfront Park (5am-10pm) reopened in 2018 as a newly redeveloped green space following decades of planning. At the riverfront promenade's center is **Grant Street Pier;** notice how the cables evoke the rigging of a ship. The pier juts out over the river and offers stunning views. For a nice stroll, head east 1 mile (1.6 km) under I-5 to connect to the **Waterfront Renaissance Trail,** which stretches 5 miles (8 km) along the river to the small **Wintler Community Park,** which has more great river views. From here, you can walk to or from Fort Vancouver via the **Vancouver Land Bridge,** a landscaped footpath that arches over busy Highway 14, featuring native plants, artwork, and interpretive panels that pay homage to the region's indigenous people and rivers. On the south side of the bridge, watch for the gated Old Apple Tree, planted in 1826.

From the Fort Vancouver National Historic Site's entrance, it's an 0.3-mile (0.5-km) walk to the bridge, and another 0.4-mile (0.6-km) walk across the bridge to the waterfront. If you'd prefer to drive, Columbia Street parallels the river and offers plenty of parking options.

Food

Known for reinvigorating historic sites in Oregon and Washington with whimsical style, McMenamins's properties always evoke a unique sense of place. Stop by **McMenamins on the Columbia** (1801 SE Columbia River Dr., 360/699-1521, www.mcmenamins.com, 11am-1am Sun.-Thurs., 11am-1am Fri.-Sat., $14) for riverside dining with stunning views. On the waterfront, the restaurant is built on the site of World War II shipyards. Grab a pint and some Cajun tots to enjoy in the sun on the patio.

For great local beer and a little pinball, stop by **Loowit Brewing** (507 Columbia St., 360/566-2323, www.loowitbrewing. com, 11am-10pm Sun.-Thurs., 11am-11pm Fri.-Sat., $10). Its 18 taps pour award-winning beer and cider, and the food menu includes burgers made from beef, elk, lamb, black beans, and boar.

Alternate Route: Barlow Road Around Mount Hood

In 1845, Sam Barlow—spurred on by impatience waiting for a raft to float down the Columbia River—forged a path skirting the impressive peak of Mount Hood, through dense forest and cliffs. In 1846, the Barlow Road opened, offering emigrants an alternative to floating the river, for a fee—wagons were charged a $5 toll (about $160 today) for passage. Some pioneers regretted their decision to follow the road, encountering deep snow and steep cliffs on the route. Even today, vehicles in winter struggle to get through the pass in snowy conditions. Nevertheless, the Barlow Road remained in operation until 1915.

The Barlow Road headed south from The Dalles to what's now the small community of **Dufur**, a route traced today by U.S. 197, before veering west on a path following today's Dufur Valley Road/ Forest Road 44 to connect with Highway 35. While drivable, the small Dufur Valley Road isn't well maintained and is closed in winter (mid-Dec.-Mar.) due to heavy snow. Most travelers today head south on **Highway 35** from **Hood River,** connecting with **U.S. 26**—which was built over much of the original Barlow Road in the 1920s—to loop around Mount Hood to **Sandy;** this route is part of the **Mount Hood Scenic Byway.** The 71-mile (114-km) drive takes 1.5 hours.

Today the old Barlow Road route is full of villages mostly geared to locals and Portlanders heading to the slopes for summer or winter fun.

TOP EXPERIENCE

Mount Hood

The snowy peak of Mount Hood is one of Oregon's most recognizable sights, visible from Portland on a clear day. It's actually a volcano and part of the Cascade Range. While it's considered dormant, scientists say there is a small possibility it could still be active and erupt someday.

The mountain is known as Wy'east by the Indigenous Multnomah people. According to legend, the two sons of the Great Spirit, Sahale, fell in love with a beautiful woman, Loowit. She loved them both, and to prove their love, the warriors, Pahto and Wy'east, fought fiercely. They burned the trees of the forest and destroyed whole villages in their rage, which angered Sahale. To stop the destruction, Sahale destroyed the great natural stone arch of Tamanawas, "the Bridge of the Gods," which fell into the river and created bubbling rapids, and he turned the three lovers into towering peaks: Loowit became the beautiful Mount St. Helens, Wy'east the proud Mount Hood, and mourning Pahto the smaller Mount Adams.

Today Mount Hood is an outdoor paradise known for summertime hiking and excellent winter sports like skiing, snowboarding, and snowshoeing. The Timberline Lodge is a top destination for overnight stays or a day trip, and the town of Government Camp has great brews and alpine-inspired eats.

Getting There and Around

From **Hood River,** drive south on Highway 35 for 39 miles (63 km), then merge onto U.S. 26. In 3 miles (4.8 km), you'll arrive at Government Camp, a base for Mount Hood. The drive takes 50 minutes.

Orientation

An alpine-style village on the slopes of Mount Hood, **Government Camp** on **U.S. 26** is the primary jumping-off point to explore the mountain, with the smaller communities of **Rhododendron, Zigzag,** and **Welches** west of town on U.S. 26.

Fees

If you plan on hiking while in the vicinity, note that most trailhead parking areas around Mount Hood require a **Northwest Forest Pass;** the day-use fee is $5 per vehicle. You can purchase it at many of the local businesses or ranger stations around the mountain, including in Dufur, Government Camp, Welches, Zigzag, and Sandy, or online (http://store.usgs.gov/forest-pass). In winter you'll need a **Sno-Park permit** ($4 per day, $9 for 3 days) instead.

Sights and Recreation

Timberline Lodge

Perched high on Mount Hood, iconic **Timberline Lodge** (27500 E. Timberline Rd., 503/272-3410, www.timberlinelodge.com/lodge) was built in 1937 as a Works Progress Administration project, and details from the handrails to the stone fireplace have been carefully handcrafted by artists—admire them as you wander around. The structure is famous for its starring role (exteriors only) in the 1980 movie *The Shining.* Even if you're not spending the night, stop by to soak up the atmosphere, warm up by the giant fireplace, or enjoy a hot chocolate or craft beer at one of the on-site bars or restaurants.

Or spend the day on the slopes behind the lodge (Nov.-Memorial Day, lift ticket $87 adults, $72 ages 15-17, $52 ages 7-14 and 65-70, free under age 7 and over age 70). In winter, **ski and snowboard equipment rentals** ($46 adults, $36 ages 5-15, $18 under 5) as well as some **snowshoes** ($20 pp) are available on-site. In summer, hop on a chairlift for the **Magic Mile Sky Ride** (opening hours subject to weather conditions, $18 pp, $54 family of four, free for children under 7), which ascends to a 7,000-foot (2,134-m) peak, where you'll find snow as well as spectacular views. The round-trip ride takes 30 minutes total, or you can walk back down; allow two hours for the one-way descent.

Pioneer Woman's Grave

In 1924 engineers were hard at work building the Mount Hood Scenic Byway, following Highway 35 south from Hood River and looping up northwest via U.S. 26, tracing much of the old Barlow Road route, when they came upon an old wooden wagon tongue and a wooden casket. It was the crude grave site of an unidentified pioneer woman who once traveled the Barlow Road. She was carefully reinterred and the site was marked by a cairn of rocks—today it's easily identifiable, and informational signs provide hints as to who she might've been.

Take an easy 2.2-mile (3.5-km) round-trip walk along the Barlow Road to see the **Pioneer Woman's Grave** via the **Barlow Road Trail,** where you'll see a sign that says "Old Barlow Road." You'll follow the old roadbed for much of the hike, which takes about an hour total, winding through Douglas firs, hemlock, and cedar, with occasional views of Mount Hood. Look for trail ruts along the way. In summer, there are plenty of fruiting huckleberry bushes. The grave is marked by a large pile of rocks—join past visitors by placing your own rock here to honor this pioneer's memory. From the grave site, look for where the road crosses the East Fork Salmon

Mount Hood

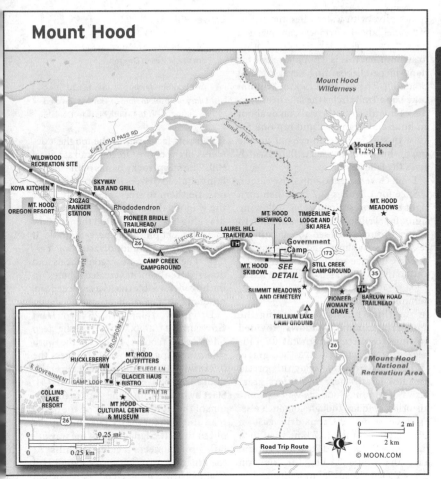

River—past the river signage, there's a small trail leading off to the right, which you can follow to find some wonderfully preserved wagon ruts.

The Barlow Road Trailhead/Sno-Park is just off Highway 35 about 5.5 miles (8.9 km) east of Government Camp. You'll need a Northwest Forest Pass ($5). You'll see the entrance to the hike on your left as you drive into the trailhead's parking lot.

If you want to skip the walk, you can drive here. From the Barlow Road Trailhead, drive 2 miles (3.2 km) west

on Highway 35 and look for a sign for the grave site. From Government Camp, drive 3 miles (4.8 km) east, just past the Highway 35/U.S. 26 junction, and look for the grave-site sign. Turn right on Forest Road 3531 and drive 2 miles (3.2 km) to the grave site parking, along the road.

Trillium Lake

Trillium Lake is a gorgeous jewel, with snowcapped Mount Hood standing tall behind it. It's a popular destination for Portlanders in summer, when the lake comes alive with water lilies and thimbleberries, and day-trippers can splash in the water and picnic lakeside. In addition to swimming, this is a popular place for stand-up paddleboarding, kayaking, and canoeing. The 1.9-mile (3-km) **Trillium Lake Loop Trail** circles the lake over a series of boardwalks; the walk takes about an hour and is an easy and fun one for kids. In spring, keep an eye out for the small white three-petaled trillium, which gives the lake its name.

From Government Camp, drive east on U.S. 26 for 1.7 miles (2.7 km), then turn right onto Forest Road 2656, following signs for Trillium Lake Trailhead. In winter, this road is closed, though still accessible to snowshoers and cross-country skiers. Continue south for 1.8 miles (2.9 km) to the Trillium Lake Day-Use Area.

Summit Meadows

In the thick forests surrounding the mountain, **Summit Meadows** provided an important stopping point for pioneers to rest, let their livestock graze, and gather strength. Today this pretty meadow is still here and offers great views of Mount Hood, as well as some historical plaques, though not much else. From Government Camp, drive east on U.S. 26 for 1.7 miles (2.7 km), then turn right onto Forest Road 2656 for Trillium Lake. In 0.5 mile (0.8 km), turn right on Perry Vickers Road. Summit Meadows is on the right in 0.4 mile (0.6 km).

Just north of the meadows off Perry Vickers Road you can find the small **Summit Meadows Pioneer Cemetery,** surrounded by a white fence. Perry Vickers, a Barlow Road toll gatekeeper 1866-1870, is buried here, along with several others. There's also the sad grave of "Baby Morgan," a five-month-old infant traveling on the Oregon Trail who died in 1847.

You can backtrack the way you came, or you can keep following the old trail route, continuing north on Perry Vickers Road to reconnect with U.S. 26.

Laurel Hill

"This is the worse hill on the road from the States to Oregon."

Absolom Harden, September 20, 1847, *Diary of Absolom Harden*. Harden traveled the trail in 1847 with his wife, Delilah.

Emigrants faced one of the toughest descents of the entire Oregon Trail at **Laurel Hill.** The steep, rocky banks of the mountain required drivers to empty their wagons, tie them to trees, and slowly lower the wagons down the hill. Others tried dragging heavy logs behind them to slow their descent on the 60 percent grade; if the ropes didn't hold, disaster was certain. The scraping of wagon wheels and dragged tree branches created "chutes" in the hillsides, visible tracks a few feet deep, proof of the wagons' descent.

Driving west along U.S. 26 as you leave Government Camp, you can see the steep hillsides the pioneers faced. On the south side of the highway, you can access the 0.5-mile (0.8-km) round-trip **Laurel Hill Chute Trail** between mileposts 50 and 51. Start by heading up stone steps to the bottom of the chute. Turn right on the paved road and look for the trail heading up the hill to the left. Signage along the way details how pioneers tackled the hills. At the junction, turn left to see Laurel Hill Chute below, a jumbled bed of rocks that wagons once edged down. You'll complete the loop and head down through switchbacks. Rhododendrons keep you company on the hike in spring—pioneers thought they were laurels, and named the hill for them.

Between mileposts 50 and 51, watch for a wooden signpost for Laurel Hill; there's a pullout on the south side of U.S. 26.

Barlow Gate

There were once five tollgates along the Barlow Road, with only one active at any given time. The first was established by Sam Barlow, who ran it for two years.

More were added by private entrepreneurs over the next 70 years in locations that best suited them. The tollgates were heavy, locked wooden gates surrounded by thick brush and trees, creating an impassable barrier for wagons on the road. After paying the fee ($5 per wagon, $0.10 per head of livestock; in today's dollars, about $160 and $3, respectively), emigrants could continue on. These tolls understandably rankled pioneers; mere days from their journey's end, many were near exhaustion or starvation.

In 1919, the last private tollgate owner bequeathed the road to the State of Oregon, which ended the tolls. No original gates remain, but at the Pioneer Bridle Trailhead you can see a **Barlow Gate replica** that was built in 1988. Near the replica you'll also find two heritage maple trees planted by Daniel Parker, gatekeeper 1883-1902. The **Pioneer Bridle Trail,** which links Government Camp and Rhododendron, 8 miles (12.9 km) west, is a popular mountain biking trail, so hikers should use caution. The entire trail stays within earshot of U.S. 26, but it's a pretty, forested path if you'd like to stretch your legs.

From Government Camp, drive 7.8 miles (12.6 km) west on U.S. 26. You'll turn left just before the Tollgate Campground into a small parking lot for the Pioneer Bridle Trailhead; an Oregon Trail sign marks the spot.

Mt. Hood Meadows
Mt. Hood Meadows (14040 Hwy. 35, 503/337-2222, www.skihood.com, lift tickets from $59) is the premier ski resort in the area and one of the largest in Oregon. With 11 lifts affording access to 2,150 acres of fun in Mount Hood National Forest, the resort has ski runs for beginners to advanced. The season depends on snowfall and runs late autumn through April or May. In summer

Top to bottom: Trillium Lake; Laurel Hill; Mount Hood from Jonsrud Viewpoint in Sandy.

visitors can enjoy the mountain with guided hikes, sunset chair rides, and geocaching fun.

Mt. Hood Skibowl

One of the best activity centers in the region, **Mt. Hood Skibowl** (87000 U.S. 26, 503/272-3206, www.skibowl.com) offers 960 acres of winter or summer fun. In winter, skiing (lift tickets $55 ages 13-64, $42 ages 65-70, $36 ages 7-13) and tubing ($28 adults, $23 children), which includes nighttime options, are the main attractions. Don't discount summer, when you can take advantage of an alpine slide, zip lines, a bungee tower, miniature golf, and a summer tube run. Also here are plenty of mountain-biking and horseback-riding trails. In summer, an Adventure Pass ($20) grants all-day access to 14 activities, including a tubing hill and slacklines; the Action Pass ($45) gives access to 7 more activities, such as the alpine slide and rock wall; and the Adrenaline Pass ($79) includes premium activities like bungee jumping and zip-lining.

Wildwood Recreation Site

A day-use site tucked up against the Salmon River, **Wildwood Recreation Site** (65670 U.S. 26, 503/622-3696, www.blm.gov, dawn-dusk daily, $5 per vehicle) has picnic tables, grills, fire pits, and shelters. The best way to enjoy Wildwood is to take a swim in the river or wander the network of trails, none more than 2 miles (3.2 km) long; the many loops and intersections mean visitors can wander without getting lost. The **Cascade Streamwatch Trail** features interpretive displays along the Salmon River and a cool fish-viewing window below the water level; in fall you can often spot spawning coho salmon. The **Wetlands Trail** is a loop with boardwalks over the marshy ground.

Rentals

Many mountain activities require equipment. Find what you need in summer or winter at **Mt. Hood Outfitters** (88661 Government Camp Loop, 503/715-2175, www.mthoodoutfitters.com, 10am-4pm Mon.-Fri., 9am-5pm Sat.-Sun.). It'll set you up with stand-up paddleboards, kayaks, canoes, mountain bikes, and backpacks in summer, and snowshoes and skis in winter. Mt. Hood Outfitters also offers a wide range of guided trips around the area, including waterfall, rock climbing, and kayaking tours. The company will deliver canoes or kayaks to local lakes.

Food

Steins line the wall at **Glacier Haus Bistro** (88817 E. Government Camp Loop, 503/272-3471, 11:30am-9pm Sun.-Thurs., 11:30am-11pm Fri.-Sat., $13), serving Czech- and German-inspired food that includes schnitzel, spaetzle, and goulash. Sandwiches, pizza, and local beer are on the menu as well.

Mt. Hood Brewing Co. (87304 Government Camp Loop, 503/272-3172, www.mthoodbrewing.com, 11am-9pm Sun.-Thurs., 11am-10pm Fri.-Sat., $16) uses glacial water from Mount Hood in each of its beers, creating delicious brews like Cascadian Pale Ale or the Cloud Cap Amber Ale, found only in Oregon. The brewery is housed in an alpine-style lodge that drips with icicles in winter, but in summer the outdoor patio shines. It also serves Swiss-style mac and cheese, great burgers, and pizza. For dessert, don't miss the cast-iron cookie or a toasted cranberry streusel.

Mere feet from the historic Barlow Road, the alpine-style A-frame of the **Huckleberry Inn** (88611 E. Government Camp Loop, 503/272-3325, www.huckleberry-inn.com, 24 hours daily, $11) serves a hearty breakfast as well as lunch. Save room for the mountain-man doughnuts and the namesake huckleberry pie.

Skyway Bar and Grill (71545 U.S. 26, Zigzag, 503/622-3775, http://skywaybarandgrill.com, 3pm-10pm Mon. and Thurs., noon-10pm Fri.-Sun., $9) offers adventurers a warm place to fuel up before or after a day on the mountain. The hearty meat-heavy menu features burgers, sandwiches, and barbecue as well as daily cocktail specials. Outdoor fire pits and live music complete the experience.

The Japanese cuisine at **Koya Kitchen** (67886 U.S. 26, Welches, 503/564-9345, noon-9pm Sun.-Thurs., noon-10pm Fri.-Sat., $12) provides a nice change from the usual burgers and beer. The tiny roadside house offers yakisoba noodles, sushi, and ramen. If it's a nice day, have a seat outside on the beautiful patio.

Accommodations

For a luxurious alpine stay and that après-ski feel any time of year, head to the ★ **Timberline Lodge** (27500 E. Timberline Rd., 503/272-3410, www. timberlinelodge.com/lodge, $150-290). Rooms are rustic and comfortable, ranging from economy options to fancier digs with wood-burning fireplaces. You have quick access to the slopes here. Keep an eye out for Heidi, the lodge's resident Saint Bernard.

The best family-friendly deals around are at **Collins Lake Resort** (88149 E. Creek Ridge Rd., Government Camp, 800/234-6288, www.collinslakeresort.com, $250-370), with chalets and lodges that sleep 6-10 people and come with kitchens and laundry.

Mt. Hood Oregon Resort (68010 E. Fairway Ave., Welches, 503/622-3101, www.mthood-resort.com, $120-250) has 157 guest rooms and offers a rustic yet modern hideaway surrounded by towering Douglas firs and leafy rhododendrons. With all the fun of the mountain, you might be hard-pressed to find time for the spa, 27-hole golf course, heated outdoor pool, and tennis and volleyball courts.

Camping

There are over 30 campgrounds in the **Mt. Hood National Forest,** many of them popular in summer, so reserve in advance. Campsites are generally open Memorial Day-September and cost $22. Call the **Zigzag Ranger Station** or reserve online (503/622-3191, www.recreation. gov). Notable campgrounds are **Trillium Lake Campground,** 3.7 miles (6 km) southeast of Government Camp, with 60 tent and RV sites at its lakeside location; the **Still Creek Campground,** 1.5 miles (2.4 km) southeast of Government Camp, with 27 reservable tent and RV sites; and **Camp Creek Campground,** 6.5 miles (10.4 km) west of Government Camp, with 24 tent and RV sites.

Information and Services

Get your local and historical bearings at the **Mt. Hood Cultural Center & Museum** (88900 E. Government Camp Loop, www.mthoodmuseum.org, 9am-5pm daily, free). It's worth a quick stop to see the tools settlers used to build log cabins, local art, old skis, and more. You can also find informational pamphlets and advice on the many trails and activities in the area, and the center offers tours and information about the local Steiner cabins, a distinct Oregon architectural style.

The **Zigzag Ranger Station** (70220 E. U.S. 26, 503/622-3191, 7:45am-4:30pm daily June-Oct., 7:45am-4:30pm Mon.-Fri. Nov.-May) offers detailed trail maps, campground information, Northwest Forest Passes, and passionate staff ready to share tips on the area. While you're here, check out the Wy'East Rhododendron Gardens that run alongside the compound; the rhododendrons bloom in spring.

Sandy

The community of Sandy grew up in the 1850s along the Barlow Road, mainly to serve emigrants making their way to Oregon City. It became one of the last stops to trade and rest before tackling the last days of the journey. Today it still serves travelers on the way to and from Mount Hood. The old Barlow Road

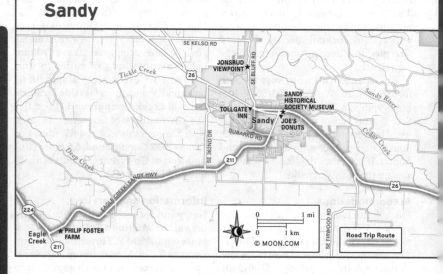

Sandy

route cuts through the small town along Pioneer Boulevard.

Getting There

From Government Camp, head west for 27.5 miles (44 km) on U.S. 26, turn left onto Strauss Avenue, and in a few hundred feet, left again onto Pioneer Boulevard for Sandy. The drive takes 35 minutes.

Sights

Sandy Historical Society Museum

The **Sandy Historical Society Museum** (39345 Pioneer Blvd., 503/668-3378, www.sandyhistory.com, 10am-4pm Mon.-Sat., noon-4pm Sun., free) is along the Barlow Road and holds many stories of pioneer history, including a breakdown of the types of wagons that emigrants took on the trail. A logging display and exhibits on 100 years of Sandy schoolhouses is here, as well as an impressive library and bookstore collection.

Jonsrud Viewpoint

One of the most spectacular views of Mount Hood, and possibly one of the best views in Oregon in general, can be found just outside of Sandy at **Jonsrud Viewpoint.** The 180-degree view encompasses Mount Hood and the Sandy River Valley. You'll also be able to see the Devils' Backbone, a ridge that spreads out to the right, which pioneers trekked over before rolling into Sandy. Sunset is a spectacular time to visit, when the sun's rays create a warm purple alpenglow on the mountain.

From U.S. 26 in Sandy, head north on Bluff Road. In just under 1 mile (1.6 km), you'll see the parking lot for the viewpoint to the right.

Philip Foster Farm

"This morning we started in good spirits, landed at Mr. Fosters, the end of our journey through the mountains . . . then drove to City and camped. Do not like Oregon yet, so far."

Elizabeth Goltra, September 28, 1853, *The Oregon Trail Journal of Elizabeth Goltra.* Goltra, 20 years old, traveled the trail from Illinois with her husband and one-year-old child. Upon arrival, she was clearly unimpressed, but she went on to have four more children and live a long life.

One of the first places in the state where Oregon Trail emigrants could get a home-cooked meal, **Philip Foster Farm** (22715 SE Eagle Creek Rd., 503/637-6324, www.philipfosterfarm.com, 11am-4pm Tues.-Sat. July-Aug., 11am-4pm Sat. May-June and Sept.-Oct., $5) was also one of the last stops on the last leg of the journey. Philip Foster partnered with Sam Barlow to finance the Barlow Road and made the strategic decision to settle near the end of the route to sell provisions to incoming emigrants. The farmhouse and accompanying store provided food, supplies, medical help, directions, and a place to rest. Many diaries report arriving in "paradise" from the welcome of Foster's family and the abundance of the farm.

The original farmhouse and barn from the 1800s still stand. There's also a reconstructed store and blacksmith shop that sold provisions and services to emigrants, and a replica log cabin rented out to weary travelers. Visitors are welcome to look inside the buildings on self-guided tours. During summer, costumed interpreters are on-site to offer glimpses into some of the pioneers' stories, and you can learn how to grind corn, build a log cabin, and scrub laundry with a washboard.

Head south on Highway 211 from Sandy for 5.8 miles (9.3 km), then turn left onto SE Eagle Creek Road to find the farm.

Food

The red-and-white-checkered exterior of ★ **Joe's Donuts** (39230 Pioneer Blvd., 503/668-7215, www.joes-donuts.com, 4am-5pm Mon.-Fri., 5am-5pm Sat.-Sun., $1.50) has been a welcome sight for locals and Portlanders on the way to the mountain since 1974. Stop in for fresh-baked treats (early birds get the best selection), including doughnuts, maple bars, and fritters, all of which go great with the hot coffee.

A kitschy throwback, the **Tollgate Inn** (38100 U.S. 26, 503/668-8456, www. visittollgate.com, 6am-8pm daily, $13) serves classic homemade diner fare. The building's facades look like an Old West town, and a covered wagon is situated at the entrance. Enjoy a big omelet and french toast for breakfast and meatloaf, steak, chicken pot pie, and burgers for lunch or dinner. The saloon boasts one of the area's largest selections of whiskey. There's also a bakery and deli for to-go treats, including from-scratch pastries, muffins, and cakes alongside deli sandwiches.

Oregon City

You've made it! Oregon City is the official ending point of the Oregon Trail, 2,000 miles (3,200 km) west of Independence, Missouri. Pioneers made their way here to formally claim land, as the city held the first federal land office west of the Rocky Mountains. It took emigrants 4-6 months to reach this spot. They would've arrived in Oregon City in October or November, when temperatures would be well into the low 40s (4-7°C), with the wet season underway. Even if it wasn't actively raining, a pervasive dampness would hang in the air. Many pioneers were destitute and walking in rags by the time they arrived, often having buried loved ones along the way; the city didn't always strike them as a paradise.

Nevertheless, it was an achievement to have made it here, and many celebrated. They arrived either by wagon via the Barlow Road or via Troutdale—where some rebuilt their rafts into wagons to continue south—or by river; some of those who had floated to Fort Vancouver chose to continue floating south via the Willamette River, which converges here with the Clackamas River.

Although Oregon City is close to Portland—just 15 miles (24 km) southeast—it has its own feel, marked by a prominent sense of pioneer history and unique terrain. The Willamette River is bordered by basalt cliffs, and the downtown's small core is nestled between. In fact, the city has operated an elevator to help residents travel between the varying levels since 1915. Main Street, on the lower level, is lined with green spaces and historic buildings. Although small, the town has some great dining and drinking options that rival Portland's. Head to the excellent End of the Oregon Trail Interpretive Center to cap off your journey, and celebrate in this waterfront town by toasting your time on the trail.

Getting There

If you followed the **Barlow Road alternate route around Mount Hood,** head south from Sandy on Highway 211, which becomes the Eagle Creek-Sandy-Highway 172. After 6 miles (9.7 km), turn right on Highway 224. In 8.6 miles (13.8 km), turn left onto Market Road/Springwater Road. After crossing the Clackamas River, turn right onto Clackamas River Drive. Follow it for 5.5 miles (8.9 km), and at the traffic circle, take the first exit onto Washington Street to continue into Oregon City. The official End of the Oregon Trail, at the End of the Oregon Trail Interpretive Center, is on the left in 0.8 mile (1.3 km). This route follows the closet approximation of the old trail from Philip Foster Farm. The 20-mile (32-km) route is a 30-minute drive from Sandy.

If you came via Troutdale along the **Columbia River Gorge,** head west on Halsey Street for 1.2 miles (1.9 km), then turn right onto NE 238th Drive, using one of the left two lanes to merge onto I-84 westbound. In 6 miles (9.7 km), take exit 9 for I-205 south. In 12 miles (19.3 km), take exit 10 and merge onto Highway 213. Stay in the right late to take a right onto Washington Street. The official End of the Oregon Trail is on the left in 0.6 mile (1 km). The route is 22 miles (35 km) and takes just under 30 minutes.

If you're coming from the Columbia River Gorge, you'll pass through **Portland** to get to Oregon City; depending on your itinerary, you might choose to stop in Portland before continuing on. From the city, you can take Highway 99E south for 12 miles (19 km) into Oregon City. Turn left onto 14th Street, then another left onto Washington Street after three blocks, to find the official End of the Oregon Trail in 0.4 mile (0.6 km). The drive takes 30 minutes.

Sights and Recreation

TOP EXPERIENCE

★ End of the Oregon Trail Interpretive Center

At the north end of Main Street, make an official end to your modern wagon journey at the **End of the Oregon Trail Interpretive Center** (1726 Washington St., 503/657-9336, http://historicoregoncity.org, 9:30am-5pm Mon.-Fri., 10:30am-5pm Sun., $13). Begin your visit in the main building; you can buy tickets, browse the gift shop for pioneer goodies like harmonicas and kits for doll-making and quilting, and get plenty of information about the local area.

The museum is designed to look like a circling of the wagons; the three oversized covered "wagons" each house a different exhibit showcasing life on the trail. Using diary excerpts and historical information, the center gives an excellent overview of the epic journey. It's especially great for kids, with lots of hands-on activities. You can practice loading your wagon in the Missouri frontier store, try on some pioneer clothing, or make a candle to take home with you.

On the grounds, a heritage garden blooms, with roses from original homesteads, and you can find the official plaque that marks the End of the Oregon Trail. The area near the museum was once called Abernethy Green, named for George Abernethy, an 1840 pioneer who built a home here. Pioneers who arrived in late fall or winter camped on his property while deciding their next steps.

If this is the end of your own journey,

the oversize covered wagons offer great photo opportunities, and a large map lets you trace your progress all the way here.

McLoughlin House

Take a free tour of the **McLoughlin House** (713 Centre St., 503/656-5146, http://mcloughlinhouse.org, 10am-4pm Fri.-Sat. Feb.-Dec., free), named for Dr. John McLoughlin, the chief factor (head trader) of the Hudson's Bay Company in Fort Vancouver. McLoughlin often took pity on the penniless emigrant families who arrived at the fort after floating the Columbia River and provided hundreds of loans, many of which were never repaid. He retired in 1846, moved to Oregon City, and built this grand home for his family. Tours begin next door at the Barclay House, which serves as the welcome center and gift shop. The 45-minute tours start 15 minutes after the hour, with the last tour at 3pm.

Municipal Elevator and McLoughlin Promenade

Oregon City is built on two levels: one along the Willamette River and the other atop the nearby basalt cliffs. Hiking trails and stairs were used between the two until the city installed a wooden elevator in 1915. In 1955, the city built a new version, and you can still find the **Municipal Elevator** (6 Railroad Ave., www.orcity.org, 7am-7pm Mon.-Tues., 7am-9:30pm Wed.-Sat., 10am-7pm Sun. June-Sept., 7am-7pm Mon.-Sat., 10am-7pm Sun. Oct.-May, free) running today. It's the only outdoor municipal elevator in the nation, and one of a handful in the world. The ride up is technically considered its own street—a vertical one!

The elevator affords access to the **McLoughlin Promenade,** a 2-mile (3.2-km) linear park along the bluffs. You'll have spectacular views of downtown,

Top to bottom: End of the Oregon Trail plaque; Oregon City Municipal Elevator; Dr. John McLoughlin, sculpted by Adrian Voisin.

the Willamette River, and Willamette Falls. It was constructed in the 1930s as a Works Progress Administration project, and the beautiful stonework showcases the craftsmanship of the era.

The promenade runs south from the elevator past a row of historic houses, and then across the highway to the **Willamette Falls Scenic Viewpoint,** offering the best views of Willamette Falls and Oregon City's mill site. For thousands of years, the massive waterfall—the second largest in volume in the United States—poured over the basalt cliffs of the Willamette River. Salmon pooled at the waterfall's base when they returned upstream to spawn, creating a natural fishing, trading, and meeting point for Native Americans from all around the region. Dr. John McLoughlin chose to settle near the falls and used them to power his sawmill. Later, the falls powered a woolen mill and then a lumber mill. The last industry, a paper mill, closed in 2011, and the huge concrete structures have been empty since, creating a scene of industrial wasteland. Today the falls provide power for the local electric company. The Willamette Falls Legacy Project has plans to reinvigorate the area by creating a river walk to connect downtown to the falls. If you'd prefer to drive to the viewpoint, there's a pullout near South 2nd Street.

Canemah Bluff Nature Park

Stretch your legs at **Canemah Bluff Nature Park** (815 4th Ave., www. oregonmetro.gov, dawn-dusk daily, free), which has some short nature trails exploring the bluffs above the Willamette River. The meadows bloom with camas lilies April-July. The 2.4-mile (3.9-km) **Canemah Bluff Loop** is an easy, hour-long walk that begins at the park's playground and follows the river, offering some great views, before heading into a forest of oak trees and bringing you to the **Canemah Pioneer Cemetery;** if the gate is open, you can go in. Look for the headstones

of Absalom Hedges and his family, who founded Canemah, a small settlement just south of Oregon City.

Paddling

The most exciting way to experience Willamette Falls is by getting up close to it. Rent a kayak or stand-up paddleboard ($25 per hour) from **ENRG Kayaking** (1701 Clackamette Dr., 503/772-1122, www. enrgkayaking.com, noon-5pm Wed.-Sat. Mar.-late May, 9am-7pm daily late May-Sept.), or hop on the fantastic 1.5-hour **Willamette Falls tour** ($60), which takes you 1 mile (1.6 km) upstream to the falls. As you paddle, you might spot some ancient sturgeons and Chinook salmon in the water. You'll learn about local history on the way, including some on the Oregon Trail. Designed for beginners and advanced paddlers alike, anyone can join in, even kids—little ones as young as four can use a tandem kayak or sit on a lap. Plan ahead in summer and sign up for one of the full-moon tours;

these popular events make a memorable evening outing.

Entertainment and Events
Bars and Brewpubs

Just down the road from the official End of the Trail, **Oregon City Brewing Co.** (1401 Washington St., 503/908-1948, www.ocbeerco.com, 11am-10pm Mon.-Thurs., 11am-11pm Fri.-Sat., 11am-9pm Sun.) has a good selection of house brews along with others on its 35 taps. Its decor includes photos of town settlers, so you can contemplate early pioneer history as you sip your suds. Sausage-mongers at Olympia Provisions Public House, based in Portland, have partnered with the brewery to offer a menu of kielbasa and frankfurters (be sure to add the house-made sauerkraut to your dog). Get nostalgic for the 1980s computer game by ordering the 8 Bit Blonde Ale while you toast a successful trip on the outdoor patio.

Run by longtime Oregon brewer Dave Fleming, **Coin Toss Brewing Co.** (14214 Fir St., 503/305-6220, www.cointossbrewing. com, 3pm-8pm Tues.-Fri., noon-8pm Sat.-Sun.) is a solid choice. Historical recipes influence the beers, such as a traditional Oktoberfest lager and a malty Settler's Red.

The Highland Stillhouse (201 S. 2nd St., 503/723-6789, www.highlandstillhouse. com, 11am-midnight Tues.-Sat., 11am-10pm Sun.) is one of the best places in the region to get a single-malt Scotch. Scottish decor highlights the authenticity of the drinks, as does a food menu offering such delicacies as a Scotch egg and bangers and mash. Live music and a variety of indoor and outdoor seating options add to the ambience.

TOP EXPERIENCE

★ Oregon Trail Brewfest

The **Oregon Trail Brewfest** (www. downtownoregoncity.org, late July, admission free, tasting $25) is a one-day

Oregon Trail Brewfest

event celebrating beer from across the Oregon Trail route. It's designed to give locals a taste of the entire trail, and while it focuses heavily on Oregon brews, you'll also find craft beer from Missouri, Kansas, Nebraska, Wyoming, and Idaho—over 40 breweries and cideries in all. Produced by Oregon City Brewing Co., who's tagline is "Beer for Pioneers," the festival is a celebration of the journey that brought the first European settlers to Oregon. Held on the lawn at the official End of the Oregon Trail, the family-friendly event boasts an all-day music lineup, lawn games, and food. Raise a glass to toast the end of the trail!

Food

A delicious and quaint bakery that rivals Portland's best, ★ **Grano** (1500 Washington St., 503/882-2980, www.granobreads.com, 7am-4pm Tues.-Sun., $10) also sells its wares throughout the region at farmers markets. At this café, you can purchase naturally leavened breads made with locally milled ancient grains, like a seeded spelt, a tangy sourdough, or a fluffy brioche. The lunch menu includes great sandwiches and soups, and there's also pastries and coffee.

Enjoy breakfast made from scratch at **Yvonne's** (818A Main St., 971/322-6613, www.yvonnes-restaurant.com, 7am-2pm Mon.-Fri., 8am-3pm Sat.-Sun., $13), in the heart of downtown. Dishes are locally sourced and include classic Benedicts, fluffy buttermilk pancakes, and a range of scrambles, all served with a hot buttermilk biscuit. If dinner and drinks is more your style, head next door to Yvonne's intimate **818 Lounge** (http://818lounge.com, 4:30pm-10pm Thurs.-Sun.), a craft cocktail lounge featuring small plates and a happy hour (4:30pm-6pm).

In a brick building on Main Street that dates to 1896, **Mi Famiglia** (701 Main St., 503/594-0601, www.mi-famiglia.com, 11am-3pm and 5pm-9pm Mon.-Thurs., 11am-3pm and 5pm-10pm Fri., noon-10pm Sat., noon-9pm Sun., $15) makes everything from scratch, and pizzas are cooked in a giant wood-fired oven. You'll find classics and something new: prosciutto and fig pizza, or salami with hot chilies. Salads, lasagna, a wine list, and a full bar round out the meal.

Ingrid's Scandinavian Food (209 7th St., 503/744-0457, noon-8pm Wed.-Sat., noon-5pm Sun., $9) offers your fix of *lefse* (crepe-like potato pancakes) with sweet or savory fillings, meatballs, and smoked salmon. It has a small dining room, or bring your food across the hall to the **Arch Bridge Taphouse** (205 7th St., 503/723-6162, www.archbridgetaphouse.com, 1pm-10pm Sun.-Thurs., 1pm-11pm Fri.-Sat.), which has 15 taps of local and regional brews, with plenty more available in bottles.

Shopping

If you're traveling with kids, **Black Ink White Rabbit** (503 Main St., 503/344-4762, http://blackink.coffee, 6am-6pm daily) café and bookshop has a nook in the back with a train set to play with, along with books and toys for sale; this will distract them long enough for you to check out the bookshelves filled with staff recommendations. Locally made goodies are also for sale and include soap, magnets, bookmarks, perfume, and cards.

Accommodations and Camping

The small size of Oregon City doesn't lend itself to lodging—the area's best can be found a 30-minute drive north in Portland. If you'd like to stay closer to town, there are a few good options.

The **Best Western Plus Rivershore Hotel** (1900 Clackamette Dr. 866/925-8648, www.bestwestern.com, $90-160) is the best stop. On the river, the 114 rooms boast balconies with water views, a heated outdoor pool and hot tub, and an on-site restaurant and lounge.

If you've come by RV, don't go to Portland with the rig—you won't find many places to park. Instead, stay at

Oregon City to Portland

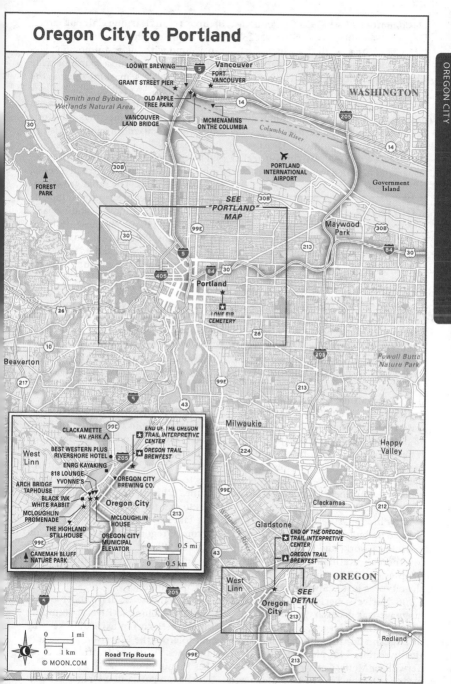

LOOWIT BREWING
Vancouver
FORT VANCOUVER
GRANT STREET PIER
OLD APPLE TREE PARK
VANCOUVER LAND BRIDGE
MCMENAMINS ON THE COLUMBIA
WASHINGTON
Smith and Bybee Wetlands Natural Area
Columbia River
FOREST PARK
PORTLAND INTERNATIONAL AIRPORT
Government Island
Maywood Park
SEE "PORTLAND" MAP
Portland
LONE FIR CEMETERY
Beaverton
Powell Butte Nature Park
Milwaukie
Happy Valley
CLACKAMETTE RV PARK
END OF THE OREGON TRAIL INTERPRETIVE CENTER
BEST WESTERN PLUS RIVERSHORE HOTEL
OREGON TRAIL BREWFEST
West Linn
ENRG KAYAKING
818 LOUNGE
YVONNE'S
ARCH BRIDGE TAPHOUSE
OREGON CITY BREWING CO.
BLACK INK
WHITE RABBIT
Oregon City
MCLOUGHLIN PROMENADE
MCLOUGHLIN HOUSE
THE HIGHLAND STILLHOUSE
OREGON CITY MUNICIPAL ELEVATOR
CANEMAH BLUFF NATURE PARK
Clackamas
Gladstone
END OF THE OREGON TRAIL INTERPRETIVE CENTER
OREGON TRAIL BREWFEST
West Linn
SEE DETAIL
OREGON
Oregon City
Redland

0   0.5 mi
0   0.5 km

0   1 mi
0   1 km

Road Trip Route

© MOON.COM

Clackamette RV Park (1955 Clackamette Dr., 503/496-1201, www.orcity.org, $25). It has 38 RV spaces, all first-come, first-served, with an RV dump and a park host. The park has nice walking trails to explore the waterfront where the Clackamas and the Willamette Rivers converge. The boat dock is a popular spot for lounging in summer, and if you keep your eyes on the ground you might find a treasure—the place is known for stirring up agate, jasper, and petrified wood.

Portland

Oregon's biggest city, Portland is a fun and convenient place to end your road trip, a 30-minute drive north of the official end of the Oregon Trail in Oregon City, and with an international airport. Although Oregon City was the official end point for emigrants, many dispersed to locations throughout the Willamette Valley, including Portland. Two Oregon Trail pioneers, Asa Lovejoy and Francis Pettygrove, established a land claim in 1843 about 14 miles (23 km) upriver from Oregon City, in a nice little clearing where ships could anchor; the village grew as more emigrants arrived, and by 1845 the two New Englanders decided it needed a name. Each man wanted to name it after their own hometowns. They decided by coin toss—Pettygrove won, otherwise you'd be visiting a West Coast "Boston" today.

Early life for settlers in Portland was focused on building log cabins, farming or finding work, and trading with the Multnomah, Kathlamet, and Tualatin peoples; in 1850, the population of the city was just 275 white settlers and 1,000 Native Americans. A common language was necessary, and the trade-based Chinook Jargon, a combination of English and Chinook, became practically required for pioneers. Charlotte Terwilliger Moffet Cartwright, who traveled the Oregon Trail in 1845 at the age of three, recalls learning Chinook Jargon better than English as she and her brother ran around with their Multnomah playmates. Fluency became a source of pride among the settlers, marking them as the "early pioneers." As late as 1910, the language was used at meetings of the Oregon Pioneer Association meetings, a historical society focused on pioneer history and lineage.

The city grew quickly due to its proximity to waterways, railroad access, and logging areas. The rapid growth attracted many people from around the world, including Chinese, Scandinavians, Eastern Europeans, Japanese, Italians, and Germans. Portland earned a reputation as a wild place for sailors to develop their vices. The 20th century brought increased growth, and today the city is known for its creative, progressive population and hipster vibe. It's a mecca for craft beer—Beervana is one of its nicknames—and celebrated for its thriving farm-to-table food scene. Portland is also celebrated for its urban planning, which has allowed for plenty of green spaces and bike-friendliness.

Getting There and Around

From Troutdale in the Columbia River Gorge, head west on Halsey Street for 1.2 miles (1.9 km), then turn right onto NE 238th Drive, using one of the left two lanes to merge onto I-84 westbound. In 13 miles (21 km), use one of the left two lanes to exit toward the city center. The drive takes 25 minutes.

From Oregon City, drive north on Highway 99E for 12 miles (19 km), and turn left onto the Morrison Bridge to reach downtown Portland. The drive takes 30 minutes.

From Vancouver, drive south on I-5 across the Columbia River, continuing 7 miles (11.3 km) to exit 300B, keeping right to cross the Morrison Bridge into downtown. Without traffic, the drive takes 15 minutes.

Although Portland is Oregon's largest

Two Days in Portland

Your time in Portland can be neatly bisected by the Willamette River, with one day spent on the west side and one on the east side. Most hotel options are on the west side, but there are options on the east side as well.

Powell's City of Books

Day 1

Enjoy brunch downtown at **Tasty n Alder** before heading to the hilly and green **Washington Park,** which encompasses the **International Rose Test Garden, Portland Japanese Garden,** and **Pittock Mansion,** the beautiful turn-of-the-20th-century home of two Oregon Trail pioneers, now a museum; even if you don't go inside the mansion, head up to its hillside perch for one of the best views of the city and Mount Hood. Enjoy lunch downtown at the **food carts** on 11th and Alder, before spending some time wandering **Powell's City of Books,** which takes up an entire city block. Stop by the **Portland Art Museum** or **Oregon Historical Society,** which has a new permanent exhibit on Oregon's various communities, from indigenous to international immigrant. The head to **Imperial** for dinner.

Day 2

Head east across the river today. Catch a hearty breakfast at the popular Southern-inspired **Screen Door,** then walk it off with a stroll through nearby **Lone Fir Cemetery,** where some of the earliest pioneers are buried. You can shop around at some of the small local stores before continuing on with a hike up **Mount Tabor** for fantastic city views. Enjoy a dinner of Russian delicacies at **Kachka.** Swing by **Cascade Brewing Barrel House** for a sour beer before ending your night with another drink or a show at the **Doug Fir Lounge.**

city, it's more like a big town than a metropolis. Its downtown is easily walkable, as are its neighborhoods, though those can be farther flung from each other. Getting around by car is easy, but parking can be challenging downtown. There are plenty of SmartPark garages—find them by looking for the big red arrows. Bus service is run by **TriMet** (http://trimet.org), which connects the entire city. TriMet also runs the **MAX Light Rail,** which connects Portland with its suburbs, including convenient transportation from Portland International Airport to downtown on its Red Line; purchase your ticket at a kiosk before

boarding. Both the bus and light rail cost $2.50 for a ticket valid for 2.5 hours and $5 for an all-day pass. For the bus, you'll need exact change. **Uber** (www. uber.com) and **Lyft** (www.lyft.com) also operate in Portland.

Orientation

Portland is easy to navigate, with "five quadrants": Southwest, Northwest, Southeast, Northeast, and North. The city is bisected east-west by the **Willamette River** and north-south by **Burnside Street.** Downtown is on the west side, while the east side is home to bustling indie neighborhoods, with businesses typically concentrated along one or two thoroughfares.

Downtown

Portland's downtown is in the **southwest** quadrant of the city. **Pioneer Courthouse Square** is something of a central plaza, and offices, hotels, restaurants, bars, and shops fan out from it. **Washington Park** is on downtown's western end, and Portland State University is on its southern end.

Northwest

Northwest Portland includes the swanky **Pearl District,** the neighborhood stretching just north of **Powell's City of Books.** It also includes the parallel, walkable **Northwest 21st and 23rd Avenues,** filled with shops and eateries.

Southeast

Southeast Portland includes the historically hippie-laden and parallel thoroughfares of **Hawthorne Boulevard, Belmont Street,** and **Division Street,** which are teeming with indie restaurants, breweries, food carts, and shops.

Northeast and North

Williams Avenue separates Northeast Portland from North Portland. Some major pockets of activity with restaurants, bars, and shops in Northeast Portland include **Burnside Street, 28th Avenue,** and **Alberta Street.** In north Portland, **Mississippi Avenue** is a small but lively thoroughfare.

Sights
Downtown
Pioneer Courthouse Square

Portland's "Living Room" is **Pioneer Courthouse Square** (bounded by SW Morrison St., SW 6th Ave., SW Yamhill St., and SW Broadway), which takes up an entire city block in the center of downtown. The site was saved from becoming a parking garage and now serves as a hub of events and transportation. The

brick-lined square has seating, food carts, chess tables, and a TriMet office (8:30am-5:30pm Mon.-Fri.) where you find maps, schedules, and buy transportation passes.

Portland Art Museum

At the **Portland Art Museum** (1219 SW Park Ave., 503/226-2811, http://portlandartmuseum.org, 10am-5pm Tues.-Wed. and Sun., 10am-8pm Thurs.-Fri., $20 adults, $17 seniors and students, free under age 18) you'll find a beautiful display of Native American artifacts on permanent exhibit, including many stone carvings from the Columbia River Gorge. The museum's permanent collection also includes European and Asian artworks. Well-known artists like Renoir, Van Gogh, Bierstadt, and Brancusi are represented.

Oregon Historical Society

The **Oregon Historical Society** (1200 SW Park Ave., 503/222-1741, www.ohs.org/museum, 10am-5pm Mon.-Sat., noon-5pm Sun., $10 adults, $8 seniors, students, and teachers, $5 ages 6-18, free under age 6) opened a new permanent exhibit in 2019 called "Experience Oregon," which brings together stories from Oregon's many communities. It traces the state's history from its original inhabitants—Native American tribes that include the Multnomah, Clackamas, Molalla, Tillamook, and others—and extends to include the experiences of women, African Americans, Chinese Americans, and Japanese Americans, urging visitors to ask hard questions of the state's history while asking "What is your Oregon experience?" Also at the museum is the penny that gave Portland its name, per the 1843 coin toss between pioneers and city founders Francis Pettygrove and Asa Lovejoy.

Mill Ends Park

Find the minuscule **Mill Ends Park** (SW Naito Pkwy., near SW Taylor St.), the smallest park in the world. Look

Black Pioneers and Enslaved Emigrants on the Oregon Trail

Historians estimate that up to 17 percent of Oregon Trail emigrants were not white, and many were free black men and women. Before the era of migration, free black people worked as fur trappers, explorers, and miners throughout the West. And some enslaved people came on the trail with their owners; Oregon Fever and the Oregon Trail got underway during the nationwide disagreement over the enslavement of African Americans, which reached its crescendo when the country descended into the Civil War in 1861.

But many white settlers—hoping to leave the issue of slavery and attendant violence behind—brought both anti-slavery sentiments as well as prejudice west with them; the Oregon territorial legislature voted in 1843 and again in 1857 to prohibit slavery while also banning free black people from living in the territory. The earliest versions of these exclusion laws included lash laws: Black people could be whipped if found living in Oregon. The laws were infrequently enforced but sent a strong message that African Americans were not welcome. While some black pioneers stayed in the state, many on the trail diverted to California or Washington once they heard about Oregon's laws.

In 1859 Oregon entered the Union as a free state, but retained the racist laws, which remained in the state's constitution until 1926; this greatly affected the diversity of the state and continues to reverberate today. In the 20th century, Oregon was home to the largest Ku Klux Klan chapter west of the Mississippi, and African Americans experienced enforced segregation and discrimination in real estate, school systems, banking, and employment. As progressive as modern Portland is, it's also been identified as the whitest large city in the United States.

The nonprofit **Oregon Black Pioneers** (www.oregonblackpioneers.org) was founded in 1993 to preserve early black history and tell the stories of pioneers through presentations, exhibits, and books.

carefully—the park is literally two feet in diameter. Its contents have changed over the years, but the latest version contains miniature roses. You'll see a tiny park sign denoting it, placed by the city.

Washington Park

Washington Park's 410 acres sprawl across the hills of west Portland, encompassing many of the city's notable sights. You could easily spend an entire day wandering here. From downtown, it's simple to enter the park via one of several access points, like SW Park Place or West Burnside Street. MAX Light Rail's Blue and Red Lines connect to Washington Park from downtown locations. It's possible to drive, but not recommended, as parking is limited and you'll pay per hour. Once inside the park, a free shuttle (May-Sept.) makes a loop connecting various attractions, although you can also just walk around.

International Rose Test Garden

Portland is known as the "City of Roses," and its love affair with the flower goes back to Georgiana Pittock, an Oregon Trail pioneer—she was nine when she traveled the trail in 1854—who established the Portland Rose Society by inviting friends to showcase their roses beside her mansion. Today the **International Rose Test Garden** (400 SW Kingston Ave., www.portlandoregon.gov/parks, 7:30am-9pm daily, free) has about 10,000 bushes that grow 600 varieties. Wander the grounds and smell the roses at your leisure to find a favorite—perhaps Orange Cream? Or join an hour-long tour (1pm daily, free); just show up 10 minutes beforehand at the Rose Garden Store.

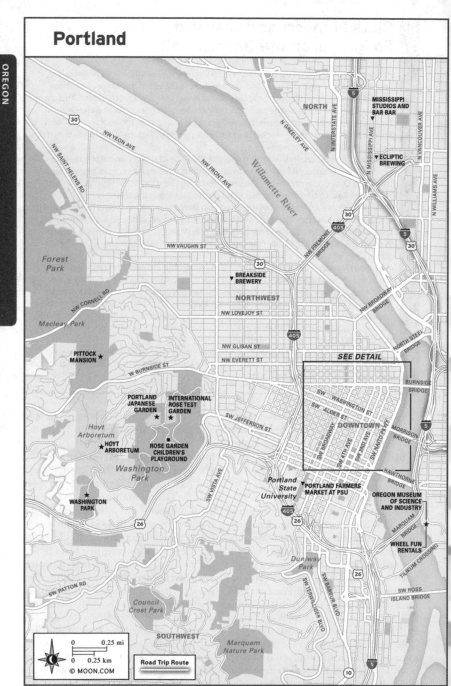

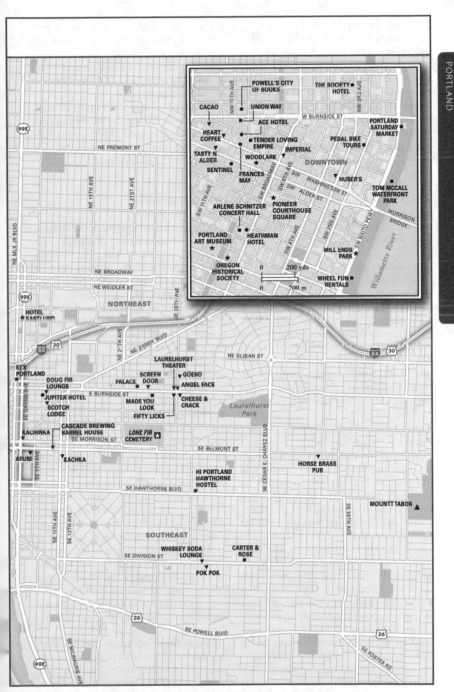

Portland Japanese Garden

Find a peaceful oasis at the **Portland Japanese Garden** (611 SW Kingston Ave., 503/223-1321, http://japanesegarden.org, noon-7pm Mon., 10am-7pm Tues.-Sun. early Mar.-Sept., noon-4pm Mon., 10am-4pm Tues.-Sun. Oct.-early Mar., $17 adults, $15 seniors, $14 students, $12 ages 6-17, free under age 6), one of the most authentic outside Japan. The carefully designed space is lovely any time of year and a favorite of photographers. Wander around the tea garden, then look for the koi in the ponds. A gallery has rotating exhibits on Japanese heritage, and you can stop in the on-site Umami Café for a snack during your visit.

Hoyt Arboretum

Visit the living museum that is the **Hoyt Arboretum** (4000 SW Fairview Blvd., 503/865-8733, www.hoytarboretum.org, visitors center 9am-4pm Mon.-Fri., 11am-3pm Sat.-Sun., grounds 5am-10pm daily, free). More than 6,000 trees are grown here in thousands of varieties. Stop in the visitors center for maps, information, and a scavenger hunt booklet for kids, then wander the extensive trail system.

Pittock Mansion

Henry and Georgiana Pittock were both Oregon Trail pioneers, but they met and married in Portland—he came from Pennsylvania, and she from Missouri. Finding success running the local newspaper, the *Oregonian,* Pittock built his mansion on this hill in 1912, and the whole family lived here for decades. Today the stunning **Pittock Mansion** (3229 NW Pittock Dr., 503/823-3623, www.pittockmansion.org, 10am-4pm daily, $13 adults, $11 seniors, $9 ages 6-18, free under age 6) is open as a museum; the house boasted the most advanced technology of its day, with central heating, an elevator, a refrigerator room, and a central vacuum system. The museum offers 50-minute tours included with admission, or you can wander at your own pace. From the grounds outside—which are free to wander—you can catch one of the best views of downtown Portland and Mount Hood on a clear day.

A popular way to reach Pittock Mansion is by hiking the **Wildwood Trail** from Hoyt Arboretum. The 2.7-mile (4.3-km) round-trip is a little steep, but it's a beautiful walk in the forest.

Southeast

Oregon Museum of Science and Industry

Keeping kids of all ages busy, the **Oregon Museum of Science and Industry,** known as **OMSI** (1945 SE Water Ave., 503/797-4000, http://omsi.edu, 9:30am-5:30pm Tues.-Sun., $15 adults, $12 seniors, $11 ages 3-13, free under age 3, parking $5) has a submarine, plenty of hands-on science exhibits, and a planetarium. You can easily fill several hours here. For adult fun, check the online calendar for the OMSI After Dark event, which blends science, alcohol, and food in various themed nights for the over-21 set.

★ Lone Fir Cemetery

A beautiful spot in a quiet neighborhood, **Lone Fir Cemetery** (SE 26th Ave. and SE Stark St., 503/797-1709, www.friendsoflonefircemetery.org, dawn-dusk daily, free) holds 25,000 graves, many of them for early pioneers, such as Aurelia Barrell, who traveled the Oregon Trail with her husband and two children and gave the cemetery its name; notorious figures like Emma Merlotin, a well-known prostitute who was murdered; and famous residents such as city founder Asa Lovejoy and Elizabeth Barchus, who painted striking landscapes of Mount Hood, the Columbia River Gorge, and the coast.

Learn about some of the fascinating stories of those buried here on the monthly cemetery tour (2 hours, $10), held at 10am the second Saturday of

A Pioneer Story: Mary Jane Holmes and Reuben Shipley

Mary Jane Holmes was three years old when her family traveled the Oregon Trail from Missouri in 1844. Mary Jane, her siblings, and her parents, Robin and Polly Holmes, were the official property of Nathaniel Ford. While Ford freed her parents a few years after their arrival in Oregon, Mary Jane and her siblings remained enslaved on his farm. Robin and Polly fought for their children's freedom in the case known as *Holmes v. Ford*. In 1853, the ruling called for the children's release—marking the last attempt to establish slavery in Oregon through the judicial system. Mary Jane was 11 years old. She remained with the Ford family as a paid servant for a time for financial reasons.

At 16, Mary Jane married Reuben Shipley, himself a formerly enslaved emigrant on the Oregon Trail. He drove his owner's team of oxen on the trail in exchange for his freedom upon arrival. Although Mary Jane had been legally freed and was technically an employee, Ford demanded that Reuben pay him $750 (about $20,000 today) for her freedom. Not wanting to face a lengthy legal battle, he paid. The couple went on to have children and run a farm south of Portland, near Corvallis, becoming respected members of the local community.

In 1861, Reuben donated some of the family's land to establish the Mount Union Cemetery, on the condition that black people could be buried there. Mary Jane outlived Reuben, as well as her second husband, R. G. Drake. She passed away in 1925 at the age of 84. All three are buried in the cemetery.

the month. Or just take a stroll around the peaceful grounds on your own. The Friends of the Lone Fir Cemetery have compiled helpful online guides and an interactive smartphone map. Be sure to visit the northwest corner of the cemetery, where you'll find the oldest headstones as well as the cemetery's namesake Douglas fir tree.

A memorial garden to Chinese immigrants, buried without headstones, is being built in the southwest corner, commemorating the integral role Chinese people played in early Portland, building infrastructure and running hundreds of thriving small businesses.

Recreation

Tom McCall Waterfront Park

Tom McCall Waterfront Park (Naito Pkwy. between SW Harrison St. and NW Glisan St., 5am-midnight daily, free) spans the west side of the Willamette River alongside downtown. In the 1970s, the park replaced Harbor Drive in one of the first freeway removals in the country, marking a big step forward in urban planning. The waterfront promenade and green space is popular with locals and visitors for walking, biking, and simply lounging. In spring, cherry blossoms bloom just north of the Burnside Bridge at the park's Japanese American Historical Plaza. Many of the city's largest events hold festivities here, including the Oregon Brewers Festival and Portland Rose Festival.

Forest Park

Forest Park (http://forestparkconservancy .org) offers 80 miles (130 km) of trails within its massive 5,200 acres. It's one of the largest urban parks in the country, somewhere you can truly escape the city within its limits. It stretches 7 miles (11.3 km) north from Washington Park and has great views of the river to the east. The park's most popular route is the **Wildwood Trail,** 30 miles (48 km) end to end; it's easy to break up into shorter jaunts, such as a 2.7-mile (4.3-km) out-and-back from Hoyt Arboretum to Pittock Mansion in Washington Park, which takes 1.5 hours.

Eastbank Esplanade

Directly across from Tom McCall Waterfront Park, on the east side of the Willamette River, the **Vera Katz Eastbank Esplanade** is a 1.5-mile (2.4-km) biking and walking trail. The esplanade runs from the Hawthorne Bridge in the south to the Steel Bridge in the north. It runs next to OMSI and connects with the Springwater Corridor multiuse trail on its southern end.

Springwater Corridor

The **Springwater Corridor** (www.portland oregon.gov/park) is a multiuse paved path that runs from Portland 21 miles (34 km) southeast to Boring (yes, that's the town's name!). The popular walking and biking path officially begins along the Southeast Portland waterfront at Ivon Street, but you can access it via the Eastbank Esplanade, continuing south on it from OMSI. In summer, wildflowers and blackberries line the Springwater Corridor.

For a nice bike ride or walk, head 2.5 miles (4 km) down the corridor from the Ivon Street trailhead to the **Oaks Bottom Wildlife Refuge** (SE 7th Ave. and Sellwood Blvd., www.portlandoregon. gov/parks, 5am-midnight daily, free), popular for birding—185 species have been recorded here. Continue on another mile (1.6 km) down the corridor to **Sellwood,** a quaint Portland neighborhood in the city's southern reaches that has some eateries and antiques shops.

Mount Tabor

Take a walk up the slopes of this dormant volcano—the only one in the United States within city limits! Located in Southeast Portland, **Mount Tabor** (SE 60th Ave. and Salmon St., www. portlandoregon.gov/parks, 5am-10pm daily, free) has forested trails, picnic areas, a playground, and an off-leash area for dogs. Enter the park from 60th Avenue and Salmon Street and head up about 0.5 mile (0.8 km) until you see a parking lot; from here you can access a network of trails that wind around and up the volcano—follow the green posts for a 1.7-mile (2.7-km) route around the base of the peak, the red posts for an alternate 1-mile (1.6-km) loop through surrounding meadows, and the blue posts for a 3-mile (4.8-km) loop up to the summit and around three of the lovely open-air reservoirs that once held drinking water for the city.

Bike Rentals and Tours

Pedal Bike Tours (133 SW 2nd Ave., 503/243-2453, www.pedalbiketours.com, 9am-6pm daily) offers rental options including city bikes ($10 per hour, $30 per day), tandem bikes ($15 per hour, $45 per day), and kids' bikes ($5 per hour, $15 per day). All rentals come with helmets, bike locks, maps, and advice. The outfitter also offers guided bicycle tours around the city, such as **Intro to Portland** ($49 pp) and the **Portland Brewery Trail** ($69 pp). The company is located downtown, close to Tom McCall Waterfront Park.

Wheel Fun Rentals (www. wheelfunrentals.com, 11am-5pm daily Mar.-Apr. and Sept.-Oct., 11am-7pm Mon.-Thurs., 8am-8pm Fri.-Sun. June-Aug.) has convenient locations at Tom McCall Waterfront Park (1020 SE Naito Pkwy., 503/808-9955) and OMSI (1945 SE Water Ave., Bldg. B, 503/802-5271), from which you can quickly hop onto bike paths. Rent a regular city bike ($10 per hour, $35 per day), tandem ($15 per hour, $45 per day), or kids' bike ($7 per hour, $20 per day). Or, if you don't mind standing out as a tourist, you can pedal the whole family in a Surrey ($25-35 per hour), a covered bike carriage with four wheels—small children fit securely in the front basket.

Entertainment
Brewpubs

Breakside Brewery (1570 W. 22nd, 503/444-7597, www.breakside.com, 11am-10pm Sun.-Thurs., 11am-11pm

Fri.-Sat.) has won multiple awards, including being selected as one of *Paste* magazine's Top 20 Breweries of the Decade. With several outposts in the city, this taproom brews on-site, and many beers can be found only in this location. The taproom is on two levels and has an outdoor patio, 16 taps, and a full food menu.

In a region that leans heavily on hops, it's refreshing to find one that focuses on unique sours, like **Cascade Brewing Barrel House** (939 SE Belmont St., 503/265-8603, www.cascadebrewing. com, 1pm-10pm Sun.-Mon., 1pm-11pm Tues.-Thurs., noon-midnight Fri.-Sat.). Often made with fresh local fruit such as cherries, peaches, or grapes, these are sour beers by way of the Pacific Northwest. Try the Kriek, a barrel-aged red ale with cherries, or the Apricot, a barrel-aged blond ale made with the namesake fruit.

Ecliptic Brewing (825 N. Cook St., 503/265-8002, www.eclipticbrewing. com, 11am-10pm Sun.-Thurs., 11am-11pm Fri.-Sat.) is in an industrial space that's a popular gathering spot in North Portland, just off Mississippi Avenue. Flagship brews include the Starburst IPA and Carina Peach Sour, and there are also plenty of seasonal releases.

With over 60 breweries in the city limits, there's no way you're going to try them all. Instead, look for a place where you can try a lot of them, all at once. **Horse Brass Pub** (4534 SE Belmont St., 503/232-2202, www.horsebrass.com, 11am-2:20am daily) is an English-style pub, but its 59 taps pour some of the region's best. Ask the knowledgeable staff about local beers on tap. It also serves solid English pub fare and good burgers.

Bars
Find a piece of Old Portland at **Huber's** (411 SW 3rd Ave., 503/228-5686, www. hubers.com, 11:30am-midnight Mon.-Thurs., 11:30am-1am Fri., 11am-1am Sat., 4pm-11pm Sun.), known for its Spanish coffee, which comes with a theatrical table-side show as it's lit on fire. While Huber's has been in its current space "only" since 1910, the business was founded back in 1879, making it the oldest bar in Portland. You'll find original fixtures like the cash registers and spittoons underneath a stained-glass skylight.

It's been described as a cocktail bar for whiskey lovers, but the **Scotch Lodge** (215 SE 9th Ave., Suite 102, 503/208-2039, www.scotchlodge.com, 4pm-midnight daily) has something for everyone. A dark, romantic cave-like atmosphere replete with warm woods and bronze accents, it's a perfect place to hide out for an evening.

You won't receive a cocktail menu at **Angel Face** (14 NE 28th Ave., 503/239-3804, www.angelfaceportland.com, 5pm-midnight Sun.-Thurs., 5pm-1am Fri.-Sat.). Instead, sidle up to the big marble horseshoe-shaped bar and whisper your desires to the bartender—who will craft a cocktail just for you. With delicate pink walls hand-painted with flowers, the space is a romantic dream.

Bye and Bye (1011 NE Alberta St., 503/281-0537, www.thebyeandbye.com, noon-midnight daily) is a bastion of Portland hipness that serves up a vast menu of cocktails. Try the signature drink—made with peach vodka, peach bourbon, cranberry juice, and soda—served in a mason jar. Homemade infusions pair well with fresh ingredients, and if you're hungry, you can't go wrong with the Southern-inspired vegan menu. Enjoy it all on one of two patios—great for people-watching on Alberta Street—or the hip indoor space.

Live Music
The **Doug Fir Lounge** (830 E. Burnside St., 503/231-9663, www.dougfirlounge. com, $10-35) combines a lodge-like feel with retro mid-century style. Order drinks and just hang out upstairs or on the outdoor patio, or head downstairs to

catch a live show—the venue attracts a rotating cast of local and national bands. It's attached to the Jupiter Hotel if you decide you want to crash for the night afterward.

Mississippi Studios (3939 N. Mississippi Ave., 503/288-3895, www.mississippistudios.com, $10-20) is one of the top music venues in town. An intimate space, it welcomes indie acts from all over on a nightly basis. It's in a renovated church, and owned and operated by musicians—so they get it. Even if you're not attending a show, stop by to hang out at **Bar Bar** (503/889-0090, 11am-2am daily), which serves up cocktails, beer, and great burgers on one of the city's best patios.

The Arts

Portland has several theaters that show second-run movies and serve up beer and food. One of the best is **Laurelhurst Theater** (2735 E. Burnside St., 503/238-4088, www.laurelhursttheater.com, $9), which shows mainstream as well as occasional classic, independent, and art films. A wide range of local microbrews is on tap, along with pizza and popcorn.

Find Broadway shows, orchestral symphonies, and world-class talent at downtown's **Arlene Schnitzer Concert Hall** (1037 SW Broadway Ave., www.portland5.com). The theater is graced by an iconic Portland sign out front. Do as the locals do and call it "The Schnitz."

Festivals and Events

A tradition for over 100 years, the **Portland Rose Festival** (www.rosefestival.org, late May-June, admission varies by event) encompasses dozens of events, like parades, a city fair, Fleet Week, dragon boat races, a rose show, a fun run, and more. The biggest event, going since 1906, is the **Grand Floral Parade,** full of colorful floats, marching bands, and dancers. The parade usually begins mid-morning, but you'll need to stake out a spot early for this popular event. Check

online for maps of the year's route. Events are centered at Tom McCall Waterfront Park and kick off around Memorial Day weekend with fireworks, signaling the start of another fantastic summer in Portland.

Every June, the streets of Portland are awash in hundreds of bicycle rides, each celebrating the city's fun, wacky bike culture. Known as **Pedalpalooza** (www.shift2bikes.org, June, free), the month-long party on wheels is a crowd-sourced mix of rides that anyone can volunteer to lead, from themed costumed rides to protest rides, family-friendly rides to adult-only dance-party rides. The month is capped off by Portland's version of the **World Naked Bike Ride,** a celebratory event that attracts over 10,000 people in all states of dress. Nudity is not required, but welcomed—and it's not as uncomfortable as you might think.

The **Oregon Brewers Festival** (Tom McCall Waterfront Park, www.oregonbrewfest.com, 2pm-9pm Wed.-Sat. late July, admission free, tasting package $20, additional tasting tokens $1) is one of the longest-running craft beer festivals in the nation, attracting up to 50,000 beer fans to Portland's waterfront. It began as a way to help publicize the small craft brewers in the state and now celebrates their wild success. Along with tasting booths, visitors will find brewing demonstrations, food trucks, games, and more. Minors are welcome.

Food
Downtown
Pacific Northwest

Run by renowned *Iron Chef* winner and critically acclaimed Portland chef Vitaly Paley, **Imperial** (410 SW Broadway St., 503/228-7222, www.imperialpdx.com, $25) serves food that's rooted in Pacific Northwest traditions and ingredients. Located inside the Hotel Lucia, the dining room has a warm, rustic lodge feel. Breakfast, lunch, and dinner are served, and it's hard to make a bad choice, from the bay scallop linguini to the rib eye with roasted mushrooms. For dinner, let them fire up the grill for a roasted half chicken with bacon brussels sprouts, and end with a warm chocolate-chip cookie.

International

Lively, tapas-style **Tasty n Alder** (580 SW 12th Ave., 503/621-9251, www.tastynalder.com, 9am-2pm and 5:30pm-close daily, $20) serves an excellent brunch, with offerings like potatoes *bravas* (fried potatoes in a spicy oil) and a merguez sausage omelet, which you'll enjoy sharing at one of the long dining tables. Dinner service continues the tour of international flavors, with a big focus on steaks like a gaucho rib eye with chimichurri or a *bulgogi* short rib with kimchi.

Coffee and Desserts

Fuel up for the day at **Heart Coffee** (537 SW 12th Ave., 503/224-0036, www.heartroasters.com, 7am-6pm Mon.-Fri., 8am-6pm Sat.-Sun., $4), a roaster and coffee shop serving pour-overs and espresso. Ask the barista about the selections of the day and you'll get a range of flavor profiles and styles. The café also serves small bites and pastries—look for the cardamom roll.

Take a break for a decadent treat at **Cacao** (414 SW 13th Ave., 503/241-0656, http://cacaodrinkchocolate.com, 10am-6pm daily, $4), a small chocolate shop with shelves full of beautifully curated and packaged chocolate bars and truffles from around the world. The main event is the exquisite drinking chocolate—a thick, velvety concoction of single-origin chocolate. It's a small slurp of heaven in a cup. Don't skimp: Try the flight of all three flavors.

Farmers Markets

The biggest **farmers market** in town happens every Saturday year-round near Portland State University (SW Park Ave. and Montgomery St., 8:30am-2pm Sat. Apr.-Oct., 9am-2pm Sat. Nov.-Mar.), where over 100 vendors come to peddle their fruit and veggies. Visitors will find the best of the season, including tender new potatoes, fragrant lavender, and juicy tomatoes as well as meat, seafood, dairy, fresh-cut flowers, baked goods, and pantry items. The market also bustles with food carts and live music, so even if you don't have a fridge to stock up on your travels, this is a great place to grab lunch and people-watch.

Southeast
Food Carts

For a great collection of food carts, head to the **Hawthorne Asylum** (1080 SE Madison St., hours and prices vary). The pod has about a dozen carts with delicious options, covered tables with seating for over 100 people, and firepits. Look for Russian dumplings from Pelmeni Pelmeni, beer and cider from BlackDagger, and award-winning brisket and ribs from Bark City BBQ. Or head around the corner to **Cartopia** (1200 SE Hawthorne Blvd., hours and prices vary), one of Portland oldest food cart pods, with an ever-changing roster of carts. A large tent provides shade or rain cover, and firepits add to the allure. Check out mainstay Potato Champion, serving fresh cut fries with various toppings, including the ever-popular poutine.

Asian

Portland's renowned Thai restaurant ★ **Pok Pok** (3226 SE Division St., 503/232-1387, http://pokpokdivision.com, 11:30am-10pm daily, $15) serves delicious food highlighting the street food of northern Thailand. Dishes are served family-style and come full of spice and zing. Don't miss out on the signature dish: Ike's Vietnamese Fish Sauce Wings—chicken wings tossed in a sticky, sweet, salty sauce and served with pickled veggies. Lines inevitably snake out the door at Pok Pok, but it's worth the wait, made more palatable by the fact that you can put your name in and then head across the street for a drink at the sister **Whiskey Soda Lounge** (3131 SE Division St., 503/232-0102, http://whiskeysodalounge.com, 4pm-11pm Sun.-Thurs., 4pm-1am Fri.-Sat., $10), where you can order from a range of cocktails, whiskey, or no-proof house-made drinking vinegars. It also has a smaller menu of bites (but no wings).

Tokyo's prized ramen restaurant **Afuri** (923 SE 7th Ave., 503/468-5001, http://afuri.us, 11:30am-2:30pm and 5pm-10pm Mon.-Fri., 11:30am-10pm Sat.-Sun., $14) opened its first international installment here in Portland. Find big bowls of expertly balanced ramen, like the bright Yuzu Shio, a broth infused with the *yuzu* citrus fruit, or the spicy Tonkotsu Tantanmen, a creamy thick pork broth, both with handmade noodles crafted in the kitchen. Ramen is the main attraction, but you'll also find dumplings, *karaage* (fried chicken), sushi rolls, and a wide choice of sake, Japanese whiskey, and *shochu,* an earthy distilled liquor made from rice, barley, or buckwheat. The large industrial dining room can get crowded on weekend nights—try it out for lunch to beat the rush.

Russian
★ **Kachka** (960 SE 11th Ave., 503/235-0059, http://kachkapdx.com, 11:30am-2pm and 4pm-10pm daily, $14) has been called one of the best Russian restaurants in the nation. Eat the Russian way with a table full of *zakuski*—Russian drinking foods like cured fish, meats, and pickled vegetables—paired with vodka (there are over 50). The sour cherry dumplings with Smetana (cream) are drool-worthy. If you're more interested in nibbling than a full meal, try the nearby café **Kachinka** (720 SE Grand Ave., 4pm-midnight daily, $9) for happy hour-style smaller bites and drinks. End with a *plombir,* a Russian-style ice cream sandwich.

Cheese and Desserts
The picture-perfect cheese board at the 20-seat café **Cheese & Crack** (22 SE 28th Ave., 503/206-7215, www.cheeseandcrack.com, 11am-10pm daily, $12) comes with house-made crackers, olives, a baguette, spoonfuls of chocolate ganache and honey, and, of course, a choice selection of cheeses. There's also a small selection of sandwiches, salads, and other snacks. Beer and prosecco are on draft, and for dessert there's espresso-dusted soft serve.

Lick your way through all the flavors at **Fifty Licks** (2742 E. Burnside St., 503/395-3333, www.fifty-licks.com, 2pm-10pm Mon.-Thurs., noon-11pm Fri.-Sun., $5), an ice cream parlor slinging fresh and unique scoops. The smooth gelato-like ice cream comes in vibrant flavors like Tahitian Vanilla, Thai Rice, and Ancho Mango. Try the Affogato Cubano, a scoop drenched in strong Cuban coffee. And good news—the vegan varieties are equally delicious!

Northeast
Southern
The popular Southern-inspired **Screen Door** (2337 E. Burnside St., 503/542-0880, http://screendoorrestaurant.com, 8am-2pm and 5:30pm-9pm Sun.-Thurs., 8am-2pm and 5:30pm-10pm Fri.-Sat., $16) has lines winding around the block on weekend mornings for brunch. If you're not up for waiting an hour, come on a weekday, or try lunch or dinner instead. The restaurant only serves its famous chicken and waffles for brunch, but for other meals you can get hushpuppies, po'boys, or shrimp and grits, as well as a huge variety of inspired vegetables.

Mexican
A food-cart turned brick-and-mortar restaurant, **Güero** (200 NE 28th Ave., 503/887-9258, www.guerotortas.com, 11am-10pm daily, $11) is known for its *tortas,* Mexican sandwiches on fresh white bread stuffed full of big flavors. You

won't find the greasy bombs of smaller outfits here—these meals are balanced and fresh. Try the classic—and messy—*torta ahogada,* or "drowned sandwich," a bolillo roll sandwich smothered in a rich spicy tomato sauce, and order a side of *esquites,* a cheesy corn salad. And don't miss the tequila and mescal-infused drinks. The bright, cheery space is decorated with colorful tiled walls, succulents, and clay pots.

Shopping
Downtown
The **Portland Saturday Market** (2 SW Naito Pkwy., 503/222-6072, www.portlandsaturdaymarket.com, 10am-5pm Sat., 11am-4:30pm Sun.) is the largest continuously running outdoor arts and crafts market in the country. Established in 1974, it runs every Saturday Sunday, rain or shine, with 350 artisans selling handmade goods and art. Find it under the Burnside Bridge.

Frances May (1003 SW Washington St., 503/227-3402, www.francesmay.com, 11am-7pm Mon.-Sat., noon-6pm Sun.) is the place to find some of Portland's best independent designers, with styles for men and women. You'll walk away with a statement sweater to remember.

Walk through **Union Way** (1022 W. Burnside St.) a shopping arcade featuring Pacific Northwest-inspired shops and restaurants. Get new boots at **Danner** (503/262-0331, www.danner.com, 11am-7pm Mon.-Sat., 11am-6pm Sun.), denim at **Self Edge** (971/271-8775, www.selfedge.com, noon-7pm Mon.-Sat., noon-5pm Sun.), or rain gear at **Bridge & Burn** (971/279-4077, www.bridgeandburn.com, 11am-7pm Mon.-Fri., 10am-7pm Sat., 10am-6pm Sun.).

Northwest
You can't visit Portland without a stop at the legendary **Powell's City of Books** (1005 W. Burnside St., 808/878-7323, www.powells.com, 9am-11pm daily).

One of the best independent bookstores in the country, selling both new and used books, Powell's has been a cultural hub since 1971. It takes up an entire block and is organized into nine color-coded rooms. Dig into literature in the Blue Room, or swing by the Red Room for a new history book. At the top is the Rare Book Room. The space can be overwhelming on your first visit—stop by the info center at either entrance for a map and directions.

Southeast
A store for handmade goods as well as a record label, **Tender Loving Empire** (3541 SE Hawthorne Blvd., 503/548-2927, http://tenderlovingempire.com, 10am-7pm daily) is quintessential Portland. Along with records, you'll find locally made jewelry, ceramics, paper goods, and baby onesies.

Carter & Rose (3601 SE Division St., 503/729-8677, http://carterandrose.com, 11am-6pm Tues.-Sun.) is housed in a beautiful light-filled space with succulents and perfectly curated goods lining the walls and shelves. Earrings, clay pots, perfumes, and more fill the store, and on Tuesday nights you can join an Open Clay Studio, where for $5 you'll have access to tools and basic guidance to create your own treasure.

If you've got kids in tow (or if you know any back home), stop by **Made You Look** (2418 E. Burnside St., 503/719-7906, http://madeyoulookpdx.com, 11am-6pm Tues.-Fri., 10am-5pm Sat.-Sun.), which has a fun collection of colorful modern toys. Kids will love crawling through the tunnel or hanging out in the tepee while you browse.

Northeast
The eclectic offerings of **PALACE** (2205 E. Burnside St., 503/517-0123, http://palacestore.com, 11am-7pm daily) include apothecary goods, bags, cookbooks, paper goods, and a wall of beautiful new and vintage clothes organized by color.

Accommodations

If you're traveling in an RV, it's best to stay just outside the city—there are good options in nearby Troutdale and Oregon City.

Under $150

★ **The Society Hotel** (203 NW 3rd Ave., 503/445-0444, www.thesocietyhotel.com, $35-49 dorm bed, $129-210 private room) is a hostel as chic as they come. In an 1881 building that was originally a boarding house for sailors, the hotel is located downtown, in Portland's Chinatown, and boasts a Wes Anderson-meets-Portland aesthetic. Coed shared bunk rooms include linens, privacy curtains, electrical outlets, earplugs, and a reading light, offering a comfortable and thoughtful stay at a fraction of a hotel's cost. Rooms come either standard with a shared bath, or with a private bath en suite. An on-site café serves coffee and sandwiches, and there's also a rooftop bar.

Quaint, eco-friendly **HI Portland Hawthorne Hostel** (3031 SE Hawthorne Blvd., 503/236-3380, www.portland hostel.org, $31-45 dorm bed, $72-80 private room) has great rates and comfortable furnishings. Some rooms have the usual bunk beds, and a few are private rooms for couples or families (kids under age 16 stay free). A full kitchen and big common spaces allow for socializing, and there's an "all-you-can-make" pancake breakfast. It's located right on lively Hawthorne Boulevard, with many restaurants, bars, and shops nearby.

Just over the river from downtown, the **Jupiter Hotel** (800 E. Burnside St., 503/230-9200, http://jupiterhotel.com, $102-180) is a motel with mid-century style. It's a fun, hip place that's been bringing life to East Burnside for years, with the connected Doug Fir Lounge and live music venue keeping the place perpetually hopping; it's a great crash pad for those who like to stay out late.

Kex Portland (100 NE Martin Luther King Blvd., 971/346-2992, www.kex hotels.com, $35-50 dorm bed, $90-210 private room), an Iceland-based hostel brand, is a fun place to chill out on the east side, close to the river and Burnside Street. The hostel has 15 shared rooms if you'd like to meet some new friends, or 14 private spaces, some with shared baths. The aesthetic is industrial-cool with warm touches, like rich hardwoods and hand-painted wallpaper. Your stay comes with a European breakfast spread that includes cured meats and cheeses, and there's a rooftop bar, an on-site restaurant, and a shared kitchen. Oh, and don't forget your swimsuit for the sauna.

$150-250

From its downtown Portland location, ★ **Woodlark** (813 SW Alder St., 403/372-1579, www.woodlarkhotel.com, $130-240) throws out hip but relaxed vibes. Rooms are bright and airy with deep green and brass touches, in-room snack packs, and even a menu of pillow options for your particular desires. You'll find minimalist design accented by live plants throughout the hotel. Be sure to stop at Good Coffee (7am-6pm daily) for a coffee and breakfast. End the day with a cocktail at Abigail Hall (3pm-11pm daily), named for Abigail Scott Duniway, who traveled the Oregon Trail in 1852 at age 18 with her family and went on to become an outspoken women's suffragist.

Get swanky at Portland's ★ **Ace Hotel** (1022 SW Stark St., 503/228-2277, www. acehotel.com/portland, $150-225), in a prime spot downtown near Powell's. Walk into the lobby to find Stumptown Coffee, a photo booth ready to capture your good hair day, and a library. Inside, the rooms are just as Instagram-worthy as the public spaces. Private and shared bath options are available.

On the east side of the river, **Hotel Eastlund** (1021 NE Grand Ave., 503/235-2100, www.hoteleastlund.com, $120-300) has 168 rooms, some with California King-size beds and all with floor-to-ceiling windows. Located near the convention center, it also offers easy access to downtown via the MAX line. Sample a glass of wine and grab a bottle to bring home at the on-site Pullman Wine Bar & Merchant (11am-7pm Mon.-Fri.).

McMenamins Kennedy School (5736 NE 33rd Ave., 503/249-3983, www.mcmenamins.com, $145-225), a 1915 elementary school lovingly restored by the McMenamins, offers lodging as well as five themed bars and restaurants, a movie theater (free for guests), and a beautiful heated outdoor soaking pool. Most of the rooms have hand-painted murals depicting local history, a shared bath, and no TV—but there's so much to do here, you won't even miss it. Even locals hang out here, and you're in close walking distance to Alberta Street.

Over $250

The beautiful downtown **Heathman Hotel** (1001 SW Broadway St., 503/241-4100, http://heathmanhotel.com, $260-350) opened in 1927, and the original decor has been polished, shined, and improved to match the excellent hospitality and service. The lobby has warm wood decor and chandeliers, and guest rooms are outfitted with sophisticated touches like marble baths, locally stocked honor bars, a pillow menu, and a French press. Enjoy perks like ice cream delivered to your room, a fitness center, and a pet-friendly menu of treats or services for your pup.

The **Sentinel** (614 SW 11th Ave., 503/224-3400, www.sentinelhotel.com, $200-350) is in two neighboring buildings from the early 1900s. The luxury hotel boasts 100 spacious rooms, many with balconies and some with fireplaces or an outdoor fire pit. Suites offer access to a private cocktail lounge for guests only, but all guests can enjoy the impeccable room service and elegant accommodations.

History

Mass Migration

The Oregon Trail is one of the largest voluntary mass migrations in world history—an entire nation shifted westward in the wagons, changing the face of the continent forever. Numbers are hard to pinpoint, but historians estimate 350,000 to 500,000 people traveled the trail when it was most active, 1843-1869. Of those, up to 1 in 10 died along the way from cholera, dysentery, accidents, or drowning.

Westward Ho

What caused so many Americans to migrate? One reason was Manifest Destiny, the belief that the United States was meant to stretch across the continent and impose its culture to remake the land. In the 1830s, crop failures, violence leading up to the Civil War, a recession in 1833-1834, and the outbreak of diseases like cholera led families to look west, hoping for something better. As time went on and reports trickled back, the West seemed to promise gold, free land, and for some, like the Mormons, escape from persecution. Most people migrating along the trail weren't trying to advance the mythic ideals of a nation but were simply looking for a better life.

The End Goal: Oregon

As the name indicates, the trail led to Oregon—at least one trail did. It has been described as a "rope with frayed ends," since cutoffs, offshoots, and alternative destinations existed the entire way. Mormons stayed with the trail until Wyoming, where they cut south for Utah. Gold-seekers and others departed the route in Idaho to head to California. Others made it to Oregon or headed north to Washington. For many, the destination was Oregon's verdant Willamette Valley. Today it's Oregon's wine country, and many family farms and orchards are still intact from pioneer times.

O'Fallon's Bluff in Nebraska

Emigrants were drawn to Oregon for a few reasons. In the 1840s politicians hoped to encourage more settlers to move to Oregon to strengthen the U.S. claims against neighboring British colonies. Guidebooks and logs full of glowing reports about the land in Oregon trickled back east. Narcissa Whitman traveled in 1836 with her husband, Marcus Whitman, to start a religious mission in the West, and her letters convinced many that it was an enjoyable trip with many wonders. John Frémont explored the trail in 1842-1843 and told his wife, Jesse Benton Frémont, extensive stories of the travels, which she helped him turn into best-selling books such as *Exploring Expedition to the Rocky Mountains in the Year 1842,* published in 1845.

From 1850-1855, the Oregon Donation Land Act allowed white male Oregon pioneers to claim 320 acres of land, and another 320 for their wives. With the gold rush in California and free land in Oregon, 1850-1852 saw the highest traffic

on the trails, with about 50,000 people each year. Subsequently, outbreaks of cholera also racked up the highest death toll in these years. Pioneers made their way to Oregon City to formally claim land; it was the site of the first federal land office west of the Rocky Mountains.

The Homestead Act of 1862 opened up vast stretches of land in not just Oregon but across western territories and states (270 million acres, or 10 percent of the area of the United States) to private ownership, distributing land to settlers—including newly arrived immigrants, women, and formerly enslaved people.

Not all the emigrants stayed in Oregon. Many were lured south during the gold rush, or went north to Washington. In 1880, Oregon's population was 175,000.

An Inhabited Land

For thousands of years, North America was home to hundreds of Native American nations and tribes. People made their homes throughout the continent and had extensive trading networks, healthy communities, and careful land management practices. In the Pacific Northwest, trading centers supported up to 10,000 people, contributing to trade networks that reached to the Southwest and what is now Minnesota. Settlements of the Mississippian culture flourished as far back as AD 1300, with echoes that survive today at Cahokia Mounds outside St. Louis.

Eastern nations like the Iroquois and Cherokee people felt the first impact from European colonists, and as the years progressed, the wave of white settlers pushed westward. In 1830 President Andrew Jackson signed the Indian Removal Act, which authorized Congress to forcibly remove the Cherokee, Crow, Chickasaw, and other peoples to new lands in the West, ostensibly where no one else lived; in reality there were Native American nations throughout the West, but not yet white settlement.

As more settlers moved west along the

Oregon Trail Timeline

♦ **1803:** Thomas Jefferson purchases the Louisiana Territory.

♦ **1804:** The Lewis and Clark Expedition reaches the Pacific and returns to the East during their two years of travels.

♦ **1824:** Fort Vancouver, a fur trading post, is started by the Hudson's Bay Company.

♦ **1825:** A few wagons make it over South Pass, Wyoming, and on to California with fur trappers William Ashley and Jedediah Smith.

♦ **1830:** President Andrew Jackson signs the Indian Removal Act, which allows the government to move Eastern nations like the Choctaw, Chickasaw, and Cherokee peoples to new land farther west in Oklahoma, past the nation's frontier and away from white settlers.

♦ **1834:** Fort William, Wyoming, is established as a fur-trading post, which eventually becomes Fort Laramie.

♦ **1836:** Narcissa and Marcus Whitman travel to Oregon to start their mission to convert the Cayuse people to Christianity.

♦ **1840:** Robert Newell and Joseph L. Meek become the first travelers to bring their wagons all the way to Oregon rather than leaving them at Fort Hall, Idaho.

♦ **1841:** The Bartleson-Bidwell Party leaves Independence, Missouri, the first emigrants to attempt the overland crossing; previously, travelers were mainly fur trappers or missionaries. The party splits up near Soda Springs, Idaho, with some heading to Oregon and the majority heading to California.

♦ **1842:** Jim Bridger establishes Fort Bridger, marking the end of the fur-trading era.

♦ **1843:** The first large wagon party heads for Oregon in what's referred to as "The Great Migration": Around 1,000 emigrants with 100 wagons set out from Independence, Missouri. Because of its notable size, the event is generally regarded as the official start of the Oregon Trail, although traffic had been building in the years before. In the same year, the Provisional Government of Oregon votes to not only ban slavery from the territory, but to ban African Americans altogether.

♦ **1844:** About 2,000 emigrants head for Oregon.

♦ **1845:** Traffic increases, with around 5,000 folks on the trail.

♦ **1846:** Sam Barlow builds his road around Mount Hood so that emigrants don't need to raft the wild Columbia River. The Donner Party travels the trail to California but is tragically trapped by heavy snows in the Sierra Nevadas.

♦ **1847:** Marcus and Narcissa Whitman are killed in the Whitman Massacre, a response to an outbreak of measles among the Cayuse people they were trying to convert.

♦ **1848:** The Oregon Territory is officially designated and recognized. Gold is discovered in California.

- **1849:** Forty-niners cause a rush on the trail, with more than 30,000 people traveling it that year.

- **1850:** Up to 55,000 emigrants travel that year, and cholera is a huge killer. California becomes a state.

- **1851:** Congress passes the Indian Appropriations Act, creating the reservation system. Native Americans on reservations are not allowed to leave without permission.

- **1854:** The Grattan Fight at Fort Laramie kicks off decades of war between the United States and the Great Sioux Nation.

- **1856:** The Mormon Willie and Martin Handcart companies lose many to terrible blizzards near Martin's Cove, Wyoming.

- **1859:** Oregon becomes a state.

- **1860:** The Pony Express begins service, running between St. Joseph, Missouri, and Sacramento, California.

- **1861:** The Civil War begins at Fort Sumter in Charleston, South Carolina.

- **1862:** Congress passes the Homestead Act, promising 160 acres of land to anyone who can stay on it for five years and "prove up."

- **1865:** The Civil War ends when Robert E. Lee surrenders to Ulysses S. Grant.

- **1869:** The Transcontinental Railroad is completed with the Golden Spike at Promontory Point, Utah, effectively ending the need for the overland trails.

- **1877:** The Nez Perce make a stand against the U.S. Army and refuse to give up their ancestral lands. The war ends with their surrender and removal, and a famous speech by Chief Joseph.

- **1890:** Fort Bridger is decommissioned by the U.S. Army, and Fort Laramie is abandoned.

- **1906:** Ezra Meeker travels the complete trail for a second time.

- **1926:** The last of Oregon's black exclusion laws, which excluded African Americans from living in the state, is officially repealed.

- **1971:** The Oregon Trail computer game is developed and later played by millions of schoolchildren.

- **1978:** The Oregon and California National Historic Trails are established by the National Park Service.

- **1982:** The Oregon-California Trails Association is established to better preserve the existing route.

The Trouble with Manifest Destiny

Manifest Destiny, a term coined in 1845, was the belief that the United States was destined and even God-ordained to span the continent. Politicians of the era were eager to push Westward Expansion, seeing it as the best way to secure the nation. Outposts along the coast of California, Oregon, and Washington were already growing, and one worry was that if the nation didn't connect itself geographically, and push other powers like Mexico and Great Britain out, California would end up as a separate nation.

President James Polk (1845-1949) was a proponent of Manifest Destiny, and when his term ended, the United States had gained Mexican land that once reached as far north as Wyoming, and had settled a truce with Great Britain to create the Oregon Territory. Now the politicians only needed the settlers to move in and finish claiming the land. While some emigrants felt a higher purpose to move, most were simply looking for economic opportunities, and took advantage of the offer of free land. The attitude of a white American destiny contributed to the reservation system that removed Native Americans from their ancestral lands.

The fierce nationalism this sparked still exists over a hundred years later as the United States acts as a world power and manages its borders. The idea of a nation that was given to the white settlers by God is hard to dislodge, and has impacts that reverberate today.

Oregon Trail, it became clear that the land wasn't going to be shared peaceably. While individual settlers may not have been pursuing the doctrine of Manifest Destiny, the U.S. government certainly believed in it, and worked to move Native Americans off their land. In 1851 Congress passed the Indian Appropriations Act, creating the reservation system as an offering of land in exchange for the areas already lost to white settlers. Slowly, Native American tribes were pushed onto reservations. Many resisted and fought back, such as various Sioux subgroups in the Sioux Wars of the 1860s-1870s, or the Nez Perce people's resistance under Chief Joseph. These conflicts are broadly known as the Indian Wars, which lasted into the late 1800s.

The Homestead Act of 1862 was another blow to Native Americans, freely giving away their ancestral lands to anyone who could plow it. Boarding schools became prevalent as the U.S. government, missionaries, and local agencies worked to separate Native American children from their cultures and remove the connection they had to their indigenous ways of life. As late as the 1970s, up to 60,000 students were enrolled in such schools. It wasn't until 1978 that the Indian Child Welfare Act was passed, which gave parents the legal right to refuse boarding school enrollment. Their legacy has left a hole in many families and Native American communities.

As of 2018 the federal government recognizes 573 tribes in the United States, both on and off reservations. Even more are recognized by the states. These communities have tribal sovereignty, the right to govern themselves. Both on reservations and in urban centers, Native American elders, scientists, artists, teachers, students, and researchers are bringing back cultural traditions, languages, traditional foodways, land and water management practices, and more while navigating the contemporary landscape. Project 562 (www.project562.com) is a photographic attempt started in 2012 to better represent the rich diversity of culture and experiences in the hundreds of Native American sovereign territories.

Who Were the Pioneers?

From 1843 to 1869, between 350,000 and 500,000 people traveled the Oregon Trail. Exact numbers are impossible to ascertain, but historians make that estimate based on written accounts. About 10 percent succumbed to disease, accidents, violence, or starvation on the route; the path was lined with gravestones. But that also means 9 out of 10 pioneers made it, successfully starting new lives in the West.

European Americans

Most settlers were European Americans from the Midwest or South. Many were farmers from the East who sold their farms to purchase supplies and move west. Some people migrated specifically to escape the volatile situation in the East, including the intense Bloody Kansas and Missouri Compromise confrontations leading up to the Civil War.

Women and Children

Women and children were a huge percentage of the traffic along the trail. The presence of families made the migration unique—previously those headed west had been fur trappers or missionaries, or on army expeditions.

Women's vital roles on the trail included cooking, cleaning, managing children, nursing the sick, and helping bury the dead. Many did it all while pregnant or with infants—often their diaries refer delicately to feeling ill, only later to say a baby was born. As the wagons were full of supplies and food, most emigrants walked—so many pregnant women were faced with walking 10-15 miles (16-24 km) a day or riding in an extremely bumpy wagon.

African Americans

Free black people moved west to find new opportunities and land. With the passing of the Homestead Act in 1862, which did not discriminate based on race, the West opened up for African Americans in a new way, with the availability of land. Many moved west and became successful farmers, ranchers, and gold seekers.

Some enslaved people traveled the trail with their owners. Oregon law gave white settlers a grace period of three years before they had to free their enslaved people.

Mormons

Mormons, in response to violent persecution in the East, traveled along a trail that closely paralleled the Oregon Trail from Nebraska, following the north side of the Platte River rather than the south. Their final destination was the Great Salt Lake Basin, chosen by Brigham Young to be their new home. The trail was active 1846-1868, parting from the Oregon Trail for the south around Fort Bridger, Wyoming. As part of the migration, many Mormon converts from Europe traveled this route.

Gold Rushers

Single men were lured west by reports of gold, especially during the California Gold Rush of 1849, which increased traffic on the trail so much it led to a cholera epidemic. The California Trail aligned with the Oregon Trail, until the California-bound began breaking off, mostly in Idaho.

The Rise of the Railroad

It took 4-6 months to get people, wagons, and supplies overland from the edge of the frontier in Missouri to the coasts of Oregon and California. If you went by ship via the Panama Canal, it could take up to a year. In order to help the country's expansion west, the idea for a transcontinental railroad arose in the 1830s, with surveyors sent west in the 1850s to look for the best routes. Congress eventually decided on the eastern point beginning at Council Bluffs, Iowa, near Omaha, and the western terminus at Sacramento. There was interest in ending the railroad in Oregon, but the gold boom and growing economy of California created a better argument for Sacramento.

In 1862, President Lincoln signed the Pacific Railroad Act, which authorized the creation of two companies, the western Central Pacific and the eastern Union Pacific. Each company, funded by government bonds, land grants, and private investment, was authorized to begin building at their starting points, eventually to meet in the middle.

Construction began in 1863 at both ends. The Civil War caused significant delays, but by 1865 construction was brisk, with rough settlements called "hell on wheels" popping up along the route. In the West, the difficult labor was done by Chinese workers, hired for long hours and little pay. They blasted through the Sierra Nevada mountain passes using dangerous nitroglycerine and gunpowder.

By 1869, both lines had decided their meeting would be at Promontory Summit in Utah, north of the Great Salt Lake. On May 10, 1869, six years after beginning, the Golden Spike was driven to join the two rail lines. The Central Pacific had laid 690 miles (1,110 km) of track from Sacramento, and the Union Pacific had laid 1,086 from Omaha. Regular service began days later. Fares were as low as $40 one-way (or $80 or $111, if passengers wanted to travel in more comfort and style), equivalent to about $630 today. The service rushed people to the West in as little as five days.

The railroad effectively ended the Oregon Trail as a major migration route. Some wagons were still traveling the route in the 1880s, but traffic declined drastically in favor of the quicker and cheaper railroad. The Northern Pacific Railroad arrived in Oregon in 1883, and the state's population quickly doubled to 300,000 by 1890. Along the route, forts were abandoned, trading posts closed down, and the ruts quietly became overgrown.

The Trail Today

After completion of the railroad, the Oregon Trail was quickly left behind by a nation eager to modernize. Paved roads and highways of the early 20th century, such as the Lincoln Highway, followed the paths of easy access, often paving over the old wagon routes, such as U.S. 26 on the Barlow Road around Mount Hood in Oregon.

Much of today's preservation efforts can be traced to Ezra Meeker, an emigrant who rode the trail in 1852, and later returned to become the first and most fervent preservationist. He went back along the trail repeatedly until his death in 1928 at age 97. Along the way he sparked nostalgia and drummed up support of local townspeople, Congress, and Presidents Roosevelt and Coolidge.

In 1968 Congress passed the National Trail System Act that included routes like the Appalachian Trail and the Pacific Crest National Scenic Trail; in 1978 a separate historic designation was added to include the Oregon Trail, the Mormon Trail, and the Lewis and Clark Trail. Even protected by law, the remains of the trail were still under threat from development. In 1982 a group of history buffs, including author George M. Franzwa, created the Oregon-California Trails Association (OCTA). The group committed itself to preserving the trail from vandalism, new highways, and development that might mar the extant portions. OCTA now has 11 active chapters and publishes a quarterly magazine, *Overland Journal*. In the 1990s several interpretive centers opened along the trail, including those in Independence, Missouri; Baker City, Oregon; and Oregon City, Oregon, attracting more visitors to the route.

Today, the trail is a cooperative effort among private, state, and federal resources, including the Bureau of Land Management and the National Park Service. Because of their combined efforts in preserving the trail, miles of the original ruts can be seen today alongside historic and natural landmarks.

Essentials

Getting There

This road trip begins in Independence, Missouri, a suburb of Kansas City, Missouri. An alternative beginning is in the travel hub of St. Louis, Missouri, to the east. You can choose to start at the other end in Portland, Oregon, an international travel destination near the trail's end in Oregon City, but you'll be road-tripping in the opposite direction as the pioneers. If you're traveling the trail in sections, you can find airports in between where you can pick up the trail, but these are typically off the route by a few hours' drive.

By Air
Missouri and Kansas
The major airport closest to the Oregon Trail's start is the **Kansas City International Airport** (MCI, 1 International Square, 816/243-5237, www.flykci.com), 15 miles (24 km) northwest of Kansas City and 30 miles (48 km) northwest of Independence, the official start of the trail. Airport transportation options to downtown Kansas City include bus 229 on **RideKC** (http://ridekc.org, 5:30am-11:15pm Mon.-Fri., 6:20am-11:15pm Sat.-Sun., $1.50), which takes about 45 minutes and runs approximately hourly, with less frequent service on early weekday mornings. From the airport you can also hail ride-sharing companies **Uber** and **Lyft** (about $30) or a **taxi** (about $50).

St. Louis Lambert International Airport (STL, 10701 Lambert International Blvd., 314/426-8000, www.flystl.com) is a major gateway and offers nonstop flights all over the country, as well as from Canada and Mexico. It's about 15 miles (24 km) northwest of St. Louis and 240 miles (386 km) east of Independence, a 3.5-hour drive west on I-70. Airport transportation options from Terminals 1 and 2 to downtown St. Louis include light-rail service via **MetroLink**

(www.metrostlouis.org, 4am-1am, $4), which takes about 40 minutes and runs approximately every 20 minutes. From the airport you can also hail ride-sharing companies **Uber** and **Lyft** (about $30) or a **taxi** (about $40).

Nebraska
Omaha Airport, or **Eppley Airfield** (OMA, 4501 Abbott Dr., 402/661-8017, www.flyomaha.com) is the biggest hub in Nebraska. From here, you can drive an hour (60 mi/97 km) southwest on I-80 to get to Lincoln, slightly off-route but a great staging point; from Lincoln you can skip the southern Nebraska section of the Oregon Trail and catch up with it in Kearney, a 125-mile (200-km) drive west on I-80, which takes about two hours. You can also fly directly to the **Lincoln Airport** (LNK, 2400 W. Adams St., 402/458-2480, www.lincolnairport.com). It's small but offers nonstop flights from Midwestern cities as well as Atlanta and Nashville. Eppley may be cheaper and offer more flight times, but factoring in mileage might make the trip more costly; the Lincoln Airport has a price comparison tool (www.lincolnairport.com) to help you decide which airport to fly into.

Wyoming
If you're planning to fly to Wyoming and rent a car, the easiest starting point is Cheyenne. **Denver International Airport** (DEN, 8500 Pena Blvd., 303/342-2000, www.flydenver.com), 100 miles (160 km) south in Colorado via I-25, is the closest major hub; it serves over 200 destinations via 20 airlines. You can also fly into small **Cheyenne Regional Airport** (CYS, 4020 Airport Pkwy. W., 307/634-7071, www.cheyenneairport.com), which has flights to Dallas several times daily. Airfares are $50-100 more to fly to Cheyenne rather than Denver, but you'll save 1.75 hours of driving time. As you continue north on I-25 from Cheyenne, you can easily go east on U.S. 26 to see one or all of

the eastern Wyoming sights, some of the state's Oregon Trail highlights, before backtracking slightly and continuing west along the Oregon Trail.

Idaho
The **Boise Airport** (BOI, 3201 W. Airport Way, 208/383-3110, www.iflyboise.com) is small but offers daily flights on seven major airlines. It's 4 miles (6.5 km) south of downtown. Airport transportation options to downtown include bus lines 2, 3, and 4 on **Valley Regional Transit** (http://valleyregionaltransit.org, 6:15am-9:30pm Mon.-Fri., 8:15am-6:30pm Sat., $1)., which runs every half hour on weekdays and every hour on Saturdays; the ride takes 15-30 minutes depending on the line (3 is the fastest, 2 is the slowest). You can also get from the airport to town via **Uber** and **Lyft** (about $15) or **taxi** (about $13).

Salt Lake City International Airport (SLC, 776 N. Terminal Dr., 801/575-2400, www.slcairport.com) has nonstop flights to over 75 cities. Heading north 125 miles (200 km) via I-15 and U.S. 89, in 2.25 hours you'll reach Garden City, Utah, a pleasant landing spot just off the route, on the waterfront of Bear Lake. From here you can connect with the Oregon Trail at Montpelier, Idaho, 30 miles (48 km) farther north via U.S. 89, an additional 40 minutes' drive.

Oregon
Portland International Airport (PDX, 7000 NE Airport Way, 503/460-4234, www.flypdx.com) has daily domestic and international flights on major airlines. It's 12 miles (19 km) north of the city center, and just 22 miles (35 km) north of Oregon City, the official endpoint of the Oregon Trail. Airport transportation to downtown Portland includes MAX Light Rail service on the Red Line run by **TriMet** (http://trimet.org, 4:45am-11:50pm daily, $2.50 one-way), which takes about 40 minutes and runs approximately every 15 minutes. From the airport you can also hail ride-sharing companies **Uber** and **Lyft** (about $30) or a **taxi** (about $40).

The **Boise Airport** actually offers a more convenient entry point if you want to begin on the eastern side of the state and head west; Ontario, Oregon, is 55 miles (89 km) northwest of Boise, less than an hour's drive.

By Bus
Greyhound (800/231-2222, www.greyhound.com) runs bus service along the route, but you'll have limited options in much of western Nebraska, Wyoming, and Idaho, and many connecting lines head through the bigger hubs of Denver and Salt Lake City, adding a lot of extra time. Relevant routes run from Chicago, Indianapolis, and Kansas City to St. Louis, Missouri; Chicago, St. Louis, and Kansas City to Lincoln, Nebraska; Cheyenne to Casper in Wyoming; Boise to Pocatello in Idaho; Boise to Portland; and Baker City to Portland in Oregon, with stops in the Columbia River Gorge.

By Train
Ironically, considering that it was the building of the railroads that eventually killed the Oregon Trail, there are no passenger rail lines serving much of the route today. **Amtrak** (800/872-7245, www.amtrak.com) runs several lines:

- The *Missouri River Runner* runs daily from St. Louis to Kansas City, Missouri.
- The *Texas Eagle* connects St. Louis with Chicago, Dallas, and San Antonio, and offers connections to Los Angeles.
- The *California Zephyr* runs from Chicago to San Francisco, stopping at Lincoln, Omaha, Denver, and Salt Lake City. It also stops 30 miles (48 km) southwest of Kearney in Holdrege, Nebraska.
- The *Empire Builder* runs between Portland and Spokane, Washington.

It stops in the Columbia River Gorge at the Bingen-White Salmon station, on the Washington side, across from Hood River.

By Car and RV

Independence, Missouri, is the official start of the Oregon Trail, and Kansas City, Missouri—10 miles (16 km) west—is the closest large city, a 20-minute drive via I-70. St. Louis, east of Independence, is within a day's drive of much of the central and eastern United States, making it a convenient place to start your trip. It's served by the major interstate highways I-55, I-70, and I-64. The 240-mile (386-km) drive from St. Louis to Independence takes about 3.5 hours via I-70.

Car Rentals

If you're renting, look for the major brands with locations throughout the country. When shopping around, be sure to look for unlimited mileage—the whole trip covers 2,000 miles (3,200 km)—and look out for out-of-state drop-off fees, which can get pricey, at over $700.

- **Alamo** (888/233-8749, www.alamo.com)

- **Avis** (800/352-7900, www.avis.com)

- **Budget** (800/214-6094, www.budget.com)

- **Dollar** (800/800-5252, www.dollar.com)

- **Enterprise** (855/266-9565, www.enterprise.com)

- **Hertz** (800/654-4173, www.hertz.com)

- **National** (844/393-9989, www.nationalcar.com)

For car rentals, you'll need to have a driver's license and be over age 21; sometimes you'll find an extra charge for those under age 26. Much of the driving will be on interstate or two-lane highways, but in many locations you'll want a car that can handle a bumpy dirt road. A full 4WD vehicle isn't necessary, but high clearance is useful.

RV Rentals

Consider renting an RV, which allows for more freedom and the comforts of home on the road. Road conditions unsuitable for an RV are rare on this route, and are noted when necessary. RV camping sites generally cost $30-40 per night, and you can also park for free, without hookups, in some parking lots and many hotels (ask first). Sites like **RVshare** (www.rvshare.com)—like an Airbnb for RVers—allow you to rent an RV directly through the owner.

Many **local RV rental companies** are near the bigger city travel hubs along the route, but be aware that you might need to make your trip a loop, as you'll likely need to return the RV to its original location. For a one-way RV road trip, your best bet may be **Cruise America** (800/671-8042, www.cruiseamerica.com), a nationwide company with convenient locations along the route that allows out-of-state drop-offs for a $650 fee, contingent on fleet availability—so inquire well ahead of time (4-6 months). Options come in four styles, from a truck camper that sleeps three to a large motorhome sleeping seven. All options come with a gas cooktop, air-conditioning, a microwave, and a fridge, and are pet-friendly. For a week, expect to pay $1,300-1,600 total, depending on mileage.

You must be at least 25 years old to rent an RV, and need only a standard driver's license—unless you want to rent a Class A motorhome that weighs over 26,000 pounds, which requires a commercial driver's license in some states along the route, including Kansas and Wyoming. However, most Class A motorhomes are under this weight threshold and shouldn't present a problem for the average renter.

Road Rules

Major Highways

The route from Missouri into Kansas is mostly along rural roads. Through Kansas, you'll largely follow **I-70** until hitting another rural stretch. In Nebraska, the route mostly follows **I-80**, then joins **U.S 26**. Once in Wyoming, you'll move from U.S. 26 to **I-25** before veering off onto various state highways, until hitting **U.S. 30** just before Idaho, which more closely follows the old trail. Soon after, you'll connect with to **I-86** and then **I-84** in Idaho. From there, you'll generally follow or parallel I-84 all the way to Oregon City.

You won't typically run into **toll roads** along the Oregon Trail route, except between Kansas City and Topeka, but it's a good idea to keep up to $10 cash in small bills on hand, especially if you're arriving from another state such as Illinois, Colorado, or Utah, where you can encounter tolls.

Highway Safety

Be safe on the roads. Wear a **seat belt** (required by law in all states). If you have **kids under 40 pounds,** they must be safely secured with a child safety system (a child car seat or booster seat). It's recommended that children under two face the rear.

Cell phone use while driving, including talking, texting, and internet use, is completely banned in Illinois, Oregon, and Washington, and texting and internet use is banned in Colorado. In other states, drivers can receive extra fines for "distracted driving" in the event of an accident.

Much of this route is in ranch country, where there is plenty of **livestock and wildlife.** While you won't encounter herds of wild bison like the pioneers, you will see many cows, which in some areas you may encounter on the road. Watch for deer and antelope as well throughout Wyoming, Idaho, and Oregon; they can jump quickly in front of cars and cause extensive damage.

If you run into trouble, pull your car over onto the shoulder and put your hazard lights on while you wait for assistance. Call 911 in the event of an emergency. Many car insurance companies, like **Geico** (800/424-3426, www.geico.com) or **Nationwide** (800/421-3535, www.nationwide.com), include 24-hour roadside assistance, as does a membership with **AAA** (800/222-4357, www.aaa.com). Some credit card companies and wireless service providers offer free assistance; check your plan before heading out. Travelers should always carry emergency gear in the car, including water and blankets.

Weather Considerations

Summer is an ideal time to travel this route, but keep in mind the heat can be intense, and summer also means **wildfire season,** which typically runs May-August. Don't contribute to the problem—keep a close eye on campfires and follow local no-burn laws. Traveling in the shoulder seasons of late fall or early spring may allow you to evade the heat, but these seasons also carry the risk of an **early or late snowstorm.** With snowmelt in spring comes **flood risk,** especially along the shallow Platte River Valley in Nebraska. Traveling the Oregon Trail route in **winter isn't recommended;** although major highways typically remain open, smaller roads are impacted by snow, and many sights are closed.

Call **511** for up-to-date travel information across the nation. Your call will be connected to the nearest service. States and some park districts operate a **Travelers Information Station (TIS)** or **Highway Advisory Radio,** which provide information on local road closures. Keeping an eye on weather reports and some flexibility in your planning can allow for a good trip even if adverse weather hits. There's nothing like a Midwest thunderstorm, so if you're lucky enough to get one, sit back and watch the show.

Fuel and Services

Fuel, rest stops, and amenities are widely available along the major highways, about every 30-40 miles (48-64 km), but there are gaps as wide as 60 miles (97 km) or more on smaller roads through Nebraska, Wyoming, and Idaho.

Motorcycles

Motorcyclists should be prepared for long distances without fuel or supplies, especially in Wyoming. Weather can be a concern at any time of year as well. The best stretches for a scenic trip are in western Wyoming, eastern Idaho, and Oregon. Be aware that helmets are always required in Missouri, Nebraska, and Oregon.

Bicycles

It's possible to bike the entire 2,000-mile (3,200-km) length of the Oregon Trail, though it's advisable to use smaller side roads rather than the interstate highways that the driving route takes. Cyclists will want local maps, a reliable hybrid bike for both pavement and dirt roads, and the know-how to fix flat tires and other problems along the way. Or consider having someone drive a support vehicle for supplies, emergency help, and luggage. Planning information and inspiration can be found at **Historical Trails Cycling** (402/499-0874, www.historicaltrailscycling.com); in past years, it has offered fully supported rides of the Oregon Trail, assuming 65 miles (105 km) a day. You might also think about tackling smaller sections at a time: The eastern plains of Kansas and Nebraska allow you to get a lot of mileage under your belt, while the higher elevations of Wyoming, Idaho, and Oregon will be slower going but offer spectacular scenery as a reward.

Tips for Travelers

Conduct and Customs

The West is a conservative but friendly place. Travelers will find gun shops and highway signs promising salvation alongside warm and welcoming people who are happy to share a story. Outside the biggest cities—St. Louis, Kansas City, Lincoln, Boise, and Portland—many shops, museums, and sometimes restaurants keep shorter hours or are closed on Sunday for religious reasons.

Traveling with Children

The Oregon Trail makes for an iconic family road trip. Not only will you head through some of the prettiest landscapes and great cities of the nation during your travels into history, you'll be able to hike, swim, canoe, camp, and tour your way through the West.

The perfect age for the trip might be grade-schoolers around 7-12 years of age, old enough to appreciate the history and sights but young enough to still want to embark on a family road trip. If you time it right, your grade-schooler may have just studied the topic in school, and the trip can be a chance to experience living history. Don't wear them out on every single museum, but choose a few every few days, especially sights with living-history demonstrations or other activities. Try to include plenty of activities, such as wagon rides, walks and hikes, or boat trips. Plenty of hotel chains along the route come with a swimming pool, so they can expend extra road-trip energy, and restaurants across the board offer kids' meals and family discounts.

If your kids are older or younger, don't despair—smaller children will have a blast at museum kids' areas and will be easy to entertain in the vast outdoor areas. For your resident bored teenagers, cherry-pick a few museums that are exceptionally interesting (the weirder the

The Oregon Trail Computer Game

In 2018 the Oregon Trail celebrated its 175th anniversary since the first large wagon train in 1843. Perhaps its most easily recognized modern-day legacy is the computer game. First developed in 1971, *The Oregon Trail* was meant to be an educational game, and often came bundled with school computer purchases. So many children played the game at school in the 1980s-1990s that "The Oregon Trail Generation" has become a term for the microgeneration of kids who came of age playing it.

The game involves a pixelated journey across the West, in which players attempt to get their family and wagon to Oregon safely—along the way they can buy supplies, hunt bison, decide when to ford rivers, and deal with medical conditions such as cholera, dysentery, and broken bones. The journey hits major landmarks along the trail, including Fort Kearny, Chimney Rock, and South Pass, and ends with a difficult run down the Columbia River before arriving at a family farm in Oregon.

It was wildly successful, selling over 65 million copies, and is now one of the 12 video games in the World Video Game Hall of Fame. For all its successes, one critique of the game is that it failed to accurately represent indigenous perspectives—Native American characters were often pushed to the side and reduced to stereotypes.

The game spawned a cadre of homages in later years, such as zombie parody *The Organ Trail,* a Facebook version, a card game, and a series of souvenir T-shirts with pixelated sayings like "You have died of dysentery." For those who once played the computer game, following the old wagon trail might feel like coming full circle, a final successful attempt at winning a game ingrained in our hearts.

facts, the better), and focus on exciting pursuits such as a climbing course, a canoe trip, or Nebraska's unique tanking tradition.

Women Travelers

Women traveling alone should rely on common sense and safety instincts as usual. Plan ahead so you know your route and have a bit of familiarity with the areas where you'll be staying. Stay mindful of your surroundings, and keep valuables in your hotel safe rather than carry them on your person.

Gay and Lesbian Travelers

It's worth noting that the Oregon Trail passes through some of the most remote and culturally conservative parts of the country; but people along the way are likely to be largely congenial. LGBTQ travelers will feel at ease in the bigger cities and college towns along the route: St. Louis, Kansas City, Lincoln, Kearney, Casper, Boise, and Portland.

Some local LGBTQ resources include the magazines *Out In STL* (http://outinstl.com) and *Camp Kansas City* (www.campkc.com). Portland's **GayPDX** (www.gaypdx.com) is an online directory of LGBTQ-friendly businesses.

Senior Travelers

Senior travelers will find plenty to enjoy on the Oregon Trail, along with folks happy to chat about local history. Restaurants and museums often offer senior rates, so be sure to ask along the way. You might also consider buying the National Park Service's **America the Beautiful Senior Pass** (www.nps.gov, $20 annual, $80 lifetime), available to U.S. citizens and permanent residents over the age of 62. It grants free entry and offers many camping discounts at over 2,000 federal recreation sites, including venues along the route such as the National Historic Oregon Trail Interpretive Center and Fort Vancouver National Historic Site. Obtain a pass in person for free at a designated federal recreation site, or order one online or via mail; note the remote applications require a $10 processing fee.

Travelers of Color

Historically, the states of Wyoming, Idaho, and Oregon have been particularly unwelcoming to people of color. While times (and racist laws) have been updated, attitudes of the past have impacted residential populations so that these three states are among the whitest in the United States; that said, people are generally friendly. The bigger cities along the route are more likely to have diverse populations.

Travelers with Disabilities

The Americans with Disabilities Act of 1990 requires all public accommodations and services (like hotels, restaurants, and retail shops) to reach minimum accessibility requirements. Some areas are still challenging to get around in, such as some monuments and historic sites. Larger chain hotels offer the best choice of accessible rooms. **Mobility International USA** (www.miusa.org) has information and advice on domestic and international travel for people with mobility needs.

The National Park Service offers the **America the Beautiful Access Pass** (www. nps.gov, free), which grants U.S. citizens and permanent residents with permanent disabilities free entry and camping discounts at over 2,000 federal recreation sites, including venues along the route such as the National Historic Oregon Trail Interpretive Center and Fort Vancouver National Historic Site. Obtain a pass in person for free at a designated federal recreation site, or order one via mail for a $10 processing fee—order two months before your trip to make sure it arrives on time.

Traveling with Pets

Many emigrants brought their dogs along with them when they struck out on the Oregon Trail, and today it's still a great road trip on which to bring your pup, with lots of outdoorsy fun. Be aware, however, that many historic sites and parks along the way do not allow pets, so you'll need to leave them in the car or skip some sights in favor of alternatives.

If you're RVing, plenty of campsites have a dog run and pet relief area. Dog-friendly hotel chains include Best Western, Motel 6, Sheraton, and La Quinta. Expect to pay $20-30 extra per night for your pet to stay with you, except at Motel 6, which doesn't charge a fee.

When traveling with your favorite furry friend, keep a collapsible water bowl on hand, and take plenty of breaks.

Information and Services

Health and Safety

The Oregon Trail was historically fraught with danger: Disease and accidents took the lives of 1 in 10 emigrants. Today's travelers don't have to deal with dysentery, but a medical issue can still ruin the trip. Drive safely and travel smart to avoid problems. Keep food and plenty of water on hand in the car, along with an emergency kit with first-aid supplies, blankets, and extra batteries. If hiking or playing outdoors, use sunscreen, carry water, and take bug spray. Hot summer weather can quickly cause dehydration and sunstroke—avoid the heat of the day by staying out of the sun when it's at its highest. Hikers should stay mindful that they may encounter rattlesnakes in Wyoming, Idaho, and eastern Oregon—if you see one, keep calm, move slowly, and give it a wide berth. In case of emergencies, dial 911.

Money

U.S. currency is accepted across the route. If you prefer using credit cards, they are widely accepted, though businesses often prefer cash to cut down on fees. When dining out, it is expected that you tip 15-20 percent of your pretax bill. Many smaller museums allow entrance "by donation"; while this technically means there's no cost, it's polite to offer some cash for your visit, usually $5-10 per person.

Time Zones

The Oregon Trail runs through six states and three time zones. It is an hour earlier as you enter each new time zone in the westbound direction. Missouri, Kansas, and half of Nebraska, near O'Fallon's Bluff between North Platte and Ogallala, are in the **central time zone.** The western half of Nebraska, Wyoming, and Idaho follow **mountain time,** and most of Oregon is on **Pacific time,** beginning 25 miles (40 km) northwest of Ontario in eastern Oregon near Farewell Bend State Park.

Cell Phones and Internet Access

In general, you'll have cell phone service—that is, the ability to place a phone call from your cell—along the paths of today's Oregon Trail, even in rural areas. Wi-Fi service on your smartphone, however, is much spottier once you're away from the major interstates and populated areas; this route travels through some of the most remote parts of the country, so expect to lose your signal, particularly through western Nebraska, much of Wyoming, and southeastern Idaho. Most hotels and RV campgrounds offer free Wi-Fi.

Maps and Visitor Information

The **National Park Service** (www.nps.gov/ oreg/planyourvisit/publications.htm) has published Auto Tour Route guides for the National Historic Trails, of which the Oregon Trail is one, along with the Santa Fe, California, Pony Express, and Mormon Trails, with which the Oregon Trail converges at various points. You can find PDFs for each state online—except Oregon, which is still in development— as well as paper copies at some locations along the route. These guides provide detailed directions on how to reach each historical marker and sight along the National Historic Trails, and you'll find helpful NPS signage along the route as well. As GPS connectivity on your cell phone can be spotty in remote locations, the NPS guides are a good resource to pair with this book, as are local and state maps found at tourism and visitors centers, hotels, and many museums. For an interactive on-the-go map, download the NPS Oregon Trail app, which provides the Auto Tour Route guides in an easy-to-use format. Be sure to go into Settings on the app and Download Content before you set out, so you can still access it offline. Google Maps, downloaded to your smartphone for offline use, are also helpful.

Accommodations

A variety of standard **hotel and motel chains** are available along the route. Many budget-friendly hotels offer a decent rate for double occupancy (or two beds for a family) and come with breakfast included. Best Western's line of Best Western Plus hotels are a good bet throughout the trip, offering similar levels of quality. Quality Inn, Holiday Inn, and Hilton Garden Inn are found in most locations and are good choices as well. **Airbnb** has great options in the cities along the route, but choices are drastically limited in smaller towns and rural areas.

Consider alternating hotel stays with tent **camping** to save money along the way; you'll be passing through some of the country's most magnificent landscapes, with incredible campgrounds, so bringing a tent along ensures better access to the wilder places, typically at $10-15 per night. Plan on using hotels in bigger cities, then camping in between. Popular locations might require reservations during the busy summer periods, but most sites have at least a few first-come, first-served options available if you arrive early enough. **ReserveAmerica** (www.reserveamerica.com) administers many public campgrounds, while **Hipcamp** (www.hipcamp.com), like Airbnb for outdoorsy lodging options, offers many privately owned options, from tent camping to glamping.

Suggested Reading

Oregon Trail History

Bagley, Will. *South Pass: Gateway to a Continent.* Norman, OK: University of Oklahoma Press, 2014. Award-winning Western historian Bagley tackles the significance of South Pass, which was the lynchpin of the entire Western migration effort.

Calloway, Colin G. *Our Hearts Fell to the Ground: Plains Indians Views of How the West Was Lost.* Boston: Bedford/St. Martin's, 1996. A collection of primary sources like speeches, myths, and oral histories on Native Americans' changing way of life from the 1700s to late 1800s.

Dary, David. *The Oregon Trail: An American Saga.* New York: Knopf, 2004. A sweeping history of the trail by a prizewinning historian, starting in Oregon in the early 1800s.

Franzwa, Gregory. *The Oregon Trail Revisited.* Tucson: Patrice Press. 1972. One of the first modern guides of the Oregon Trail from a passionate historian.

Karson, Jennifer. *Wiyaxayxt—As Days Go By—Wiyaakaa'awn: Our History, Our Land, and Our People—The Cayuse, Umatilla, and Walla Walla.* Pendleton, OR: Tamástslikt Cultural Institute, 2006. The history of the Confederated Tribes of the Umatilla Indian Reservation by community members, working together with elders, students, and nonnative scholars.

Katz, William Loren. *The Black West: A Documentary and Pictorial History of the African American Role in the Westward Expansion of the United States.* New York: Harlem Moon, 2005, 2019. A tale of the long-overlooked stories of the African American men and women in the West, told with fascinating pictures and firsthand accounts.

Stegner, Wallace. *The Gathering of Zion: The Story of the Mormon Trail.* Lincoln, NE: University of Nebraska Press/Bison Books, 1964, 1992. The eminent Western historian tells about the Mormon migration along the trail in a touching saga of purpose and American discipline.

Trail Narratives

Buck, Rinker. *The Oregon Trail: A New American Journey.* New York: Simon & Schuster, 2016. The author departs on a modern-day covered-wagon trip, complete with mules, and on the way weaves a touching personal narrative interspersed with historical facts.

Parkman, Francis. *The Oregon Trail.* (Elmer N. Feltskog, ed.) Lincoln, NE: University of Nebraska Press/Bison Books, 1994. (First published serially in *Knickerbocker's Magazine* in 1847-1849 and as a book in 1849). Francis Parkman journeyed the Oregon Trail on horseback in 1846, which lives on in history as one of the best descriptions of the way West.

Schlissel, Lillian. *Women's Diaries of the Westward Journey.* New York: Schocken Books, 1982. A collection of primary sources from women's diaries on the trail and how they cooked, cleaned, and braved the wilderness.

For Kids

Erickson, Paul. *Daily Life in a Covered Wagon.* New York: Puffin Books, 1997. Explore what life was like in a wagon train to the West in this fun book for ages 5-8.

Hill, William E. *Reading, Writing and Riding along the Oregon-California Trails (An Educational Activity Book)*. Independence, OR: Oregon California Trails, 1993. This activity book is targeted at grade-schoolers and is filled with maps, puzzles, word searches, and emigrants' stories, making a great addition to an Oregon Trail road trip.

Hopkinson, Deborah. *Apples to Oregon: Being the (Slightly) True Narrative of How a Brave Pioneer Father Brought Apples, Peaches, Pears, Plums, Grapes, and Cherries (and Children) Across the Plains*. New York: Aladdin, 2008. Kids six and under will enjoy this clever tale of a young girl's wagon train and the fruit trees her father brought with them.

Internet Resources

General Information
Oregon-California Trails Association
www.octa-trails.org
The official website of the volunteers who help celebrate, preserve, and protect the historic overland trails.

National Park Service Auto Tour Guides
www.nps.gov/oreg/planyourvisit/trail-brochures.htm
The National Park Service has designated the Oregon Trail a National Historic Trail. It's also published a series of Auto Tour Route Interpretive Guides to direct travelers to sites along the route, which can be downloaded from the website or found at many tourism centers along the way. Guides are provided for Missouri and Kansas, Nebraska, Wyoming, and Idaho, but Oregon is still in development. You can also download an NPS Oregon Trail app to your smartphone

for a helpful on-the-go guide featuring an interactive map.

Missouri and Kansas
Visit Missouri
www.visitmo.com
The state's official guide for traveling in Missouri offers maps and information on attractions, places to stay, and events.

Explore St. Louis
http://explorestlouis.com
St. Louis's official tourism website offers lists of things to do and where to eat and enjoy nightlife.

Visit KC
www.visitkc.com
Kansas City's official tourism website offers lists of things to do and where to eat and enjoy nightlife.

Travel Kansas
www.travelks.com
The state's official guide for traveling in Kansas offers information on adventures and events around the state.

Visit Topeka
www.visittopeka.com
Topeka's official tourism website offers tips on where to eat, drink, stay, and have fun in the capital city.

KanDrive
www.kandrive.org
The Kansas Department of Transportation offers information on road conditions and closures, with live camera feeds and travel alerts.

Nebraska
Visit Nebraska
www.visitnebraska.com
The state's official guide for traveling in Nebraska offers planning tips, itineraries, and regional highlights.

Nebraska Department of Transportation
www.511.nebraska.gov
The Nebraska DOT offers information on road conditions, and you can download the 511 on-the-go app to view snowplow trackers, find traffic events, and see weather conditions.

Wyoming
Travel Wyoming
http://travelwyoming.com
The state's official guide for traveling in Wyoming offers road trip itineraries, seasonal events, and hidden gems.

Visit Casper
www.visitcasper.com
Casper's official tourism website offers tips on local hot spots.

Wyoming Department of Transportation
http://wyoroad.info
The Wyoming DOT offers an interactive online map with weather forecasts, road conditions, and closures, sortable by city or region.

Idaho
Visit Idaho
www.visitidaho.org
The state's official guide for traveling in Idaho offers maps, travel tips, itineraries, and festival coverage.

Boise Convention & Visitors Bureau
www.boise.org
Boise's official tourism website offers lists of things to do and events.

Idaho Department of Transportation
http://ow.511.idaho.gov
The Idaho DOT offers information on road construction and closures and winter conditions. You can also download an app.

Oregon
Travel Oregon
www.traveloregon.com
The state's official guide for traveling in Oregon offers information on the state's top attractions, bicycling itineraries, and ideas for exploring the Oregon Trail.

Travel Portland
www.travelportland.com
Portland's official tourism website offers information on city neighborhoods as well as nearby areas including the Columbia River Gorge and Mount Hood.

Trip Check
www.tripcheck.com
The Oregon Department of Transportation offers information on road conditions sortable by region, with traffic updates and live cameras.

INDEX

LIST OF MAPS

PHOTO CREDITS

MOON NATIONAL PARKS

ACADIA
NATIONAL PARK

HILARY NANGLE

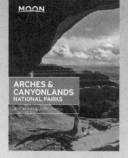

ARCHES &
CANYONLANDS
NATIONAL PARKS

BANFF
NATIONAL
PARK

HIKE · CAMP · KAYAK

ANDREW HEMPSTEAD

DEATH VALLEY
NATIONAL PARK

GLACIER
NATIONAL PARK

GRAND
CANYON

KATHLEEN BRYANT

GREAT SMOKY
MOUNTAINS
NATIONAL PARK

HIKE · BIKE · CAMP

JASON FRYE

MOUNT RUSHMORE
& THE BLACK HILLS

LAURA L. DUNNELL

ROCKY
MOUNTAIN
NATIONAL PARK

HIKE, CAMP,
SEE WILDLIFE

ERIN ENGLISH

In these books:

- Full coverage of gateway cities and towns
- Itineraries from one day to multiple weeks
- Advice on where to stay (or camp) in and around the parks

MOON ROAD TRIP GUIDES

Share your adventures using **#travelwithmoon**